TURNER'S WESSEX

ARCHITECTURE AND AMBITION

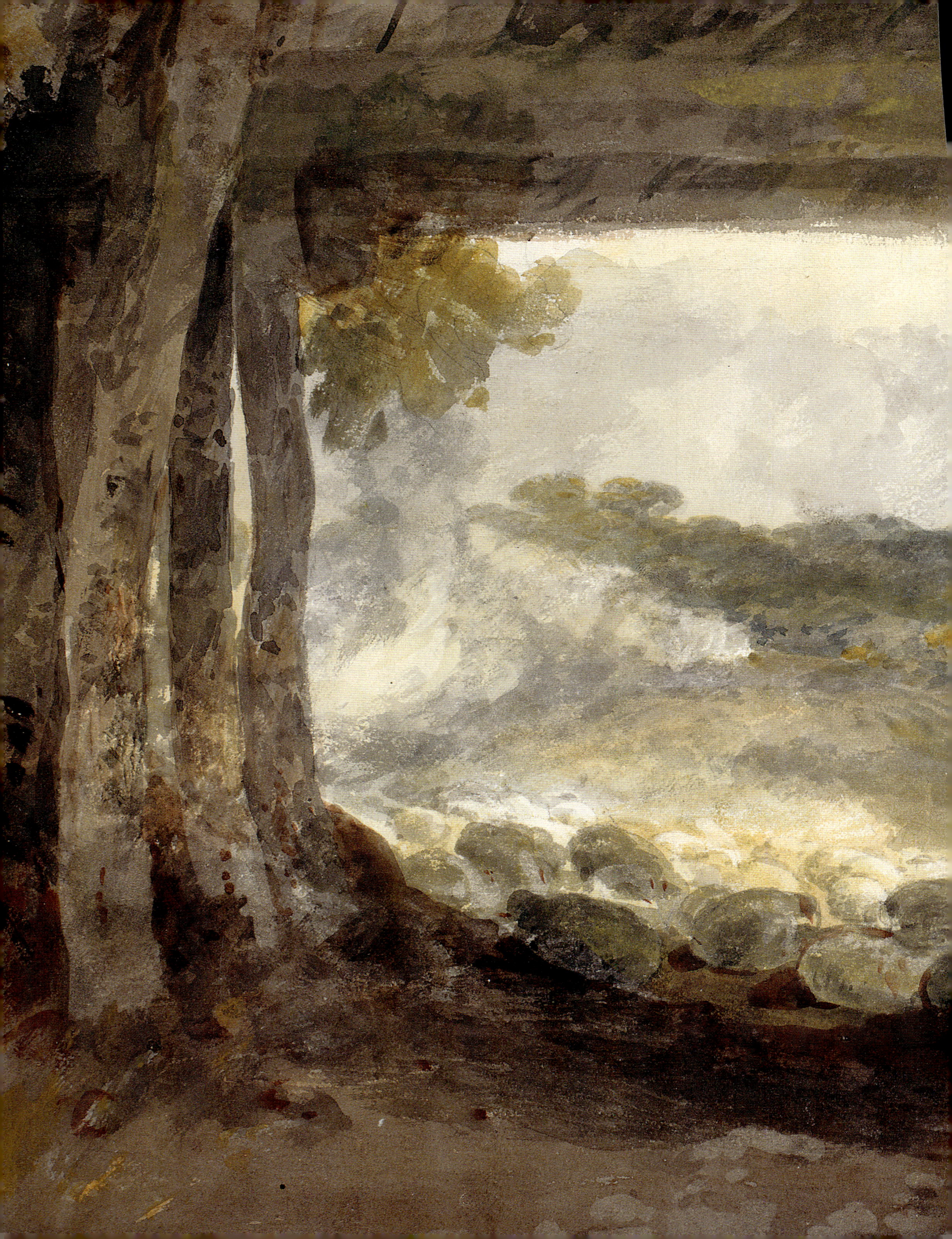

TURNER'S WESSEX

ARCHITECTURE AND AMBITION

IAN WARRELL

SCALA

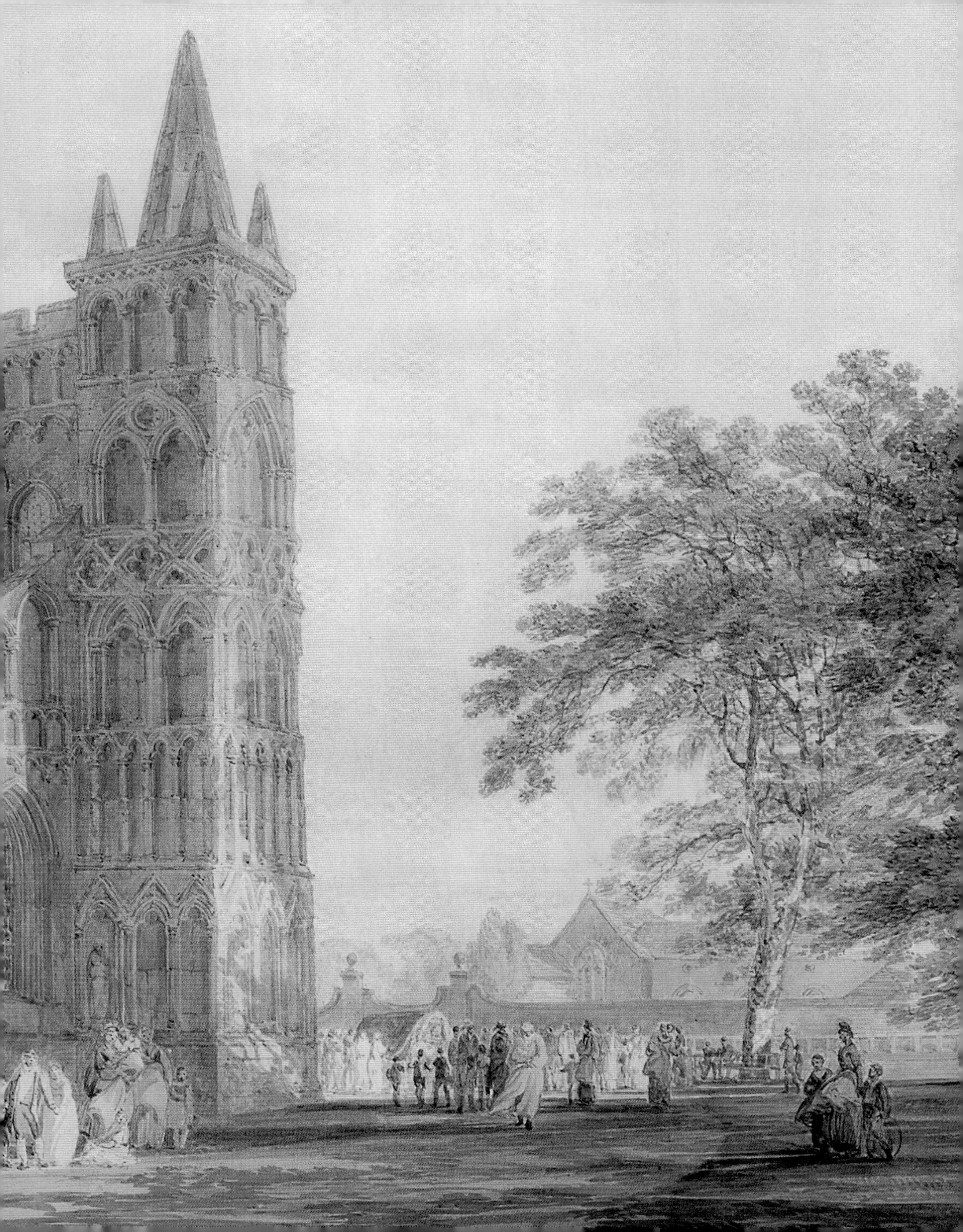

CONTENTS

Sponsor's Foreword 6

Foreword 7

1 Architecture and Ambition: The Rising Star 8

2 Sir Richard Colt Hoare and Stourhead 20

3 The Salisbury Commission: 'Poems in Stone' 40

4 William Beckford, and the Rise – and Falls – of Fonthill Abbey 76

5 Westward Ho! Turner and the Picturesque Coast of Southern England 120

6 Stonehenge and History 140

7 Castles Old and New: The Isle of Wight 156

Appendix 184

Notes 196

Selected Bibliography 199

List of Works in the Exhibition 200

Acknowledgements 203

Photographic Credits 204

Index 205

SPONSOR'S FOREWORD

Woolley and Wallis is delighted to sponsor this exhibition, which focuses on Turner's views of Wessex. We are also very pleased to continue our association with The Salisbury Museum, which began with our sponsorship of the *Constable and Salisbury: The Soul of Landscape* exhibition in 2011.

Turner's precocious talent was evident from a young age and he was only 15 when he first exhibited at the Royal Academy. There is little doubt that from early on he recognised his potential for greatness – when he was 21 he painted a watercolour of the interior of Westminster Abbey with his own name and date of birth inscribed on a tombstone. He may have anticipated the wrong location – he is buried in the crypt at St Pauls – but he was clearly aware of his own genius.

It was in the mid-1790s that Sir Richard Colt Hoare, who lived at Stourhead, commissioned Turner to paint a series of watercolours of Salisbury Cathedral. In May 1799 Turner visited the London home of that extraordinary aesthete and reprobate William Beckford (where incidentally he first saw the works by Claude acquired from the Altieri collection, which had such a deep impact on his artistic development) and was commissioned to create a series of pictures of Fonthill Abbey, the gothic folly that Beckford was building in Wiltshire. Both these commissions are well represented in this exhibition.

Short of stature, dishevelled in appearance, gruff and at times coarse and rude, Turner was all these things. But he was also that rarest of men, someone who like Titian before him and Picasso after him redefined the very boundaries of art, and in doing so had a profound influence on generations of artists that were to follow.

How fortunate we are that this beautiful corner of England, which includes Salisbury, Stourhead and Stonehenge, forms the heart of this exhibition and gives us the opportunity to see for the first time together these works painted by one of the greatest artists who ever lived.

Paul Viney
Chairman
Woolley and Wallis
Fine Art Auctioneers

FOREWORD

We are privileged to live in a landscape that has attracted some of Britain's greatest artists. *Turner's Wessex: Architecture and Ambition*, the fifth major exhibition in Salisbury Museum's flourishing programme, centres on the Wiltshire drawings and paintings of Joseph Mallord William Turner. The rapid development of both his technique and vision in the 1790s can be seen clearly in his drawings and watercolours of this county.

This exhibition is the first to be devoted to Turner's drawings and paintings of Salisbury Cathedral, the city and its surroundings. Considered together, these works will illustrate how the ambitious young artist succeeded in winning the admiration of two of the most influential collectors in Britain, and the crucial role his depictions of Salisbury played in his campaign to establish himself as the pre-eminent artist of his generation.

To mount an exhibition of this nature we have been fortunate in having the cooperation of a number of generous lenders, both public institutions and private collections, all of whom are named in the List of Works. The exhibition has been supported by substantial loans from the Tate collection.

We owe a huge debt of gratitude to our sponsors, without whom it would be impossible to continue our efforts to offer exhibitions of such stature to the local community and to the many foreign visitors who come to the Cathedral Close. Once again, we offer our appreciation to the Foyle Foundation, sponsors of this exhibition and of our 2011 Constable exhibition. A full list of our sponsors is listed at the end of the book but we extend particular thanks to The Golden Bottle Trust and to Woolley and Wallis Fine Art Auctioneers.

As Salisbury Museum continues to further its reputation as a place for the curious and engaged visitor, I would like to thank the team who have masterminded this exhibition. In the Directorship of Adrian Green, the Chair of the Exhibitions Committee Richard Morgan and the Exhibitions Officer Kim Chittick, we are most fortunate.

Finally, I must thank our curator, and author of this book, Ian Warrell. Ian is one of the leading scholars working in the field of Turner and the English landscape. His *Turner and Venice* exhibition at the Tate in 2003 and *Turner Inspired: In the Light of Claude* at the National Gallery in 2012 were two landmark exhibitions in the history of Turner scholarship. We are delighted that he has been willing to lend us his knowledge and expertise and we offer him our sincere thanks.

S.M. Denniston
Chairman of the Trustees
The Salisbury Museum

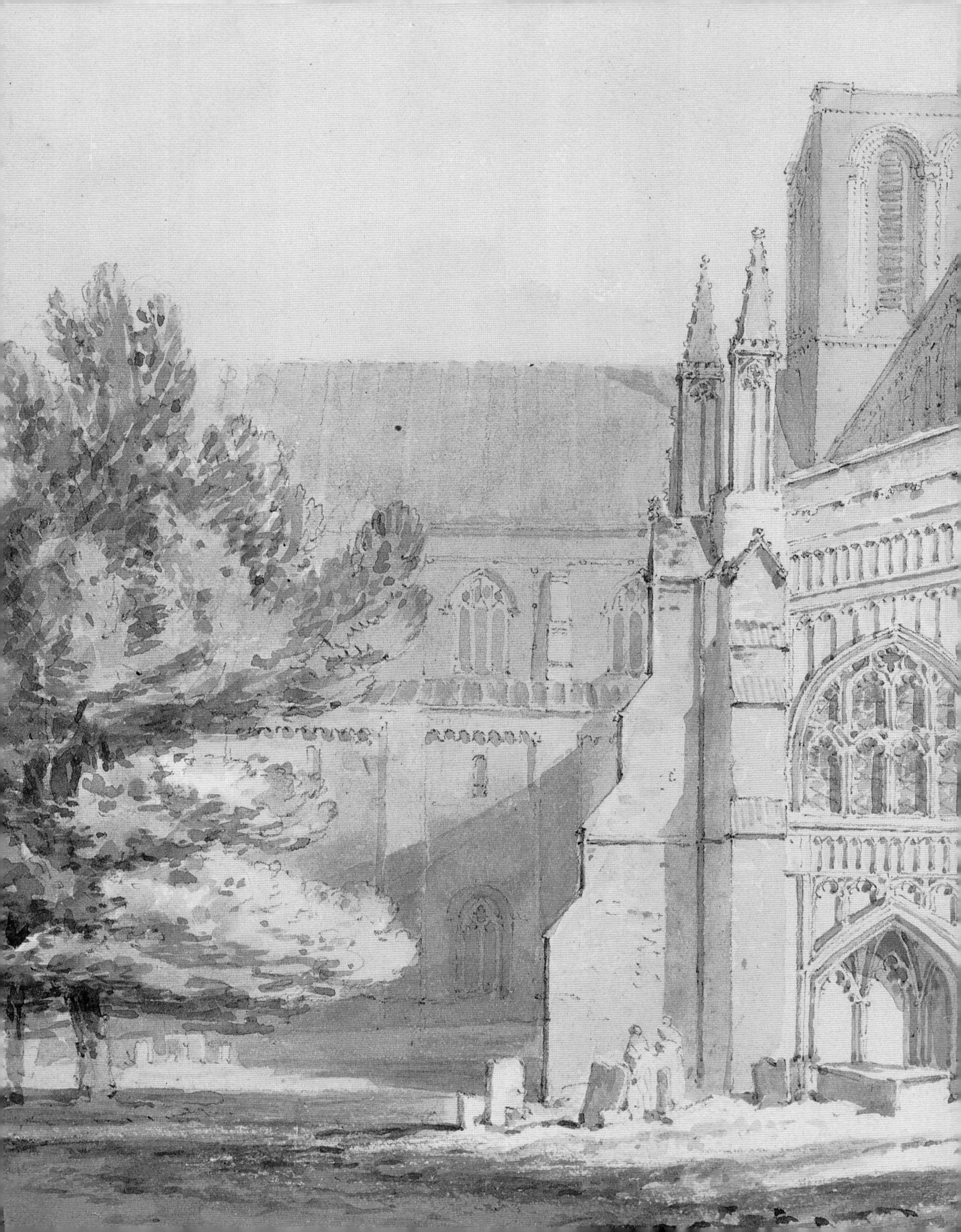

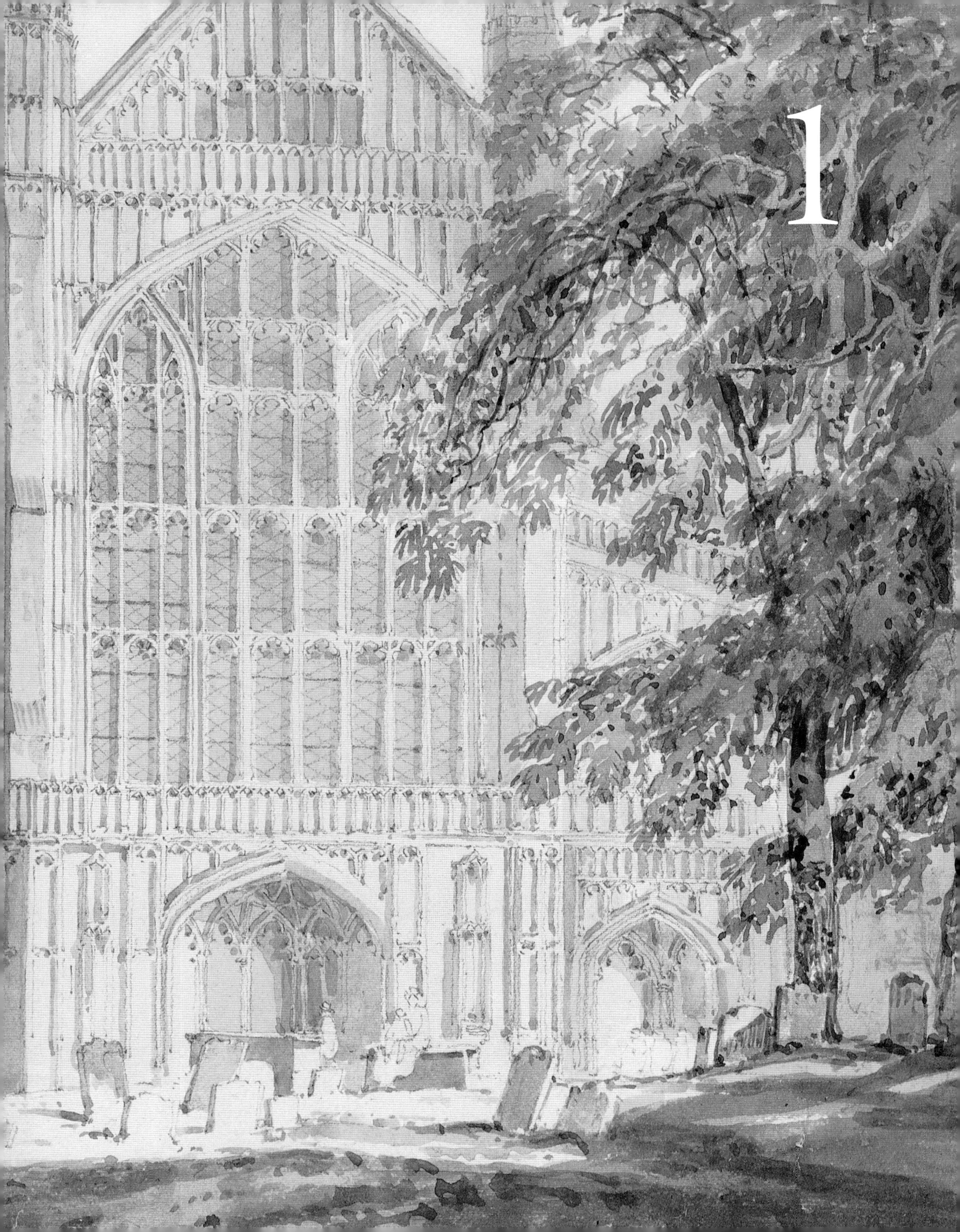

1

ARCHITECTURE AND AMBITION: The Rising Star

FOR MANY OF US, the most pervasive image we have of Joseph Mallord William Turner (1775–1851) is of him in later life, at the dawn of the Victorian era: a short, stocky man in a top hat; his clothes slightly shabby; his speech taciturn; his behaviour guarded and eccentric – just like his final paintings. This was indeed how his contemporaries and his first biographers had seen and remembered the great artist in his declining years. But the pathos of that image is a lifetime away from how Turner depicted himself in his well-known *Self-Portrait* (*c.*1799, Tate), or the way he was captured in a surreptitious sketch of him at work at the home of Dr Thomas Monro (fig. 1). Both of these portraits date from the second half of the 1790s, when Turner had only recently entered his twenties and was still forging his way in the London art world. In each he is elegantly (but not flamboyantly) dressed. His father, a Covent Garden barber, had presumably attended to his hair, which is powdered and pulled back in a neat ponytail. The overall impression is of a presentable and self-possessed young man, clearly aware of the image he was projecting, even when engrossed in his painting. This is the individual that we will be concerned with in most of the following chapters, and these early portraits provide an invaluable sense of Turner at this crucial stage of his career, when his character sometimes proves elusive. His actions and sayings were occasionally reported by others but, for the most part, the period up to 1800 lacks any documentation in his own voice.

Although still emerging as a notable talent, he had already attracted favourable reviews in the press by 1794, and with each year he was becoming a stronger presence in the annual exhibitions at the Royal Academy of Arts in London. Such precocious success was undoubtedly founded on soaring ambition, but was coupled with a dogged capacity for hard work, both within the training available at the Academy, as well as in opportunities pursued primarily for purely commercial ends. One of Turner's earliest commissions earned him tuppence per image for the 70 plates he coloured by hand of an edition of Henry Boswell's *Historical Descriptions of New and Elegant Picturesque Views of the Antiquities of England and Wales, &c* (1786).[1] The task required only basic watercolour skills, but was a great opportunity for the aspiring artist, probably not yet a teenager, enabling him to become familiar with historic sites across the nation, introducing many places that he would later visit himself. One of these was Stonehenge, which looms massive and mysterious above the visitors in Thomas Hogg's image (fig. 2).

Other extra-mural studies undertaken before and in tandem with his time in the Academy

PREVIOUS PAGES:
The West Front of Winchester Cathedral (detail) (see fig. 10)

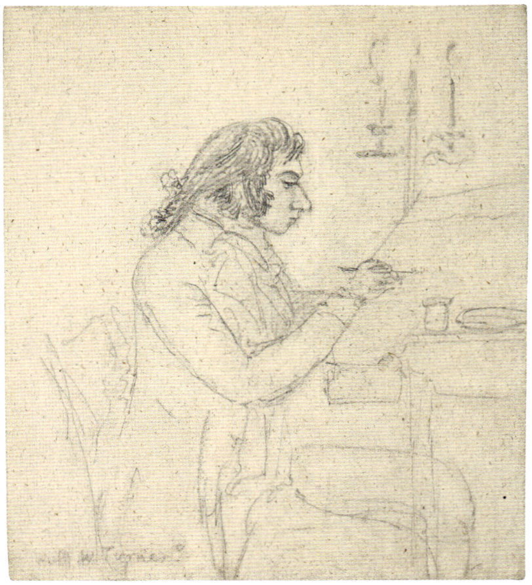

Fig. 1
DR THOMAS MONRO (1759–1833)
Turner Working at a Drawing Table, probably at Dr Monro's Home
c.1795–96
Pencil and wash on paper, 18.1 × 15.6 cm
Indianapolis Museum of Art (1996.155)
Bequest of Kurt F. Pantzer

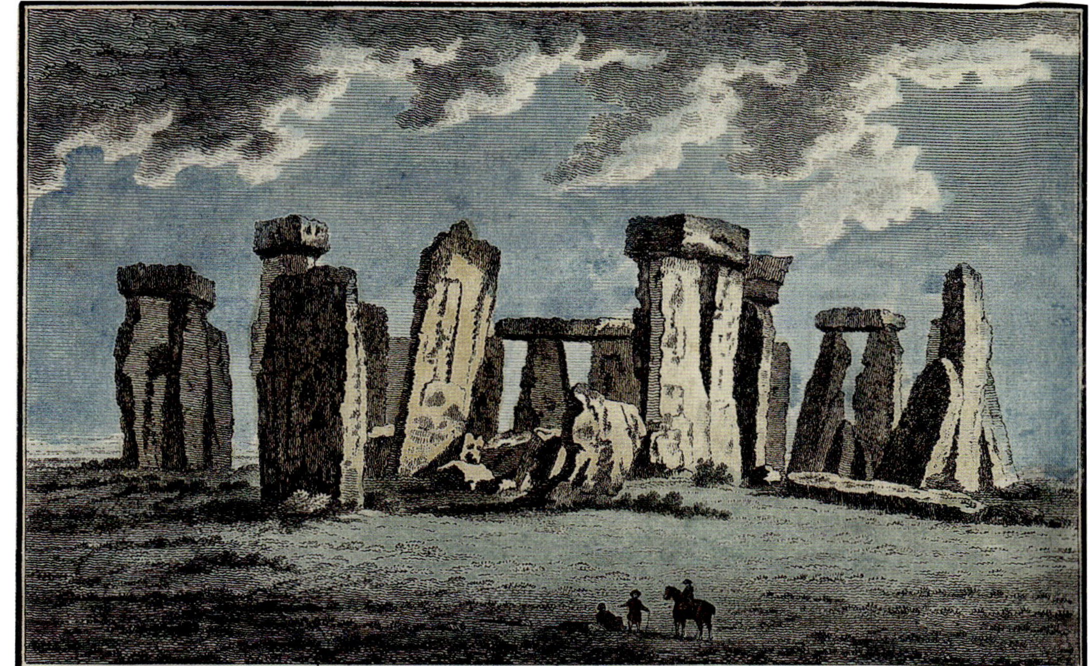

Fig. 2
WILLIAM TOMKINS PELTRO (1759–1840) engraving after THOMAS HOGG, possibly hand-coloured by TURNER
Stonehenge
1786
From Henry Boswell, *Historical Descriptions of New and Elegant Picturesque Views of the Antiquities of England and Wales, &c*, 1786
Hounslow Library

schools involved working as a draughtsman with the architects William Porden (*c.*1755–1822) and Thomas Hardwick (1752–1829), and later with the topographical artist Thomas Malton Jr (*c.*1751/2–1804).[2] As well as learning the ability to present architectural ideas vividly and tangibly on paper, within a professional framework, the connections with these men, and their clients, can only have advanced Turner's reputation. While his extraordinary ability to define complicated interlocking spaces in his watercolours was its own recommendation, it clearly won him influential friends, and it has perhaps been overlooked that the discipline of this early architectural work proved to be the foundation for his later endeavours. Moreover, as this book will demonstrate, the work he did in and around Salisbury contributed materially to his first success among his peers.

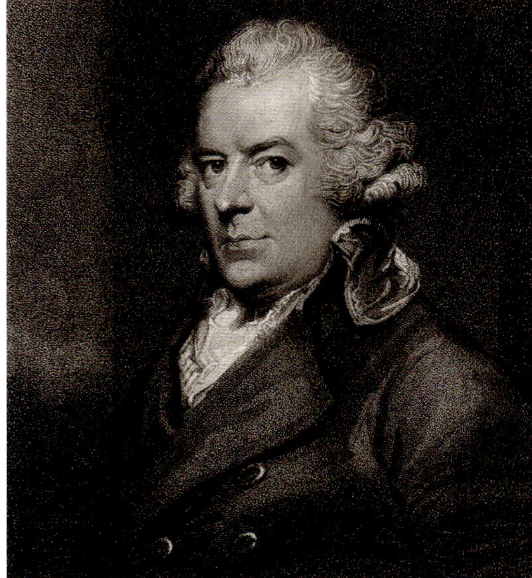

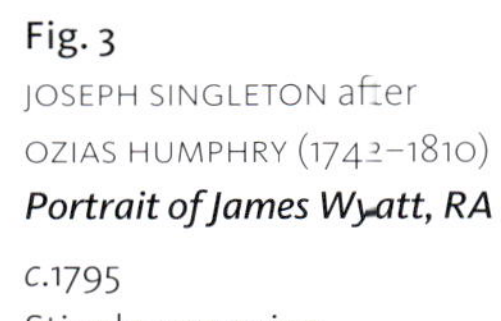
Fig. 3
JOSEPH SINGLETON after OZIAS HUMPHRY (1742–1810)
Portrait of James Wyatt, RA
*c.*1795
Stipple engraving, 15.4 × 10.8 cm
National Portrait Gallery

It may have been the link with Porden that provided the means by which Turner eventually became acquainted with James Wyatt (1746–1813; fig. 3), who had been Porden's teacher and was one of the most prolific and sought-after architects in Britain.[3] Turner recorded many of Wyatt's buildings, but given their significance in their own right, this may be coincidental. Unfortunately, the loss of the architect's correspondence and his office's paperwork hinders a true sense of whether there was a working relationship; even so, they ultimately shared many mutual friends and patrons, most notably William Beckford of Fonthill (see p. 79).[4] In addition to his designs for town houses and country mansions, Wyatt worked for King George III at Windsor, which added to his contemporary prestige. But it was his restorations – some would describe them more politely as interventions – to the fabric of several of the country's cathedrals that earned him a lasting notoriety as 'The Destroyer', or 'The Vandal'.[5] His proposals for Durham in 1795–97, for example, were vigorously challenged at the Society of Antiquaries, frustrating his attempt to demolish features like the Galilee Chapel, or to add an octagon and spire to the central tower.[6] Temperamentally Wyatt was a classicist, who absorbed the aesthetics and details of gothic only in mid-career. He was, nevertheless, ahead of the prevailing taste, which still found the battered and neglected remains of gothic architecture crude or barbaric, and in need of being tidied up. As recently as 1771 Tobias Smollett had written that cathedral architecture was:

> displeasing to the eye of every man who has any idea of propriety and proportion, even though he be ignorant of architecture as a science; and the long slender spire puts one in mind of a criminal impaled, with a sharp stake rising up through his shoulder. … I would vote for their being distinct from the body of the church, because they serve only to make the pile more barbarous, or Saracenical.[7]

In spite of such opinions, a concern for a fuller understanding of earlier buildings was established and grew in the eighteenth century to encompass sympathetic repairs and attempts at preservation. These concerns were characteristic of the arcane enquiries of antiquarians, whose requirement in a drawing of any subject was for precision in its record of appearances; but the appreciation of the past was also popularised in picturesque, and therefore essentially artful, depictions of ruined abbeys and castles. At Somerset House in London both appetites could be appeased because the Royal Academy and the Society of Antiquaries were housed in adjacent rooms. Inevitably there must have been some overlap between the two bodies. The Wiltshire collector and antiquarian Sir Richard Colt Hoare (fig. 15), for example, had been elected a fellow of the Society in 1792, but was also alert to developments in contemporary art.

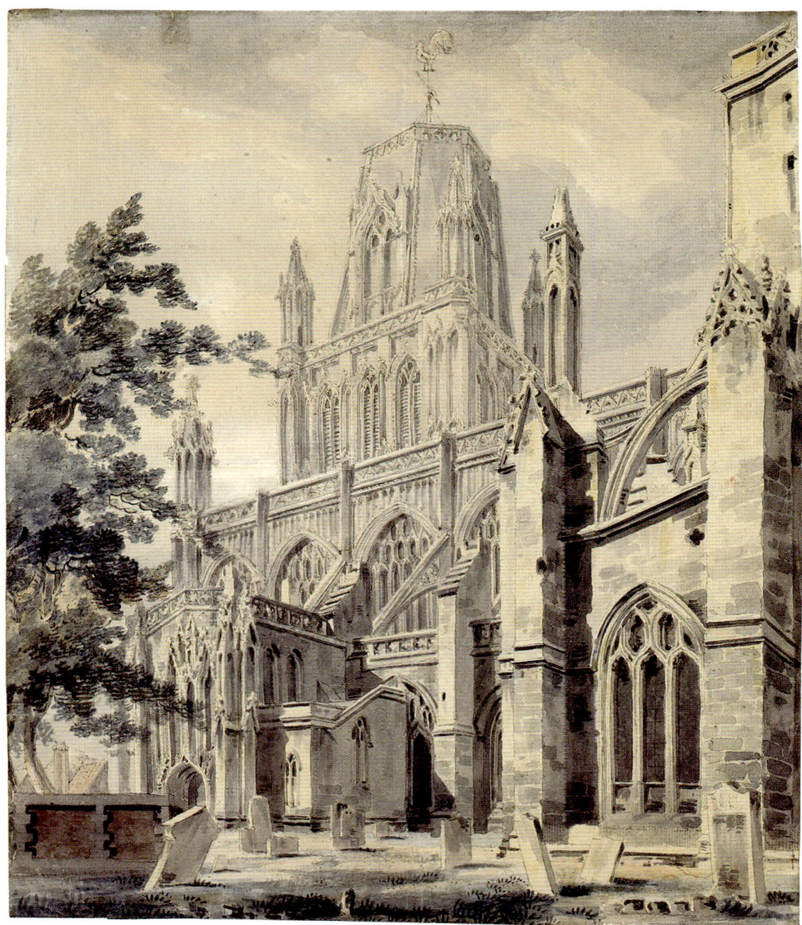

Fig. 4
South Porch of St Mary Redcliffe, Bristol
1791–92
Pen, brown ink and watercolour, 35.6 × 29.8 cm
City Museum and Art Gallery, Bristol (K347; W16)

As a consequence of all of these factors, a market grew up for images that addressed this fundamentally patriotic interest. Boswell's published sequence of picturesque views has already been mentioned, but it had been preceded by Francis Grose's six-volume work, *The Antiquities of England and Wales* (1772–76, 1777–87). Many subsequent projects focused on individual counties or building types, such as James Moore's *Monastic Remains and Ancient Castles in England and Wales* (1791), which was based on designs by Edward Dayes (1763–1804).

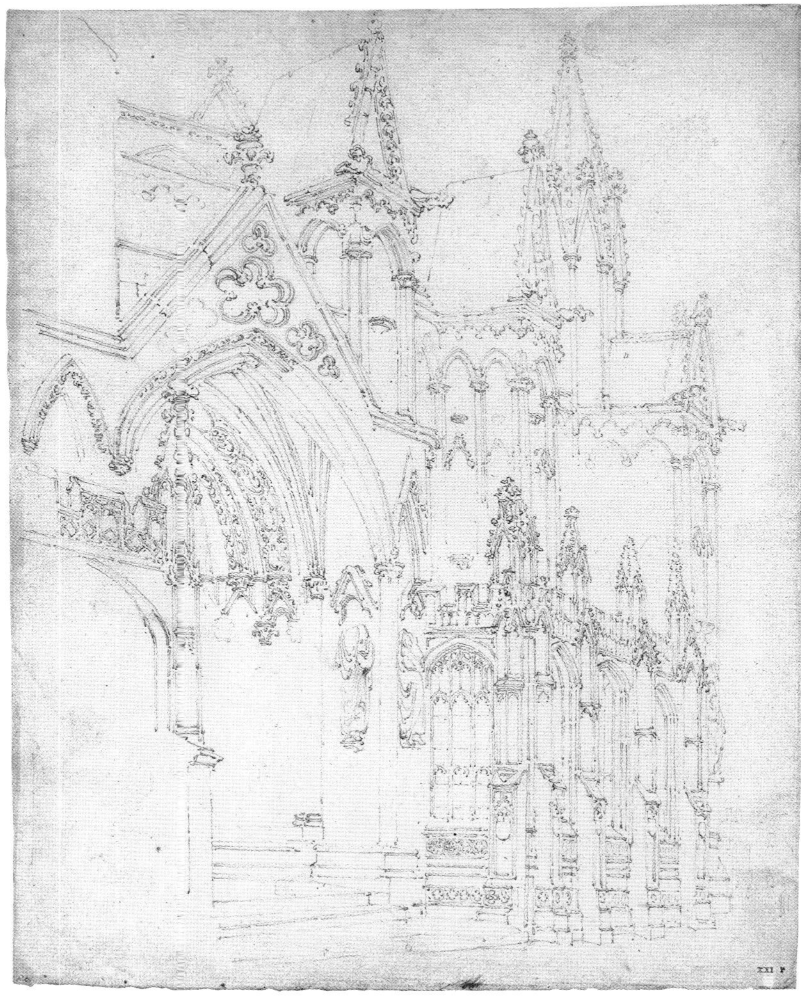

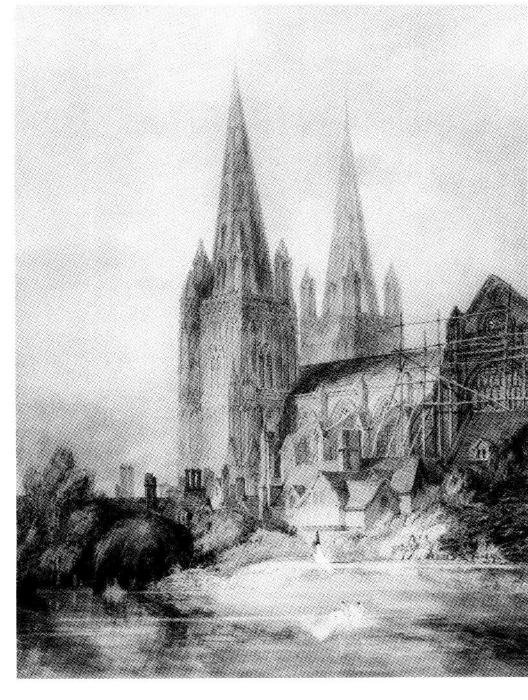

Fig. 5
Lincoln Cathedral: the South-East Porch with the Chantry Chapel of Bishop Russell (study for ***'St Hughe's the Burgundian's Porch at Lincoln Cathedral', exhibited RA 1795)***
1794
Pencil on paper,
27.7 × 21.4 cm
Tate (D00343 / TB XXI P)

Fig. 6
Lichfield Cathedral from the Minster Pool
1794
Watercolour,
30.8 × 22.5 cm
Private collection (W80)

At the outset of his career, Turner would have been aware of these bodies of images and they shaped his approach as he gained in proficiency as a draughtsman. His earliest tours from London took him to stay with friends of his father's in Bristol, and while there, as well as scrambling over the rocks of the Avon gorge, he composed challenging views of the cathedral and St Mary Redcliffe (fig. 4).[8] In these watercolours the buildings are studied from low vantage points that exaggerate individual details in relation to the whole, even while being factually correct.

The charming gaucheness of these adolescent efforts was rapidly surpassed, so that by the time Turner made an extensive tour of the Midlands in 1794, he was much more accomplished in his mark-making and able to instil a taut, purposeful quality to his line (fig. 5). His route that year took him to sites popular with artists in north Wales, like Valle Crucis, but its essential focus seems to have been the cathedrals of Lichfield, Lincoln, Peterborough and Ely, with a coda in the fan-vaulted splendour of King's College Chapel in Cambridge. At Lichfield his sketch, and the resulting watercolour, of the south side of the cathedral includes the scaffolding then in place (fig. 6). This was part of Wyatt's upgrade of the building, which entailed adding a pair of buttresses to the south transept. A year earlier Turner had seen Wyatt's revisions to the nave and west front at Hereford, so he would have been well aware of the gathering controversies about such improvements.

At Ely there were comparable recent changes and additions, involving a new octagon and the organ screen (or *pulpitum*), this time by James Essex (1722–1784), all of which Turner transcribed on a large sheet in pencil in his most

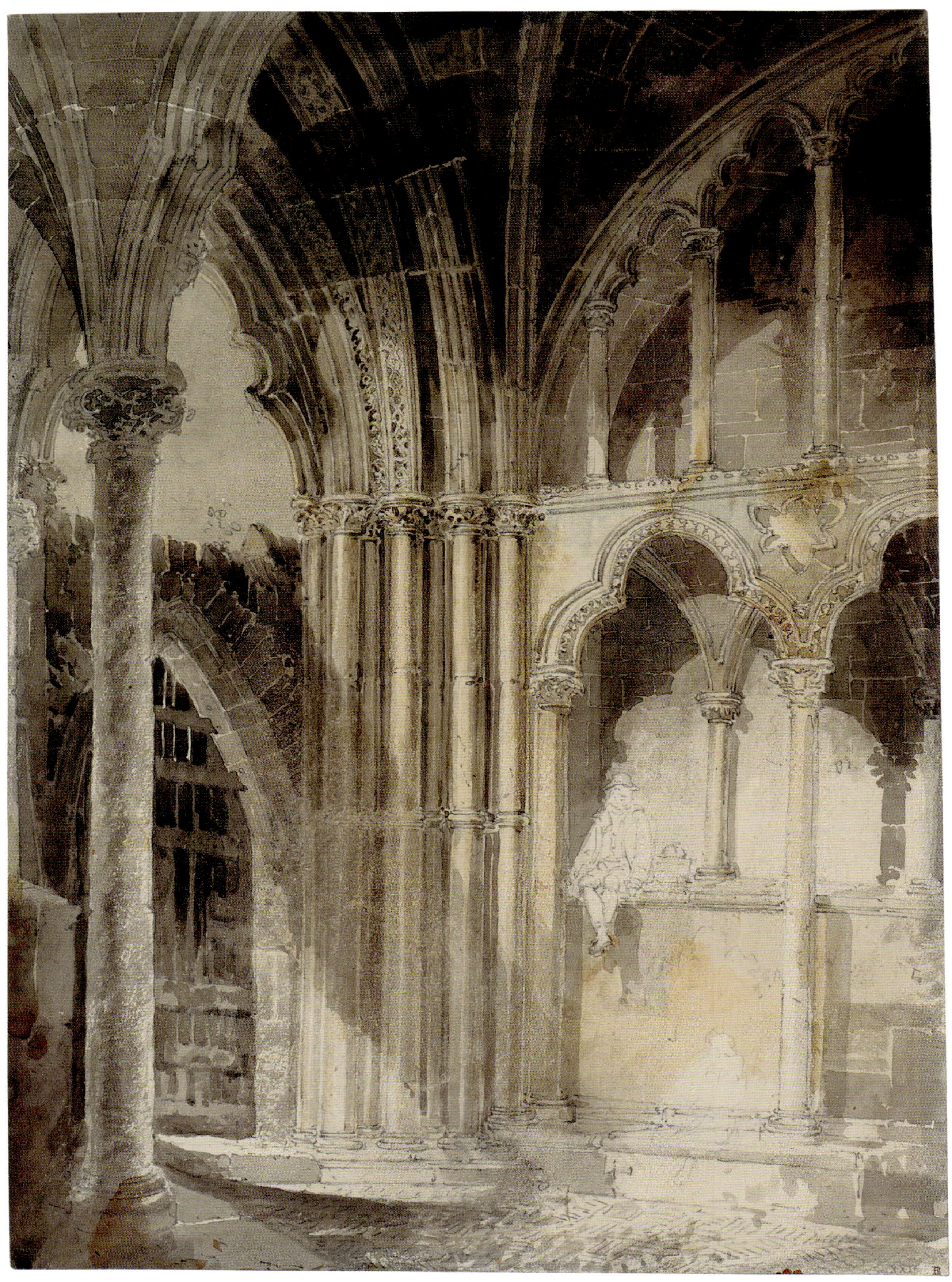

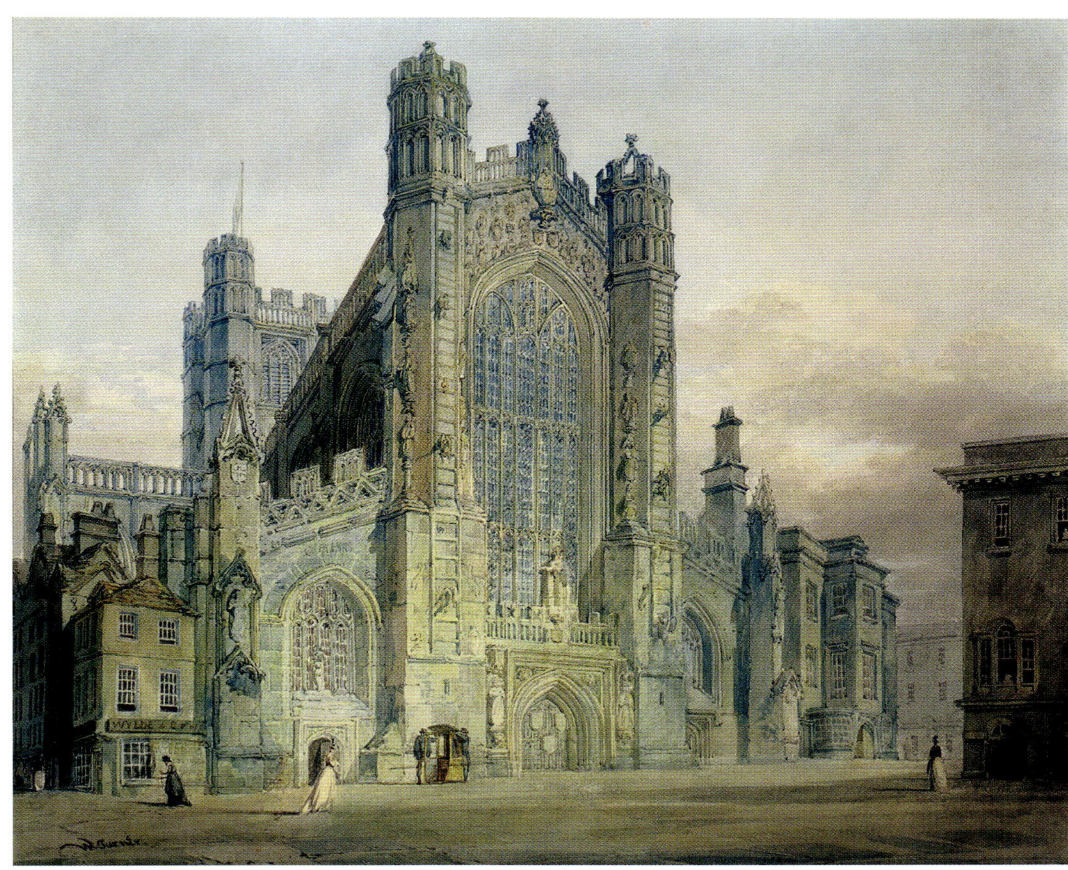

Fig. 8
West Front of Bath Abbey
Exhibited RA 1796
Watercolour, 23.5 × 23. cm
Victoria Art Gallery, Bath
(W145)

astounding depiction of a soaring cathedral interior to date.[9] Another of Turner's views of Ely Cathedral shows the Galilee Porch (fig. 7). The strong lighting falling across the walls adds a drama to what is otherwise a meticulous antiquarian record. To the left it is possible to see the unusual outer portal, which had survived till then in its original form, although evidently in a dilapidated state. By 1801 Wyatt was employed at the cathedral and he oversaw many changes to the Galilee, which resulted in the loss of the portal and other features recorded by Turner.[10]

Turner would next encounter Wyatt's work in the cathedral at Salisbury in 1795. As part of his streamlining of the building, the architect had controversially removed the medieval bell-tower to the north, as well as two porches and a couple of the chantry chapels (see fig. 35 and p. 184); objections to his methods were then a matter of animated discussion at the Society of Antiquaries.[11]

The year 1795 may not have been Turner's first stay in the city; he could easily have broken his journeys there while travelling westwards either in 1791 or 1792. However, no earlier sketches are known to survive. A couple of months before arriving in Salisbury in 1795, he had exhibited two views of Lincoln Cathedral, one of Peterborough and a depiction of the interior of King's College, Cambridge.[12] The success of these watercolours no doubt encouraged him to focus on similar subjects during his travels that summer. At Bath, Wells, Llandaff, St David's, Hereford, Gloucester, Winchester and Salisbury, Turner created very precise outline studies of each cathedral (or abbey), concentrating on the architecture of the west front in almost all cases (figs 8–10).[13] It is as if he was undertaking his own comparative analysis of the unique character of each building. He gave full reign to differences in stone type or surface detail in the watercolours he made shortly afterwards of Wells and Bath, and for each he had selected viewpoints that allowed him to showcase his improving skills in perspective.

At Salisbury, however, his pencil sketches of the façade were less complete than at the other

OPPOSITE: **Fig. 7**
The Interior of the Galilee Porch, Ely Cathedral
1794
Pencil and watercolour,
27.1 × 19.5 cm
Tate (D00358 / TB XXI E)

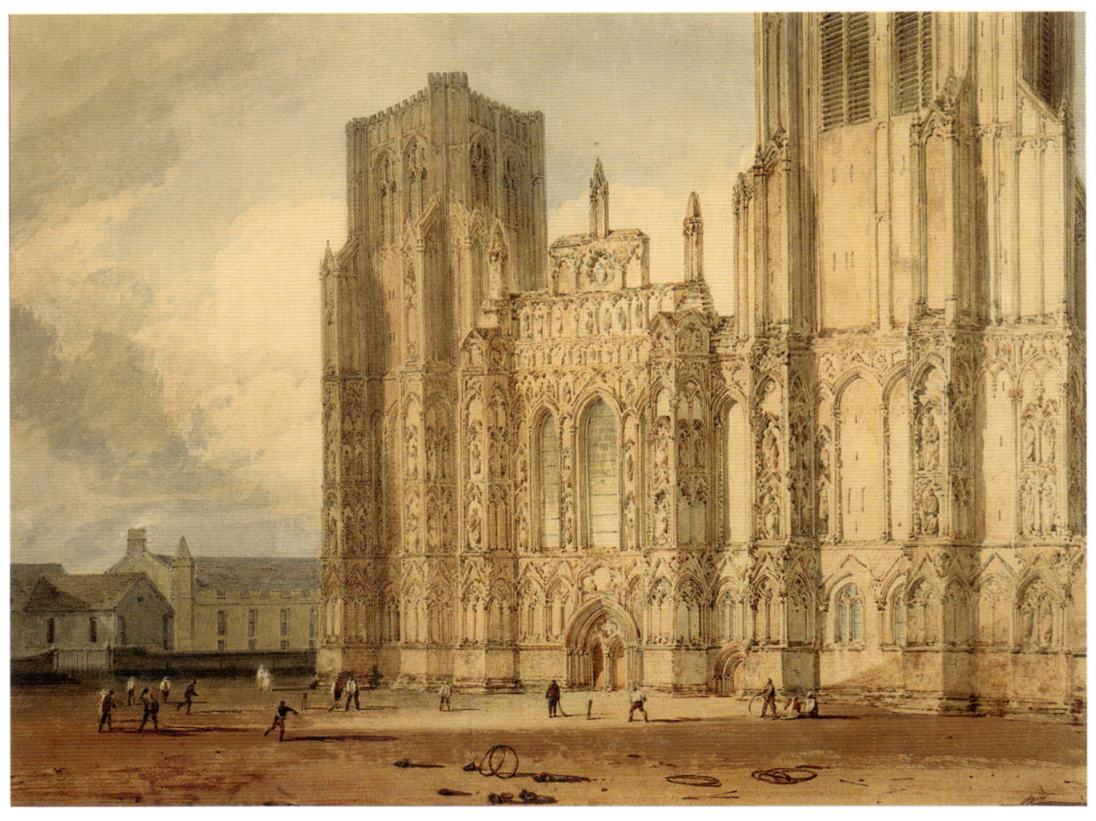

Fig. 9
West Front of Wells Cathedral
c.1795
Watercolour, 41.3 × 54 cm
Lady Lever Art Gallery, Port Sunlight (W134)

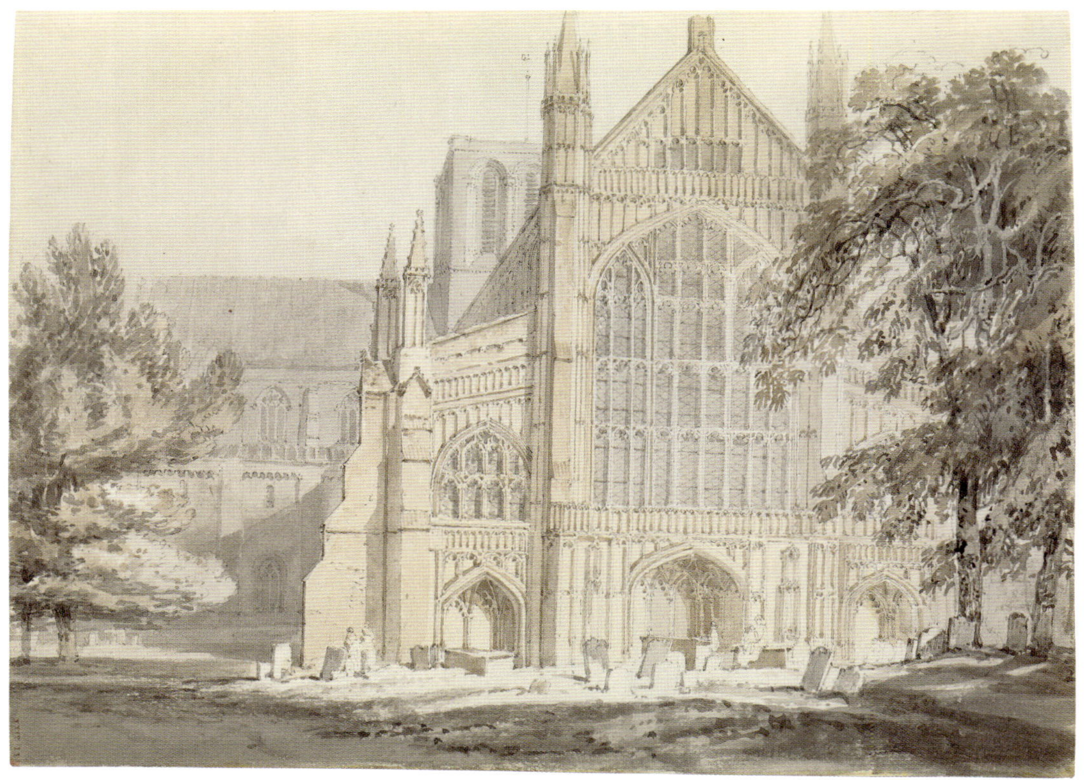

Fig. 10
The West Front of Winchester Cathedral
1795
Pencil and watercolour, 20.4 × 26.4 cm
From the 'Isle of Wight' sketchbook
Tate (D00417 / TB XXIV 11)

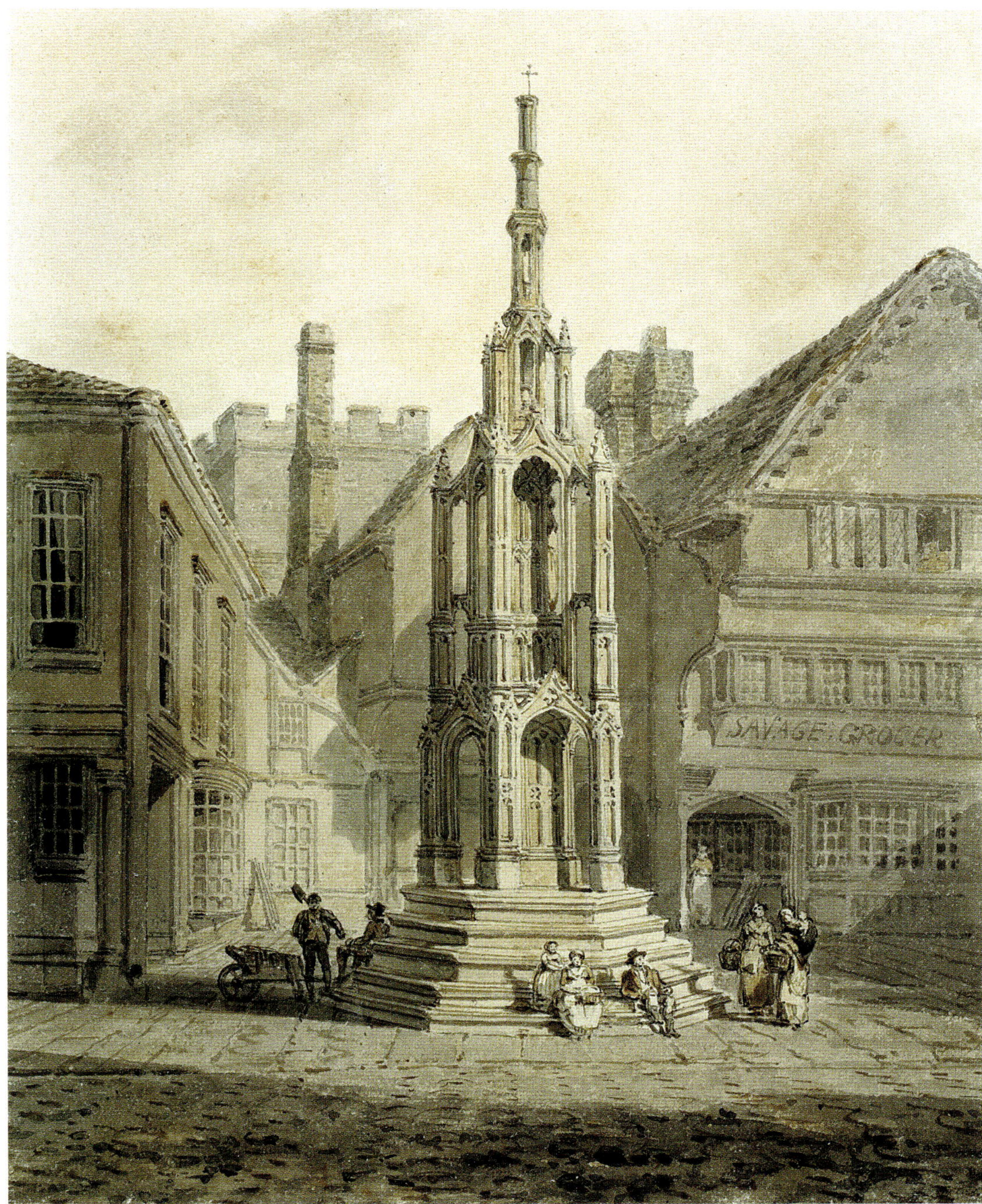

Fig. 11
The Butter Cross, Winchester
1795
Watercolour, 22.3 × 17.3 cm
Probably from the 'Isle of Wight' sketchbook
The Whitworth, The University of Manchester
(D.84-1892; W164)

cathedrals (see fig. 40). This can be attributed to a recognition that, where there was symmetry, it saved time to record a part of a pattern only once. It is a habit that comes from experience, when time is short, and is noticeably different from his practice elsewhere that year.[14] This development has a bearing on the order in which the two large sketchbooks that Turner filled in 1795 were used, confirming that the Salisbury scenes in the 'Isle of Wight' sketchbook were made *after* the more elaborate cathedral studies in the 'South Wales' sketchbook.[15]

Turner's round trip from Bristol through Wales took at least three weeks, to judge from the number of inns he highlighted in the itinerary of his planned route. The same notes indicate that after re-crossing the Severn he intended to head back from Bristol via Salisbury.[16] However, following a detour to Hereford and then slightly north to Hampton Court, the country home of

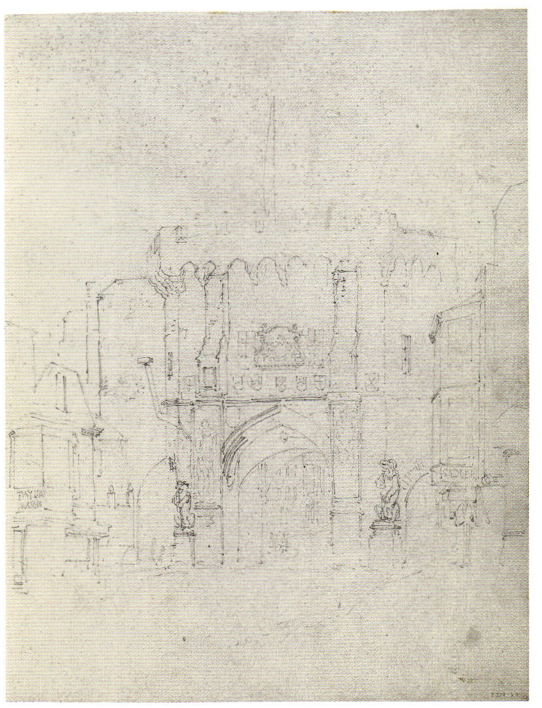

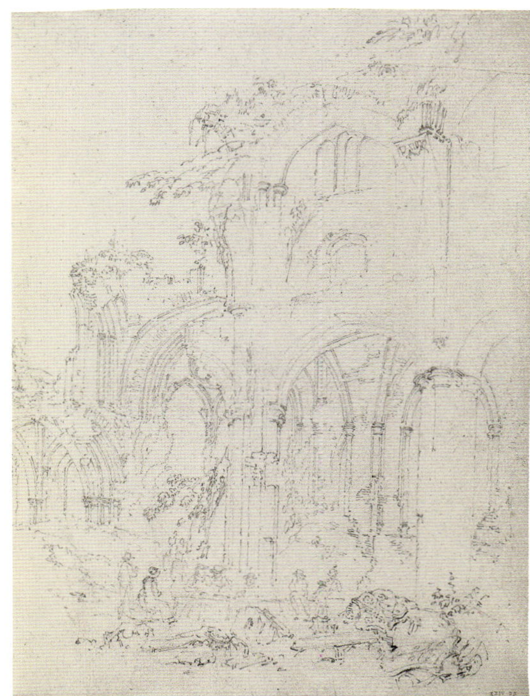

Fig. 12
The Bargate, Southampton
1795
Pencil, 26.3 × 20.4 cm
From the 'Isle of Wight' sketchbook
Tate (D00416 / TB XXIV 10)

Fig. 13
Netley Abbey: The Interior of the Ruins
1795
Pencil, 26.4 × 20.4 cm
From the 'Isle of Wight' sketchbook
Tate (D00430 / TB XXIV 23)

Viscount Malden (1757–1829), Turner decided to abandon his original idea of repeating the picturesque voyage down the Wye from Chepstow. Instead, he cut across to Gloucester and from there, with a third of his sketchbook still unused, he returned to London, via Oxford, where he sketched Christ Church.

How soon afterwards he returned to southern England is not documented, but the trees that Turner recorded throughout the 'Isle of Wight' sketchbook are in full summer growth. Therefore, the visit is most likely to have taken place in either July or August. The details of the excursion to Wiltshire, Hampshire, and the Isle of Wight will be considered in due course (see figs 11–13 and Chapter 7). For present purposes, Turner's time in Winchester and Salisbury in 1795 enabled him to resume his cathedral studies and probably also brought him into the orbit of Colt Hoare, who lived less than 30 miles from Salisbury at Stourhead. The art collection there, especially works by Rembrandt and Piranesi, seems to have influenced some of the pictures that Turner developed from his field notes over the winter, most obviously the celebrated *Fishermen at Sea* (1796, Tate), which blends his recollections of the Isle of Wight with the effects in Rembrandt's moonlit picture (fig. 20).[17]

Another of his finest exhibits in 1796 was a view of the interior of Westminster Abbey (fig. 14). This is a stunning tour de force of ingenuity and dexterity, combining the plunging perspective on the left with intersections across and through the picture plane that heighten the interplay of light and shade, while also lending visual drama to the rich variety of architectural styles. Turner was evidently satisfied with his achievement here, and instead of merely adding his signature in the foreground, as he sometimes did, he inscribed his name on one of the tomb slabs. It is both a humorous and a subversive gesture that reveals the ambitions of the artist, undaunted by his modest background, to be ultimately worthy of being accorded such a distinguished burial place.

Even though he was unable to charge much for this impressive watercolour at this stage of his career, as a demonstration of his abilities it had done the trick. Before a year was over he had won important commissions from Edward Lascelles (by then the purchaser of the Westminster subject[18]) for depictions of Harewood House, and he was also at work for Colt Hoare on a series of watercolours of Salisbury and its cathedral.

Fig. 14
St Erasmus in Bishop Islip's Chapel, Westminster Abbey
Exhibited RA 1796
Watercolour, 54.6 × 39.8 cm
British Museum
(1958-7-12-402; W138)

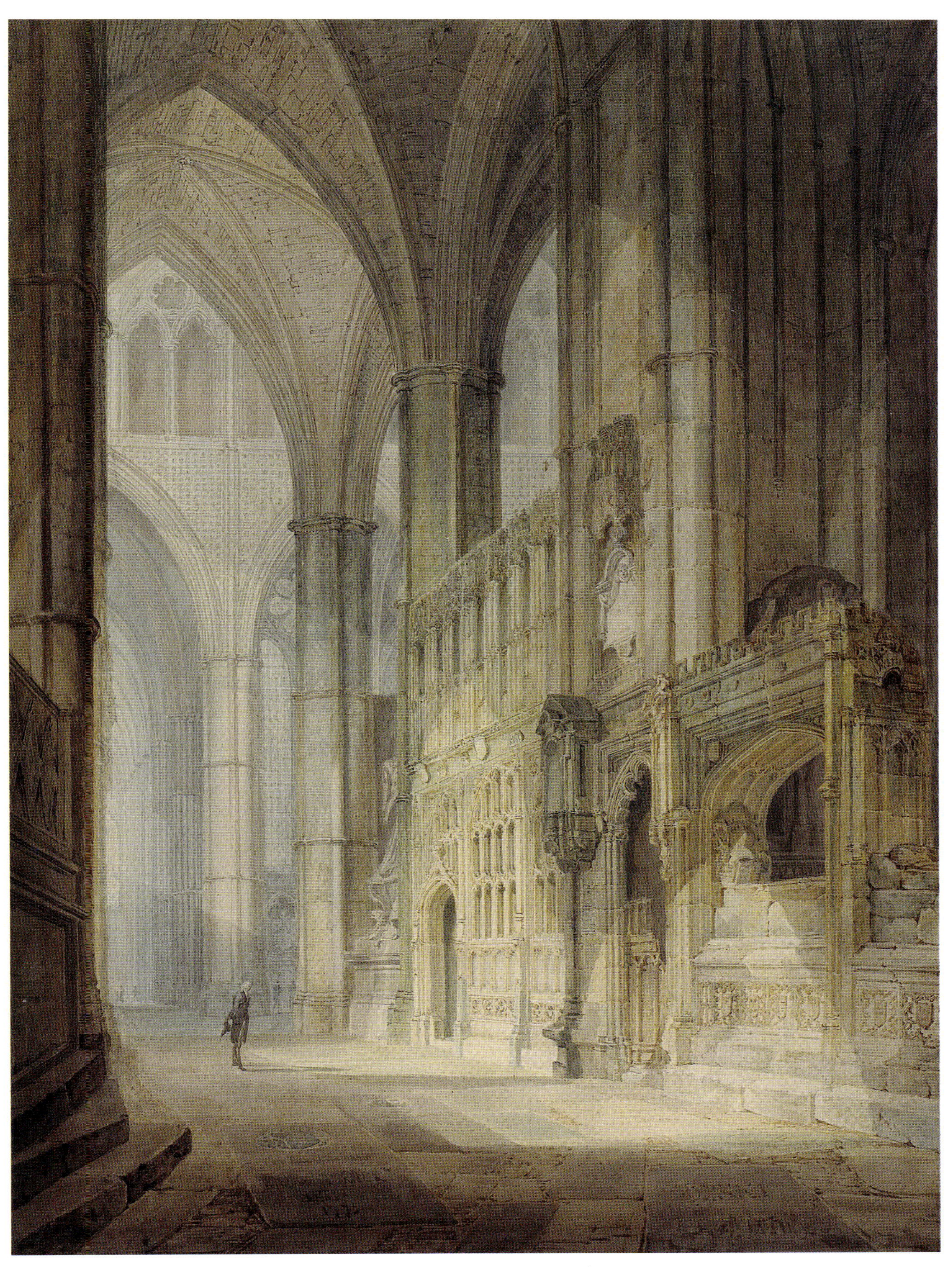

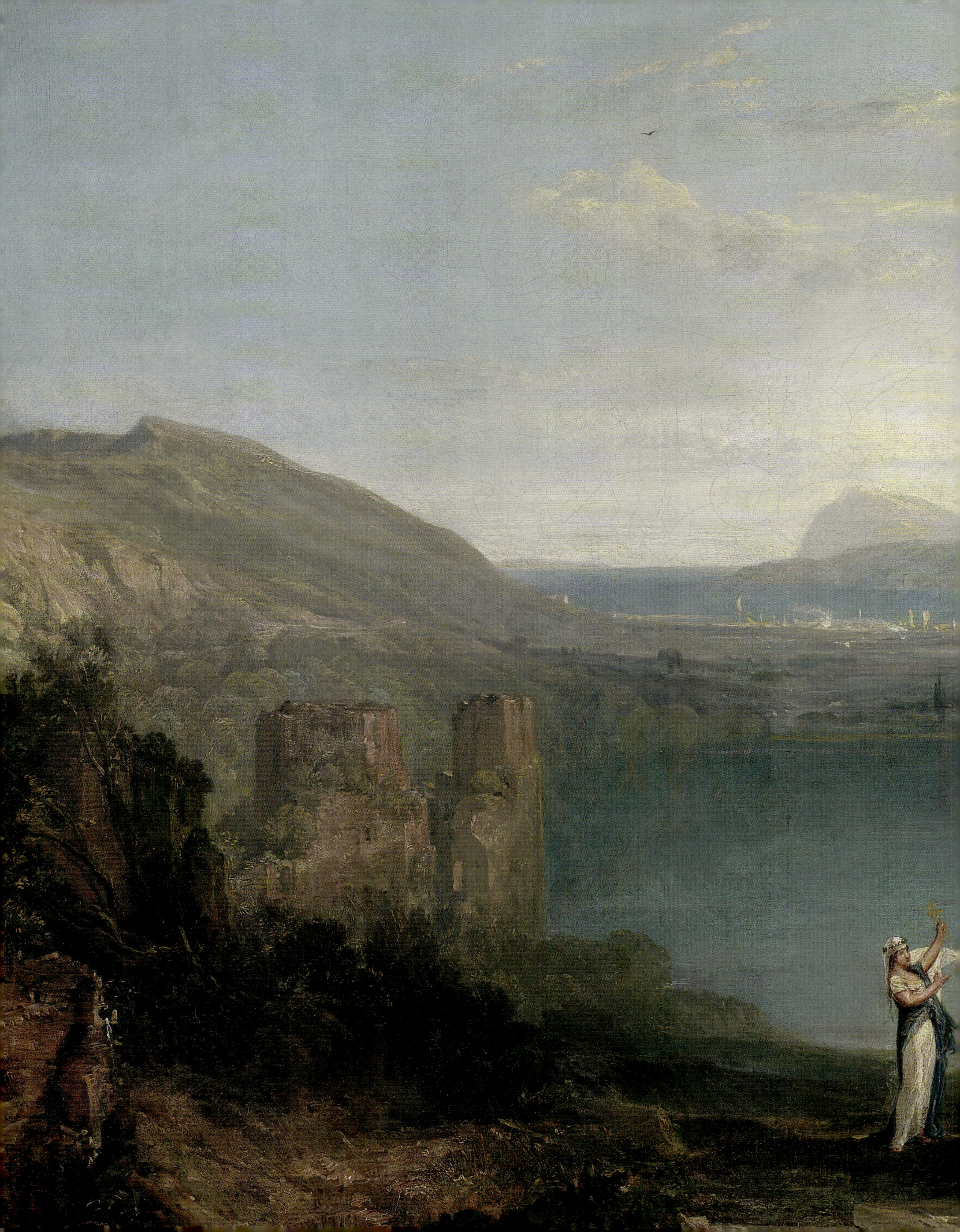

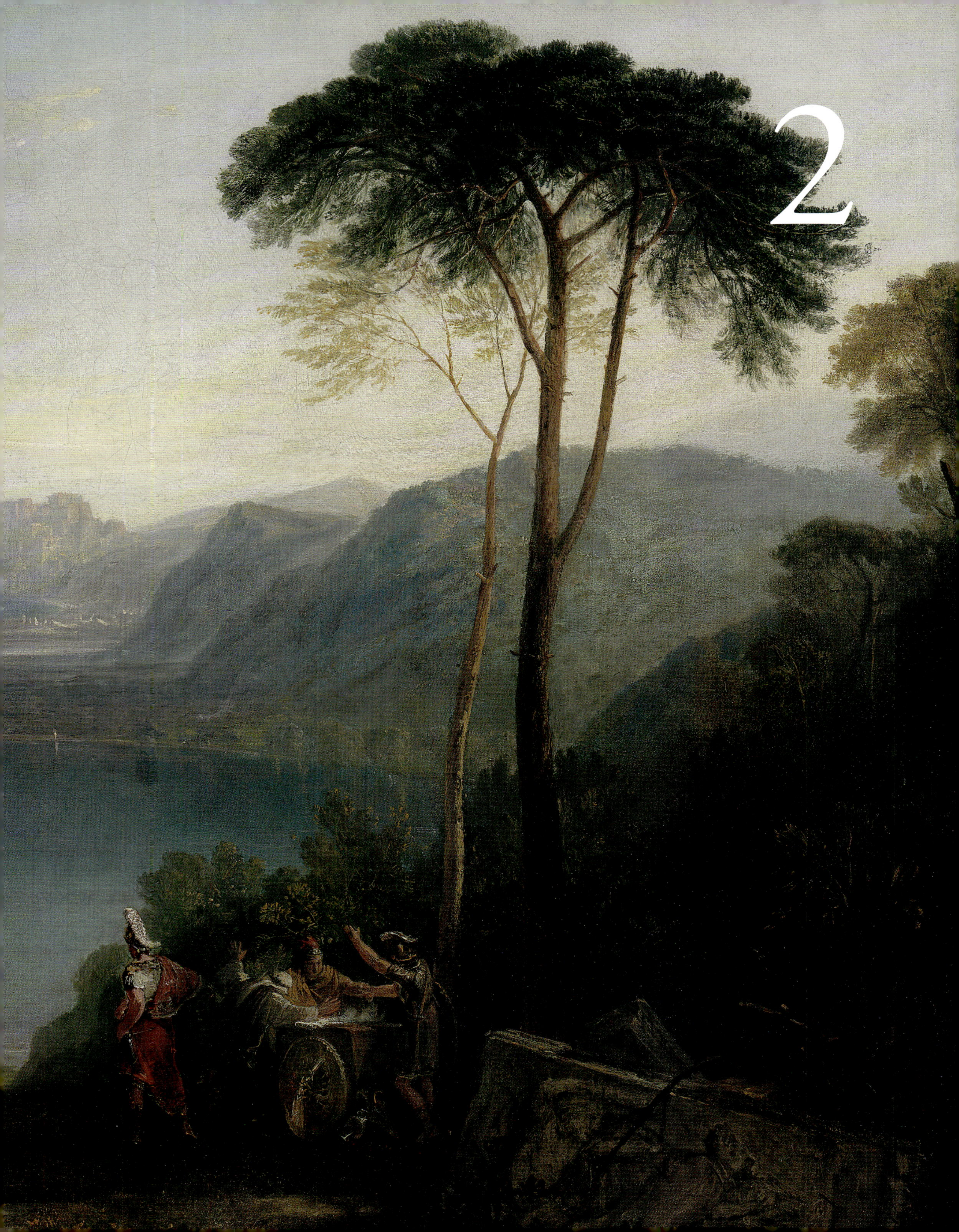
2

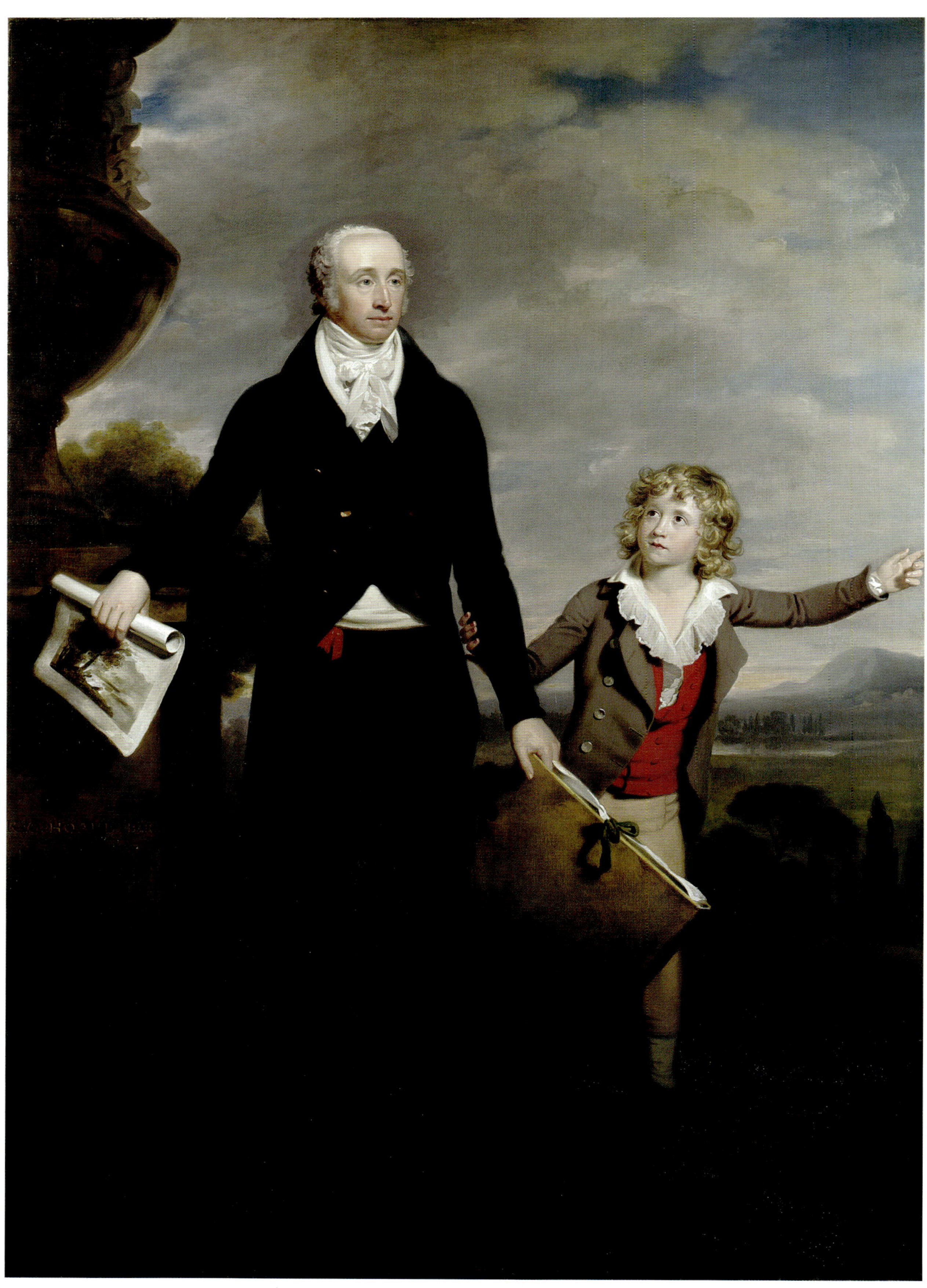

SIR RICHARD COLT HOARE AND STOURHEAD

PREVIOUS PAGES:
Lake Avernus: Aeneas and the Cumaean Sibyl (detail)
(see fig. 29)

Fig. 15
SAMUEL WOODFORDE
(1763–1817)
Sir Richard Colt Hoare (1758–1838) with Henry (1784–1836), his Son
1795–96
Oil on canvas, 254 × 168 cm
Stourhead, National Trust

Fig. 16
LOUIS DUCROS (1748–1810)
The Valley of the Nera
c.1788–93
Watercolour and gouache, 78 × 118 cm Stourhead, National Trust

Sir Richard Colt Hoare (1758–1838) inherited the Stourhead estate when he was only 25. It was passed to him by his grandfather, Henry Hoare ('the Magnificent'), who from the 1740s onwards had created the celebrated Stourhead garden, with its serpentine lake, bordered by grottoes and temples, in the valley below the Wiltshire country house. The family's wealth came from the eponymously named private bank, founded in London in 1672. But rather than pursuing the family tradition, for which he had little aptitude, Colt Hoare was prevented from taking an active role in the running of the bank by his grandfather's decision to resign Stourhead in his favour. Accordingly, he was provided with the rents from the 11,000-acre estate, sometimes estimated at between £9,000 and £10,000 a year.[1]

In August 1785, just a month before his grandfather's death, Colt Hoare's wife of only two years died following a difficult childbirth, leaving him with one surviving son: Henry. Hester had been a vivacious counterpoint to his own earnest character and he was naturally devastated. So, as a distraction from his grief, he set out on a Grand Tour to Italy.

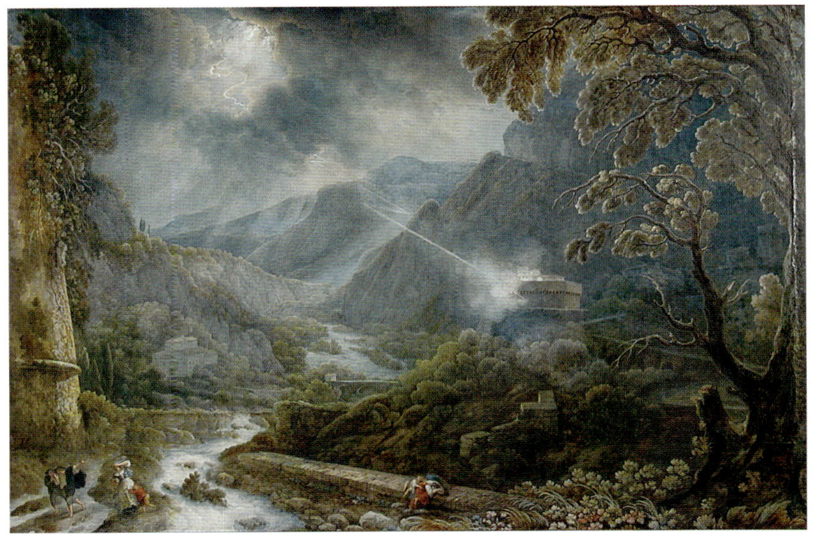

During this first spell away from Britain, he was primarily based in Rome and Naples, from where he explored the surrounding countryside for its historic associations. Repeatedly he sought out landscapes described in classical literature. While in Rome he inevitably encountered topographical artists, ready to provide views of favourite scenes. In addition to Jackob Philipp Hackert (1737–1807) and Carlo Labruzzi (1748–1817), there was the Swiss landscape painter Louis Ducros (1748–1810), from whom he would acquire at least 13 watercolours (fig. 16), and who offered guidance for Colt Hoare's own efforts at painting.[2] Colt Hoare also met up with Samuel Woodforde (fig. 15), then an aspiring artist from Somerset, whose studies at the Royal Academy and in Italy had been sponsored by Henry Hoare. Many years later, Woodforde would describe his travelling companion as a 'shy man to strangers, but liberal and steady in his attachments'.[3] He had grounds for being grateful to Colt Hoare, who continued Woodforde's annual stipend of £100 thereafter.[4]

Another important future connection came from Colt Hoare's meeting with Sir John Fleming Leicester (1762–1827), 5th Baronet and afterwards 1st Baron de Tabley. Leicester, too, enjoyed sketching during his travels and was later to become one of the foremost patrons of contemporary British art: he commissioned or acquired many of Turner's boldest works in the first decade of the nineteenth century.[5] Leicester was great friends with the Prince of Wales (later King George IV), then in his dissolute youth, so he must have introduced some animation into Colt Hoare's rather studious existence.

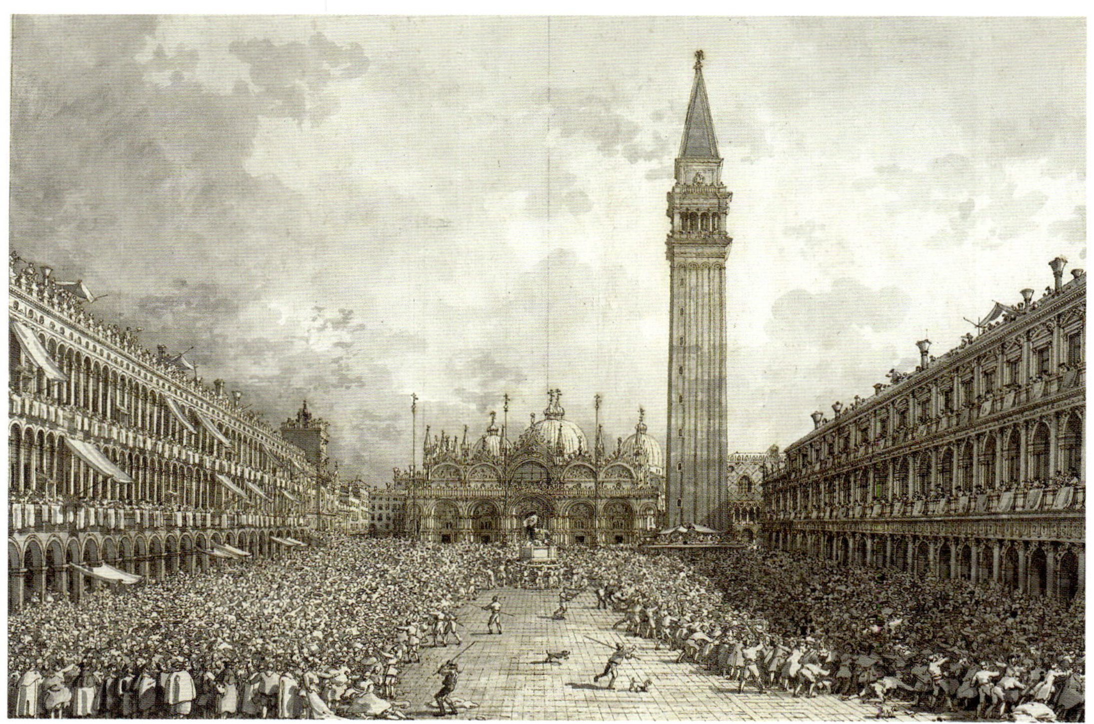

Fig. 17
CANALETTO
(GIOVANNI ANTONIO CANAL;
1697–1768)
The Doge Carried Around St Mark's Square, Venice, Before his Coronation
*c.*1763–66
Pen and brown ink with grey wash, heightened with white over black and red chalk, 37.9 × 55.2 cm
British Museum
(1910,0212.18)

Perhaps resisting such distractions, instead of accompanying Leicester to Venice for Carnevale, Colt Hoare went northwards to the Alps, with an unusual side trip to Barcelona, followed by another sojourn in Rome. Before heading home he spent two weeks in Venice, where he was fortunate in his discovery of a cache of ten drawings by Canaletto (fig. 17).

This first Italian tour came to an end in July 1787. Colt Hoare's return to Stourhead was followed a couple of months afterwards by the death of his father, which conferred on him the title of 2nd Baronet. But he was still restless and within a year he embarked again from Dover, staying abroad this time until the spread of the French Revolution made it difficult to continue in Italy.

On the way south in the summer of 1788 his route took him through the Netherlands and Germany, across to Prague and Vienna, and then down to Venice by November. Over the ensuing three years, he deepened his knowledge of Italy and became familiar with the kind of byways that were still neglected by other Grand Tourists. He lingered in Siena in 1789 to explore Etruscan settlements (an interest stimulated by the engravings of Piranesi); he toured the island of Elba; and also visited the Greek temples at Paestum. In 1790 he spent eight months in Sicily, with a side trip to Malta. As elsewhere, the sites that resonated most profoundly with him had links with ancient history, such as Mount Eryx in western Sicily, where Virgil had described Aeneas landing on his way to Italy.[6] In his later account of his time in Italy, Colt Hoare explained that 'every scene bears a classic character, and every district acquires double interest from the recollections it calls forth'.[7] The rich associations he enjoyed were similar to those that Turner would later embed in his pictures and were typical of poetic ideas of the period.[8]

By August 1791, the unsettled state of Europe meant that Colt Hoare was back at Stourhead, where he set to work restoring and simplifying his grandfather's garden. His travels in Italy had enriched his understanding of the underlying significance of the ornamental temples and their interrelationship, which had been conceived and positioned to evoke Aeneas's journey around the Mediterranean to found ancient Rome.[9] Colt Hoare was soon also adding rooms to the house in the form of the Library and the Picture Gallery in order to accommodate purchases made on his travels. Construction of the latter seems to have

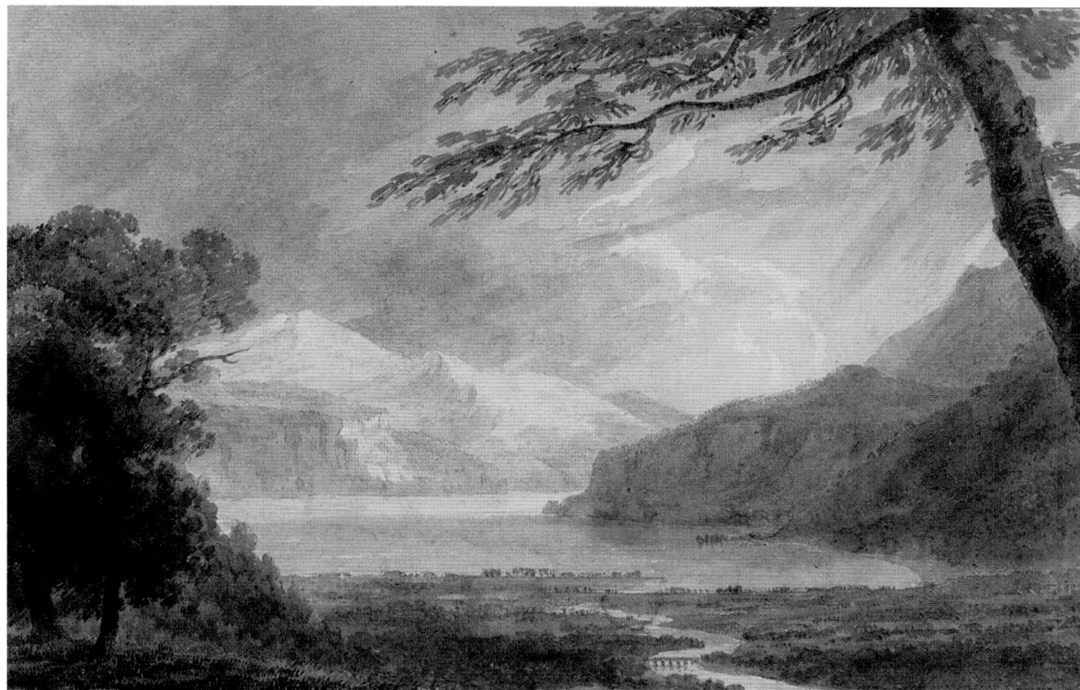

Fig. 18
JOHN ROBERT COZENS
(1752–1797)
Fluelen on the Lake of Lucerne
c.1777–79, or later
Pencil, watercolour and gouache, 32.2 × 43.3 cm
Tate (D36669 / TB CCCLXXX 20)

been under way by 1795, but the decoration and provision of fittings for both spaces continued until around 1805.[10]

This phase of rearranging his domestic setting coincided with the period of his most direct contact with Turner. Their respective positions in late eighteenth-century British society, combined with Colt Hoare's instinctive reserve, would have ensured that the relationship was one of patronage bestowed, rather than a friendship of equals.[11] At its start, if Turner did visit Stourhead during the summer of 1795, as seems very probable, he would have been only 20, nearly 17 years younger than the widely-travelled landowner. While members of the family invariably referred to the older man as 'Colt', the letters addressing him from Turner follow the deferential and more standard format of 'Sir Richard'.

How the connection between the two came about remains uncertain. Some scholars assert that Colt Hoare's friend Sir John Leicester was the means of the introduction.[12] However, he is not known to have purchased anything by Turner until after 1800 and no other link is documented prior to that. In fact, it is much more plausible that it was Colt Hoare who forged a link for Leicester.[13]

Other possible intermediaries range from Dr Thomas Monro or Viscount Malden, to the Wiltshire topographer John Britton. The first of these was physician at the Bridewell and Bethlem hospitals for the insane, a role in which he had apparently treated Colt Hoare's brother-in-law, George.[14] Dr Monro was also a collector of drawings by Old Masters and contemporary topographers, and between 1794 and 1798 Turner was a weekly guest at his home at Adelphi Terrace, near the Strand, London. There he was paid to copy drawings in the collection (see fig. 1), sometimes in collaboration with Thomas Girtin. Many of the designs were by John Robert Cozens, the innovative watercolour artist, whose frayed mental health had drawn him into Monro's custody by 1794. Colt Hoare, too, owned works by Cozens: some possibly commissioned directly, but most acquired from the artist's sale in 1805. He could have encountered Cozens in Bath or London in the early 1780s, or later between his two sojourns in Italy. Intriguingly, the view of Lake Lucerne by Cozens that Turner later owned was inscribed by Colt Hoare (fig. 18).[15] But in either case, there are insufficient grounds for viewing Monro or Cozens as the likely introduction between Colt Hoare and Turner.

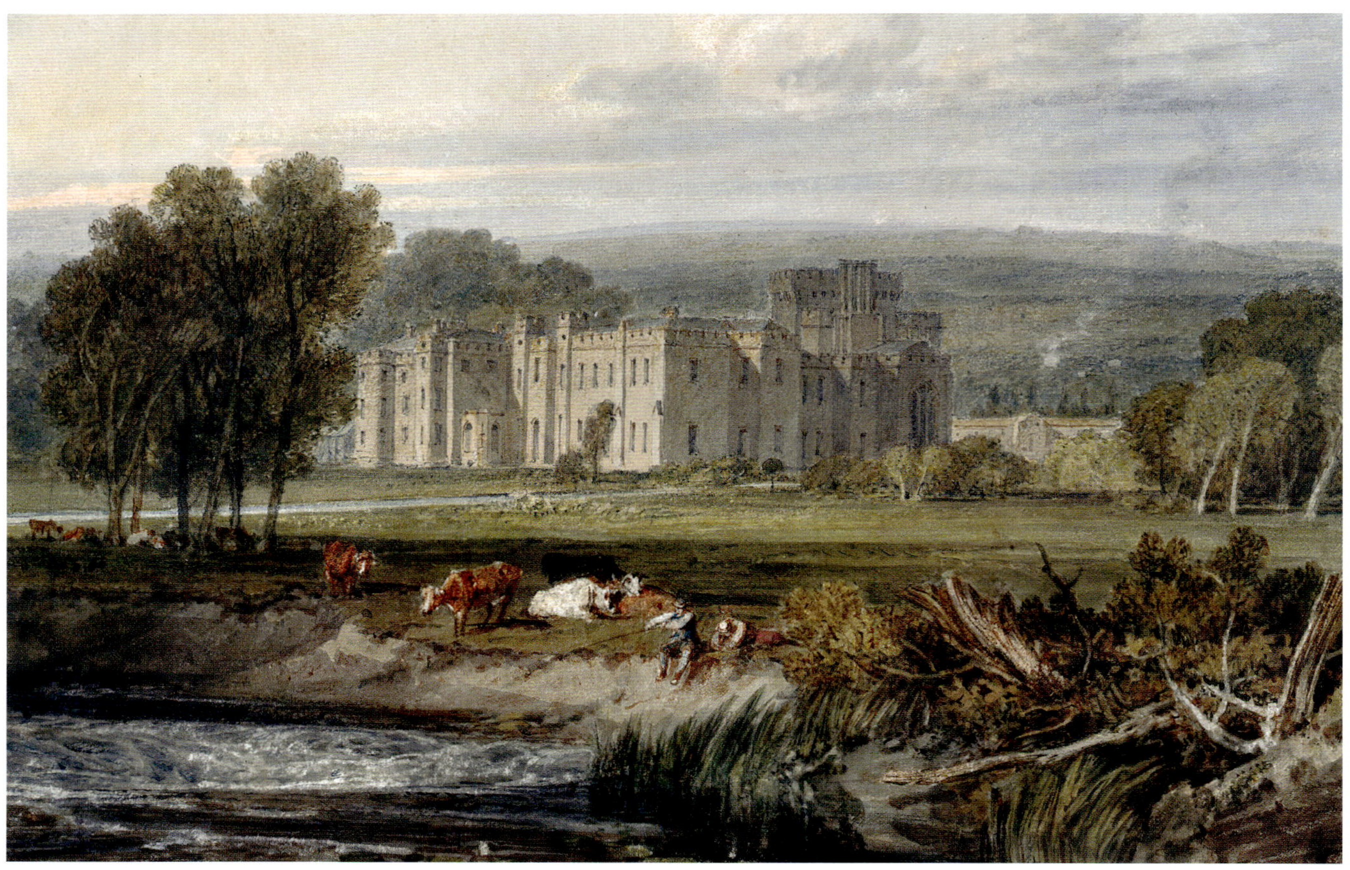

There are other overlaps among Turner's early collectors that point to George Capel-Coningsby, Viscount Malden, as potentially a more significant early patron than has been assumed. As we have seen, Turner visited his Herefordshire estate of Hampton Court at the end of the Welsh tour in 1795, making sketches for a set of five commissioned watercolours, which were developed over the following winter.[16] A list of 'Order'd Drawings' in the 'South Wales' sketchbook, containing the sketches made on the spot, includes a further commission for repetitions of two of the Hampton Court subjects.[17] These bear the name of 'Sir Richard Hoare' and this request has often been seen as the start of his patronage, seemingly taking place in 1795, while Turner was at Stourhead. Contradicting this conclusion, however, is the inscription itself, which was clearly written after the main group of orders was drawn up, indicating it arose later, but not when. Furthermore, although Malden may plausibly have encouraged Edward Lascelles Jr to acquire works by Turner in 1796–97,[18] nothing in the existing documentation supports the idea of there having been any contact between Colt Hoare and Malden at this time; quite the opposite. During a tour of Wales in June 1797 Colt Hoare paused at Hampton Court, evidently for the first time, and it is not even certain that he visited the house.[19] It might, nevertheless, be presumed that this experience was the stimulus for the commissioned works. However, an even later date for the origin of these watercolours is discussed below.

A final candidate as the conduit between Colt Hoare and Turner, perhaps the most improbable, should also be considered. This is the writer and artist John Britton (1771–1857), who had begun preparing his illustrated two-volume work, *The Beauties of Wiltshire* (1801), before 1796.[20] As a fellow topographer, he would have been aware of Turner's abilities and might just have recommended him to Colt Hoare, or passed on an introduction to his ambitious colleague. They certainly knew each other, although evidently

Fig. 19
Hampton Court, Herefordshire, from the South-East
*c.*1806
Watercolour, 20.3 × 30.5 cm
Yale Center for British Art, New Haven (W216)

an element of friction quickly grew up between them.[21] One anecdote, recorded after both men were dead, alleges that Britton surprised Turner by appearing in his studio unannounced, acting as an intermediary for Viscount Malden, who wanted to know how the drawings he had ordered were coming along.[22] Caught off guard, Turner is reported to have snapped, 'You shan't see 'em', and his blunt behaviour is explained as having been motivated by a fear that Britton was there chiefly to spy on his methods. The date of this incident is not given, but it might at first be assumed to refer to the winter of 1795–96, when Turner is known to have been working on the five watercolours of Hampton Court mentioned above (one of which is dated '1795').

Another possibility is that this encounter took place a few years afterwards, perhaps as late as 1800. By then Turner was struggling to keep up with orders he had taken on. Two of these were for Viscount Malden, who from March 1799 was known as the 5th Earl of Essex. Once again he had commissioned watercolour views of Hampton Court, following Turner's second visit there in 1798.[23] One of the pair was engraved in 1801 for a huge project that Britton oversaw in collaboration with Edward Wedlake Brayley: *The Beauties of England and Wales*. Britton's personal involvement with this concern, in tandem with the Earl's commission, gives this later date more weight as the probable origin of the comical narrative. So, while this conclusion diminishes the substance of the connection in 1795 between Turner, Malden and Colt Hoare, Britton was clearly a factor common to each of them.

Nevertheless, in the light of the uncertainties for each of these putative channels between Turner and Colt Hoare, the most obvious conclusion is that the patron simply introduced himself, possibly at the Royal Academy exhibition in the spring of 1795. Colt Hoare's experiences with artists in Italy meant that he was comfortable with interacting with creative individuals. Moreover, his desire to improve his abilities as an amateur artist would have led him to identify a new talent from whom he could benefit in ways similar to his painting studies with Ducros. But it is unlikely that the invitation he presumably extended to Turner to visit Stourhead constituted a formal arrangement, involving paid lessons, even though the mid-1790s was exactly the period when the young artist was most active as a drawing master.

Turner had already painted the country homes of various minor members of the gentry, but the experience of staying in such a building was still comparatively novel and exciting. Apart from the hope that a visit of this kind would generate work, another important attraction was the opportunity to study notable picture collections prior to the establishment of a public art gallery in London. Stourhead may not have been as richly endowed with as many genuine treasures as some of the houses Turner later frequented, but it clearly left a profound impression. One of the most potent images for him seems to have been Rembrandt's *Landscape with the Rest on the Flight into Egypt* (fig. 20). As well as having an almost immediate impact on the first oil Turner prepared for the Royal Academy – *Fishermen at Sea* – and some related scenes on panel, Rembrandt's magical combination of cool and warm light effects lodged itself among his favourite images, and became a reference point throughout his career. For example, over 15 years later, he described the painting passionately in one of his lectures as Professor of Perspective at the Royal

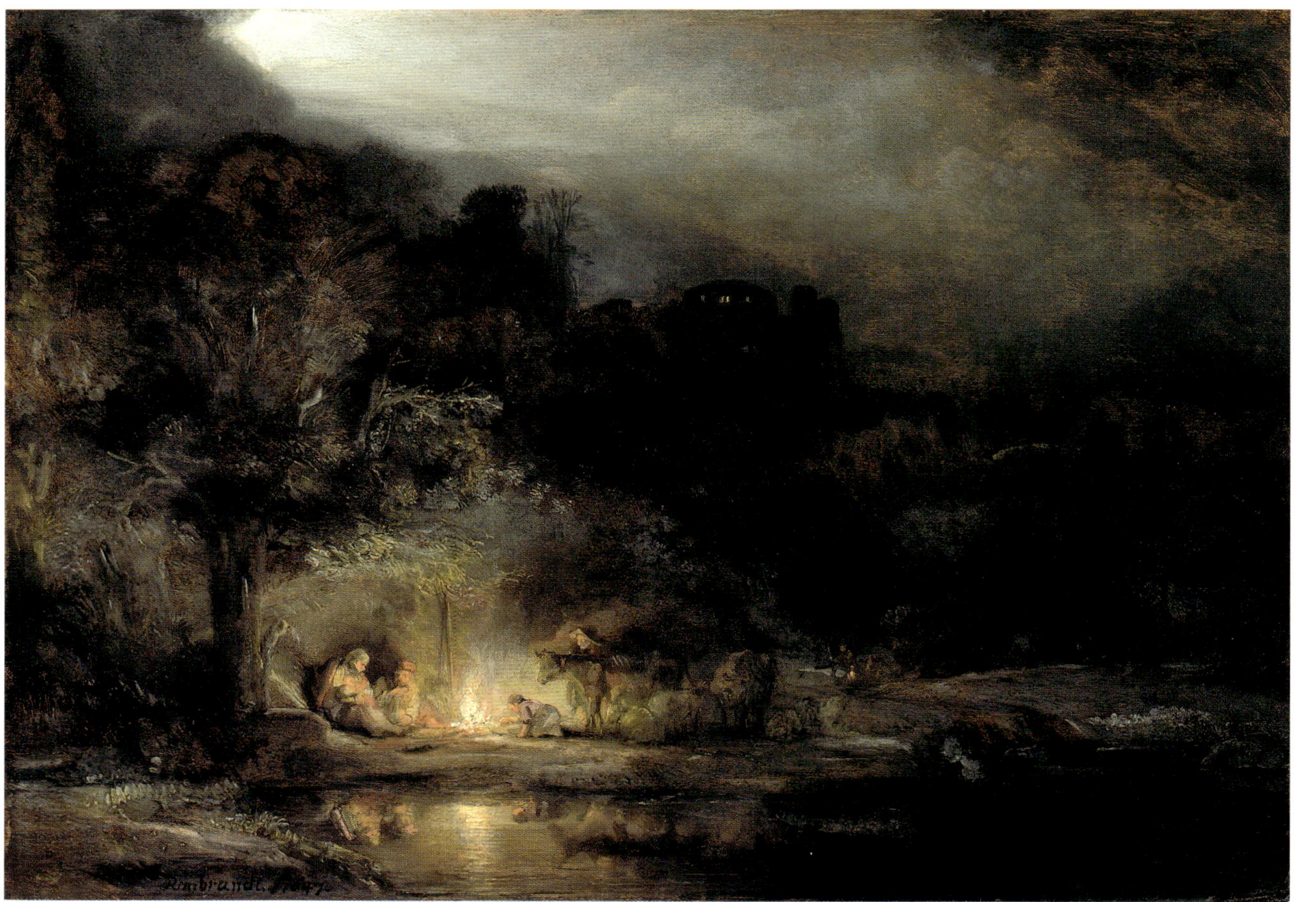

Fig. 20
REMBRANDT VAN RIJN
(1606–1669)
Landscape with the Rest on the Flight into Egypt
1647
Oil on wood, 34 × 48 cm
National Gallery of Ireland, Dublin (NGI.215)

Academy, claiming, 'In no picture have I seen that freshness, that negative quality of shade and colour that aerial perspective enwrapt in gloom ever attempted but by the daring hand of Rembrandt in his Holy Family Reposing.'[24]

A first attempt to assimilate Rembrandt's lessons can perhaps be detected in one of the watercolour views Turner made of the Stourhead garden, depicting the sun rising and its reflection (fig. 22). Although this and two related studies have been dated to 1798–99, the style and colouring is more consistent with the work Turner produced around 1795–96.[25] It seems that he planned two contrasting views of the lake: one looks across to the Pantheon from the Bristol Cross, with long afternoon shadows (fig. 23); the other surveys the landscape towards the previous viewpoint, with the Temple of Flora on the left, the stretch of the Lower Water, below the dam, running across the right side of the image (now known as Turner's Paddock), and rising above it the hillside on which the Temple of Apollo stands, though it is unseen here (fig. 22). Neither of these works is complete, although the latter is more fully developed and somewhat larger. The third work in the group (fig. 21) is a pared down version of the sunrise scene, set out merely as a grey and blue tonal structure. It is comparable in size to the Bristol Cross watercolour, but that design is more developed through the additional use of warm ochre and greens.

Curiously, there are no finished works related to these watercolours and no record of a commission. One possibility is that they were made during the visit as a means of demonstrating to Colt Hoare the 'scale practice' that Turner habitually employed when building up his images.[26] His method was to work across his sheets, applying successive shifts in tone to build up the image from light to dark, simultaneously retaining the white of his paper for highlights. The process was directly comparable to that he was deploying for the copies he created at Dr Monro's at this time. An illustrative sequence would have

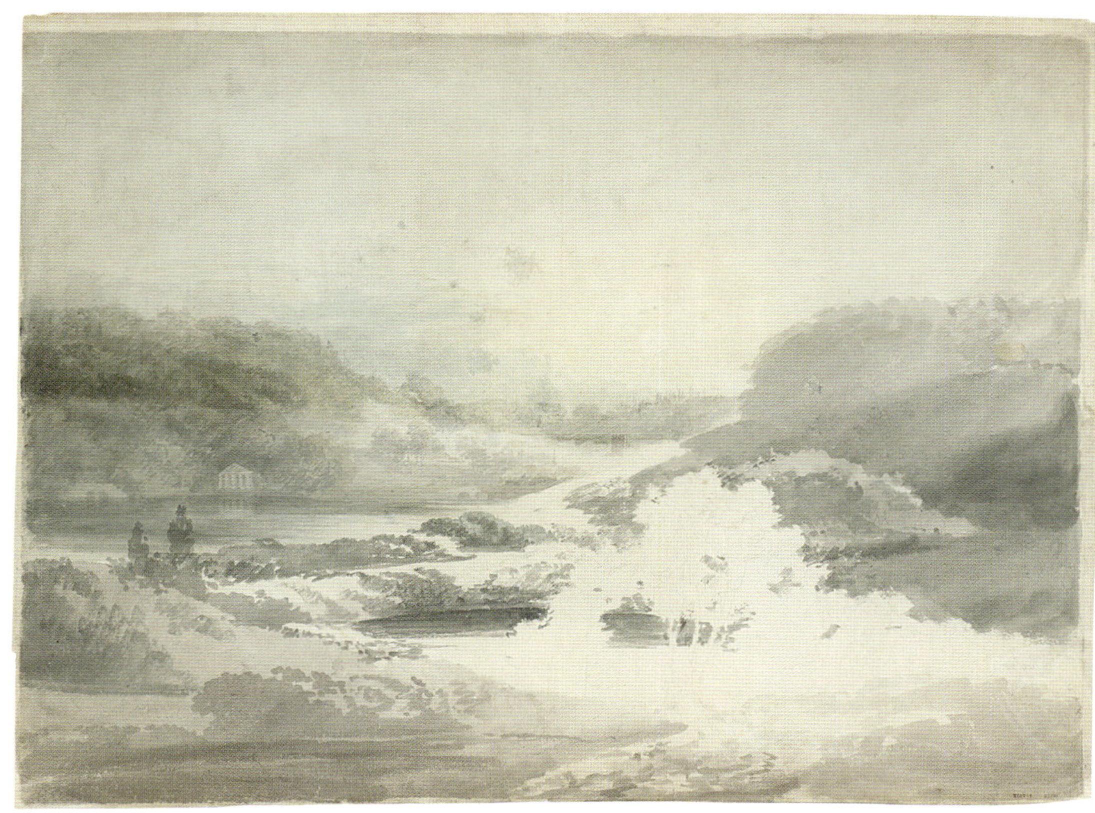

Fig. 21
Study for 'View over the Lake at Stourhead'
*c.*1795–96
Pencil and watercolour,
41.9 × 55.3 cm
Tate (D01908 / TB XLIV f)

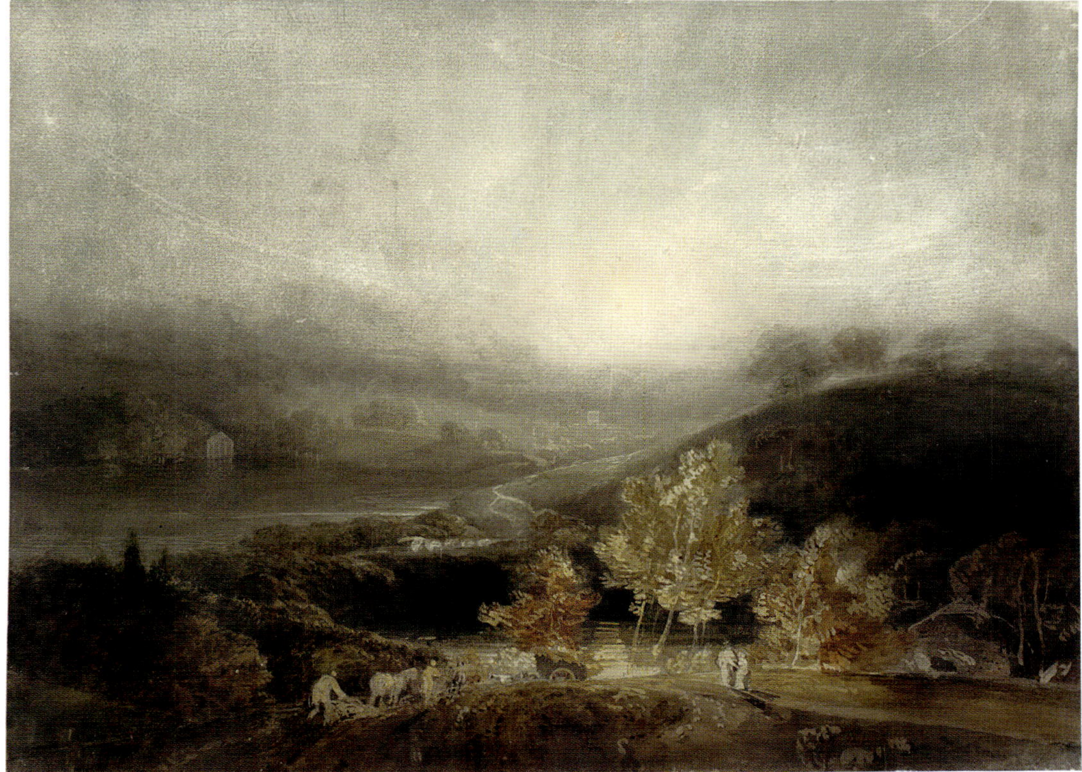

Fig. 22
View over the Lake at Stourhead, from the South-West
*c.*1795–96
Pencil and watercolour,
52.8 × 78.1 cm
Tate (D01909 / TB XLIV g)

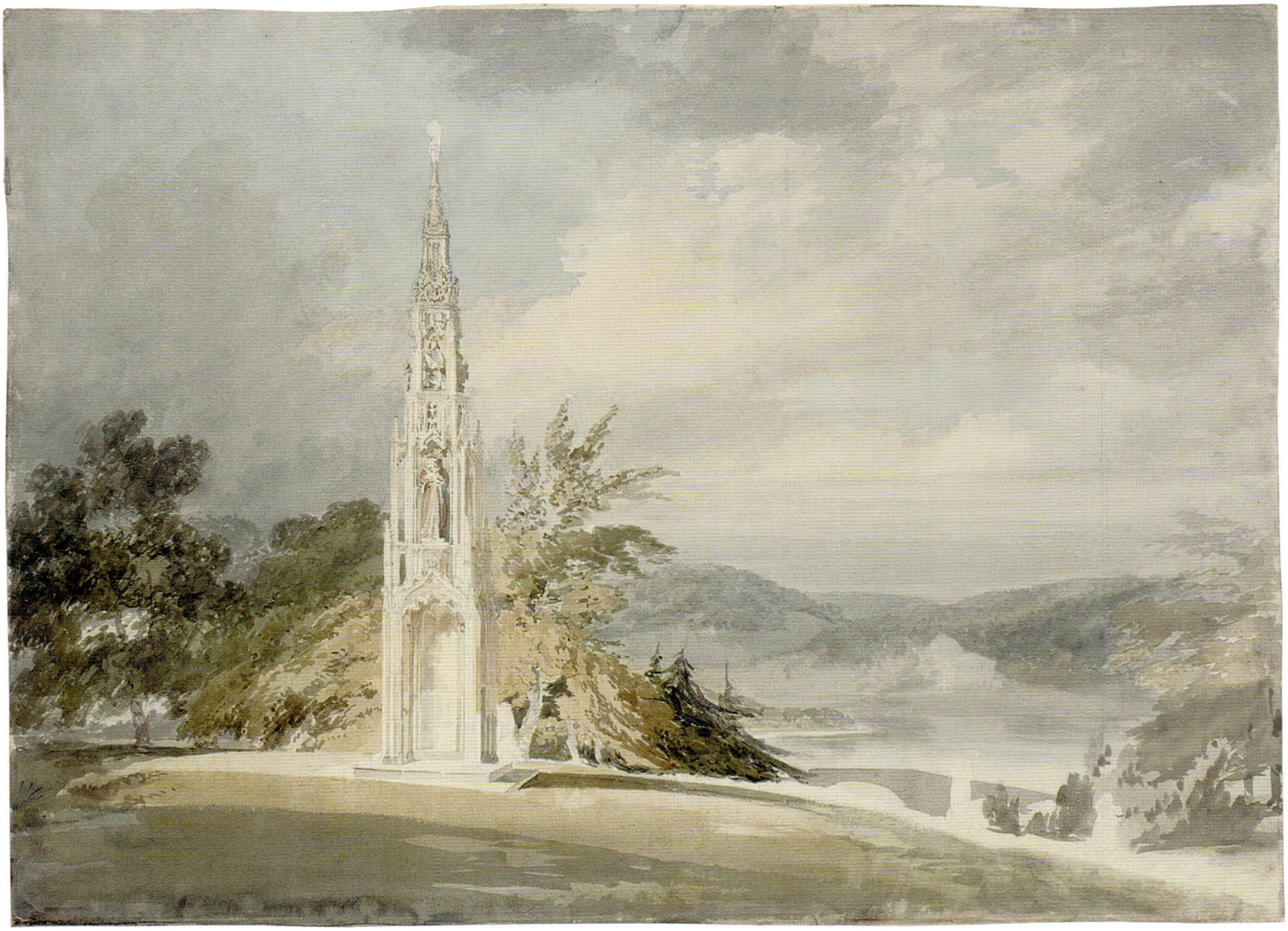

Fig. 23
The Gothic Cross Above the Lake at Stourhead, with the Pantheon in the Distance
c.1795–96
Pencil and watercolour, 40 3 × 54.1 cm
Tate (D01907 / TB XLIV e)

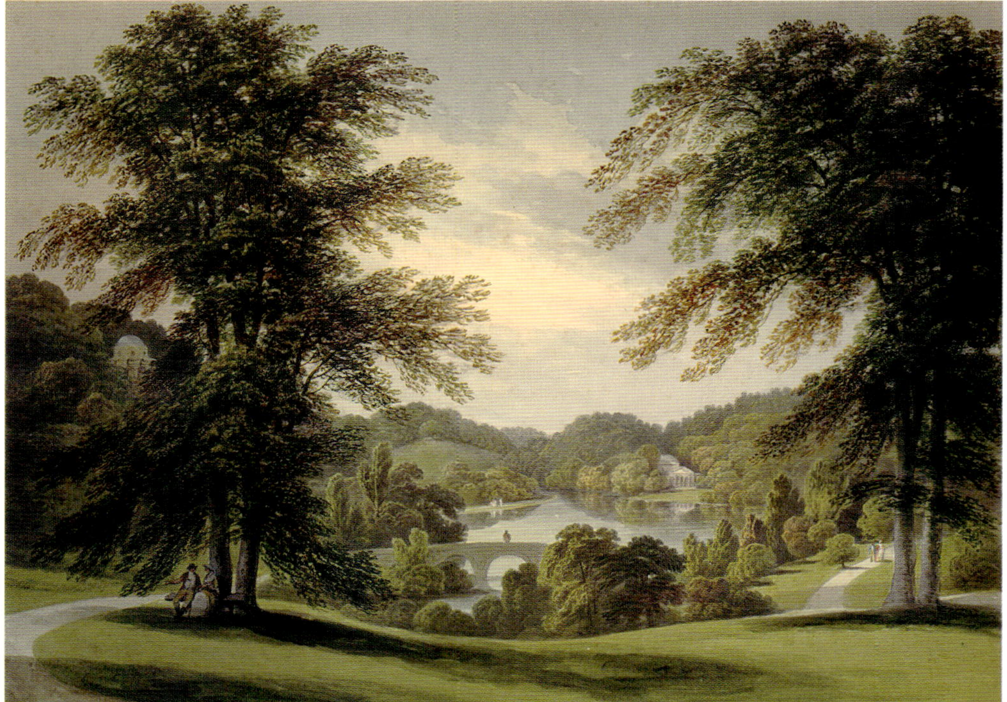

Fig. 24
FRANCIS NICHOLSON
(1753–1844)
View of the Lake and Bridge at Stourhead, with the Temple of Apollo and the Pantheon
c.1813
Watercolour, 40.4 × 55 cm
British Museum
(1944,1014.138, donated by Miss M.H. Turner)

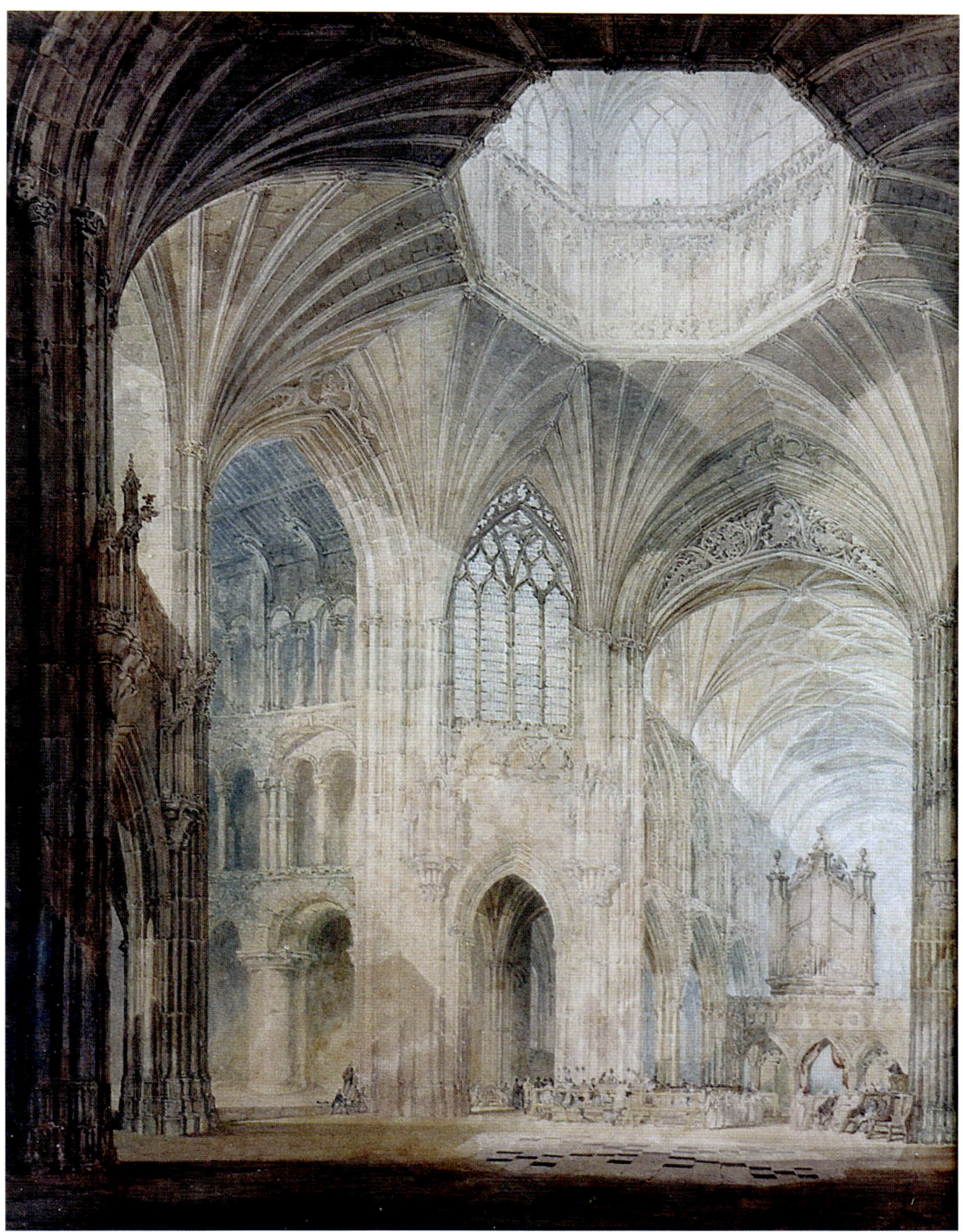

Fig. 25
Ely Cathedral, South Transept
?exhibited RA 1796
Watercolour, 62.5 × 48 cm
James Methuen Campbell, Corsham Court (W154)

started with the basic view looking toward the dam and continued with the more coloured study of the gothic cross. Turner then transferred the first design to a larger sheet, bringing the image close to completion so that only details like the architecture, figures and the sky required greater definition. It is also possible that, in his realisation of dawn, he was rising to a challenge from Colt Hoare to match the diverse skills in the watercolours of Italy by Ducros, which were by then on display in the Column Room (see fig. 16).

Colt Hoare was fiercely proud of these works. When acquiring the first of them from Ducros in 1787 he had anticipated that they would 'put all our English artists, even [his teacher] the great Mr [John 'Warwick'] Smith to the blush'.[27] Much later, in 1822, once Turner's reputation as a leading figure in the development of watercolour

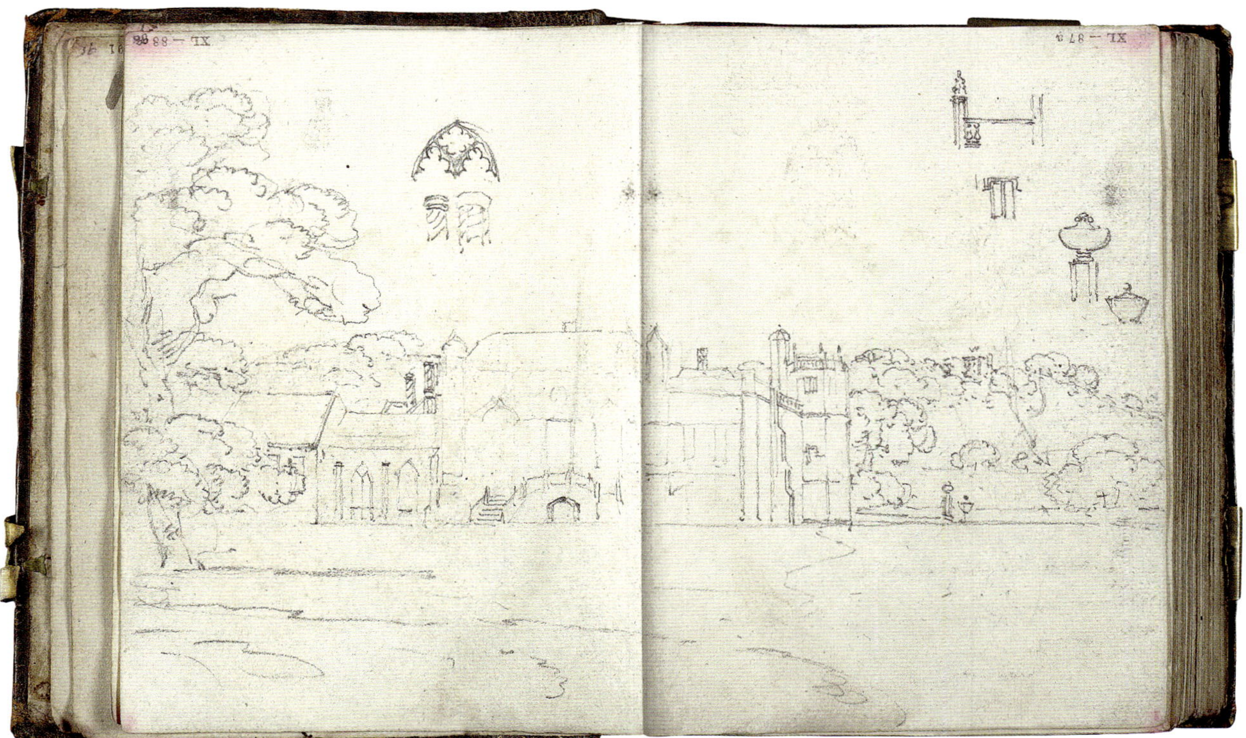

Fig. 26
Lacock Abbey: the Entrance Front
1798
Pencil, 13.1 × 9.5 cm
From the Dynevor ('Dinevor') Castle sketchbook
Tate (D01613, D01614; TB XL 87a, 88)

in Britain had been fully established by the recent exhibitions of the collection of Walter Fawkes (1769–1825), Colt Hoare offered a slight corrective in his account of the works by both Ducros and Turner that he owned. It was actually the former, he claimed, who had been most instrumental in the advancement in Britain,

> from *drawing* to *painting* in water-colours … His works proved the force, as well as consequence, that could be given to the unsubstantial body of watercolours, and to him I attribute the first knowledge and power of water-colours. Hence have sprung a numerous succession of Artists in this line.[28]

This assertion, of course, also allowed him to bask in the significance of the watercolours at Stourhead. But Turner certainly absorbed much from Ducros's large and technically assured views. The greater monumentality of his architectural subjects from 1796 onwards, for example, including the interiors of Ely, Salisbury Cathedral and Ewenny Priory, can be traced back to the model provided by Ducros.

Another influence from Turner's Stourhead studies was Piranesi, whose engravings of Rome and imaginary prisons were well represented in the volumes in Colt Hoare's impressive library.[29] An early drawing by Turner of the Pyramid of Caius Cestius in Rome seems to be loosely based on the image by Piranesi in his *Vedute di Roma*, and he would borrow its form once more for the 1800 painting, *The Fifth Plague of Egypt* (fig. 98).[30]

The prize Canaletto drawings at Stourhead would also linger in Turner's memory and were among the most important formative shapers of his ideas of Venice. Although the scene was familiar in other formats, it is possible that the celebrated view of St Mark's Square (fig. 17) was a lurking influence on *Juliet and her Nurse*, the controversial painting Turner exhibited in 1836 (Coleccion de Arte Amalia Lacroze de Fortabat, Buenos Aires).

Despite the obvious links between the pictures of Claude Lorrain and the garden at Stourhead, the collection possessed no genuine work by the artist whose paintings would afterwards prove so important to Turner's idea of the potential of landscape. There is, however, a pair of full-scale copies of pictures in the Doria-Pamphili Gallery

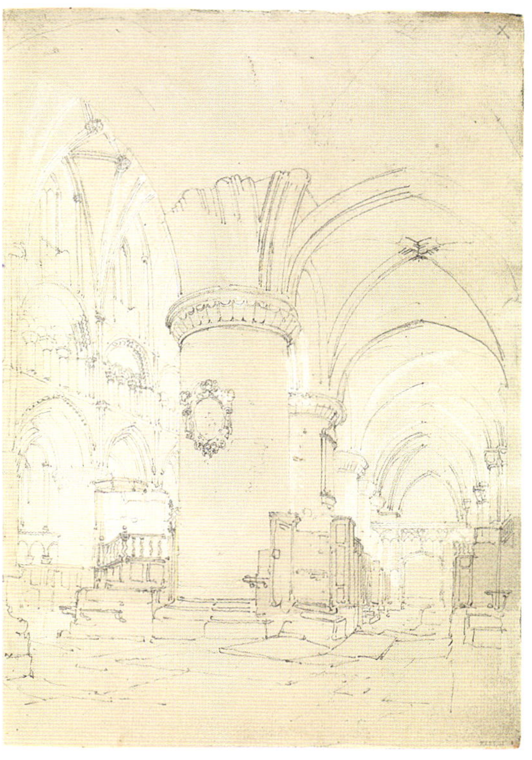

Fig. 27
The Interior of Malmesbury Abbey from the South Aisle
1798
Pencil, 33.2 × 22.5 cm
From the 'Hereford Court' sketchbook
Tate (D01253 / TB XXXVIII 4)

in Rome, including *The Mill*, which was an image Turner cherished in the version that entered the National Gallery, London, in the 1820s.

One final picture that Turner clearly examined is a small panel painting by David Teniers and Herman Saftleven showing a *Barn with a Still Life of Kitchen Utensils and a Sleeping Cook*. A clear parallel with the sombre interior and its glittering pots and pans can be felt in a watercolour Turner exhibited in 1796 as *Internal of a Cottage, a Study at Ely* (Tate).[31] The topographical location specified in the title suggests it was painted earlier, maybe actually during the 1794 Midlands tour. But it was one of three watercolours related to that journey that he prepared for the 1796 exhibition, so the composition feasibly evolved after seeing Teniers's painting at Stourhead. Alternatively, it may be that this validated for Turner a work he had painted merely as an exercise in the spirit of Flemish art.

The other image of Ely exhibited in 1796, a view across the space under the octagon inside the cathedral (fig. 25), has a direct connection with the Salisbury watercolours that Colt Hoare eventually owned. That series is considered in detail in the next chapter, but it is significant here to note that the pre-1797 order for two of the watercolours in the 'Isle of Wight' sketchbook specifies that they be the 'Size of Ely'.[32] The reference has been taken to indicate that Colt Hoare had acquired the perspective-defying and enveloping scene now at Corsham Court. However, there is no record of it having been at Stourhead and the early history of the drawing remains unclear.[33]

Other than a bill recording Colt Hoare's payment for the first two Salisbury watercolours, no other documents have been unearthed to chart what was plainly an ongoing connection with Turner between 1796 and 1798. In early August of the latter summer Turner set out on his most extensive tour of Wales, a journey lasting seven weeks. His route to Bristol would have offered the chance to revisit both Salisbury and Stourhead, but once again, if he did so, this is based more on reasonable speculation than hard fact. There are, however, as will become clear, sketches to support his presence in Wiltshire at some stage in 1798.

Another relevant detail is that the early days of his tour coincided neatly with the only period of two weeks, between 24 June and 10 September, when Colt Hoare was actually at Stourhead. This interval allowed the baronet to return from a fishing trip in North Wales before he set off again, this time for the south-eastern corner of Wales.[34] Of course, this short residence at Stourhead may be entirely fortuitous, but one further factor indicates that the two men almost certainly met at this time: this lies in the route Turner took before he got to Bristol as recorded in his sketchbooks. Instead of going directly to the port, he visited Lacock Abbey (fig. 26) and Malmesbury (fig. 27), both of which lie in a northerly line from Stourhead.[35]

The resulting sketches need to be considered in conjunction with one of the few letters to survive from the artist to his patron, written over seven years later.[36] In this text Turner attempted to assert that his visit to the north Wiltshire market town had arisen from a specific request by the baronet; he consequently charged Colt Hoare five guineas for expenses (quite a considerable amount at that time). Had there been a definite arrangement between them, it is all the more remarkable that Colt Hoare refused to be 'overcharged' (as he put it) and declined to pay this sum. The implication is that Turner was mistaken in his understanding and his expectations.

This is puzzling because at some stage between the visit in August 1798 and March 1806, when the letter was written, five of the detailed pencil outlines of Malmesbury in the 'Hereford Court' sketchbook were annotated with Colt Hoare's name (fig. 27), implying he had selected them as subjects he wished Turner to develop as watercolours. This process could have taken place fairly soon after the tour, because it is known that Turner was showing the sketchbook to others towards the end of year in order to win approval.[37] However, there was no obvious reason for Colt Hoare to request them around 1798. Indeed, it was not until about 1802 that he directed his antiquarian interests to his native county, moving on from his work for William Coxe's *Historical Tour of Monmouthshire* (1801) to support the barrow excavations at Stonehenge by William Cunnington.[38] Then, in February 1805, Colt Hoare was appointed High Sheriff for Wiltshire, the oldest secular office in England and Wales, which would have regularly required his presence in Salisbury, and it was significantly early that year that he nudged Turner towards completing the set of watercolours of the city. Addressing this long-running commission may have prompted him to think about depictions of other places in Wiltshire, and if the Malmesbury drawings had been sanctioned earlier, he may have chased these up too. On the other hand, the first reference to them in the existing correspondence does not occur until the letter of 1806, where they are mentioned in conjunction with the delivery of the newly completed pair of views of Hampton Court (fig. 19). The context here is so partial and ambiguous that it is not possible to be certain whether the discussion arises from a new commission or part of ongoing negotiations. Either way, perhaps exhausted by Turner's protracted delays in completing the Salisbury set, ultimately Colt Hoare decided not to commit to the Malmesbury views, and so they were put aside, undeveloped until the 1820s (see fig. 130). Curiously, however, one of Britton's engravings of the abbey of 1807 is taken from exactly the same viewpoint as Turner's sketch of the interior (fig. 28). Perhaps there really were grounds for Turner's suspicions about this rival?

The last surviving letter between patron and artist is dated April 1806, but Turner seems to have revisited Stourhead a year or two after that.[39] They evidently remained in contact, not least because Colt Hoare's great friend, Leicester, was rapidly building up one of the most important collections of Turner's oil paintings at his London home, as well as commissioning in 1808 a pair of views of his country house, Tabley, where Colt Hoare was a regular guest. Surprisingly, however, the latter was noticeably absent from the long list of subscribers for Turner's mezzotint of *A Shipwreck* in 1807, and the library at Stourhead seems never to have included Turner's ambitious mezzotint series

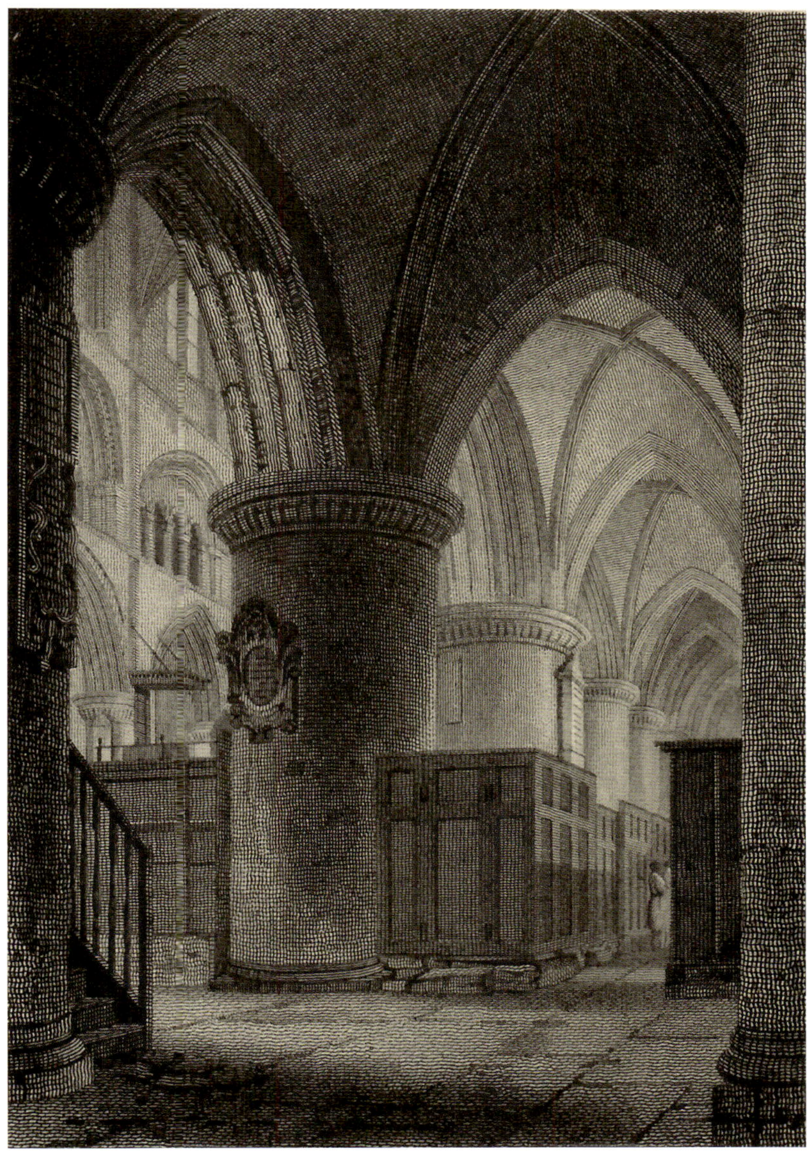

Fig. 28
J.C. SMITH after
JOHN BRITTON (1771–1857)
Malmesbury Abbey-Church, South Aisle &c, Wiltshire
1807
For the *Beauties of England and Wales*
Engraving, 15.3 × 10.2 cm
British Library, London

Liber Studiorum. Nevertheless, Colt Hoare did acquire copies of the *Views in Sussex* (1819), *Picturesque Views on the Southern Coast of England* (1826) and other publications featuring Turner's works, such as *Britannia Depicta* and the 1808 *Oxford Almanack*. Even so, there was possibly a cooling between them, which the founding of the British Institution in 1805 can only have increased.

As a rival exhibiting body to the Royal Academy, the Institution was established by members of the gentry as a patriotic endeavour to encourage aspiring artists to learn by studying the Old Masters. This ambition was conservative in spirit and was in conflict with a move away from earlier models at the radical edges of British art, towards a greater naturalism, as best expressed by John Constable.[40] The annual exhibitions of earlier masters, however, were a positive contribution to London life, even though their purpose was primarily to permit students to undertake copies. There were prizes for new works, but the bias of the awards was towards submissions that slavishly repeated pre-existing formulas, a detrimental step in the opinion of contemporary artists, who were excluded from the committee of the British Institution. Many of Turner's patrons, including Colt Hoare, had been founder-members, and although he occasionally participated in the British Institution exhibitions, Turner was clearly unhappy about this development. In his own work he recognised the benefits of studying past achievements, but he resented anything that imposed dictates on the brotherhood of artists.

Throughout the 1800s Turner's paintings irritated and then antagonised one of the British Institution's Directors, namely Sir George Beaumont, who was both inflexible in his ideals and libellous about artists of whom he did not approve. This situation simmered until 1814, when Turner exhibited a picture that was almost a direct copy of a landscape belonging to Lord Egremont, effectively thereby mocking the aims of the Institution. Attitudes in the art world were polarised still further the following year when a *Catalogue Raisonné*, lampooning the views of the connoisseurs, was published anonymously.[41]

These developments provide the background for Colt Hoare's final purchase from Turner, the classical landscape *Lake Avernus: Aeneas and the Cumaean Sibyl* (fig. 29), which was, during its time at Stourhead, paired with Richard Wilson's *Lake of Nemi, or Speculum Diana* in the Cabinet

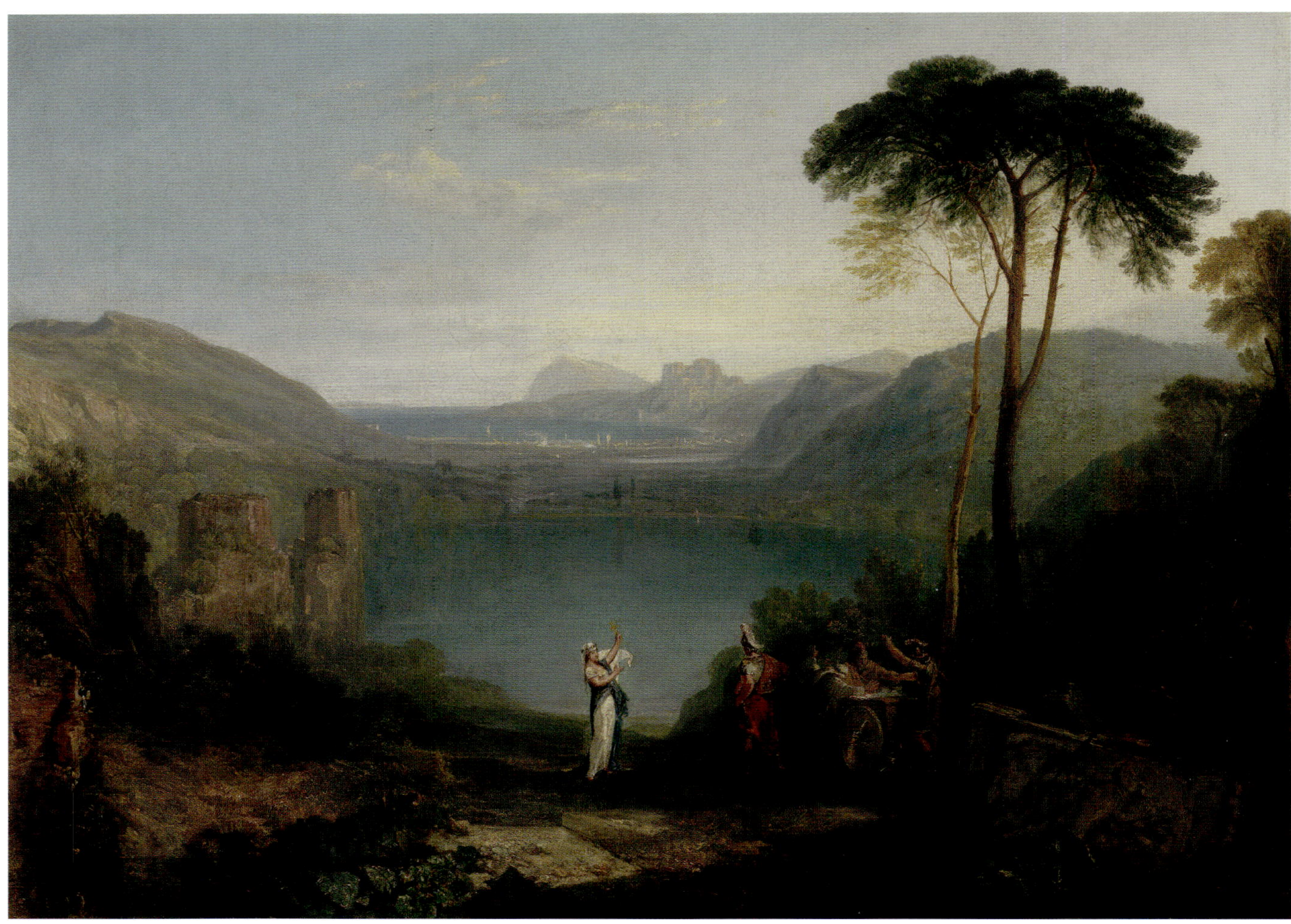

Fig. 29
Lake Avernus: Aeneas and the Cumaean Sibyl
c.1814–15
Oil on canvas,
71.8 × 97.2 cm
Yale Center for British Art, New Haven (B1977.14.78; B&J 226)

Room, perhaps in order to replace a view of Lake Avernus by Wilson that had left the collection (Turner would have liked the fact that the Rembrandt was also displayed in this room).[42] In 1814, the year Turner must have been at work on *Lake Avernus*, he had just exhibited his evocation of Dido and Aeneas setting out on the hunt that inaugurates their passion for each other, although that work probably dates from several years before (Tate).[43] So, while the subject of Aeneas is of obvious relevance to the associations that had shaped the Stourhead garden, it was not necessarily determined by the collector. Turner had painted another version of the composition at least 15 years earlier, probably not long after the 1798 visit mentioned above. That canvas remained with Turner and there is no record of it ever having hung in the Wiltshire house (Tate),[44] yet it must have evolved through collaborative dialogue with Colt Hoare.

The starting point for both of Turner's paintings was a drawing made on the spot at Lake Avernus on 4 February 1786.[45] Colt Hoare later catalogued the scene as 'The lake of Avernus near Naples, comprehending the Temple on its banks, the Monte Vuovo, the Lucrine lake, the Castle of Baiae, the promontory of Misenum, and the distant island of Capri'.[46] For anyone steeped in the classics, the volcanic crater was believed to be the way to the underworld, but in visiting the site for himself Colt Hoare saw that the lake was connected by a cavernous passage to Cumae, the dwelling place of the Sibyl. None of these associative details are apparent in his drawing, nor in the transcription Turner made from it,[47] though the story of Aeneas's visit to the Sibyl could have been readily located in Virgil's *Aeneid*, which would have been Turner's source in creating the foreground narrative in his painting.

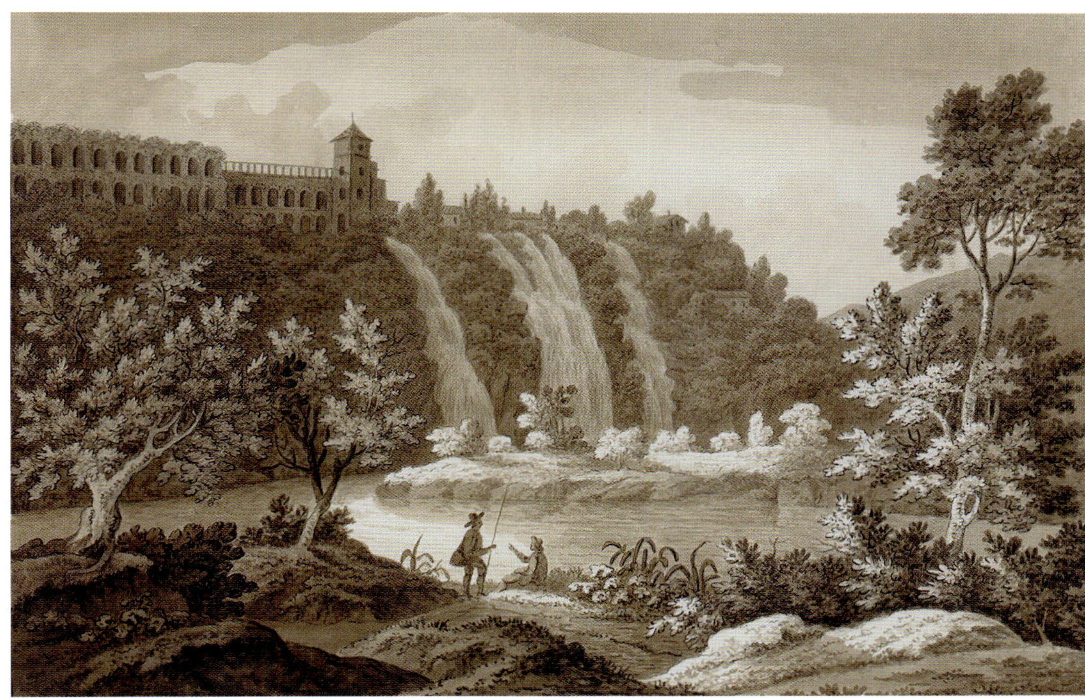

Fig. 30
SIR RICHARD COLT HOARE
(1758–1838)
Villa of Maecenas at Tivoli
*c.*1786–90
Pencil, pen and brown ink, with brown wash on cream paper, 24.9 × 51.1 cm
Yale Center for British Art, New Haven (B1977.14.2769)

Turner did not exhibit a history painting at the Royal Academy until 1800, so his first version of *Lake Avernus* may have been a tentative private exercise that also carried the hope of inducing a sale by flattering his patron's interests. It has been described rather dismissively as resembling 'a student's self-conscious effort to produce an ersatz Old Master'.[48] But in creating the picture at that moment, Turner was in tune with the reassessment of Richard Wilson's Italian landscapes, which was at its peak in the last years of the 1790s. One aspect of Wilson's work that provoked much debate was his loose handling of paint, which also became a controversial characteristic of Turner's works from this point on.[49] Another canvas found in Turner's studio, possibly though not necessarily by him, is a broadly painted version of Wilson's *Lake Nemi*, which could imply that the idea of pairing his own picture with that work was actually his suggestion.[50] However, as far as we know, this remained an entirely theoretical proposition until the beginning of 1815, when on 25 February Colt Hoare paid 150 guineas for the delivery of the second version.[51] This was by then a price only slightly more than Turner was charging for his largest watercolours and seemingly reflects the damage to his marketability caused by Beaumont's criticisms. But the amount may also have been reduced to accommodate Colt Hoare's opinion, as published in the *Annals of the Fine Arts*, that the cost of 'historical painting' was not affordable for most private collectors.[52]

During the previous few years Colt Hoare, then in his 50s, had been nostalgically reviewing his experiences in Italy, which resulted in a catalogue of his immense collection of books about Italian history and topography, and several volumes of recollections of his travels. In 1817 he reworked, in collaboration with

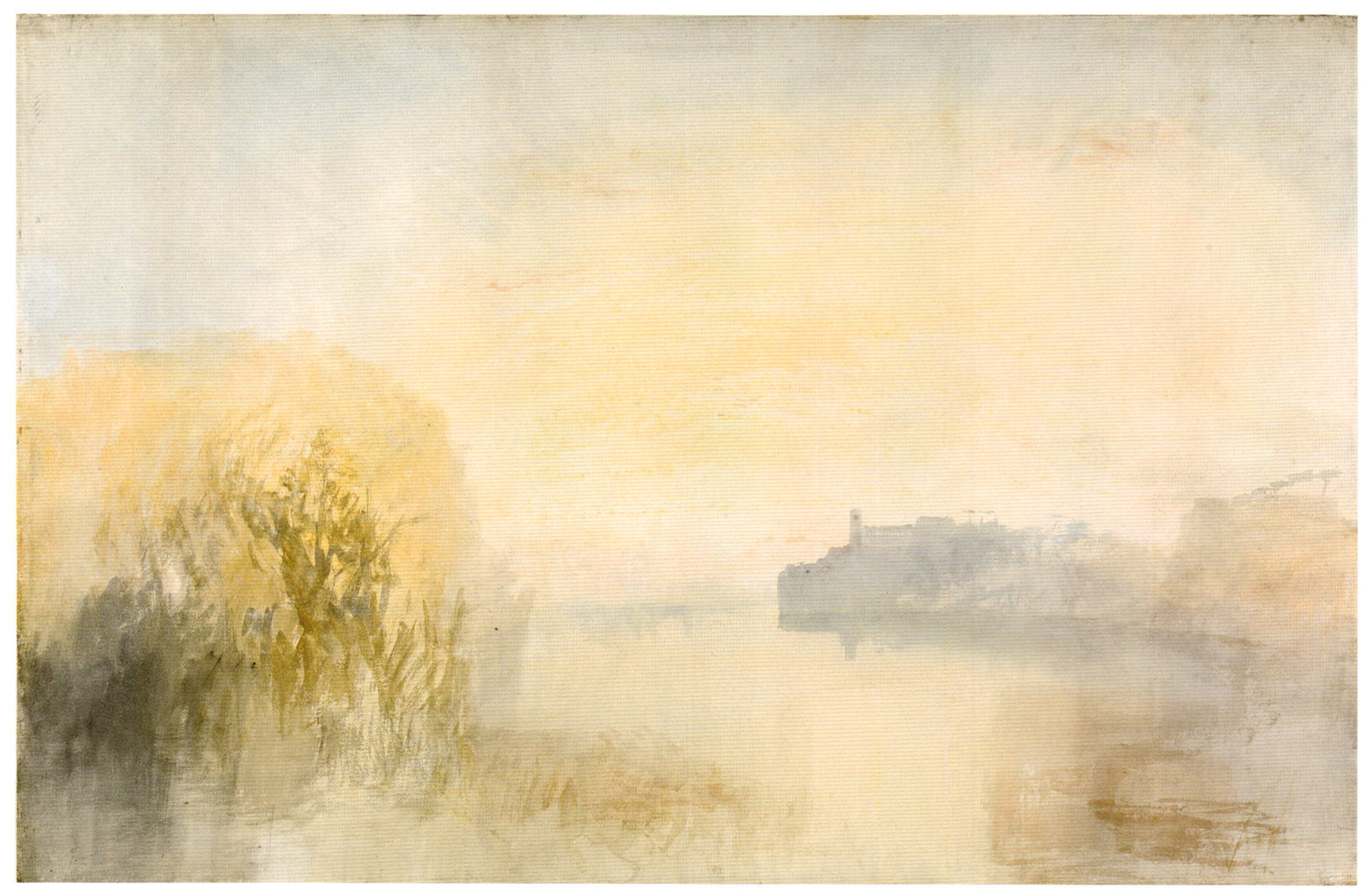

Fig. 31
Lake with Distant Headland and Palaces; Study for 'Rise of the River Stour at Stourhead'
c.1824–25
Watercolour, 67.3 × 100.5 cm
Tate (D36320 / TB CCCLXV 29)

John 'Warwick' Smith, 50 of his sketches for an album of 'Select Views' (see fig. 30). Prior to this he had commissioned new renderings of some of his Italian sketches from Francis Nicholson, the watercolour artist who had recorded the Stourhead gardens around 1813 (fig. 24). One of the images Nicholson repeated some time between 1813 and 1815 was the same sketch of Lake Avernus that Turner had worked from around 1798, corroborating that it was a scene especially cherished by Colt Hoare.[53] Consequently his acquisition of Turner's second version fits into a pattern of retrospective reflection at a time when the decades of turmoil in Europe were at last coming to an end. The painting's ravishing use of light and colour pre-dates Turner's travels to the Mediterranean by a few years, and is instead derived from his appreciation of Claude's paintings. These were also the principal influence on his exhibits for the following years, but his realisations of ancient Carthage presumably also benefited from discussions with Colt Hoare.[54]

The latter's guiding hand has been detected in the preparations Turner was making by 1818 for his own trip to Italy.[55] As well as possessing a copy of Colt Hoare's *Hints to Travellers in Italy* (1815), which must have had rather limited value given the long interval since the baronet had himself been there, the artist consulted the Revd John Chetwode Eustace's *Tour through Italy*, and the 72 *Select Views in Italy* by John 'Warwick'

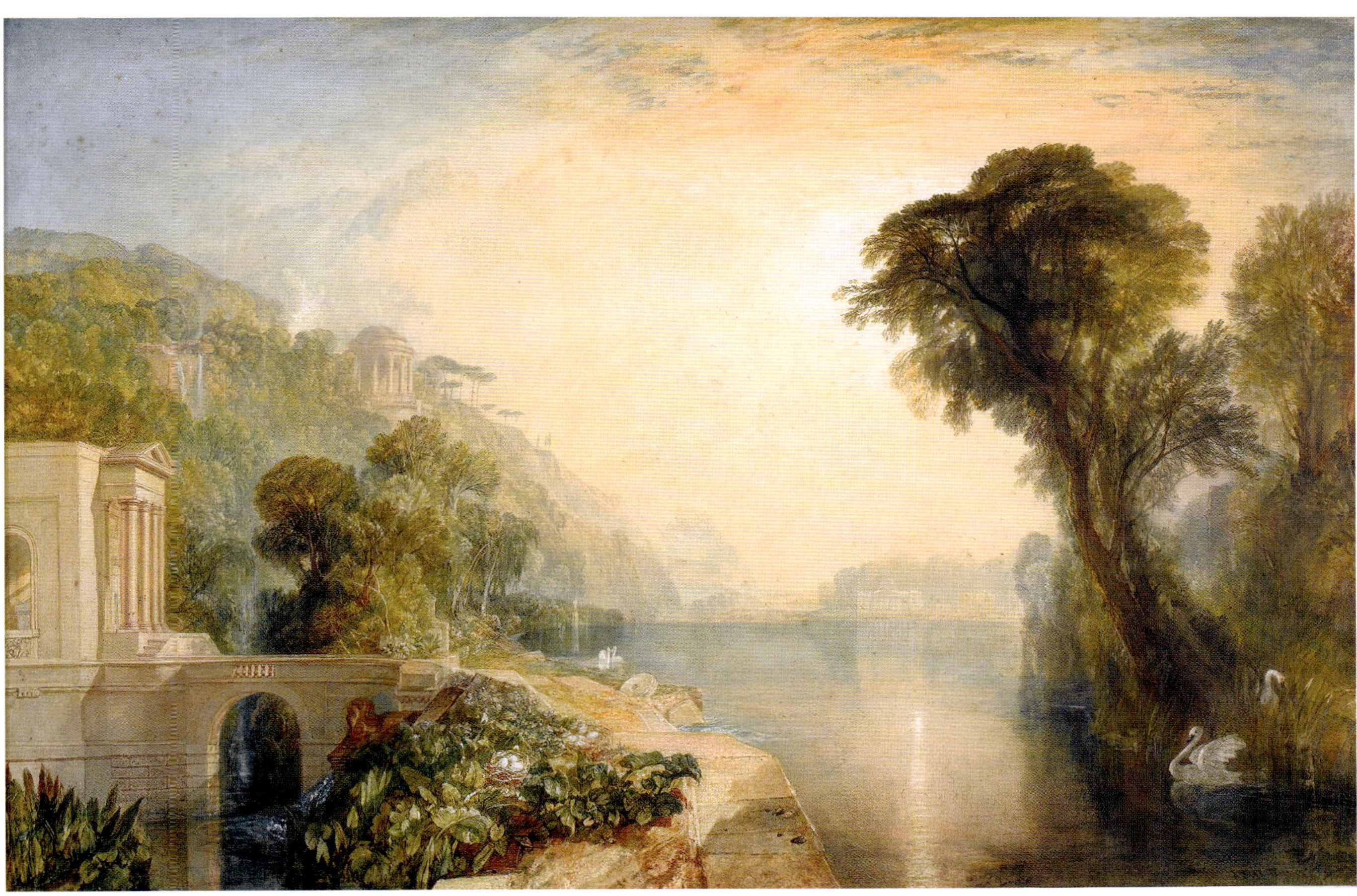

Fig. 32
Rise of the River Stour at Stourhead (also known as ***The Swan's Nest***)
Exhibited RA 1825
Watercolour,
67.3 × 102.2 cm
Trustees of the Walter Morrison Collection, Sudeley Castle (W496)

Smith. The renewed association with Stourhead presumably also gave him access once again to the numerous Italian scenes around the house.

There was clearly a fusing in Turner's mind of Italy with Stourhead that is readily appreciable in his largest depiction of the famous garden (fig. 32). This was one of the last watercolours he exhibited at the Royal Academy, where it was shown five years after he returned from Italy. Visitors to Stourhead will struggle to align the Temples of Flora, Apollo and the Pantheon into the compressed panorama Turner created, which has the character of a classical capriccio. The light pervading the lake and the treetops also feels stylised and Italianate; it had begun as a more diluted, almost sunrise effect in one of his experimental large colour studies (fig. 31).[56] In composing his scene in this way, Turner was taking a lead from Henry Hoare's iconographic programme for the garden. The result was to designate the river that rises there as the source of harmony and renewal. This message of rebirth is underlined by the presence of a swan's nest in the foreground. We do not know whether the watercolour was ever owned by Colt Hoare, whose health kept him chiefly at Stourhead after 1820, but he would surely have recognised it as a warm tribute from the artist, who had gained so much from their association.

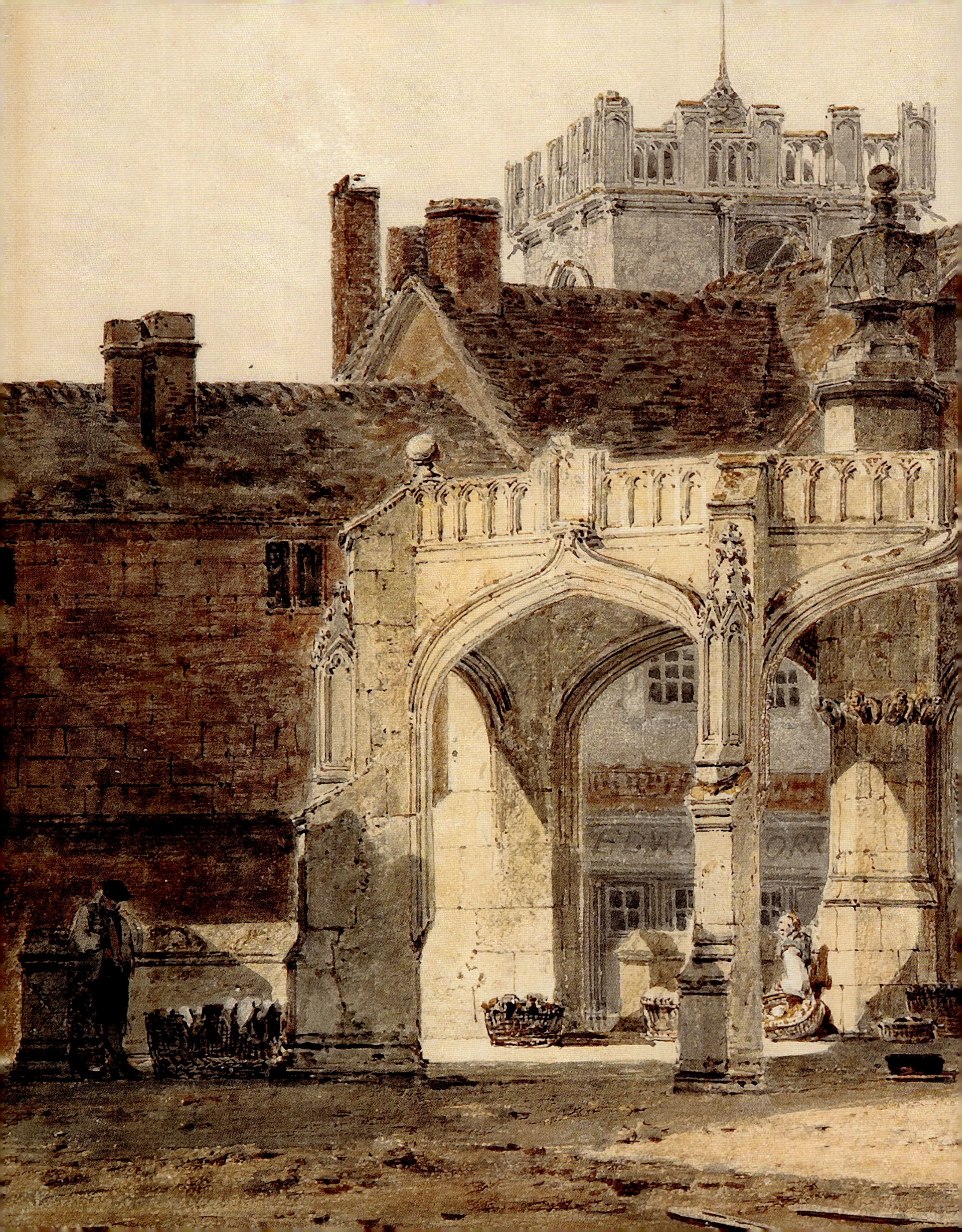

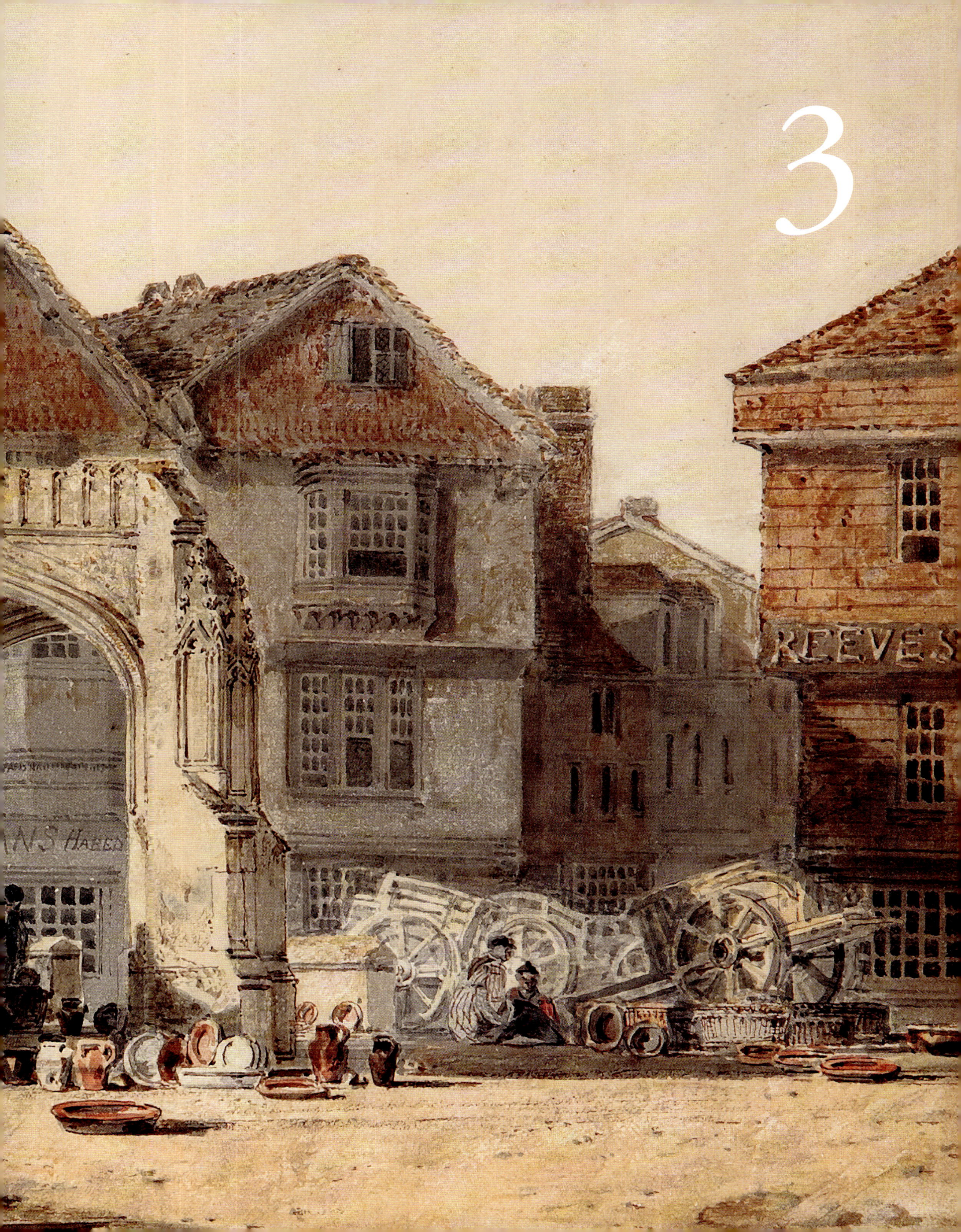

3

THE SALISBURY COMMISSION: 'Poems in Stone'

THE 17 VIEWS of Salisbury that Turner painted for Sir Richard Colt Hoare between 1795 and 1805 have been described as the 'most important topographical commission' of the first decade of his working life.[1] Dr John Gage, who made this claim, proposed that they are comparable in both their artistic significance, and their variations around a specific theme, with the groups of watercolours Turner later created of the Alps (after 1802) or during his excursion on the Rhine (1817).

Like the first of these, the Salisbury series was produced over a lengthy period, in this case one that commenced with Turner's earliest successes at the Royal Academy and continued a few years beyond his election to that body in 1802. Throughout this decade Turner made dramatic stylistic advances, both in his oils and watercolours, although these are less observable in the Salisbury designs, where there was presumably a desire by the artist and his important client to maintain a harmonious relationship within the group. The antiquarian nature of the subject matter also dictated that factors such as the precise rendering of architectural detail were of greater consequence than atmosphere, which was increasingly a feature in other areas of Turner's artistic output.

By 1795, when Turner first sketched at Salisbury, his ability to re-create the chiselled and carved lines of gothic architecture had been recognised and acclaimed critically for the 'profusion of minute parts massed with judgment and tinctured with truth and fidelity'.[2] These qualities would have assuredly recommended his work to Colt Hoare by the summer of 1796. Although his connection with Turner almost certainly began the previous year, the origins of the Salisbury commission initially evolved in a piecemeal way around this time. There is, however, an incomplete record of bills and a paucity of correspondence charting Turner's progress. Attempts at understanding the commission were further hindered by the sale of the group of watercolours from Stourhead in 1883 by Colt Hoare's heirs, after which they became widely dispersed. It is only comparatively recently that art historians have been able to assess the sequence in its entirety, to attempt to date individual works within the series, and to consider how the whole enterprise was determined and shaped.[3] In the meantime, some erroneous theories have developed about the purpose of the watercolours, including a belief that the designs were primarily commissioned to be engraved for Colt Hoare's *History of Modern Wiltshire* (1822–44), a notion for which there is no contemporary evidence.[4]

An important factor that has not previously been considered is the question of Colt Hoare's opinion of the recent restoration of the cathedral by James Wyatt and whether that determined the focus of the commission in any way. In fact, it is readily apparent from Colt Hoare's journals that he had a strong aversion to much that had been done. As he travelled to other medieval cathedrals, he voiced his disapproval of 'modern alterations & improvements', specifically those of Wyatt, describing the scraping of the stones at Durham as presumptuous and as bad as a modern painter retouching 'a picture of Raphael or of Claude Lorrain'.[5] Given these views, his desire to engage Turner to paint Salisbury Cathedral while controversies still simmered is striking; except that, as an antiquarian, he would have recognised the importance of documenting the appearance of historic monuments exactly as they were for the benefit of posterity.

PREVIOUS PAGES:
The Poultry Cross, with the Tower of St Thomas's Church, Salisbury (detail) (see fig. 54)

Fig. 33
Gateway to the Close, Salisbury Cathedral
Exhibited RA 1796
Pencil and watercolour, 50.8 × 37.5 cm
Newnham College, Cambridge (W210)

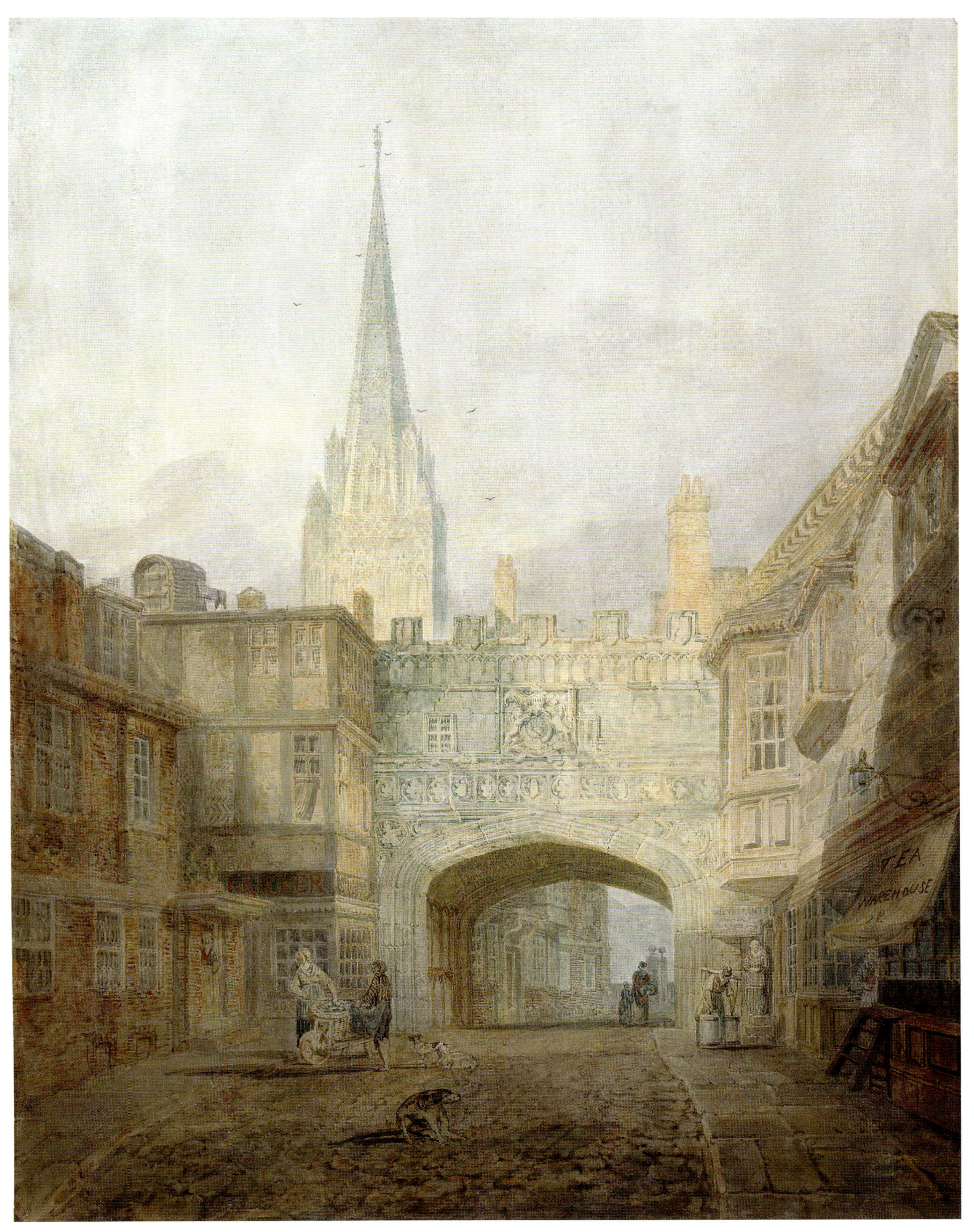
FRICKER
ALL VAGRANTS
TEA
WAREHOUSE

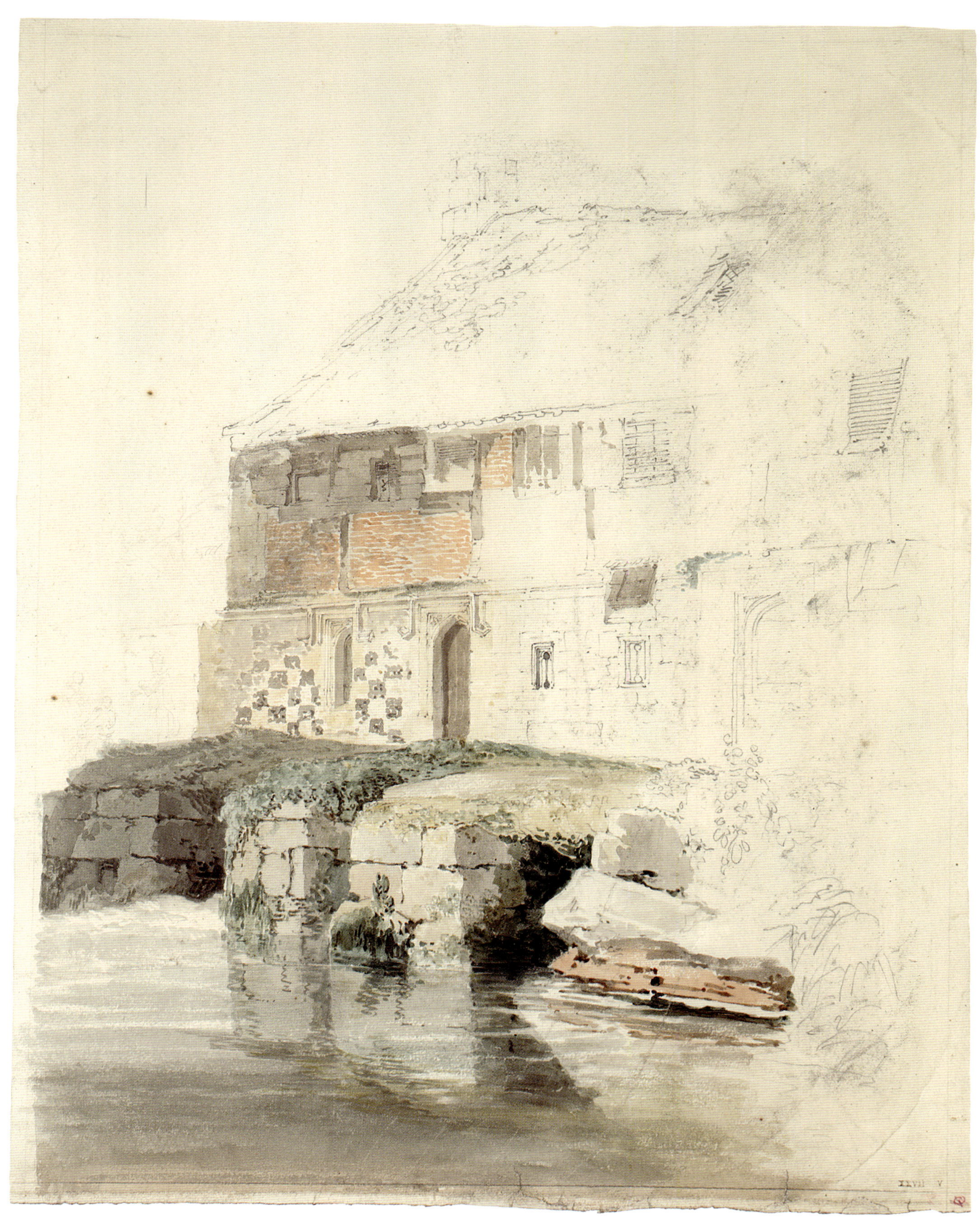

OPPOSITE: **Fig. 34**
Harnham Mill, Salisbury
c.1795
Pencil and watercolour,
35.1 × 27.7 cm
Tate (D00683 / TB XXVII V)

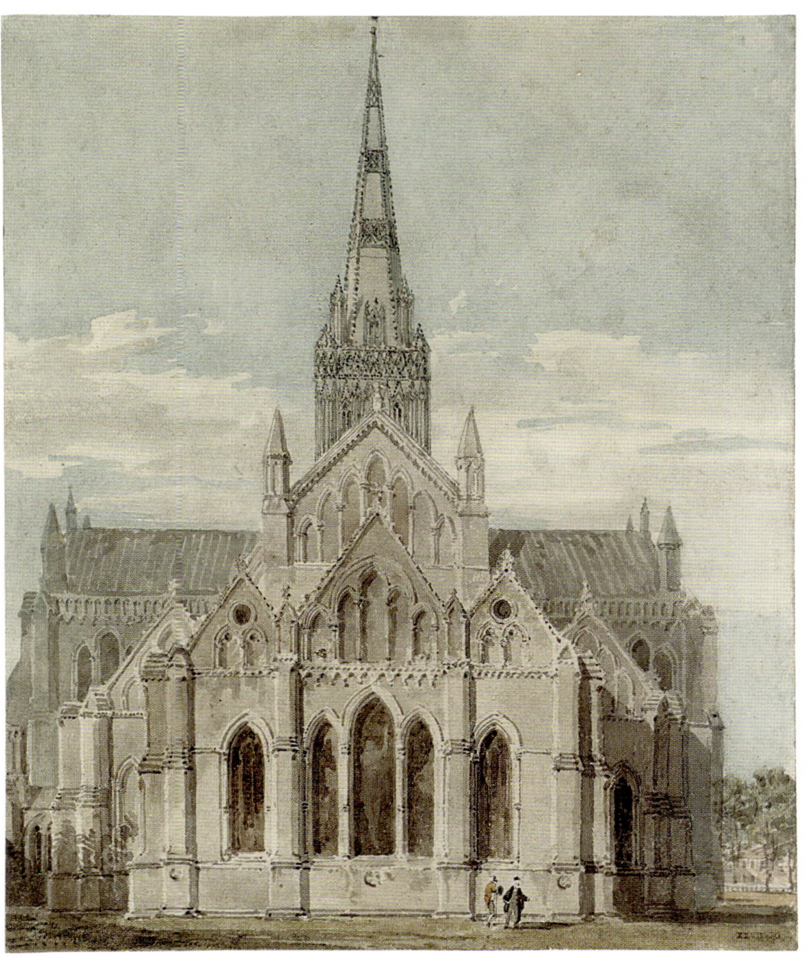

Fig. 35
Salisbury Cathedral from the East
c.1795–96
Pencil and watercolour,
28 × 23 cm
Tate (D00668 / TB XXVII G)
(see p. 184)

The first hint of the project lies in a list of orders in the 1795 'Isle of Wight' sketchbook, where views of 'Salisbury Porch' and 'Front of Salisbury' are noted as having been selected by 'Sir Richard Hoare' to be executed to the 'Size of Ely. 13'.[6] As noted previously, this last allusion has generally been assumed to refer to the large watercolour of the interior of Ely Cathedral that was exhibited in 1796 (fig. 25). The number '13' might seem to refer to the proposed size, but unlike other dimensions in Turner's list, it is set to one side. So a plausible interpretation is that this represents the amount he proposed to charge for each watercolour. This tallies with his contemporary pricing: 13 guineas would be only slightly more than the 10 guineas he received for each of the smaller views of Harewood completed in November 1797. In fact, an entry in Colt Hoare's private account book for 5 September 1797 records that he paid Turner £15 for each of the first views of Salisbury – £2 more than seems to have been agreed at the time of the commission.[7]

As well as the Ely watercolour, the 1796 Royal Academy exhibition featured Turner's first view of Salisbury, a depiction of the Close Gate (fig. 33). Even though it was acquired by an unknown collector, rather than Colt Hoare, its inclusion among that year's exhibits further supports a case for this being the most opportune moment for him to have requested Salisbury views for himself.

Little is known of Turner's movements in 1796, so it is not impossible that he revisited Salisbury once more that summer. However, during the previous year he had recorded six pencil outlines of the city in his sketchbook, all but one of which he would develop for Colt Hoare over the following decade, although it was not until the late 1820s that he returned to his view from Old Sarum (see fig. 131). The other subjects were the two cathedral views (figs 36 and 40), the Close Gate, the appealingly picturesque Poultry Cross, and the dilapidated Old Council House. In addition to these pages in the notebook, he clearly used several loose sheets during his stay. One of these depicts the east end of the cathedral (fig. 35), seen from the Walk to the Bishop's Palace. Another was a pencil sketch of the new Council House, where building work continued (fig. 60), and a third study, charming but regrettably incomplete, shows Harnham Mill on the River Nadder, near the Water Meadows to the west (fig. 34).

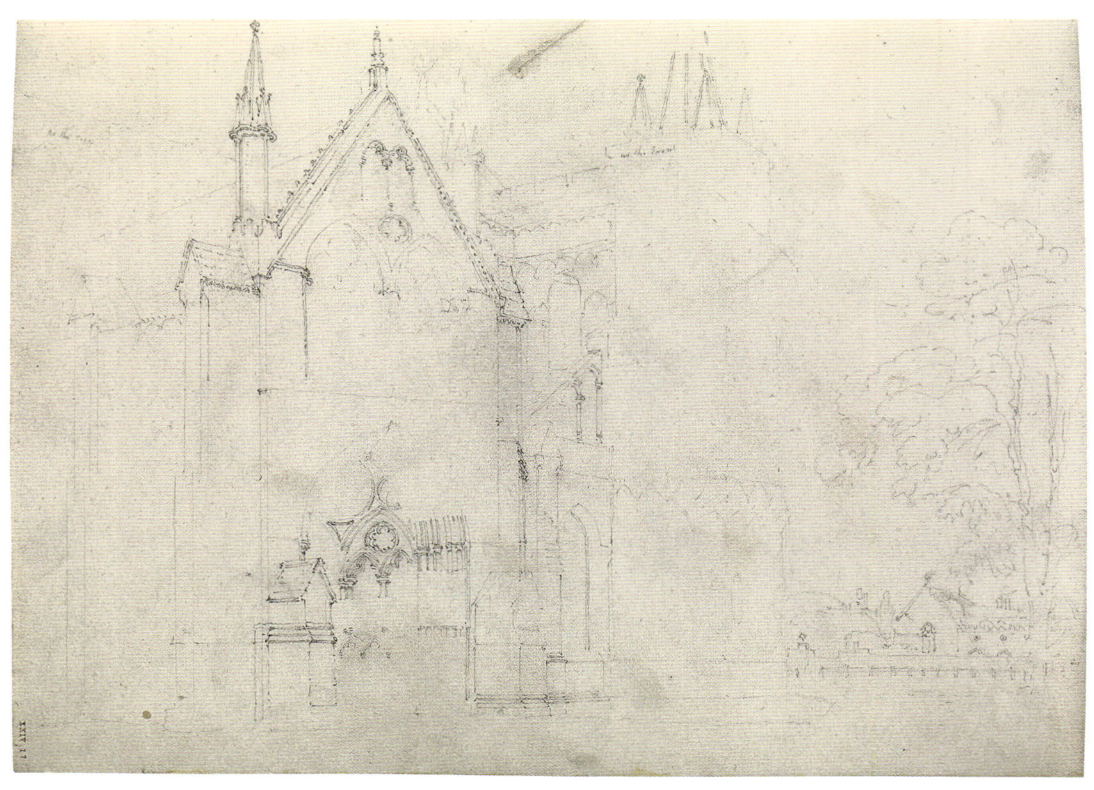

Fig. 36
The North-West Corner of Salisbury Cathedral
1795
Pencil, 20.4 × 26.4 cm
From the 'Isle of Wight' sketchbook
Tate (D00424 / TB XXIV 17)

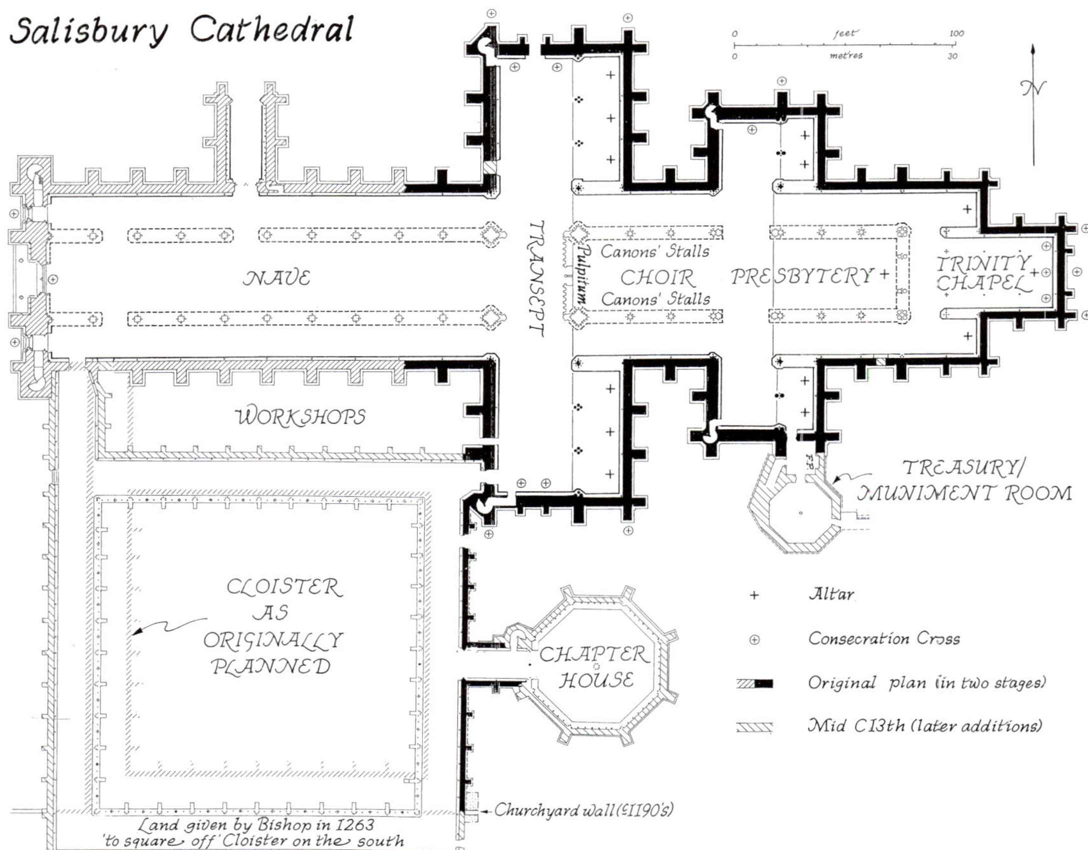

Based on a plan published in Tim Tatton-Brown and John Crook, ***Salisbury Cathedral: The Making of a Medieval Masterpiece***, 2009

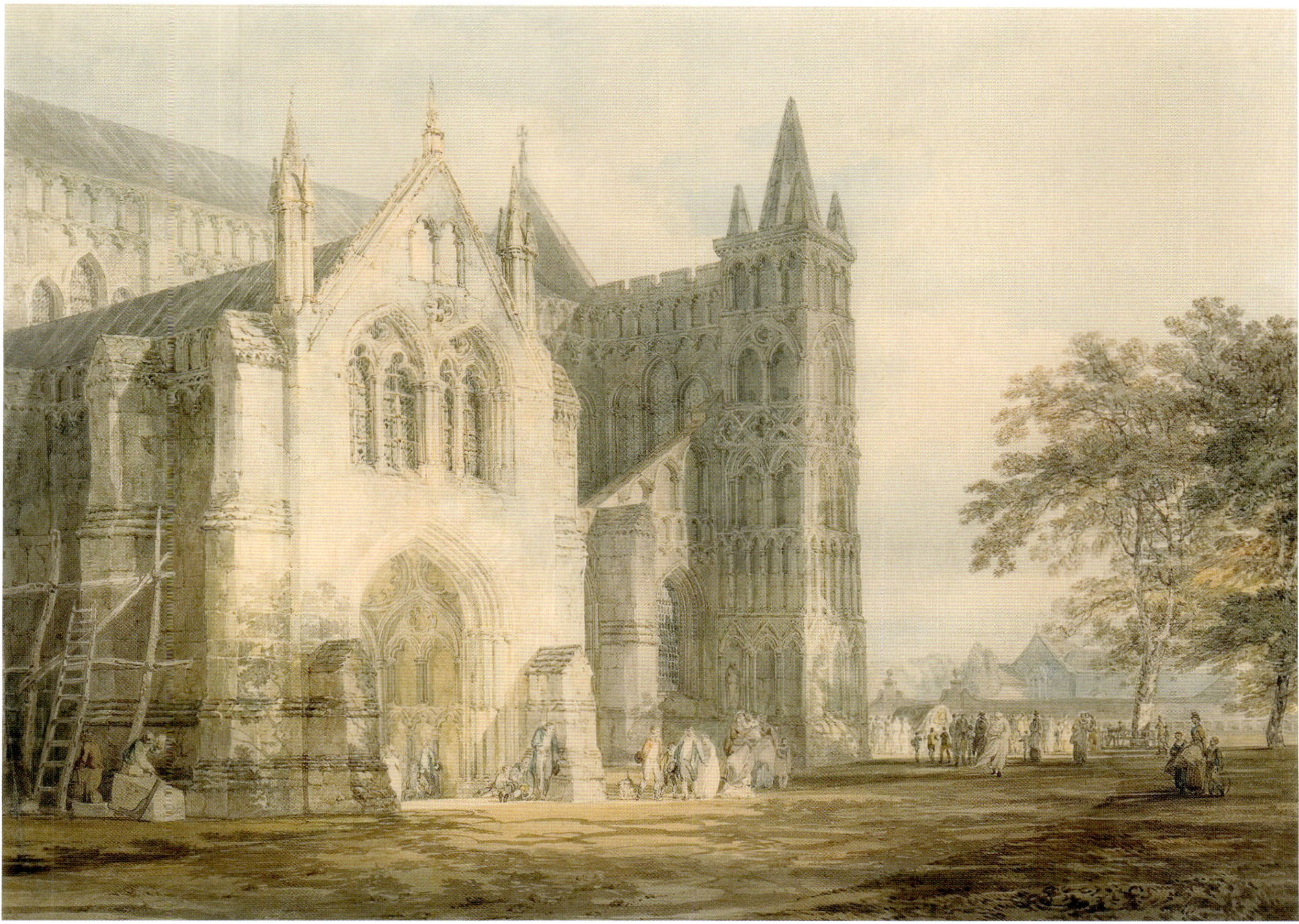

Fig. 37
North Porch of Salisbury Cathedral
Exhibited RA 1797
Watercolour, 50 × 65 cm
The Salisbury Museum
(W196)
(see p. 184)

Despite the documented order for two views of the cathedral, Turner had pressed ahead with only one of these by May 1797, when his large watercolour of the North Porch was shown at the Royal Academy (fig. 37). Instead of pairing it with the commissioned view of the West Front, it was accompanied in the exhibition by an ingeniously composed view of the Choir and Lady Chapel (fig. 39). Such a complicated architectural study was dependent on painstaking observations akin to those Turner had undertaken when sketching the crossing below the octagonal lantern at Ely (fig. 25). As on that occasion, he had first worked on the spot by pinning one of his largest sheets of paper to a sketching board, and had then diligently measured out the space in a network of pencil lines, adding colour only as an aide memoire for the stained glass (fig. 38). The finished version of the watercolour was worked up some time later in his studio. Turner was used to travelling with cumbersome sketching materials, so he could have made this sketch in 1795, at the same time as the others. It may be relevant, nevertheless, that he used a similar piece of paper for a view of Chichester Cathedral in 1796 (British Museum).[8]

The back of the Chichester sheet was inscribed many years later with one of the three lists that provide the only real record of how Turner and Colt Hoare planned the Salisbury series. The earliest of these three documents is the most comprehensive, revealing that the full commission was envisaged as 20 views that were to provide a thorough survey of the Wiltshire city: ten of the cathedral, and ten of buildings in and around Salisbury. These are hereafter referred to as the Cathedral and City sets (see also Appendix, pp. 184–93). The subjects were listed in ink as follows, with some pencil annotations (Tate; TB CCCLXVIII A; D36332):

No. 1 Bishop's Palace
2 St Thomas's Church
3 Ancient Arch in Mr Wyndham's Garden
4 Close Gate
5 Ancient Market Place
6 New Council Rooms
7 Church
[added in pencil 'St Ed'
and 'by the Market place']
8 Wilton House
[and in pencil]
9 St Edmund's Church
10 Poultry Cross

X 1 Chapter House
Pd X 2 D°
3 Cloisters
4 General View of Church
from Bishop's Garden
5 East Front
Pd X 6 West D°
Pd X 7 North D°
8 Transept
Pd X 9 Choir – Audley Chapel
10 Entrance from West Door

The list is headed 'Size of the drawings at Salisbury for Sir Richard Hoare', but as this sheet measures 54.5 × 38 centimetres (21½ × 15 inches), it does not correspond to the dimensions used for either set of views (though the overall sheet is approximately the size of two City views placed one above the other). This tends to indicate that it was drawn up while ideas about the series were still in flux, something that the muddle over church names for the subject of no. 7 (resulting in the omission of St Martin's) and the later additions of nos 9 and 10 to the City set also supports. However, the annotations to the list of Cathedral subjects, indicating which items had been completed and paid for ('Pd'), demonstrate that the list was a working document around 1801, when the second watercolour of the Chapter House had been exhibited but Turner had not yet received his remuneration.[9] More surprising is the absence of recorded payments for any of the City views, although several must have been completed by that date, judging from the simple 'W Turner' format of the signatures on them. The other thing to note from this list is that three of the subjects stipulated were never actually realised for Colt Hoare: two were to have depicted the cathedral – the East Front (no. 5) and a view looking down the Nave from the West Door (no. 10) – while St Thomas's Church was never painted for the City set.

Before considering the two other lists, which reflect the later stages of the project, we

Fig. 38
The Choir of Salisbury Cathedral, looking East towards the Lady Chapel
c.1796–97
Pencil, 69 × 56 cm
Tate (D02345 / TB L D)

Fig. 39
The Choir of Salisbury Cathedral
Exhibited RA 1797
Watercolour,
64.8 × 50.8 cm
The Salisbury Museum
(W197)
(see p. 185)

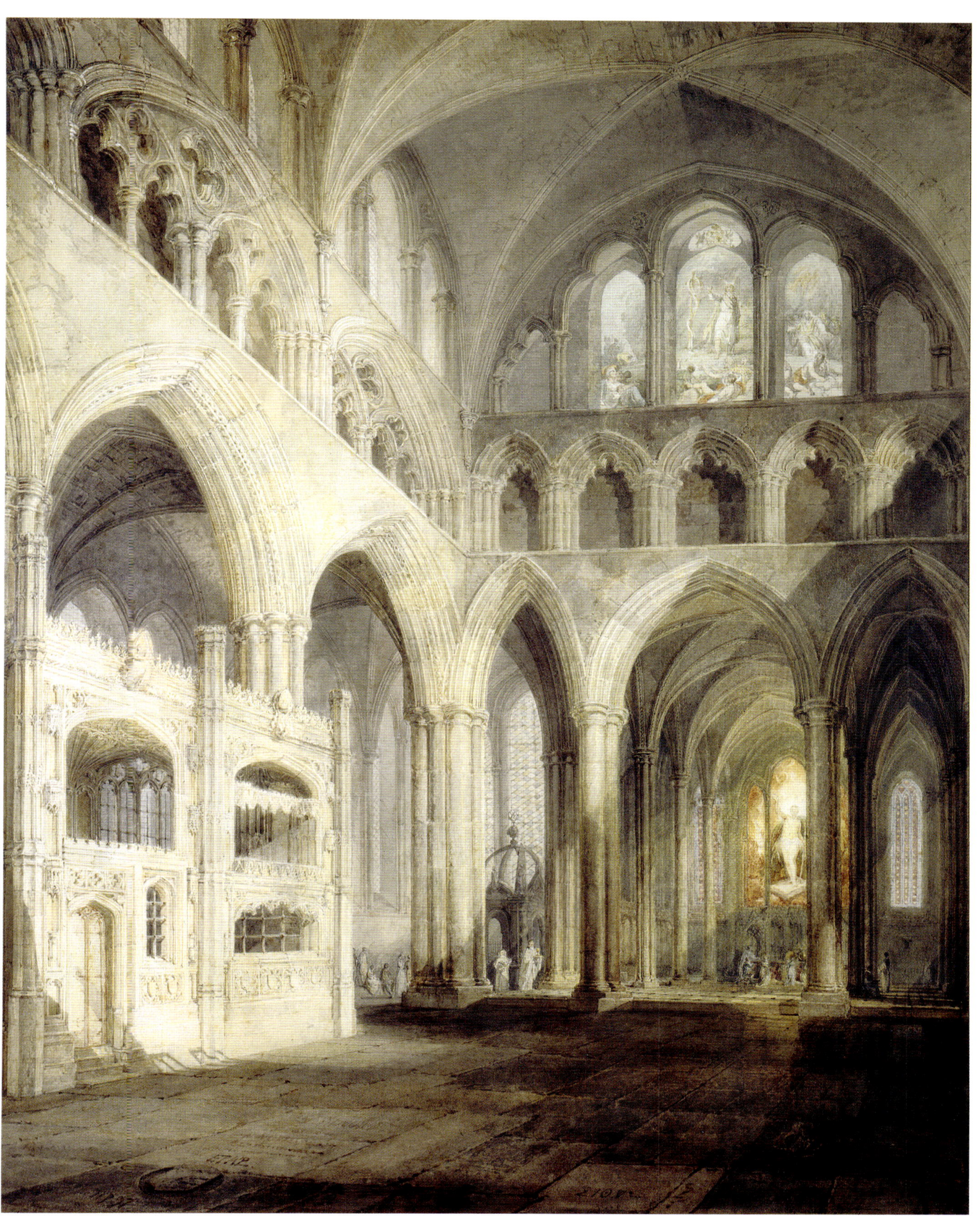

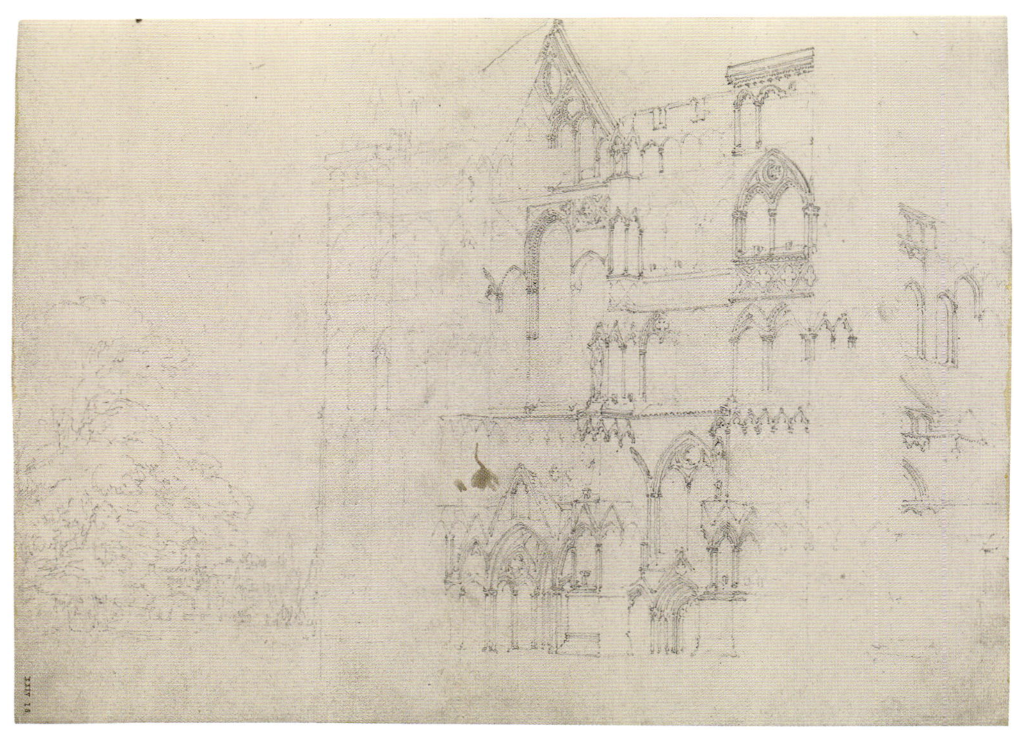

Fig. 40
The West Front of Salisbury Cathedral
1795
Pencil, 20.4 × 26.4 cm
From the 'Isle of Wight' sketchbook
Tate (D00423 / TB XXIV 16)

Fig. 41
The West Front of Salisbury Cathedral
Exhibited RA 1799
Watercolour, 48.5 × 66 cm
Harris Museum and Art Gallery, Preston (W198)
(see p. 185)

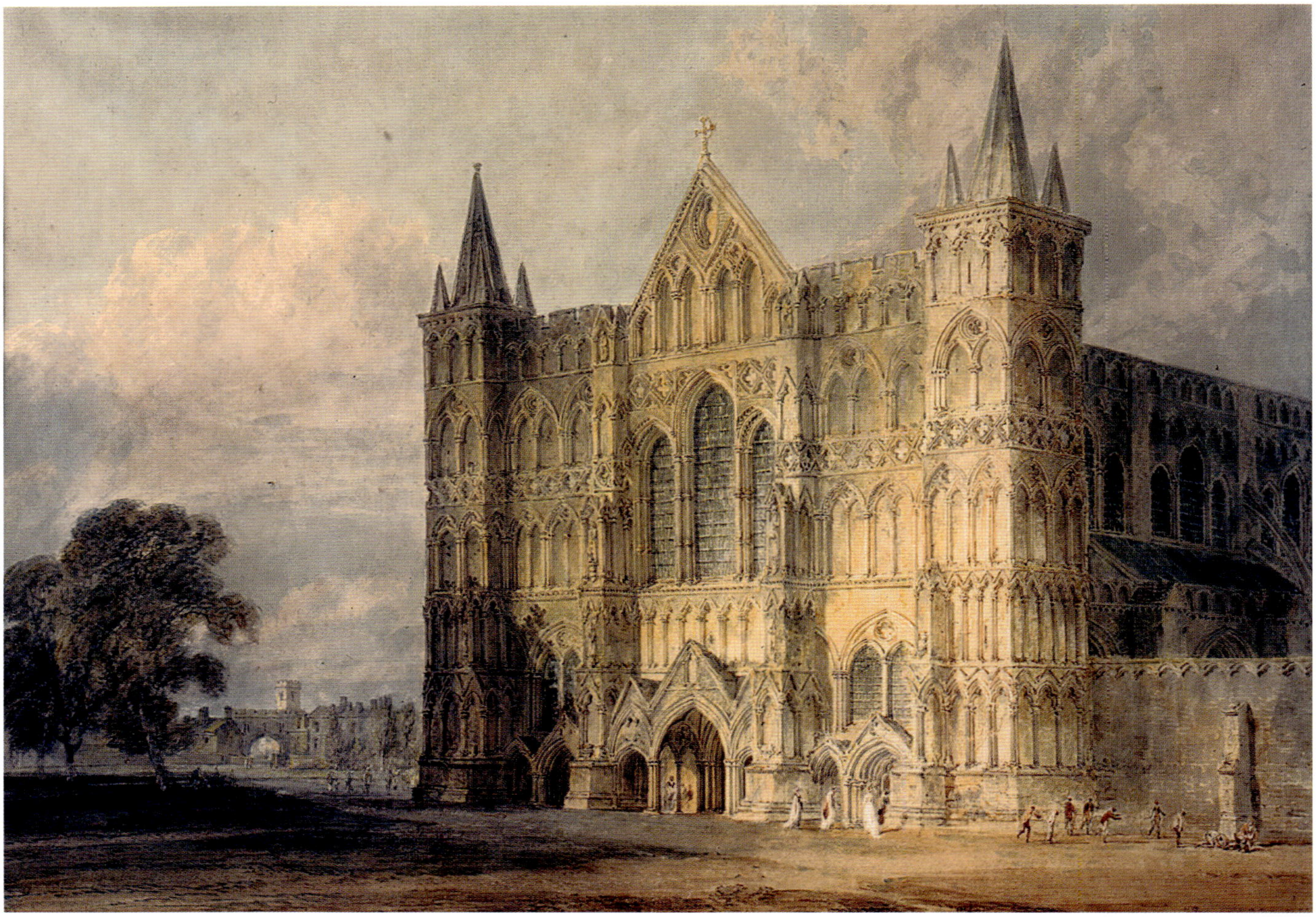

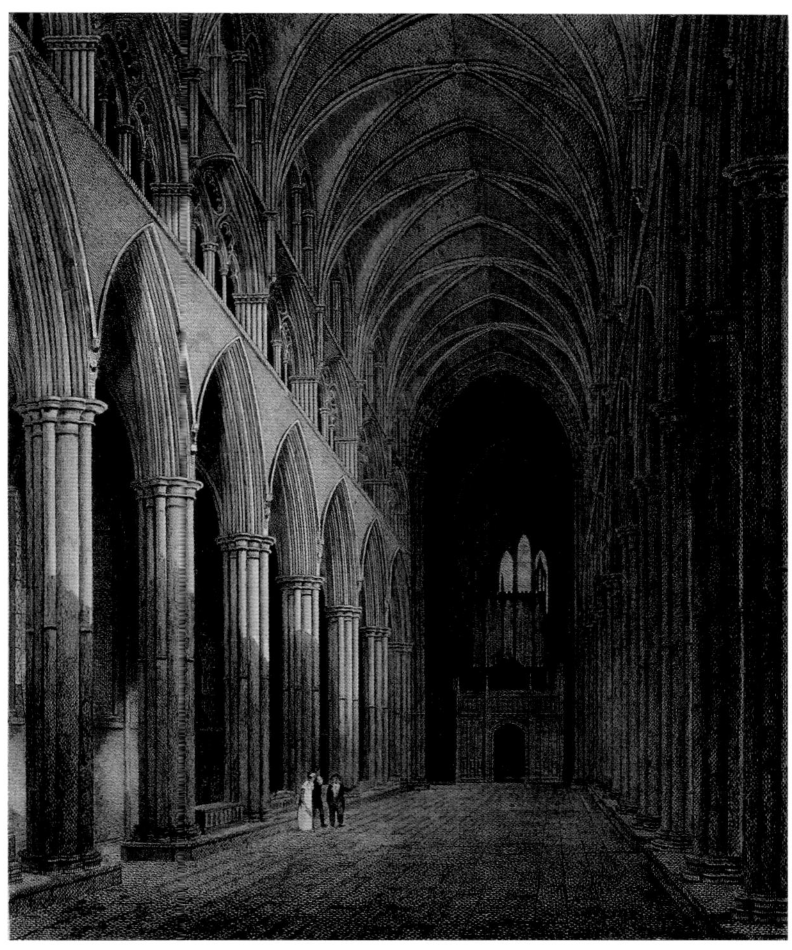

Fig. 42
WILLIAM WOOLNOTH (1780–1837) after FREDERICK NASH (1782–1856)
The Interior View of Salisbury Cathedral from the West Entrance
1814
For Dodsworth, *An Historical Account of the Episcopal See and Cathedral Church of Sarum, or Salisbury*
Engraving, 21.7 × 16.6 cm
British Library, London
(see p. 186)

need to return to 1798. The traditional dating of the *Chapter-House, Salisbury Cathedral* at Manchester (fig. 44), which has been linked with Turner's 1799 exhibit of the same name, would require him to have spent time in Salisbury in 1798 in order to make the related studies (figs 45–46). While this is entirely possible, it requires redating the contents of the 'Salisbury' sketchbook (TB XLIX), a solution that is unsatisfactory because Turner's passage through Wiltshire on the outward stage of the 1798 tour is charted in the Swans sketchbook (TB XLII), a volume of roughly the same dimensions. The 'Salisbury' book was also annotated by Turner late in 1799 with his new address on Harley Street, implying that it was more likely to have been in use that year, when we know he visited Salisbury from Fonthill. So if Turner was not able to call on these sketches for the 1799 view of the Chapter House, his exhibit can only have been the alternative view, now in the Victoria and Albert Museum and previously dated to 1801, which also shows the interior but from the lobby (fig. 43). There are no preliminary designs for this composition, but it could have been developed over an elaborate sketch, made on the spot, like that for the view of the Choir. Indeed, there are areas of under-drawing clearly visible through the washes. It also has a stronger affinity in its stylisation of the figures and its range of colour with the 1799 view of the West Front (fig. 41). This conclusion means that the titles and dates of the Chapter House subjects have been mistakenly exchanged since the nineteenth century; a further detail that confirms this emerges in a letter from Turner that is discussed below.

Following the exhibition of the two views at the Royal Academy in 1799, Turner received a further payment from Colt Hoare of £32.11s, yet again securing an increase on the original terms.[10] He would subsequently charge around 25 guineas for the remaining views of Salisbury Cathedral, but there is no correspondence to pinpoint how he went about inflating his prices – or Colt Hoare's reaction to that much sharper rise.

During the summer of 1799 Turner announced to Joseph Farington his plans to go back to Salisbury while working nearby at Fonthill.[11] The pencil sketches already mentioned reveal him again in the cathedral, as well as conscientiously recording buildings that

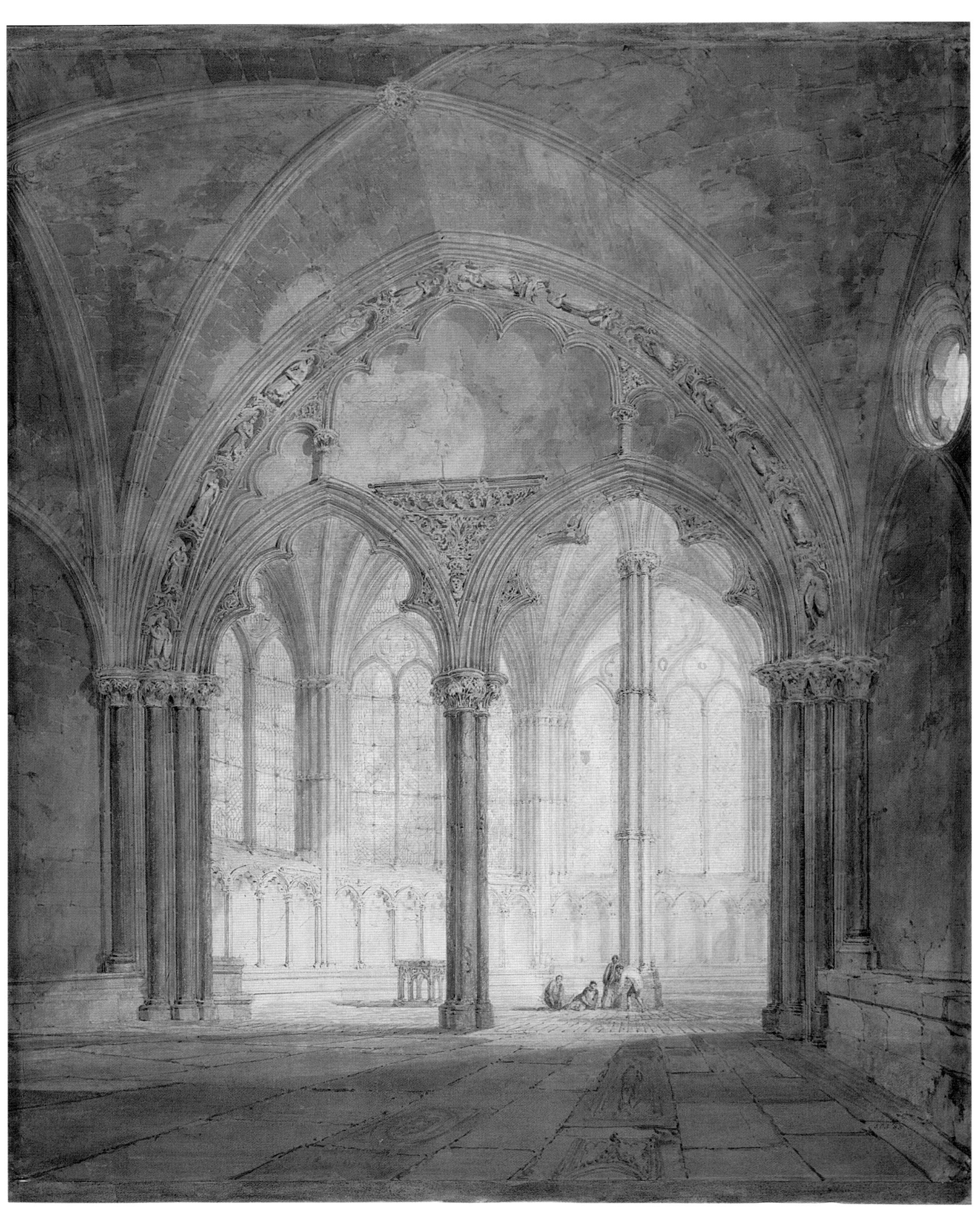

appear on the list of approved City subjects, such as St Thomas's Church (fig. 53), and he also made an excursion up Harnham Hill (fig. 132). Other City subjects included the churches of St Martin's (fig. 55) and St Edmund's (fig. 50), the nearby gothic arch in the garden of the antiquarian Henry Penruddocke Wyndham (an associate of Colt Hoare's and Member of Parliament for Wiltshire since 1795; fig. 52), and the completed Council House (figs 60–62). There was a further opportunity to visit Salisbury (and Stourhead) from Fonthill during the autumn of 1800, but after the second watercolour of the Chapter House was exhibited in 1801 there was no further public manifestation of any work on the project.

Turner was establishing his range as an attention-grabbing painter in oils during this period, but did not abandon topographical commissions, with their guarantee of regular payments. In fact, he was deluged with this kind of work. So much so that even by the end of 1798 he was boasting to Farington, that he 'had more commissions at present than he could execute & got more money than He expended.'[12] After 1798 he created views of the Brocklesby Mausoleum (designed by James Wyatt) for Lord Yarborough, a series of illustrations for Thomas Dunham Whitaker's *History of the Parish of Whalley* in Lancashire (1800), the large watercolours of Fonthill for William Beckford (see pp. 93–103), and began meeting the exacting requirements of the publishers of the annual *Oxford Almanack*.[13] The greater confidence he acquired in his depiction of architecture as a result of this workload fed noticeably into the final works in the Salisbury sequence, where there is a broader handling and an audacious, almost playful way of framing his chosen subjects.

Fig. 43
Inside of the Chapter-House of Salisbury Cathedral
Exhibited RA 1799
Watercolour, 66 × 50.8 cm
Victoria and Albert Museum, London (W201)
(see p. 186)

Colt Hoare would have undoubtedly monitored these developments and could have been concerned, if not frustrated, that the formerly regular trickle of Salisbury watercolours had dried up, even though half of the listed Cathedral subjects and apparently all the City views were still to be done. Until now, the lack of any documentation would have justified this interpretation. However, a previously unpublished bill – currently one of the earliest existing letters from Turner – sent from his second residence at Norton Street, documents his latest delivery to Colt Hoare:

6 Small drawings of Salisbury	42 Guineas
Interior of the Chapter House Salisbury	25 Guineas
	67 – 67
	3 7
	£70 -

Mr Turner will be particularly oblig'd to
Sir Richard Hoare could he show him
a small pair [or 'piece'] of Scipica to make use of
in the Trancept

Norton St. Nov 21 1801.[14]

This bill covers almost all of the City set (figs 49–50, 52, 54–55, 57), but, more significantly, it also relates to the Chapter House view of 1801. Turner's own description of this later exhibit as the 'Interior' subject further supports the theory that the Manchester watercolour has been mistitled and dated (fig. 44). Colt Hoare settled his account on the same day that the invoice was submitted.[15] It is not clear whether this took place in London or at Stourhead; the payment in 1799 was definitely made in London. After the expense of his long tour of Scotland earlier in the autumn

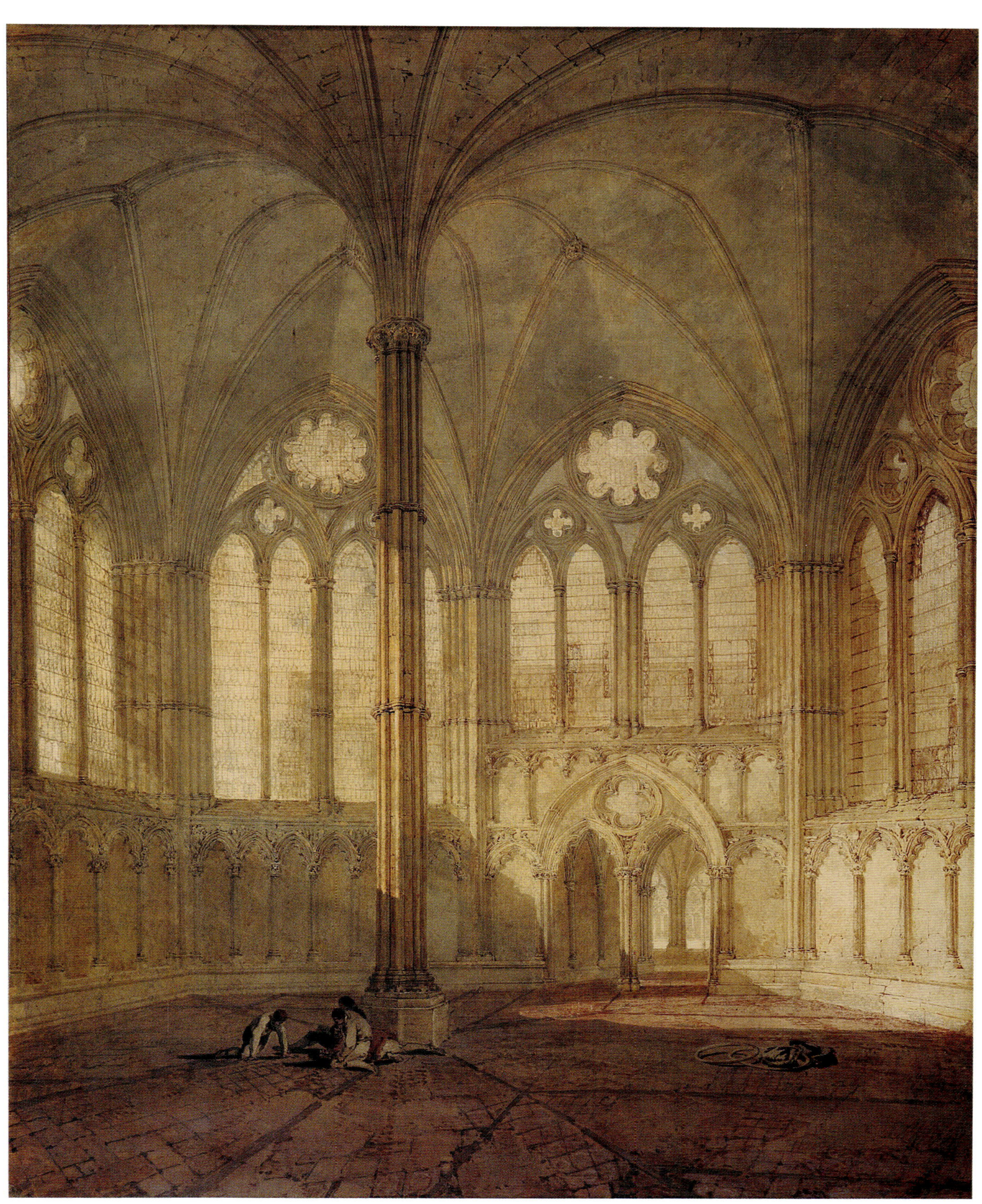

Fig. 45
Studies of the Sculptural Frieze in the Chapter House of Salisbury Cathedral: Joseph and his Brothers; Moses and the Exodus
c.1799
Pencil, 15 × 12.3 cm
From the 'Salisbury' sketchbook
Tate (D02334 / TB XLIX 79a)

Fig. 46
A Capital in the Chapter House of Salisbury Cathedral
c.1799
Pencil, 15 × 12.3 cm
From the 'Salisbury' sketchbook
Tate (D02332 / TB XLIX 78a)

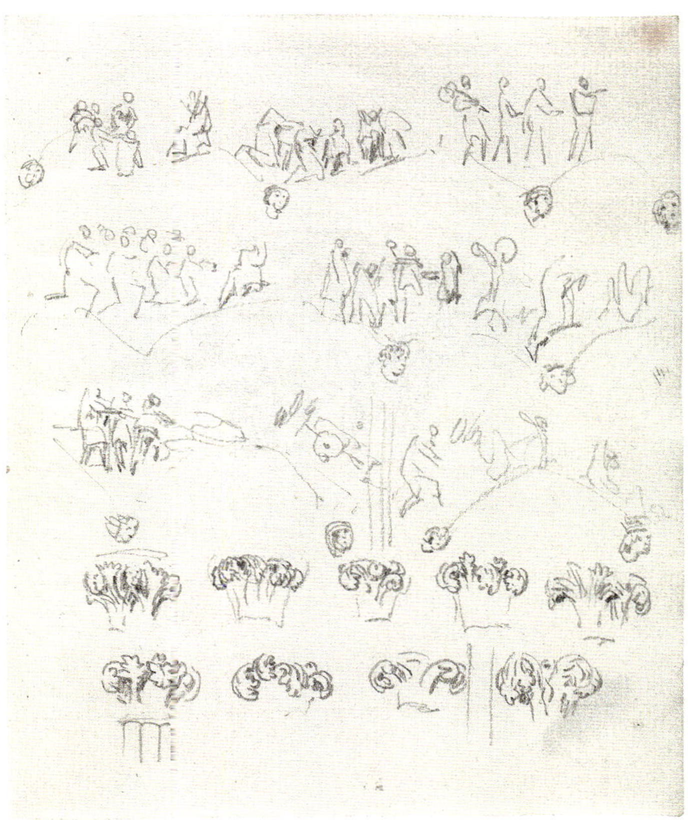

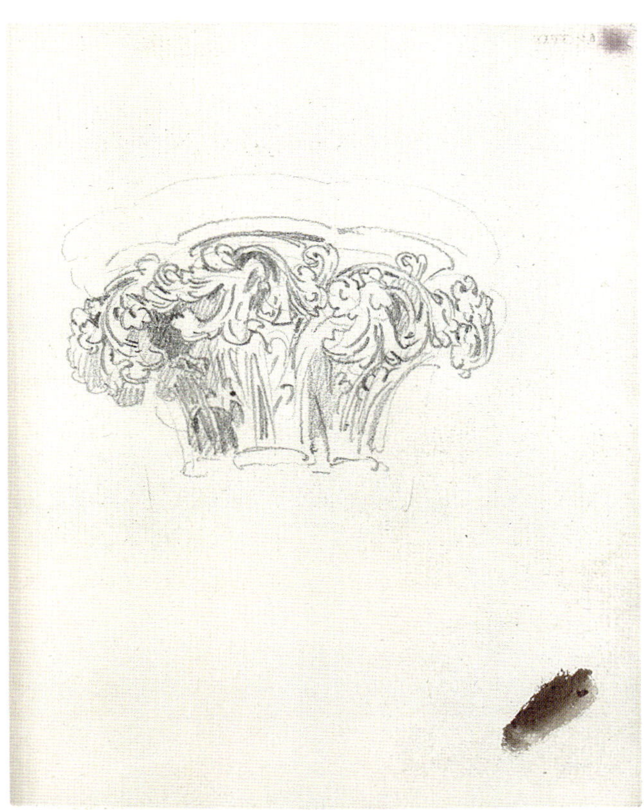

of 1801, Turner would have been glad to chase up outstanding payments.

Strangely, despite the indication in the invoice that Turner was researching the view of the Transept, there appears not to have been an immediate resumption of labour on the Salisbury subjects still to be done. Instead, between 1801 and early 1805, there was yet another hiatus. But some time before April of the latter year there had at last been some progress and four more watercolours were ready. Perhaps significantly, Turner's laggardly manner in executing these was met with a similar dilatoriness in paying for them by Colt Hoare, who evidently told Turner he would not be able to remunerate him before a certain day. Something of that order explains the cool, businesslike tone in Turner's first surviving letter to Colt Hoare. Writing on Saturday 6 April 1805, the artist began with the words, 'The Time being past when Sir Richard Hoare mention'd that I was to send my account of the Drawings finished I now take the liberty of so doing.'[16] After this he proceeded to list the works he had completed and their diverse prices, which ranged from 30 guineas for his most ambitious view of the cathedral's Transept interior (fig. 68), to 25 for the other two large 'outside' works (figs 63 and 66), and 10 for the repetition of his 1796 exhibit of the Close Gate (fig. 59; a rise of 3 guineas above the rate paid for the City subjects). There

Fig. 44
Chapter-House, Salisbury Cathedral
Exhibited RA 1801
Watercolour, 64 × 51 cm
The Whitworth, The University of Manchester (W199
(see p. 187)

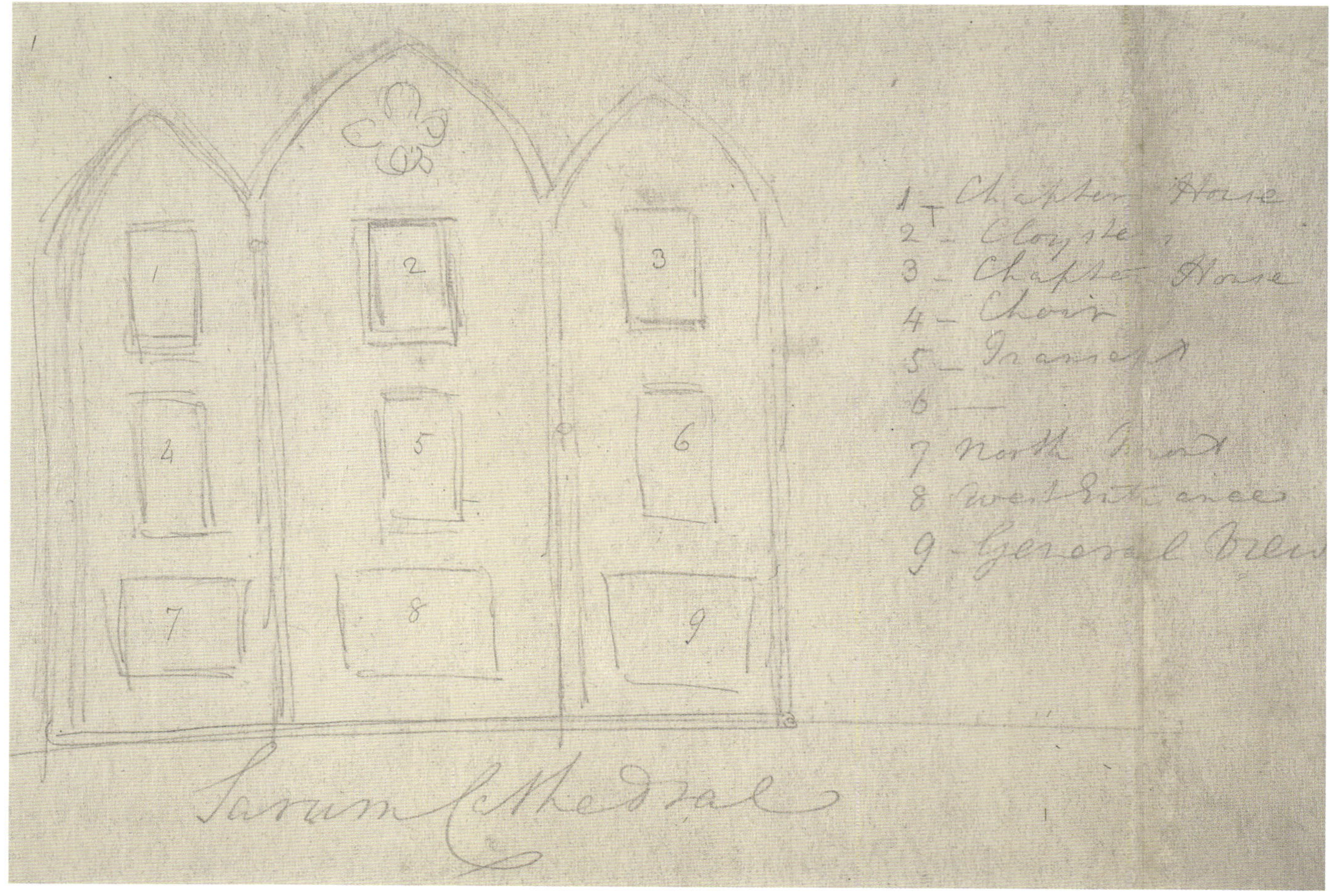

Fig. 47
Design for a Gothic Frame for Nine Drawings of Salisbury Cathedral
c.1805
Pencil, 47.6 × 62.6 cm
British Museum
(1949,0627.1)

appear to be no outline sketches related to the three larger watercolours. Turner could either have been back to Salisbury some time in 1804 to research these subjects, working directly onto the sheets, or he could have unearthed earlier outlines, as in the view of the Choir (fig. 38), and brought them to a more finished state.

In addition to the valuable nuggets of information about Turner's prices, another important detail in the letter reflected a new understanding between patron and artist that only two additional watercolours were now considered necessary to 'complete the set'. Turner hoped he might have time to send them to Stourhead by the end of the summer, after a proposed trip to Devon, but qualified this by saying, realistically, that they were likely to be with Colt Hoare somewhat later. These newly curtailed limits for the Salisbury group imply a body of earlier correspondence, now missing, perhaps even a meeting. Colt Hoare generally spent the first months of the year in London, so they could then have discussed a way of resolving the Salisbury series.

He was evidently in London in 1805 just days after Turner wrote his letter, because he attended the sale on 10 April of the 'Capital and Truly Valuable Collection of Original High-Finished Drawings … by that Eminent Artist, The Younger Cozens'. This group of over 90 works came from the collection of 'An Amateur of Distinguished Taste', the person in question being William Beckford, Colt Hoare's near neighbour at Fonthill. Very few of the watercolours sold for more than £10, but the most expensive lot at £21 was a view of Rome from the Villa Madama, which was one of seven bought by Colt Hoare. The records of the sale do not specify a name for the buyer of lot 35, which sold for only £2.12s.6d, and followed the first of the baronet's purchases. Perhaps it did not reach its reserve and a deal was done subsequently,

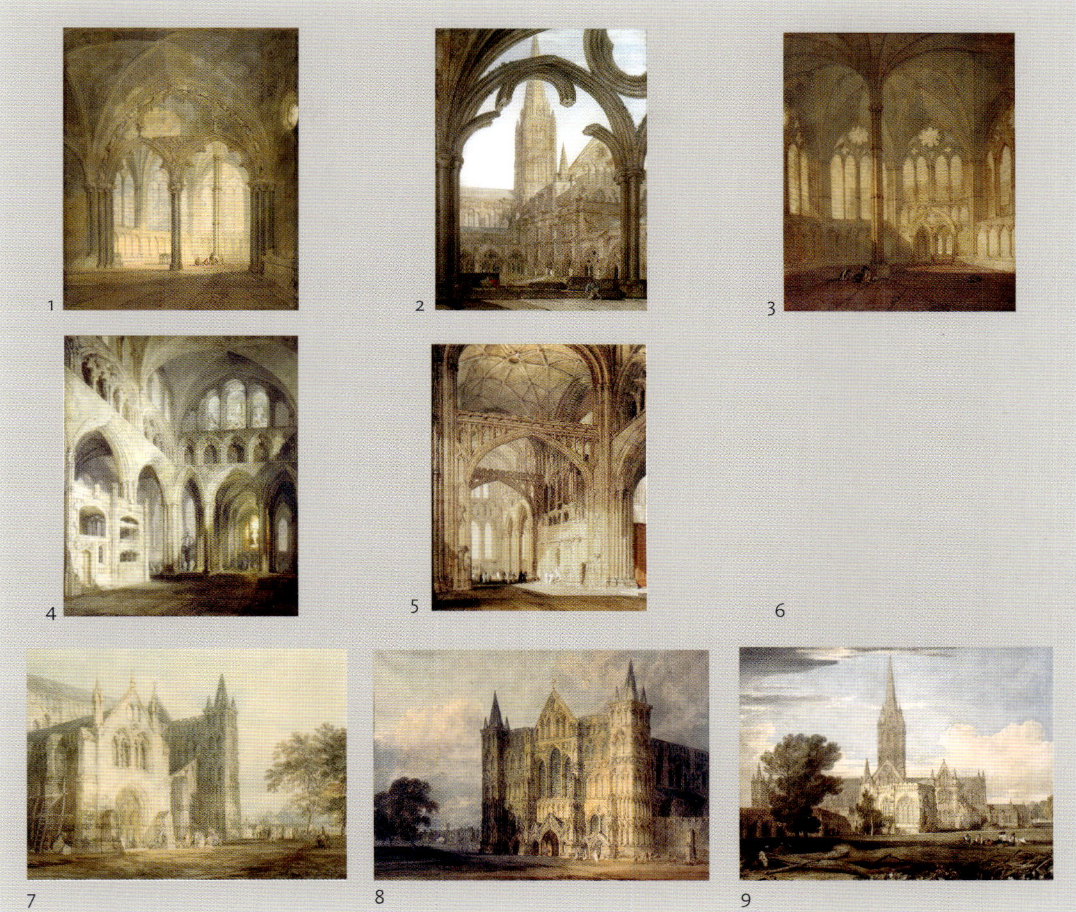

Fig. 48
Turner's Cathedral set, arranged according to the picture hang in fig. 47:

1. Chapter House (fig. 43)
2. Cloister (fig. 63)
3. Chapter House (fig. 44)
4. Choir (fig. 39)
5. Transept (fig. 68)
6. No image listed for this space
7. North Front (fig. 37)
8. West Entrance (fig. 41)
9. General View (fig. 66)

but it is a matter of some significance, because the item belonged to Turner shortly afterwards. This was the 'View near Fluelen in the Tyrol – a delicate and beautiful Drawing in manner, and exquisitely finished' (fig. 18).[17]

At some point in the next days or weeks, the two men met once more and totted up the present composition of the Cathedral set, making a list on the back of the Cozens watercolour that reads: '2 chapter / 2 inside / 1 Cloyster / 2 outside / 1 general'.[18] Alongside this there is a faint outline of a gothic arch, divided into two sections. These elements were given fuller treatment on the third list, on the back of the view of Chichester, mentioned above (fig. 47). The same works were numbered and enumerated yet again to relate to a more elaborate gothic structure, this time divided into three long panels resembling the cathedral's lancet windows, each containing three watercolours arranged vertically, below which Turner wrote 'Sarum Cathedral'.

This may have been a proposal for a special setting to display the watercolours, envisaged for Stourhead. In considering a possible function for the Cathedral set, the year 1805 is significant because of the role Colt Hoare played once he became High Sheriff of Wiltshire in February; as both a civic dignitary and a local antiquarian, he would naturally have wanted to be able to display the watercolours at Stourhead to demonstrate to guests his strong affiliation with the county and its principal city. What Turner's schema helped to identify was the awkwardness inherent in attempting to present the existing drawings as a planned set: three of them are landscape format; the other five are uprights. These can be arranged in only so many permutations to form satisfactory patterns suitable for a picture hang (see fig. 48). The diagram highlighted a way of getting round this, proposing the need for one more upright cathedral subject – no. 6 – which would ideally have been the view from

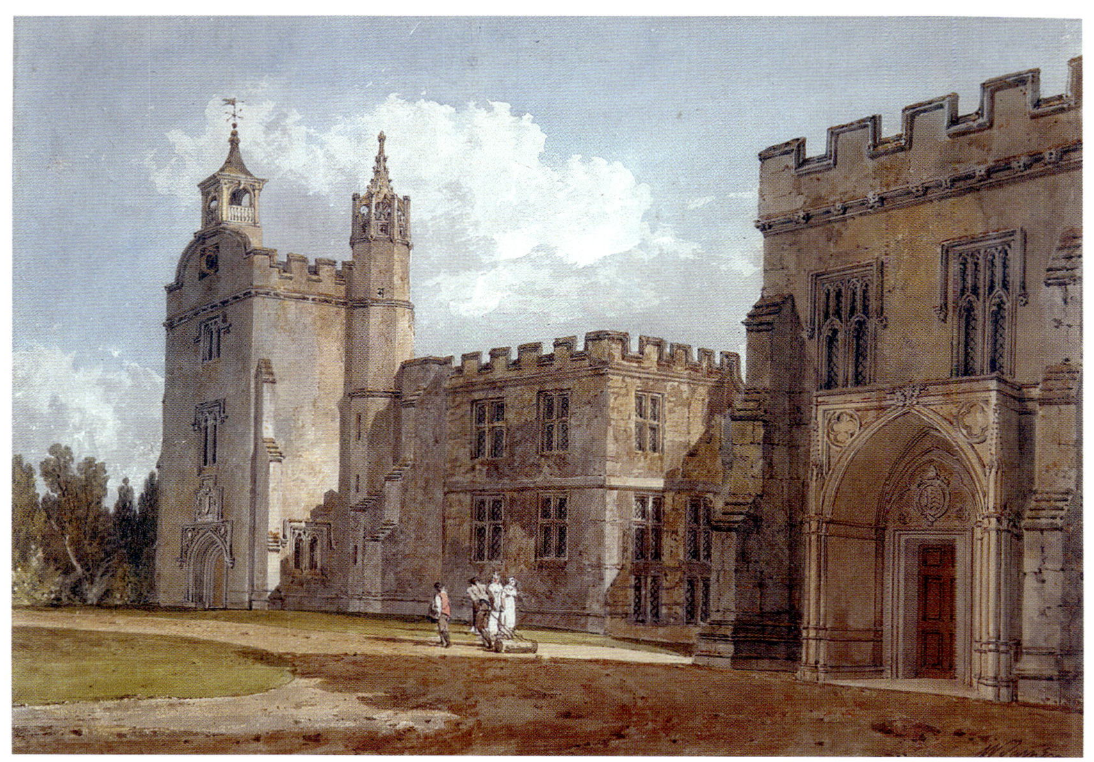

Fig. 49
The Bishop's Palace, Salisbury
c.1799
Watercolour, 28.4 × 35.9 cm
The Higgins, Bedford
(W204)
(see p. 189)

the west entrance on the original list. But having made this case, it seems neither Colt Hoare nor Turner pressed for any further additions, and soon afterwards the Cathedral watercolours were installed as a group in the Column Room, opposite the prized Italian views by Ducros.

Nevertheless, payment for the last of these, as requested by Turner in his letter in April 1805, had still not been forthcoming seven months later, and so on 23 November a further invoice was submitted, which was paid soon after.[19] This also specified the final two City views that had just been delivered on 21 November (figs 58 and 62), apparently face to face, when there had also been some discussion of a further commission related to a 'History of Marden'. The reference has puzzled scholars because none of Colt Hoare's published writings touch on the Herefordshire district. In fact, the relevant 'History' was much older and something of great value to Colt Hoare as a bibliophile. The library at Stourhead contained one of the exceptionally rare copies of the *Account of the Manor of Marden*, written by Thomas, Earl Coningsby of Hampton Court (1657–1729), running to 720 pages, which the house catalogue lists as having been 'Illustrated with additional Drawings and Prints'.[20] Turner, it seems, was to provide designs to supplement this copy. In his November letter he mentioned that he possibly had a sketch of 'Lord Coningsby's Monument' (which can be found in the church of Hope-under-Dinmore), but he seemed very half-hearted about the value of developing such a subject, effectively

Fig. 50
St Edmund's Church, Salisbury
c.1799
Watercolour, 38.4 × 27 cm
British Museum (W205)
(see p. 189)

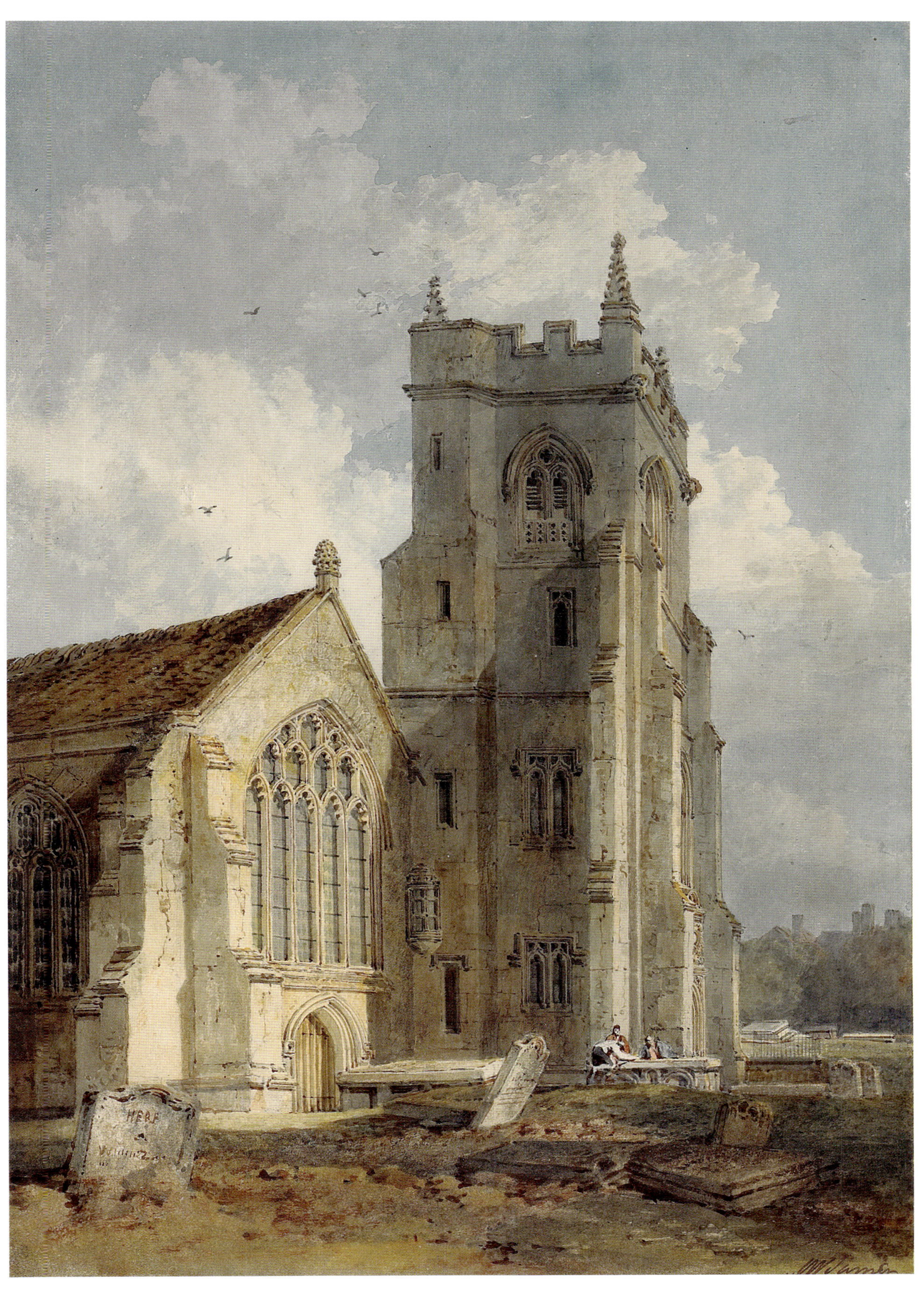

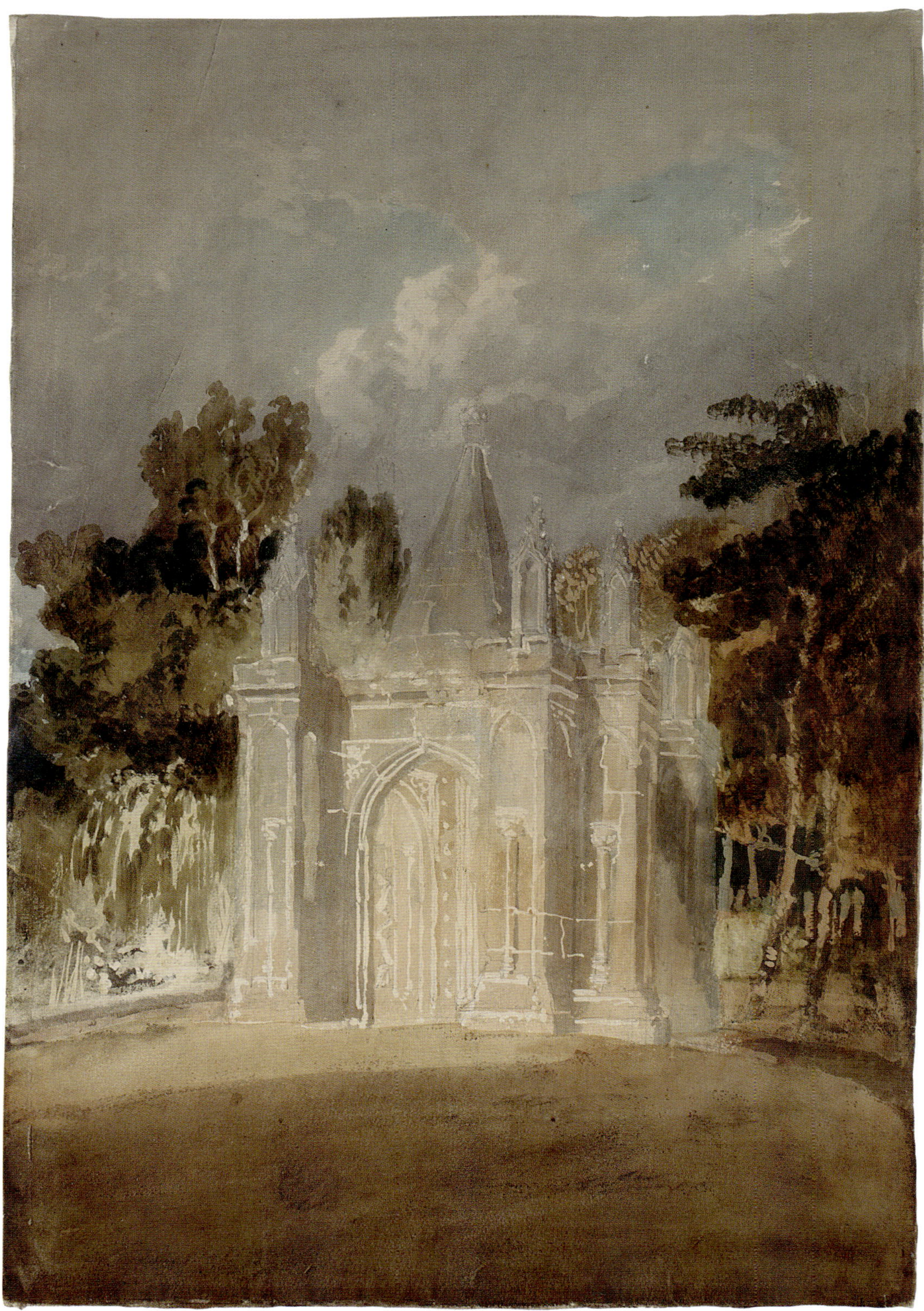

Fig. 51
A Study of the Arch in Mr Wyndham's Gardens, Salisbury
c.1799
Pencil, watercolour and gouache, 47.7 × 32.9 cm
Tate (D02350 / TB L I)

OPPOSITE: Fig. 52
The Ancient Arch in Mr Wyndham's Garden, Salisbury
c.1799
Pencil and watercolour, 37.9 × 29.3 cm
British Museum (W206)
(see p. 190)

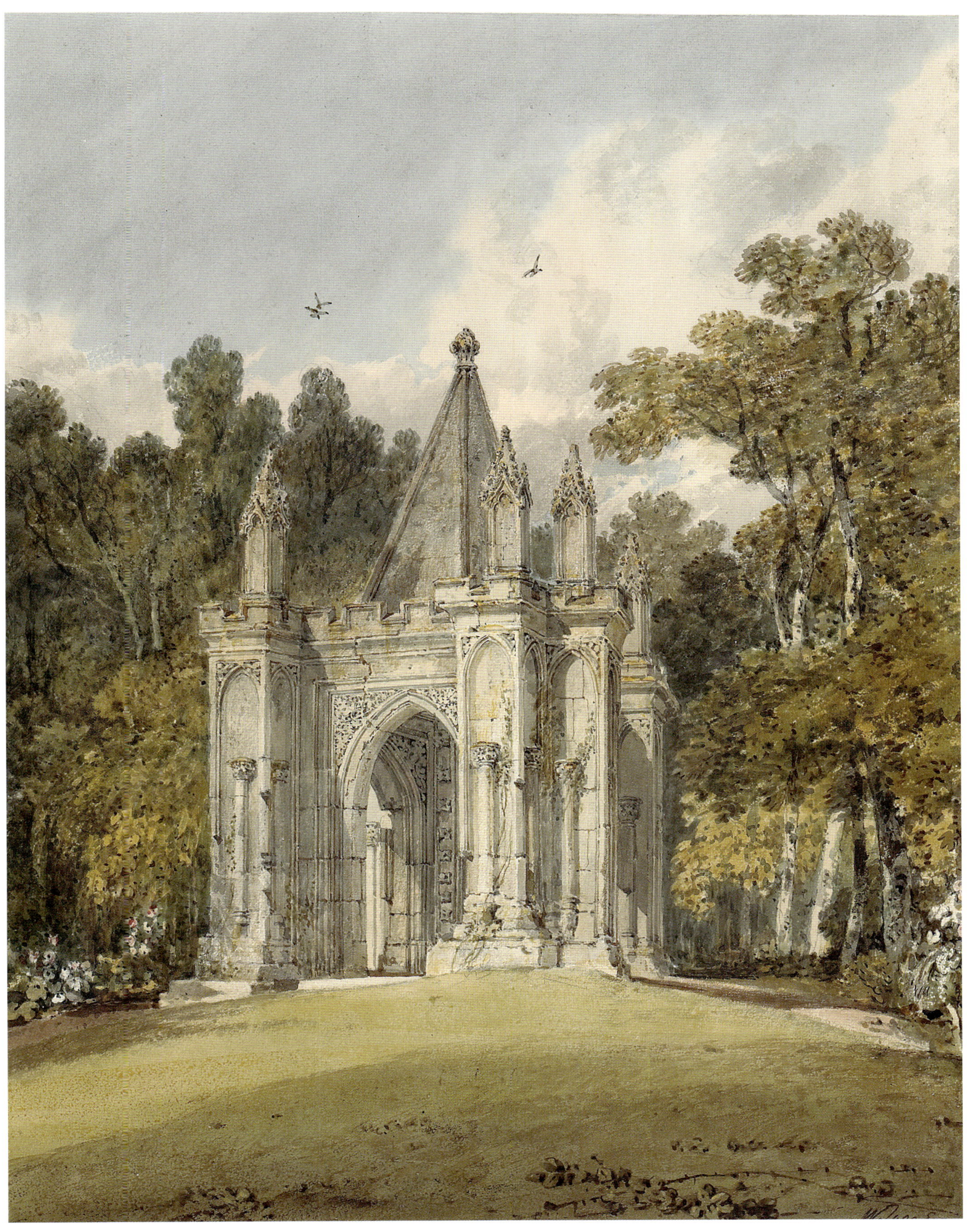

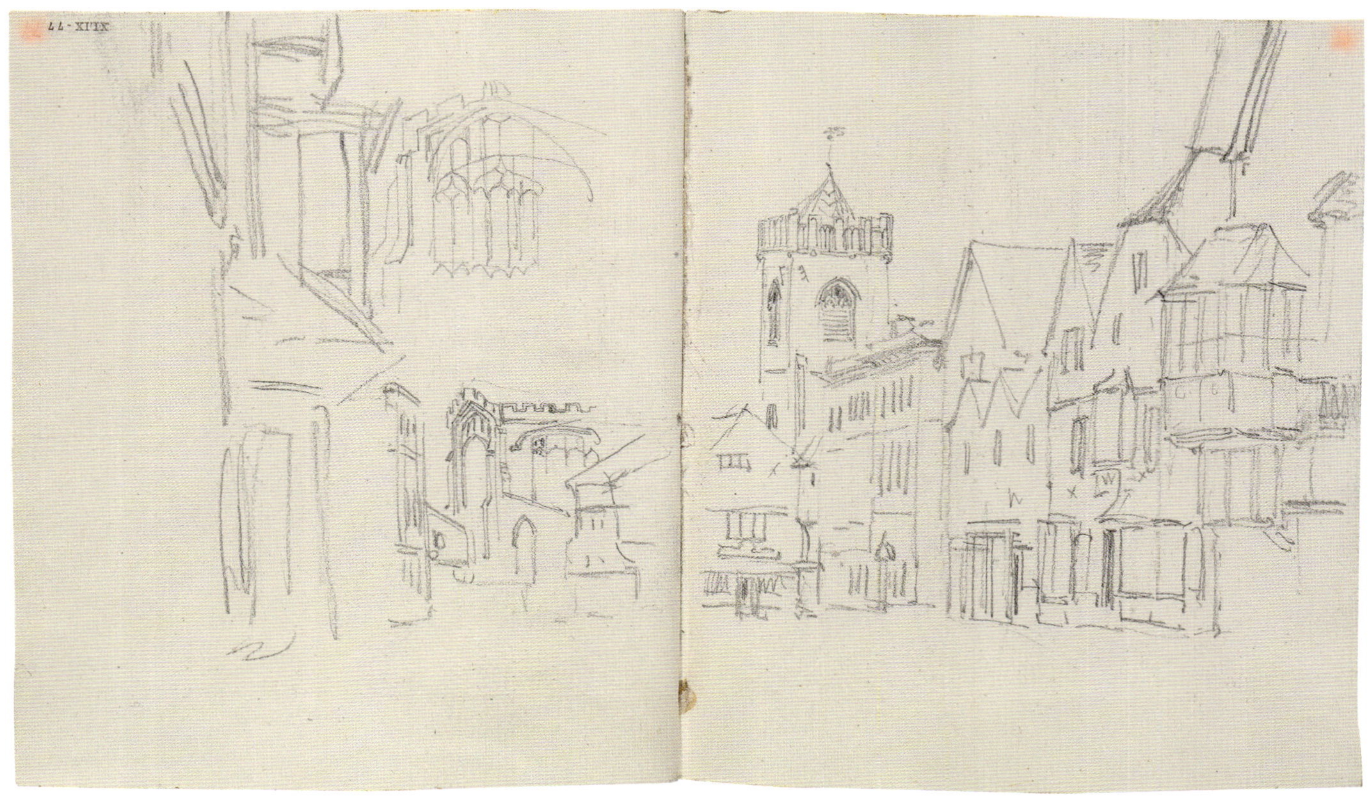

Fig. 53
St Thomas's Church from the High Street, looking North

c.1799
Pencil, 15 × 12.3 cm
From the 'Salisbury' sketchbook
Tate (D02329, D02330 / TB XLIX 76a, 77)
(see p. 190)

discouraging Colt Hoare's interest. His tactics presumably worked and resulted instead in the commission for the two views of Coningsby's home, Hampton Court, which are listed in the 'Hereford Court' sketchbook and were sent to Stourhead at the beginning of March 1806 (see pp. 26–27 and pp. 34–35; fig. 19). The November 1805 conversation could also have been the moment when Colt Hoare's name was inscribed on the various views of Malmesbury (fig. 27), although in the end nothing came of that group.[21] It would be several more years before Colt Hoare embarked on his detailed researches into the history of his own county.

These matters brought to a close the long period of Turner's involvement with Colt Hoare's topographical interests. Once complete, the City set was mounted and bound up in an album for the library, a process that helped to preserve the original colours until they left Stourhead, after which some works were better protected from bright light than others. By binding them in a volume Colt Hoare also determined that they were primarily for his own reference, or for favoured guests. The Cathedral set, on the other hand, hung prominently in the Column Room, where they could be seen by visitors to the house and became among the most valued of Colt Hoare's acquisitions from a contemporary artist. He described them proudly as some of the finest achievements of recent watercolour painting, 'the acme of perfection' (though he remained doubtful as to whether artworks in watercolour could be considered 'worthy of being included in

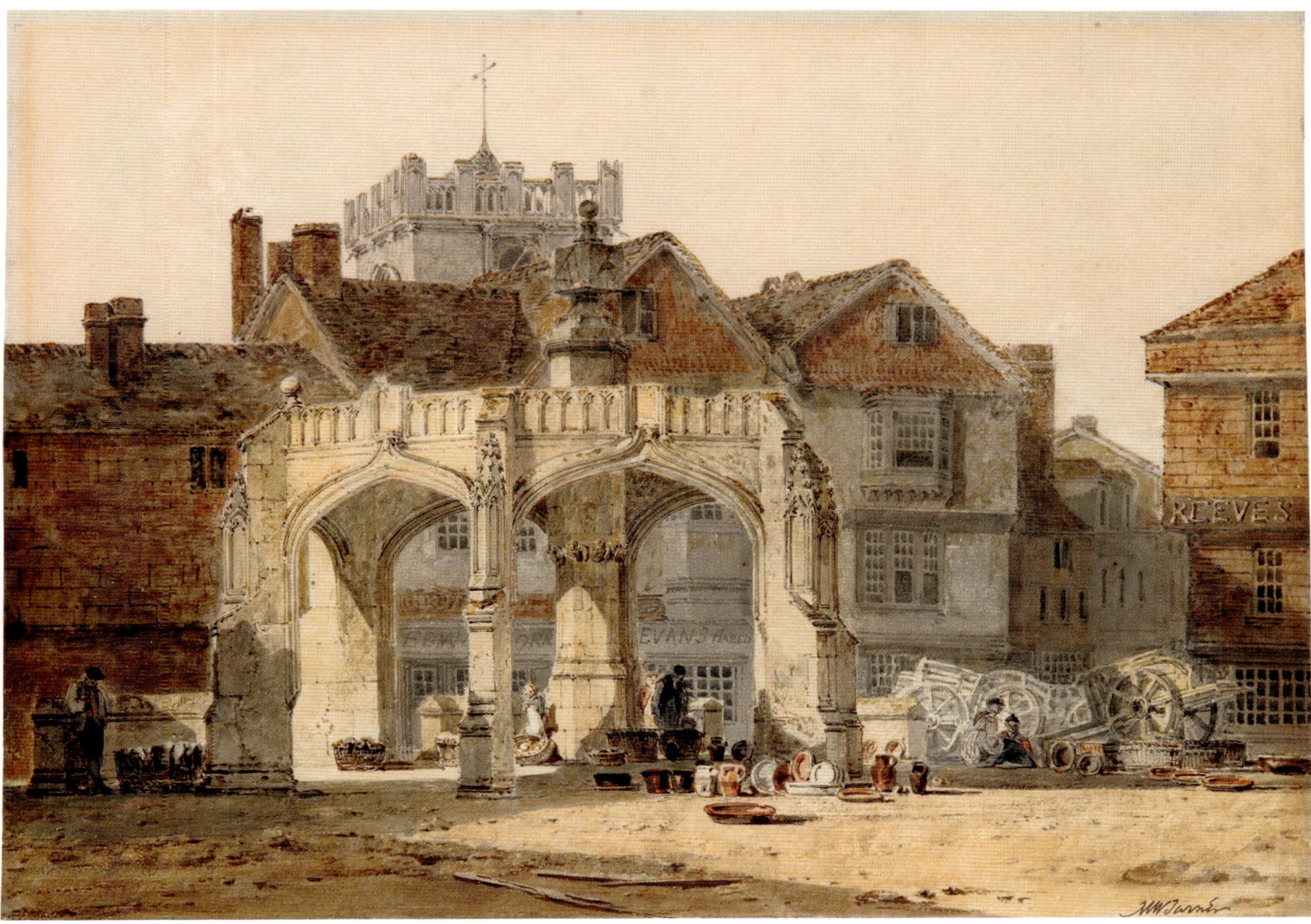

Fig. 54
The Poultry Cross, with the Tower of St Thomas's Church, Salisbury
*c.*1799
Watercolour, 36.2 × 48 cm
Israel Museum, Jerusalem (W211)
Gift of Sam Weisbord, Los Angeles, to American Friends of the Israel Museum, in loving memory of his mother, Goldie Weisbord
(see p. 191)

the *higher* class of painting'). In time, the drawn-out process of their creation had been forgotten and he was ready to question whether they could 'ever be surpassed'.[22]

Other artists certainly saw them and took note. John Constable, for example, must have studied them during his visit in October 1811, when he would no doubt have been intrigued to see that Turner had anticipated the viewpoint of one of his sketches of the cathedral from the Bishop's Garden (Victoria and Albert Museum).[23] The influence of Turner's watercolours can also be detected in several of the illustrations by Frederick Nash (1782–1856), engraved for the 1814 history of the cathedral written by the verger William Dodsworth, particularly those of the Chapter House and the Transept. John Britton's rival publication, also published in 1814, included views that are patently derived from Turner's series (fig. 65). Even in the 1830s, Thomas Shotter Boys (1803–74) composed his view of the North Porch in exactly the same way as Turner's earlier depiction.[24]

Both of Turner's sets of Salisbury watercolours remained at Stourhead until 1883, when the costs of maintaining the estate led Sir Henry Ainslie Hoare to sell off many important heirlooms, including a large number of the best paintings and the vast library devoted to British history and topography. The top price among the Cathedral series was reached for the inventive depiction of the Chapter House (fig. 44), but two of the cheapest works went straight into the national collection at the Victoria and Albert Museum (figs 43 and 63). Curiously, the album

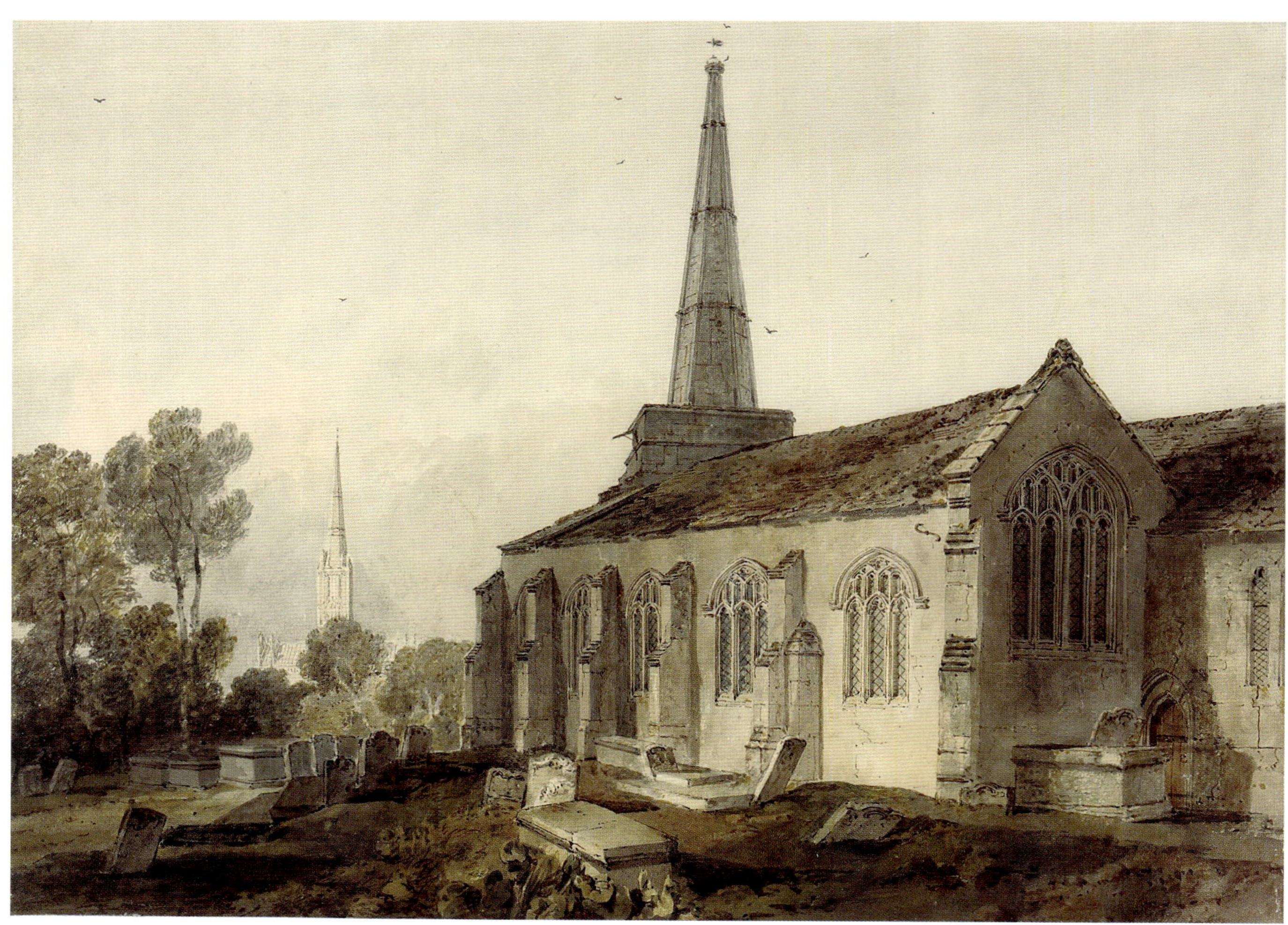

Fig. 55
St Martin's Church, Salisbury
c.1799
Watercolour, 31.8 × 43.2 cm
British Museum (W207)
(see p. 192)

of City views did not appear in the official sale catalogue, but was subsequently acquired by the Revd J.A. Ellis of the local village of Stourton, 'who knew the Library well'.[25] After the album left his collection it was broken up in a sale in 1927, and since then the whereabouts of some of the watercolours remained unknown until very recently.

The Cathedral views, however, continued to resonate with artists and the wider public, speaking to the patriotism that promoted watercolour as a uniquely British (often defined more narrowly as an 'English') achievement. In the last decades of the Victorian era, the Royal Academy occasionally included large groups of Turner's watercolours in its annual winter exhibitions of Old Masters. In 1887 the exhibition was slanted towards earlier works and featured two of the Salisbury set: the Choir (fig. 39) and the Transept (fig. 68). These were seen by the young Frederick H. Evans (1853–1943), who went on to become a celebrated architectural

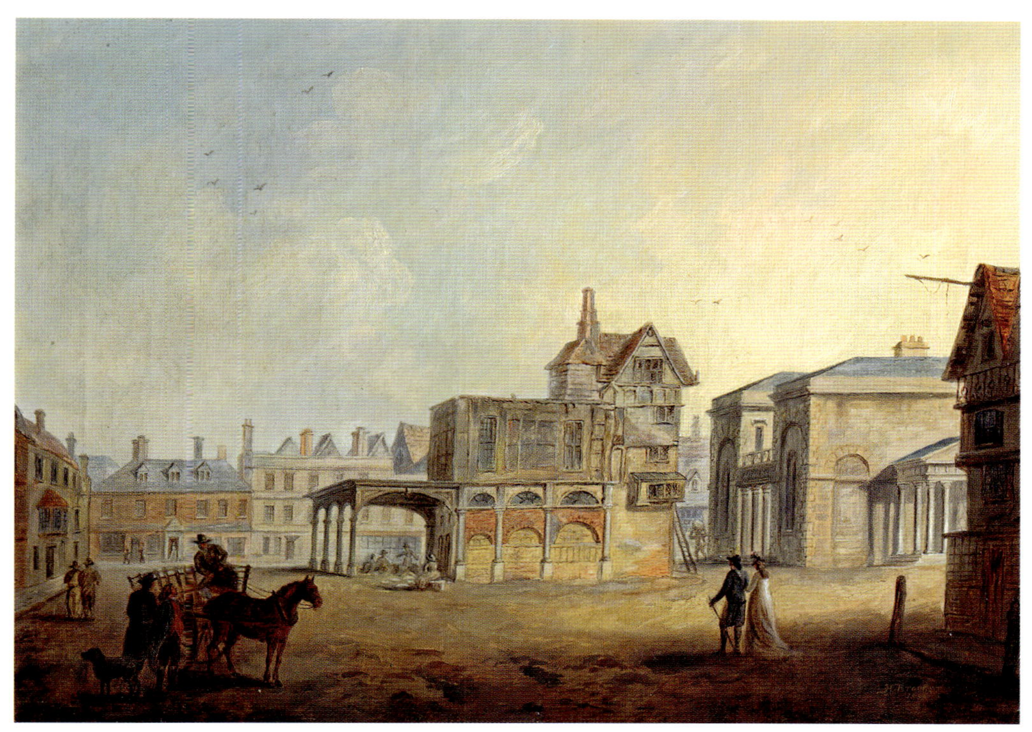

Fig. 56
HENRY BROOKS
Salisbury Guildhall from the Square
1795
Oil on canvas, 34 × 47 cm
Salisbury City Council

Fig. 57
The Old Council House, the Market Place, Salisbury
*c.*1799
Watercolour, 28 × 38.5 cm
Cooper Gallery, Barnsley
(W212)
(see p. 191)

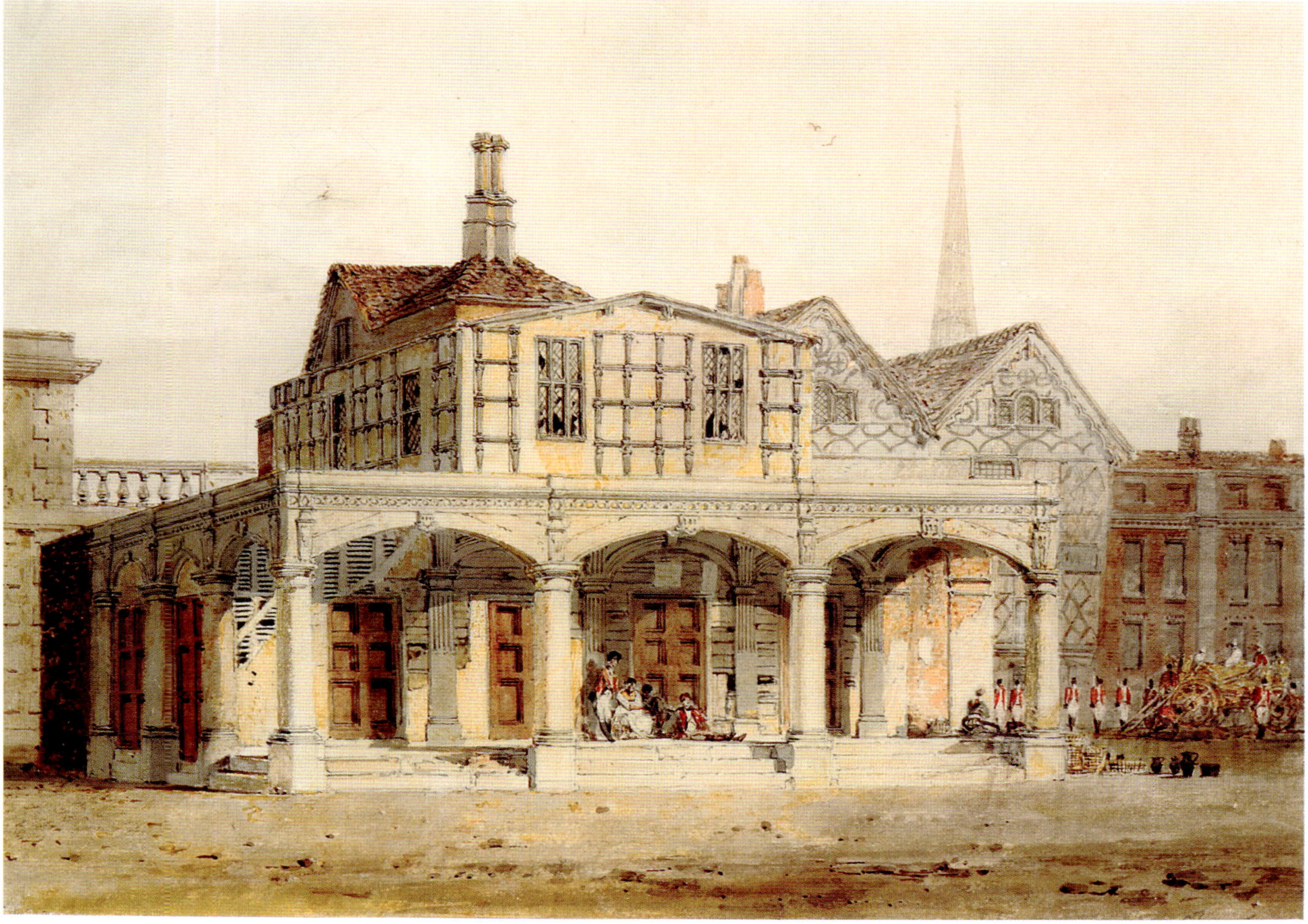

OPPOSITE: **Fig. 59**
Gateway to the Close, Salisbury
1802–5
Watercolour, 45.6 × 31.5 cm
Fitzwilliam Museum, Cambridge (W208)
(see p. 192)

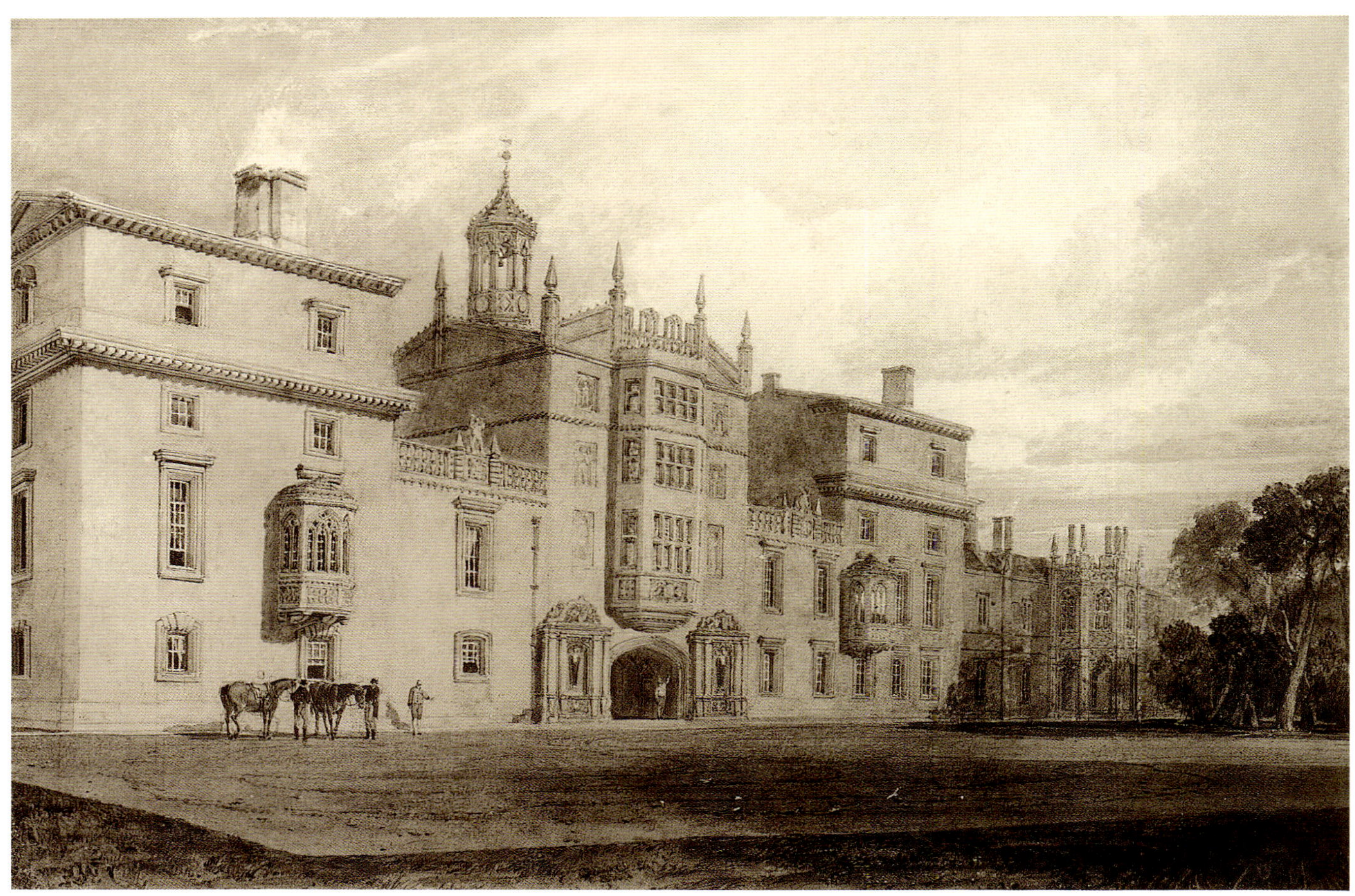

Fig. 58
The East Front of Wilton House
1805
Watercolour, 32 × 46 cm
Engraved by Thomas Higham (1795–1844) for Colt Hoare, *History of Modern Wiltshire*, 1825
Private collection, whereabouts unknown (W214)
(see p. 193)

photographer and for whom they were a revelation: 'What impressed me most was the superb sense of height, bigness, light, atmosphere, grandeur that this incomparable artist had managed to suggest with the few inches that comprise these small pictures.'[26] The experience led him to visit Salisbury for himself, to 'see what a cathedral looks like'.[27] Curiously, however, none of his photographs of Salisbury appear to have survived. But from 1888 onwards he was producing images at Gloucester (fig. 64), which was the start of a process that eventually took him to most of the English cathedrals Turner had recorded around a century earlier. Evans's ability to capture light and shade, and his notable use of daring or overlooked compositions, position him as one of Turner's most successful followers. Although Turner's watercolours had been produced at a time when antiquarian interest in historical or architectural information was paramount, he imbued his views with a more imaginative flavour. It was this openness to the subjective response of each viewer that Evans described as an ambition for his photographs, and his hope of making each a 'record of emotion' or a series of 'poems in stone'.[28]

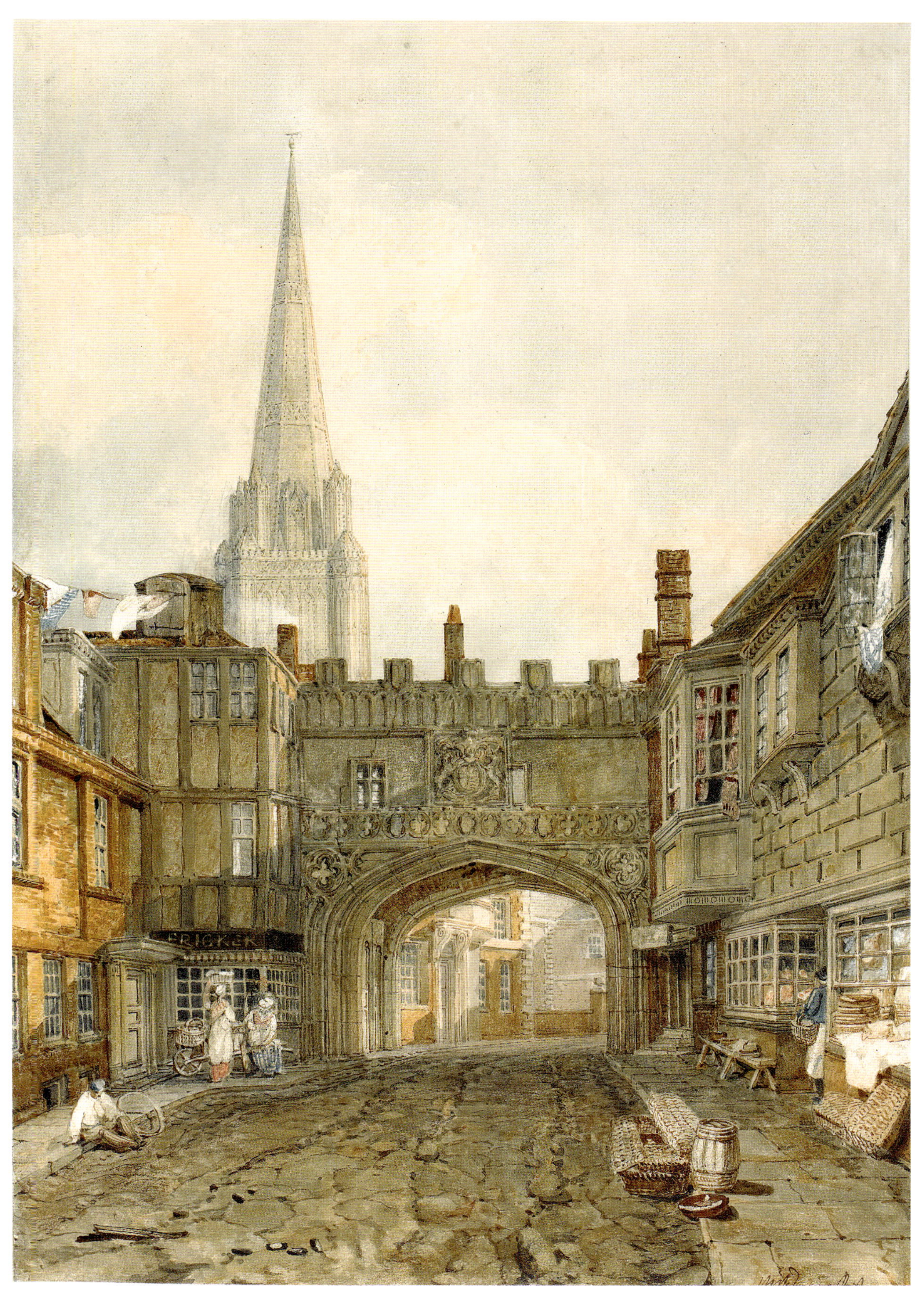
FRICKER

Fig. 60
The New Council House, Salisbury
c.1795
Pencil, 23.1 × 28.2 cm
Tate (D02356 / TB L O)

Fig. 61
The New Council House, Salisbury
c.1799
Pencil and watercolour, 28.4 × 43.1 cm
Tate (D02357 / TB L P)

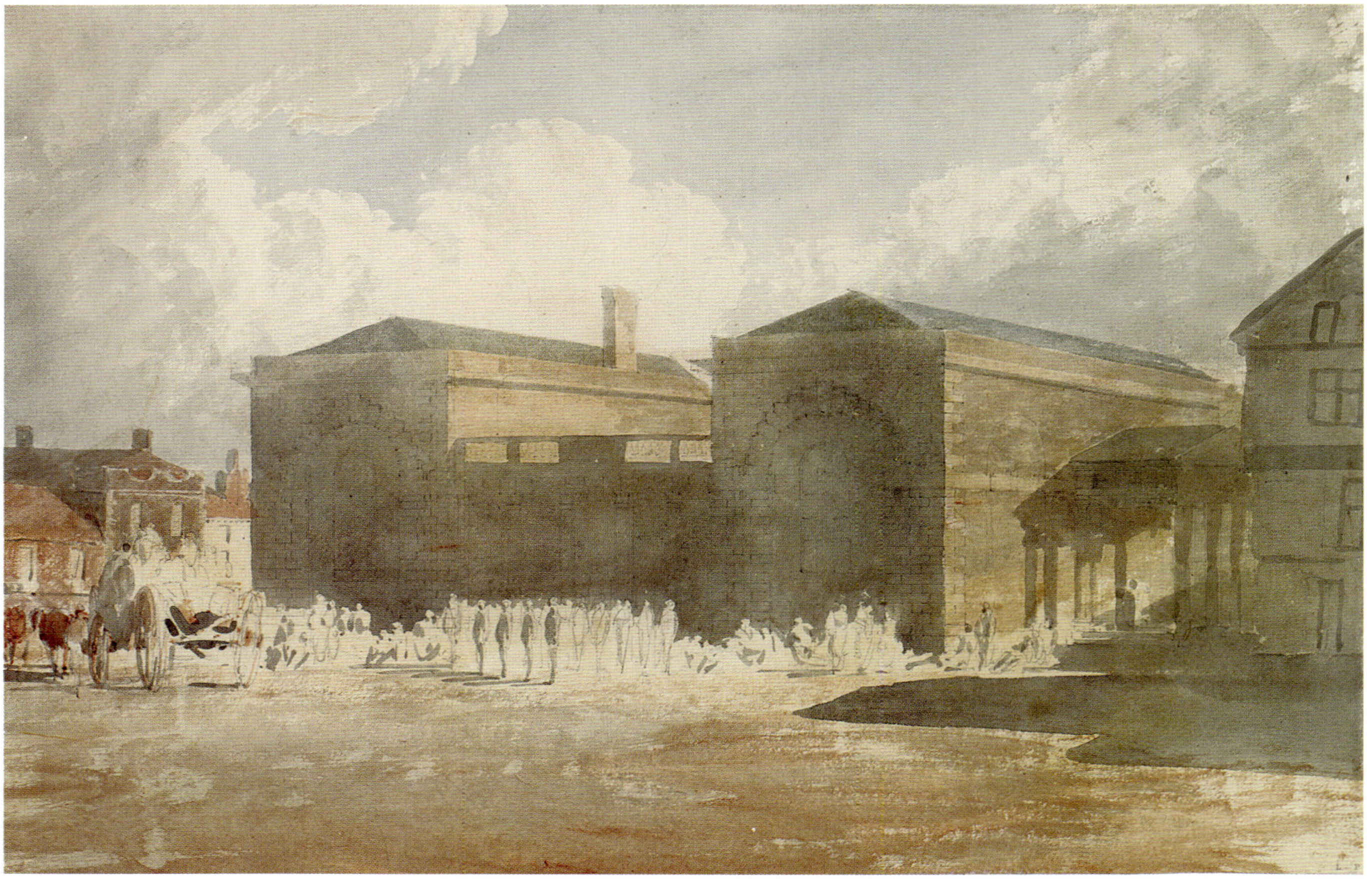

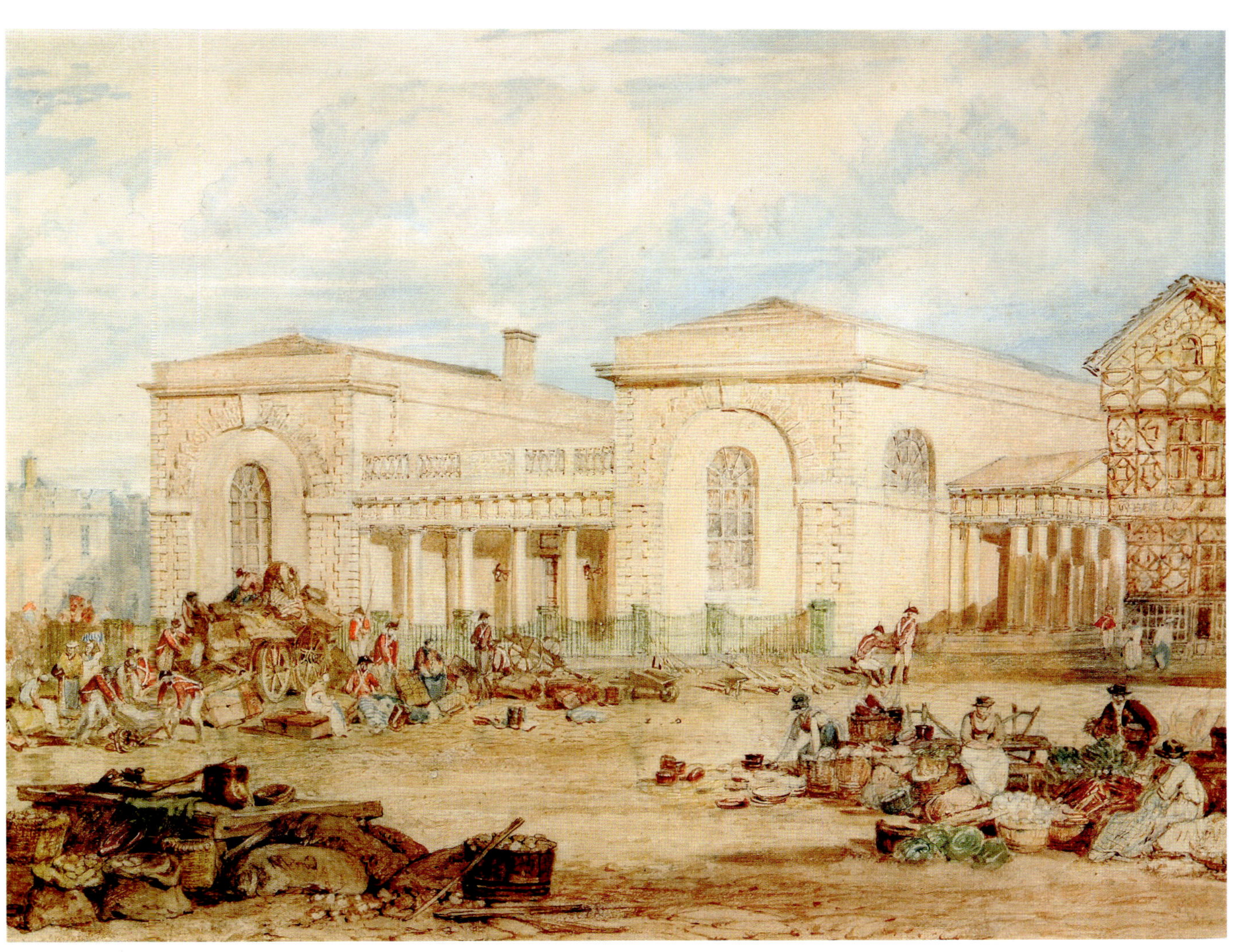

ABOVE AND DETAIL ON FOLLOWING PAGES:

Fig. 62

The New Council House (or Guildhall), Salisbury

c.1805
Watercolour, 30 × 39 cm
Cooper Gallery, Barnsley
(W213)
(see p. 193)

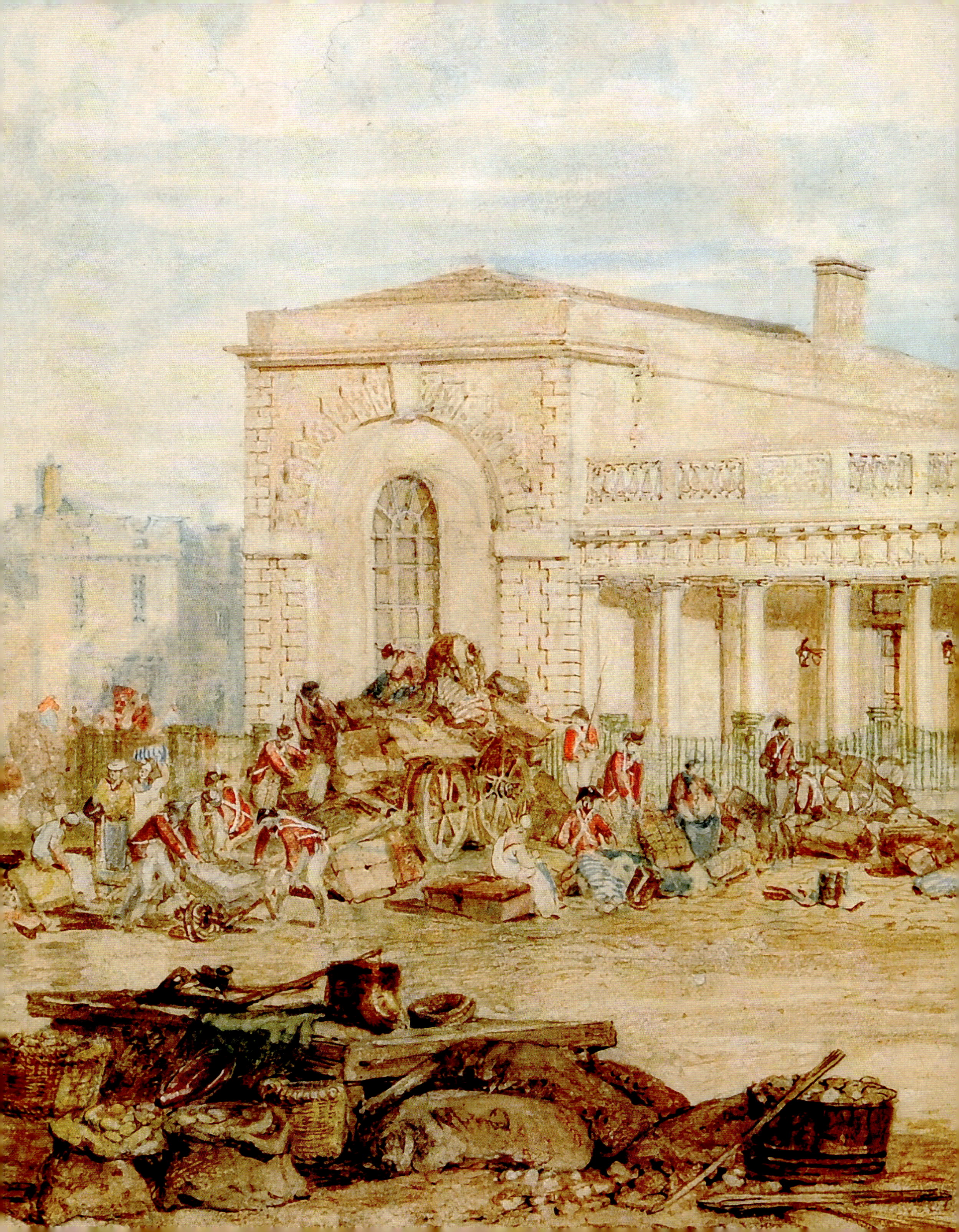

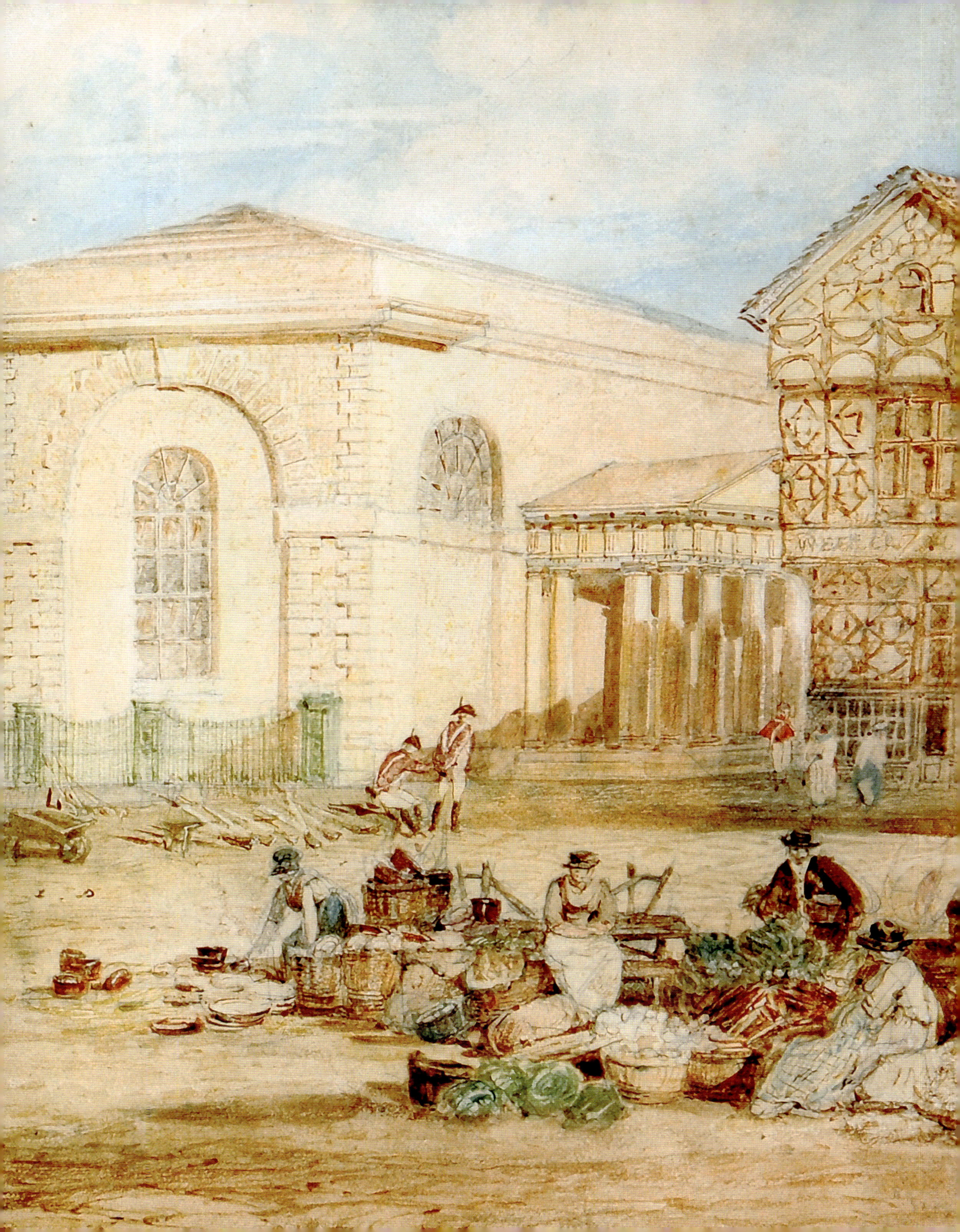

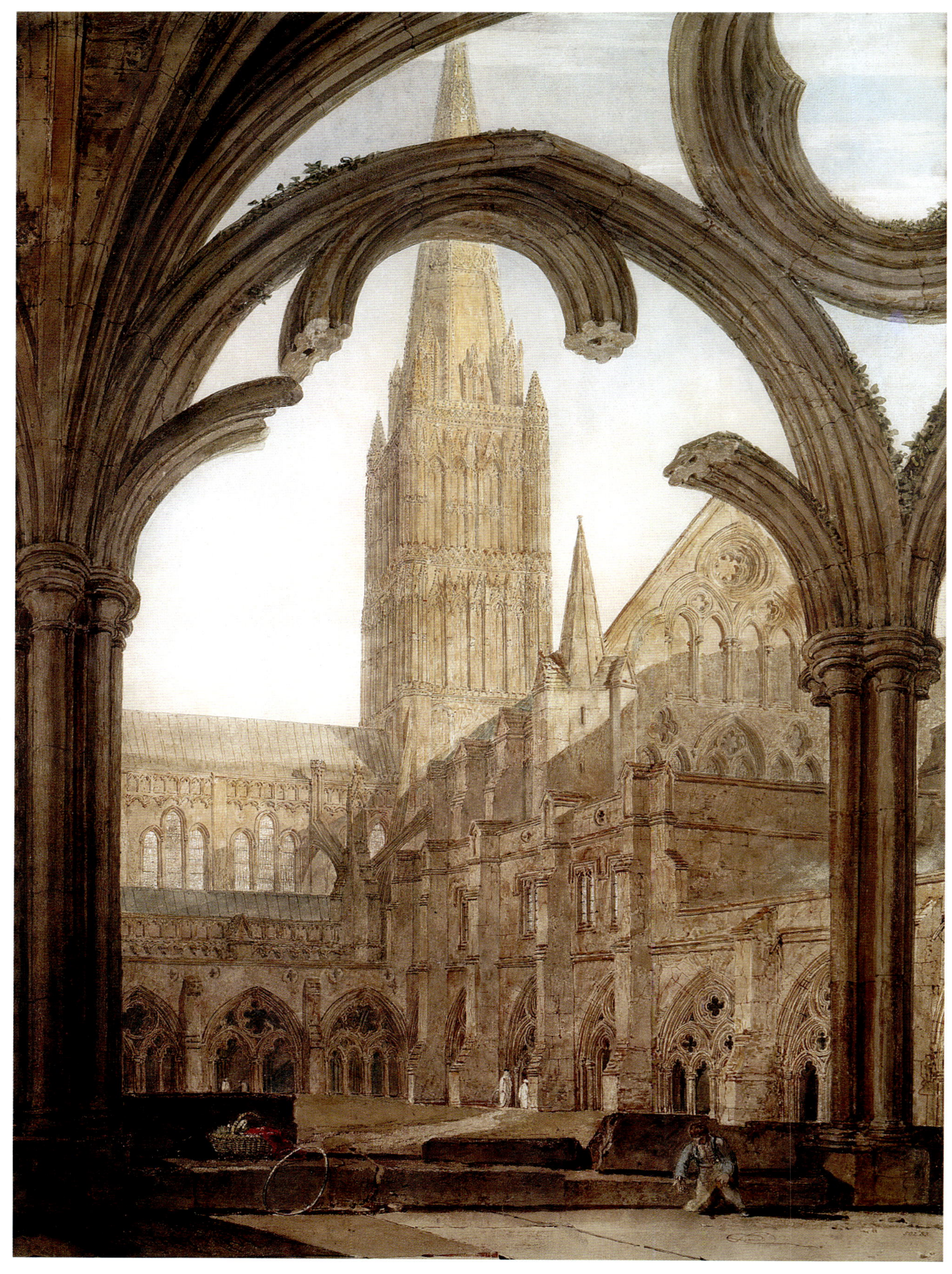

OPPOSITE: **Fig. 63**
Salisbury Cathedral from the South Side of the Cloister
*c.*1801–5
Watercolour,
68 × 49.6 cm
Victoria and Albert Museum, London (V202)
(see p. 187)

BELOW: **Fig. 64**
FREDERICK EVANS (1853–1943)
Gloucester Cathedral: The Cloisters
*c.*1903
Platinum print,
21.6 × 25.4 cm (image)
Philadelphia Museum of Art (1970-31-27)

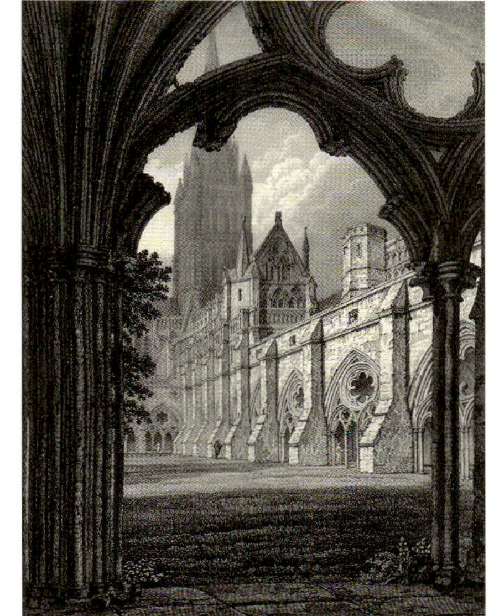

Fig. 65
JOHN LE KEUX (1783–1846) after FREDERICK MACKENZIE (C.1787–1854)
View from the Cloisters
1814
From Britton, *The History and Antiquities of the Cathedral Church of Salisbury*
Engraving, 23 × 16.1 cm
British Library, London

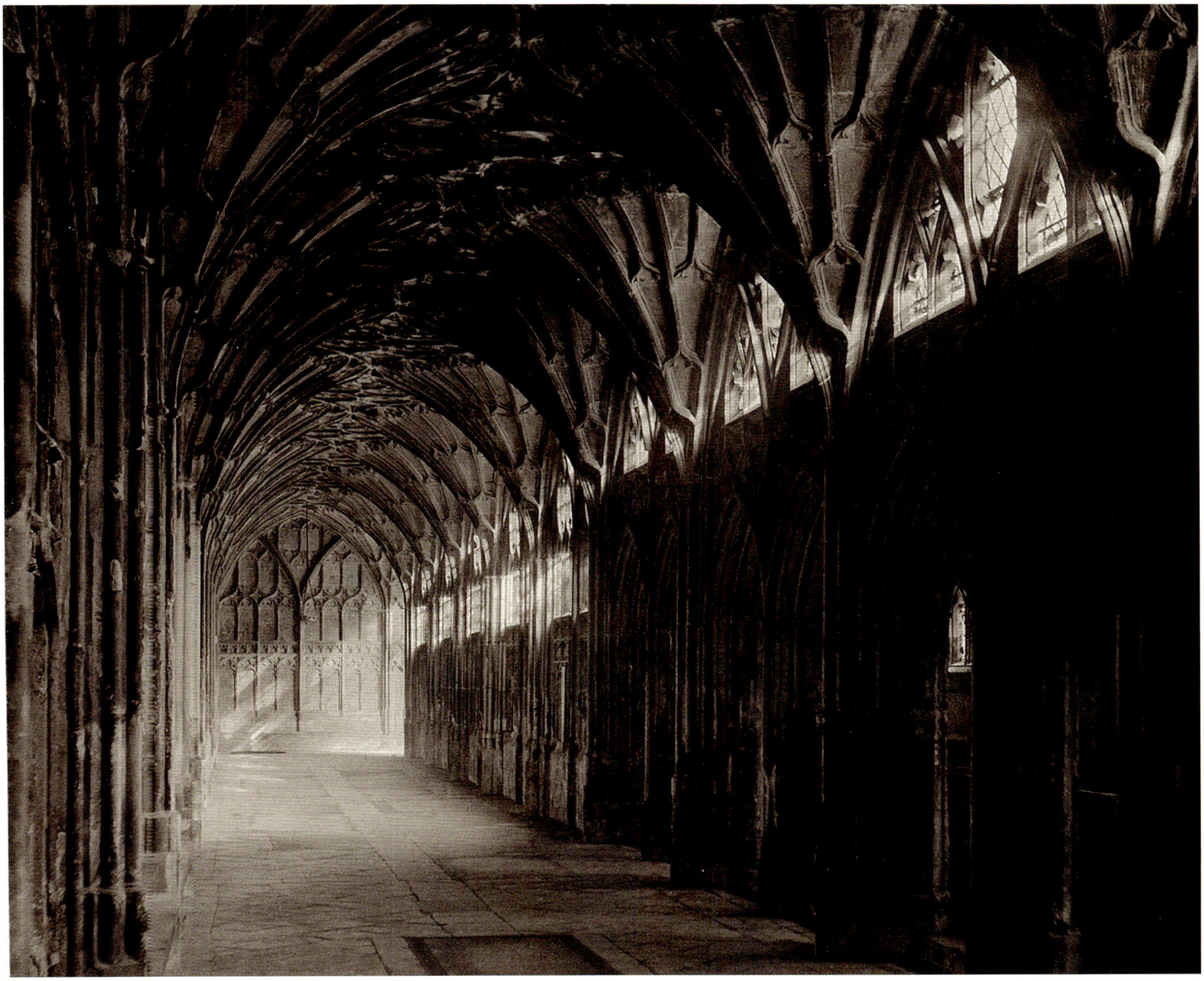

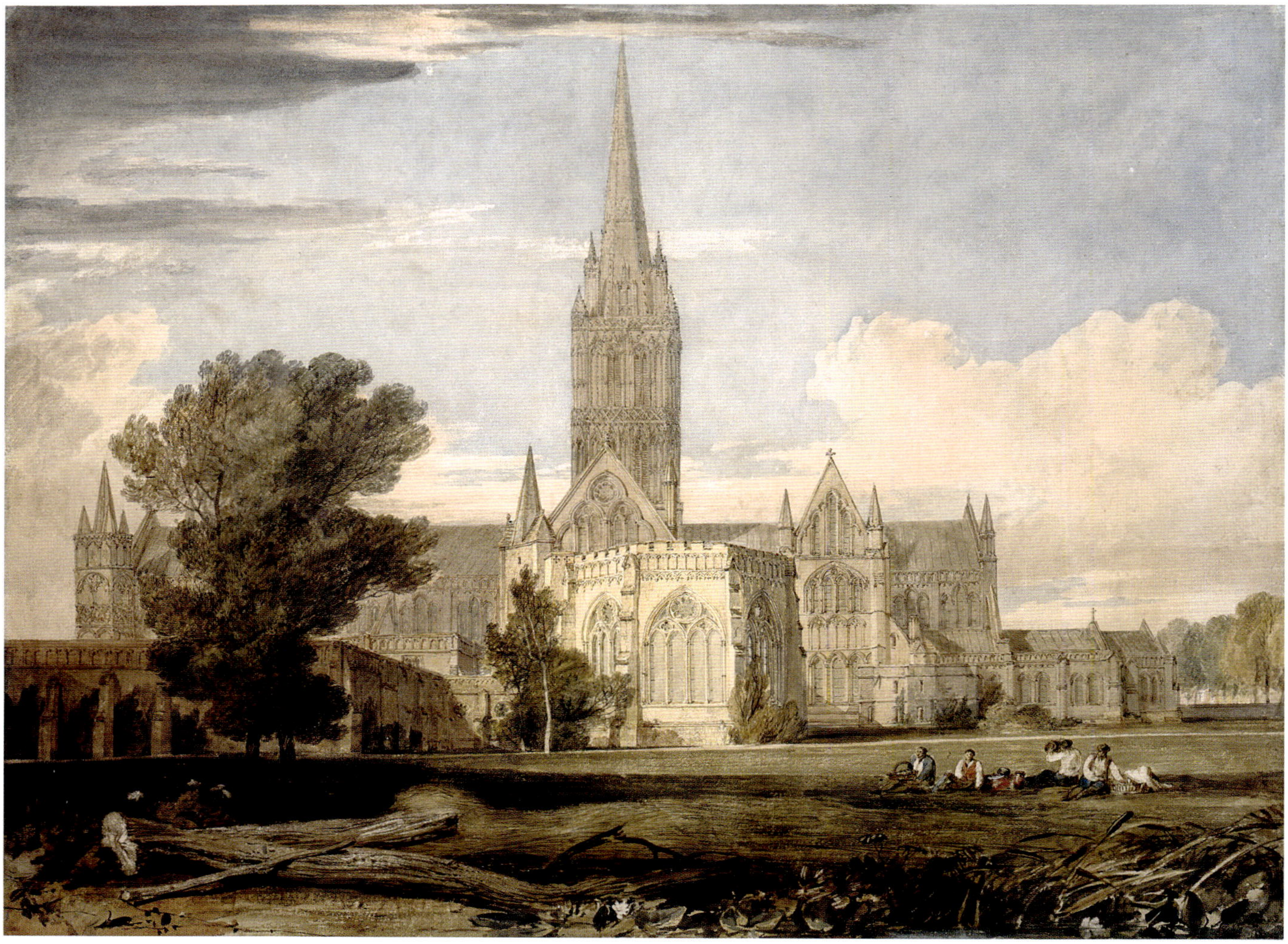

Fig. 66
A General View of Salisbury Cathedral from the Bishop's Garden
c.1801–5
Watercolour, 51.3 × 67.8 cm
Birmingham Museum and Art Gallery (W200)
(see p. 188)

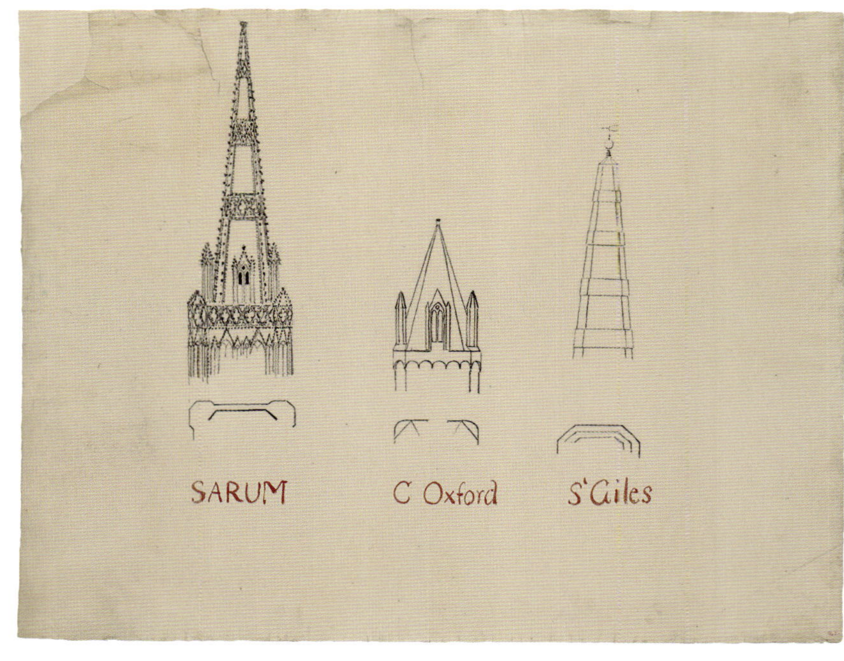

Fig. 67
Lecture Diagram. Various Steeples: Salisbury; Christ Church, Oxford; St Giles, London
c.1810–28
Pencil and watercolour, 65.8 × 83.2 cm
Tate (D17113 / TB CXCV 142)

Fig. 68
Interior of Salisbury Cathedral, looking towards the North Transept
c.1801–5
Watercolour, 66 × 50.8 cm
The Salisbury Museum (W203)
(see p. 188)

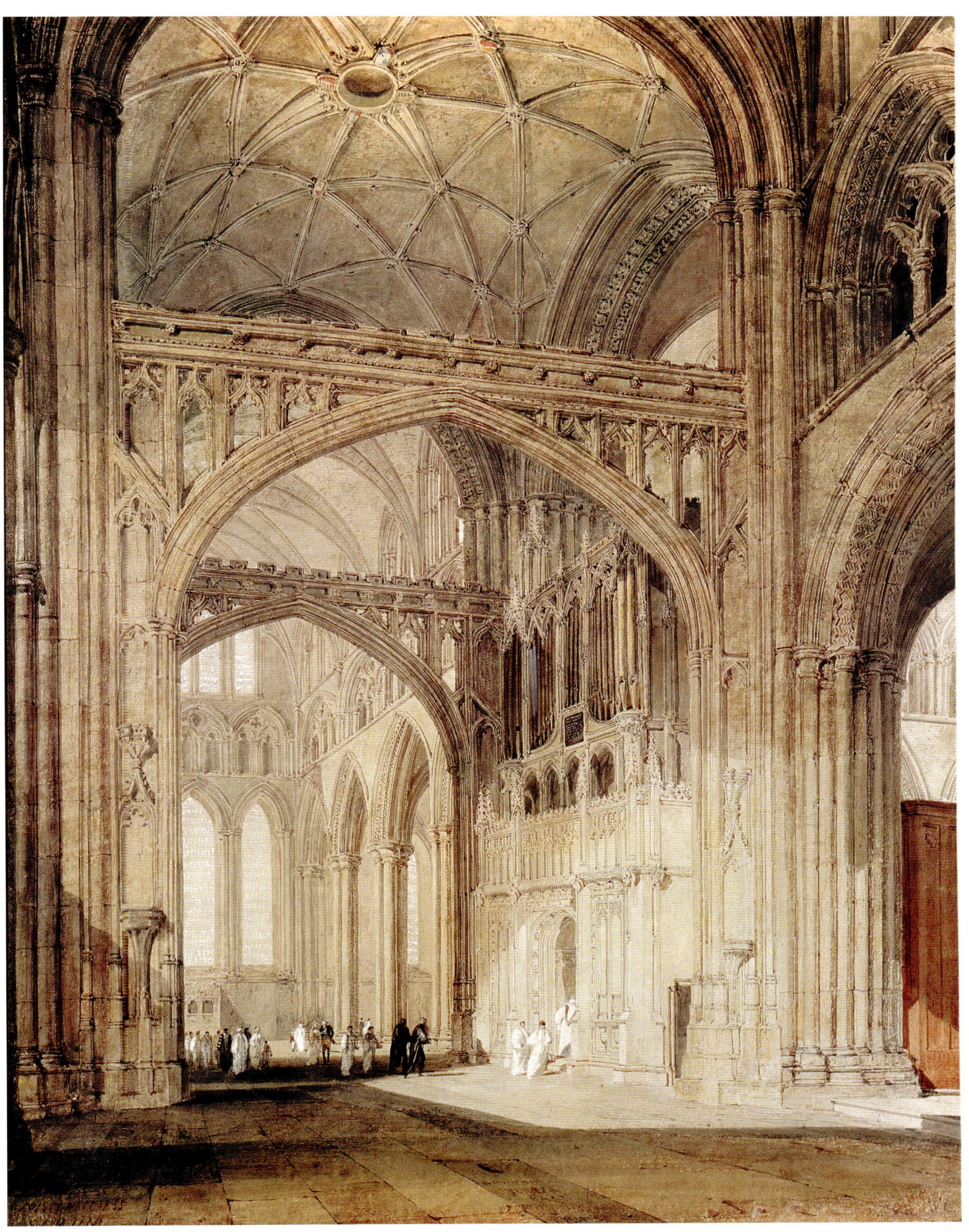

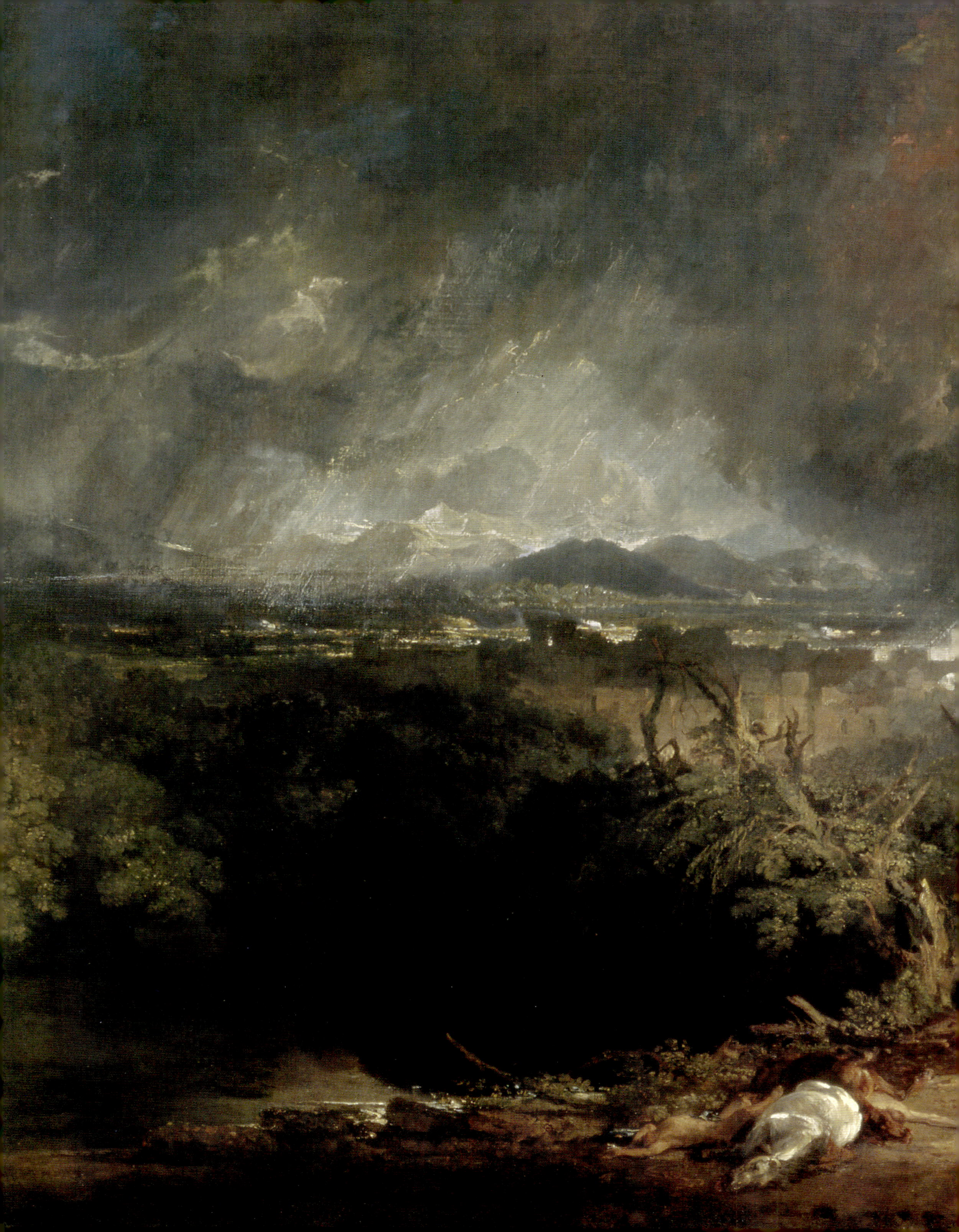

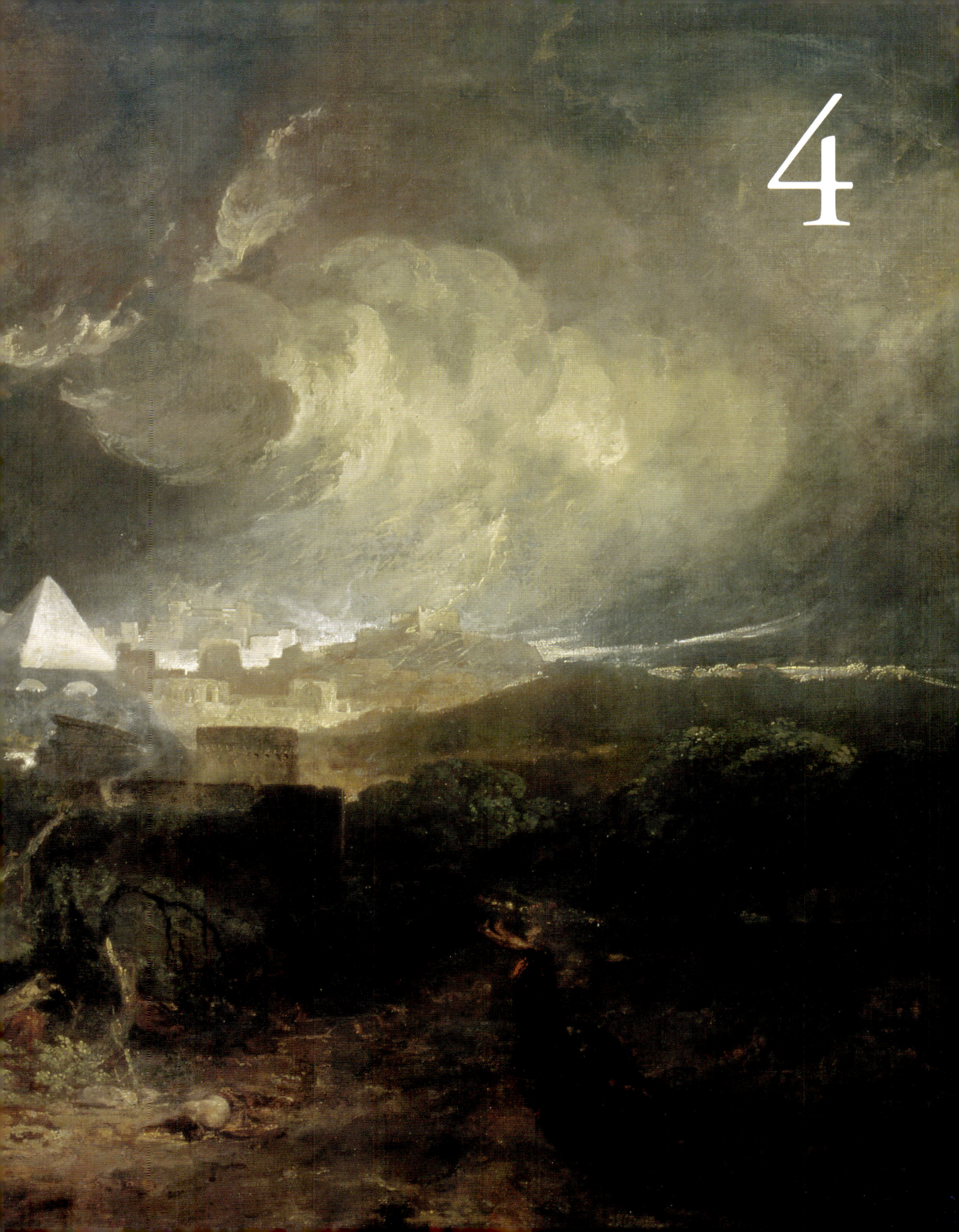
4

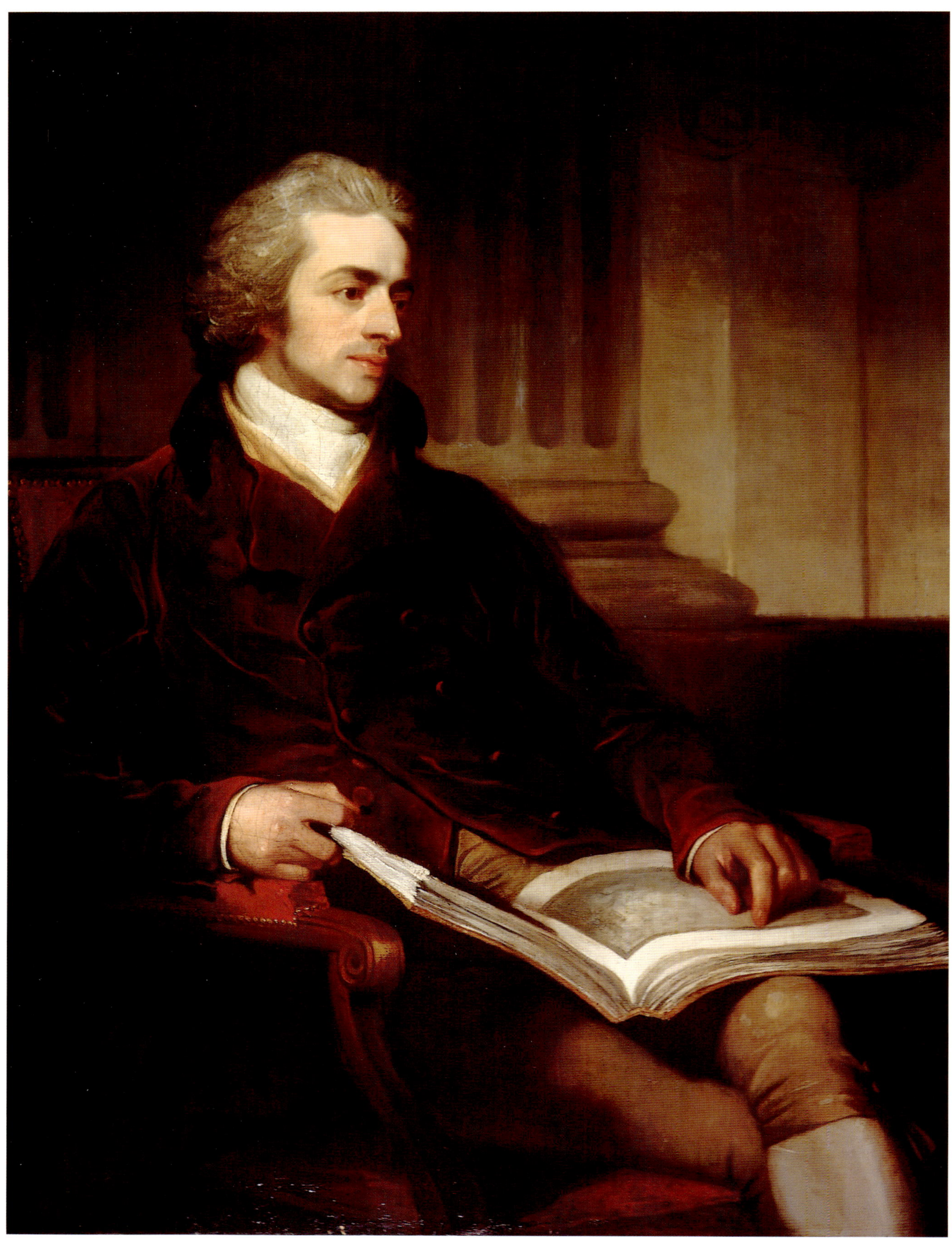

WILLIAM BECKFORD, AND THE RISE – AND FALLS – OF FONTHILL ABBEY

Turner's work at Salisbury for Colt Hoare coincided exactly with the period when he was also documenting the construction of Wyatt's neo-gothic abbey nearby at Fonthill for its owner, William Beckford (1760–1844; fig. 69). Although the estates at Stourhead and Fonthill are separated by scarcely ten miles, there was little sympathy and only rarely any communication between the two landowners.[1] Ironically, both men were favourably placed financially as the descendants of practically-minded money-makers, and they both also possessed a sensitivity to history and literature, art and nature. However, rivalry, snobbery and scandal prevented them from forging a meaningful connection. Working for both, Turner would have needed to sharpen his skills as a diplomat, particularly with reference to Wyatt's work. As we have seen, the architect's iconoclastic approach to the decluttering of the cathedral was disliked by traditionalists, such as Colt Hoare. Beckford, on the other hand, had subscribed to the alterations and became increasingly dependent on Wyatt after 1796, as their collective architectural fantasy began to rise at Fonthill.

Long before Turner was introduced to Beckford, the conspicuous wealth and notoriety of his employer would have ensured an awareness of certain elements of his earlier life. Beckford may well be revered now as 'an icon of Romanticism and a sexual and architectural Lucifer',[2] but the air of mystery he generated around himself and his home at Fonthill was simultaneously fascinating and alarming to his contemporaries.

He was the son of Alderman William Beckford (1709–1770), a politician who had skilfully exploited the vast stake that the buccaneering merchants of his family had established in sugar production in the West Indies, amounting to many hundreds of slaves and an annual income of between £30,000 and £100,000.[3] After being sent back from Jamaica to London in 1723, Beckford's father gained a prominent place in the City, further securing his position by marrying Maria Hamilton, granddaughter of the 6th Earl of Abercorn, in 1756. By then he had already bought the estate at Fonthill Gifford and was at work on the construction of a new house having recently lost the original one to fire. Designed in the Palladian style to emulate Houghton Hall in Norfolk, the result was eventually called Fonthill Splendens, reflecting its grandeur and its ostentatious furnishings (fig. 70).[4] Continuing his steady social ascent, the Alderman became Mayor of London for the first time in 1762, but two years before that, his wife had delivered William, his first and only legitimate heir (accounts vary between 7 and 30 for the number of his illegitimate offspring).[5]

Even before his father's death in 1770, the younger William lived a sheltered life at Fonthill. His mother's fears of losing the estate if anything happened to him ensured an overly protective upbringing and no school. Instead, he was tutored by the rather diffident Revd John Lettice. Instruction in drawing and aesthetics came from Alexander Cozens (1717–1786), famous for his technique of developing images from 'blots', resulting in Beckford nicknaming him 'Mr Dingy Digit'. Through 1777 to 1778 Beckford went to live with his mother's brother in Geneva, exploring the Alps from there. A longer Grand Tour of Italy ensued in 1780, during which he was the guest of Sir William Hamilton and his wife in Naples.

Back in Britain, the following year he officially came of age, which brought with it an inheritance

PREVIOUS PAGES:
The Fifth Plague of Egypt (detail)
(see fig. 98)

Fig. 69
JOHN HOPPNER (1758–1810)
William Beckford
*c.*1800
Oil on canvas, 124 × 99 cm
Salford Museum and Art Gallery, on loan to Beckford's Tower, Bath

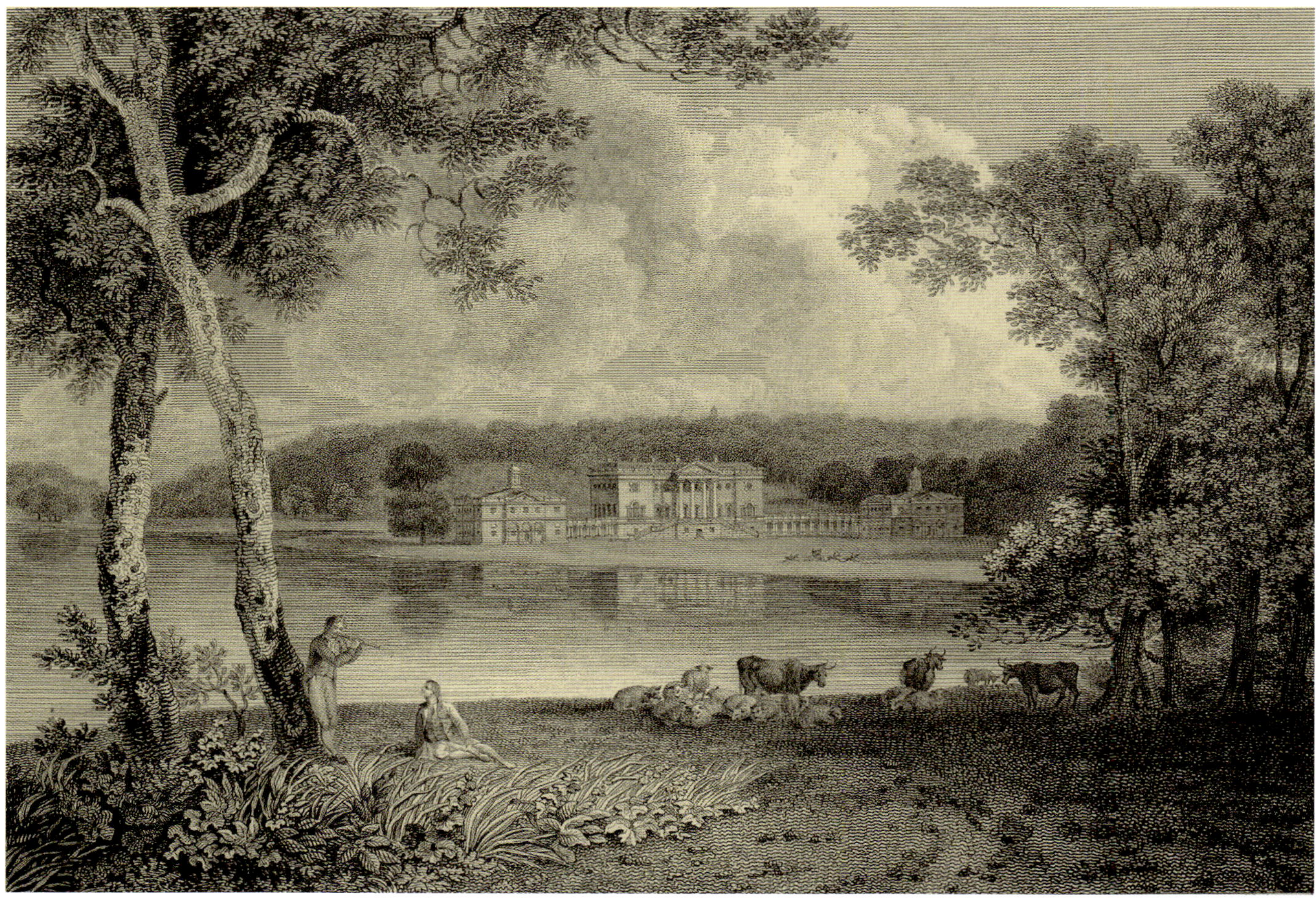

Fig. 70
WILLIAM ANGUS (1752–1821)
after J.M.W.TURNER
Fonthill House in Wiltshire, the Seat of William Beckford Esqr. (from *Principal Seats of the Nobility and Gentry in Great Britain and Wales, in a Collection of Select Views*)
1800
Engraving,
13.2 × 18.8 cm (image)
Private collection (R 62; based on W334)

of more than £1 million, plus an annual income of around £100,000. This made him one of the richest people in Europe, so it was with good reason that Byron would later deem him 'England's wealthiest son' (even though by that stage Beckford's wealth was much diminished).[6] A series of lavish entertainments took place to mark his birthday and to celebrate Christmas 1781. The latter event was a private affair, principally staged for Beckford's younger friends, and has acquired a legendary status for its supposed debauched revelry, though it seems likely to have been tamer than Beckford wanted people to believe.[7] The highlight was the magical light installation created by the theatre designer and painter Philippe-Jacques de Loutherbourg (1740–1812), presumably derived from his *Eidophusikon,* a sequence of changing atmospheric pictures, which had stunned Londoners earlier in the year. Another of the guests was the 13-year-old William Courtenay (later 9th Earl of Devon) and it was his presence that subsequently lent the occasion its scandalous notoriety.

More immediately, Beckford's imagination was charged by de Loutherbourg's evocative transformation of the halls of Fonthill Splendens and he responded by beginning to write his novel *Vathek*, an oddly compelling fusion of his oriental and gothic interests that has remained in print since it was first published in 1786 (both in his original French version and the translation by the Revd Samuel Henley). Beckford's emotions, meanwhile, were divided between his cousin's wife, Louisa, and – much more dangerously – the young Courtenay. To distance himself from his dilemma, he returned again to Italy in the summer of 1782, travelling with such an impressive retinue (including the artist John Robert Cozens) that he was apparently mistaken for the emperor of Austria.

His decision to marry Lady Margaret Gordon in May 1783 demonstrated a resolve to move on

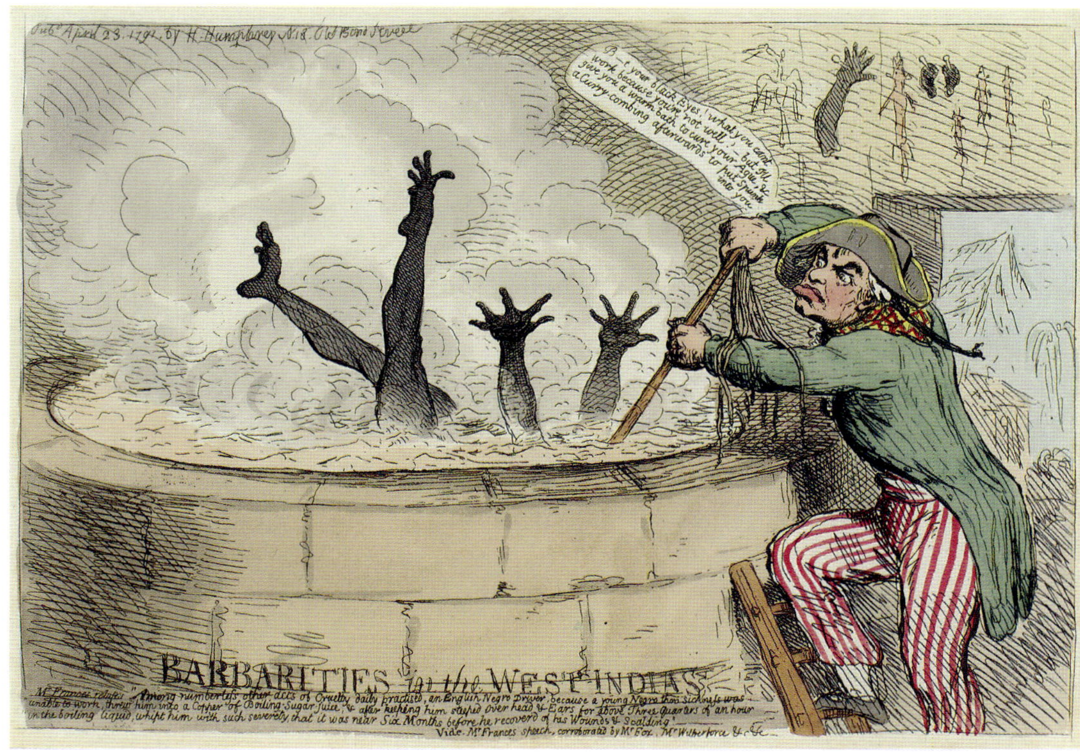

Fig. 71
JAMES GILLRAY (1756–1815)
Barbarities in the West Indies
23 April 1791
Hand-coloured etching, 25 × 34.7 cm
National Portrait Gallery
The disembodied limbs in this image possibly influenced the way Turner represented the bodies of drowning slaves in the foreground of his painting *Slavers* (1840, Museum of Fine Arts, Boston).

and, like his father, he clearly had hopes of social advancement, with the prospect of a peerage on the horizon. But the likelihood of this coming to pass was suddenly imperilled during a visit to Powderham Castle in September 1784, when Beckford was compromised while alone with Courtenay. What actually happened behind closed doors can be surmised, though naturally was never explicitly confirmed, but it was soon the stuff of pointed comment in the *Morning Herald*.[8] With his wife beside him, Beckford initially withstood the damaging scandal, but after the birth of their first daughter they were eventually compelled to seek exile on the shores of Lake Geneva. Sadly, in May 1786, barely a year later, Margaret died shortly after the delivery of a second girl. The young widower returned the children to England and then embarked for Jamaica, but he sailed only as far as Lisbon, where he remained for two and half years (the first of three residences in Portugal).

By 1790 Beckford was back at Fonthill, where he began encircling part of the estate with a 12-foot-high wall, extending for seven miles.[9] Inside this was the secluded hillside above Splendens, where he conceived a plan to construct a tower on Stop's Beacon, although he also looked for a means of manifesting his devotion to Saint Anthony of Padua and the Catholicism he had imbibed abroad. The eventual result would be Fonthill Abbey: 'a cathedral of contradictions or a palace of paradox'.[10] Wyatt was then at work in nearby Salisbury and was soon enlisted to develop designs, which were in circulation by 1792.[11] But Beckford's finances were less secure than they had been as a result of the Revolutionary War, compounding the losses he sustained at the hands of those ostensibly managing his interests in Jamaica. These were also the years in which the principle of slavery itself was at last challenged and threatened by abolitionists such as William Wilberforce and Thomas Clarkson (fig. 71).

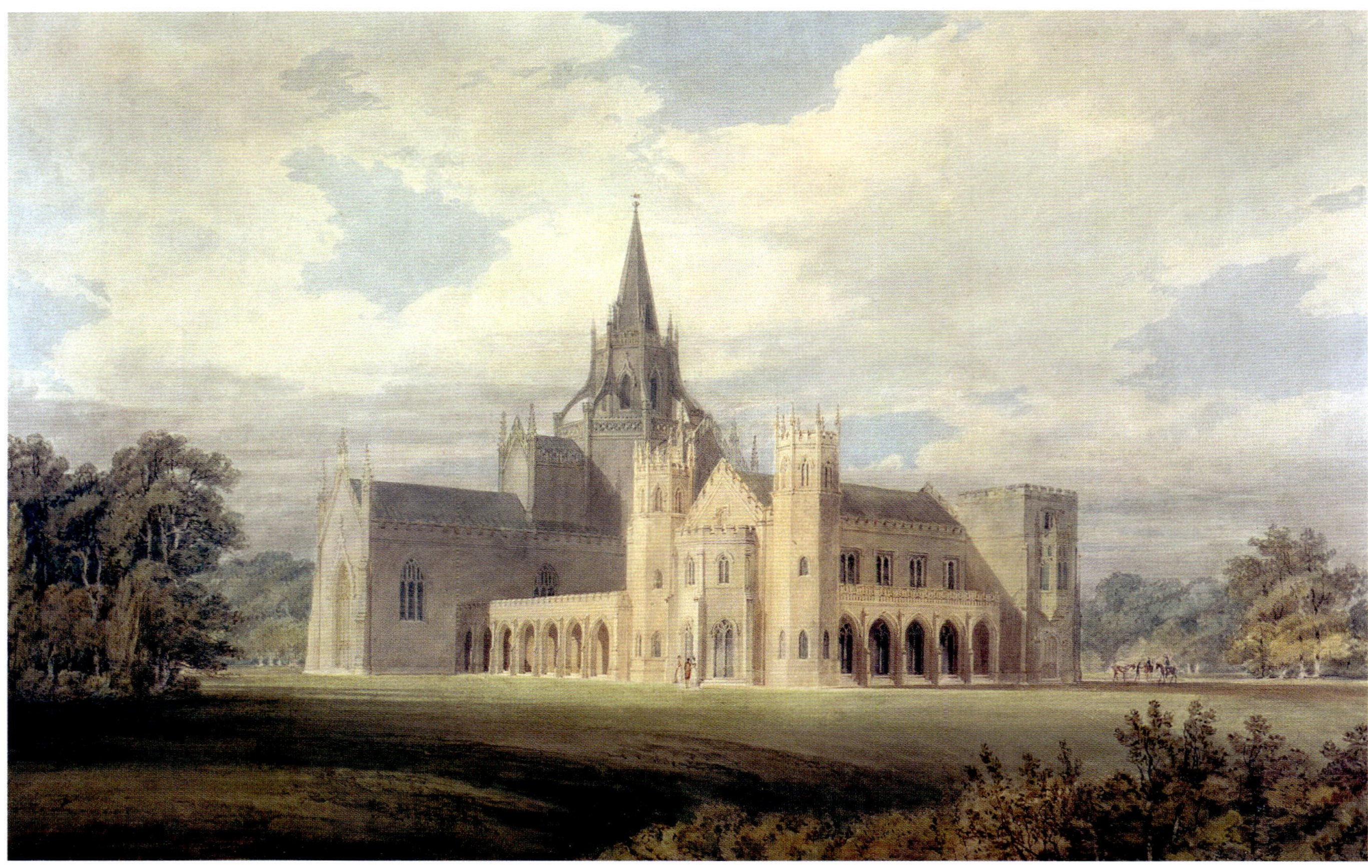

Fig. 72
Perspective View of Fonthill Abbey from the South-West
*c.*1797, possibly exhibited RA 1797
Watercolour, 49.3 × 75.8 cm
Bolton Museum and Art Gallery (W332)

Theirs was an heroic endeavour because so many aspects of Britain's economic life were inextricably ensnared in the far-reaching tentacles of the slave trade. Indeed, Beckford was not the only one of Turner's patrons whose wealth came from the West Indies. Shamefully, as late as 1805, Turner himself invested in a scheme that blatantly sought to make a profit from slave labour in Jamaica.[12]

While these factors caused a halt in Beckford's ambitions to build at Fonthill, the delay was as much attributable to his further travels in Europe. During his time in Portugal he visited the gothic monastery at Batalha, very likely encouraged to do so by Wyatt, although the architect only knew the mausoleum at second hand through drawings belonging to his client William Burton Conyngham of Slane.[13] However, in constructing Lee Priory in Kent (1785–1790), Wyatt had incorporated an octagonal library, inspired by the buttressed lantern at Batalha. So by the time Beckford returned in 1796, the Portuguese monastery coloured their collective ideas of what they wanted to achieve. Regrettably, for Beckford, Wyatt became Surveyor-General and Comptroller of the Office of Works in 1796, a prominent administrative post that made many demands on his time, keeping him away from Fonthill in London or Windsor, but in which he was ultimately found wanting because he was 'dilatory, negligent and irresponsible'.[14]

It was during this year that building work at Fonthill started. Beckford initially described it as 'the Abbey in the Woods', implying that it was planned as a garden folly, suitable for a picturesque landscape.[15] However, by November he was talking about the front of the abbey having a span of 200 feet and boasting that most of the ground floor was already in place, something that, if true, indicates how little time had gone into preparing proper foundations. By February 1797 the 'half finished' building had apartments in 'the most gorgeous Gothic style' fitted with painted glass. The design centred on a chapel measuring 66 feet in diameter and 72 feet

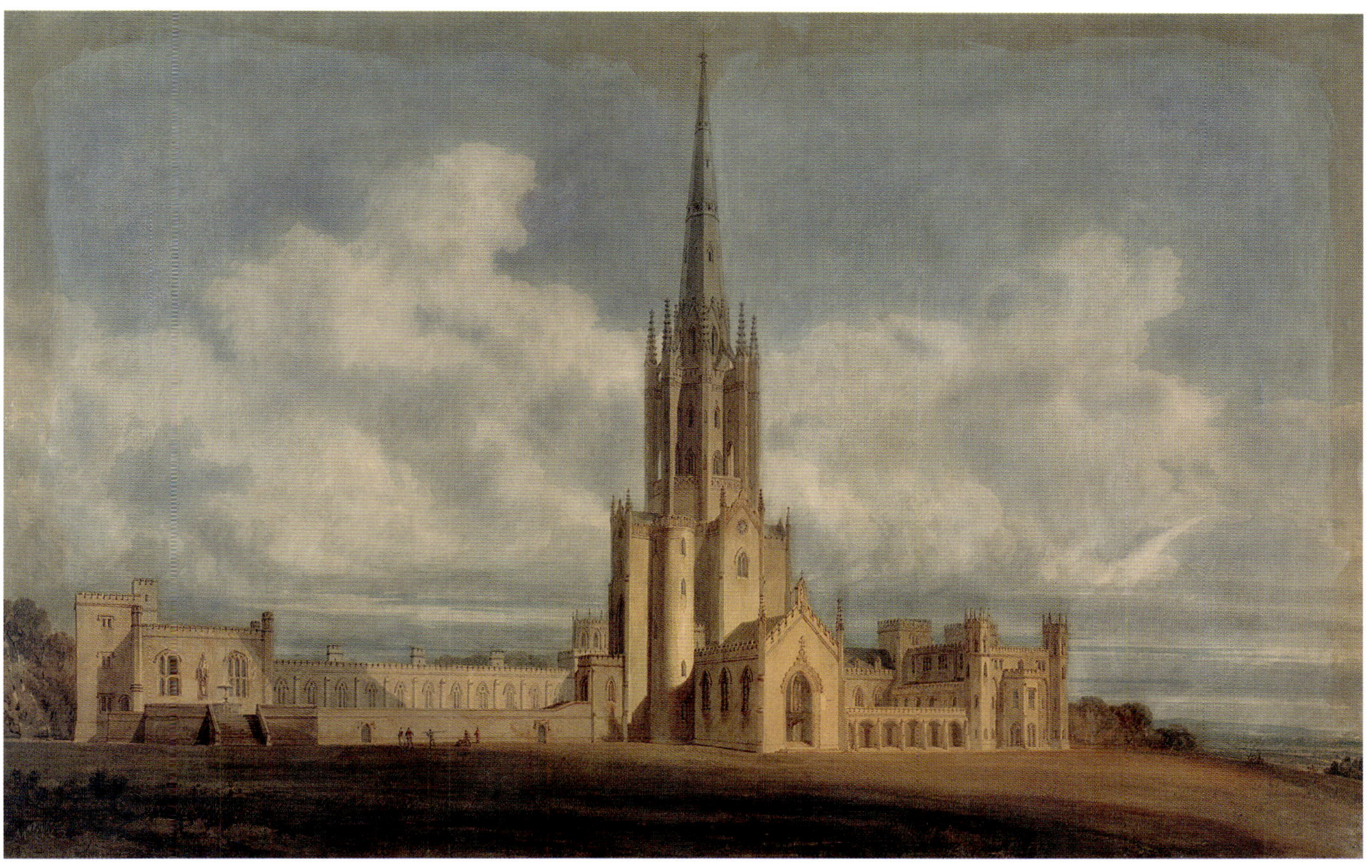

Fig. 73
JAMES WYATT (1746–1813)
and TURNER
Fonthill from the North-West
Exhibited RA 1798
Watercolour, 67 × 105.4 cm
Yale Center for British Art, New Haven (W333)

high, with 'a gallery 185ft in length and a tower 145 feet high'.[16]

A sense of how the abbey was intended to look at this stage can be gleaned from a watercolour by Turner, where the building has a close kinship with Wyatt's Lee Priory (fig. 72).[17] This seems likely to be the first of the three designs of 'a building now erecting at Fonthill, the Seat of William Beckford, Esq., in the style of a Gothic Abbey' that were exhibited at the Royal Academy between 1797 and 1799.[18] All appeared under Wyatt's name, but Turner's talent and his links with the architectural world would have made him an obvious person to enlist to showcase this important project.[19] Other more established artists, such as the sculptors Joseph Nollekens, John Flaxman, John Charles Felix Rossi and Richard Westmacott, received commissions for Fonthill, as had the President of the Academy, Benjamin West (1738–1820), who was paid a stipend to produce a series of paintings evoking the apocalypse. These were intended to decorate the Revelation Chamber in the abbey, in which Beckford planned to be buried.[20]

Beckford's pride in all this was premature, however, for during the winter of 1796–97 part of the tower was brought down by a gale.[21] It is not known how severe the damage was, but by August Joseph Farington was shown Wyatt's latest, 'much enlarged' design, which evidently included revisions to the tower, causing work on it to be temporarily suspended.[22] Towards the end of the year Farington recorded that the tower was to be topped by a spire rising to 300 feet – a blatant attempt to rival neighbouring Salisbury Cathedral.[23] Turner incorporated this new element in another large watercolour that was exhibited at the end of April 1798 (fig. 73). As well as the obvious addition of the spire, the Western Transept is longer in this design, perhaps indicating that this arm of the abbey had been rethought because repairs were needed after the spring crash. Similarly, the pitched roof of the southern wing, a more-or-less self-contained perpendicular gothic villa, has been raised by an attic storey and taller towers.

Building at Fonthill continued throughout 1798 and on into 1799, even after Beckford left once more for Portugal. His new ambition was for an even taller spire that would soar 17 feet higher than St Peter's in Rome.[24] Another notable addition to the plan at this stage was a substantial Eastern Transept, conceived as a Choir, but which eventually accommodated vast drawing and dining rooms. Wyatt displayed a design of this third variant of the abbey at the Royal Academy in 1799, but there is no surviving candidate for this exhibit by Turner; however, a watercolour by Charles Wild (1781–1835) preserves the revised proposal (?1799, Victoria and Albert Museum).[25]

Soon after Wyatt's design appeared at the annual exhibition, Turner was among a gathering of distinguished members of the art world at Beckford's London home in Grosvenor Square. Their host was still away in Portugal, but before setting off he had instructed his agents to monitor and then acquire two newly-imported landscapes by Claude Lorrain, whose pictures were the most coveted among British connoisseurs (both are now at the National Trust property Anglesey Abbey). They were undoubtedly exceptional by any standards, but the negotiations resulted in a record price for them of 7,000 guineas (although this sum also brought four smaller works).[26] Inevitably, there was much excitement about this acquisition combined with a curiosity to see the pictures; hence the crush at Grosvenor Square in early May 1799. Turner was then in the first flush of his passion for Claude's light-filled pastorals and harbour scenes, and visited the pictures on consecutive days. The general consensus preferred *The Father of Psyche Sacrificing at the Temple of Apollo* (1662) and this was most likely also the painting that made Turner 'both pleased and unhappy while He viewed it, – it seemed to be beyond the power of imitation'.[27] However, the potent theme of the founding of Rome in the pendant picture (1675) induced Turner to transcribe its composition, either then or more probably in 1800, by which date the pair by Claude were hanging in the Grand Saloon at Fonthill Splendens (fig. 76).

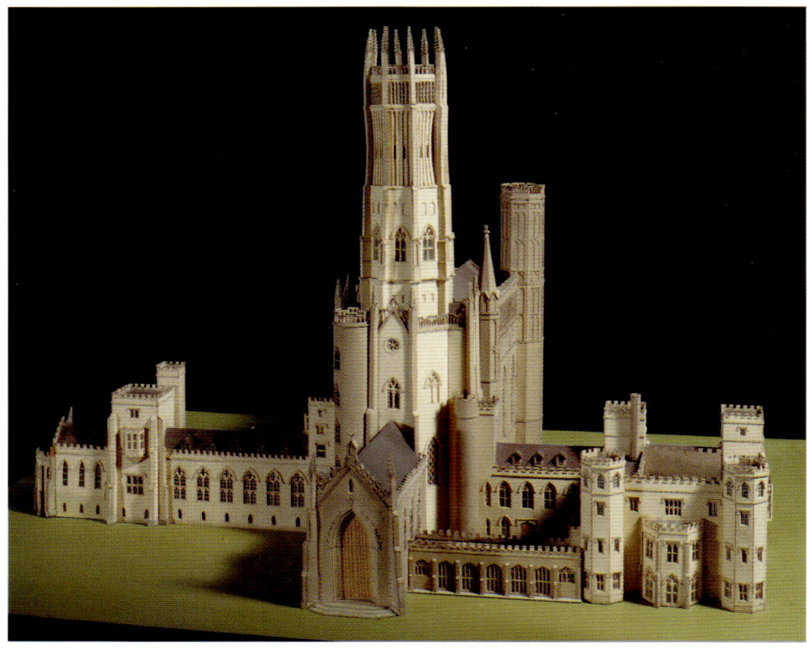

Fig. 74
Model of Fonthill Abbey
?1806
The Estate of the late Niel Rimington, courtesy of the Beckford Tower Trust

At the end of May 1799 Turner received a request from Beckford to go to Fonthill later in the year. Curiously, the letter did not specify what was required, but Turner recognised the trip would provide another opportunity to continue his work for Colt Hoare on the Cathedral series.[28] Although Turner had by then become very fashionable, and he was able to pick and choose among his clients (even declining the terms offered by Lord Elgin to record his

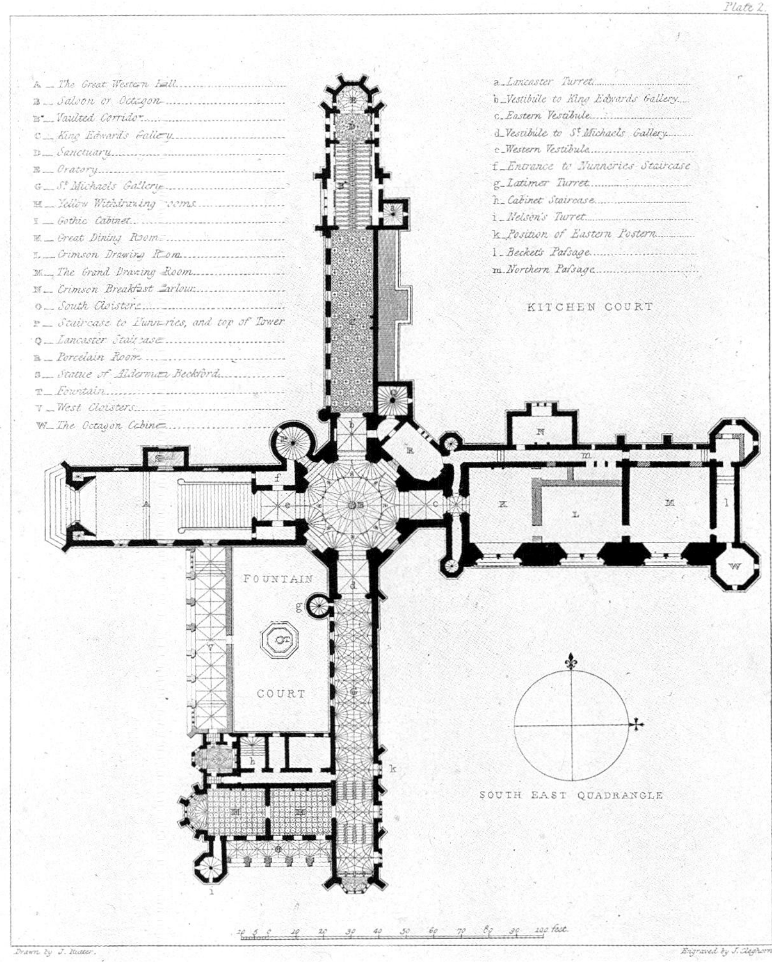

Fig. 75
Ground plan of Fonthill Abbey
From John Rutter, *Delineations of Fonthill and its Abbey*, 1823
British Library, London

momentous trip to Greece), Beckford's approach almost certainly stemmed from an awareness of Turner's demonstrable skills in giving shape to Wyatt's ideas in previous years.

By late July Beckford was once more at Fonthill and arrangements were soon afterwards in place for Turner to go there in mid-August.[29] This has generally been assumed to be his first visit, but, in fact, that seems unlikely to have been the case. A drawing in Turner's Swans sketchbook shows the rising abbey from the south-west.[30] Since that book was otherwise used on the tour of Wales in 1798, it appears to indicate that Turner made a detour along the Nadder Valley from Salisbury on his way to Stourhead that year. If that is correct, his sketch of the tower reveals that work on the abbey was not much further ahead than he was to find it in 1799. It is possible that some of it had fallen just a couple of months prior to his visit that year.[31]

Another of Turner's views of Fonthill that seems to pre-date his prolonged stay is the engraving of Splendens and the lake, with its rather knowing inclusion of a boy demonstrating his skill on the flute to his seated companion (fig. 70). The print was issued in March 1800 and Turner's name is augmented below the image with the status of Associate, which he won on 4 November 1799; though either the market-savvy artist or his publisher would have updated this detail on an existing image from some years earlier. Given the widespread curiosity about the construction of Fonthill, news of which regularly featured in the newspapers, the most striking absence in the image is the abbey's tower, which should be visible. Instead, the hill above Splendens is marked merely by a stump, which may be the beacon erected by Beckford's father. It would be reasonable to suspect that the publication of the image in 1800 was simply opportunistic by William Angus, its engraver and publisher, since most of the other views in his series were already quite old. Perhaps the now untraced watercolour on which it is based dates from 1795, when Turner first visited Salisbury.

What Turner actually saw at Fonthill in August 1799 also needs to be examined more rigorously. The principal record of the time he spent there comprises his large, portfolio-sized 'Fonthill' sketchbook (Tate; TB XLVII). The pencil outlines and colour studies it contains are supplemented by the very brief report he gave Farington on 11 September, soon after returning to London:

> He has been at Fonthill 3 weeks, – [Henry] Tresham, West, [William] Hamilton & Wyatt there part of the time. – He is to make several drawings, – views

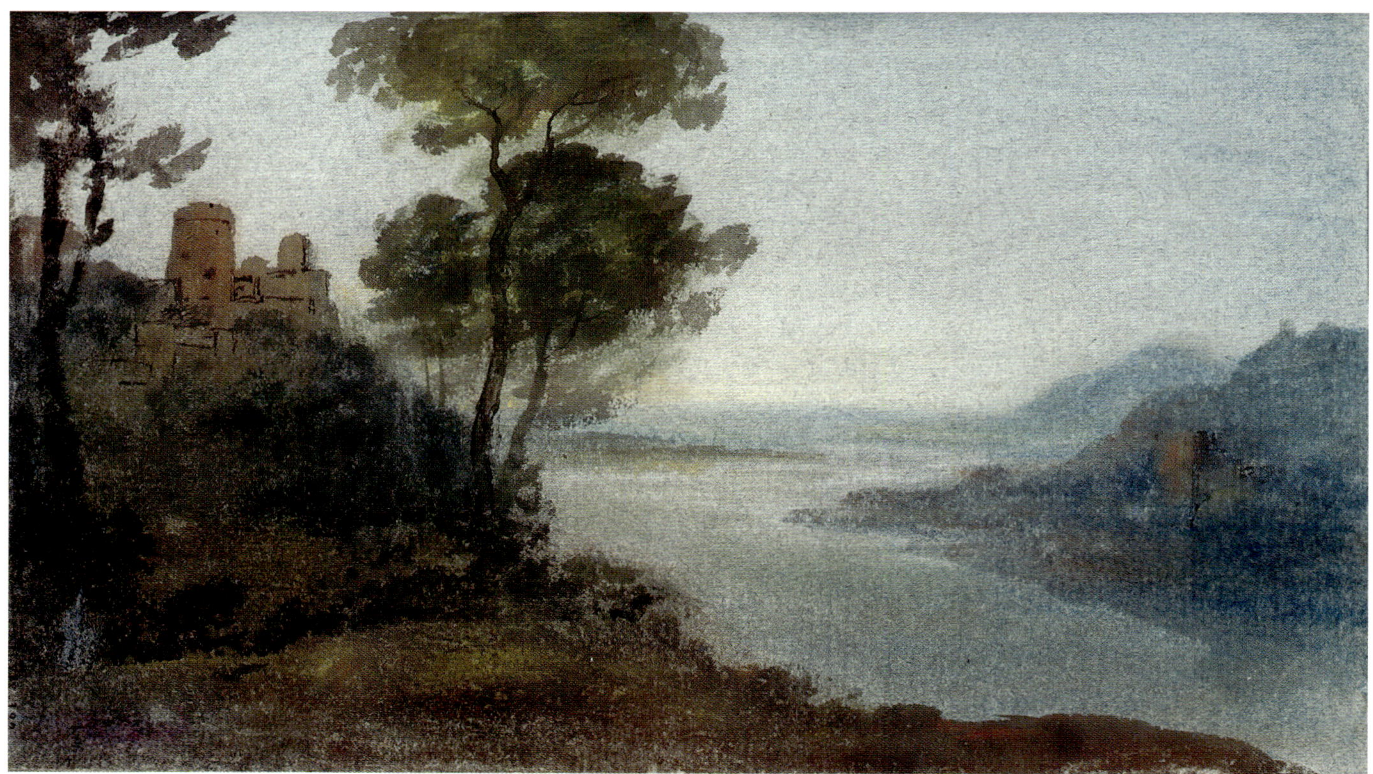

Fig. 76
Study of the Composition of Claude's 'Landscape with the Arrival of Aeneas before the City of Pallanteum'
c.1800
Watercolour on blue paper, 13.8 × 21.5 cm
From the 'Studies for Pictures' sketchbook
Tate (D04139 / TB LXIX 122)

> near the Abbey &c. They breakfasted with [the steward, Captain Nicholas] Williams at nine – Beckford himself at Eleven as He rides out before breakfast – dined at 4 – Walked out at 6, tea at 8 – supper at 10 – Beckford retired abt 11 or little after.[32]

Clearly Turner's appetite was gratified by this regular supply of refreshment, but Farington's summary of their conversation provides scant detail about such a long stay. We have no idea what Turner thought of Beckford, his collections or the new abbey, and the details of the commission are similarly intangible. The fault lies as much with Farington, who as Wyatt's confidante had already established his own views on Fonthill and its owner. Although it was over 15 years since the scandal of Powderdam Castle, rumours continued to circulate about the true nature of what had taken place, which no doubt required leaving much unreported, for the sake of business if nothing else.[33] Indeed, it should be noted that for a young artist, like Turner, whose reputation was still insecure, there must have been an inherent risk in working for someone tainted by infamy, however prominent and wealthy.

Other stories about Turner's time at Fonthill emerged posthumously, which inevitably means they should be treated with caution. Turner's early biographer, Walter Thornbury, writing in 1862 records a tale he had heard from a 'well-known picture-dealer, now living', who claimed to have been at Fonthill while Turner was sketching there. Apparently Beckford summoned his minions to erect a tent so that an impromptu luncheon could take place on the spot where Turner had been at work.[34] This is picturesque, but it would mean that the dealer in question had lived well into his 80s.

Compared with second-hand narratives like this, Turner's outline sketches constitute a much more dependable source of documentary information. Superficially, the meticulously precise use of pencil appears to be consistent throughout Turner's 'Fonthill' portfolio. However, the range of subjects contained therein reflects a time span of around six years, so there is no stylistic reason to suppose that the sketches record only one visit to Fonthill. In fact, we

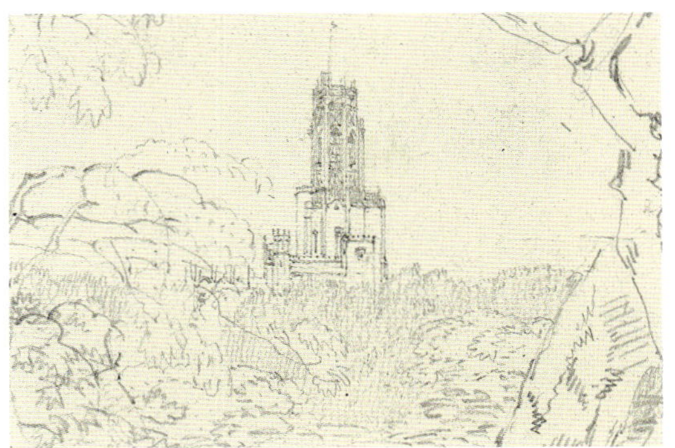
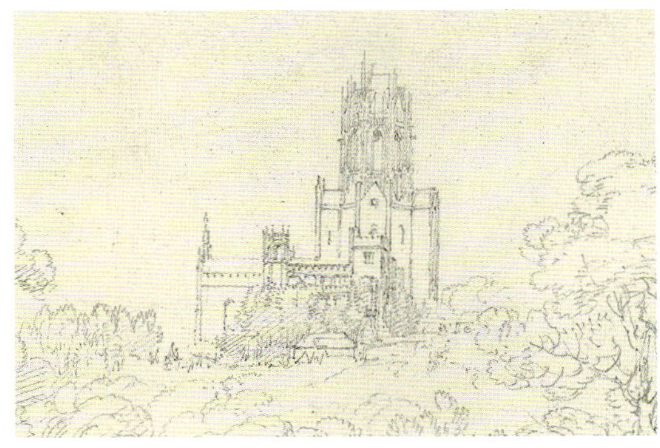

Details of figs 90 and 103, showing the different stages of work on the tower of Fonthill Abbey.

know that Turner stayed at Splendens yet again in the autumn of 1800, although not for how long.[35] Looking closely at the sketches, it has not previously been noticed that there are glaring discrepancies in the way the abbey is delineated, particularly in the form of its tower, and as a result it is possible to create two distinct batches: in some the tower is nearing completion;[36] in others, it is much lower and fragmented.[37] This striking difference can be accounted for by the fact that on 17 May 1800, between Turner's visits, a strong south-westerly wind toppled much of the hastily-constructed tower for the second (or perhaps the third) time.[38] The disaster caused Beckford to employ even more labourers to rectify the damage; one source even alleges he took on 'nearly five hundred men' working in shifts, day and night.[39] To speed the rise of the tower upwards, Wyatt had decided to construct it around a wooden core, using brick and Roman, or compo-cement. Permanence was evidently not as important a consideration as visual impact. Time was short because Beckford was seeking to impress Lord Nelson, for whom a special entertainment was staged at the abbey in December 1800.[40]

The crucial key to separating out which sketches relate to which visit lies in the five watercolours Turner exhibited at the Royal Academy from April 1800 – and in fact they were on the walls of the Academy when the tower fell, fortuitously creating the kind of topical frisson Turner often sought (figs 81, 85, 87, 89, 91). These were by far the largest works in watercolour he had yet displayed, a fact that is itself a measure of the ambitions he lodged in this project. Regrettably, they were exposed to too much sunlight in the nineteenth century, and none of them now retains the subtle range of greens and blues that can be found in the view of Caernarvon Castle, which was also exhibited in 1800 (Tate).[41]

Studying the representation of the abbey in each of the watercolours highlights a peculiarity in the appearance of the Western Transept, which was evidently not roofed and clearly not even fully erected in August 1799. This is confirmed by going back to the pencil outlines from which the exhibited watercolours were derived, where the same architectural shortcomings can be found. Other sheets in the 'Fonthill' notebook record a more fully advanced building on the western side, and a battered tower, and must therefore relate to the visit over a year later (figs 102–3, 104, 106).

In addition to the large 'Fonthill' sheets, in 1799 Turner carried with him a slender pocketbook made up of blue paper. A couple of the pen and ink studies it contains capture the impact the abbey would have made on visitors approaching it for the first time, perched high above the Nadder valley, and towering over the woods that surrounded it (fig. 77). Another quick jotting records a closer view of the abbey, where, yet again, it lacks the Western Transept.[42] As in the exhibited watercolours, the tower is topped by the long wooden pole from which the hubristic Beckford impatiently flew his own flag, even before the structure was truly sound.

The flagpole can also be seen on a sheet that comes from another album of assorted subjects, known as the Smaller Fonthill sketchbook.[43] Although most of its pages were used during a tour of Scotland in 1801, a handful relate to the

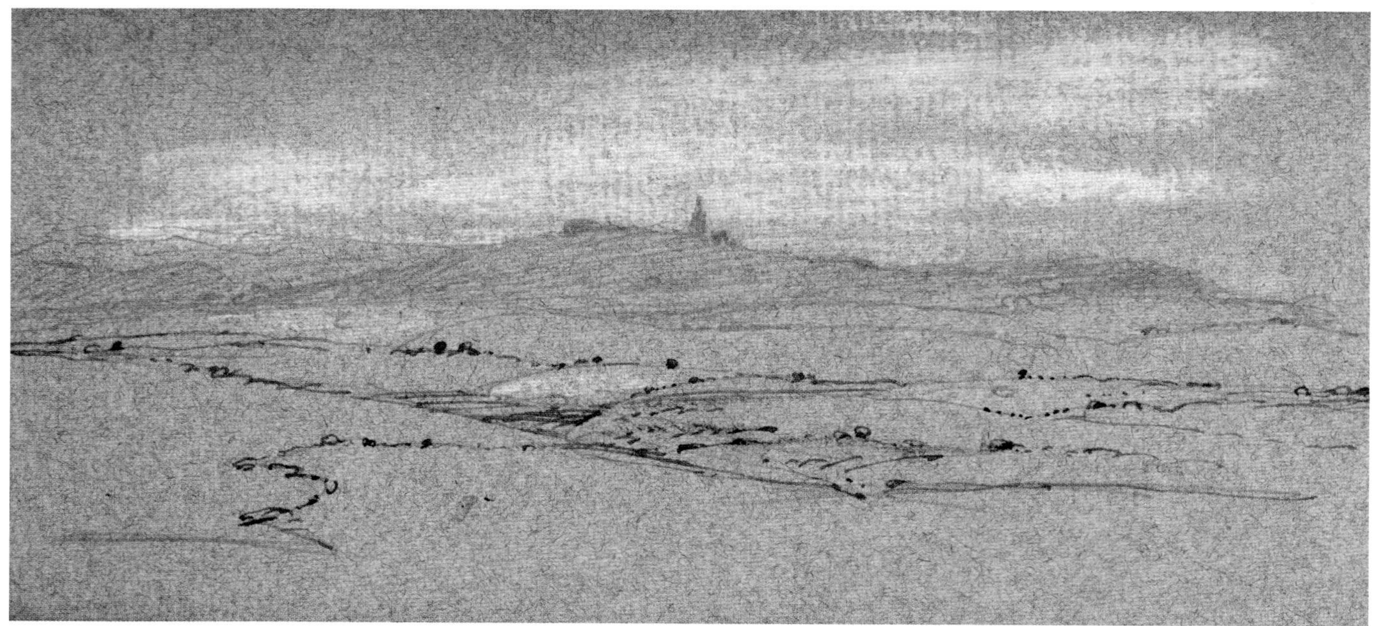

Fig. 77
View Towards Fonthill Abbey from the South
1799
Pen and ink, with white highlights, on blue paper, 8.2 × 16.6 cm
From the Egyptian Details sketchbook
Tate (D03963 / TB LXVI 125a)

1799 visit to Fonthill, the period when Turner was also recording views of Oxford, including Wyatt's new Canterbury Gate at Christ Church.[44] The verso of this sheet depicts a group of workmen at Fonthill using a wooden tripod to lift stone.[45]

Groups of labourers also fill the foreground in one of two monochrome studies from the same book (fig. 78).[46] This drawing provides a fascinating snapshot of the number of men working on the site and the nature of their activity. In addition to the builders, horses and carts are being used to convey materials. On the right, there are indications of the temporary accommodation erected to house this workforce. Frustratingly, however, Turner composed his image to show only the southern part of the abbey, which was the most completely furnished, although Beckford would not inhabit it fully until several years later. It is possible that Turner recorded the central tower on other sheets, now missing; or perhaps the omission of it was tactful, given its recent troubles.

It is certainly notable that, during his 1799 visit, Turner chose not to record the total effect of the abbey more precisely, other than from a distance. This shortcoming was seized on by one of the reviewers of the 1800 Royal Academy exhibition, who proposed that the series of watercolours 'appear too much alike', despite being observed from different positions of the compass, recording different times of day. Instead of creating variety, the sequence left the critic frustrated: 'There should have been some point taken where the building was decidedly the object.'[47]

Turner's views of Fonthill followed the format of country house portraiture by setting the property in its landscape, but there was possibly a deliberate attempt to disguise the incomplete state of the abbey by not getting too close. Presumably Beckford himself was complicit to this decision, since he would have selected the sketches he wanted Turner to develop more fully. One of these was eventually left unfinished (fig. 83), a circumstance that is striking because it would have highlighted precisely the western side of the building where work was still under way. For his part, Beckford was reported to have believed Turner's views were 'rather too poetical, too ideal, even for Fonthill. The scenery there is certainly beautiful, but Turner took such liberties with it that he entirely destroyed the portraiture, the locality of the spot.'[48] However, this was a later observation, after he had left Fonthill and sold all but one of the five exhibits (fig. 85). Even so, Beckford was correct in noting a tendency towards idealisation in the watercolours that sometimes distorts the true scale of the building in relation to its landscape.

Another anomaly that has not been investigated is the discrepancy between the contemporary references to a sequence of 'seven' views of the abbey compared with the five that were actually completed and displayed. To reiterate: Turner had specified in September 1799 that Beckford had commissioned 'several' watercolours, and he repeated the information with the precise number when he reviewed his success at the 1800 exhibition with Farington on 10 July.[49] At this stage he was hoping to charge Beckford 40 guineas for each watercolour, although he eventually secured only 35 apiece.

Obviously the five preliminary sketches for the finished watercolours account for most of the set. Significantly, all of these are numbered in ink in the lower corner of the design, as is one other

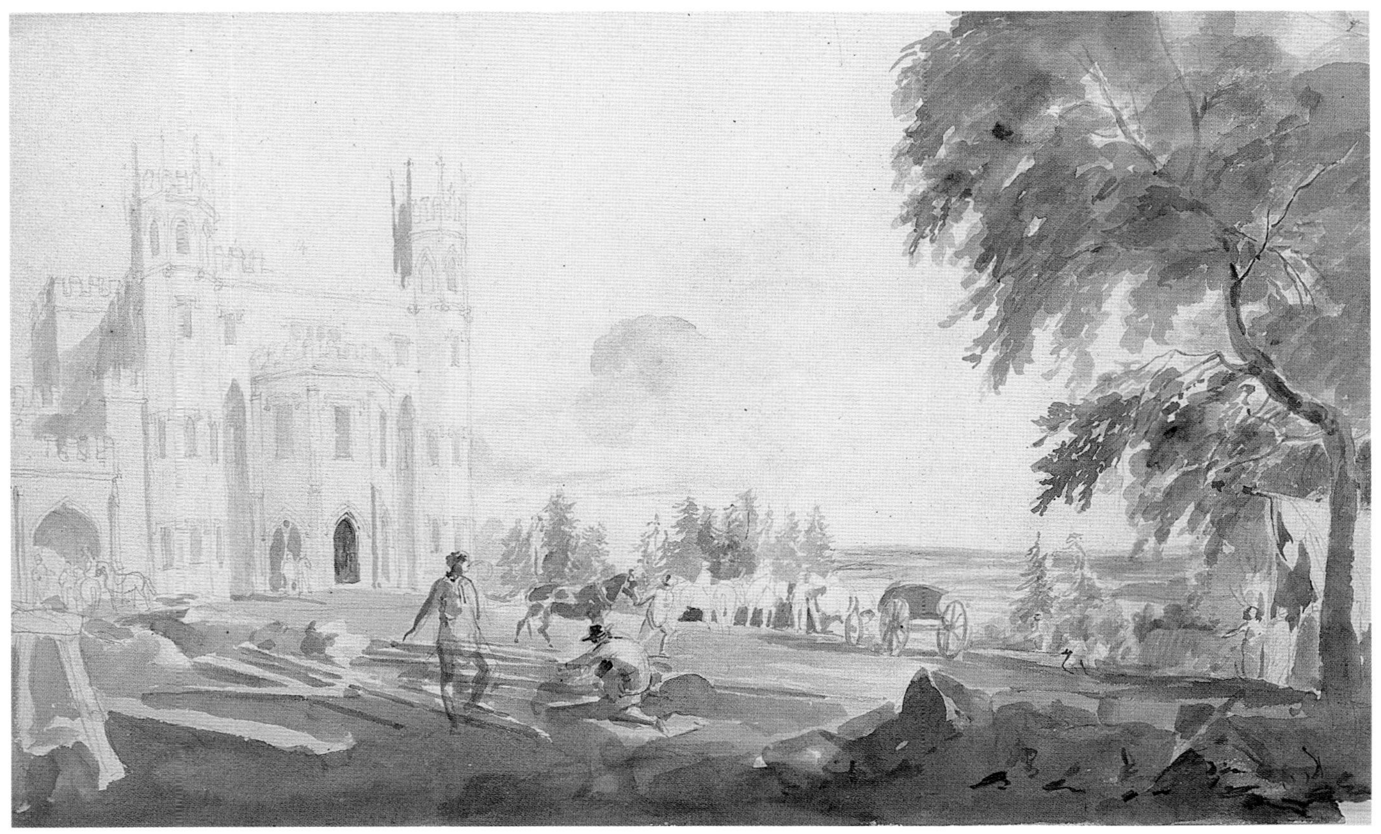

Fig. 78
Builders Working on the Construction of Fonthill Abbey
1799
Pencil and grey wash,
25 × 40.5 cm
Trimmed sheet from the Smaller Fonthill sketchbook
Private collection

sketch, which leaves the identity of just one of the seven subjects uncertain. Their specific places in this numerical sequence reconstruct the passage of time, from dawn to evening:

1. Sunrise or Dawn: no finished work can be linked with this subject
   study: ?TB XLVII 47 (fig. 79)
2. 'Morning' from the South-West, exh. RA 1800 (Council Room), no. 341 (fig. 81)
   study: TB XLVII 12 – inscribed '2' (fig. 80)
3. Mid-Morning: Unfinished design (fig. 83)
   study: TB XLVII 10 – inscribed '3' (fig. 82)
4. 'Noon' from the East, exh. RA 1800 (Antique Academy), no. 663 (fig. 85)
   study: Leeds Art Gallery; apparently not inscribed (fig. 84)
5. 'Afternoon', exh. RA 1800 (Council Room), no. 328 (fig. 87)
   study: TB XLVII 11 – inscribed '5' (fig. 86)
6. 'Sunset' from the North-East, exh. RA 1800 (Antique Academy), no. 680 (fig. 89)
   study: TB XLVII 7 – inscribed '6' (fig. 88)
7. 'Evening' from the South, exh. RA 1800 (Antique Academy), no. 566 (fig. 91)
   study: TB XLVII 13 – inscribed '7' (fig. 90)
   Andrew Loukes has identified TB LXX U (D04172) as an intermediate study for the finished work.

The first thing this list reveals is that the titles of the exhibited views of 'Afternoon' and 'Sunset' have been wrongly exchanged in the past, something that resulted from their shared early histories in the Morrison collection, near Fonthill, once they had left Beckford's collection (see pp. 194–95).[50] The full title of 'Sunset' stipulates a view from the North-East, which is that from the east side of the lake, near the picturesque boathouse (on the right), and although Turner took liberties in working up his sketch, he did include the disc of the setting sun and its reflection in the lake.[51]

The two subjects that were not exhibited were both intended to depict morning light: the first would have been a dawn or sunrise scene. The strongest candidate for this is the wonderfully atmospheric study of a shepherd turning out his flock as the early morning mists lift off the hillside (fig. 79).[52] However, the bold human interest here, which juxtaposes humble rural life with extravagant aristocratic folly, as epitomised by the abbey's distant tower, may have been too poignant for Beckford. Other possibilities for the first design could be a view from Old Wardour Castle, though the herdsman here appears to be rounding up his cattle, a theme more suitable for later in the day (fig. 94). Finally, there is a variant of the 'Sunset' view of the abbey tower seen from near Fonthill Lake, which includes an aqueduct or viaduct, perhaps an ornamental feature inspired by Beckford's travels in Italy, or an imaginative embellishment by Turner (fig. 93). Indeed, if this structure ever existed in the vicinity of Fonthill, there appears to be no record of it in print or local memory. The *contre jour* shading of the tower suggests it was also observed in the afternoon or evening, thus ruling it out as an appropriate study for the first design.

Luckily, the third subject, a view of the abbey from Bitham Lake, was identified by the addition of a numerical inscription (fig. 82), but it is unusual in being the only upright composition, and its place, not absolutely in the middle of the sequence, would have made this format even

A partial plan of the Fonthill Estate. From John Rutter, *Delineations of Fonthill and its Abbey*, 1823
British Library, London

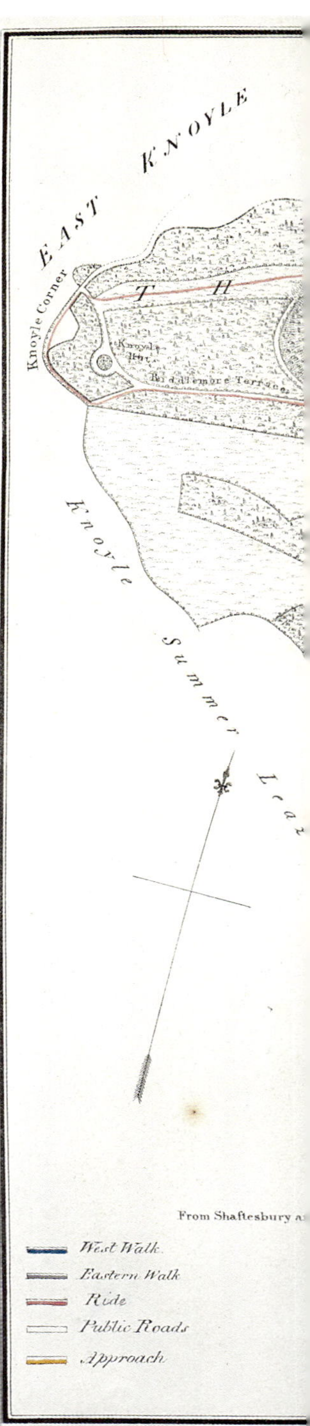

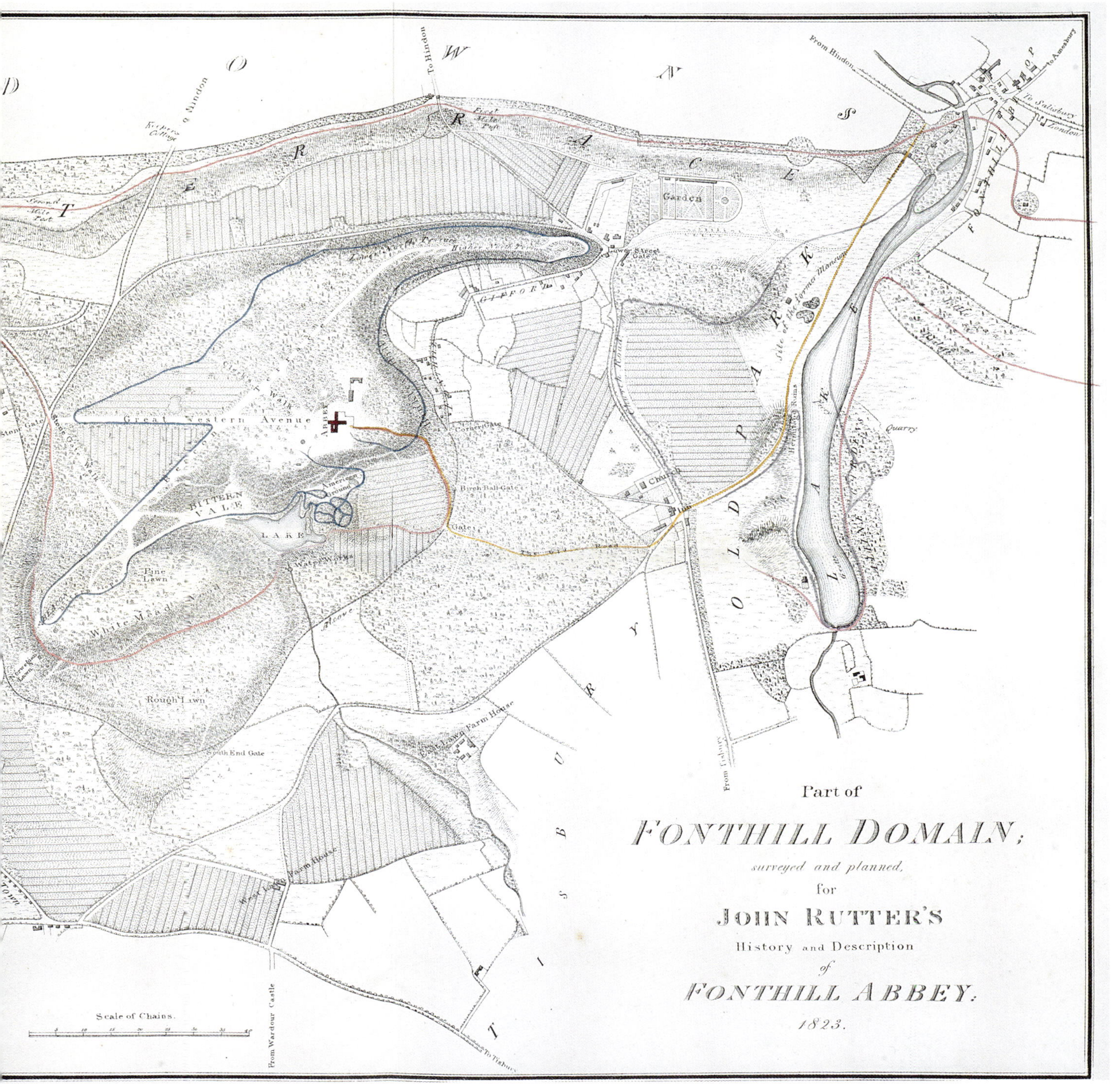
Part of
FONTHILL DOMAIN;
surveyed and planned,
for
JOHN RUTTER'S
History and Description
of
FONTHILL ABBEY.
1823.
To Hindon
From Hindon
To Salisbury
London
Garden
Lower Street Gate
Great Western Avenue
Abbey
Lake
Pine Lawn
Rough Lawn
South End Gate
Corner Gate
Birch Ball Gate
Quarry
From Tisbury
From Wardour Castle
To Tisbury
Scale of Chains.

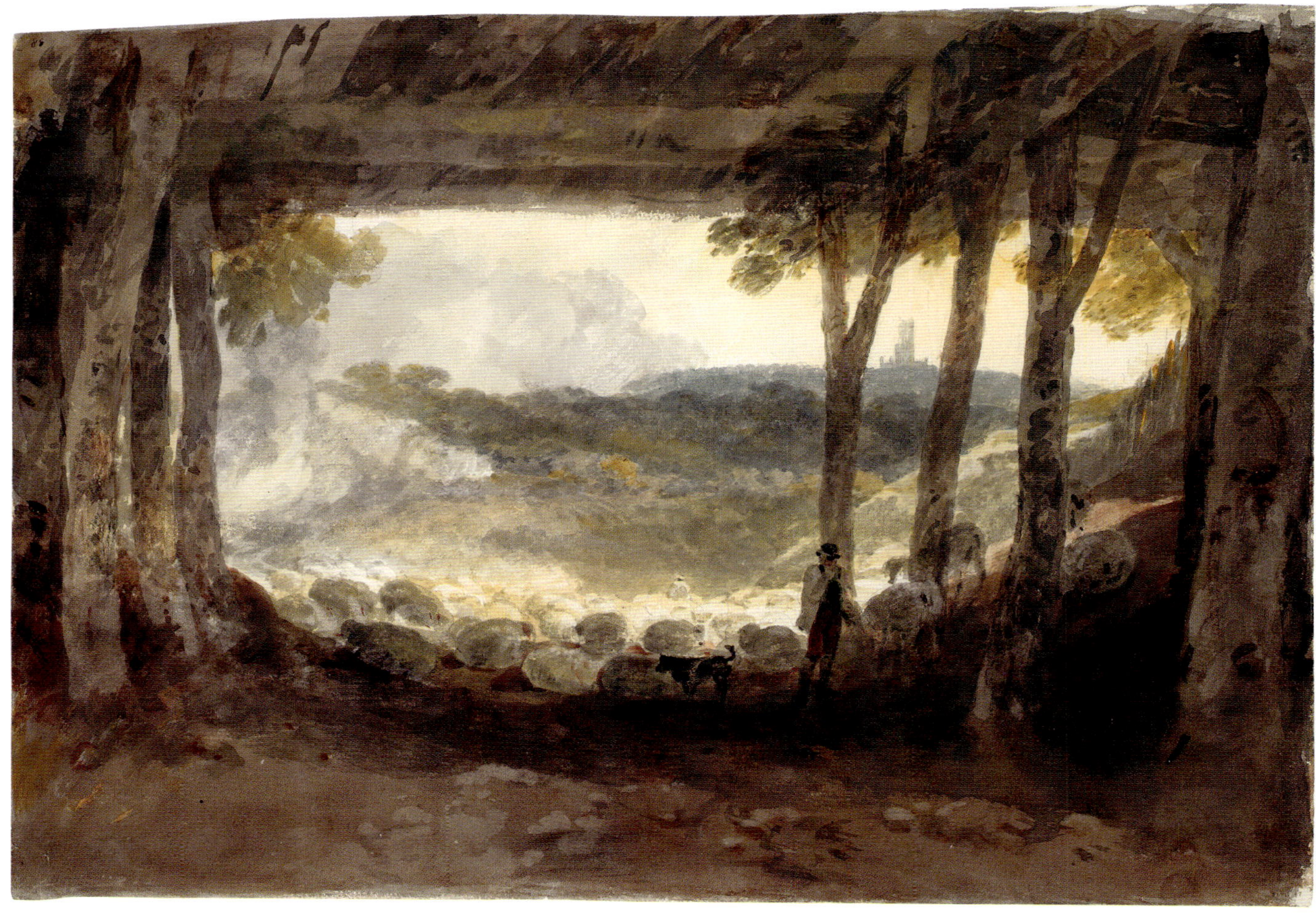

more conspicuous. In addition, the walls of the abbey in the study have a rosy tint, reflecting the setting sun. These factors possibly had a bearing on why the large colour study developed from it was never completed (fig. 83). But it was clearly in contention for a while. A sketchbook used by Turner later in 1799 includes quick memoranda of four of the Fonthill designs, including this unresolved one (fig. 95), which would suggest that discussion about the constitution of the group ensued some time after Turner's visit.[53] Although the selection was then pared down to five views for the 1800 exhibition, Turner had evidently not dismissed the idea of finishing this and a seventh work as late as July 1800.[54]

Contemporary records indicate that the weather during Turner's stay in August 1799 was not always fine, but he would in any case have wanted to spend time indoors studying the painting collection at Fonthill Splendens. The smallest sketchbook he took with him includes a handful of figure studies that may, in part, have been stimulated by the Egyptian décor in the hall (fig. 96).[55] Individually, however, they are derived from various plates of Bernard de Montfaucon's *L'Antiquité expliquée et représentée en Figures* (1719, Paris), which was available in Beckford's library.[56]

This focus on Egyptian subject matter while actually at Fonthill could imply that there had already been an expression of interest from

Fig. 79
A Wooden Shelter, with a Shepherd and his Flock of Sheep; Fonthill Abbey in the Distance
c.1799
Pencil and watercolour, 33.3 × 46.8 cm
From the 'Fonthill' sketchbook
Tate (D02224 / TB XLVII 47)

Fig. 80
Fonthill Abbey from the South-West; Study for 'Morning'
1799
Pencil, 33.5 × 43.3 cm
From the 'Fonthill' sketchbook
Tate (D02189 / TB XLVI 12)

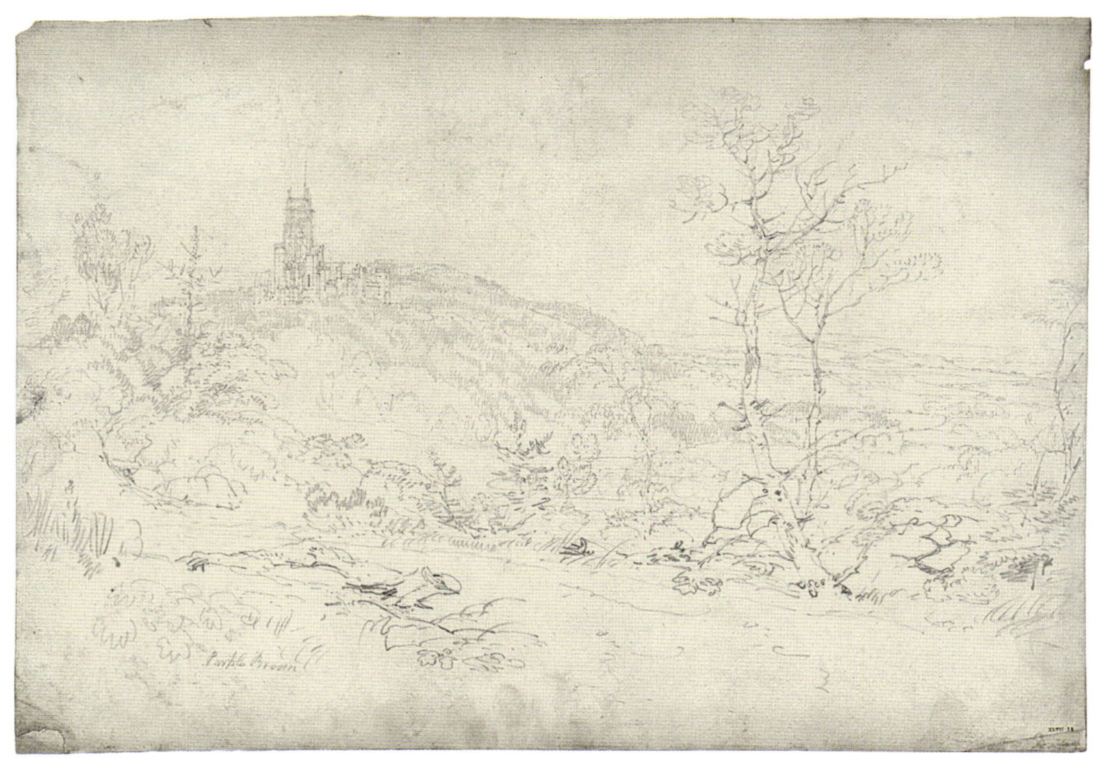

Fig. 81
South-West View of a Gothic Abbey (Morning), Now Building at Fonthill, the Seat of W. Beckford, Esq.
Exhibited RA 1800 (341)
Pencil and watercolour, 69.4 × 102.9 cm
Art Gallery of Ontario, Toronto (W336)
Bequest of John Paris Bickell, Toronto, 1952 (51/39)
(see p. 194)

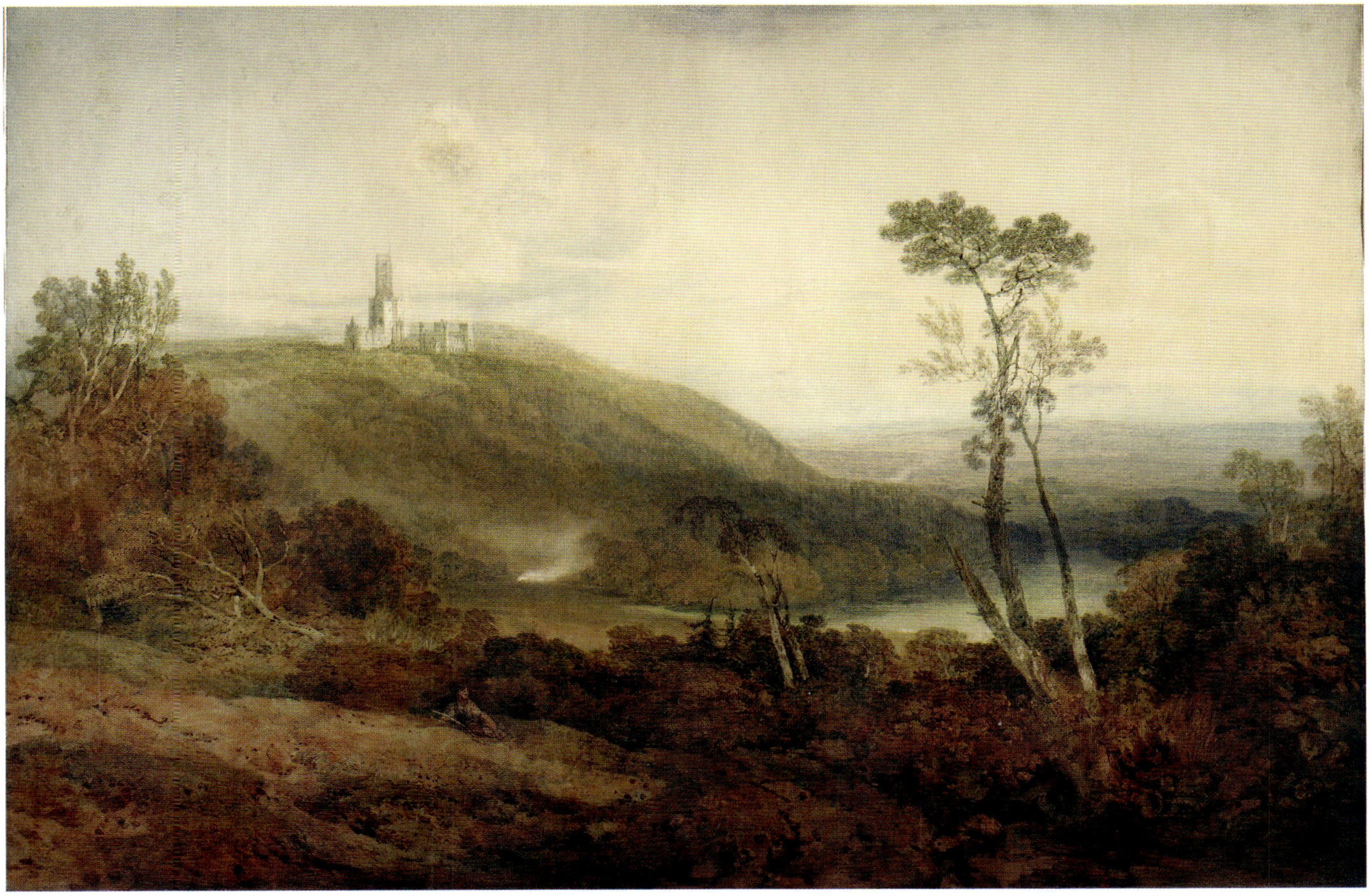

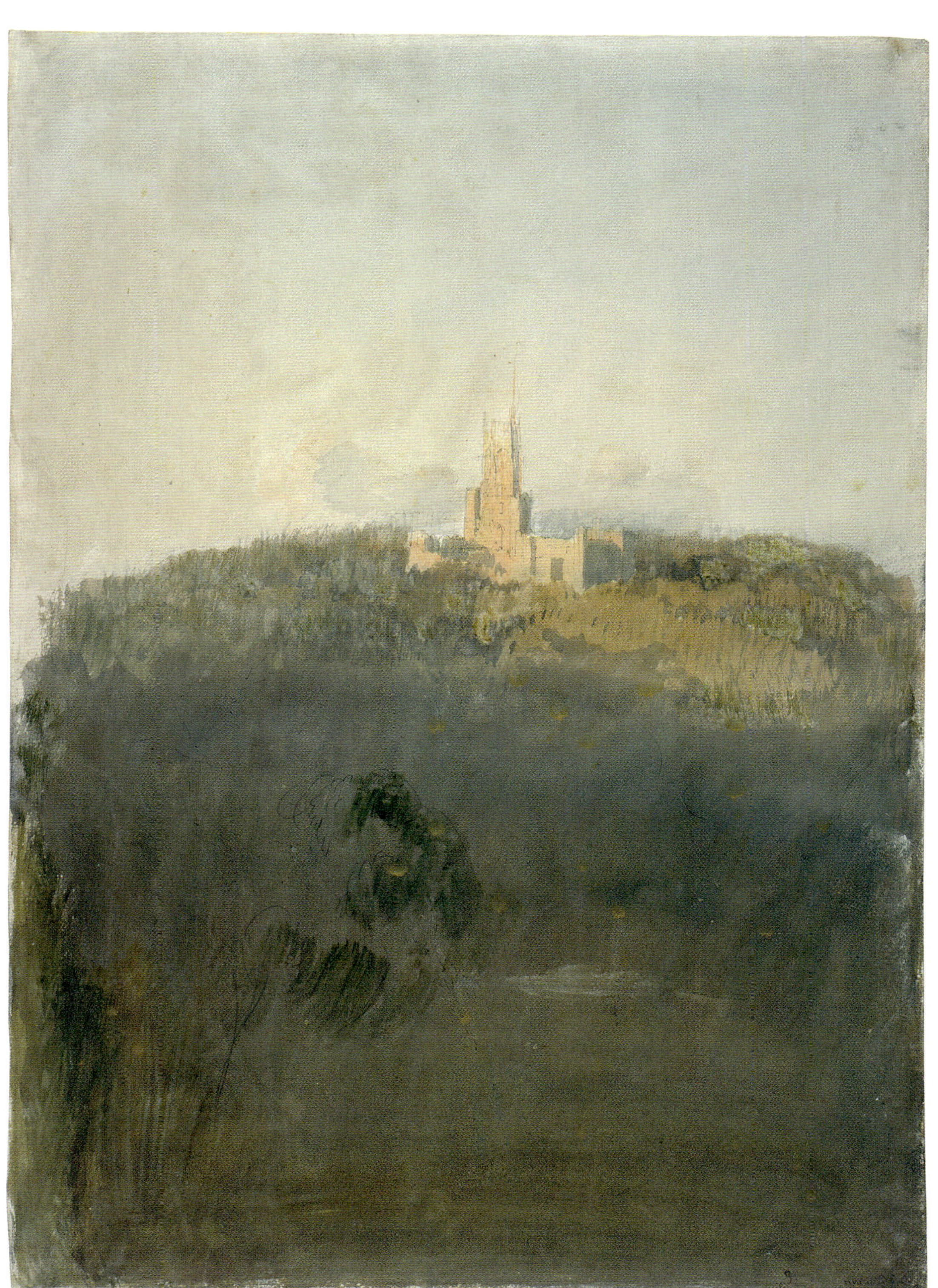

Fig. 82
Fonthill Abbey; from the South-West
1799
Pencil, watercolour and gouache,
46.8 × 33.1 cm
From the 'Fonthill' sketchbook
Tate (D02187 / TB XLVII 10)

OPPOSITE: **Fig. 83**
An Unfinished View of Fonthill Abbey, with Bitham Lake
c.1799–1800
Pencil and watercolour,
104.5 × 71.2 cm
Tate (D04167 / TB LXX P)

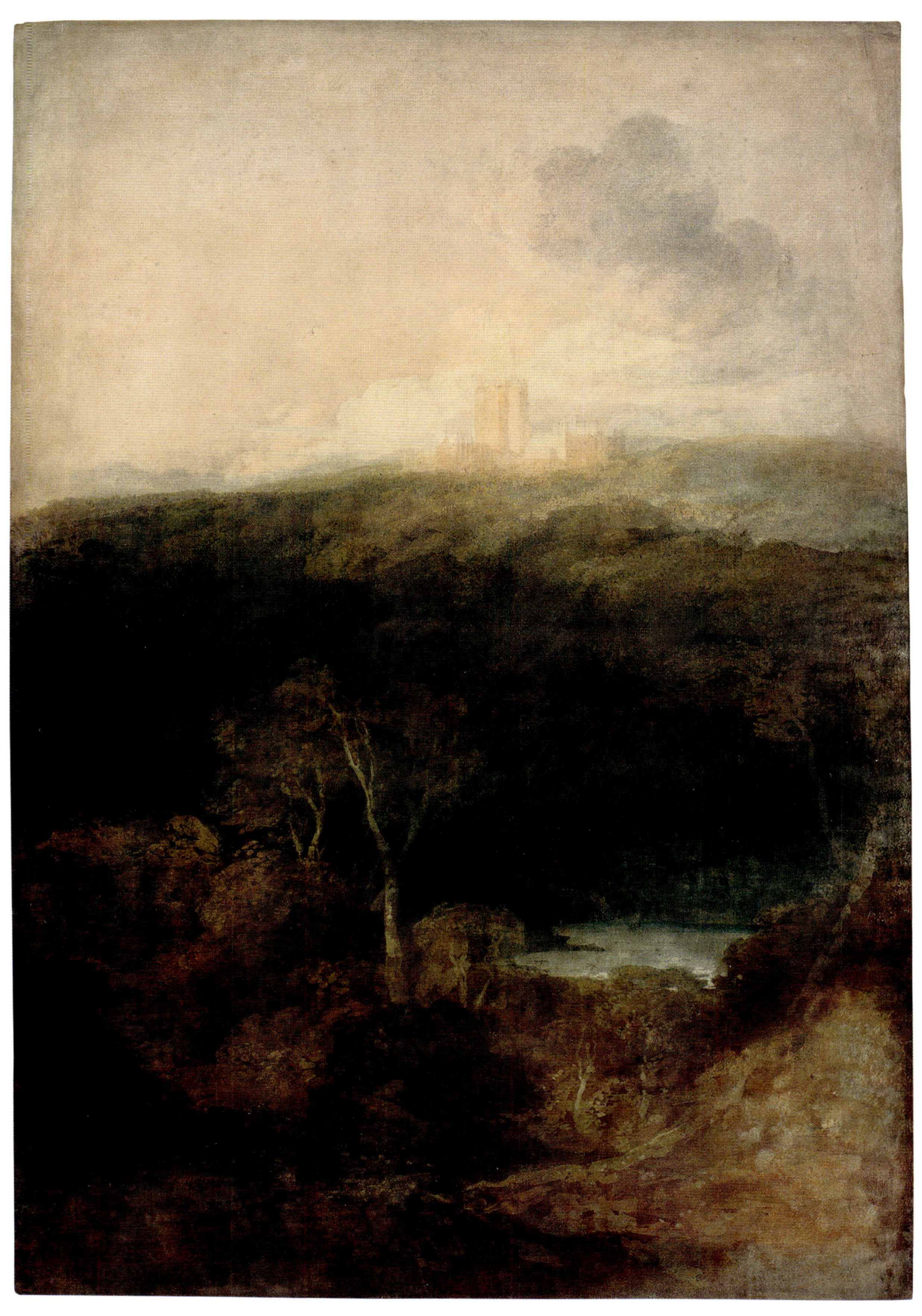

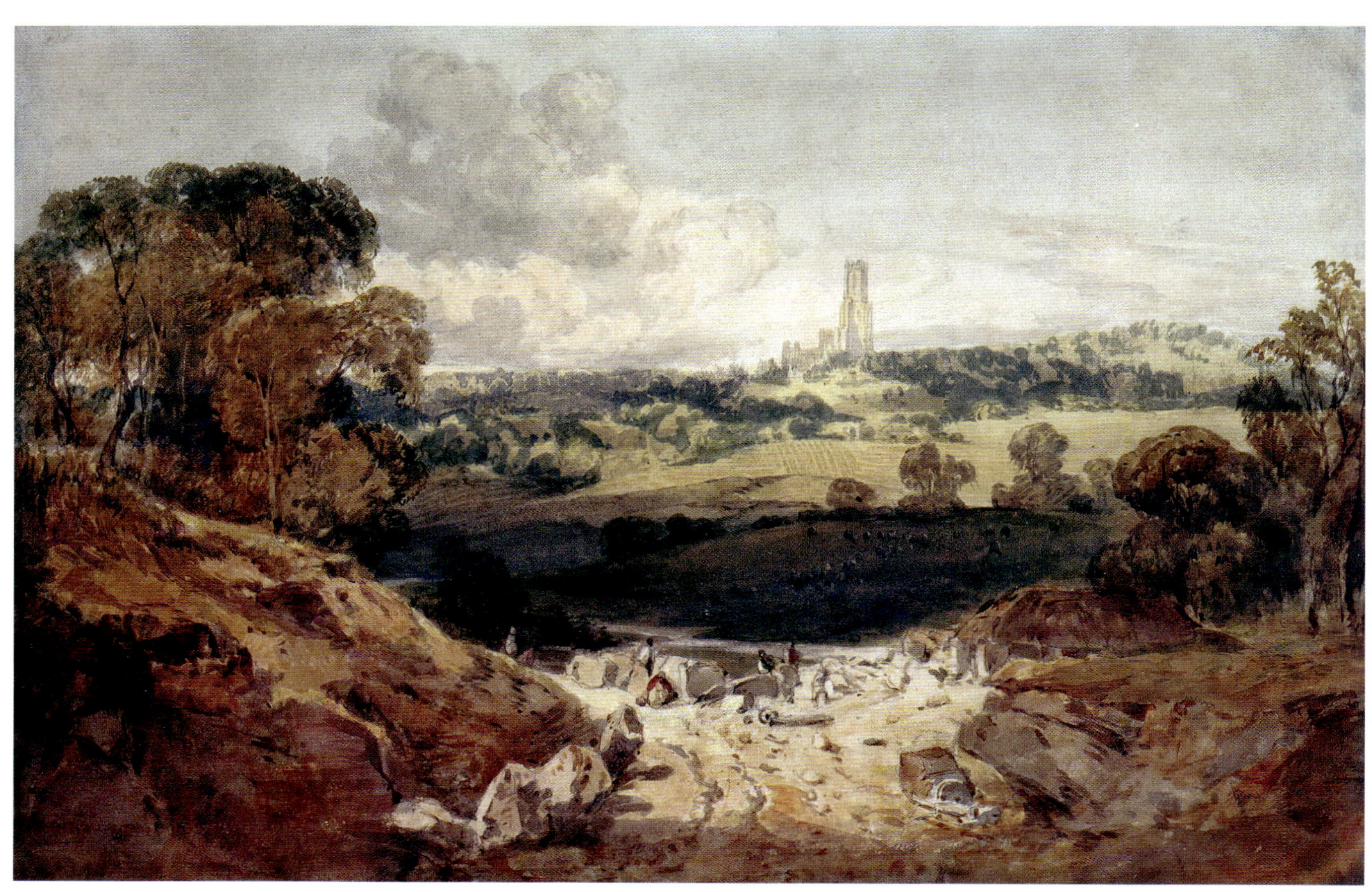

Fig. 84
View of Fonthill Abbey from a Stone Quarry near Chilmark; Study for 'Noon'

1799
Pencil and watercolour,
30 × 44.2 cm
From the 'Fonthill' sketchbook
Leeds Art Gallery (W340)

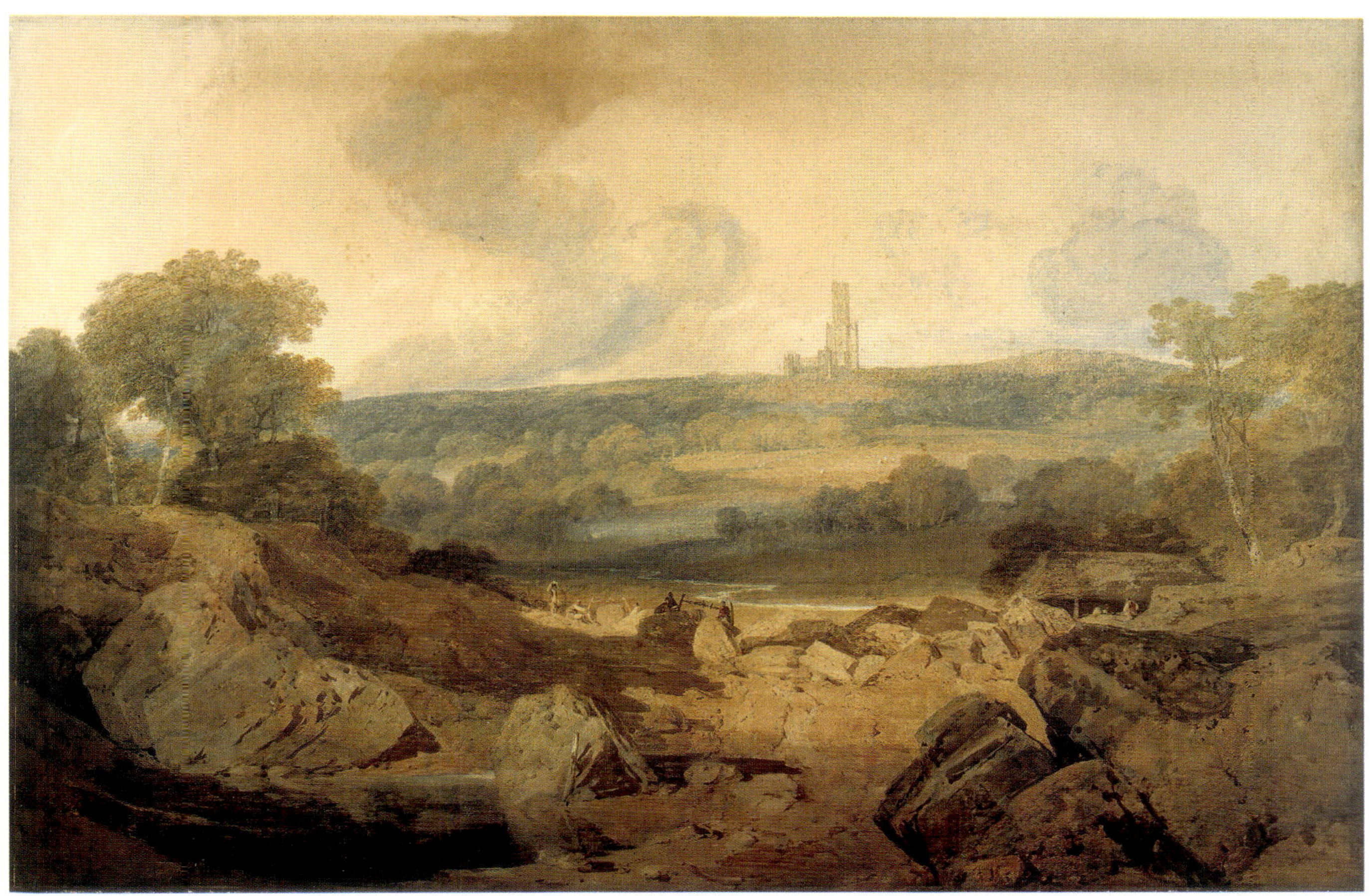

Fig. 85
East View of the Gothic Abbey (Noon) Now Building at Fonthill, the Seat of W. Beckford
Exhibited RA 1800 (663)
Watercolour,
68.5 × 103.5 cm
National Gallery of Scotland, Edinburgh (W338)
(see p. 194)

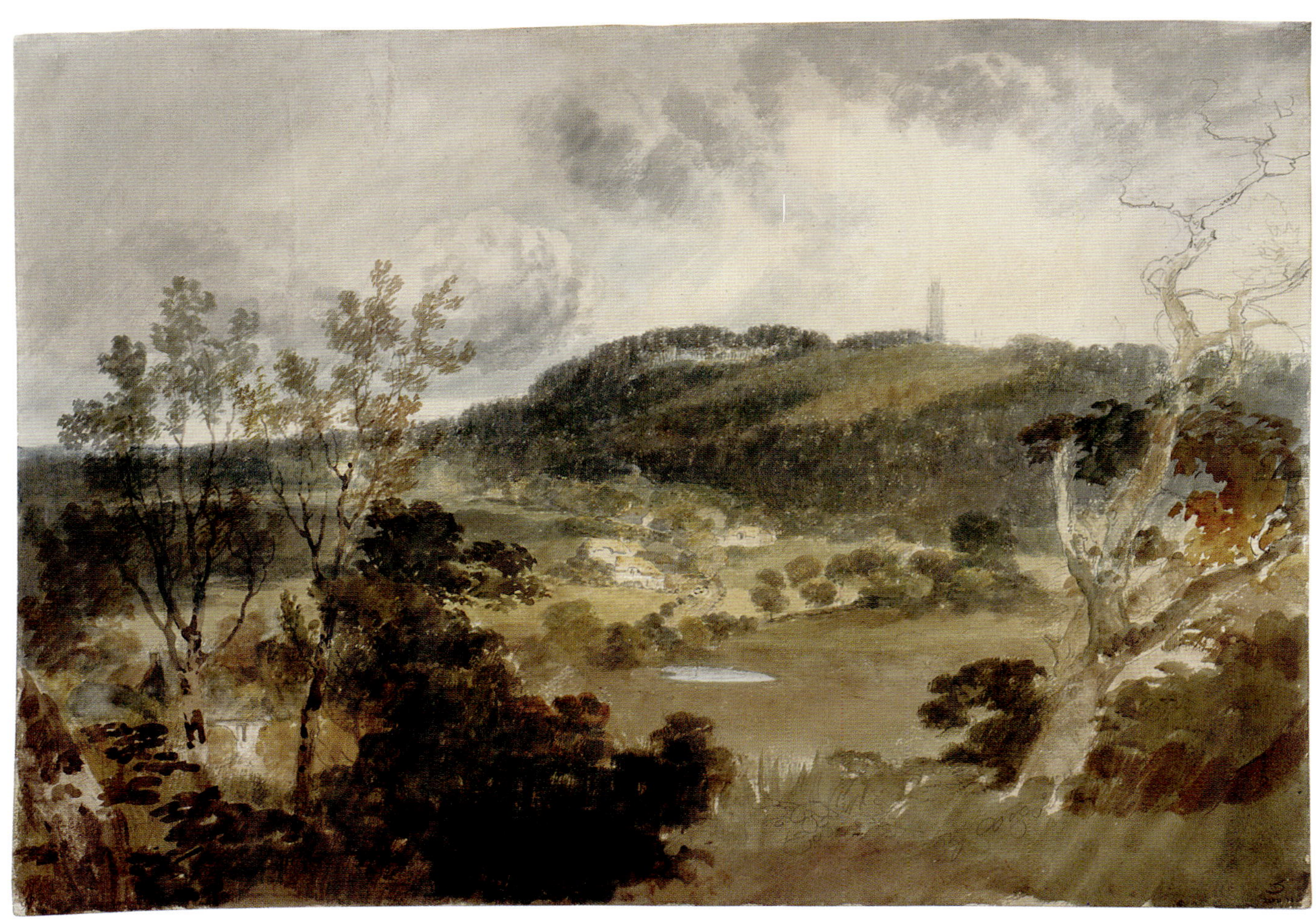

Fig. 86
Fonthill Abbey from the North, with the Village of Fonthill Gifford; Study for 'Afternoon'

1799
Pencil and watercolour, 33.2 × 46.9 cm
From the 'Fonthill' sketchbook
Tate (D02188 / TB XLVII 11)

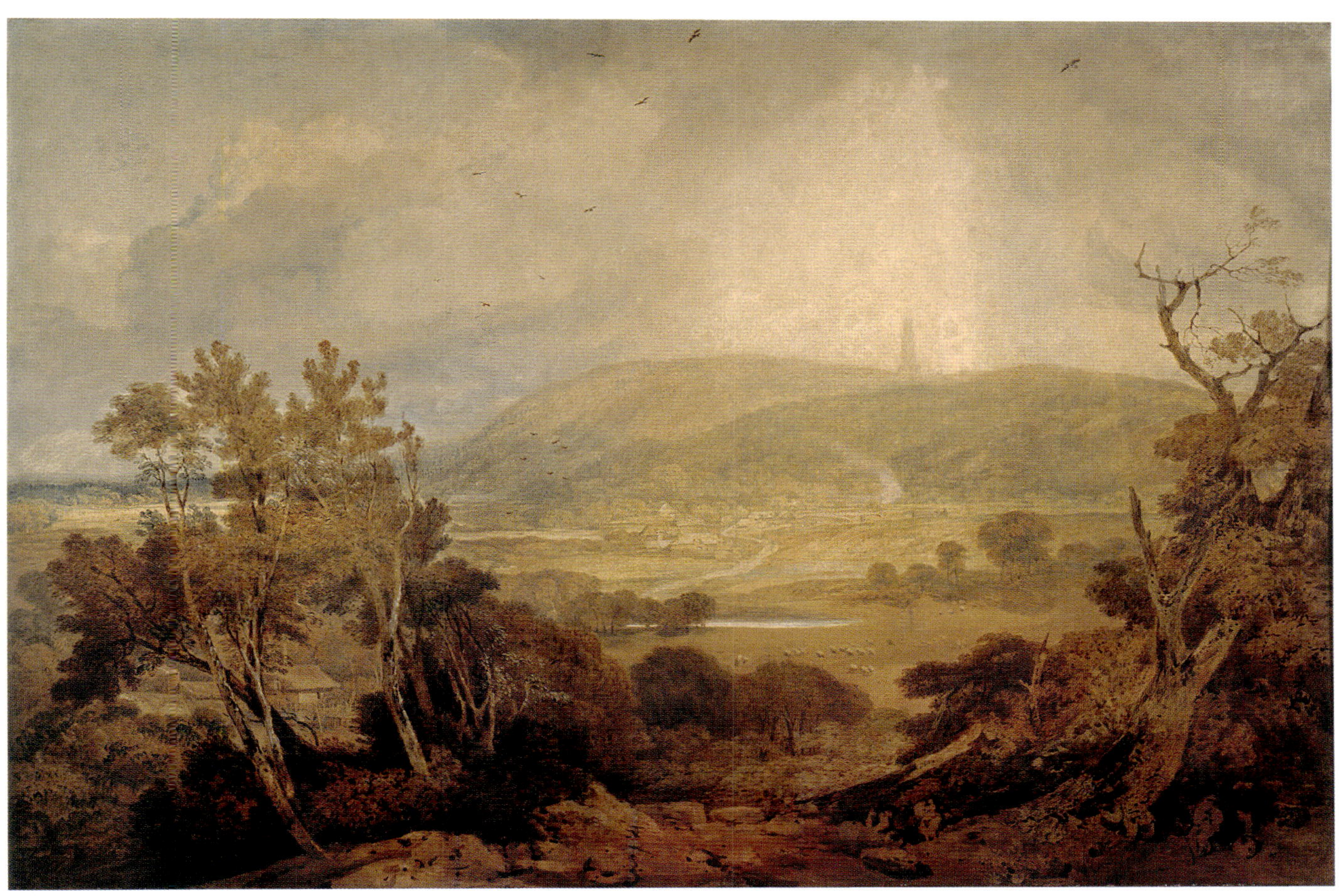

Fig. 87
View of the Gothic Abbey (Afternoon) Now Building at Fonthill, the Seat of William Beckford
Exhibited RA 1800 (328)
Watercolour,
69.5 × 103.5 cm
The Whitworth, The University of Manchester (W339)
(see p. 194)

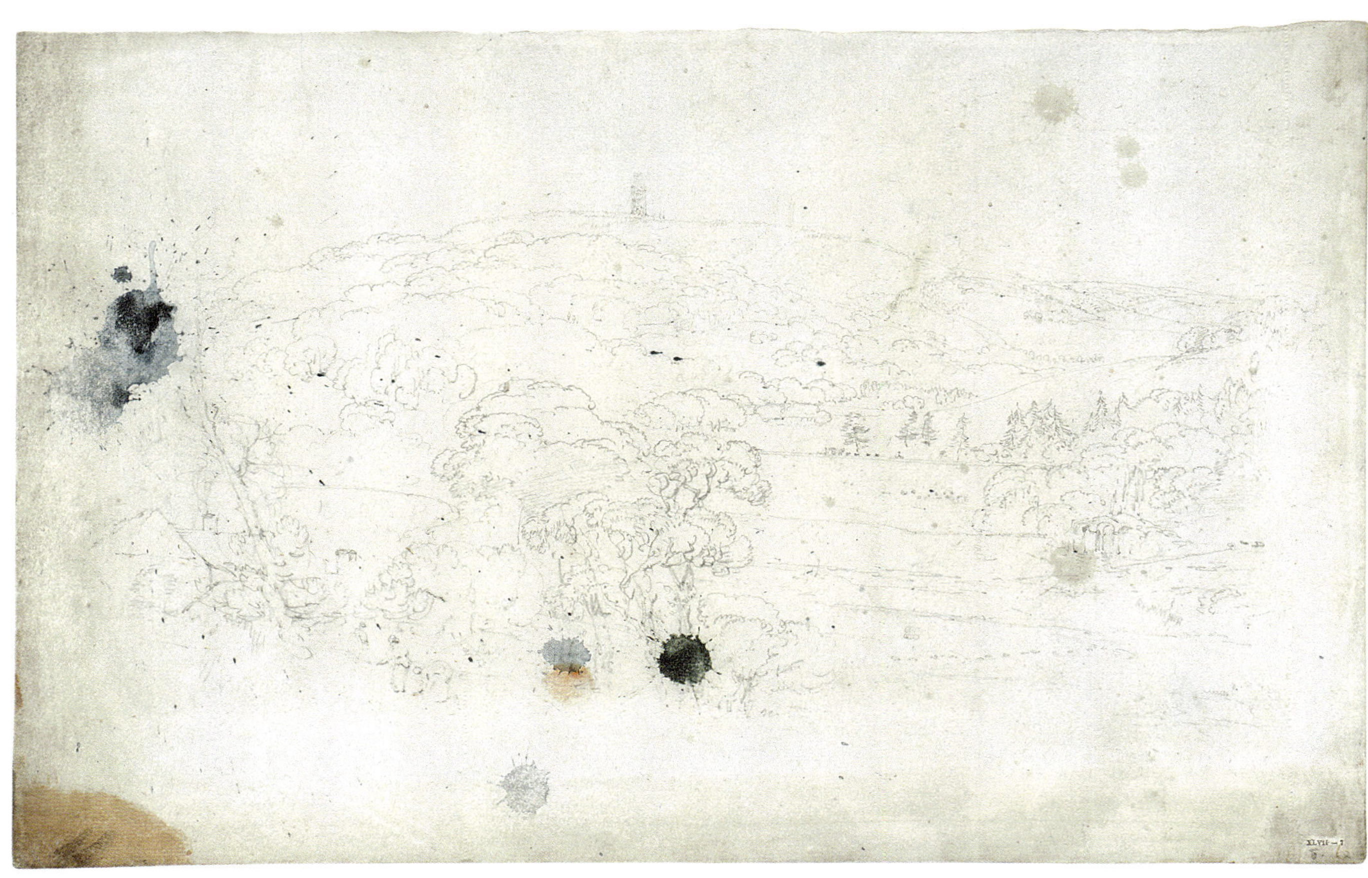

Fig. 88
Fonthill Abbey from the North-East; Study for 'Sunset'

1799
Pencil, 33.5 × 43.3 cm
From the 'Fonthill' sketchbook
Tate (D02184 / TB XLVII 7)

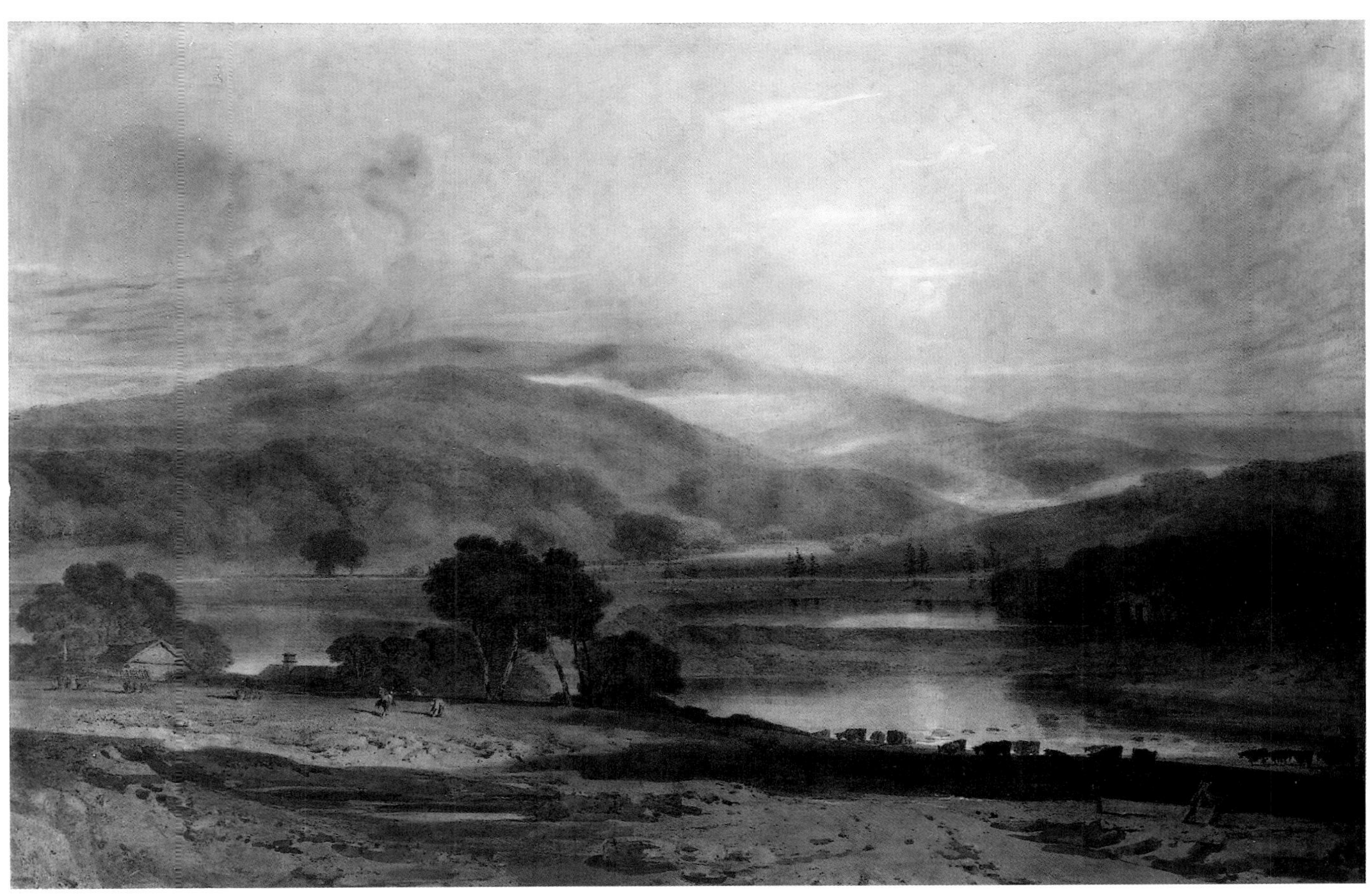

Fig. 89
North-East View of the Gothic Abbey (Sunset), Now Building at Fonthill, the Seat of W. Beckford
Exhibited RA 1800 (380)
Watercolour,
70.4 × 105.3 cm
Private collection (W335)
(see p. 195)

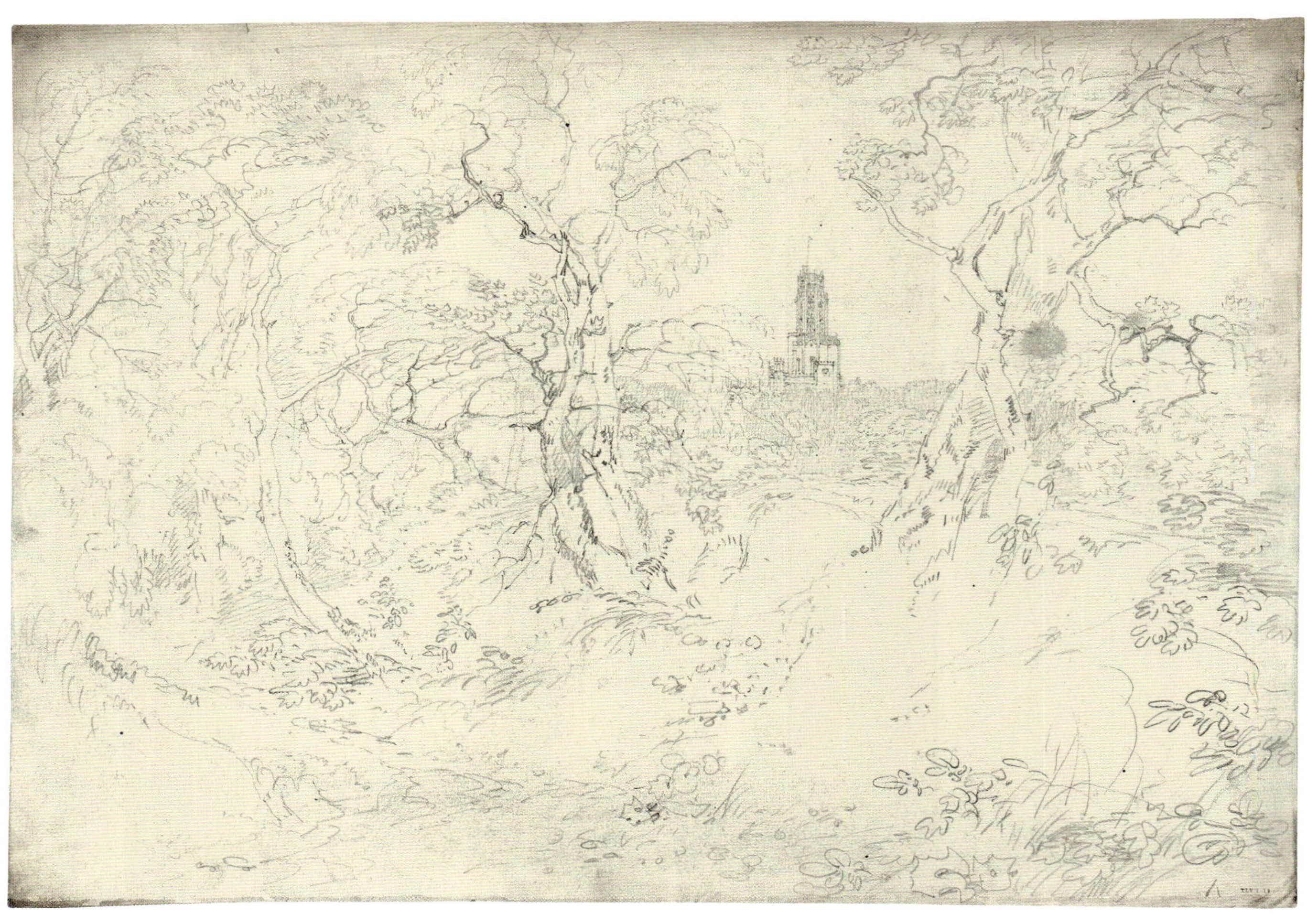

Fig. 90
Fonthill Abbey seen through Trees from the South; Study for 'Evening'
1799
Pencil, 33.5 × 43.3 cm
From the 'Fonthill' sketchbook
Tate (D02190 / TB XLVII 13)

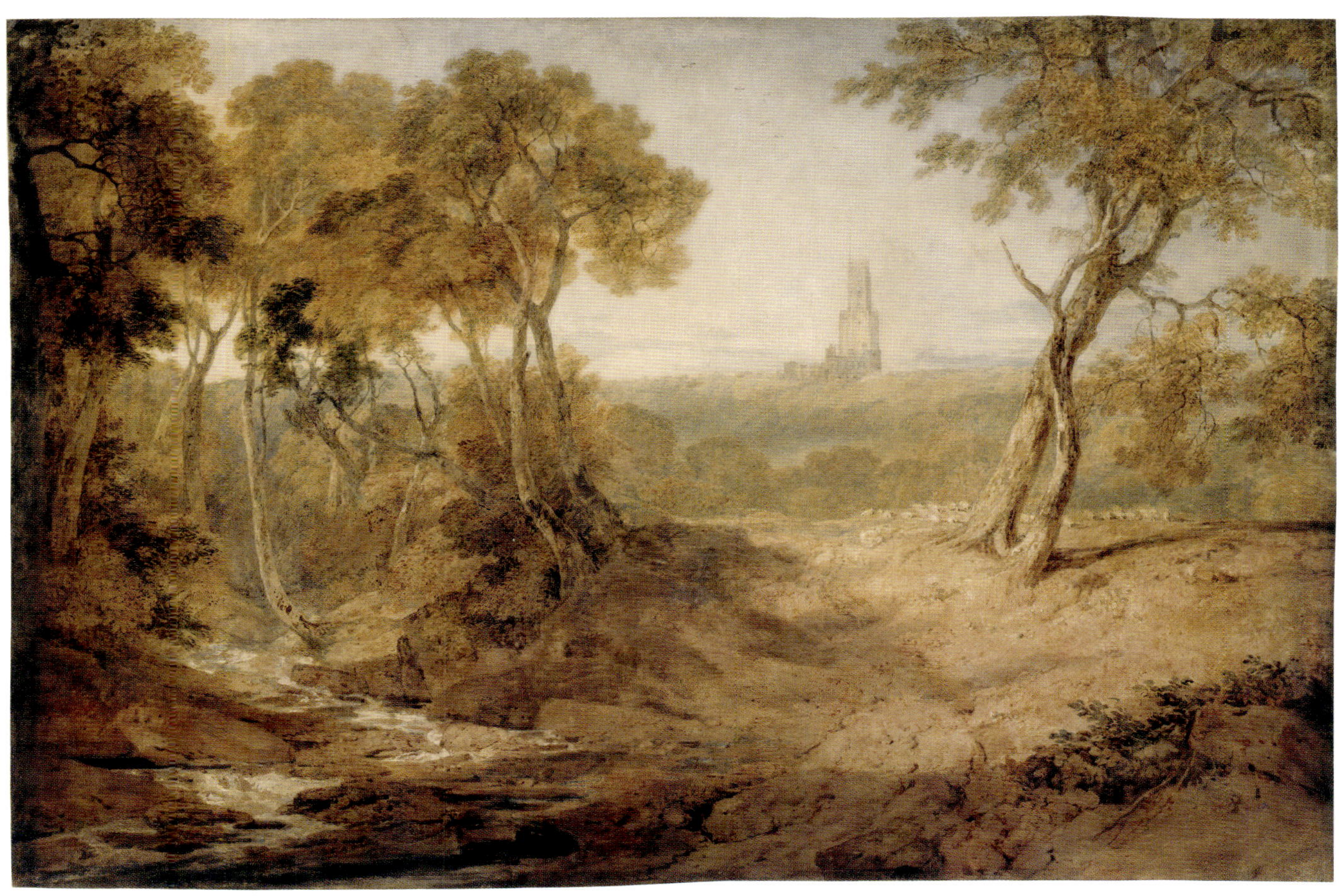

ABOVE AND DETAIL ON FOLLOWING PAGES:

Fig. 91

South View of the Gothic Abbey (Evening) Now Building at Fonthill the Seat of W. Beckford

Exhibited RA 1800 (566)
Watercolour,
70.5 × 104.4 cm
The Montreal Museum of Fine Arts, purchase, Horsley and Annie Townsend Bequest (1963.1385) (W337)
(see p. 195)

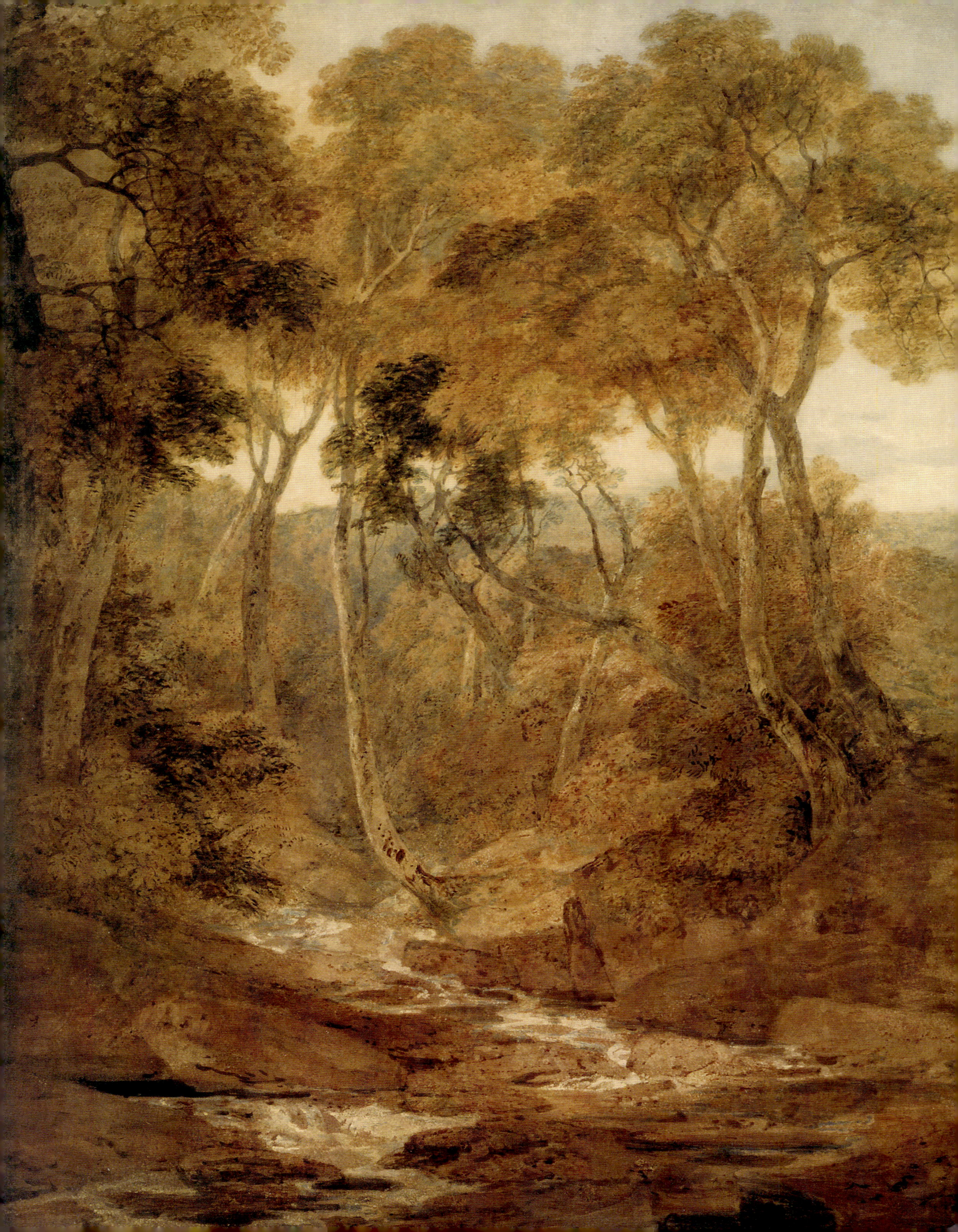

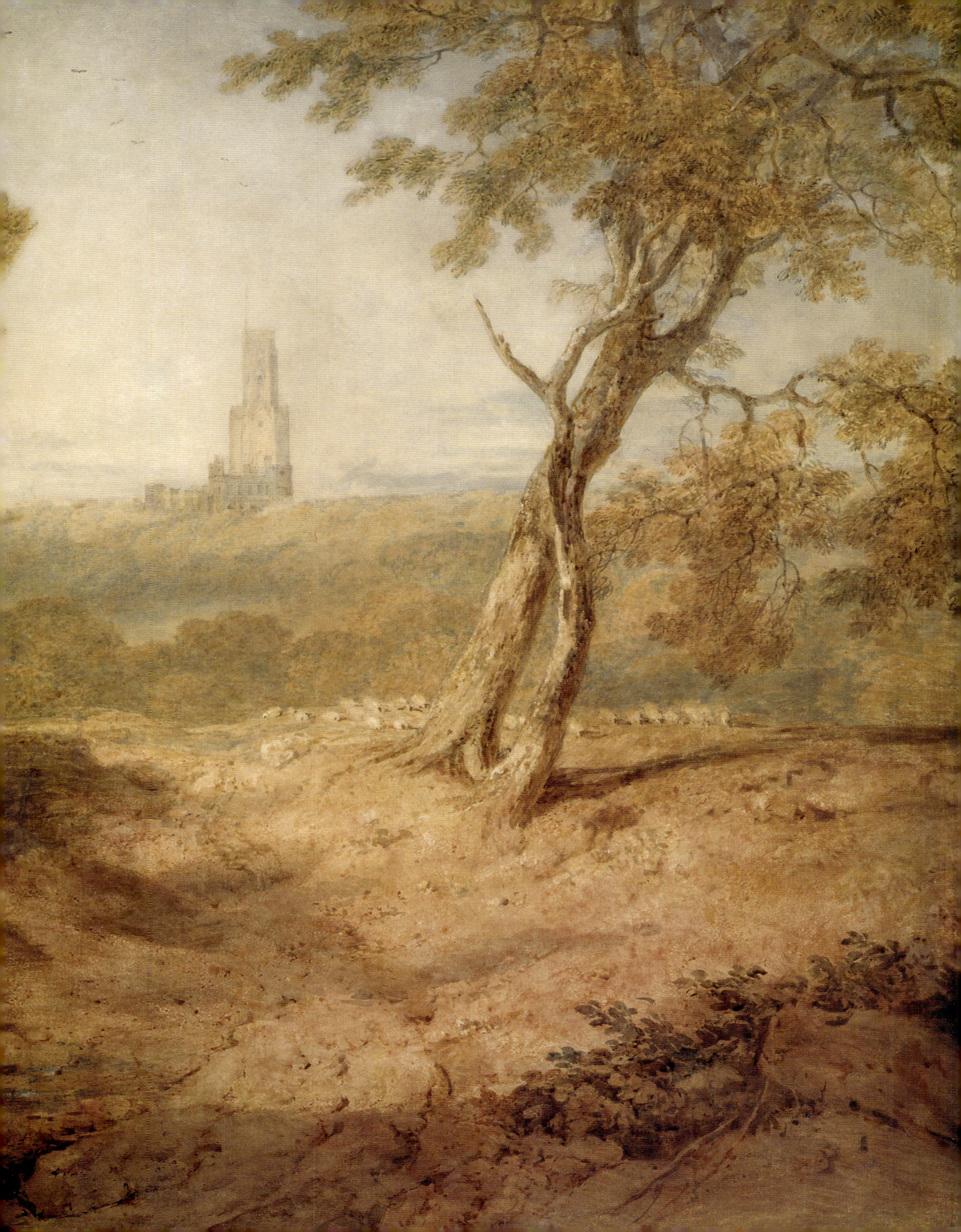

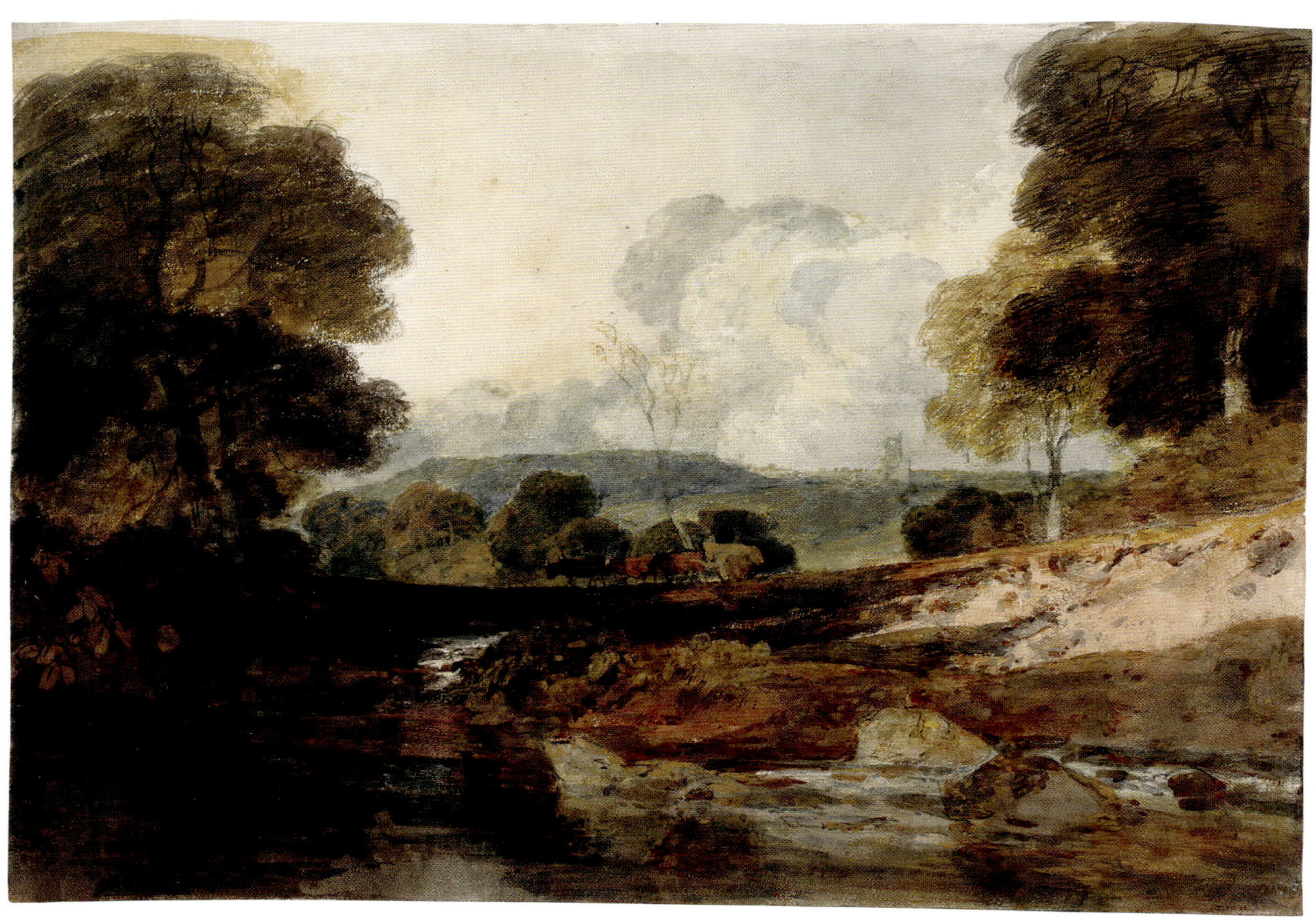

Fig. 92
Fonthill Abbey from the South

*c.*1799
Pencil and watercolour, 33.5 × 43.3 cm
From the 'Fonthill' sketchbook
Tate (D02223 / TB XLVII 46)

Fig. 93
Distant View of Fonthill Abbey, from the North-East, with an Aqueduct

1799
Pencil, 33.2 × 46.8 cm
From the 'Fonthill' sketchbook
Tate (D02183 / TB XLVII 6)

Fig. 94
The Ruins of Old Wardour Castle, with Fonthill Abbey in the Distance

1799
Pencil, 33.5 × 43.3 cm
From the 'Fonthill' sketchbook
Tate (D02186 / TB XLVII 9)

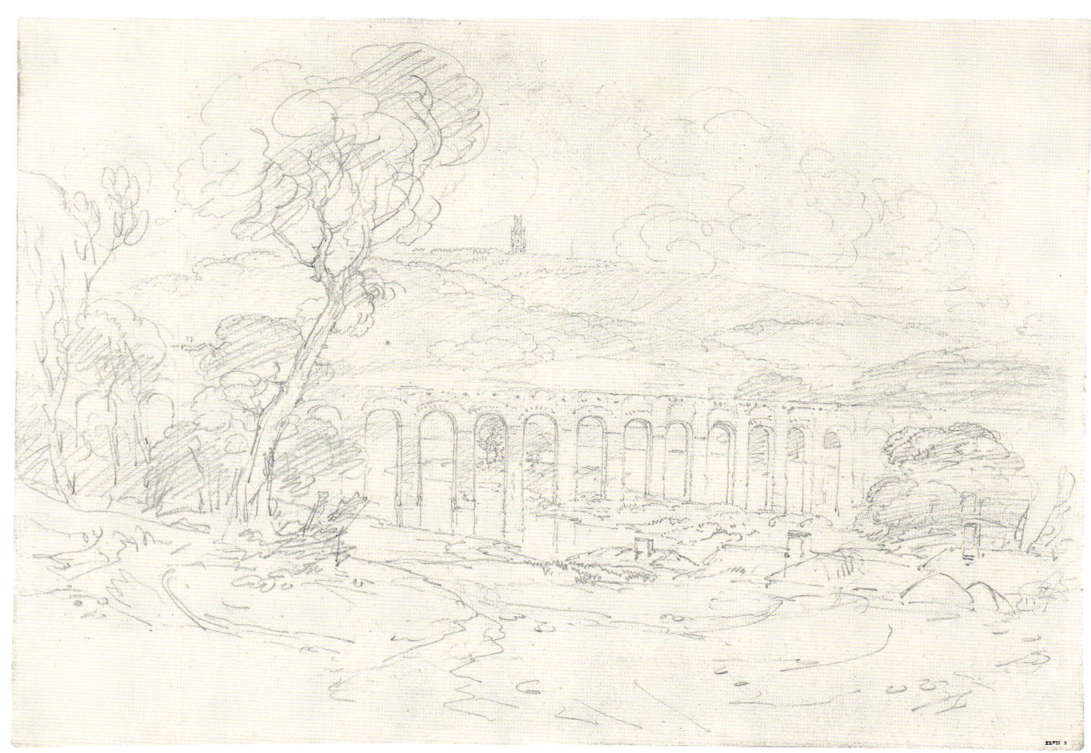

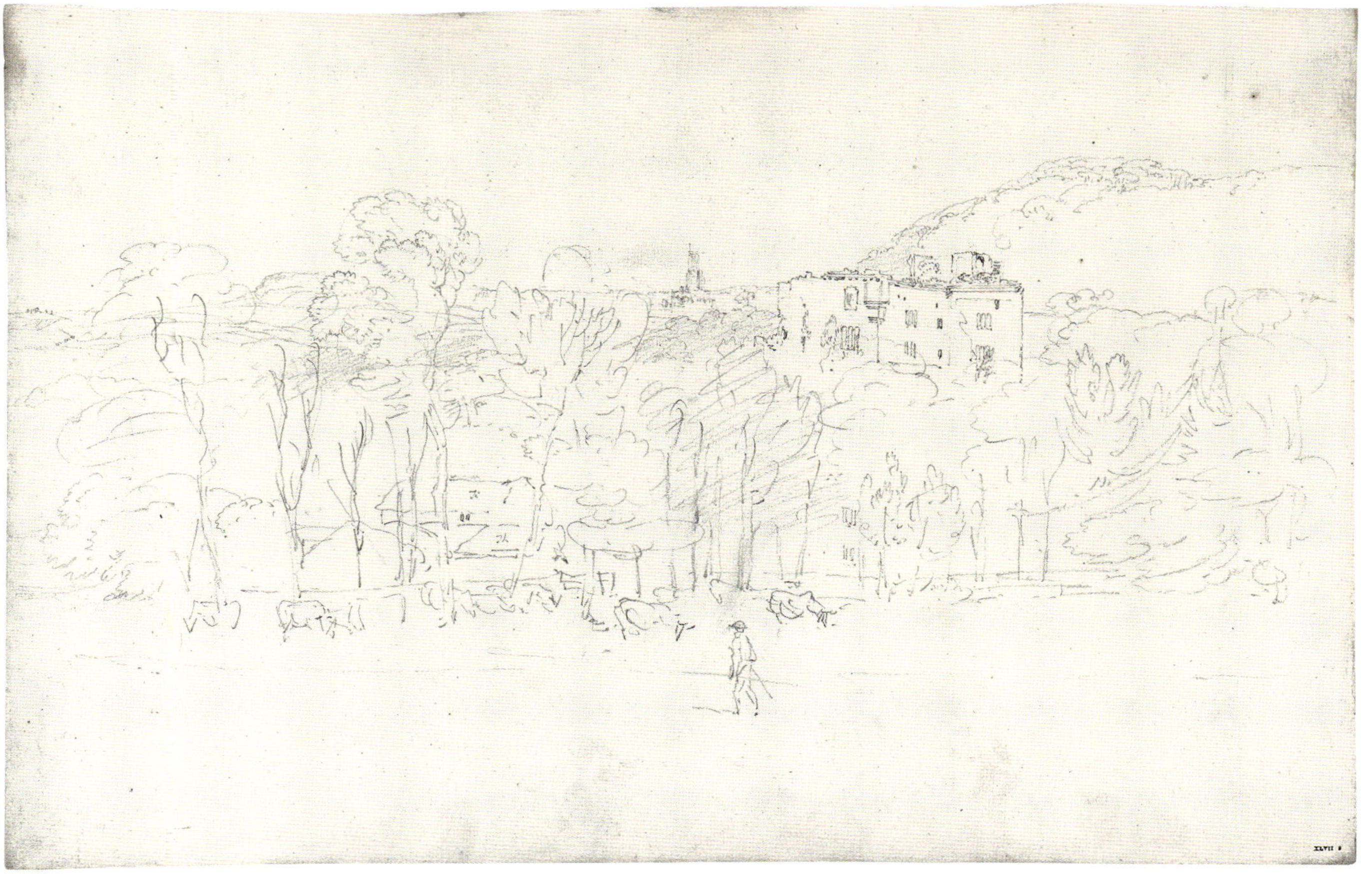

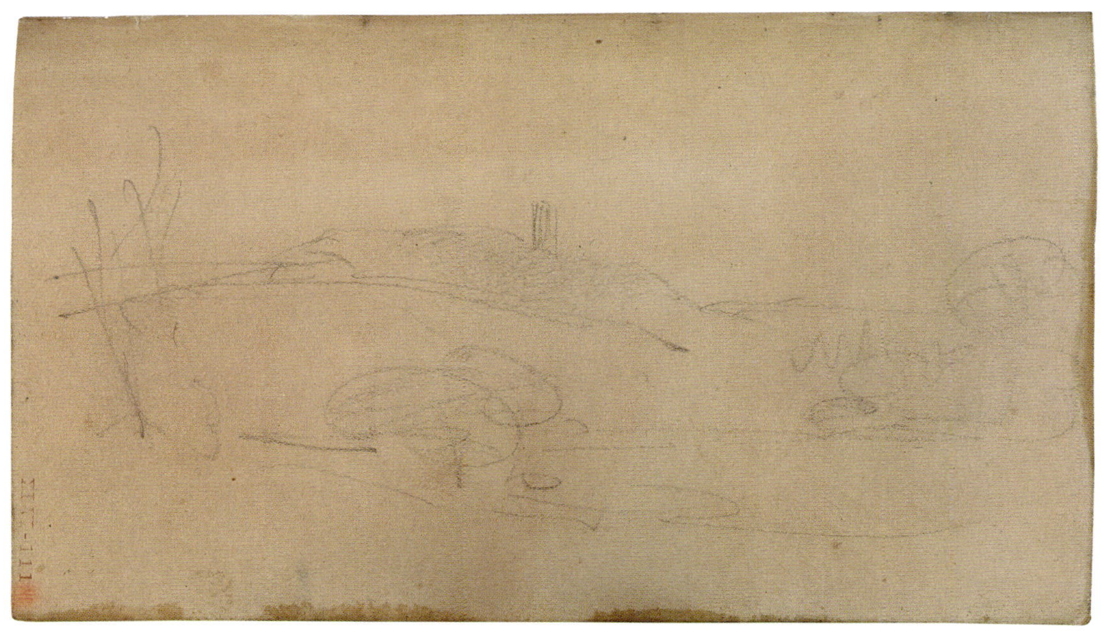

Fig. 95
Transcription of the Study for 'View of the Gothic Abbey (Sunset), Now Building at Fonthill, the Seat of W. Beckford'
c.1799
Pencil, 7.8 × 13.1 cm
From the Dolbadarn sketchbook
Tate (D02158 / TB XLV 111)

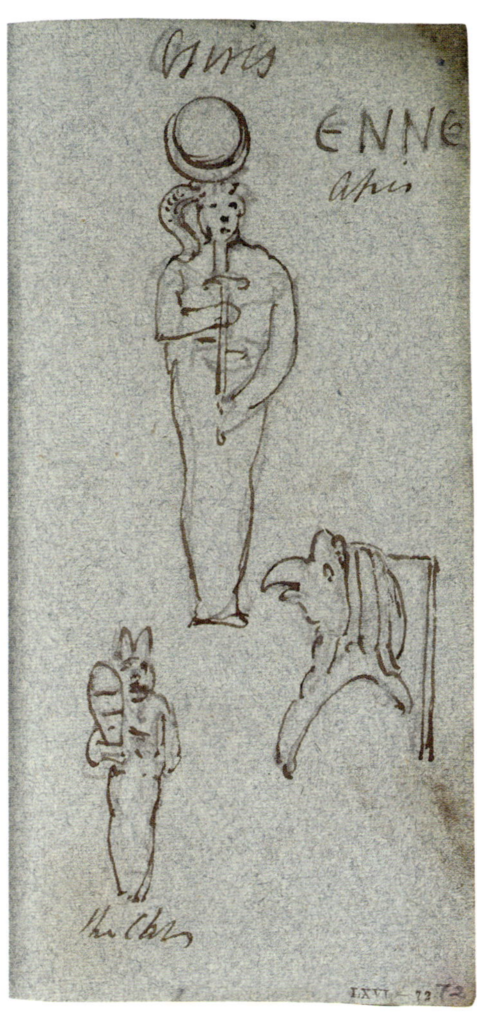

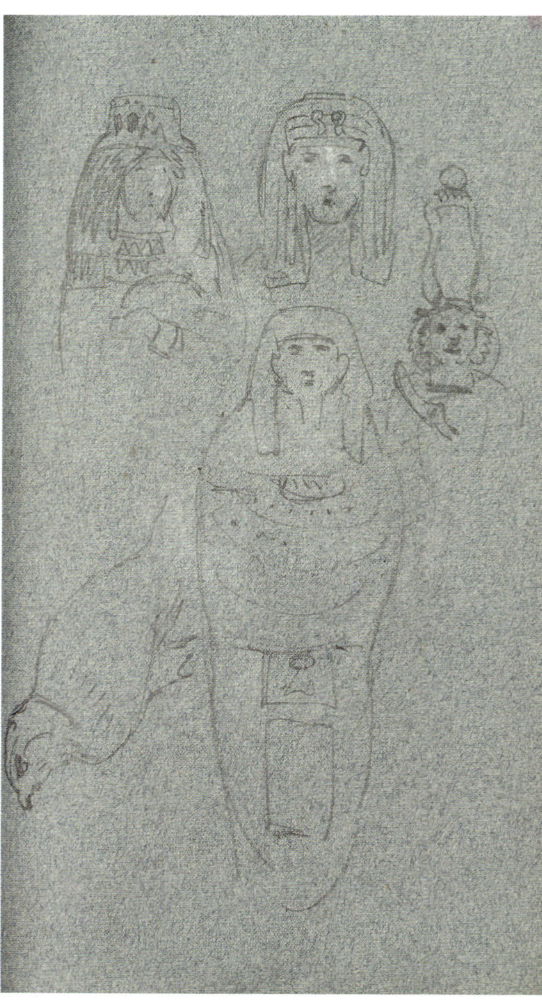

BELOW LEFT: Fig. 96
Studies of Egyptian Gods, copied from Bernard de Montfaucon's 'L'Antiquité expliquée et représentée en Figures'
1799
Pen and ink on blue paper, 16.6 × 8.2 cm
From Egyptian Details sketchbook
Tate (D03906 / TB LXVI 72)

BELOW RIGHT: Fig. 97
Studies of Egyptian Figures, copied from Bernard de Montfaucon's 'L'Antiquité expliquée et représentée en Figures'
c.1799–1800
Pencil and chalk on blue paper, 21.5 × 13.8 cm
From 'Studies for Pictures' sketchbook
Tate (D04074 / TB LXIX 65a)

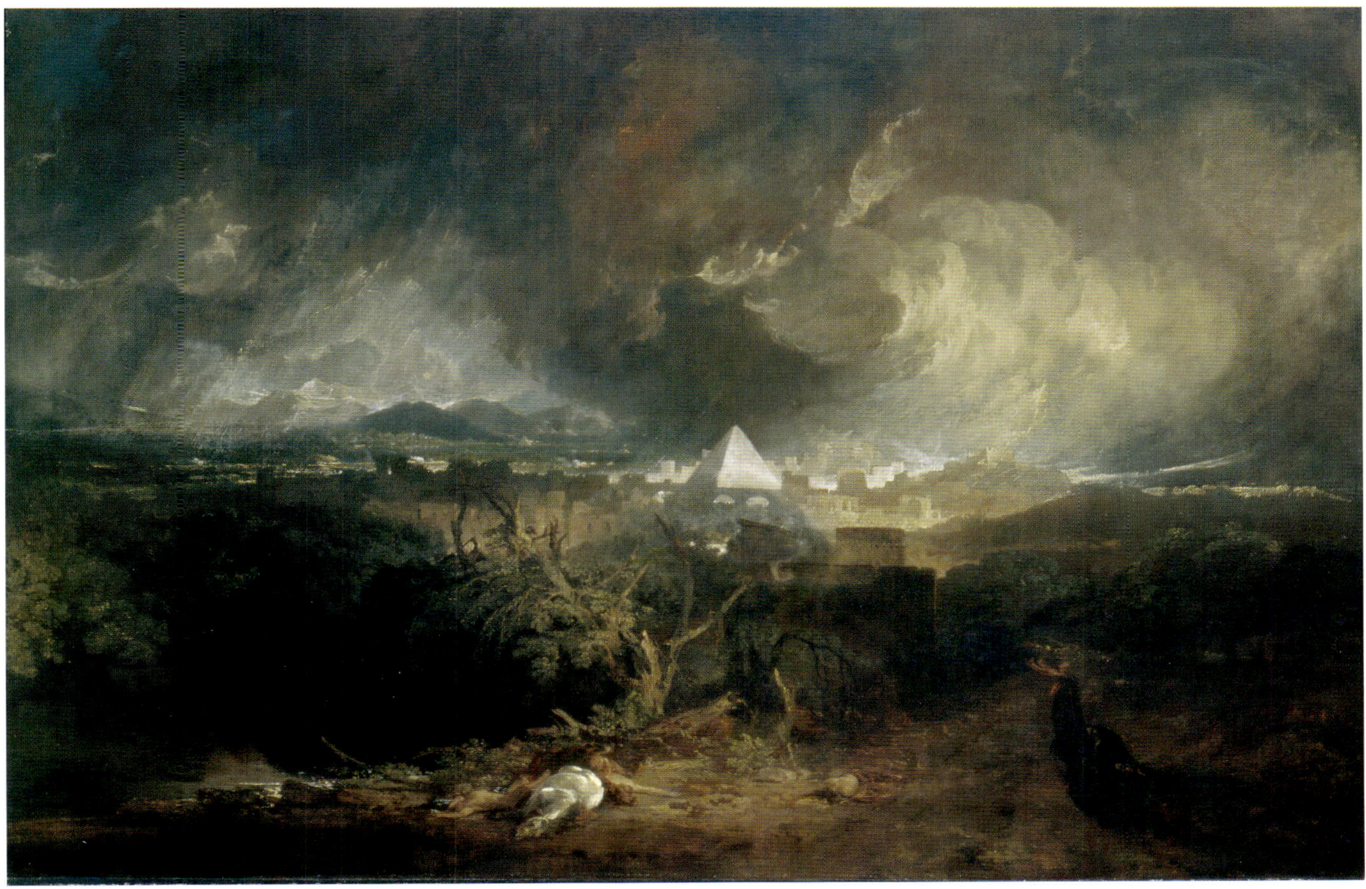

Fig. 98
The Fifth Plague of Egypt
Exhibited RA 1800
Oil on canvas,
124.4 × 183 cm
Indianapolis Museum
of Art (B&J 13)
Gift in memory of
Evan F. Lilly (55.24)

Beckford in the major exhibit Turner prepared for the 1800 exhibition, *The Fifth Plague of Egypt* (fig. 98). Although Beckford had commissioned apocalyptic subjects from Benjamin West (who was increasingly out of favour), Turner's abilities as a history painter were still an unknown quantity, so he did not commit himself to purchase the picture until it was exhibited. But it would be typical of Turner's opportunistic nature to exploit his patron's taste for scenes of cataclysm or devastation to his own advantage. In developing the composition, he possibly made use of Piranesi's views of Rome nearby at Stourhead, although they could also be found in the Fonthill library. Turner's finished image is a conflation of the Pyramid of Caius Cestus in Rome (fig. 100), with studies made during his travels in Wales in 1798 and 1799.[57] Highlighted in the foreground is a pair of dead horses and their fallen riders, which have apparently been struck down by the disease, or murrain, if it was indeed Turner's intention to illustrate the fifth of the plagues visited on the Egyptians. However, in consulting chapter 9 of Exodus, Turner read on to its conclusion and eventually selected a quotation from verse 23 to append to his title. This text confusingly suggests the picture was illustrating the seventh plague, which is also implied by the introduction of dramatic thunderclouds and lightning, apparently representing the storms of fire summoned by the gesticulating figure of Moses (Turner presumably despaired of representing the plague of boils that falls in between the fifth and seventh). Such details mattered little once the picture was on display at the Academy, where it was the

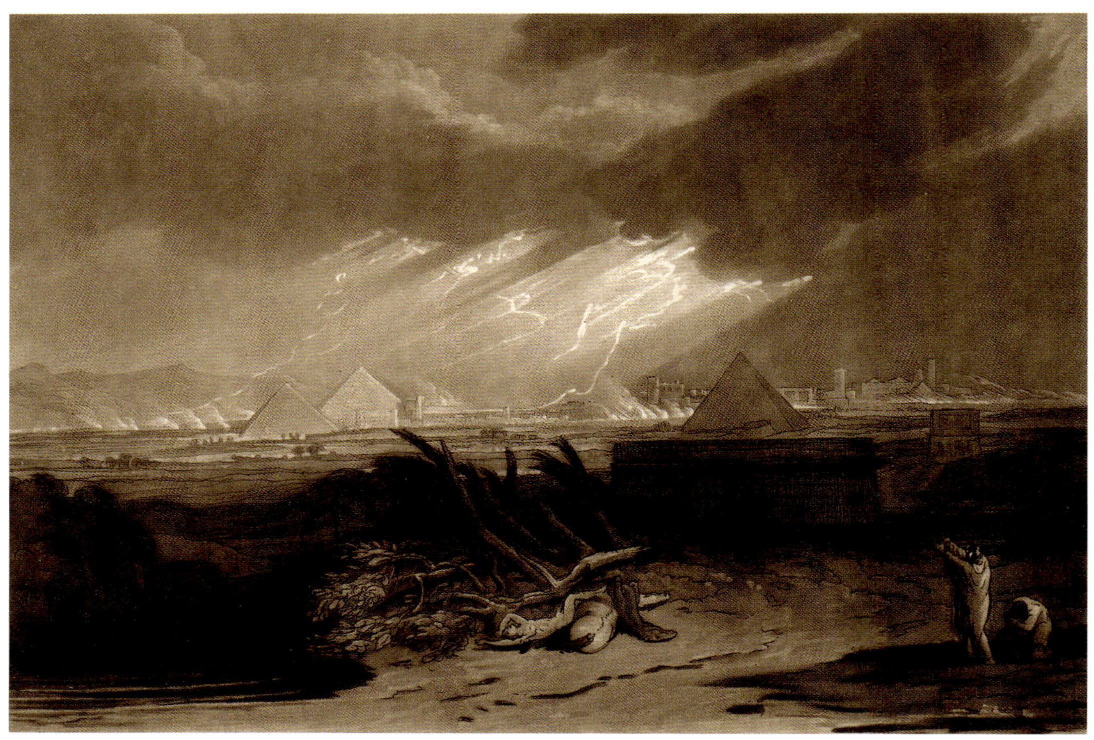

Fig. 99
CHARLES TURNER (1774–1857)
after J.M.W. TURNER
The Fifth Plague of Egypt
(from *Liber Studiorum*;
plate 16)
1808
Etching and mezzotint,
18 × 26 cm
British Museum
In this version of the image, the pyramids on the left replace the Welsh mountains found in the original painting.

sensation of that year's exhibition.[58] If anyone pointed out the disparity between text and image, Turner stuck to his guns, and he retained the title when he engraved the image for his *Liber Studiorum* in 1808 (fig. 99). A year before that Beckford had been in need of funds to continue building and so had sold the picture among the contents of Fonthill Splendens.

But in September 1800 *The Fifth Plague* was hanging in the Music Room, where Turner would have seen it a month or so later, if he did not travel down to oversee it being installed. It may have been during this visit that he conceived two further paintings he anticipated Beckford might buy: *The Army of the Medes Destroyed in the Desart by a Whirlwind – Foretold by Jeremiah* (1801, untraced); and *The Tenth Plague of Egypt* (1802, Tate). The latter was obviously related to his 1800 exhibit, but is of larger dimensions, so does not work as a pendant. However, it might have played a part in a putative decorative scheme, comparable to the Revelation Chamber. Beckford's name occurs in a list in one of Turner's Welsh sketchbooks in conjunction with his order for a painting. The reference has been assumed to relate to *The Fifth Plague*, but in fact the inscription reads 'X Plague of Egypt', confirming that *The Tenth Plague* does indeed have a connection with Fonthill.[59]

Similarly, while a number of studies for the *Army of the Medes* image have been identified in sketchbooks used around 1799–1800,[60] there are several sheets in the 'Fonthill' book that feature whirling clouds, blasted trees and tumbling

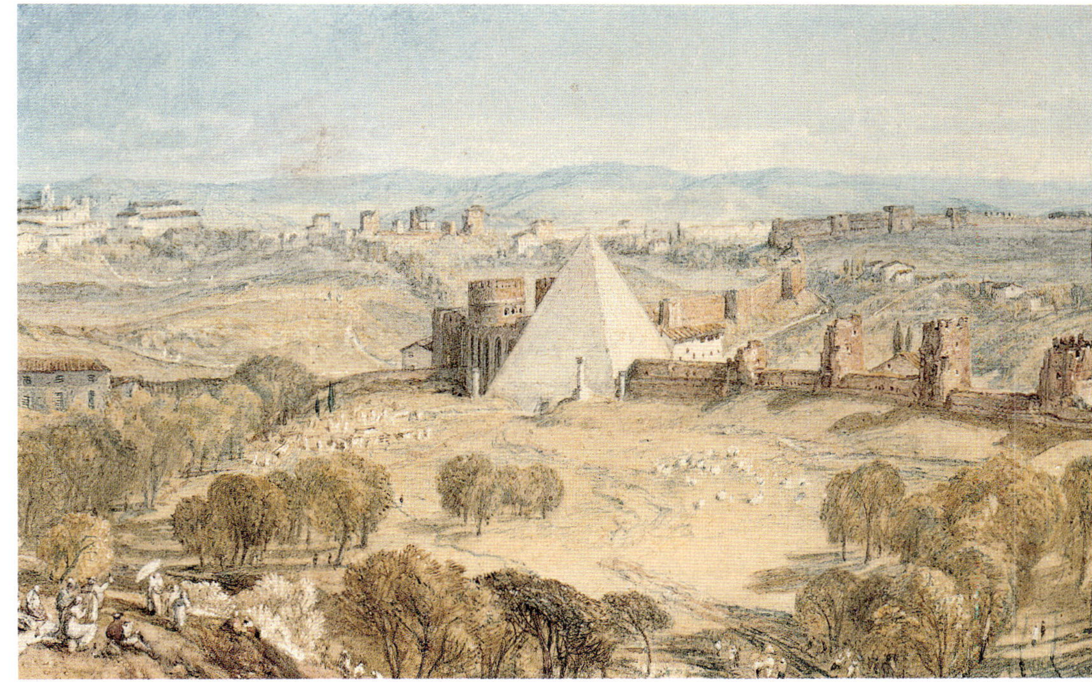

Fig. 100
Rome from Monte Testaccio
1818
Watercolour,
14 × 21.6 cm
Private collection (W707)

Fig. 101
The Tenth Plague of Egypt
Exhibited RA 1802
Oil on canvas,
143.5 × 236.2 cm
Tate (N00470; B&J 17)

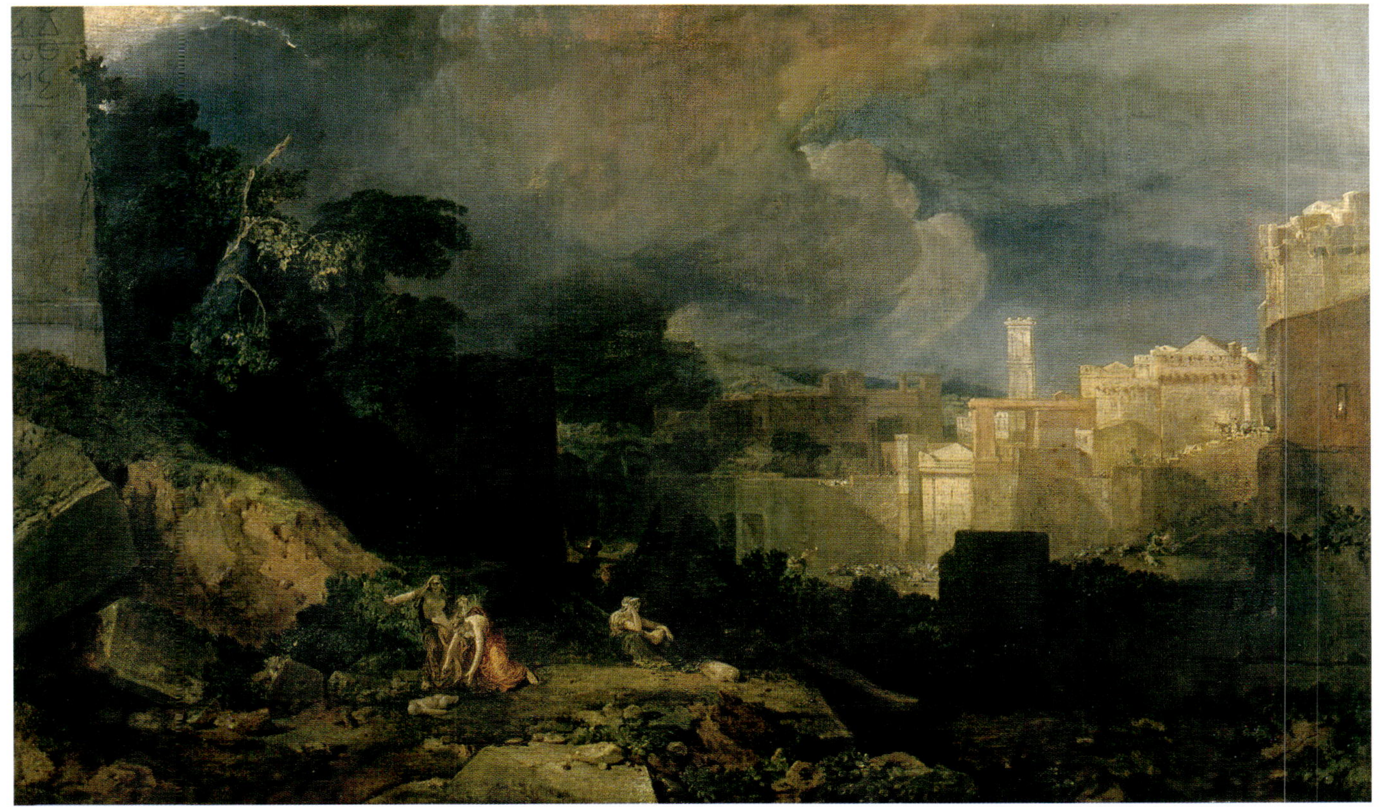

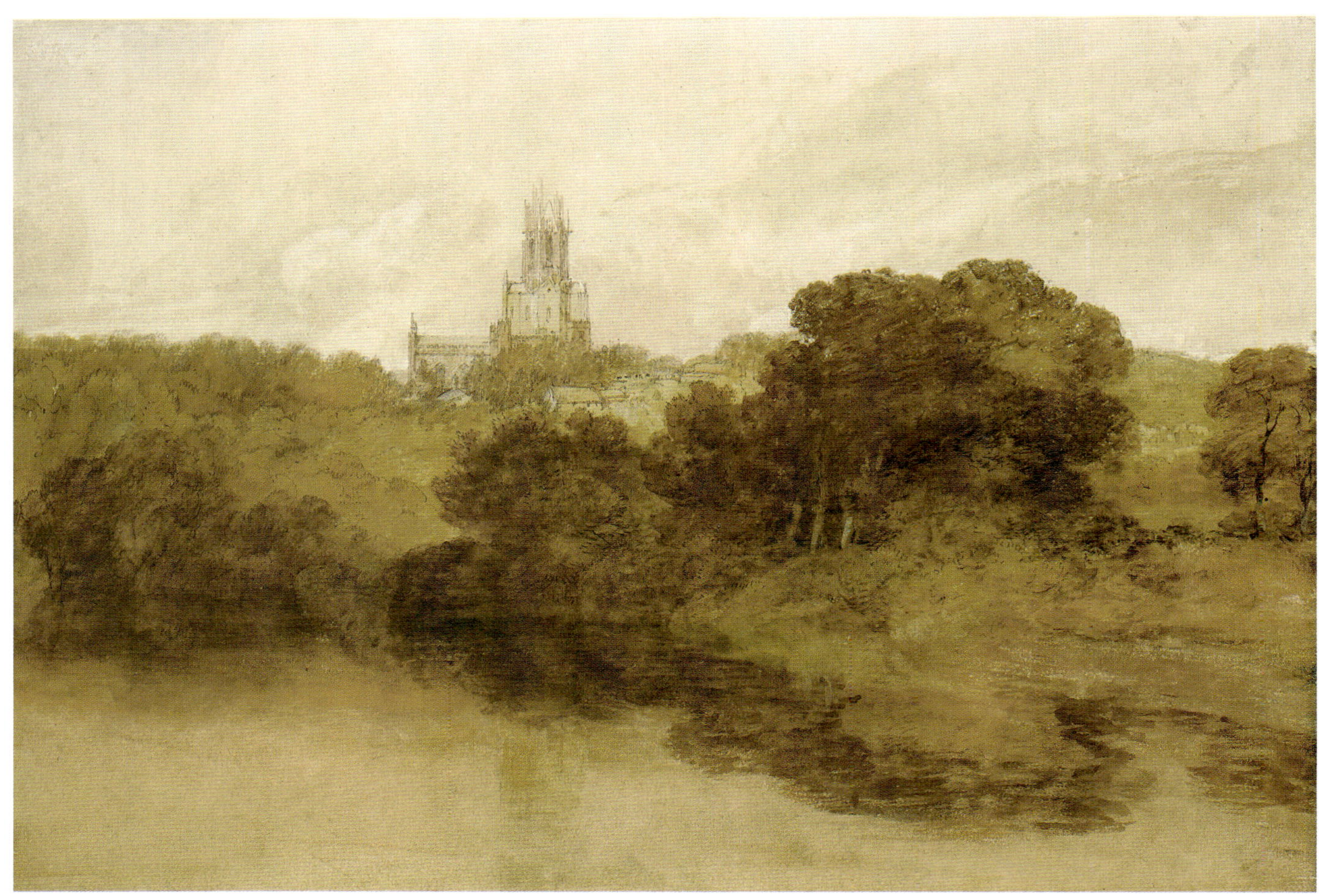

Fig. 102
Fonthill Abbey from Bitham Lake
1800
Pencil and watercolour, 31.5 × 45.5 cm
From the 'Fonthill' sketchbook
Private collection, c/o Philip Mould (W341)

bodies, which may also be connected with the development of this composition.[61] Nothing is known of the finished picture after it was exhibited in 1801.

Back in the autumn of 1800, Turner's visit provided an opportunity to assess progress on the abbey since the devastating fall of the tower around 16 months earlier. At least seven of the pencil sketches from the 'Fonthill' book document this visit. Most of them depict the profile of the abbey from the south, thereby showcasing the projecting Western Transept. In one of these a line of sheep trek steadily ahead of their shepherd down into the valley (f.8). A more distant view, probably from the north-east, shows the reconstructed tower cradled against the hillside (f.16).

Two nearer sketches record the tower from the fishpond known as Bitham Lake, where Beckford swam regularly (figs 102–3): the watercolour may have been worked up from the upright study away from the motif. Another sketch, which it is not possible to link definitively with either visit, shows a group of labourers napping under a fallen tree at the edge of the lake (fig. 107). Just out of reach, but within earshot, a group of swans squabble, providing the kind of incident Turner often recalled in his finished watercolours.

Fig. 103
Near View of Fonthill Abbey from the South, with Bitham Lake in the Foreground
1800
Pencil, 43.3 × 33.5 cm
From the 'Fonthill' sketchbook
Tate (D02181 / TB XLVII 4)

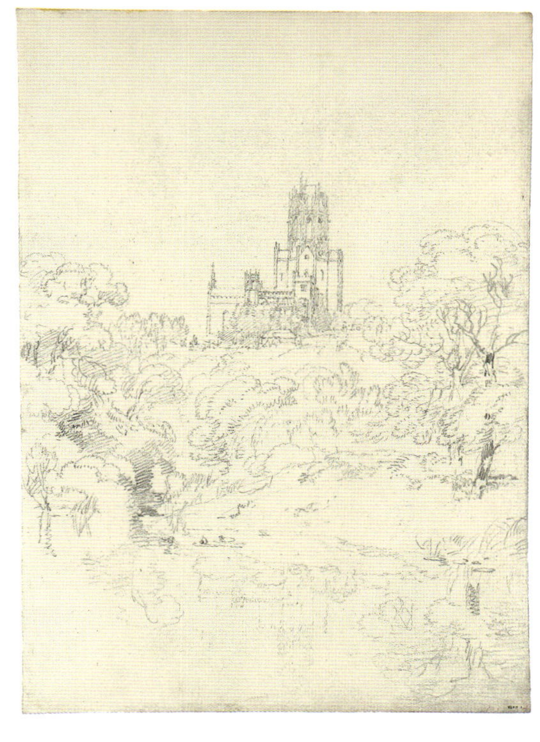

Fig. 104
Fonthill Abbey from the South-West, with the Reconstructed Tower
1800
Pencil, 33.4 × 46.6 cm
From the 'Fonthill' sketchbook
Tate (D02182 / TB XLVII 5)

In the remaining sketches the building team remains a discernible if ghostly presence and the men are generally dwarfed by the immensity of the tower they are reconstructing (figs 104 and 106). Turner shows them balancing on scaffolding or negotiating the roof tiles. This attention to human activity is a side effect of his concentrated response to the architecture of the abbey, which he delineated with an almost photographic precision in these close-up studies. After its recent history, he would have appreciated the documentary value of what he

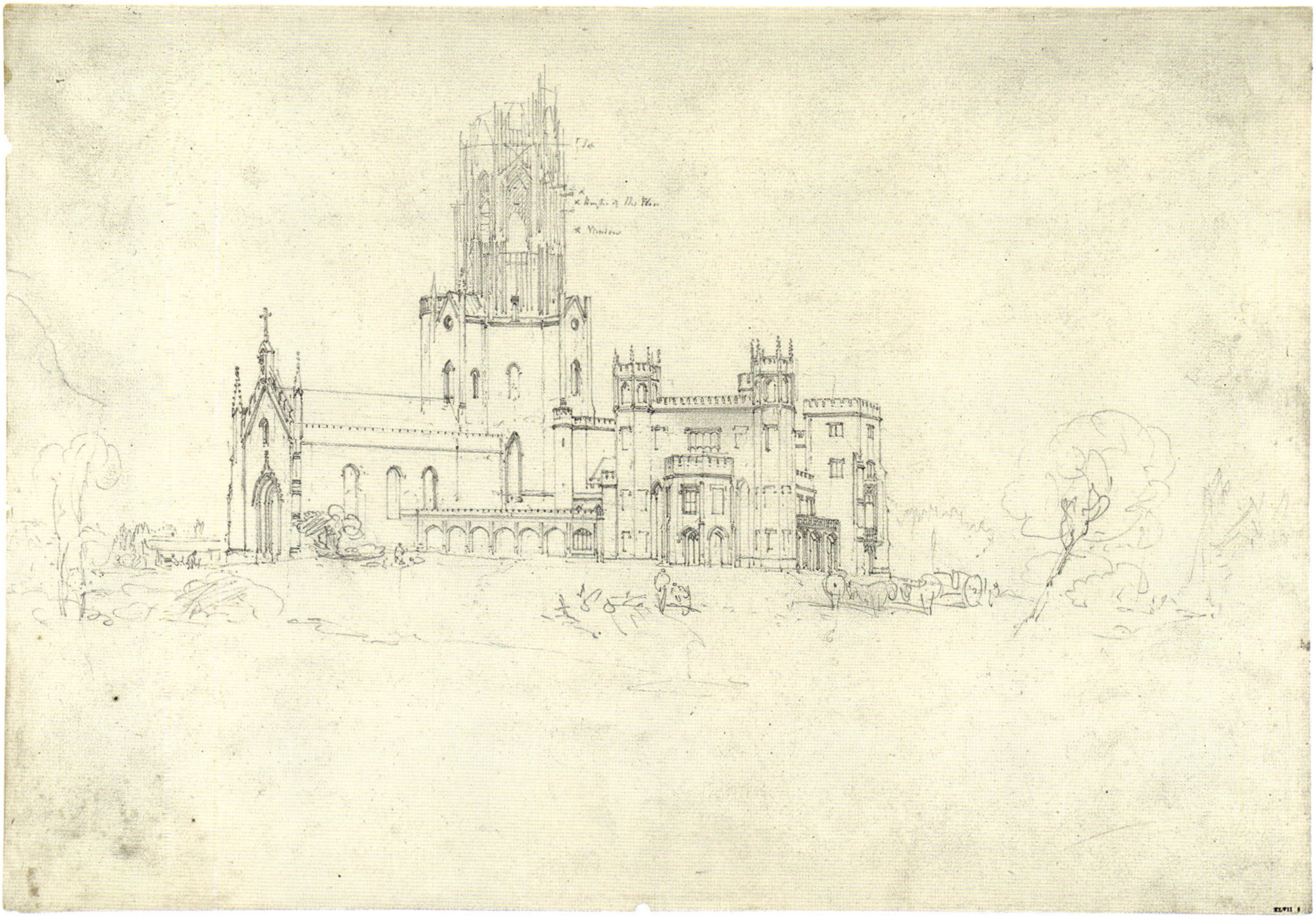

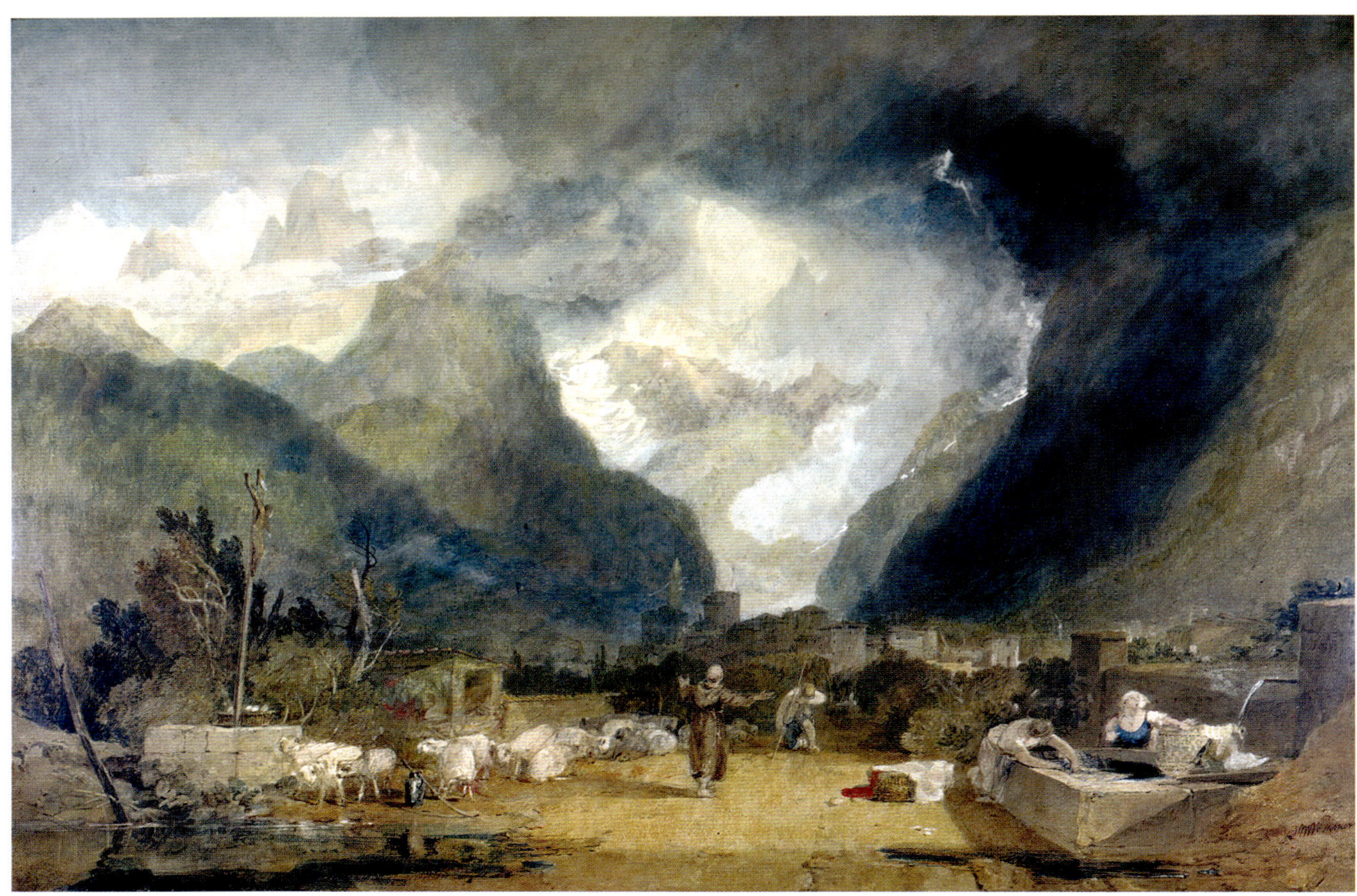

Fig. 105
St Huges Denouncing Vengeance on the Shepherd of Cormayer, in the Valley of d'Aoust
Exhibited RA 1803
Watercolour, 67.6 × 106 cm
Sir John Soane's Museum, London (W364)

recorded, but he could also have been reacting to the press criticism of his exhibited watercolours and seeking to gather data for any further commissioned views Beckford demanded.

Aside from the history paintings already noted, Beckford may have been the intended target for one of the Alpine subjects Turner exhibited in 1803, a year after his first continental tour (fig. 105). The precise subject of the large watercolour remains unclear, but rather than Saint Hugo of Grenoble, as has been suggested, it is likely that the scene recalls an incident in the first half of the life of the better-known Saint Hugh of Lincoln (*c.*1135/40–1200).[62] The Carthusian had been trained in the austere and pious Grande-Chartreuse monastery before moving to England. There he was appointed prior of the Charterhouse at Witham in Somerset by King Henry II, subsequently being translated to Lincoln as bishop, where he oversaw substantial building works (see fig. 5). Much of this was of direct interest to Beckford, for his father had acquired the dilapidated remains of Witham, where he retained the ranges of the old monastery. This personal connection gained Beckford tremendous kudos when he stayed with the monks in the Grande-Chartreuse.[63] It seems likely that they would have regaled him with anecdotes about Saint Hugh during his stay, which he may have relayed to Turner, perhaps in Paris at the end of his Alpine tour, if not before.

By then, however, Beckford's finances were becoming rocky. It was thought that he had already spent £242,000 on Fonthill Abbey by May 1801 and it was estimated that he might spend 'near as much more to complete it'.[64] Over the next few years he was forced to sell pictures, including those commissioned from de Loutherbourg, and so it was no longer realistic that he could continue as an active collector. *The Fifth Plague*, as we have seen, was sold on 22 August 1807 for a negligible profit of only 5 guineas more than the 150 Beckford had paid for it in 1800, and the celebrated paired canvases

OPPOSITE: Fig. 106
The South Front of Fonthill Abbey, with the Reconstructed Tower
1800
Pencil, 46.6 × 32.8 cm
From the 'Fonthill' sketchbook
Tate (D02178 / TB XLVII 1)
The left-hand edge of this image was continued on the verso of f.3 (D41264).

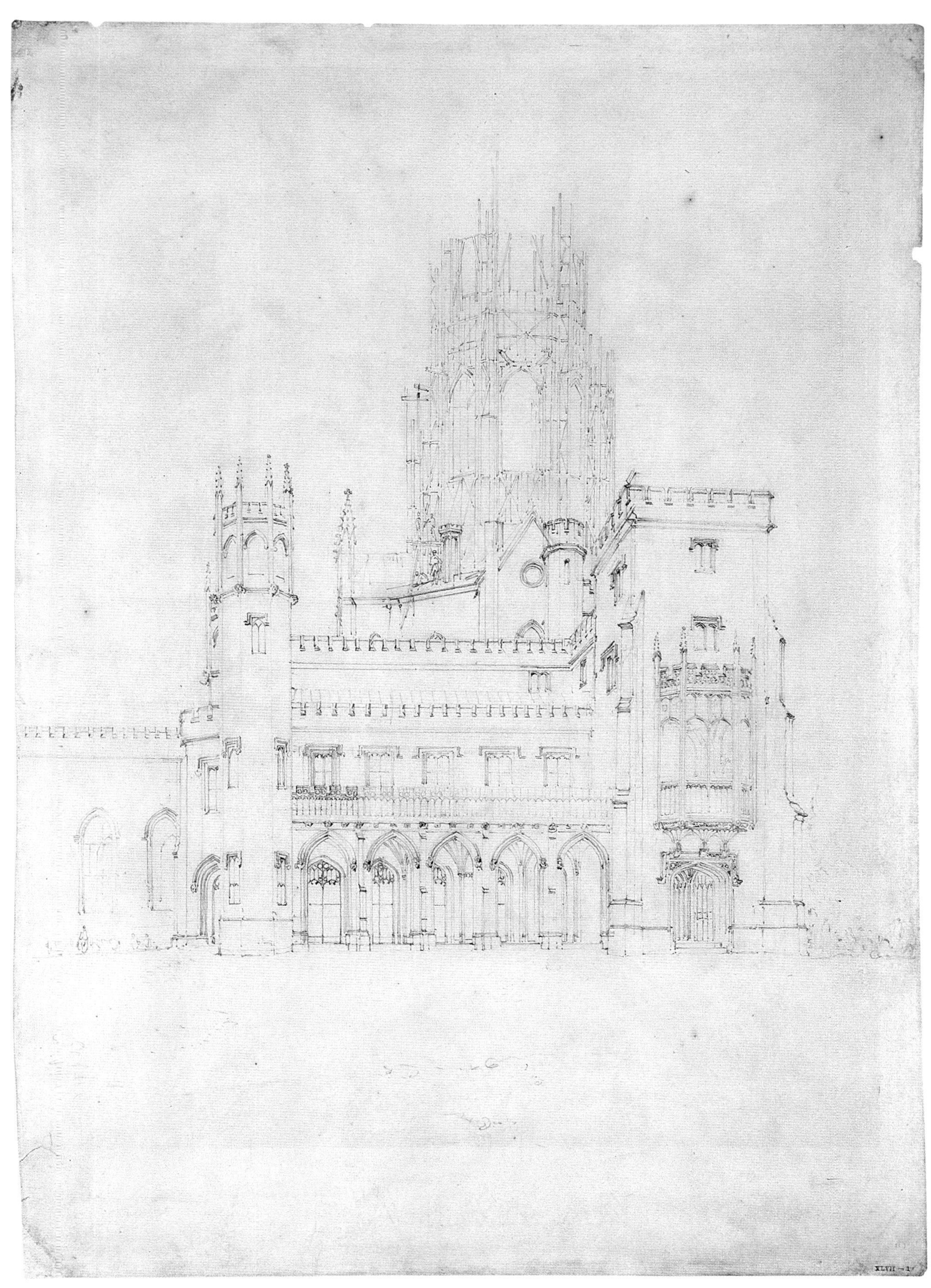

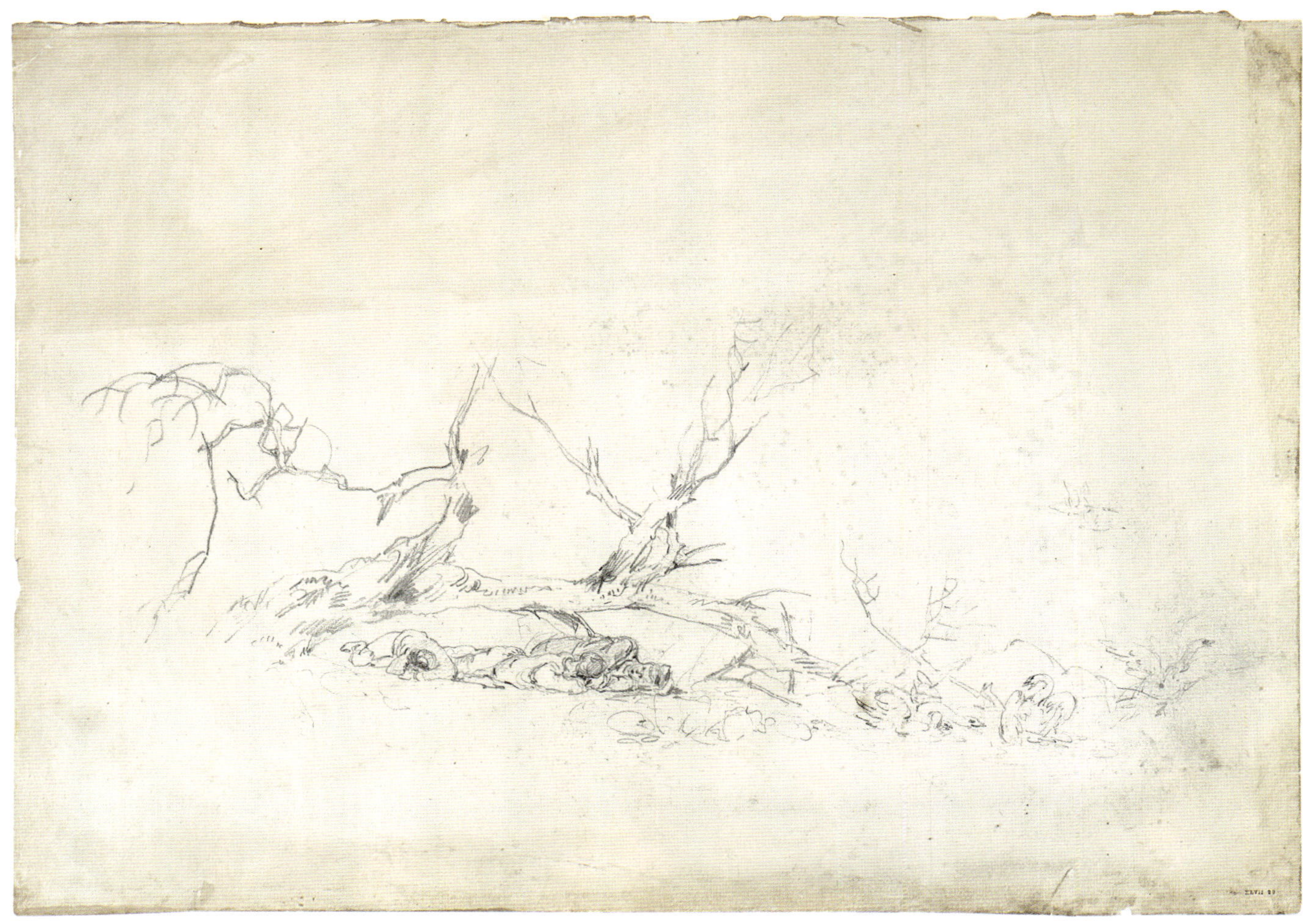

Fig. 107
Labourers Sleeping under a Fallen Tree, with Swans Fighting
*c.*1799–1800
Pencil, 33.5 × 43.3 cm
From the 'Fonthill' sketchbook
Tate (D02197 / TB XLVII 20)
Compare the tree here with the blasted one in fig. 98.

by Claude followed a year later, realising a more respectable total of 10,000 guineas. Turner may perhaps have recorded the images on a sheet of the 'Fonthill' sketchbook that has since been lost. This is suggested by one of the remaining pages on which Turner drew a statue of a River God, formerly in the park at Fonthill (f.19) – on the back of this page he subsequently transcribed pictures by Claude that came on the market in 1804 using a blue-grey wash.[65] Another study, painted in the same limited tones, shows a fallen tree, perhaps at Fonthill (fig. 110), and alludes to Turner's admiration for Claude's British follower, Richard Wilson, whose canvases, especially a pair of views of Ariccia, he appears to have studied at Wilton House when painting his watercolour of its exterior for Colt Hoare (fig. 58).

If Turner and Beckford maintained a connection after 1807, any evidence of it has now been lost. Beckford became a captive of his own ambition, driven to shore up and complete the precarious tower at all costs. Other than occasional trips to London, he withdrew to Fonthill. But when in London, he had no excuse for not dropping in on Turner, whose gallery at 64 Harley Street was just blocks away from his own home at 6 Upper Harley Street. The depredations of his former riches, however, resulted in the sale of that house and its contents over three days in May 1817. Had Turner inspected the property prior to the auction, he would have seen his five watercolours of Fonthill marked up for sale, but he was not tempted to bid on them.[66]

Public perceptions of Beckford had by now shifted from the envy implicit in Byron's reference to his former wealth, to the more mocking phrase 'The Fool of Fonthill'. Although the abbey was complete, Beckford found no peace there and in 1822 he managed to sell it privately for £300,000, thereby cheating

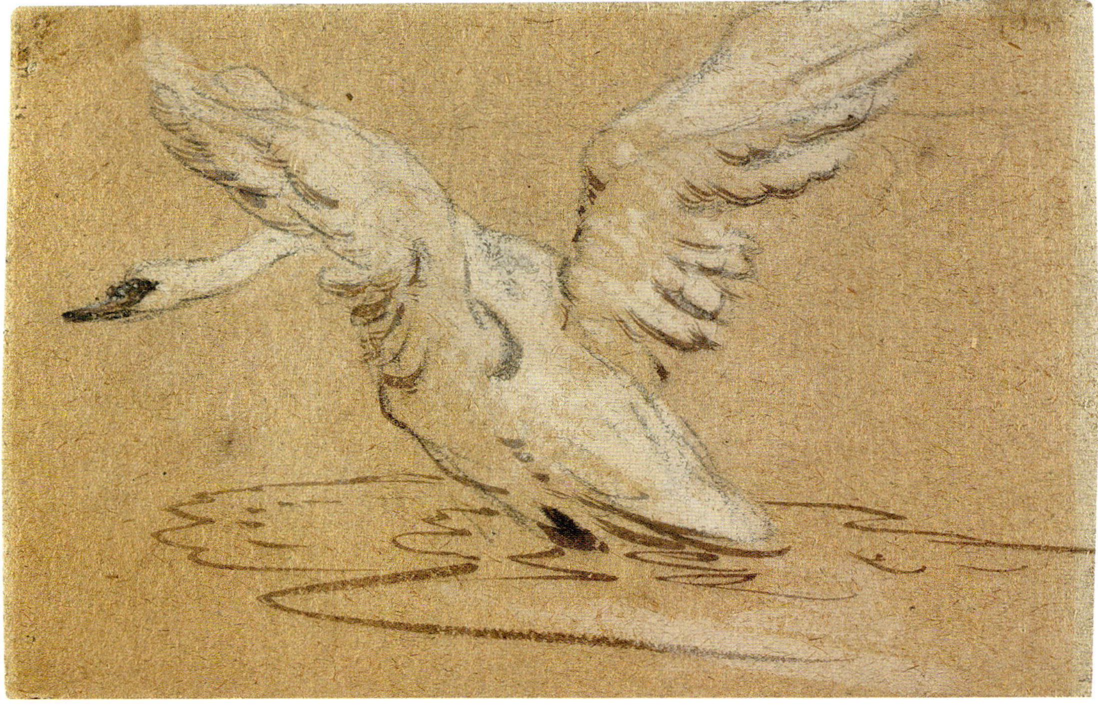

Fig. 108
Study of a Swan Risi[illegible]g from the Water
c.1798
Pen and gouache on toned paper, 12.5 × 17.4 cm
From the Swans sketchbook
Tate (D01689 / TB XL[illegible] 14)

Christie's of a promised sale, but enabling him to relocate to Bath. This proved to be just in time, for on 21 December 1825 the 276-foot tower, the physical manifestation of wasteful exploitation and extravagance, came crashing down for the final time. Ironically, in the process it created the kind of romantic ruin Beckford had perhaps envisaged when he began his construction (fig. 111).[67]

Beckford had always been known for his sharp tongue and pithy judgements, and these characteristics colour his last documented link with Turner. The source of this anecdote is one of a series of 'Conversations with the Late W. Beckford, Esq.', which were published by the *New Monthly Magazine* during the months after his death in 1844, feeding the continuing appetite for details about the 'Caliph of Fonthill'.[68] In this instance, the recipient of Beckford's reminiscences was a young artist from near Bath, who is identified only as 'H'. In his first article he looked back to when he met Beckford in 1831. After a tour of the collection in Lansdown Crescent, they came to the only one of Turner's five Fonthill views still with Beckford (fig. 85). When the visitor tentatively commented, 'He does not paint like that now', Beckford replied, 'Oh! gracious God! No! He paints now as if his brains and imagination were mixed up on his palette with soapsuds and lather. One must be born again to understand his pictures.' It is not difficult to imagine the 69-year-old Turner reading this article with acute interest, having outlived his patron, and spluttering 'Soapsuds and whitewash!' to himself in indignation (or amusement).

The latter phrase has long been claimed to have been among the immediate criticisms of his 1842 masterpiece, *Snow Storm – Steamboat off a Harbour's Mouth* (Tate), but despite exhaustive

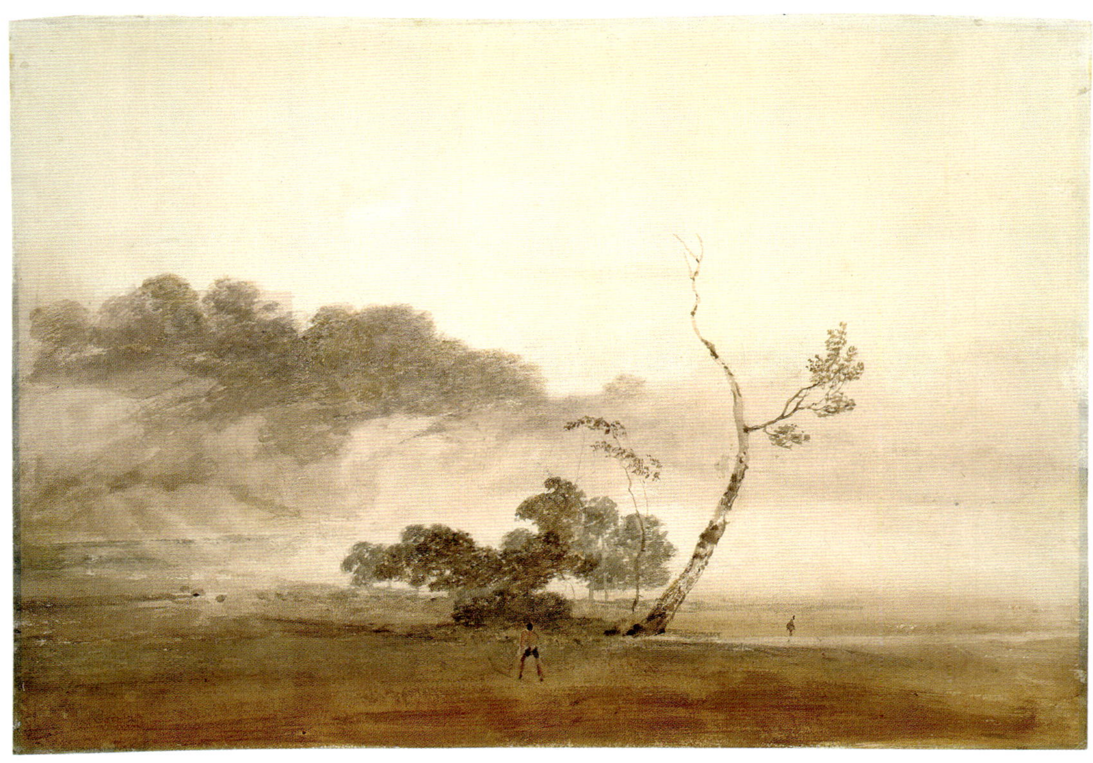

Fig. 109
Autumn Morning near Fonthill
*c.*1799–1800
Pencil and watercolour, 32.1 × 46.2 cm
From the 'Fonthill' sketchbook
The Whitworth, The University of Manchester (W342)

Fig. 110
A Fallen Tree, perhaps at Fonthill
*c.*1800–5
Pencil and watercolour, 33.5 × 43.3 cm
Tate (D02225 / TB XLVII 48)

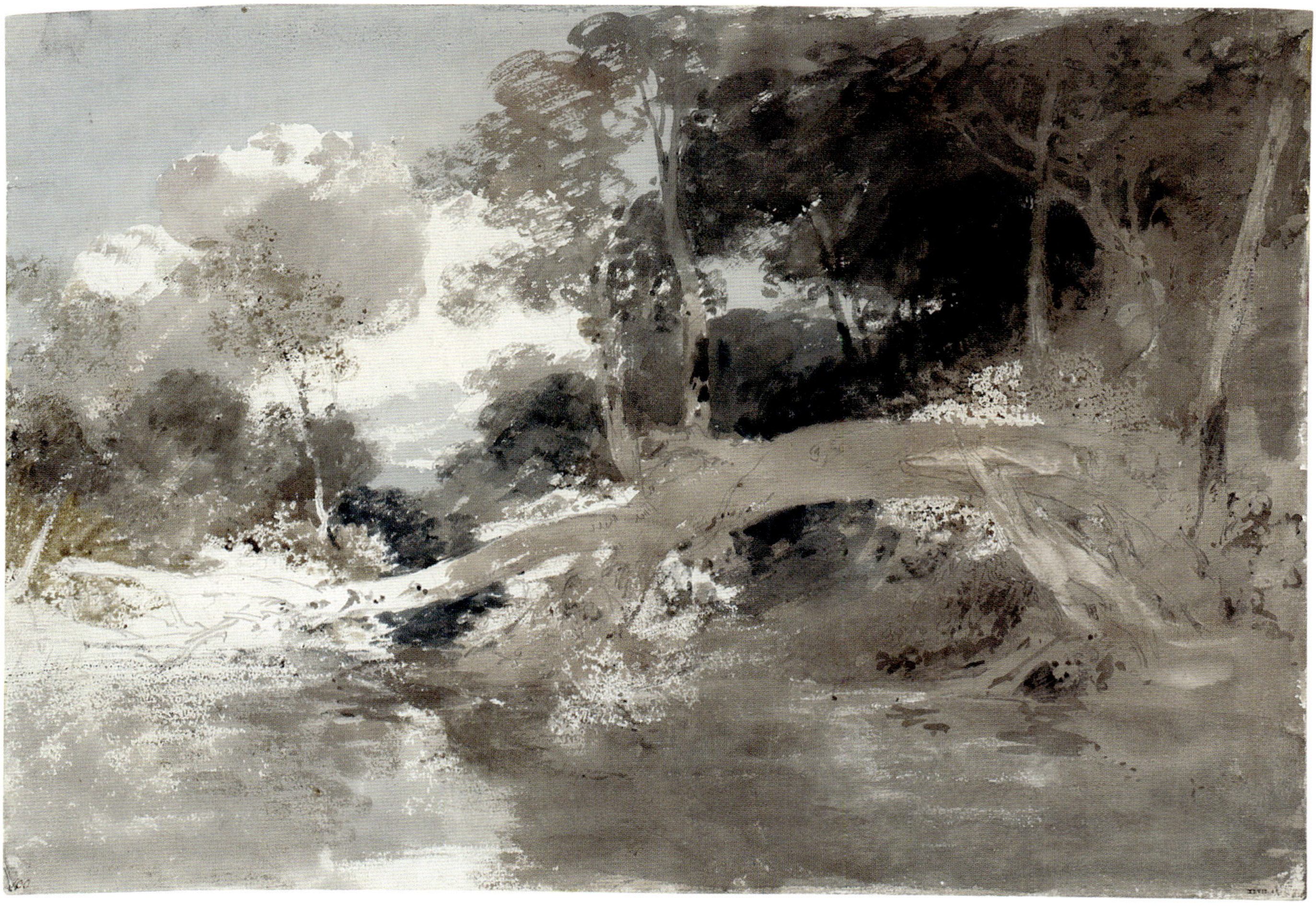

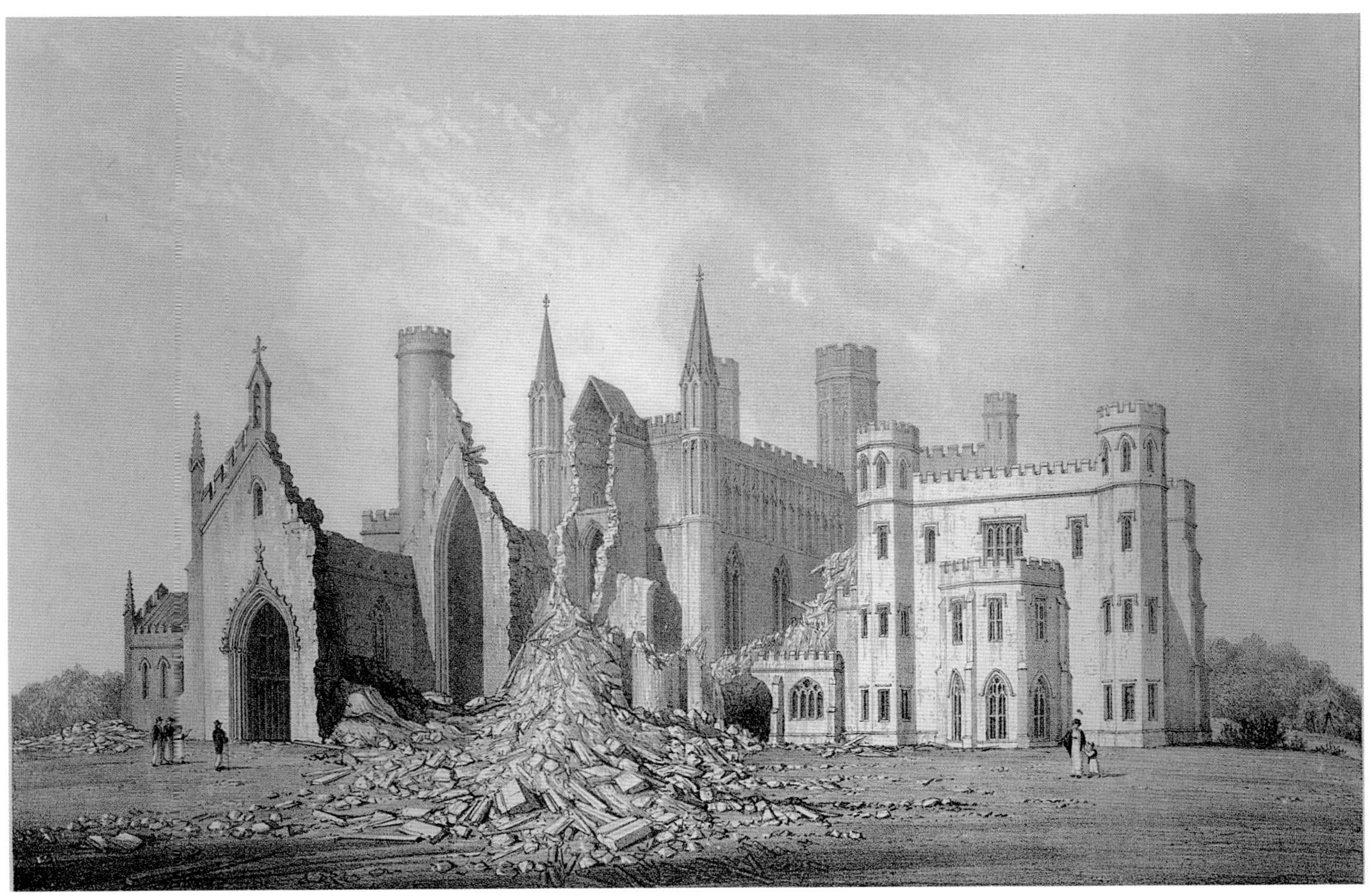

Fig. 111
WILLIAM WESTALL (1781–1850) after JOHN BUCKLER (1770–1851)
Ruins of Fonthill Abbey: The Tower fell 21st December 1825: 'And thus this unsubstantial Fabric falling left a sad wreck behind!'
1825
Lithograph, 26.5 × 38.7 cm
British Museum

searches, no evidence for a contemporary source has ever come to light. In fact the earliest record of the comment comes from John Ruskin's *Notes on The Turner Collection* (1857), where Turner's anger at the taunt is supposed to have taken place 'at my father's house on the day this criticism came out'.[69] Since the Ruskins do not seem to have entertained Turner at home in 1842, it is worth considering the year in which the Beckford anecdote appeared in print. Turner was away in September 1844 when the relevant edition of the *New Monthly Magazine* was published, so his first opportunity of seeing it would not have been until mid-October. It was at this time that Turner met Ruskin and thanked him – for the first time – for undertaking the publication of *Modern Painters* (1843) on his behalf. Fourteen years later, Ruskin might well have misremembered the precise circumstances. Perhaps Turner did grumble about Beckford's comment. Certainly the slightly garbled version served Ruskin's purposes in 1857, when the battle to gain greater understanding of Turner's later works had been won, allowing Ruskin to play up his outrage at earlier critical mockery and incomprehension, which had come to a head in responses to the *Snow Storm*. This would confirm William Powell Frith's contemporary belief that the source of this phrase was indeed Ruskin himself.[70] If this well-known critique of Turner's later seapieces did emerge in this fashion, it means that the original comment refers not to *Snow Storm*, but to a much earlier picture. In fact, in 1831, when Beckford offered his fulminations on Turner's most recent works, the painting he presumably had in mind would have been *Life-Boat and Manby Apparatus going off to a Stranded Vessel making Signal (Blue Lights) of Distress* (Victoria and Albert Museum), a canvas on which rough waves churn up the foreground sea into bands of lathery, almost abstract impasto. But, as with so many aspects of Beckford's life, there must remain a degree of uncertainty and ambiguity about this deduction.

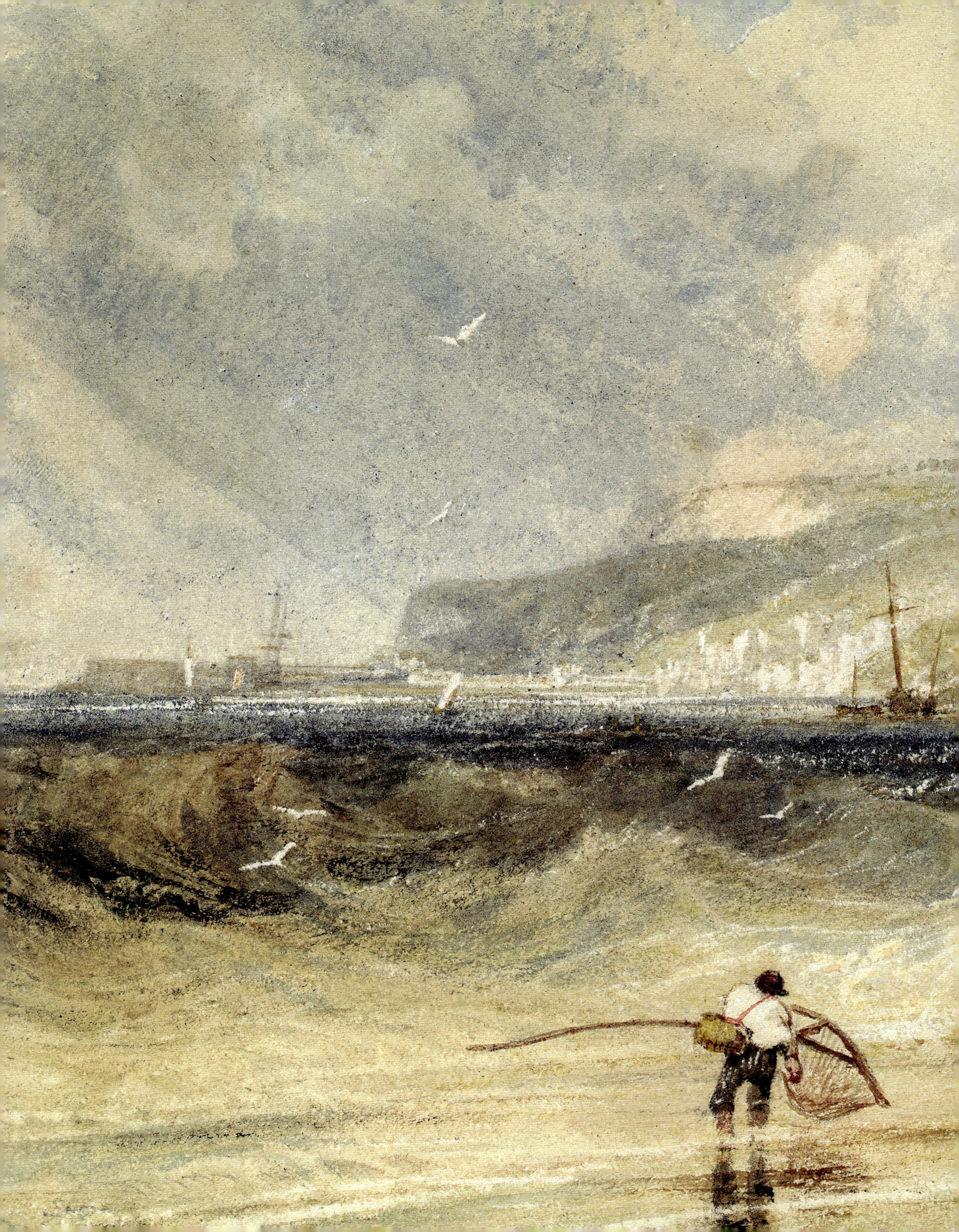

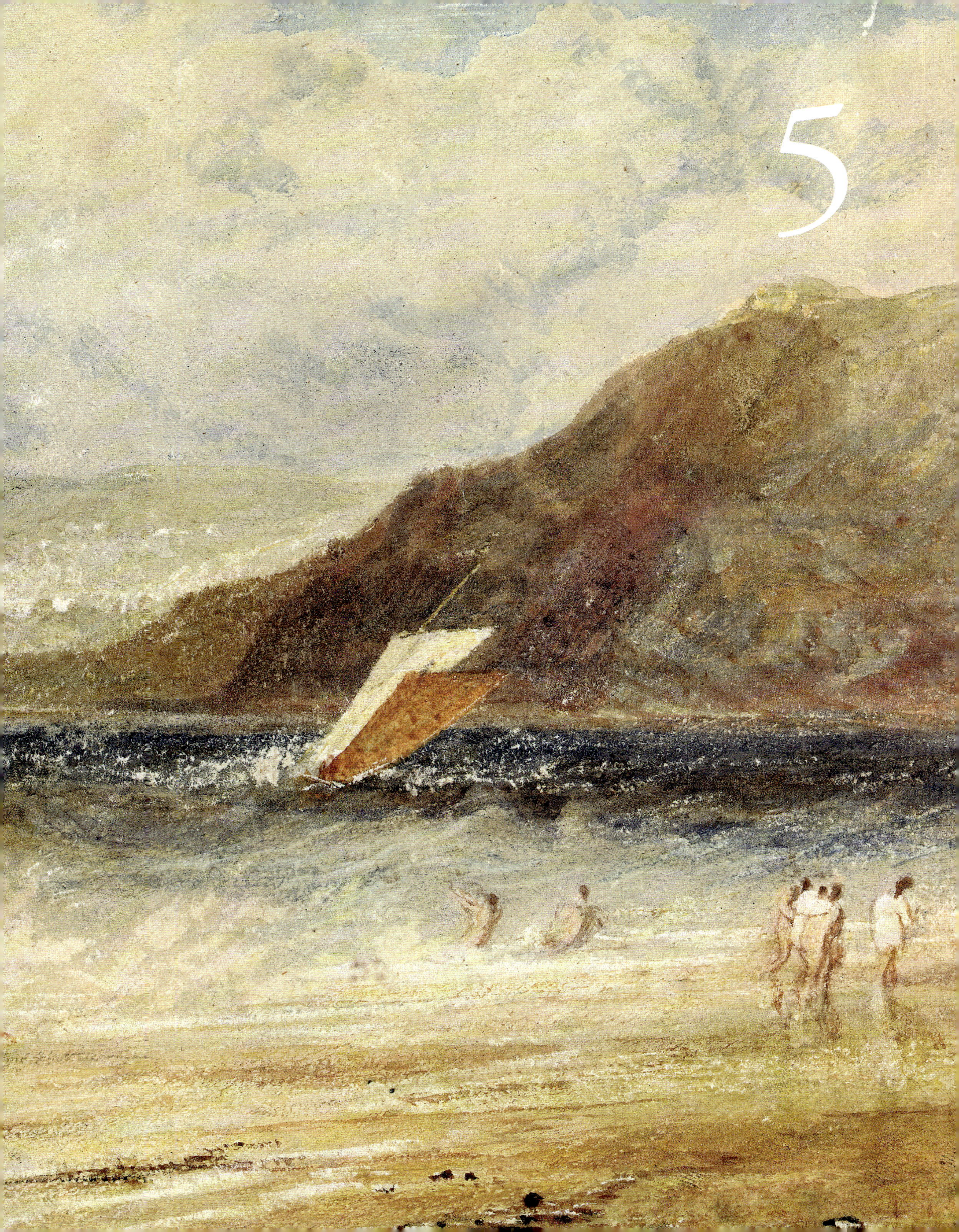
5

WESTWARD HO!
Turner and the Picturesque Coast of Southern England

Turner had become very familiar with Salisbury by the time he finished his series of views for Colt Hoare towards the end of 1805. During the next decade the city proved a useful place to break the journey on his way to Stourhead, or as he travelled to and from Devon, which became the focus of his topographical interest between 1811 and 1814.

By 1811 Turner had established his pre-eminence as a landscape painter. In addition to his exhibits at the Royal Academy and his own gallery, he aimed at reaching a wider public by issuing a series of mezzotints called *Liber Studiorum*. At the same time, his skills as a topographer were beginning to be called on by publishers, who recognised his ability to capture the essence of specific locales in small but dynamic images. Turner's first important undertaking of this kind was for the engravers William Bernard Cooke (1778–1855) and his brother George (1781–1834), who devised a plan to create a set of engravings illustrating the most significant places all around the British coast.[1] Recognising the ambitious scale of their endeavour, they wisely embarked on the project in a more limited way, promoting their venture as *Picturesque Views on the Southern Coast of England*. As well as Turner, a handful of other artists were commissioned to make watercolours as the basis for the black and white engravings, although his were to prove the main attraction. Once this was clear, around 1814 Turner was able to renegotiate the terms of his contract so that the Cooke brothers increased their payments for his watercolour designs from £7.10s to 10 guineas.

It was the need to gather visual data for this work that brought Turner back to Salisbury in mid-July 1811, in the early stages of his longest tour of the westernmost counties of England. This expedition kept him away from London for around two months and, untypically, he travelled at a comparatively leisurely pace. For example, he seems to have lingered at Andover prior to reaching Salisbury, perhaps indulging his passion for angling there with a lazy day by the clear waters of the River Test (see p. 177).[2] From Salisbury he followed the Avon down to Christchurch (fig. 112).[3]

On this journey he recorded his impressions in notebooks measuring around 15 × 20 centimetres, but he also carried with him a smaller pocketbook. This was actually a copy of Nathaniel Coltman's *British Itinerary* (1811), which had been customised to Turner's needs by being rebound and interspersed with well over a hundred blank pages that he used not only to record the places he visited but also for drafts of poetry. In these texts he reflected on what he saw, the character of the landscape and its people and their occupations.[4]

PREVIOUS PAGES:
Lyme Regis, Dorsetshire (detail)
(see fig. 125)

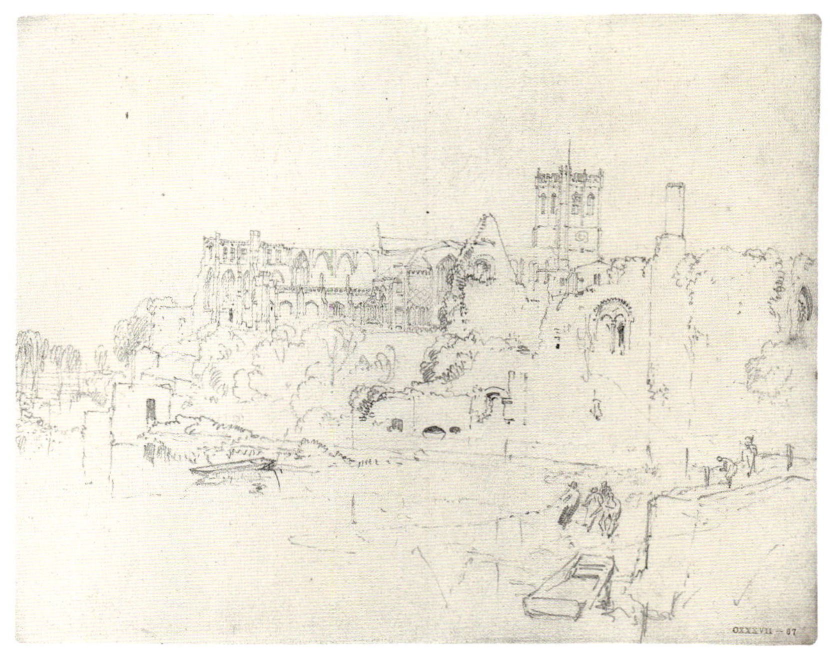

Fig. 112
Christchurch: the Ruins of the Constable's House, with the Priory Beyond, from the Avon Bridge
?1811
Pencil, 18.1 × 22.8 cm
From the Vale of Heathfield sketchbook
Tate (D10310 / TB CXXXVII 67)

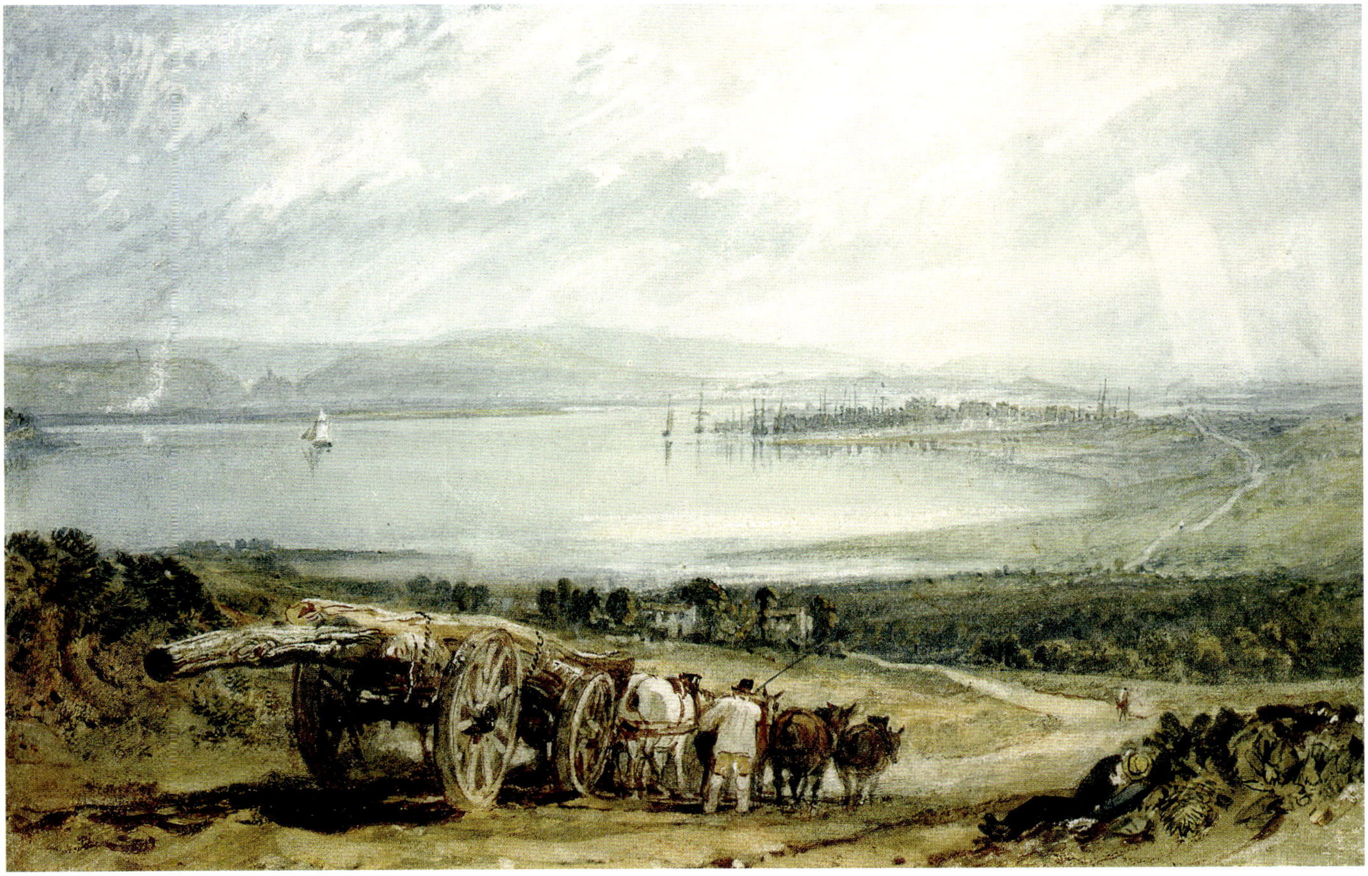

Fig. 113
Poole, Dorsetshire

*c.*1812
Watercolour, 13.9 × 21.9 cm
For *Picturesque Views on the Southern Coast of England*
Private collection (W446)

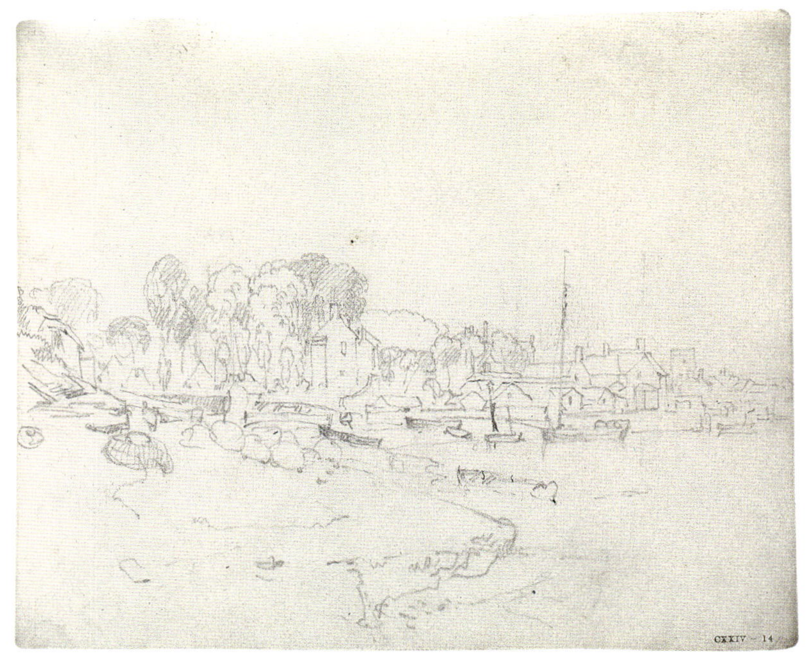

Fig. 114
Swanage Harbour

1811
Pencil, 17 × 20.9 cm
From the 'Corfe to Dartmouth' sketchbook
Tate (D08821 / TB CXXIV 14)

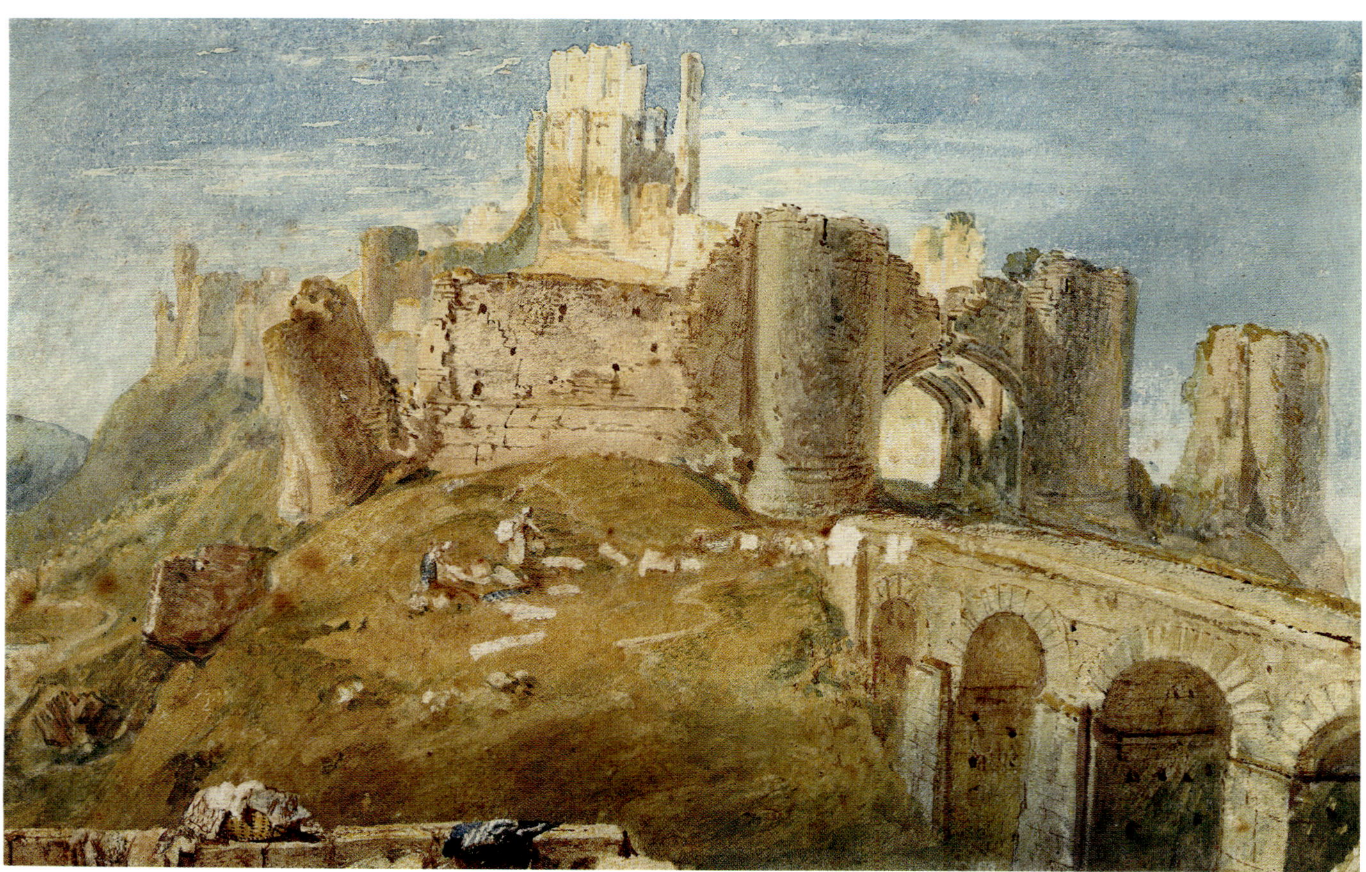

Fig. 115
Corfe Castle, Dorsetshire
*c.*1812
Watercolour, 14.1 × 21.3 cm
For *Picturesque Views on the Southern Coast of England*
Fogg Art Museum, Harvard, Cambridge, Mass. (W450). Anonymous Gift in memory of Richard Wheatland, Class of 1895 (1986.533)

In this raw state it would be hard to claim it as a piece of great literature, fascinating though it is for its insights into Turner's attitudes about what he saw. He subsequently completed a more polished version, which he envisaged as an accompanying commentary for his images, but Cooke decided it was not something he could credibly publish, and sadly it is now lost.

Having sketched the medieval priory at Christchurch, and the view across to the Isle of Wight, Turner covered the short distance to Poole, which was the subject of one of the earliest of his watercolours for the *Southern Coast* project (fig. 113). He described the town in rather unflattering terms as 'a little headland in a marshy lake', but the watercolour offers an appealing vista over Poole Harbour to Corfe in the distance on the left.[5] Throughout his series Turner indicated the status of the coast as a military frontline, which was obviously then a matter of anxiety and patriotism. Here, for example, the timber being transported down to Poole alludes to shipbuilding, while also resembling a canon.[6]

Over on the Isle of Purbeck, Turner visited Swanage (fig. 114), but he was more impressed by the location of the nearby ruins at Corfe Castle, set between 'two lofty downs', and made many sketches there.[7] In the watercolour he created for the *Southern Coast*, he shows the outer walls from the south (fig. 115), but as in his views of the Close Gate at Salisbury (figs 33 and 59), the former power of the stronghold is undermined by the prosaic use of its earthworks for the drying of washing. Technically, the scene is realised through an assured layering of only a limited range of colours that re-creates the effect of brilliant summer sunshine.

Turner found a darker subject nearby on the cliffs at St Alban's Head, where the 'unhappy Halsewell', a fully laden East Indiaman, had been wrecked on 6 January 1786. The loss of all but 74 of the 240 crew and passengers had shocked the nation, resulting in commemorative poems, prints and a representation of the shipwreck at de Loutherbourg's *Eidophusikon*. While in Dorset Turner meditated on the fate of the ship in his

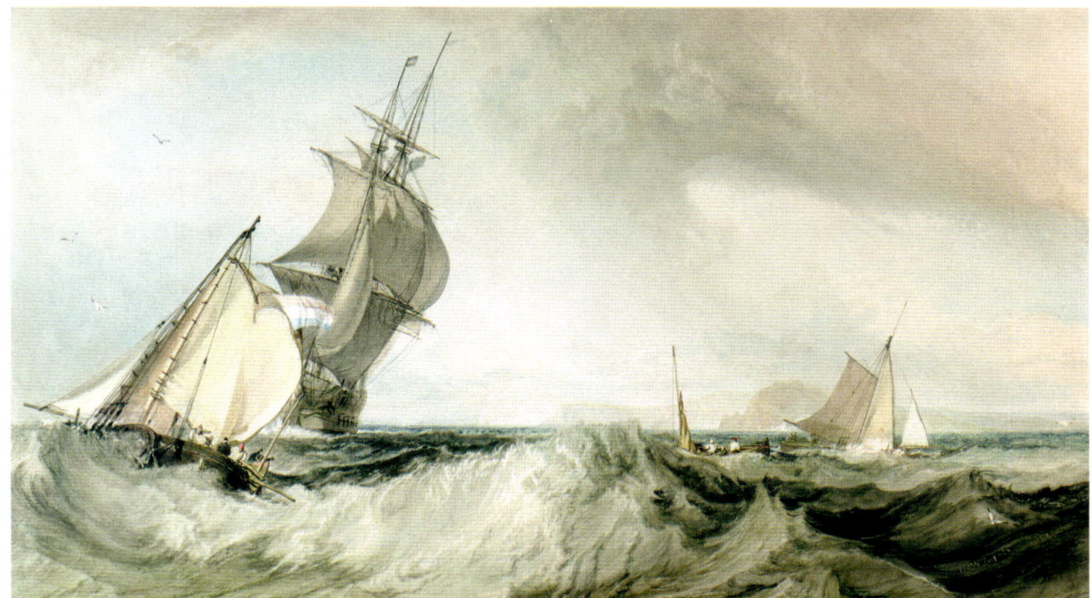

Fig. 116
Off St Alban's Head
*c.*1818–22
Watercolour, 39.5 × 67.4 cm
Mercer Art Gallery, Harrogate

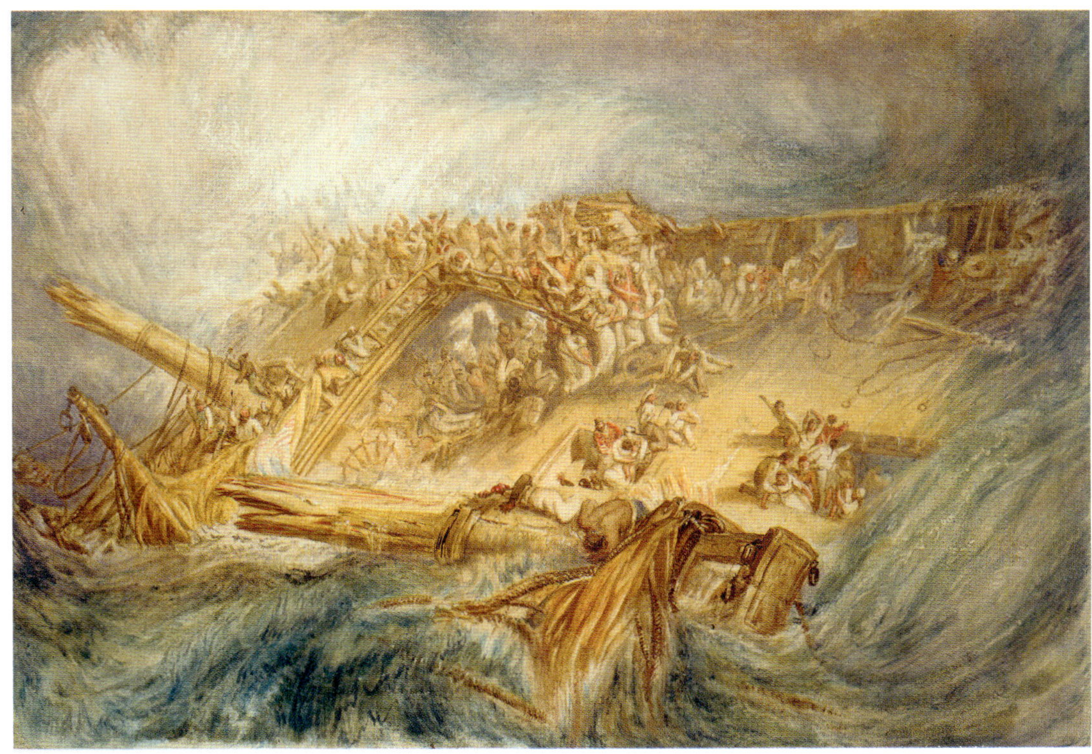

Fig. 117
Loss of an East Indiaman
*c.*1818
Watercolour, 28 × 39.5 cm
The Higgins, Bedford
(W500)

poetic notes.[8] But it was not until some years later that he attempted to give visual form to its final moments in one of a pair of images he summoned from his imagination for Walter Fawkes at Farnley Hall (1818, The Higgins, Bedford; see fig. 117).[9] Both of these watercolours are tightly cropped to exaggerate the scale of the ships that protected Britain and linked it with its Empire, but a more complete sense of one of them, under full sail, can be found in the slightly later watercolour that depicts the coastline from St Alban's Head to Portland Bill (fig. 116).[10] Despite its breezy energy, dark clouds hover near the centre of the image, directly above the fatal cliffs.

Further along the Dorset coast, Turner's next important subject was the striking geological

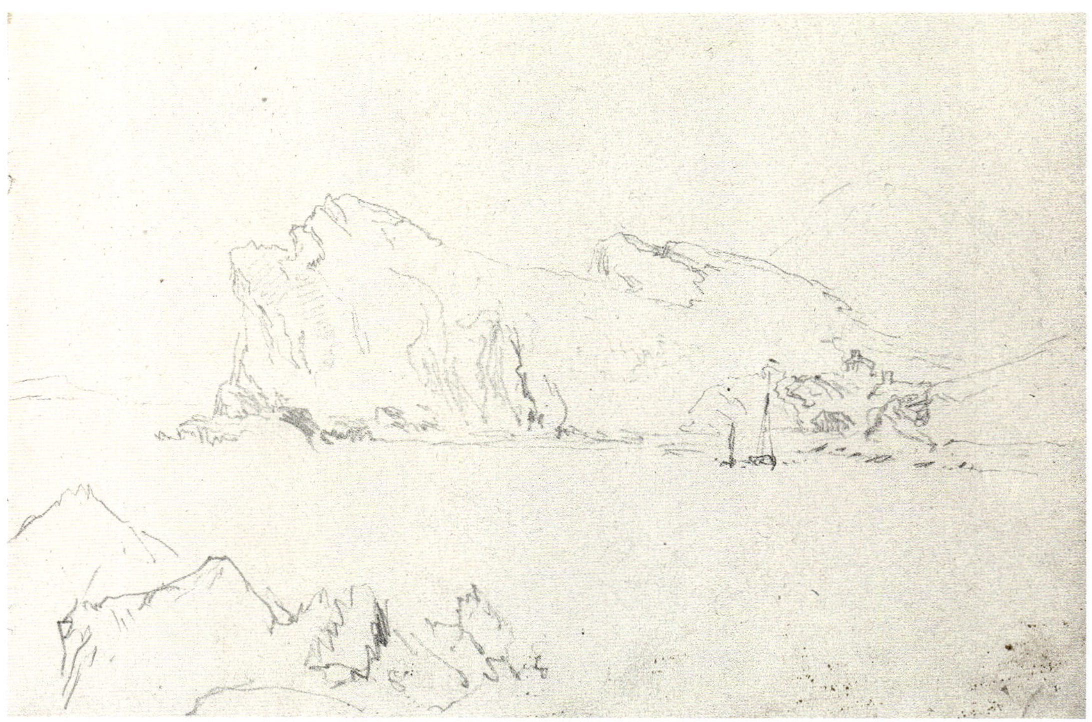

Fig. 118
Lulworth Cove, with the Isle of Portland Beyond
1811
Pencil, 17 × 20.9 cm
From the 'Corfe to Dartmouth' sketchbook
Tate (D08830 / TB CXXIV 20a)

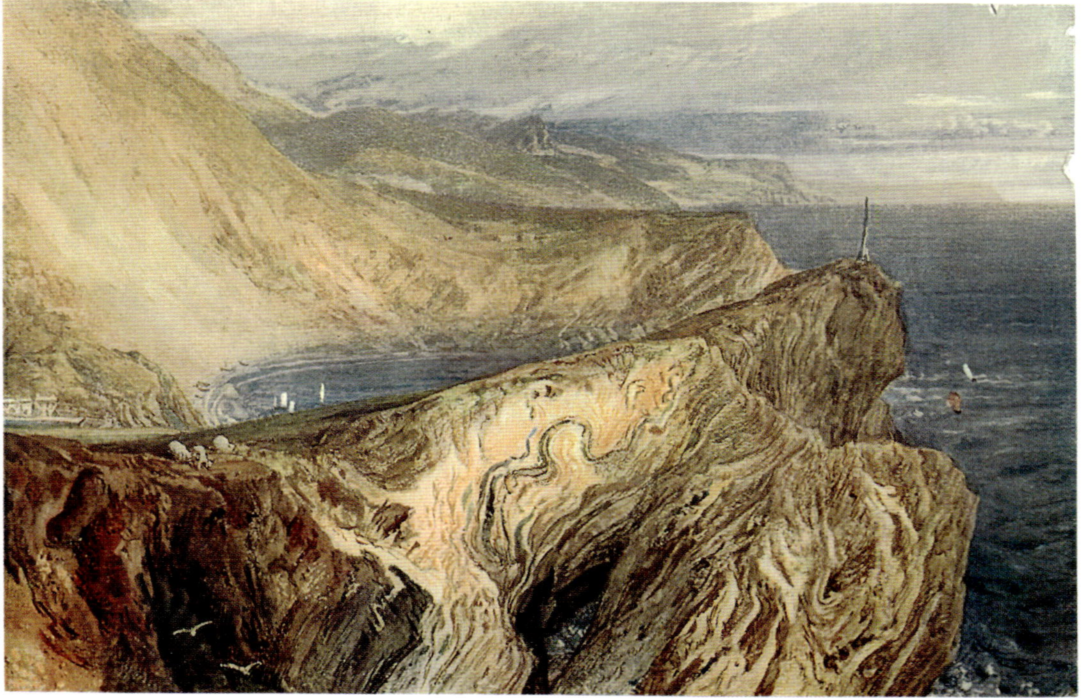

Fig. 119
Lulworth Cove, Dorsetshire
c.1811
Watercolour, 14.7 × 20.3 cm
For *Picturesque Views on the Southern Coast of England*
Reproduced from the illustration in *The Studio*, 1909
Private collection (W449)

phenomenon that is Lulworth Cove (figs 118–19). This natural feature was created by erosion of the clays behind the bands of Portland and Purbeck limestone, which are thrown up into dramatic folds on the west side of the cove. Turner found the ideal spot from which to showcase these, but in translating his on-the-spot pencil sketch into watercolour, he exaggerated and distorted the actual form of the limestone curves, making them wilder and more sinuous.[11] This shortcoming is surprising, given his friendship with members of the Geological Society, who

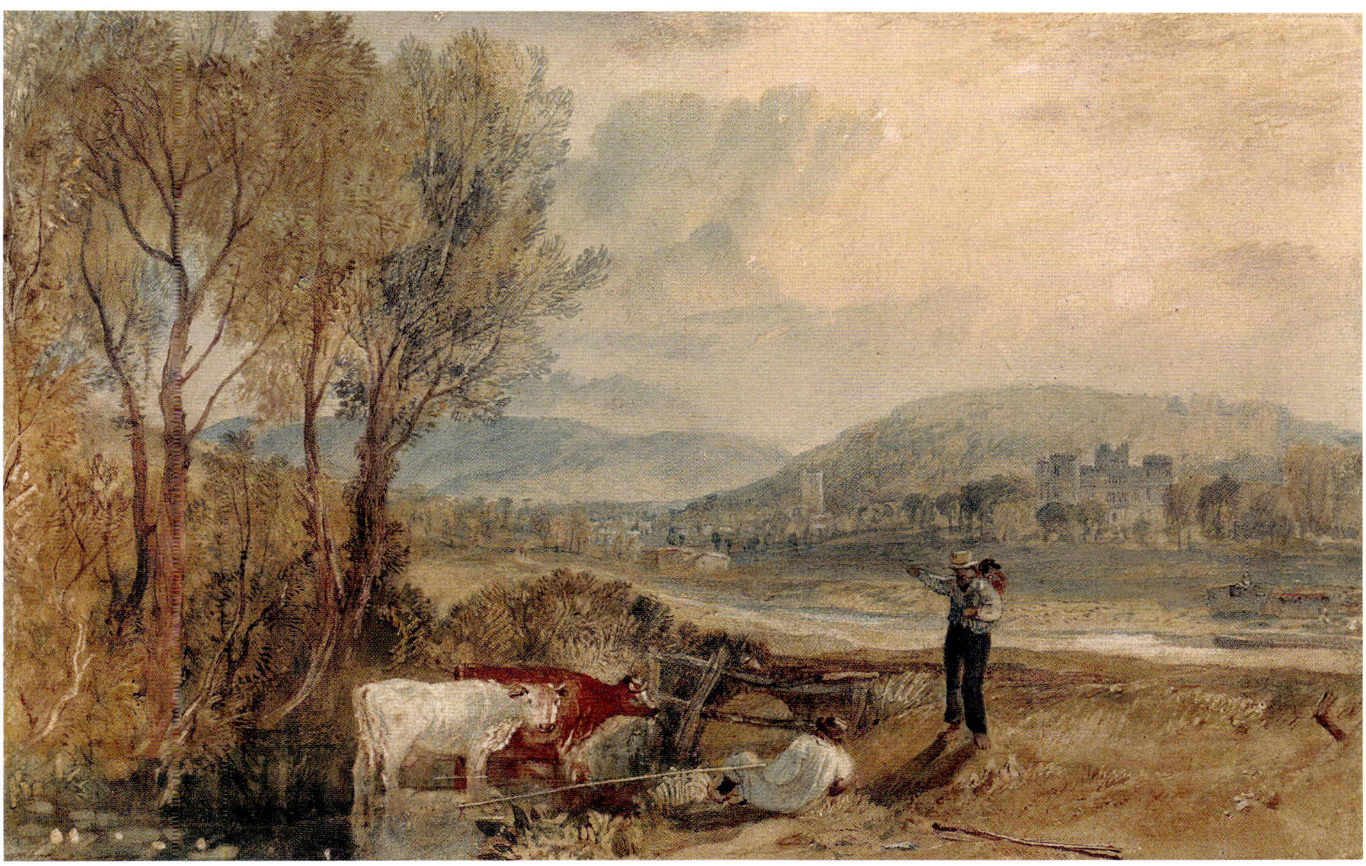

Fig. 120
Lulworth Castle, Dorsetshire
*c.*1820
Watercolour, 15.5 × 23.7 cm
For *Picturesque Views on the Southern Coast of England*
Yale Center for British Art, New Haven (W467)

insisted on precision in their own records, but it highlights Turner's tendency towards effect at the expense of accuracy. Here a clue to his approach occurs in his verse, where he discerned a resemblance between the strata of the 'bristling rocks' and 'vitrified scoria', a type of volcanic rock, presumably because the undulating bands of limestone reminded him of lava flows.[12]

Inland Turner sketched Lulworth Castle from the north-east (fig. 120). It was owned by the Weld family, noted Roman Catholics, for whom Turner had recorded Stonyhurst College in Lancashire after it was presented to the Jesuits by Thomas Weld.[13] Curiously it was not until around 1820 that Turner developed his sketches of Lulworth for the *Southern Coast* series, by which point the serial publication was just a few years from completion. The inclusion of the castle in the sequence is also striking because it is one of only two in which the shore cannot be seen (the other being Corfe Castle; fig. 115).

But this deficiency in the Lulworth image was fully compensated for in the view Turner made a little further west of the great sweep of Weymouth bay, where the gently rolling waves sparkle as they catch the midday light falling above the town in widely spaced crepuscular rays (fig. 121). In the foreground Turner depicts some of the many bathers who had been attracted to Weymouth by its fashionable associations with health and royalty, following George III's first recuperative visit there in 1789. He also notes, beyond the end of the tapering line of townhouses, the distinctive headland of the Isle of Portland.

Turner explored the island himself, evidently curious about this celebrated source of limestone, which had been used by Sir Christopher Wren at St Paul's Cathedral. So instead of focusing on Pennsylvania Castle, another of Wyatt's neo-gothic country houses (which can be glimpsed under the arch on the right), Turner's attention was drawn to the quarry below the remains of the medieval Rufus Castle (nicknamed 'Bow and Arrow' because of the narrow openings designed to be used by archers; fig. 122). In his pencil sketch of the setting he had only noted

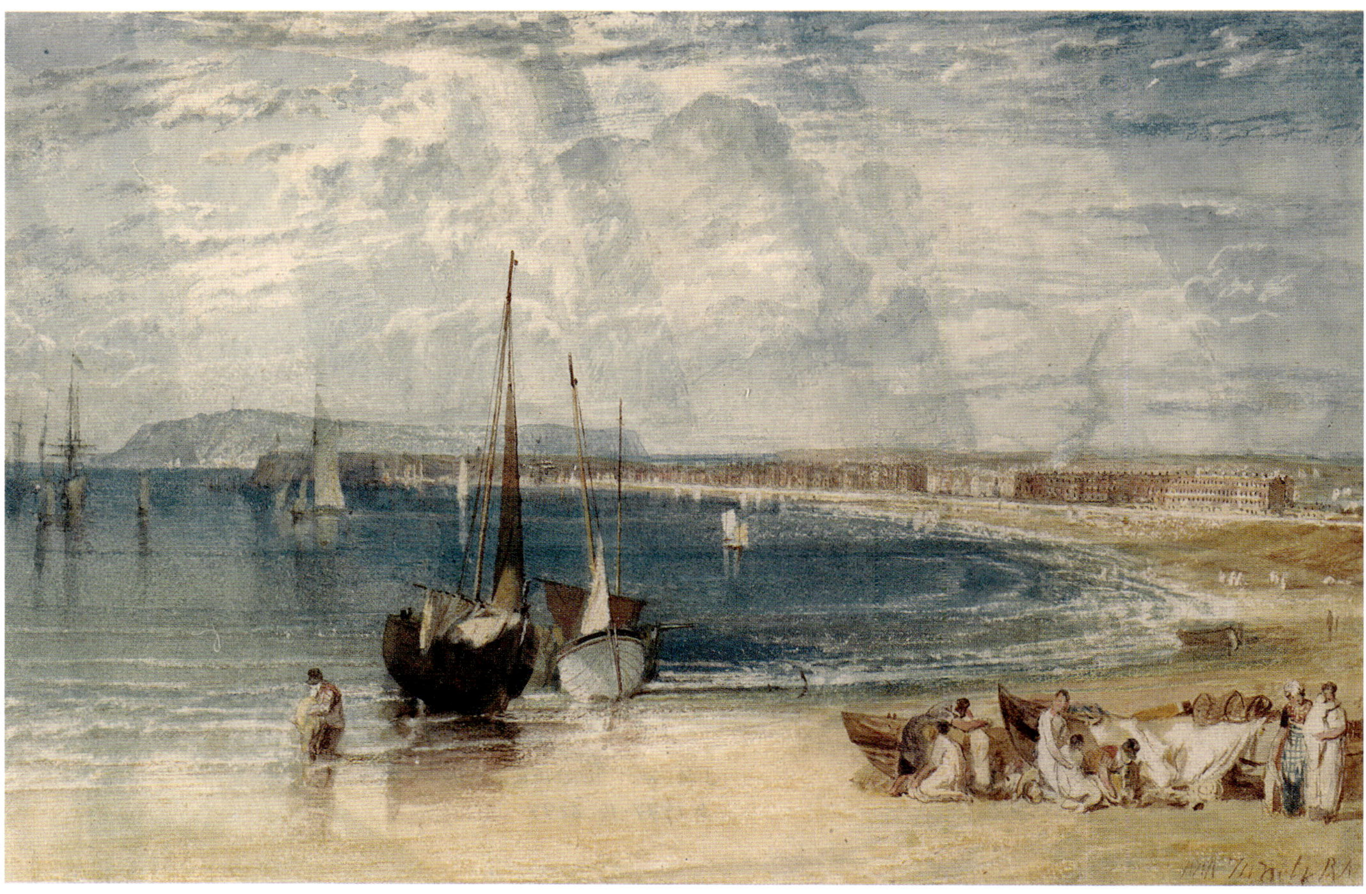

Fig. 121
Weymouth, Dorsetshire
*c.*1812
Watercolour, 14 × 21.3 cm
For *Picturesque Views on the Southern Coast of England*
Yale Center for British Art, New Haven (W448)

the placing of a few blocks, but he was able to amplify the scene with his recollections of the masons measuring and cutting the stone.[14]

North of Portland Turner stopped at Dorchester (fig. 123). While there he evidently saw Maiden Castle, the vast Iron Age fort to the south-west; he made no sketches, but his attempts to sum up the place in verse reveal certain misconceptions about its age (he thought it was 'The work of Norman prowess'). More poetically, he lauded it for 'Defying the hand of Time and stormy skies' (in terms similar to those he also used to evoke Old Sarum), but had he realised how much older it was, he would have felt the greater truth of his words.[15] From his contact with Colt Hoare, he knew something of the current research into the ancient barrows dotted across the landscape, but, in reality, the archaeological understanding of these traces of earlier civilisations was still in its infancy.

Back on the Jurassic coast near Bridport, Turner celebrated the town's renown as a producer of rope for the navy by showing a team of men securing a brig offshore at West Bay (fig. 124). The ship is positioned to the west of the two piers that marked the entrance to the narrow harbour, but is saved from the dangers of the impending blustery weather on this rocky coast by the collective endeavour and the reliability of the local product.

Further on, at Charmouth, Turner made sketches that provided the basis for the distant view of Lyme Regis, with a squall driving in from sea (fig. 125). He had insufficient information to draw on to re-create the specific topographical details of the little town spilling down the hillside, but he relied on the wall of the harbour, known as the Cobb, as his distinctive marker of the place.[16] His design had been skilfully translated into a black and white line engraving by W.B. Cooke by the end of 1814 and so could have been familiar to Jane Austen when she was plotting her novel *Persuasion* (1817), with its decisive events at Lyme Regis.

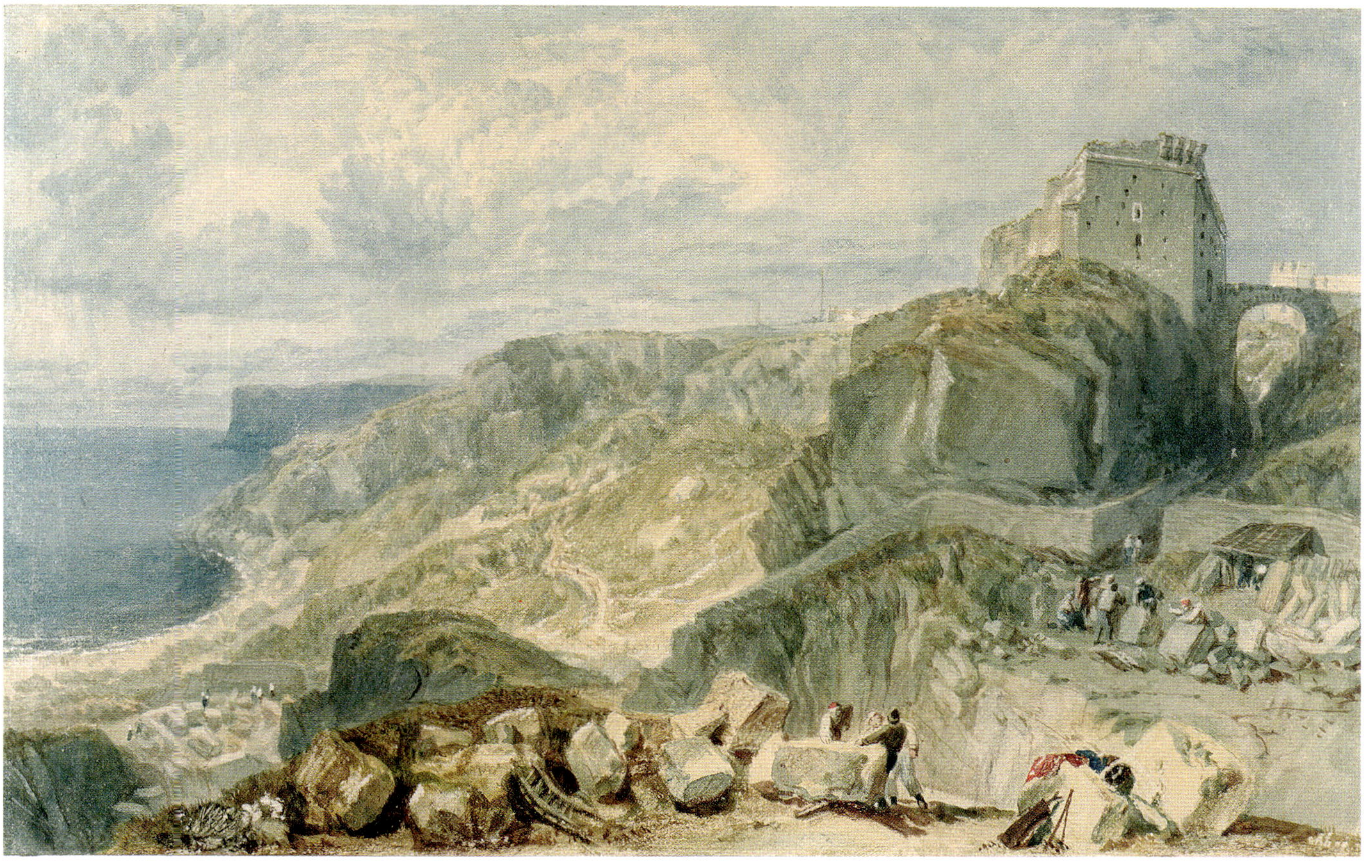

Fig. 122
Bow and Arrow Castle, Isle of Portland
*c.*1815
Watercolour, 15.2 × 23 cm
For *Picturesque Views on the Southern Coast of England*
University of Liverpool
(W459)

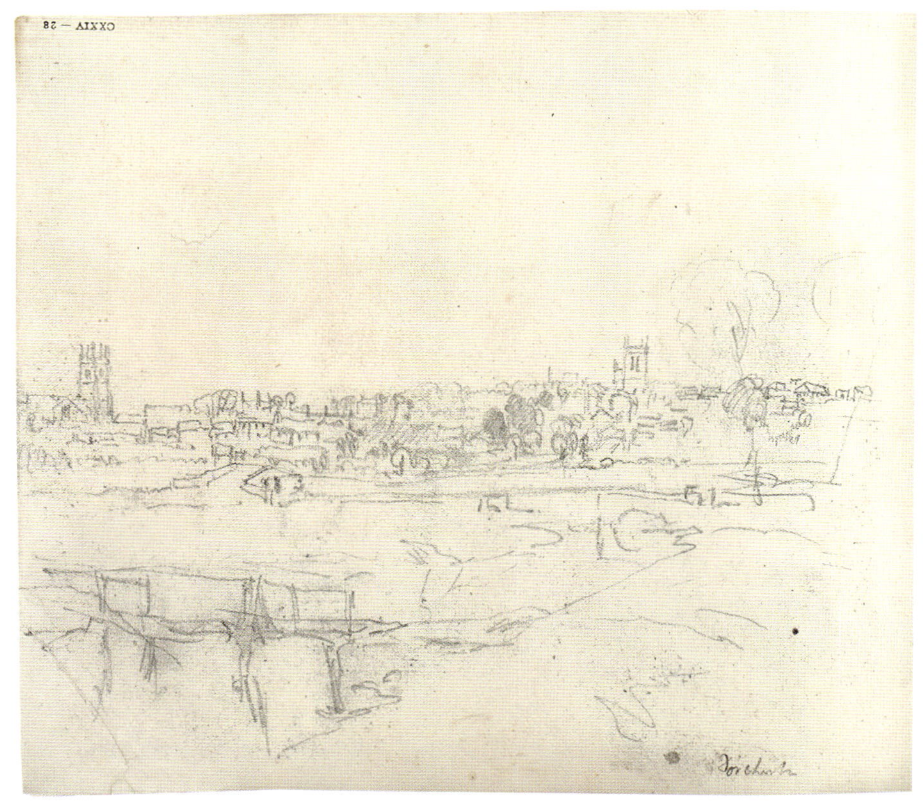

Fig. 123
Dorchester from the Frome Valley
1811
Pencil, 17 × 20.9 cm
From the 'Corfe to Dartmouth' sketchbook
Tate (D08834 / TB CXXIV 23)

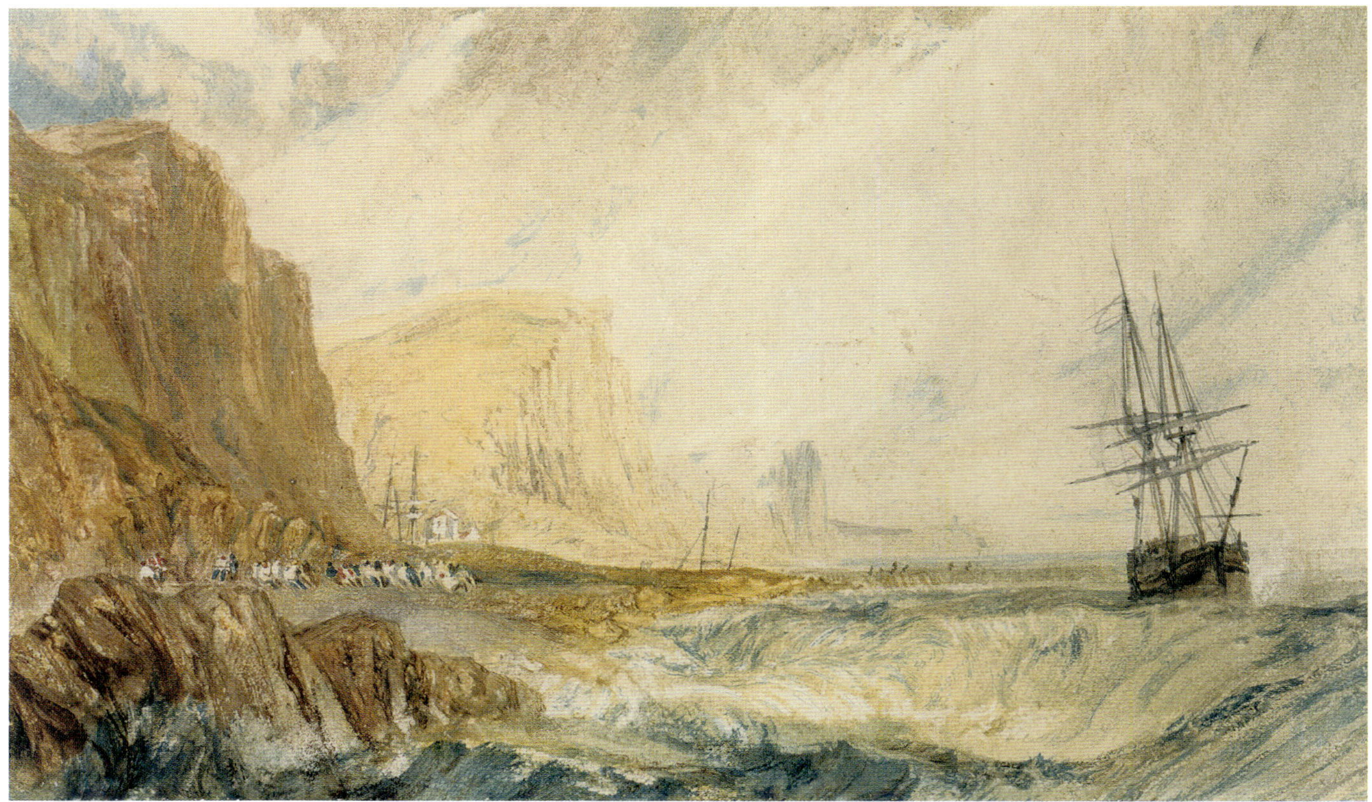

Fig. 124
Bridport, Dorsetshire
*c.*1818
Watercolour, 15.2 × 23.5 cm
For *Picturesque Views on the Southern Coast of England*
Art Gallery and Museum, Bury (W465)

It was early August 1811 by the time Turner reached Lyme Regis and he continued from there as far as Land's End. After exploring the cliffs and bays of north Cornwall, Devon and Somerset, he would have reached Glastonbury by September (fig. 126). From there it was a short walk to Wells, where he sketched the cathedral and its Chain Gate yet again. Just to the north he investigated Wookey Hole and beyond there he made a detour to Cheddar Gorge. A day or so later, as the afternoon waned, he arrived at Stonehenge (see p. 142), and after staying the night at Salisbury or Amesbury he could have been back in London in just a couple of days. It had been an incredibly productive journey, creating a stockpile of rudimentary images that he was able to draw from over the following decade. Neither of the tours of the ensuing years was as far reaching, but the journeys in 1813 and 1814 brought Turner back through the southern counties of England once more; it is probable that during the later one he stayed again at Stourhead, thereby prompting the commission for the picture of Lake Avernus (see fig. 29).

By the mid-1820s the *Southern Coast* series was almost complete. Chasing up some subjects he had not yet depicted, in 1824 Turner visited Portsmouth and Brighton. He had, of course, been to Portsmouth before, having recorded the arrival of captured Danish ships at Spithead in 1807; and then on 25 June 1814 he had watched the review of the fleet staged to commemorate the Treaty of Paris, which was attended by the Prince Regent and the Allied Sovereigns.[17] It is odd, therefore, that he felt he had insufficient reference material from which to compose a view of the harbour. When making his sketches in 1824 he concentrated on the landmark towers rising above the waterfront: the cathedral of St Thomas, the Admiralty Semaphore, Burridge's Folly and the Dockyard Semaphore. In his finished watercolour, these towers lead the eye from the right steadily into the port, beyond the bulky defences of Fort Blockhouse on the left (fig. 127).

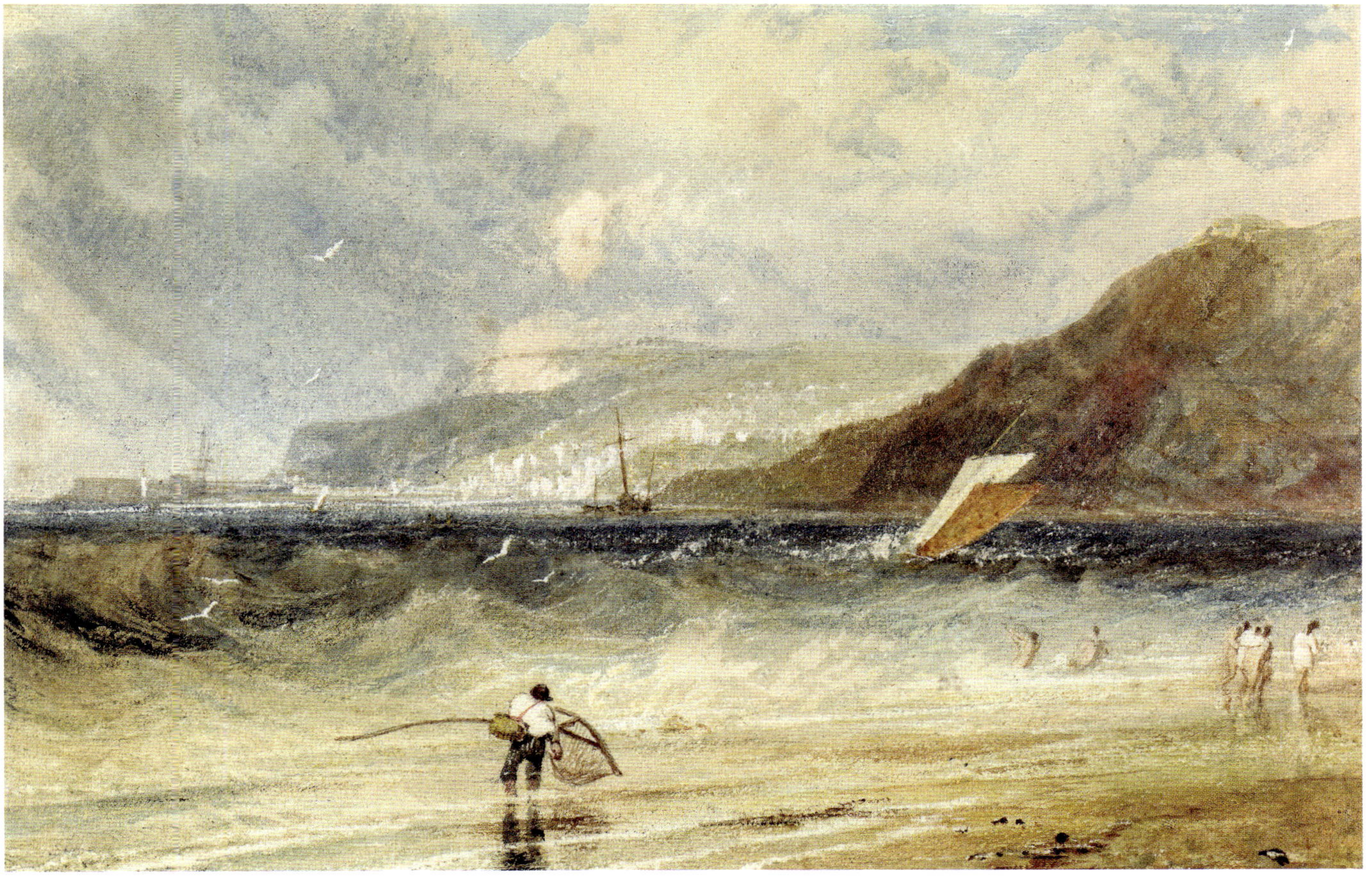

Fig. 125
Lyme Regis, Dorsetshire

*c.*1812
Watercolour, 15.3 × 21.7 cm
For *Picturesque Views on the Southern Coast of England*
Glasgow Art Gallery (W451)

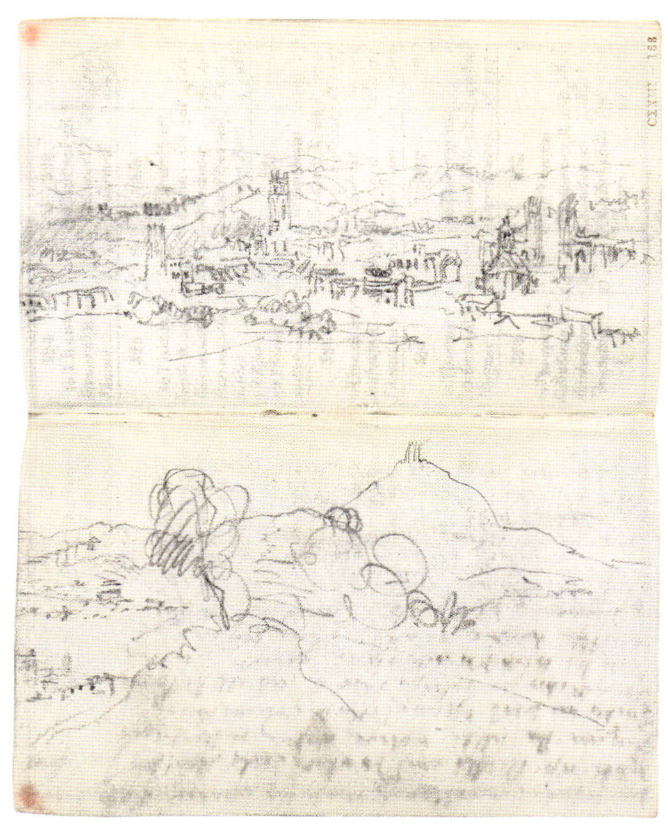

Fig. 126
Glastonbury: the Abbey and Town, with another study of the Tor, from Wearyall Hill

1811
Pencil, 7.5 × 11.7 cm
From the Devonshire Coast No. 1 sketchbook
Tate (D08681, D08632 / TB CXXIII 167a, 168)

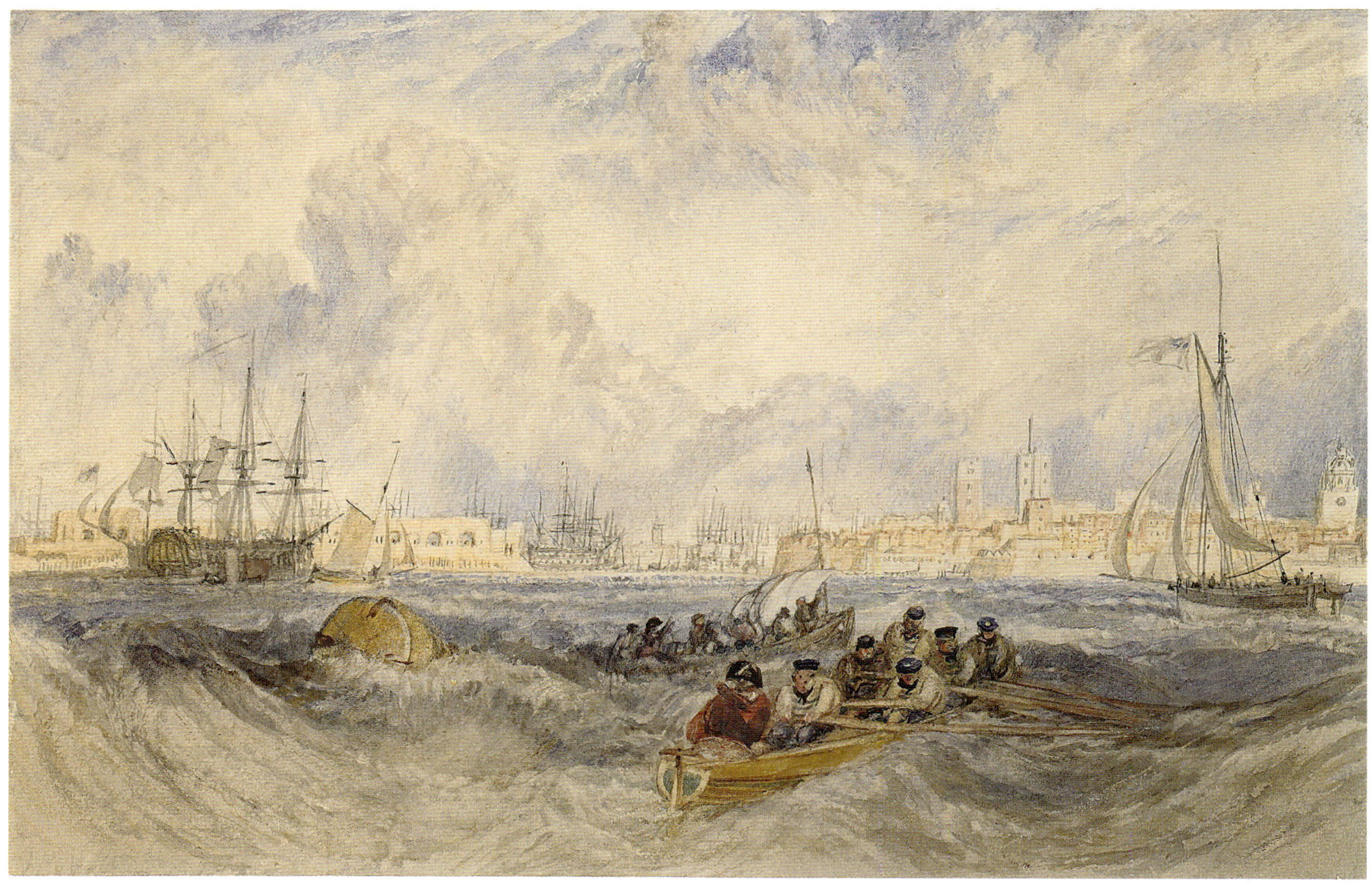

The image subtly conveys the scale of the harbour and its busy waters. Turner was evidently pleased with his composition, and more or less repeated it for another project that he was working on with Cooke, *The Ports of England* (fig. 128). If anything, this design, with the centrally placed battleship, is even more powerful. Once again, there is a diagonal recession along the line of towers, which alludes to the rapid communication achieved by the semaphore system they operated. A further link in this visual chain is the waving sailor in the foreground boat, who indicates the Admiralty tower with his hat.

Just a year or so after producing these watercolours, Turner embarked on a new topographical part-work with Charles Heath (1785–1848). Designed along the same lines as those series he had known as a child, *The Picturesque Views in England and Wales* would eventually comprise over 90 scenes illustrating Regency Britain.[18] Although the series was inherently nostalgic, making use of sketches Turner had recorded as far back as the 1790s, it presented the contemporary state of the nation both incidentally and directly, including industry, travel and urban expansion, as well as the traditional rural life. Inevitably the coast also features significantly and, once again, Turner repeated his view of the entrance to Portsmouth harbour (fig. 129). This time, however, he shifted his focus to the battery guarding it at Gosport, with the masts of a crowded harbour beyond.

Three more of the *England and Wales* views depicted settings familiar from Turner's earlier travels in Wiltshire (figs 130, 134, 154). For the view of Malmesbury he unearthed the group of sketches that he believed he had made for Colt Hoare (see p. 34). The composition focuses on the ruined abbey, which had suffered the collapse of both its spire and its western tower in the sixteenth century. Turner surveyed the building from every angle, but here he combined two of his sketches from the north, both of which are marked with the yellow colour used in the

Fig. 127
Portsmouth, Hampshire
1824
Watercolour, 15.2 × 21.8 cm
For *Picturesque Views on the Southern Coast of England*
Lady Lever Art Gallery, Port Sunlight, Liverpool (W477)

OPPOSITE ABOVE AND DETAIL ON PAGES 182–83:
Fig. 128
Portsmouth
1824
Watercolour, 16 × 24 cm
For *The Ports of England*
Tate (D18152 / TB CCVIIII S / W756)

Fig. 129
Gosport, Entrance to Portsmouth Harbour
*c.*1829
Watercolour, 28.5 × 41.9 cm
For *Picturesque Views in England and Wales*
Portsmouth Museum (W828)

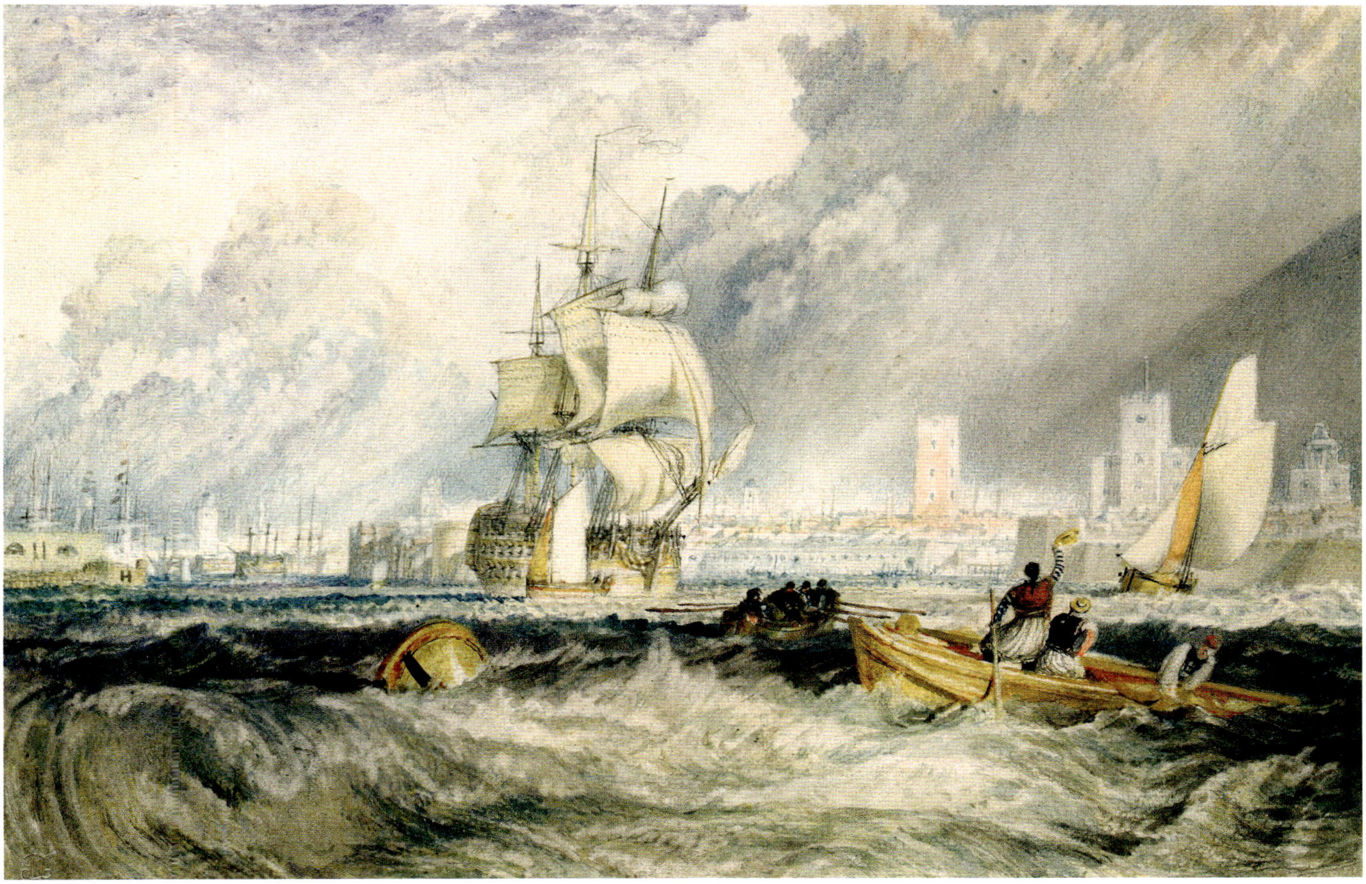

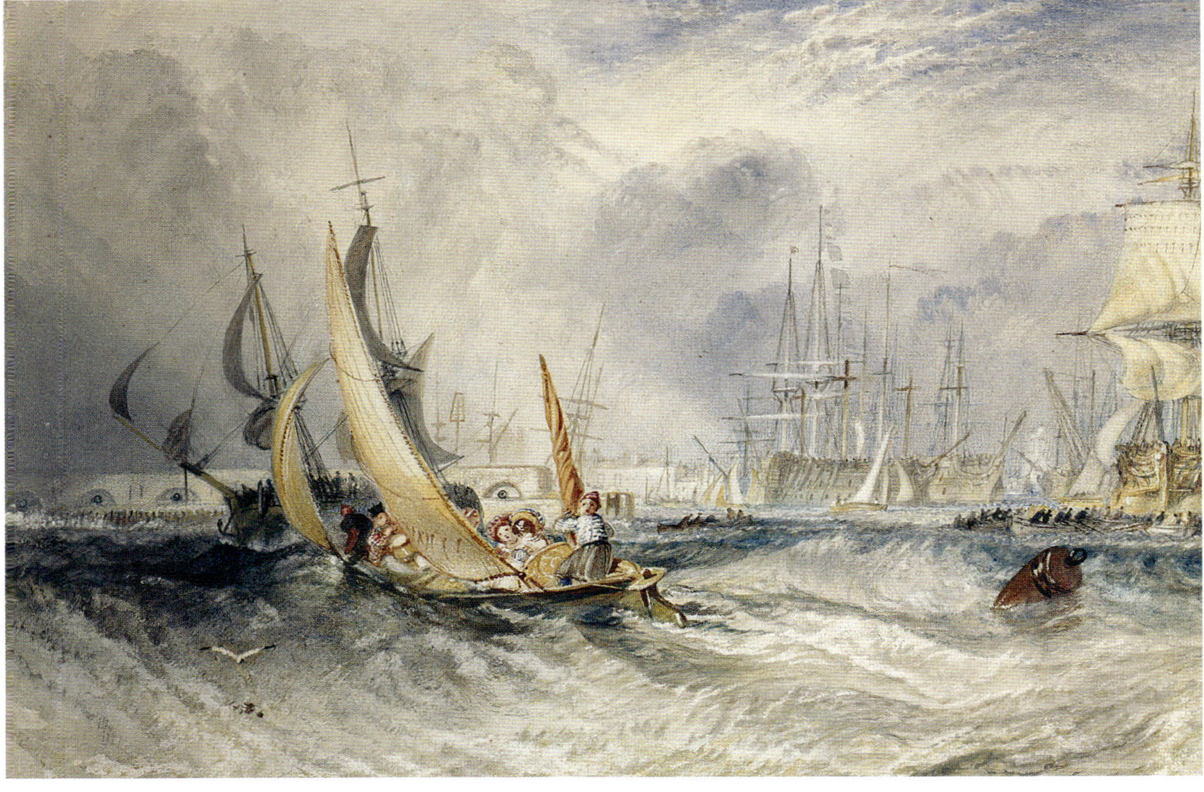

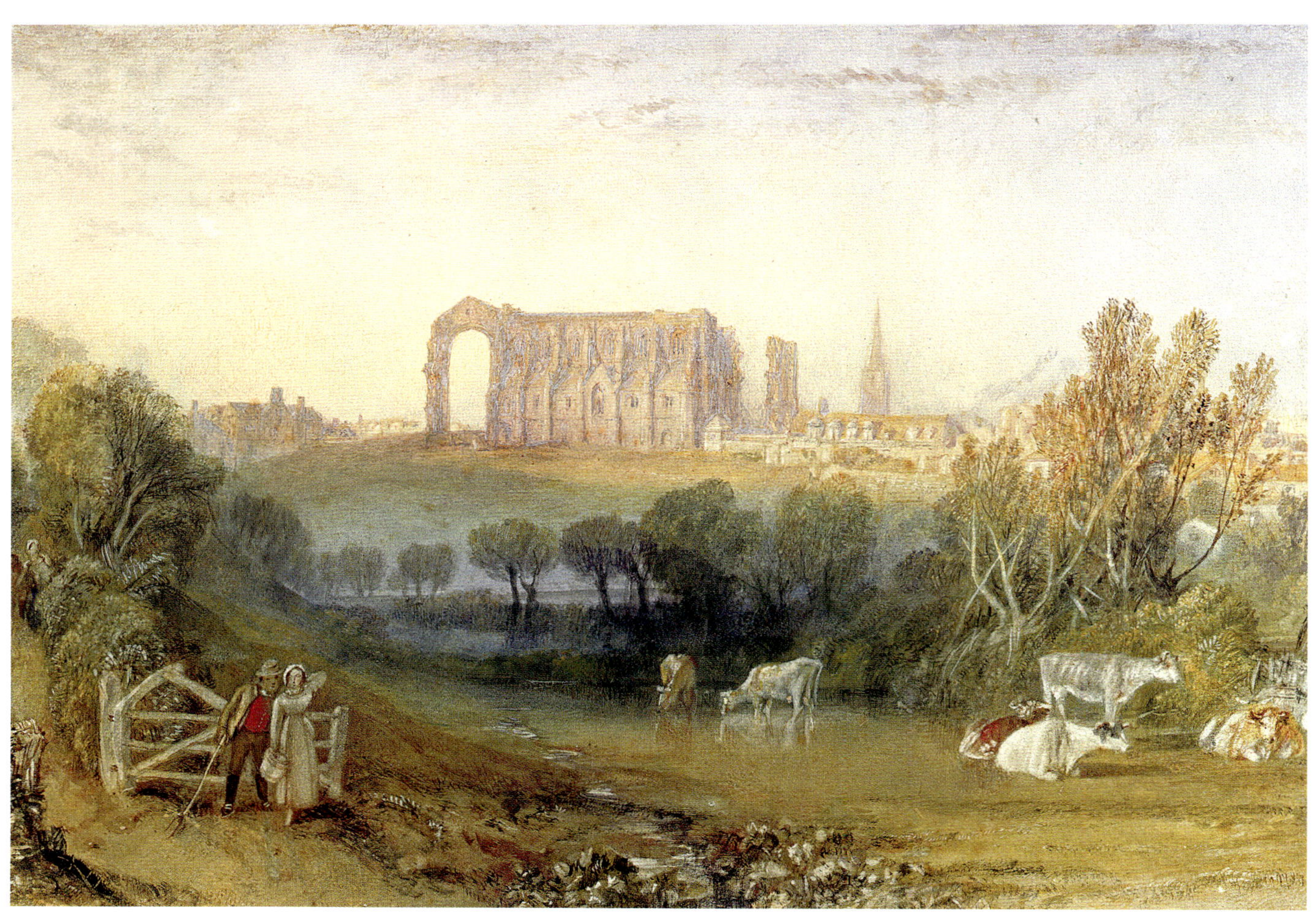

Fig. 130
Malmesbury, Wiltshire
c.1827
Watercolour, 28.9 × 41.6 cm
For *Picturesque Views of England and Wales*
Private collection,
c/o Peter Johnson (W805)

design to create the rising sun.[19] The scene is a perfect pastoral, inhabited by contented cattle, but Turner has updated the kind of classical idyll that would have been familiar to Colt Hoare by introducing an ungainly suitor wooing the milkmaid, much to the amusement of some children, eavesdropping from the bushes.

His foregrounds in the views of Salisbury (fig. 134) and Stonehenge (fig. 154) are similarly enlivened with human interest, and it is likely that he developed these watercolours as a pair, using the same range of colours to build up both designs simultaneously. They were exhibited with others from the series in June 1829 at the Egyptian Hall in Piccadilly, promoting the latest *England and Wales* engravings, and must have been painted a year or so earlier. Common to both is a shepherd and his herd, although his presence in each image has different resonances. In the view of Salisbury, seen from its historic origins at Old Sarum, the shepherd has been interpreted as a symbol of the Christian Church looking after its flock, and there is indeed a visual echo of the standing figure in the spire of the distant cathedral.[20] Turner's steadfast and stoic shepherd perhaps also alludes to the pious

Fig. 131
Distant View of Salisbury from Old Sarum, to the North

1795
Pencil, 26.3 × 20.4 cm
From the 'Isle of Wight' sketchbook
Tate (D00421 / TB XXIV 14b)

Fig. 132
View of Salisbury, from Harnham Hill

*c.*1799
Pencil, 15 × 12.3 cm
From the 'Salisbury sketchbook
Tate (D02249, D02250 / TB XLIX 6a, 7)

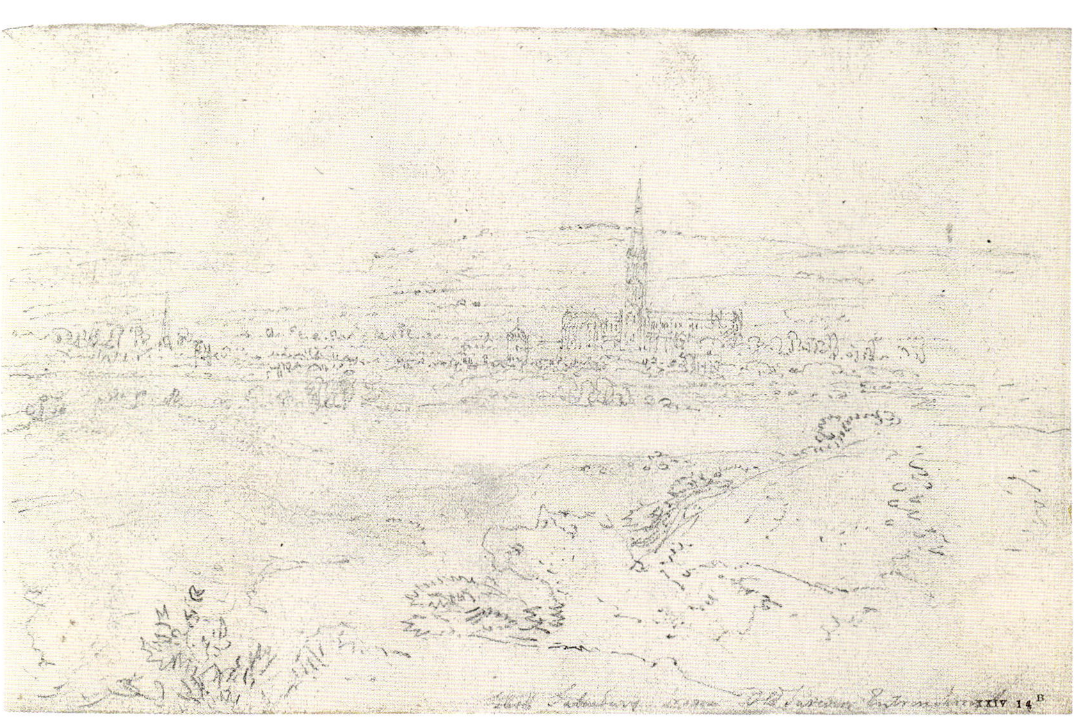

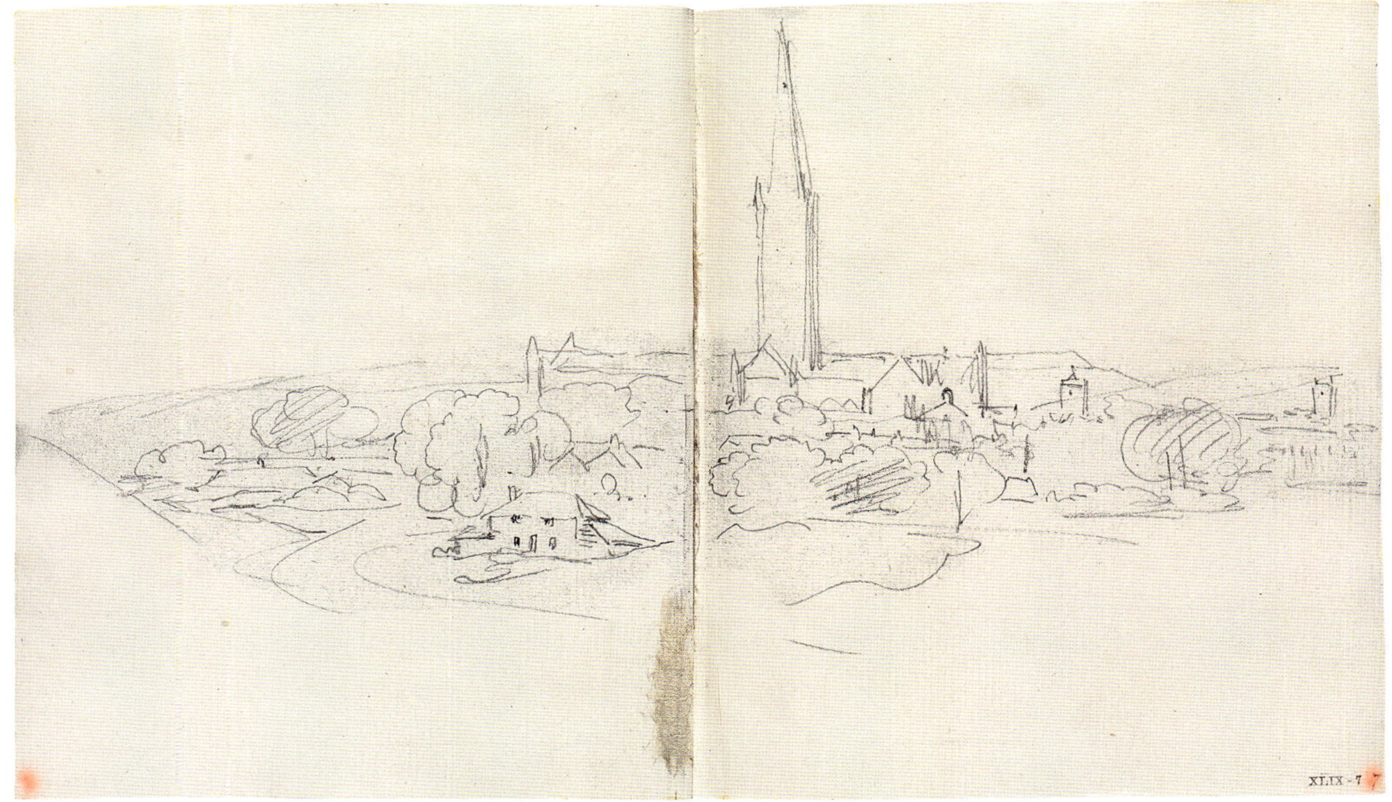

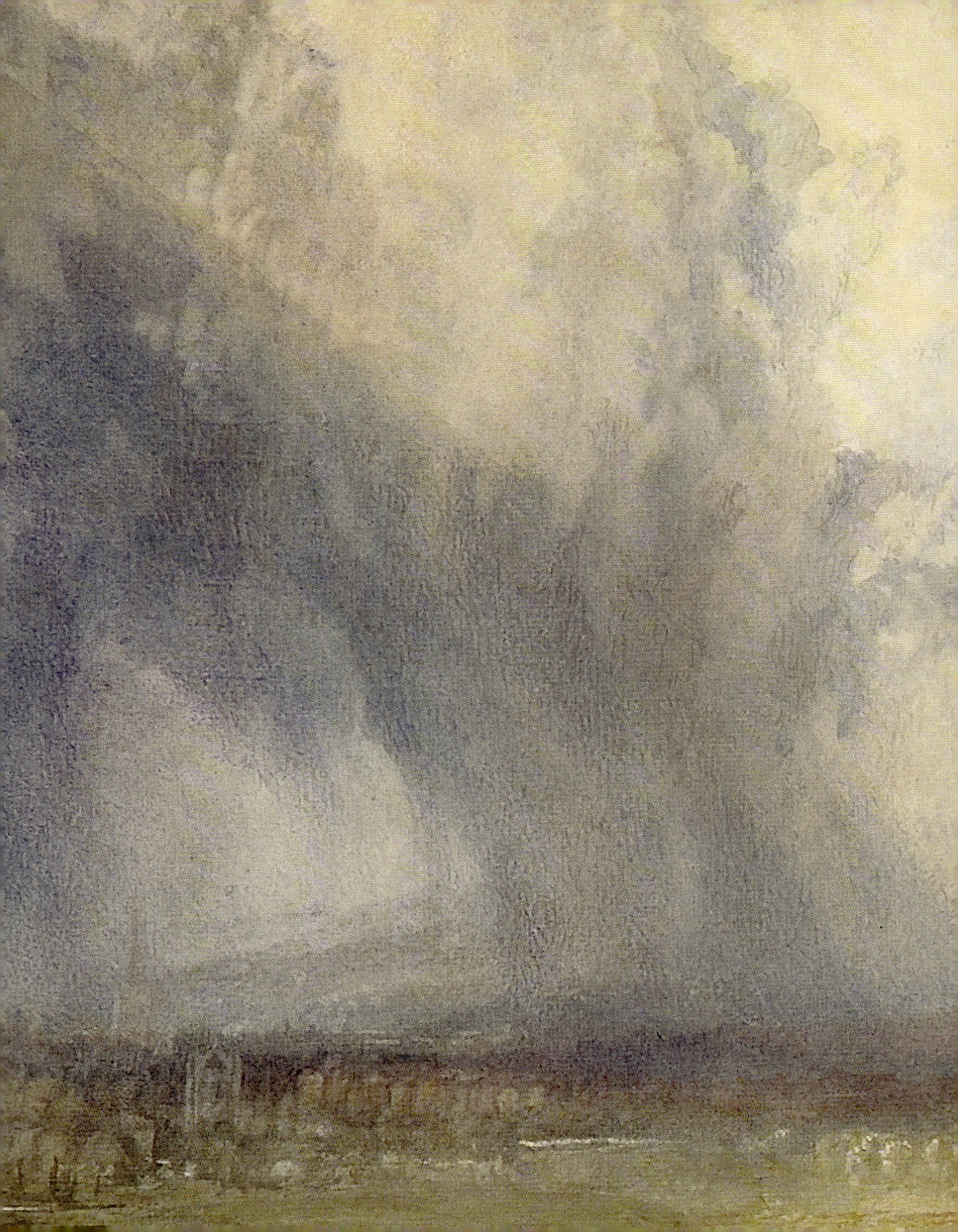

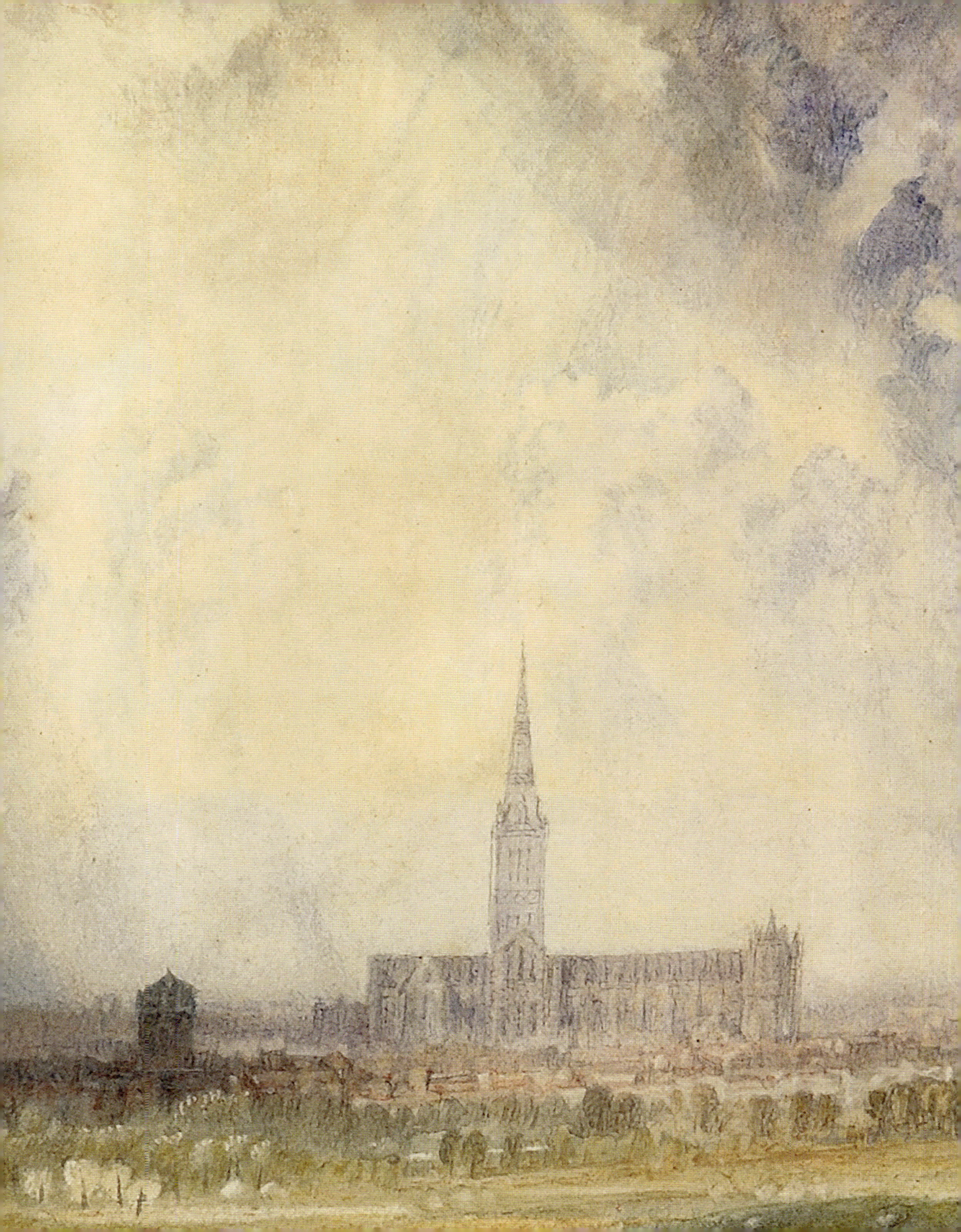

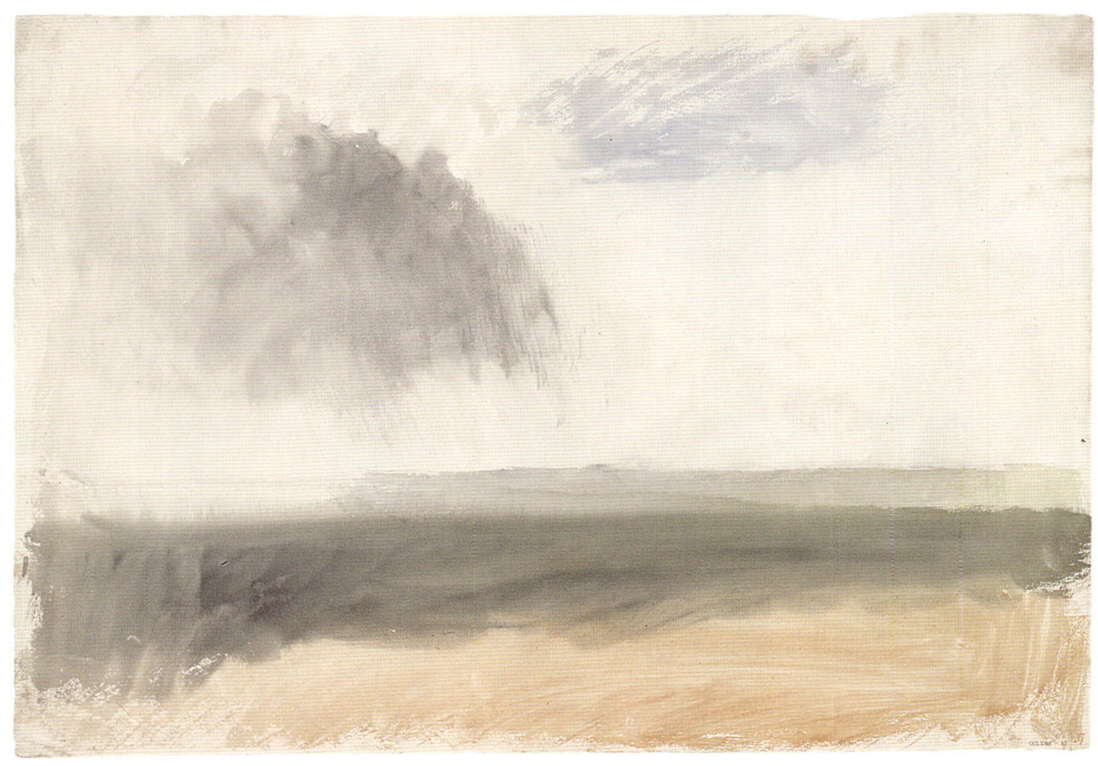

Fig. 133
Salisbury from Old Sarum, with a Raincloud: Preparatory Study
*c.*1827–28
Watercolour, 34.3 × 48 cm
Tate (D25159 / TB CCLXIII 37)

BELOW AND DETAIL ON PREVIOUS PAGES: **Fig. 134**
Salisbury, from Old Sarum
*c.*1827–28
Watercolour, 27.2 × 41 cm
For *Picturesque Views of England and Wales*
The Salisbury Museum (W836)

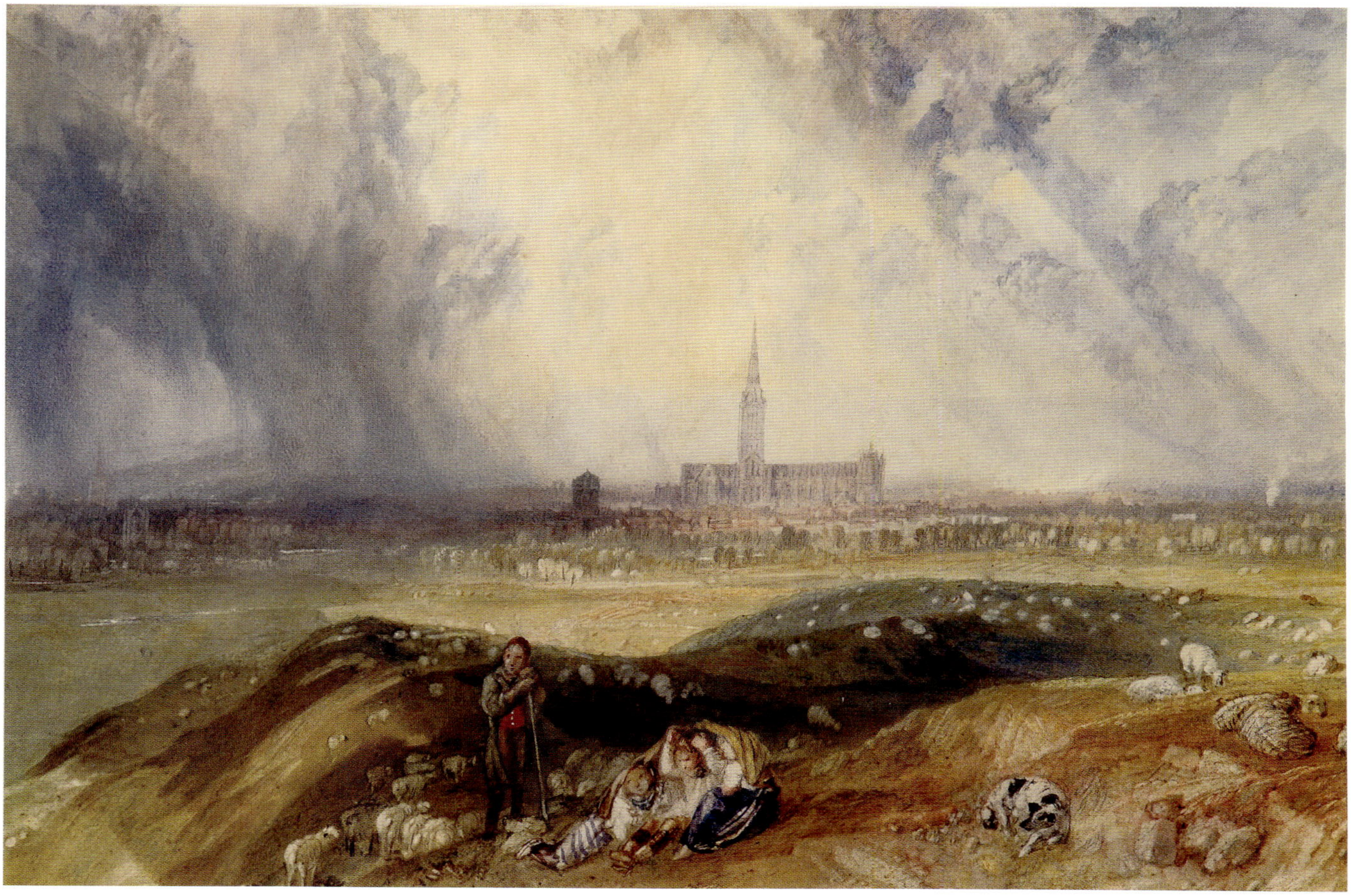

protagonist in Hannah More's hugely popular tract, *The Shepherd of Salisbury Plain* (1795).

This was a period in which the Anglican Church was under increasing pressure, caused by the drive for Catholic Emancipation, which was achieved in April 1829. Consequently the traditional bond between Church and State seemed much less secure. In Turner's watercolour the majestic outline of Salisbury Cathedral appears mirage-like and otherworldly, irradiated among rain clouds, and he would adopt a similar means of representing the cathedrals of Ely, Coventry and Lichfield in the ensuing years. Visitors to the Egyptian Hall in 1829 would have looked at the Salisbury watercolour (the inescapable first work in the show) and seen an image that dramatised the storms then threatening to engulf the Church, and not only the Church. By utilising his much earlier sketch of Old Sarum just then, Turner tapped into the wider discontent about the iniquities of the electoral system. Old Sarum was one of the most infamous and ridiculed of the 'rotten boroughs', an essentially uninhabited 'Green Mound' that returned two representatives to Parliament (fig. 135). For satirical printmakers, its name alone served as a metaphor of the need for reform, a divisive sentiment that gathered momentum in the following years, ultimately finding a kind of resolution in the Great Reform Bill of 1832. Given this charged atmosphere, it is interesting to note that, although the engraving of the view of Salisbury was complete by June 1830, it was not published until February 1832, when there was at last hope that Lord John Russell's Bill would pass through the House of Lords.

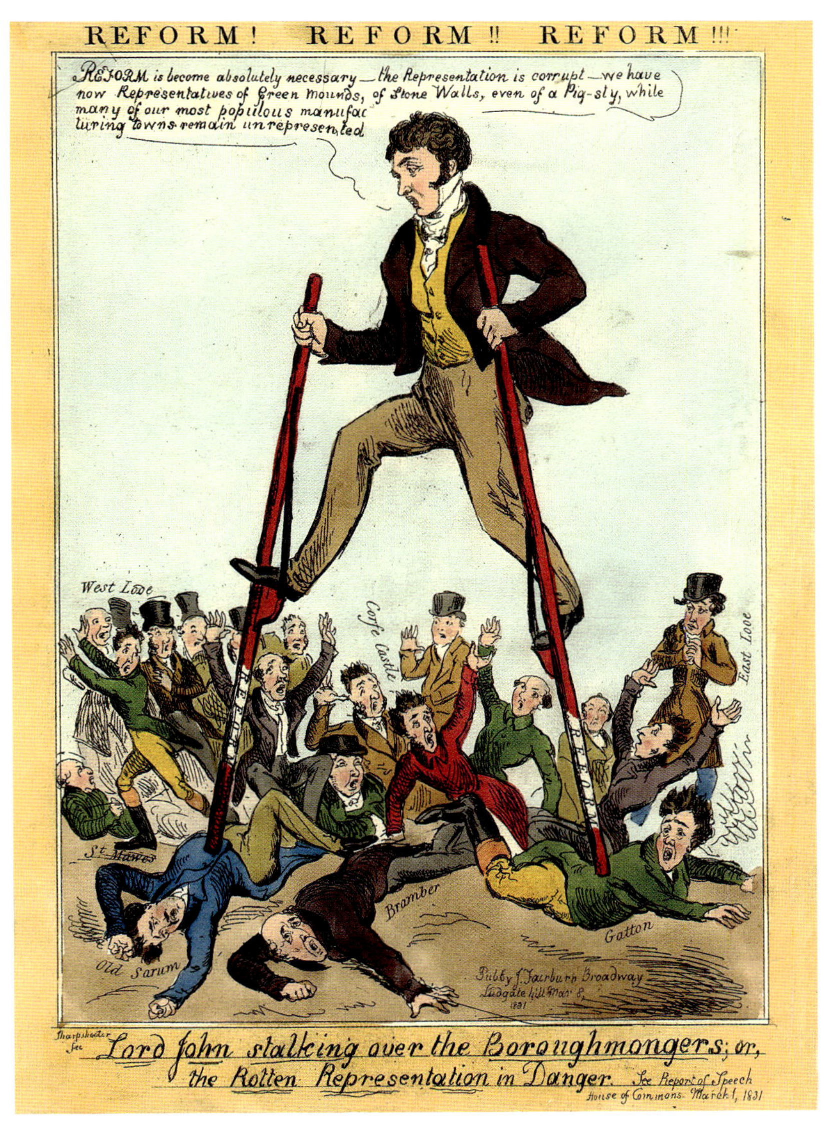

Fig. 135
UNKNOWN ARTIST
Reform! Reform!! Reform!!! Lord John Stalking Over the Boroughmongers, or, the Rotten Representation in Danger
8 March 1831
Hand-coloured etching, 34 × 24 cm
British Museum (1985,0119.242)

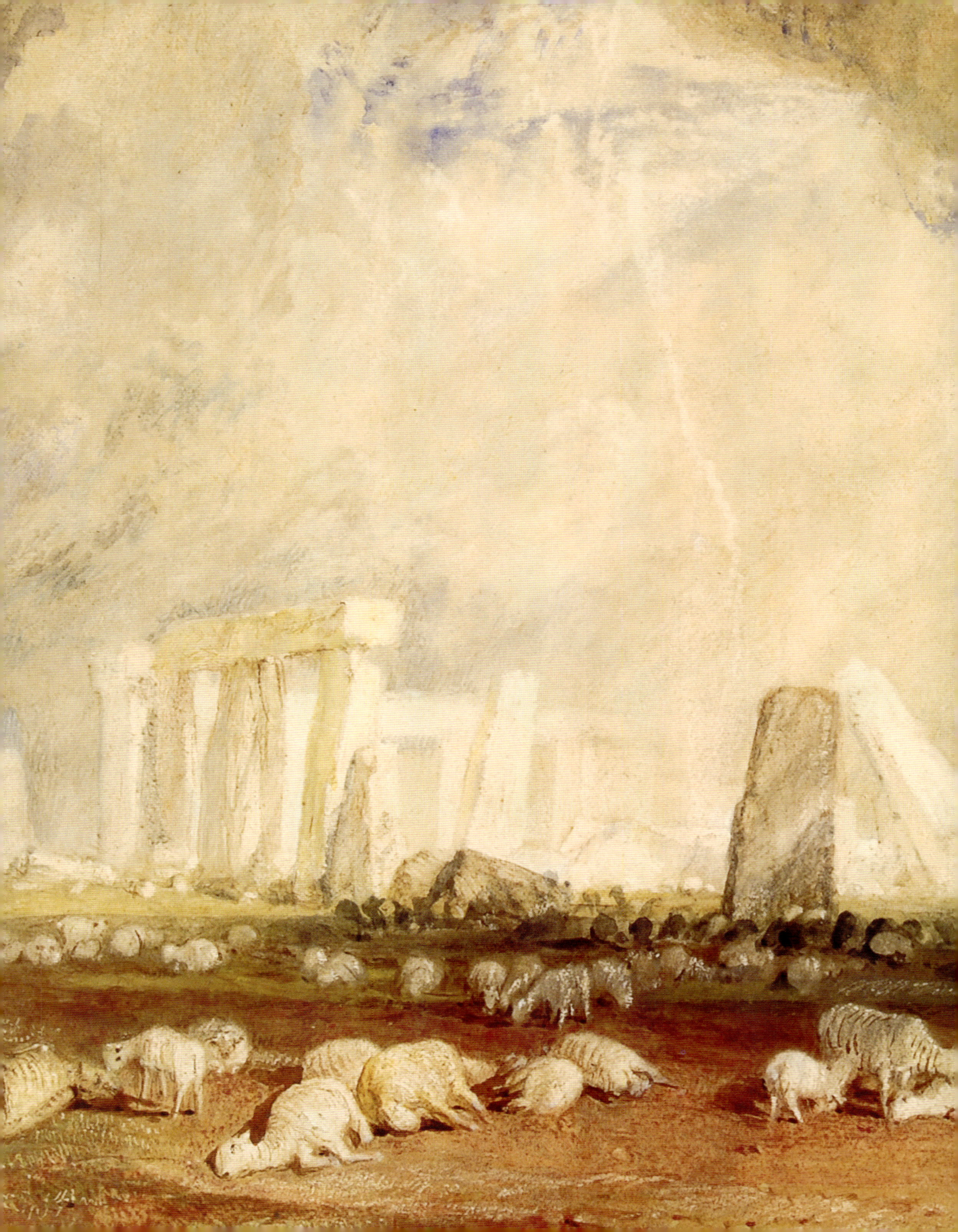

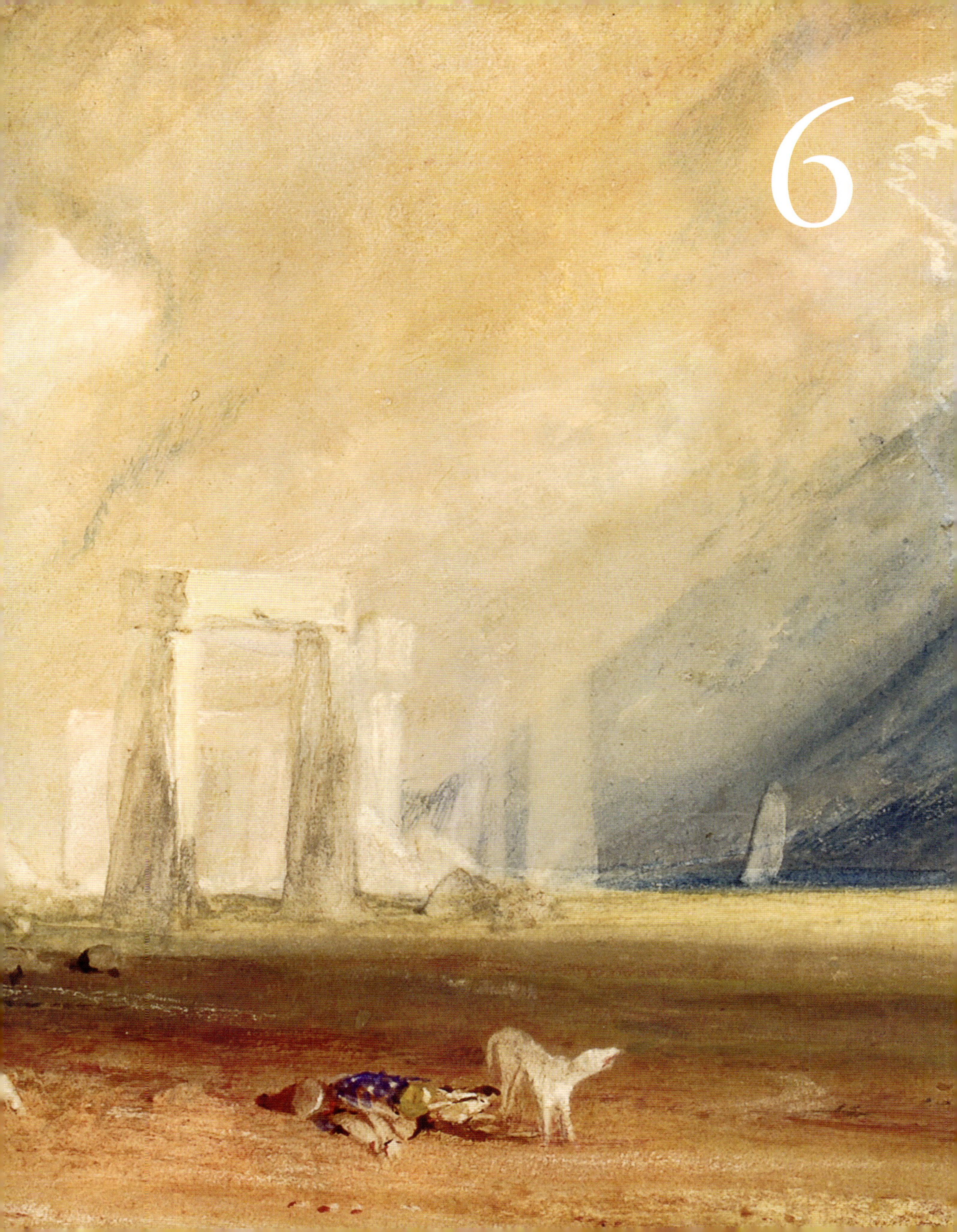

6

STONEHENGE AND HISTORY

PREVIOUS PAGES: *Stonehenge, Wiltshire* (detail) (see fig. 154)

TURNER WAS NOT THE FIRST to contrast Salisbury Cathedral with Stonehenge. In the summer of 1783 the great Dr Samuel Johnson visited the stone circle, doing so in the spirit of amateur antiquarian enquiry that had become established since the publication of William Stukeley's book *Stonehenge* in 1740. For Johnson, it was utterly logical to view the circle and the cathedral as the antithesis of each other: both were 'eminent monuments' in the development of architecture, but whereas the gothic church should be considered the 'last perfection' in its art, Stonehenge appeared much more crude and primitive, merely 'the first essay'.[1] He no doubt aired these views during a meeting with Edmund Burke, who also visited Stonehenge that summer. Many years earlier Burke had published *A Philosophical Enquiry into the Origin of our Ideas of the Sublime and Beautiful* (1757), a celebrated treatise which described and legitimised the more instinctive response to the natural world that characterises late eighteenth-century sentiment and is an element of Romanticism.

A combination of these overlapping outlooks pervades the views Turner produced of Stonehenge. It was for him both a curiosity of an obscure age and a man-made structure rich in imaginative possibilities. Given his concern for the plight of the Welsh Bards, he would have been interested in Stukeley's idea that the stones had been an ancient Druid Temple.[2] For, although this theory had been discredited in some circles, it continued to provide 'a fog-bank of mystification'.[3] However, Turner's connection with Colt Hoare meant that he was also alert to the new archaeological investigation that began around 1801, which attempted to provide a more factual account of the stones' history and purpose. How much of this Turner knew in detail remains a matter for speculation.

More certainly, it is clear that Turner visited Stonehenge on at least two occasions: first, while at Fonthill, in either 1799 or 1800 (more probably the latter); and then at the end of his West Country tour of 1811. Curiously, he does not seem to have travelled the short distance north from Salisbury to Stonehenge in 1795, when he was otherwise assiduous in noting potentially marketable subjects for pictures. Had he gone then he would have had the chance to see a more complete Stonehenge. Just two years later, on 3 January 1797, one of the inner trilithons – the paired sarsen uprights topped by a horizontal lintel – had crashed down, leaving a gap until it was resurrected in 1958. The trilithon in question can be seen in the centre of a dramatic depiction by Turner's associate Thomas Girtin (fig. 136), probably worked up from an outline by James Moore, the first owner of the watercolour. To animate his scene, Girtin introduced a crackle of lightning ricocheting into the heart of the circle, which illuminates the facing stones as if by a flare; it is an effect that is truly Sublime, epitomising the 'physic menace' that has been identified as a quality of Romantic representations of Stonehenge and its sense of oblivion.[4] Looking at the image, it is difficult to believe that Turner did not have it in mind when developing his own watercolour many years later.

Turner's first attempts to record the monument do not entirely escape the jumbled appearance of a 'stone quarry', which was Constable's damning assessment of many earlier representations of Stonehenge.[5] This is largely attributable to his use of pen and ink on blue paper, which fails to re-create a sense of actual space (figs 137–38). Indeed, the sketches possess

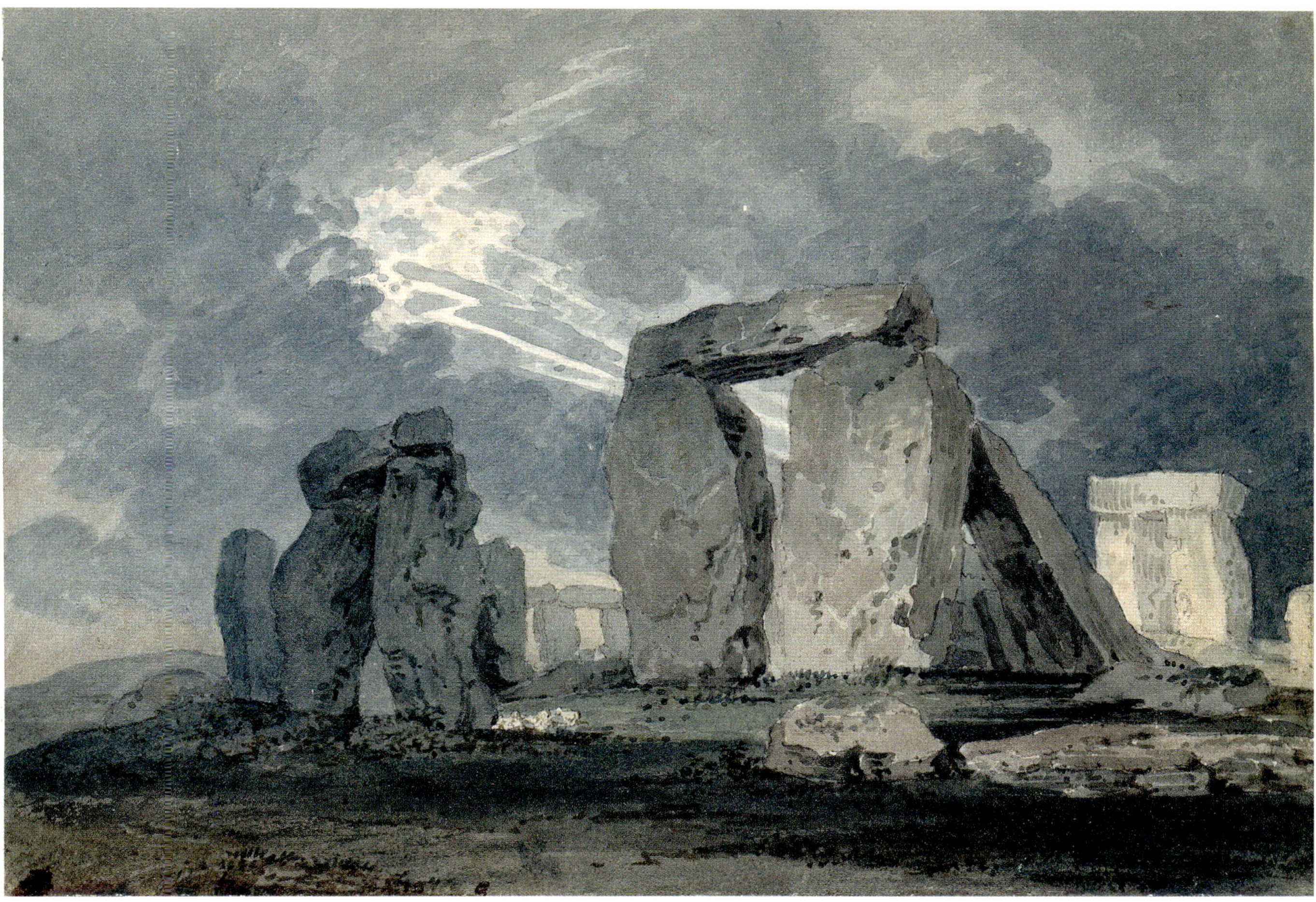

Fig. 136
THOMAS GIRTIN (1775–1802)
Stonehenge During a Thunderstorm
c.1794
Pencil and watercolour, 10.4 × 14.7 cm
Ashmolean Museum, Oxford (WA 1916.8)

several of the faults that Christopher Chippindale has perceptively analysed as common to many views of Stonehenge: a sense of confusion about the interrelationship of the stones that is unintelligible to anyone who has not visited the site; no depth of perspective; and an absence of scale.[6] The latter was often overcome by introducing ridiculously small figures, as in the engraving after Thomas Hogg for Boswell's *Picturesque Views* (see fig. 2).

Both of Turner's sketches show Stonehenge from roughly the south/south-west side, near where the trilithon had fallen, which was one of the most popular viewpoints. They were included in a notebook that Turner filled with ideas that generally found an outlet in his exhibited works around 1800–2; however, he is not known to have featured Stonehenge in any of his paintings in this period.

When he returned there in 1811 he made a much fuller survey on eight sheets in a medium-sized sketchbook (figs 140–47), as well as a handful of thumbnail sketches in the pocketbook he had used throughout the tour for his poetic ideas (fig. 139). Although they are little more than rudimentary memoranda, they provide a valuable record of the position of the stones at this date, several of which have since been returned to their 'original' positions, such as the eye-catching slanting sarsen, one of the inner horseshoe. In a couple of the sketches Turner got right up close to the sarsens, using their bulk to define his compositions (figs 139–40). More often, he recognised that the location of the stone circle in the surrounding landscape contributed substantially to its visual potency. It is apparent in these wider vistas that his visit coincided with the arrival of sunset. In one sketch the moon, looking fairly full, rises behind clouds that make it impossible to see precisely what stage in the cycle it has reached (fig. 146). Turner would have been at Stonehenge in 1811 towards the beginning

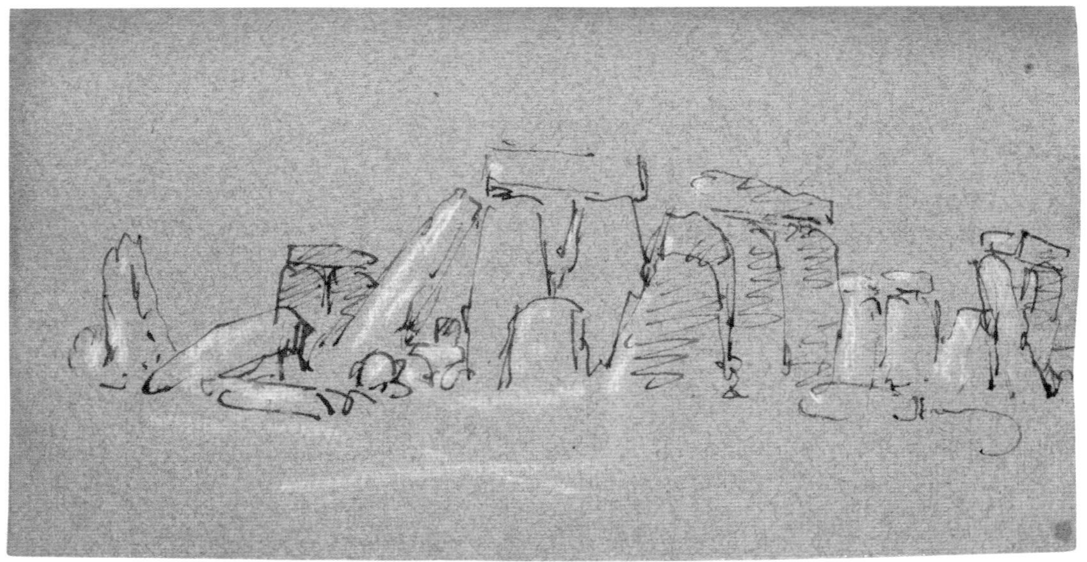

Fig. 137
Stonehenge from the South-East
*c.*1799–1800
Pen and ink on blue paper, 13.8 × 21.5 cm
From the 'Studies for Pictures' sketchbook
Tate (D04092 / TB LXIX 80a)

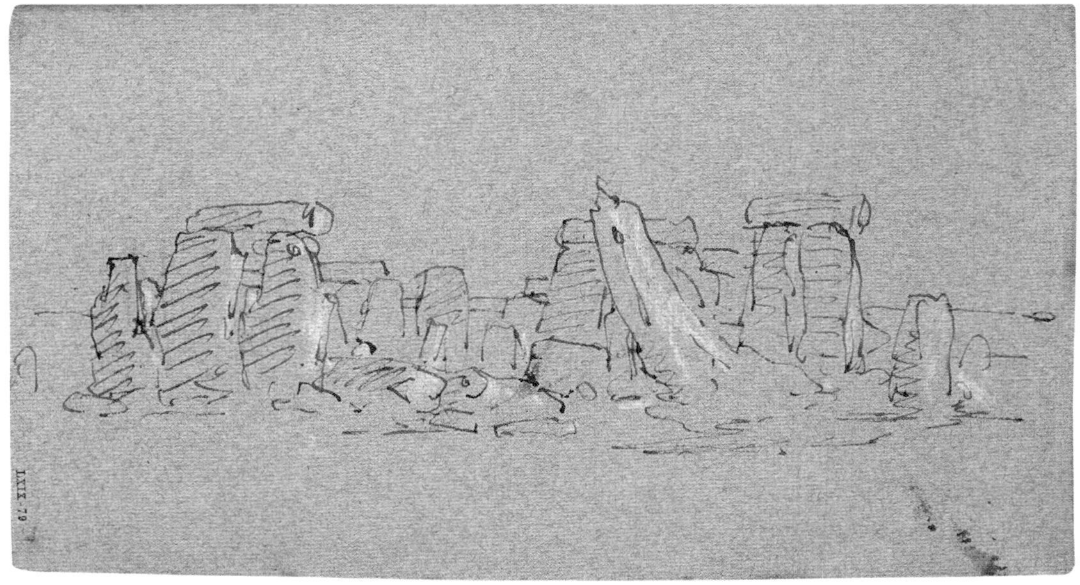

Fig. 138
Stonehenge from the South-West
*c.*1799–1800
Pen and ink on blue paper, 13.8 × 21.5 cm
From the 'Studies for Pictures' sketchbook
Tate (D04090 / TB LXIX 79)

of September, when the full moon would have risen on the 2nd around 10.35pm.[7] Whether on that day, or one close to it, the presence of this detail indicates that Turner was, as usual, working as late as the light would permit.

Witnessing the sunset at Stonehenge, followed by the onset of twilight, was a deeply formative experience, as we shall see. Turner made an incidental note of the effect in his pocketbook when recording the view back to the stones from above the junction of the main road towards Exeter with that to Shrewton and Devizes.[8] Some time later he gave this idea fuller expression on one of the remaining blank leaves of the larger sketchbook (fig. 147). Here the sun has already disappeared below the horizon, its last rays silhouetting the lintels, while the details of the foreground sink into the indistinctness of dusk. Down the road a lone figure stands near the signpost at the junction. It is a haunting and somewhat bleak impression of Stonehenge, known to thousands because of its use by Penguin books as the cover to *Tess of the d'Urbervilles* (1889): Turner's Stonehenge transformed into Thomas Hardy's Wessex.[9]

Although it naturally lay on his way back to London, Turner's visit in 1811 may have been stimulated by the ongoing publication of

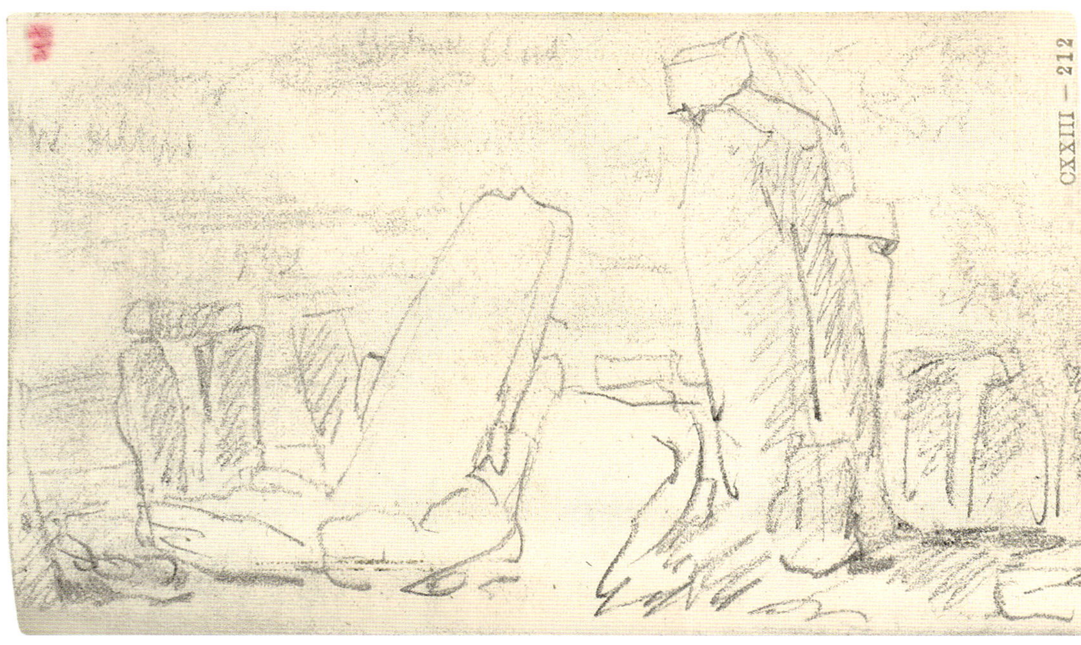

Fig. 139
Stonehenge; the Inner Sarsen Horseshoe from the South
1811
Pencil, 7.5 × 11.7 cm
From the Devonshire Coast No. 1 sketchbook
Tate (D08750 / TB CXXIII 212)

The Ancient History of South Wiltshire (1810–12), the first of Colt Hoare's exhaustive accounts of his county, which documented the excavations he had paid for of the ancient barrows around Stonehenge and elsewhere. These were actually undertaken and directed by William Cunnington (1754–1810), but after his death, during the process of preparing the research for publication, it was inevitably Colt Hoare's text that received the praise of the critics. *The Quarterly Review*, for example, considered that his work on Stonehenge demonstrated the 'sobriety, modesty and discretion which become a modern antiquary in treating a subject of such difficulty'.[10] One of the most urgent questions that had required addressing about Stonehenge was its age. In his rival publication, John Britton claimed it was Roman – an assertion that Colt Hoare and Cunnington had been able to disprove. However, the lack of a useful system of quantifying and stratifying ancient history would, for that entire generation of archaeologists, prove an obstacle to the proper understanding of the monument's true antiquity. Current research suggests Stonehenge was an active ritual site for 1,400 years from 3000 BC, but the construction of the stones is still contentiously assigned to the period between 2600 and 2300 BC.[11]

The question of the ordering of time and history was something that preoccupied Turner's great friend Walter Fawkes, the former Whig MP and Yorkshire landowner, with whom he frequently stayed between 1808 and 1824. Fawkes created a number of albums for which Turner provided watercolours, including a 'Book of Birds' and a set of 'Historical Vignettes' charting the period between the Reformation and the Glorious Revolution, and celebrating particularly the part played by family-member the Parliamentarian Thomas Fairfax. Another

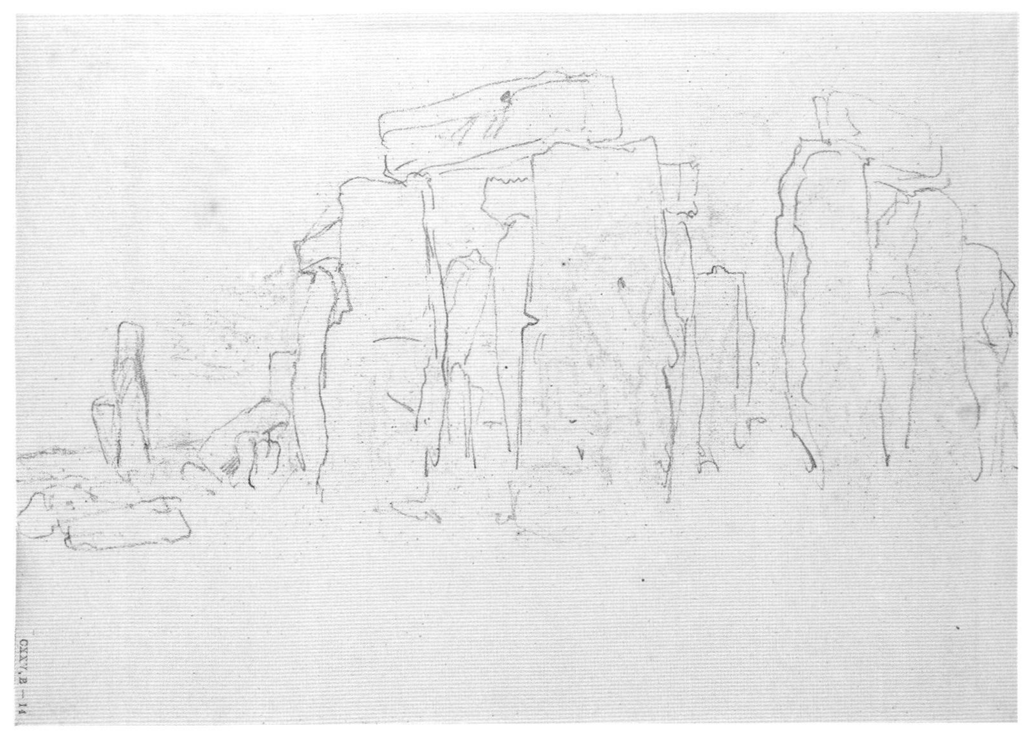

Fig. 140
Stonehenge from the South-East
1811
Pencil, 18.2 × 22.2 cm
From the Stonehenge sketchbook
Tate (D41387/ TB CXXVb 14)

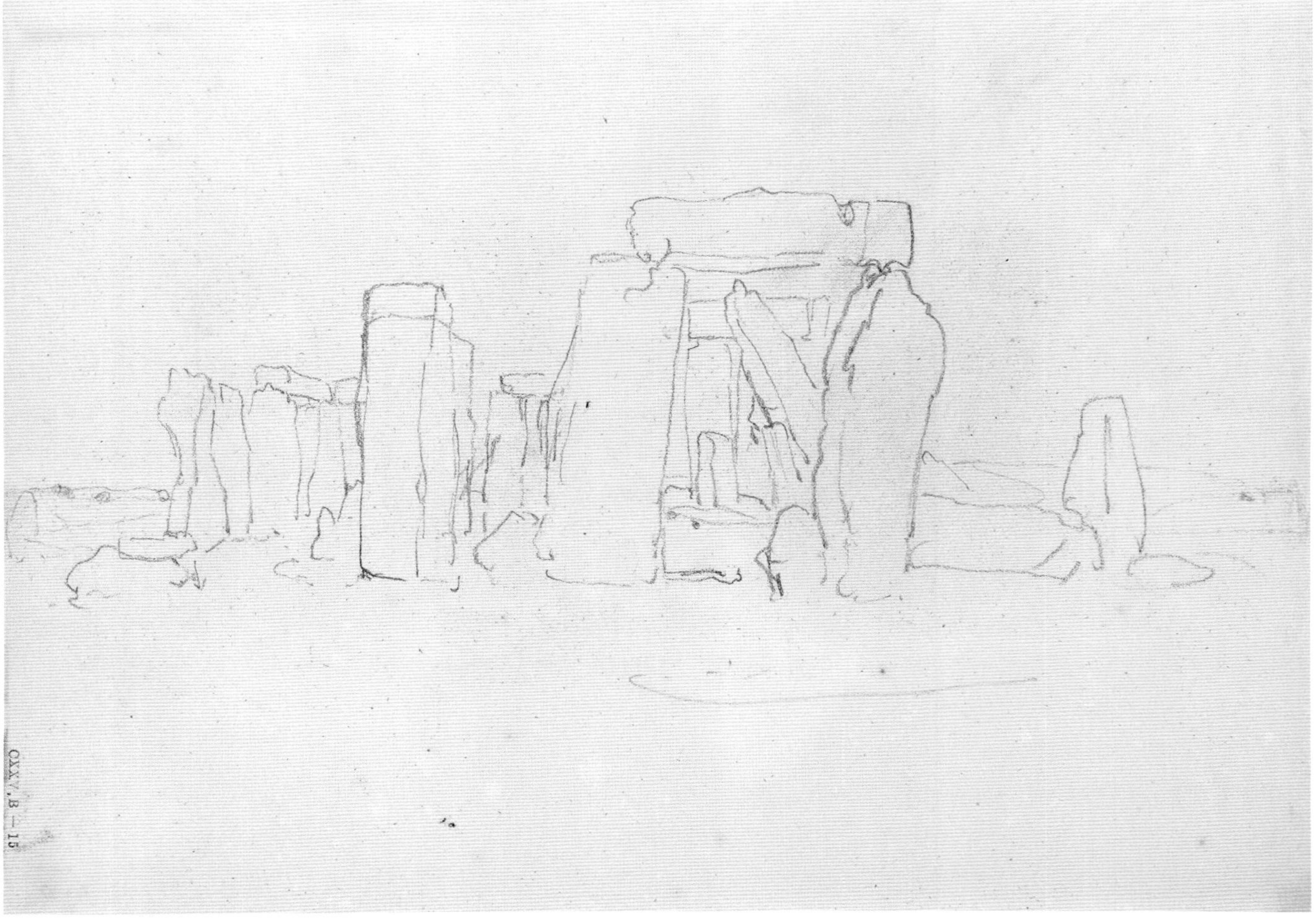

Fig. 141
Stonehenge from the North-West
1811
Pencil, 18.2 × 22.2 cm
From the Stonehenge sketchbook
Tate (D41388 / TB CXXVb 15)

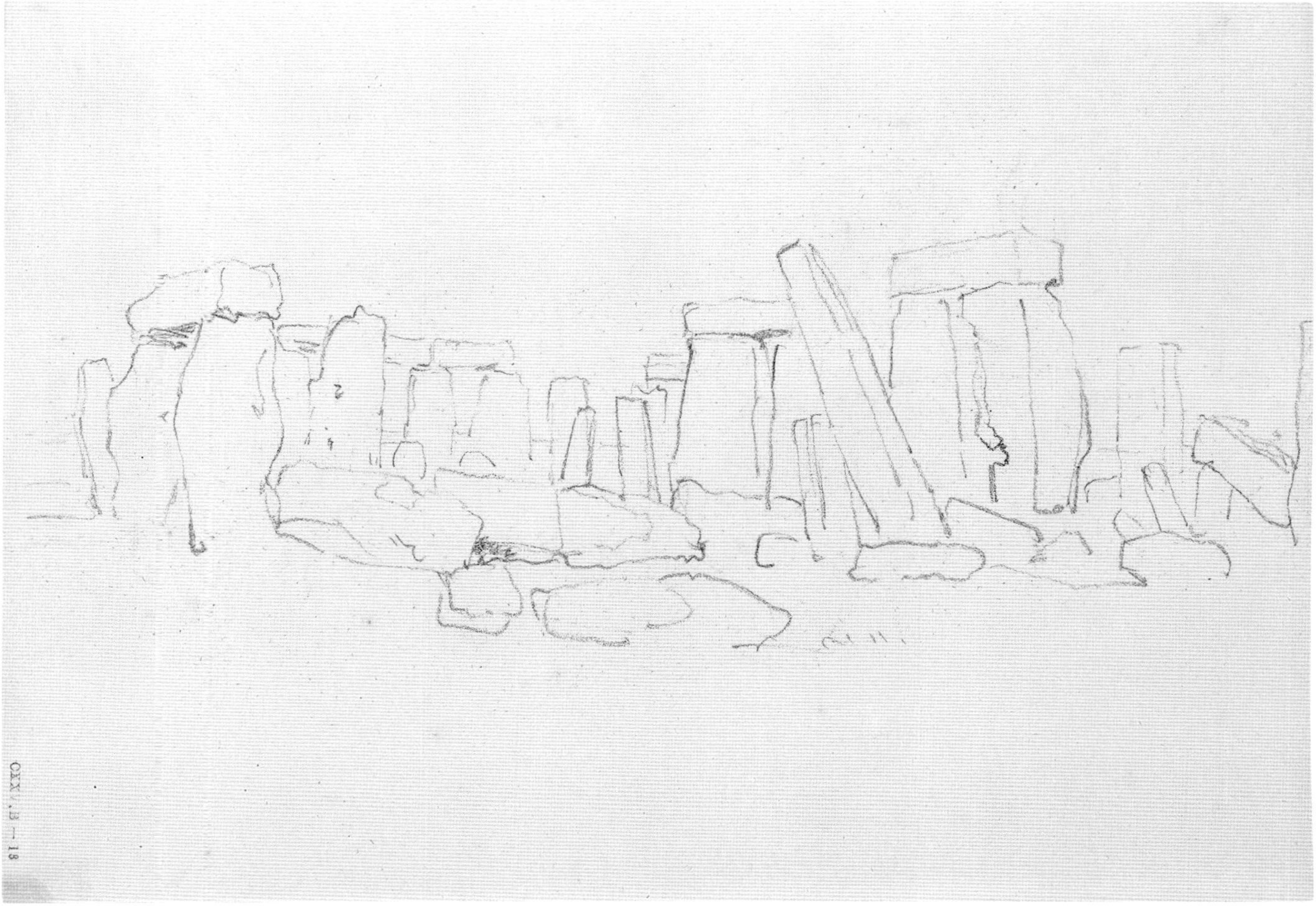

Fig. 142
Stonehenge: the Inner Sarsen Horseshoe from the South-West
1811
Pencil, 18.2 × 22.2 cm
From the Stonehenge sketchbook
Tate (D41386 / TB CXXVb 13)

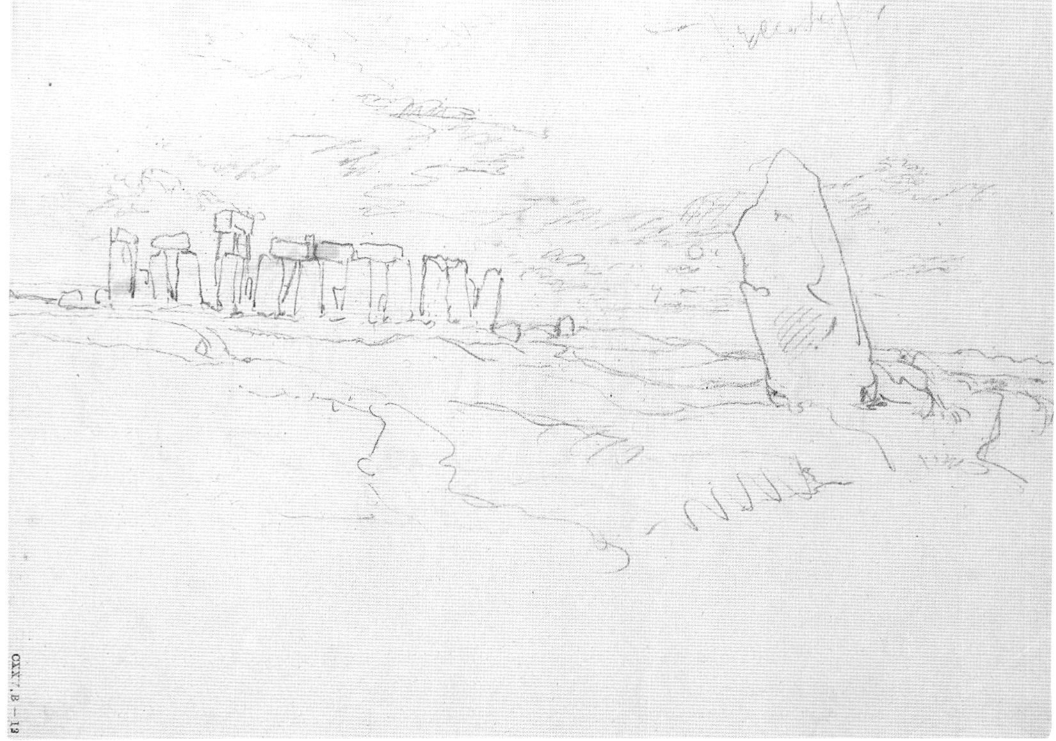

Fig. 143
Stonehenge from the North-East, with the Setting Sun Beyond the Heel Stone
1811
Pencil, 18.1 × 22.2 cm
From the Stonehenge sketchbook
Tate (D41385 / TB CXXVb 12)

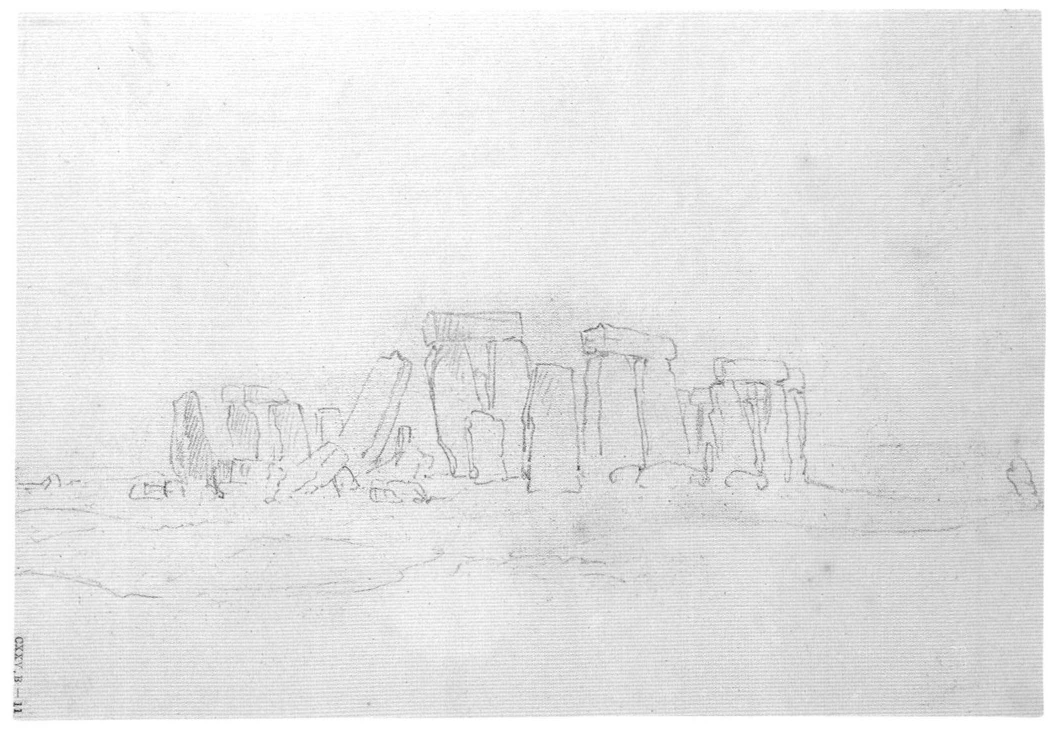

Fig. 144
Stonehenge from the South, with the Heel Stone Beyond
1811
Pencil, 18 × 22.2 cm
From the Stonehenge sketchbook
Tate (D41384 / TB CXXVB 11)

Fig. 145
Stonehenge from the South-East, with the Setting Sun
1811
Pencil, 18 × 22.2 cm
From the Stonehenge sketchbook
Tate (D41383 / TB CXXVB 10)

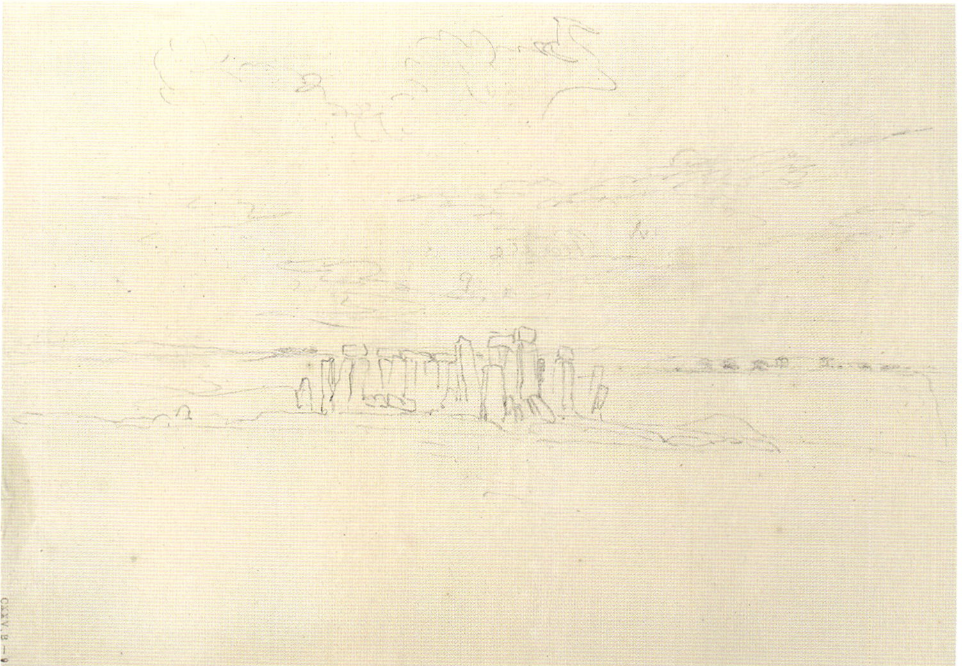

Fig. 146
Stonehenge from the West, with the Heel Stone Beyond
1811
Pencil, 18 × 22.2 cm
From the Stonehenge sketchbook
Tate (D41382 / TB CXXVb 9)

Fig. 147
Stonehenge at Sunset
1811
Watercolour, 17.2 × 22.3 cm
From the Stonehenge sketchbook
Private collection

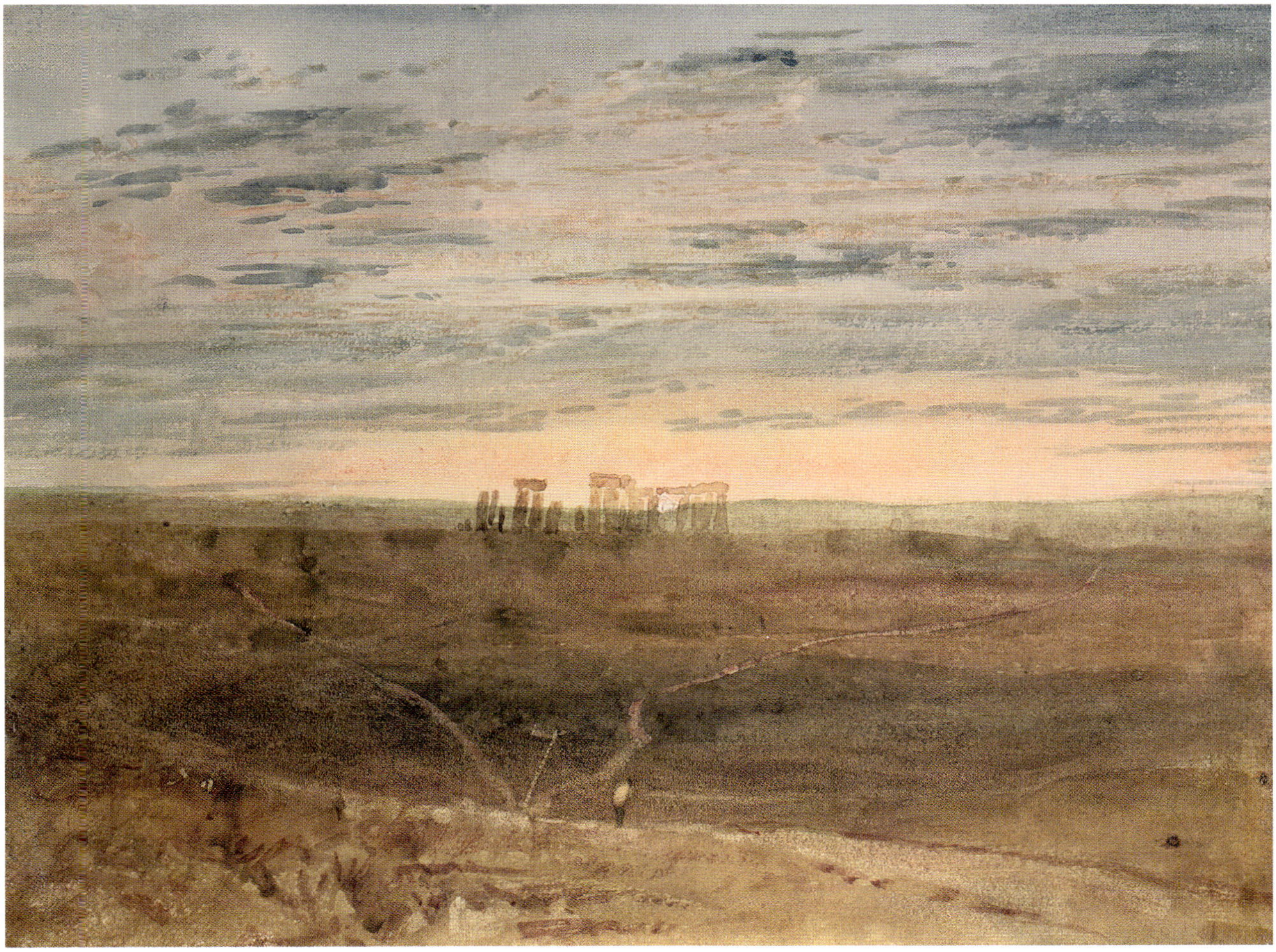

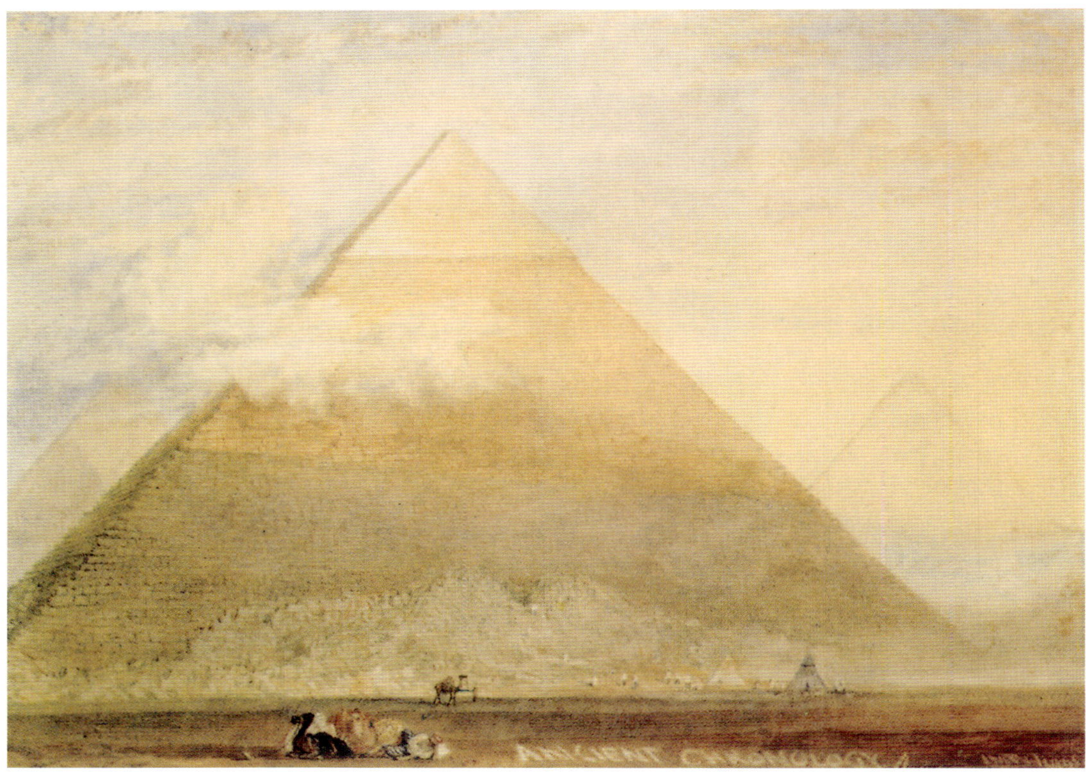

Fig. 148
The Pyramids: Ancient Chronology
c.1822
Watercolour, 20.6 × 27.7 cm
Private collection

of these projects was an 'Ancient and Modern Chronology', although evidently nothing like the all-consuming endeavour undertaken by Edward Casaubon in George Eliot's *Middlemarch* (1871–72). Fawkes had, in fact, actually published his *Chronology of the History of Modern Europe* in 1810. Over ten years later, around 1822, Turner painted two watercolours to act as frontispieces for the family albums: a view of the Great Pyramid of Khufu at Giza for the 'Ancient' part (fig. 148); and one of Stonehenge for the more 'Modern' (fig. 149). This will no doubt amuse contemporary historians, now that the pyramid is thought to date from roughly the same sort of timeframe as the sarsen stone circle at the British monument. But it highlights the misconceptions then still shaping the common idea of Stonehenge.

Turner's design is a very stylised rendering, restoring and extending the lintel-topped sarsen circle; yet its origins lie in the sketch he made from the south-east (fig. 137). The introduction of a 'listless shepherd' and his flock was already a standard trope in Stonehenge imagery and literature, from Hannah More to William Wordsworth.[12] More striking is the position of the sun in relation to the stones. During the early nineteenth century artists began to reflect the theory of Stonehenge's alignment to the rising sun on the summer solstice.[13] So the crimson sky of Turner's sunset perhaps also introduces a cautionary symbolism beyond the associations of the old saying:

> Red sky at night, shepherd's delight;
> Red sky in the morning, shepherd's warning.

He would develop the idea of menace a few years later in the well-known *England and Wales* watercolour (fig. 154).

Before then he painted a pair of studies that do repeat the sunset effect he had seen back in 1811 (figs 151–2). The first depicts the approach of a coach on the main road, with Stonehenge in the background, perhaps recalling Turner's experience after he had finished sketching. The related sketch shows the scene closer to Salisbury, where the cathedral is silhouetted

OPPOSITE ABOVE:
Fig. 149
Stonehenge: Modern Chronology
c.1822
Watercolour, 20.9 × 26.6 cm
Private collection, c/o Lowell Libson

OPPOSITE BELOW:
Fig. 150
JAMES BASIRE (1730–1802) after PHILIP CROCKER (1780–1840)
West View of Stonehenge
1826
Engraving, 24.2 × 36.3 cm
From Colt Hoare, *History of Modern Wiltshire*
British Library, London

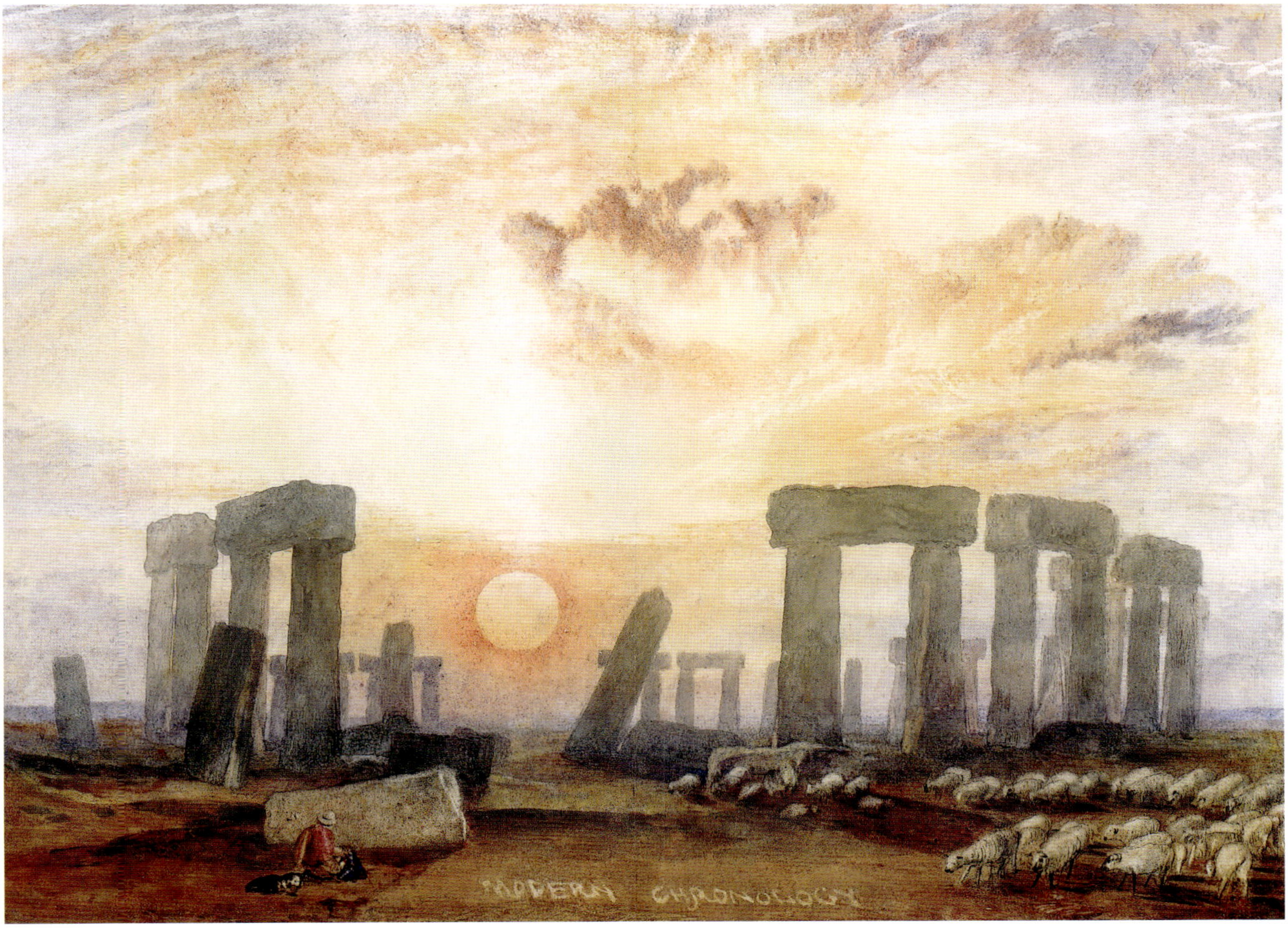

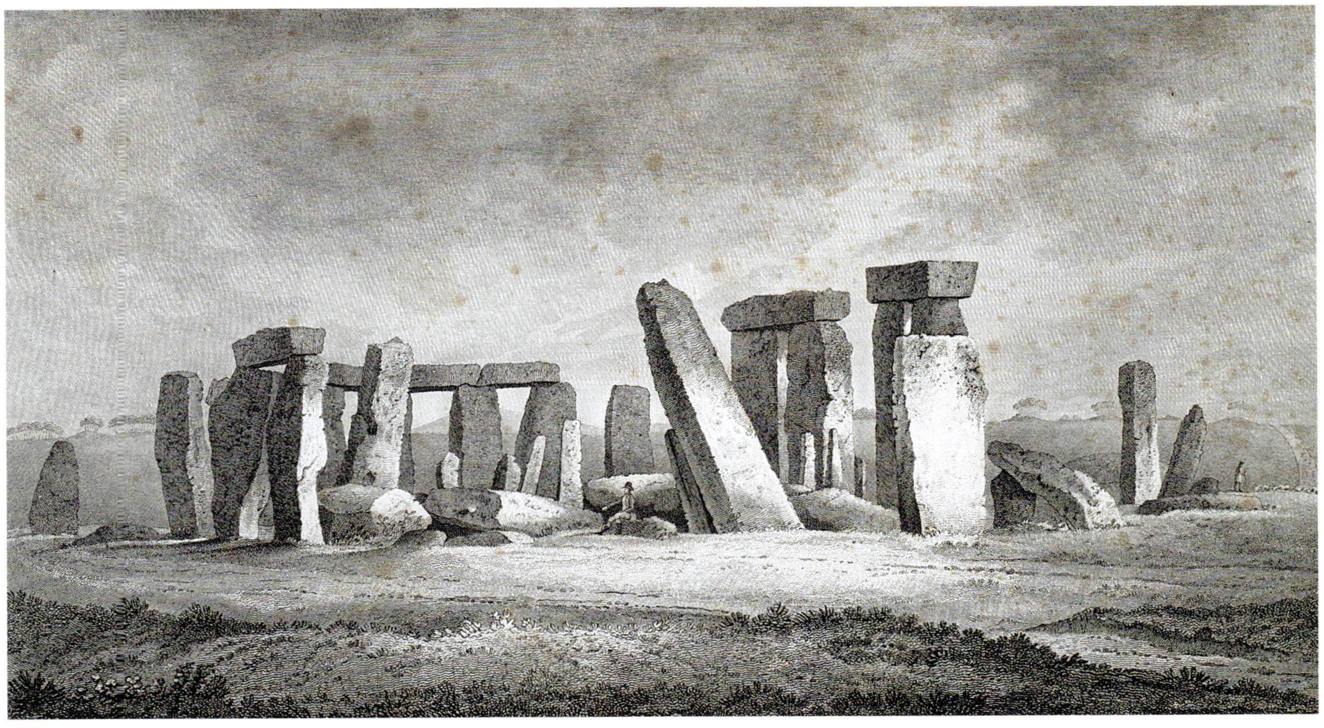

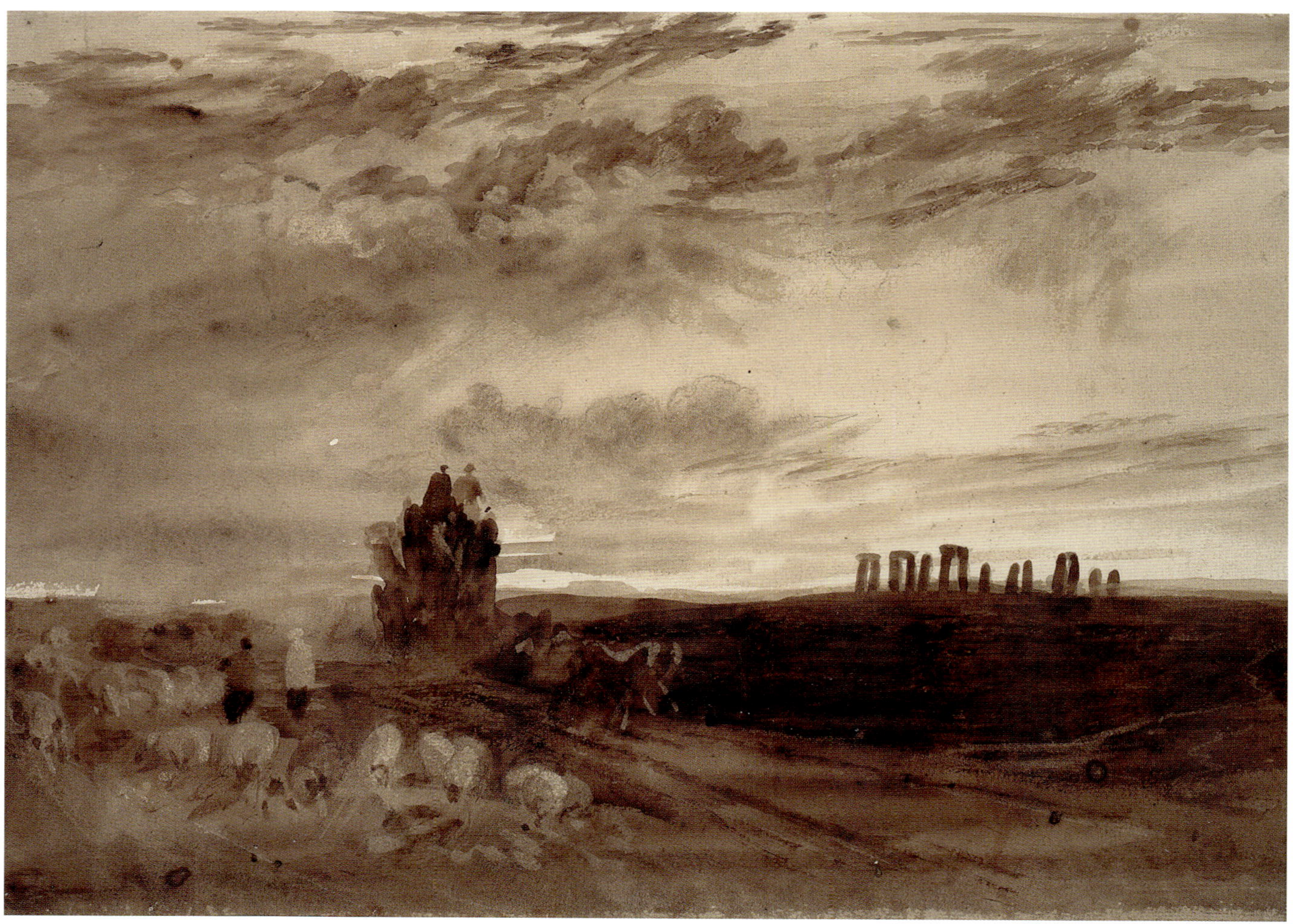

Fig. 151
Stonehenge at Sunset
c.1824
Pencil and watercolour, 19.4 × 27 cm
Probably from the Farnley-Munro sketchbook
Museum of Fine Arts, Boston, Anonymous Gift (59.795)

against the sky.[14] These were made in a sketchbook that was in use in 1824, the year Stonehenge was acquired from the Marquess of Queensberry's heirs by Sir Edmund Antrobus. Turner was still occasionally working in monochrome or sepia washes of the kind he deployed when producing designs for his *Liber Studiorum*. This was a period of innovation in the engraving process, with the introduction of new steel plates, and Turner tested their capability to reproduce extremes of light and shade in a series of designs featuring stormy occluded skies, generally known as the Little Liber. He was almost certainly assisted in this experimentation by the engraver Thomas Lupton (1791–1873), who is assumed to have created the unpublished mezzotint of the Stonehenge view.[15]

The only image of Stonehenge Turner actually published was that already mentioned, for the *England and Wales* series (fig. 154). Although it is clearly related to the view of Salisbury, they were deliberately published in different parts, separated by three years. There appears to have been some initial distaste by Turner's publisher for the Stonehenge view, although it was the first to appear.[16] In the letterpress that accompanied engraved impressions, H.E. Lloyd provided a summary on current thought about Stonehenge, but did not offer any comment on the scene unfolding in Turner's image. Yet this is arguably the most troubling image in the entire series, showing a dead shepherd, recently struck down by the lightning storm that continues its path of destruction through the flock, striking now at the heart of the stone circle. Writing about the picture in the final volume of *Modern Painters* (1860), John Ruskin described this effect as

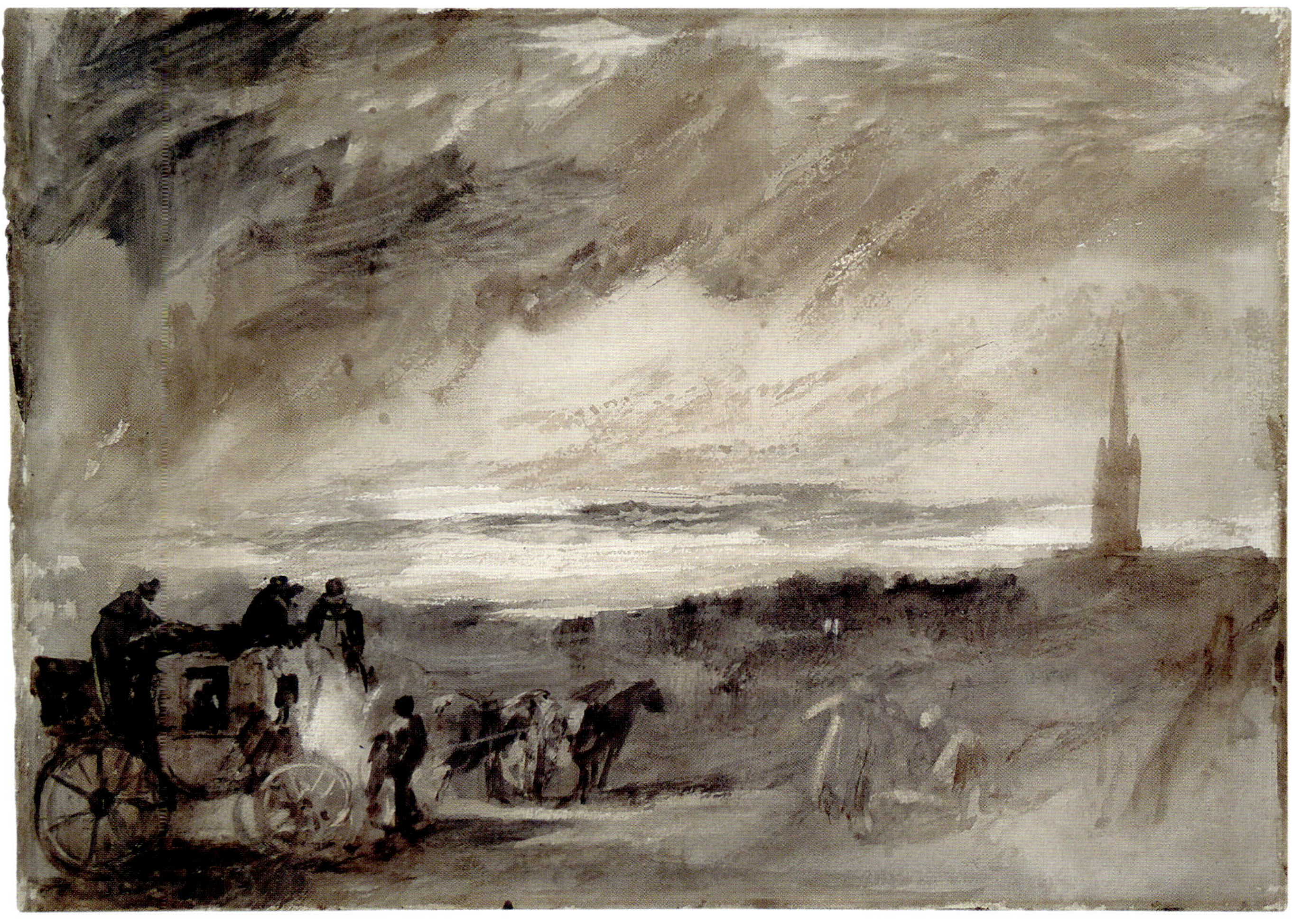

Fig. 152
Passengers Beside a Coach near Salisbury
*c.*1824
Pencil and watercolour, *c.*19.5 × 27 cm
From the Farnley-Munro sketchbook
Private collection

the 'cloud of judgment', and interpreted the devastation caused by the lightning as righteous punishment visited on the former Druid temple, an interpretation based on a paternalistic reading of the related watercolour of Salisbury.[17] This certainly provides a neat contrast, but Turner was evidently thinking specifically about the Christian religion when preparing both works and his study for Stonehenge is inscribed 'XRS', alluding to the Greek word 'Christos'.[18] Set against the turmoil in the Church in the late 1820s, the death of the shepherd at Stonehenge could perhaps therefore be read as a lament for the loss of leadership and stability that the Church had traditionally provided. Alternatively, the fallen body, watched over by the baying sheepdog, might constitute a kind of desolate pietà that is succeeded by the more consoling image of Salisbury with its guardian shepherd. At any rate, death by lightning was an occasional hazard of rural life that was reported in the papers throughout the 1820s. Coincidentally, the phrase 'lightning before death' was also used in June 1828 to describe the troubled state of Ultra-Toryism, which was then considered to be in its death throes.[19]

As a topographical record of the site the watercolour has been criticised by some as, at best, 'a potent, sublime vision, whose light and colours owe little to Wiltshire', and at worse, 'hopeless'.[20] Once again, the composition harks back to one of the two early pen and ink sketches (fig. 138), but a more recent influence would have been James Basire's 1826 engraving after Philip Crocker's design for Colt Hoare's *History of Modern Wiltshire* (fig. 150). Moving between the two sources, Turner remained unsure of the actual form of the circle to the right of the

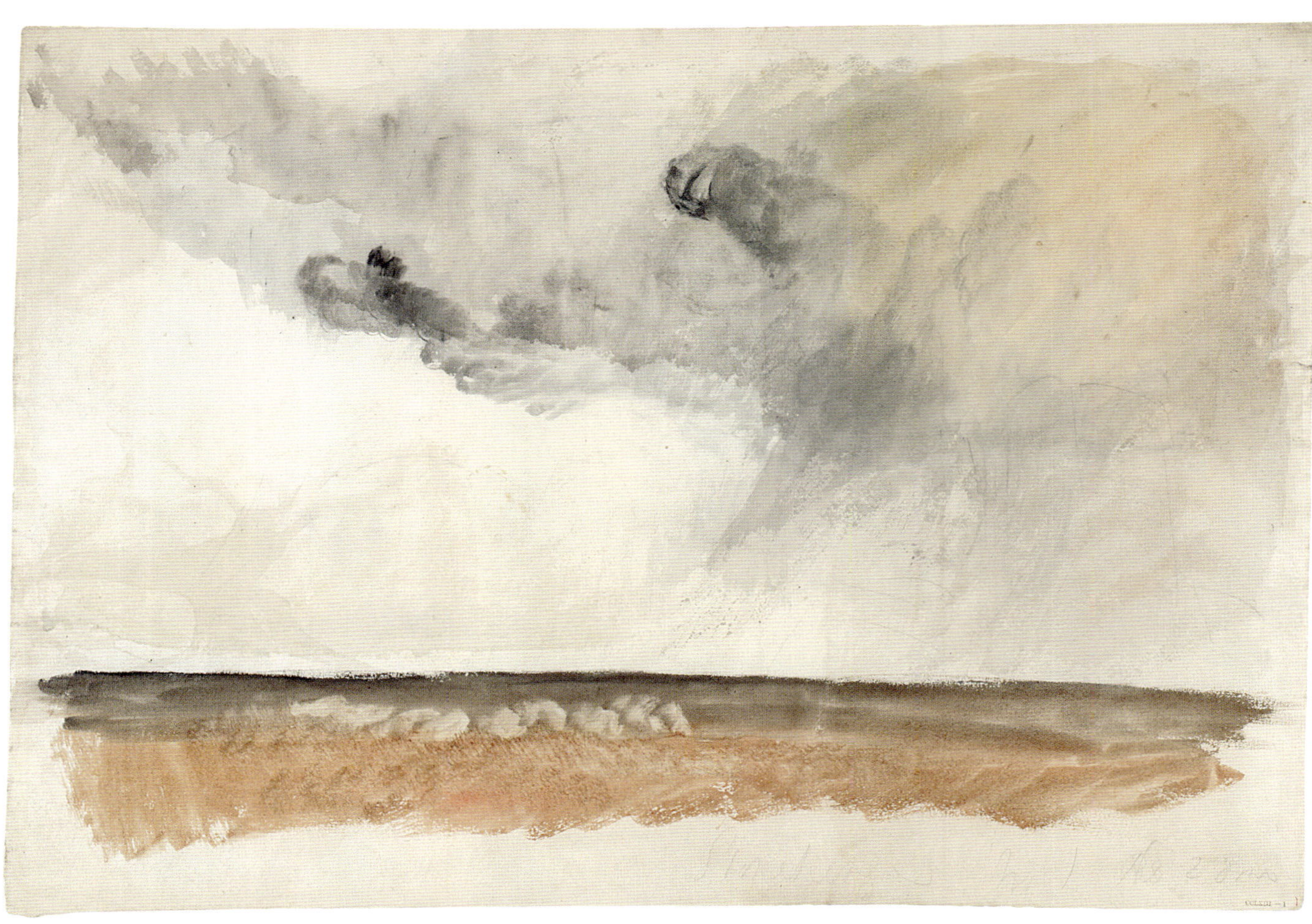

Fig. 153
Stonehenge: Preparatory Study
c.1827–28
Watercolour,
34.6 × 48.8 cm
Tate (D25123 / TB CCLXIII 1)

trilithon pair and began to introduce stones like those in the Crocker image, but then left them undeveloped. (However, his own engraver, Robert Wallis, attempted to make sense of this fudged detail in the printed version.)

Turner's evocation of the blasted heath of Salisbury Plain is possibly best appreciated for its sky, which Ruskin praised as 'the standard of storm-drawing, both for the over-whelming power and gigantic proportions and spaces of its loud forms, and for the tremendous qualities of lurid and sulphurous colours which are gained in them.'[21] The scene represents the culmination of the troubled, menacing and darker associations of Stonehenge that colour the Romantic period. By 1829, when the engraved version was published, the site was becoming the popular tourist destination that we know today. Visiting it that year, the future photographer William Fox Talbot grumbled about the carriages and the people enjoying their picnics.[22] It was, of course, still possible to meditate on the history and purpose of the stones. Something of their sublimity, however, had been tamed and lost.

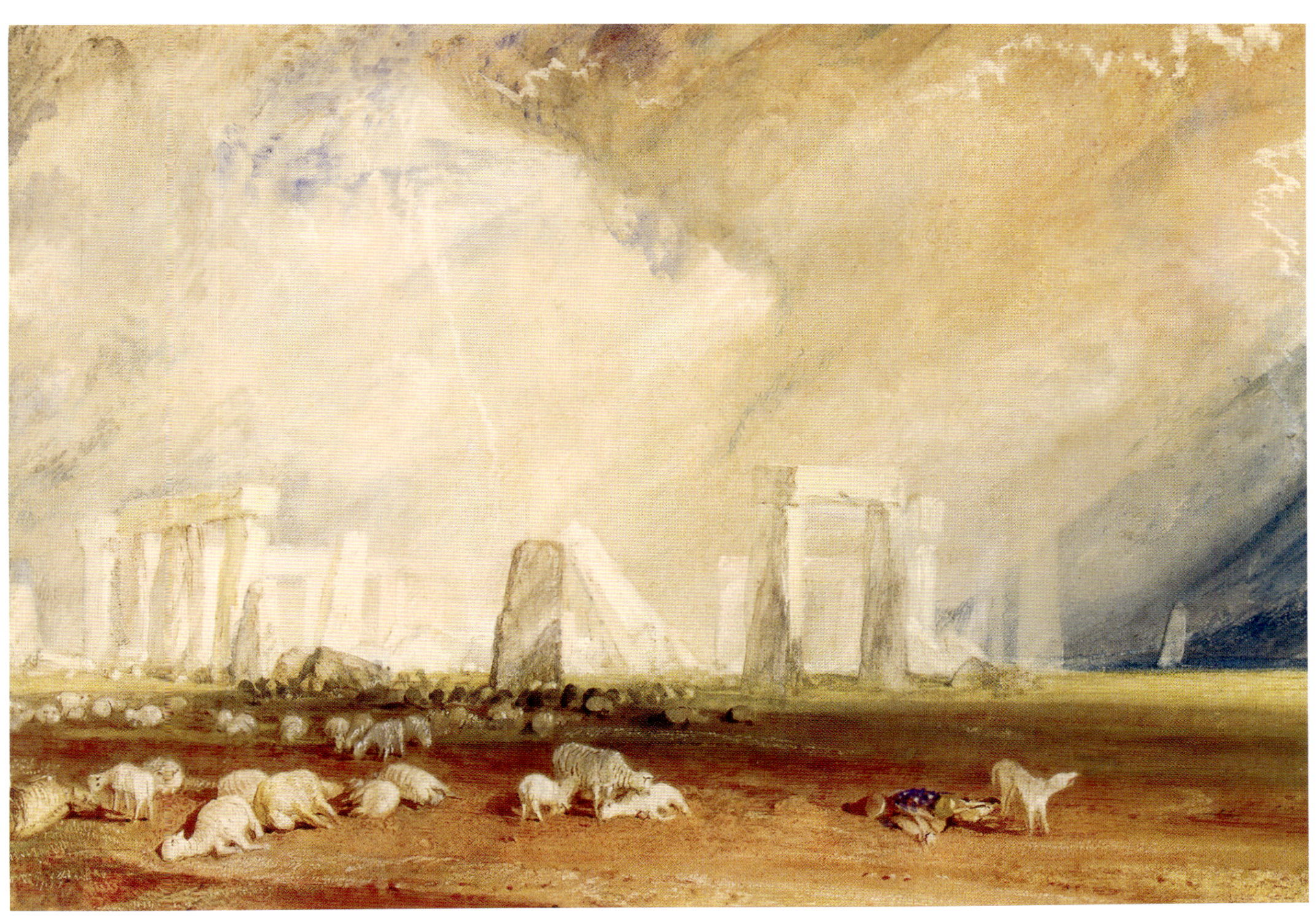

Fig. 154
Stonehenge, Wiltshire
*c.*1827–28
Watercolour,
27.9 × 40.4 cm
For *Picturesque Views in England and Wales*
The Salisbury Museum
(W811)

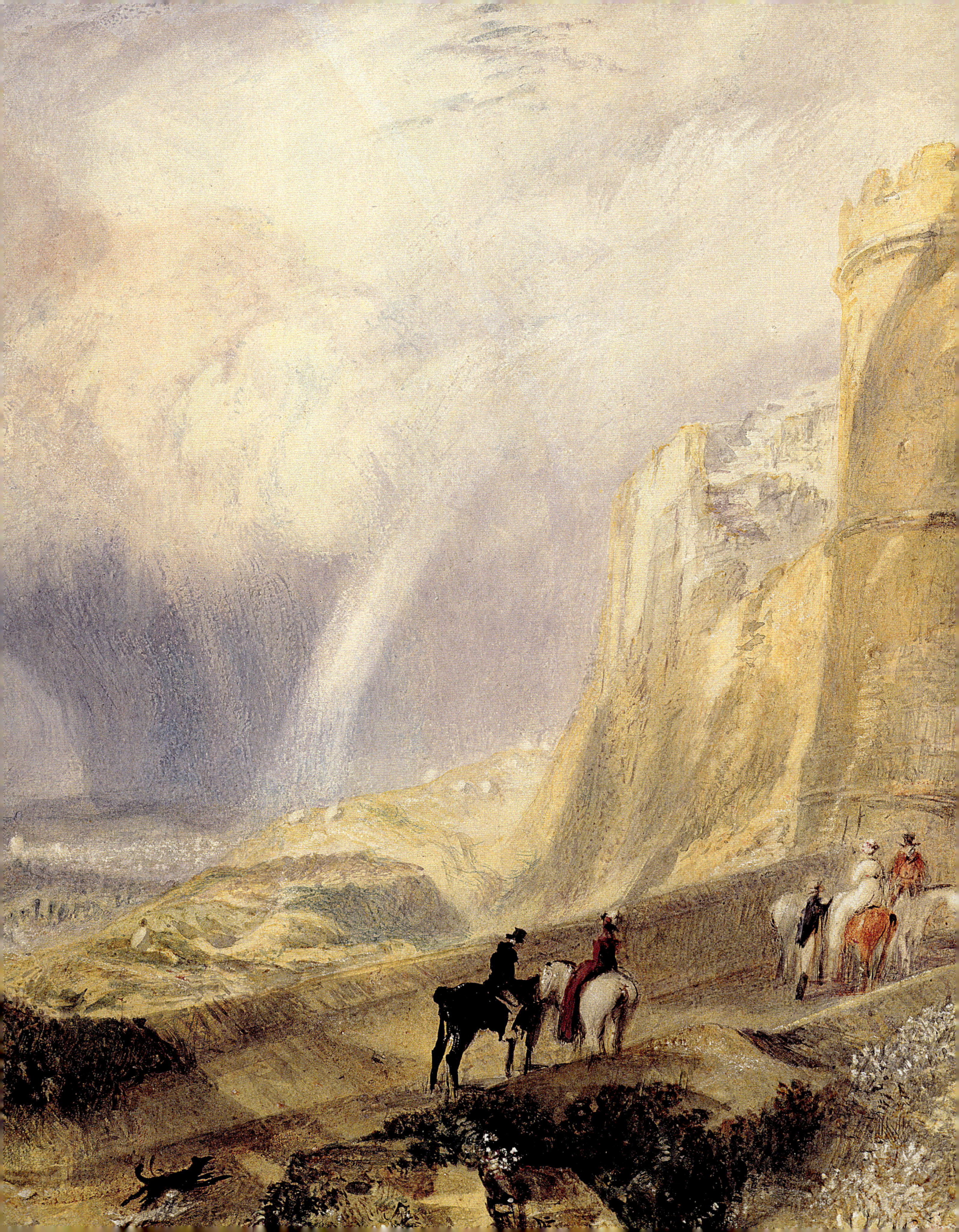

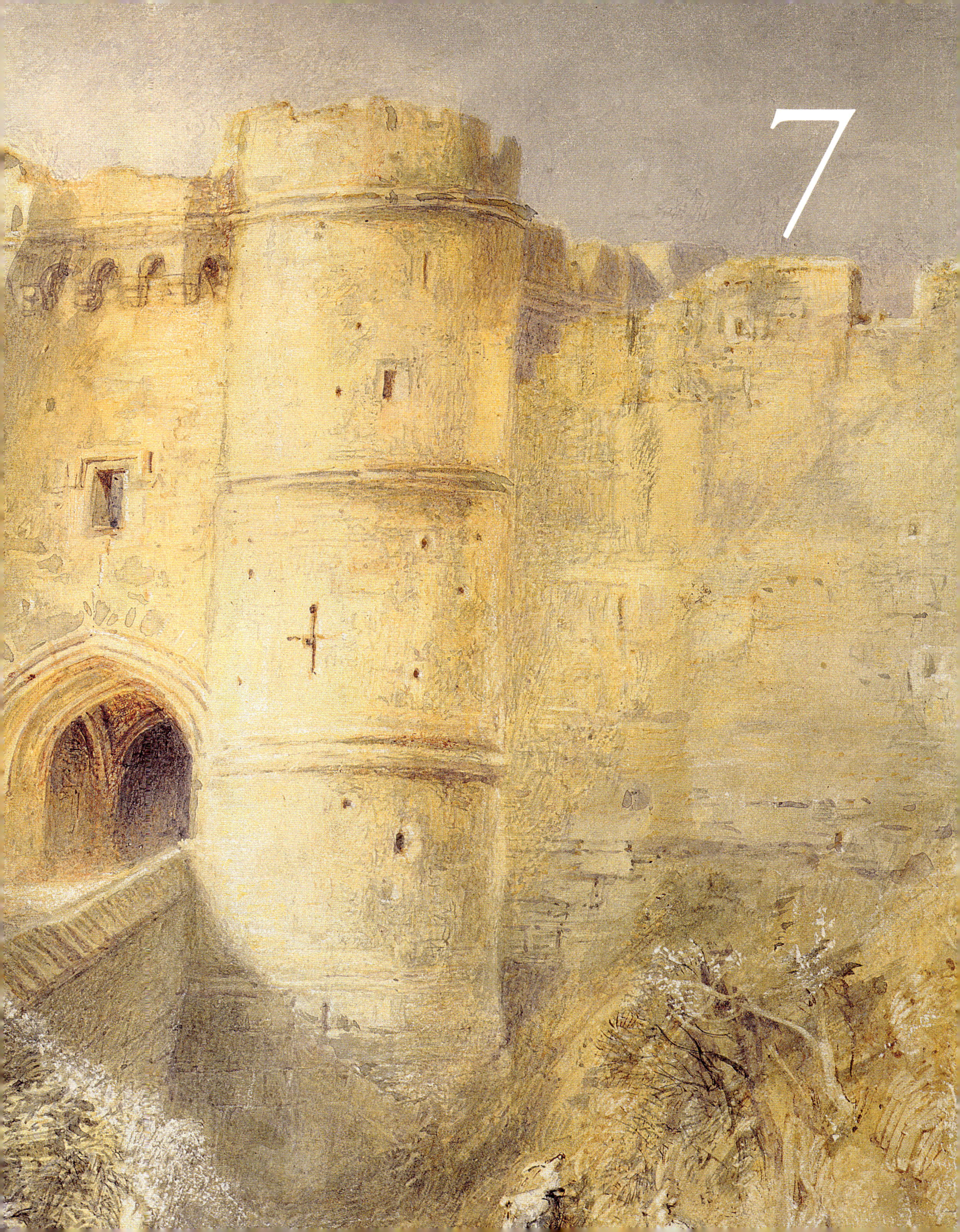

7

CASTLES OLD AND NEW: The Isle of Wight

PREVIOUS PAGES: ***Carisbrooke Castle, Isle of Wight*** (detail) (see fig. 161)

The gentle beauties of the Isle of Wight had only recently begun to attract artists when the Revd William Gilpin (1724–1804), the influential, self-appointed arbiter of taste in matters of landscape, got round to assessing them in 1798.[1] Contradicting what the picture-makers themselves had discerned, he pronounced the island *un*-Picturesque. Apart from its rocky coast, he dismissed much of the island as 'a large garden, or rather a field'.[2]

Turner's first visit to the Isle of Wight in 1795 pre-dates these judgements by Gilpin, the Prebendary of Salisbury, and was very much concerned with traditionally Picturesque material. His guide may have been the *Tour of the Isle of Wight* by John Hassell, which combines descriptions of Winchester (see figs 10–11), Southampton (see fig. 12) and neighbouring Netley Abbey (see fig. 13), as well as the excursion across the Solent.[3] But a more personal influence for the trip came from the versatile artist de Loutherbourg, who had toured the island a year earlier. The young Turner evidently admired de Loutherbourg's painting techniques and aimed to match them at the Royal Academy exhibition of 1796 in his *Fishermen at Sea*, the impressive moonlit marine scene set in the waters off the western end of the Isle of Wight.[4]

The 1795 tour concentrated primarily on Newport, plus the south and west of the island, and cannot have lasted more than a week; it occupies only around 30 pages of the sketchbook Turner was using that summer. These reflect his usual habit of recording churches, castles and any other notable historic buildings that would be of topographical interest (figs 155–56, 159), but also reveal his increasing confidence in purely landscape subjects, such as the island's characteristic coves and bays (fig. 158). These latter sketches induced John Landseer to commission a series of watercolours that he intended to have engraved, although this never fully came to pass.[5]

There is only one sketch of anything on the east side of the island, showing the windmill at Bembridge, which may hint that it was the last study Turner made before crossing the Solent back to Portsmouth. Another subject that appealed to Turner's sense of the Picturesque was Chale Farm (fig. 157), which he developed as an exhibition watercolour (now very faded).[6]

Turner also made a distant view of the nearby estate of Sir Richard Worsley and evidently sketched Appuldurcombe House itself, according to his list of 'Order'd Drawings'. Both the sketch and any watercolour derived from it are now untraced, but it is probable that the relevant sheet was detached and then worked up, like the view of the Butter Cross, Winchester, now at The Whitworth, The University of Manchester, which must once have been part of the sketchbook (see fig. 11). Appuldurcombe had been enlarged in the mid-1770s by the seemingly ubiquitous James Wyatt.[7] After Worsley's death in 1805, it passed to his niece, Henrietta, who married Charles Anderson-Pelham (1781–1846); he will reappear later in this chapter.

In the years after his visit, Turner adapted some of his Isle of Wight sketches as watercolours for his pupils to copy. One subject was Cowes Castle, the sixteenth-century round blockhouse on the west side of the mouth of the River Medina (fig. 155). He collaborated on a version of this with the talented Julia Bennet (1797–1867), something she commemorated by inscribing the sheet, 'First with Mr Turner, 1797'.[8] She appears to have been one of his most promising students and remained a good friend; her sister subsequently married Sir John Swinburne,

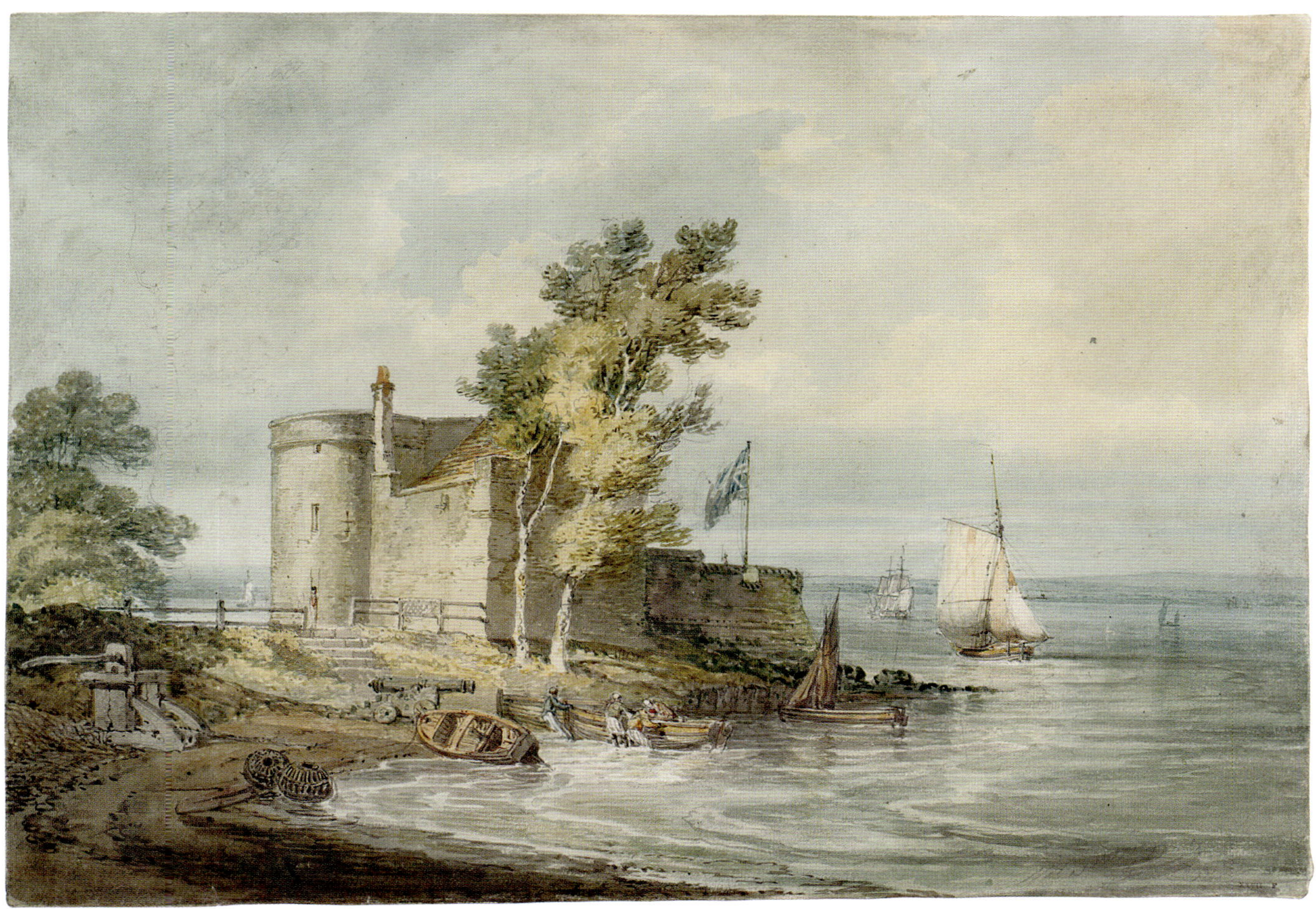

Fig. 155
West Cowes Castle, Isle of Wight
*c.*1796
Pencil and watercolour, 30.5 × 43.1 cm
Tate (D00667 / TB XXVII F)

who became a Turner collector, proving that the female links of sisters and wives, although less obvious, were just as important in securing artistic patronage.

Another scene that Turner used in teaching was the island's chief historic monument, Carisbrooke Castle, which even Gilpin conceded was 'an object perhaps the best worth seeing of any in the island'.[9] The castle occupies a hillside beyond Newport, so made an impression as visitors arrived (fig. 156). At some point after 1807 Turner revisited the view he had made of the castle from the south-west (fig. 159).[10] The impetus for returning to the subject then seems likely to have been his involvement in the business of printmaking, possibly spurred by the publication of a view of the gateway at Carisbrooke by de Loutherbourg a couple of years earlier.

Turner would make his own depiction of the gateway around 1827–28, for the series of engraved *Picturesque Views in England and Wales* (fig. 161), but before then he had returned again to Carisbrooke (fig. 160). While there he produced a group of five colour studies, painted in lush verdant colours, with rosy, mauve shadows, suggestive of full summer: three are in the Tate Collection; the other two are at the Fitzwilliam Museum in Cambridge.[11] In each of them the width of what is now the meagre trickle of Lukely Brook is exaggerated so that it looks more like a significant river. These watercolours had previously been linked with various other locations, but were identified as Carisbrooke by William Fox in 2003.[12] The dating of these works remains to be resolved and may be connected with a watercolour of the city of Trier (or Trèves) on the River Mosel (Moselle), painted on a similar sheet, using the same range of colours, which must date from after 1824 (Private collection).

There are, however, grounds to believe that they relate to a previously unknown trip to the

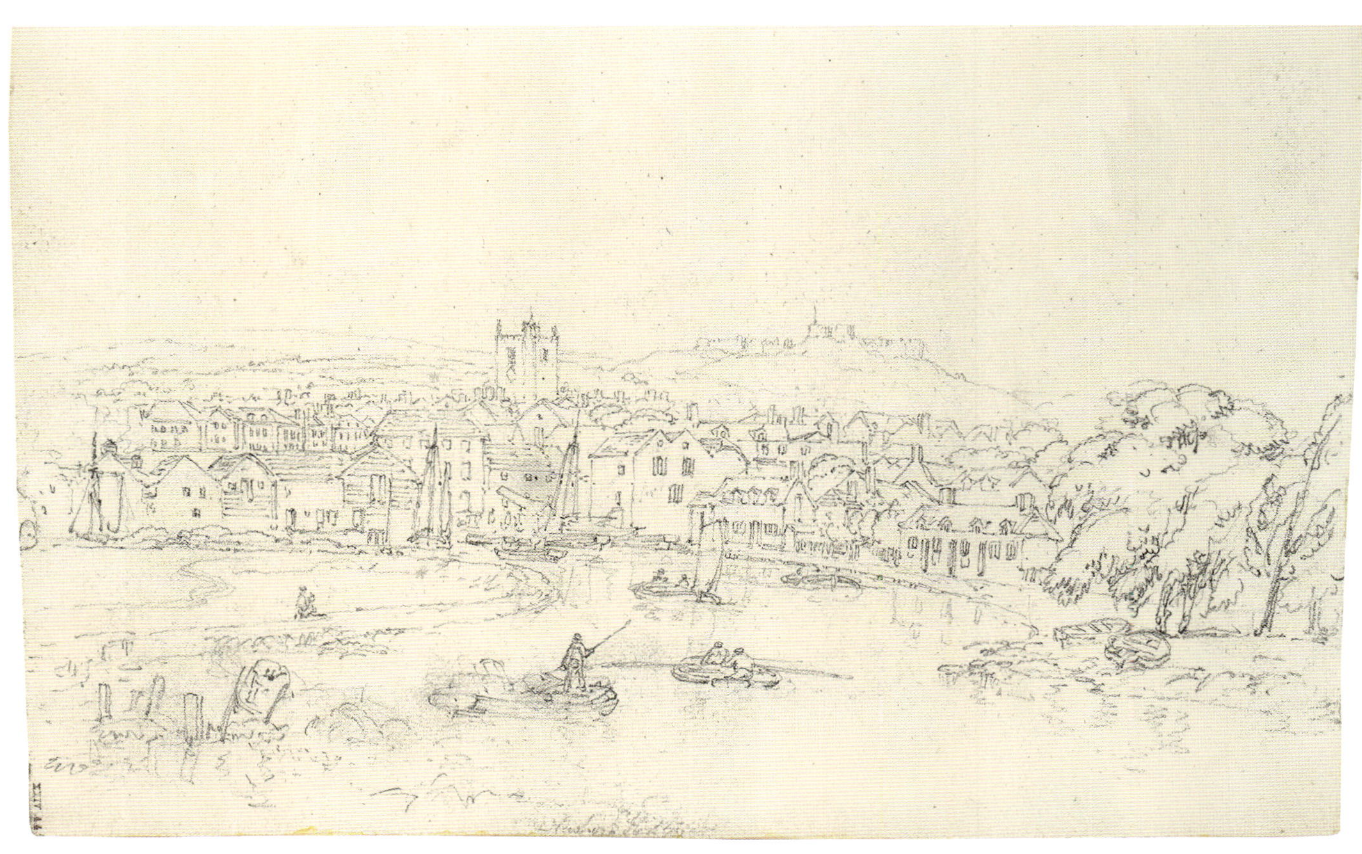

Isle of Wight that Turner appears to have made in the summer of 1826. That year he exhibited a small canvas entitled *View from the Terrace of a Villa at Niton, Isle of Wight, from Sketches by a Lady* (Museum of Fine Arts, Boston).[13] This is an unusual picture, one of several that Turner developed from existing images by other people. In this case, the person in question was his old pupil Julia Bennet, by then Lady Gordon, following her marriage in 1805 to Colonel James Willoughby Gordon (1772–1851). The couple lived at The Orchard, above the cliffs to the east of St Catherine's Point, and the 1826 picture would prove to be the first of a group of three by Turner that they acquired. The others are: *Scene in Derbyshire* (exhibited Royal Academy 1827; Musée national des beaux-arts du Québec), which may represent Gordon's native village of Risley; and *The Banks of the Loire* (exhibited Royal Academy 1829; Worcester Art Museum). After the 1826 Academy exhibition closed, Turner probably took the picture down to the Isle of Wight himself. An entry in Gordon's account book for 20 July records a payment of £105 for the picture; this exchange could have taken place in London, but it is just as likely to confirm Turner's presence on the Isle of Wight at that date.[14] Turner's movements over the summer of 1826 are not well documented until his departure for his tour of Normandy, Brittany and the Loire at the start of

Fig. 156
Newport, Isle of Wight, with Carisbrooke Castle in the Distance
1795
Pencil, 20.4 × 26.4 cm
From the 'Isle of Wight' sketchbook
Tate (D00452 / TB XXIV 44)

OPPOSITE: **Fig. 157**
Chale Farm
1795
Pencil, 26.4 × 20.4 cm
From the 'Isle of Wight' sketchbook
Tate (D00436 / TB XXIV 28)

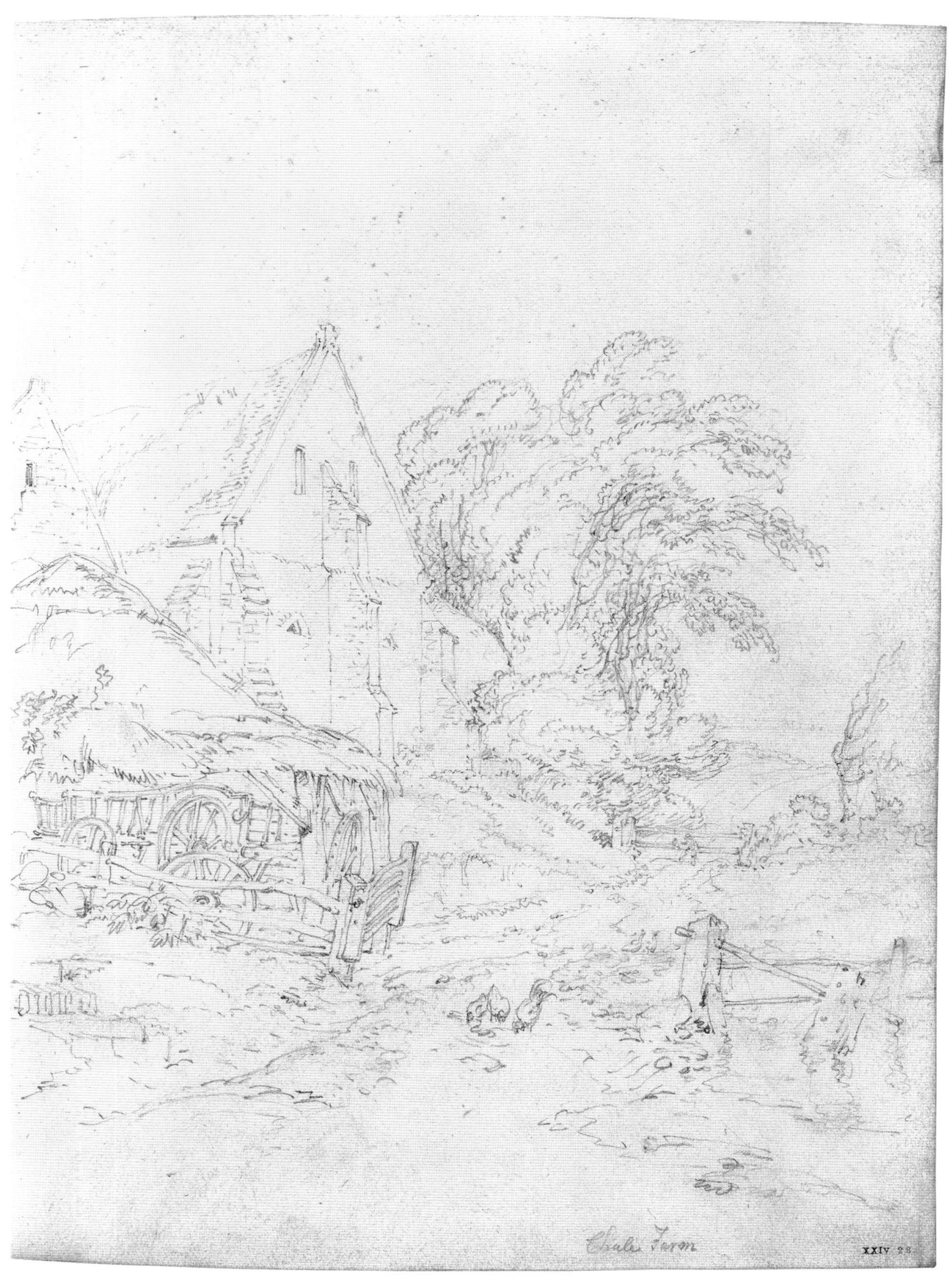

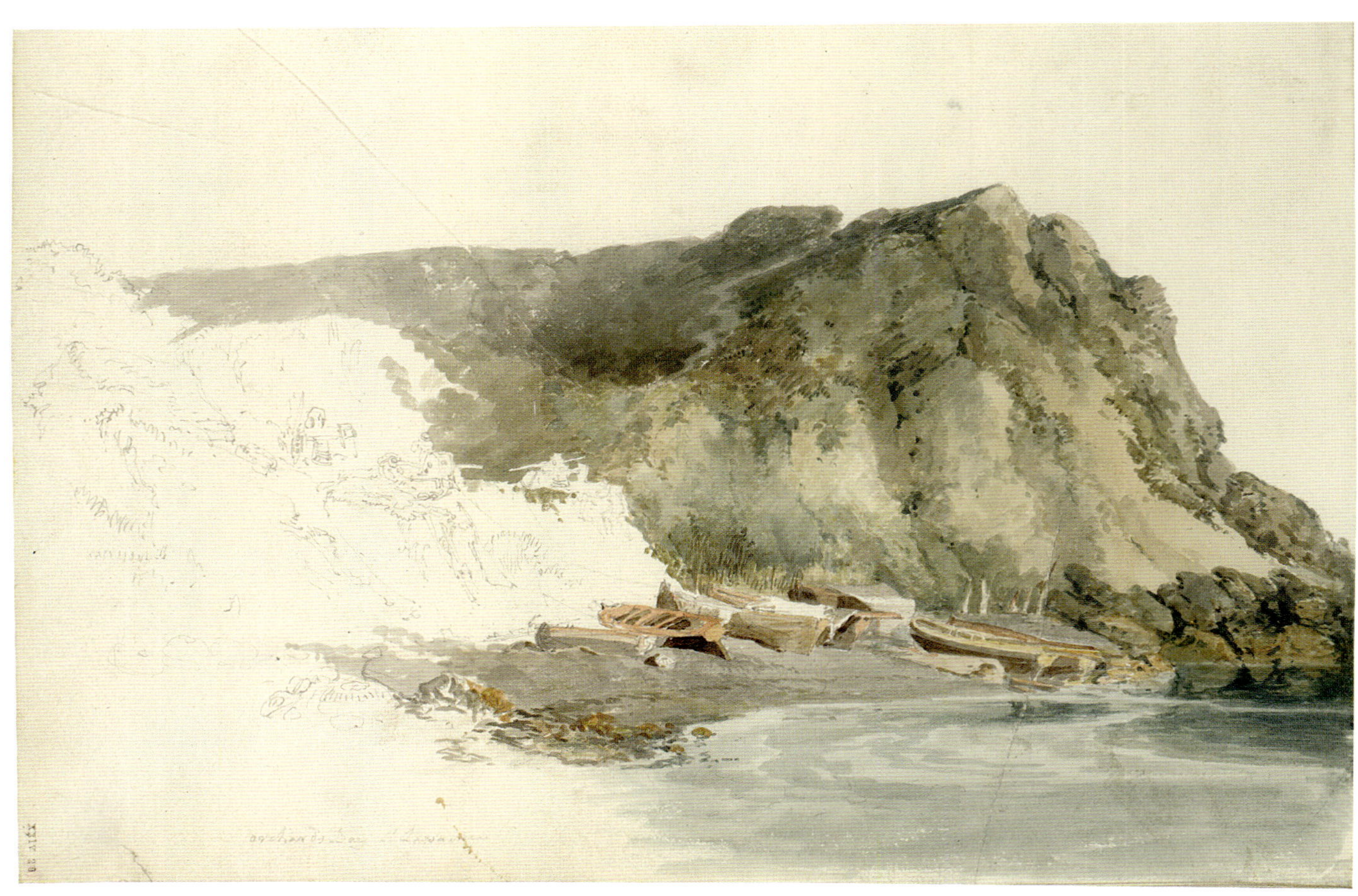

Fig. 158
Fishing Boats in Orchard Bay
1795
Pencil and watercolour, 20.4 × 26.4 cm
From the 'Isle of Wight' sketchbook
Tate (D00437 / TB XXIV 29)

September. So there was time to squeeze in a trip to the Isle of Wight, where the very first Cowes Regatta, organised by Charles Anderson-Pelham, took place on 10 and 11 August.[15]

When painting his *England and Wales* view of Carisbrooke (fig. 161), Turner was able to rework a sketch of the gateway from 1795 (in reverse), conflating it with his recollections of a more recent riding party arriving at the castle (maybe an excursion from Niton). The view was paired in the series with one of the anchorage off Cowes, seen just after the sun had set behind the tower of St Mary's church (fig. 162). To paraphrase the lines from Byron's *Childe Harold* that Turner often selected to complement his paintings: the moon is up but it is not yet night.[16] In the foreground two officers are rowed ashore; one points or waves to the battleship on the right, while his companion slumps, possibly injured. Compared with most of Turner's views of Cowes, it is a very tranquil image, recalling the golden-hued river scenes by Aelbert Cuyp that Turner admired in the early 1800s.

A broader prospect of the Cowes Roads can be found in one of the series of oil sketches that Turner made in 1827, although this looks eastwards, with a contrasting view of sunrise (fig. 163). Turner stayed for part of that summer

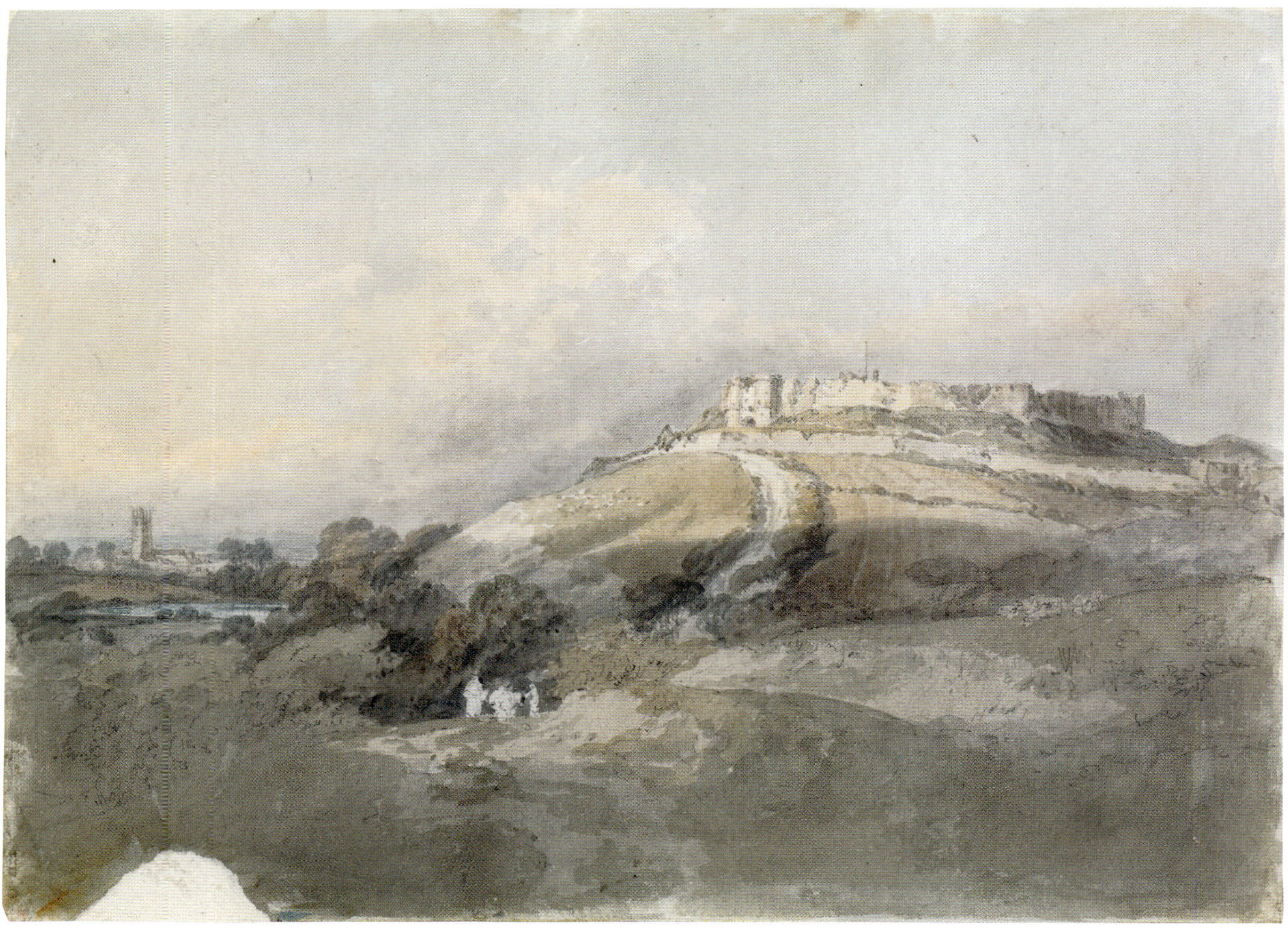

ABOVE AND DETAIL ON FOLLOWING PAGES:
Fig. 159
Carisbrooke Castle from the South-West, with the Church of St Mary's in the Distance
1795
Pencil and watercolour, 20.4 × 26.4 cm
From the 'Isle of Wight' sketchbook
Tate (D00432 / TB XXIV 25)

as the guest of John Nash (1752–1835), the celebrated architect then at the peak of his reputation with his works for King George IV and in the midst of his transformation of central London. On the Isle of Wight he had designed the new church of St Mary (1816), as well as his own neo-gothic castle on the east headland above Cowes, begun in 1798, a year before neighbouring Norris Castle, which Wyatt had planned for Lord Henry Seymour.[17] It is not known exactly how Turner and Nash became acquainted: during the 1820s Turner continued to socialise with other architects, such as Sir John Soane (1753–1837) and C.R. Cockerell (1788–1863); and, like Nash, Turner had briefly worked for George IV in 1823–24.

Turner's correspondence indicates that he was established at East Cowes Castle by August 1827. However, he may have spent a few days before then with the Gordons at Niton. Another entry in their account book records the receipt of *Scene in Derbyshire* on 26 July, again for the sum of £105. As in 1826, this picture was small enough for Turner to have delivered it personally. How long he stayed with them is unclear.

Less than a week later, as July ended, Turner was among those watching the first of the two Cowes Regattas of that year. The initial races

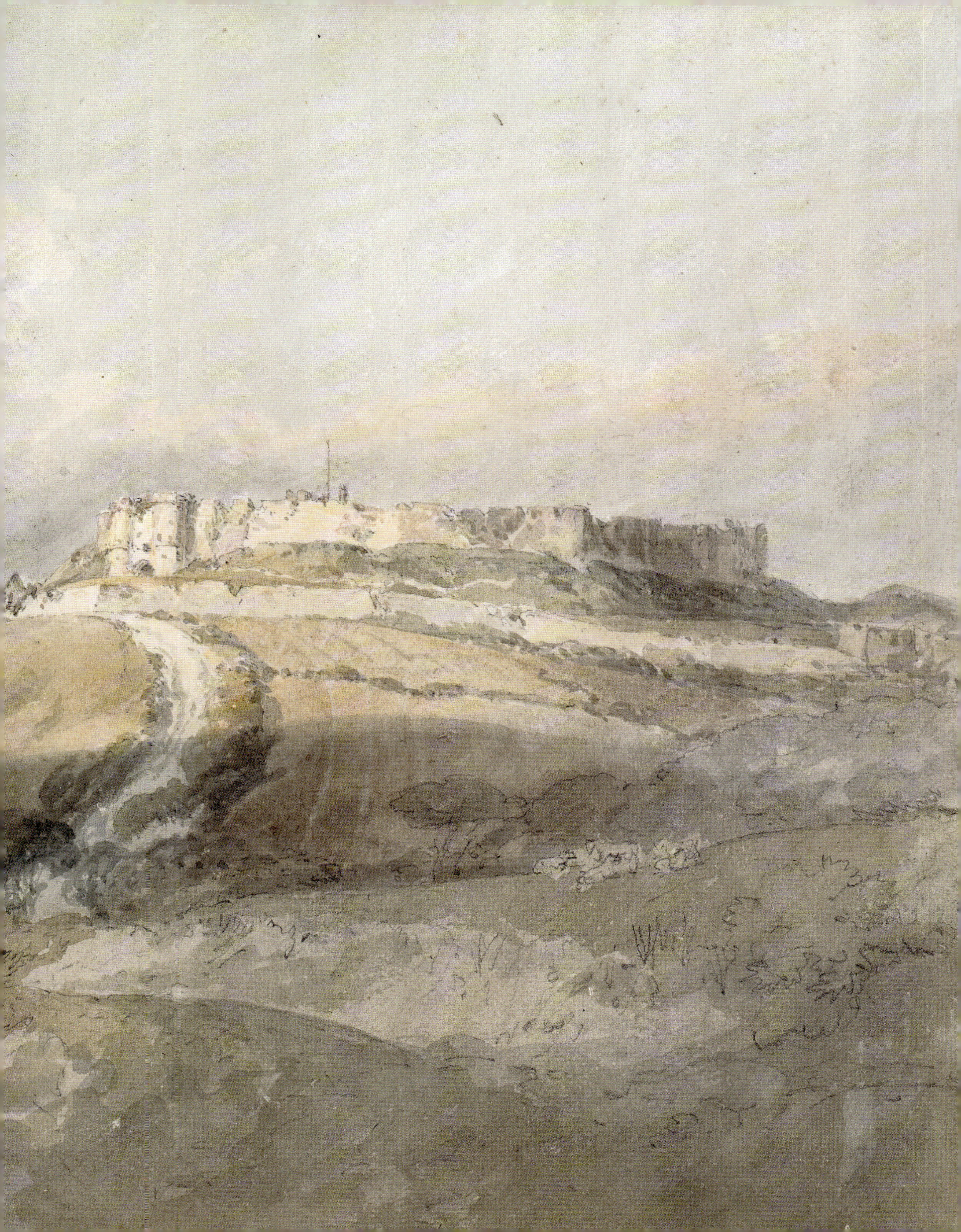

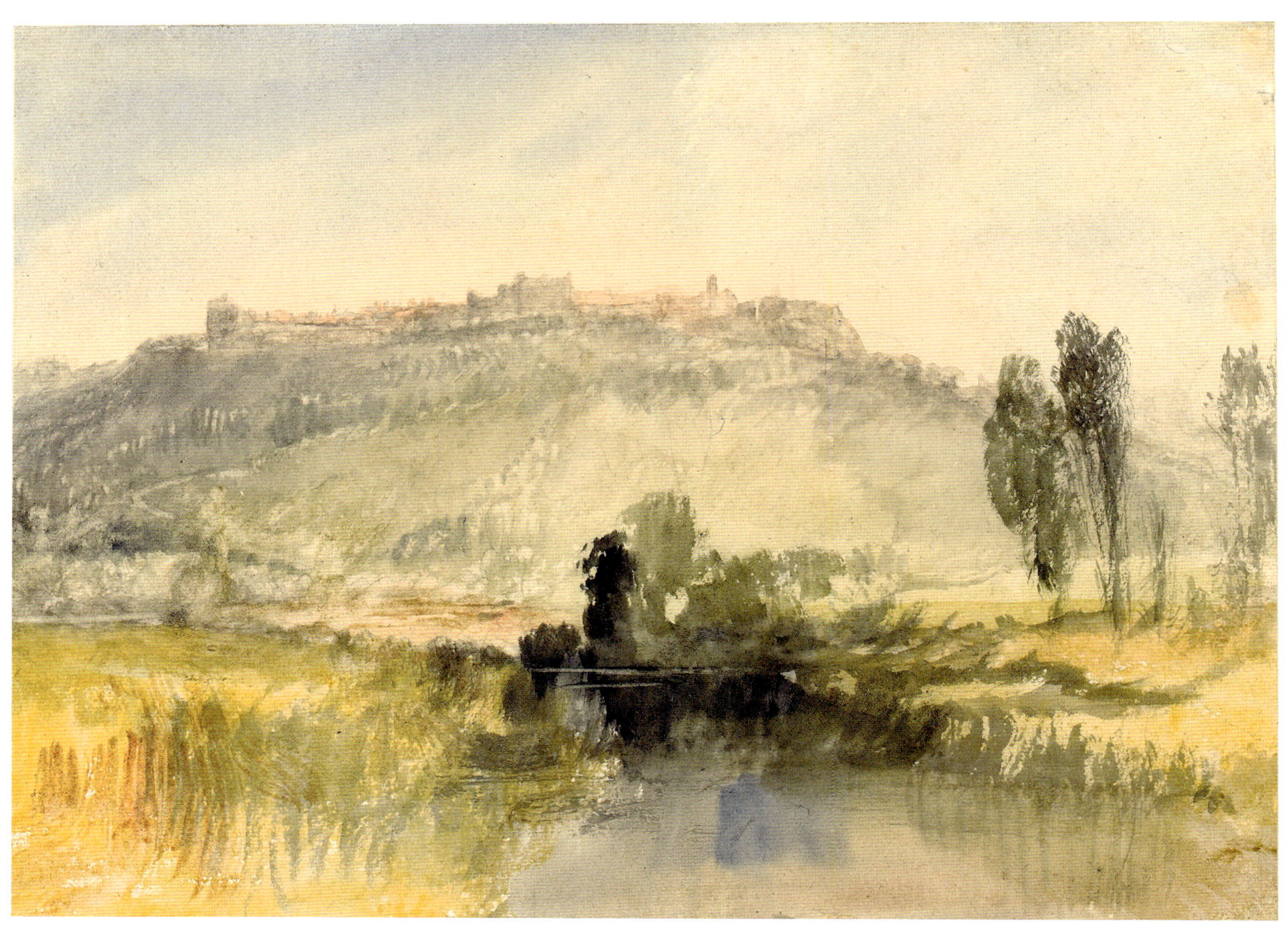

Fig. 160
Carisbrooke Castle, Isle of Wight (formerly identified as Chateau d'Arques)
*c.*1826
Watercolour, 16.7 × 22.8 cm
Fitzwilliam Museum, Cambridge (W421)

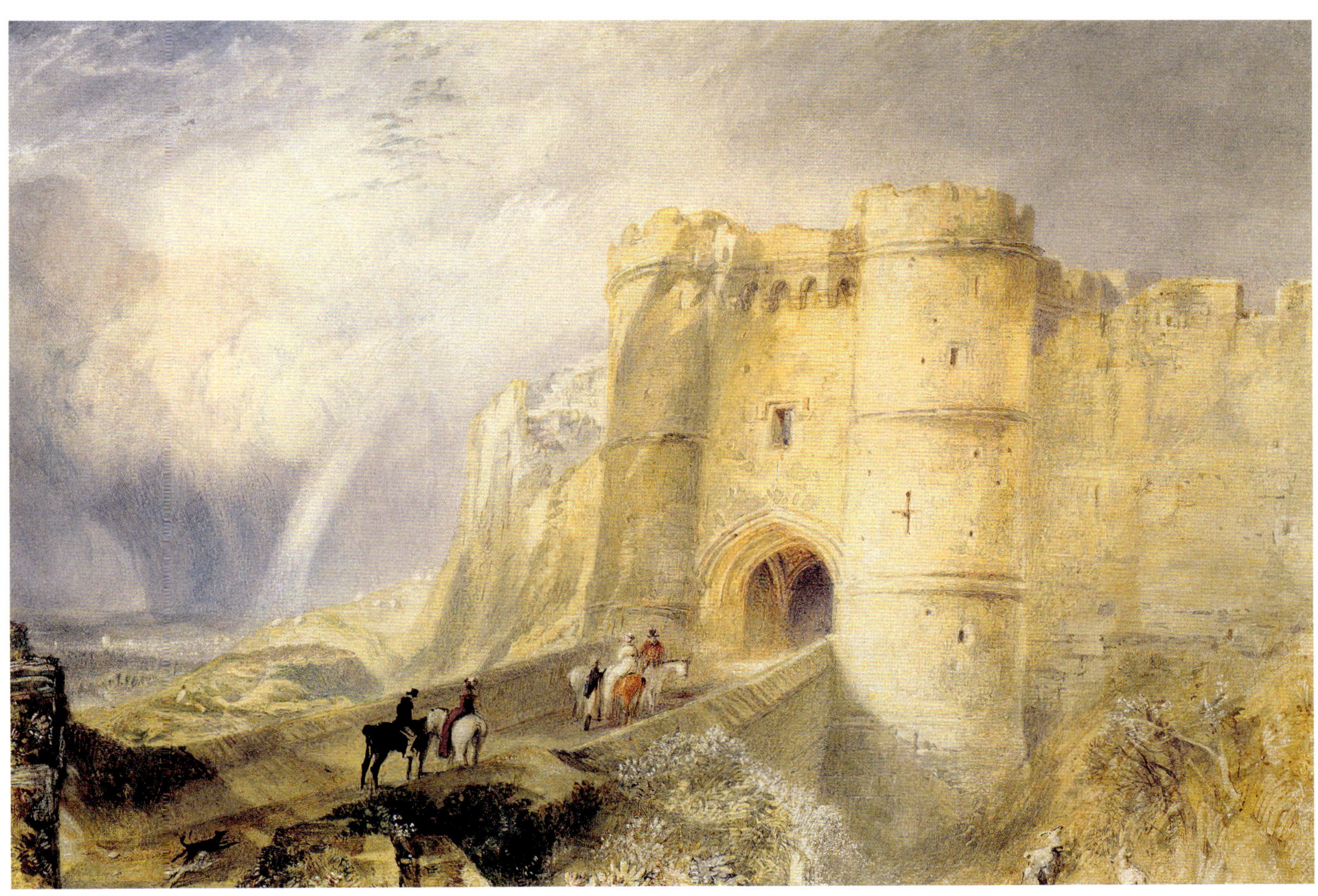

Fig. 161
Carisbrooke Castle
Isle of Wight

*c.*1827–28
Watercolour, 29.2 × 41.2 cm
For *Picturesque Views in England and Wales*
Carisbrooke Castle,
Isle of Wight (W81[illegible])

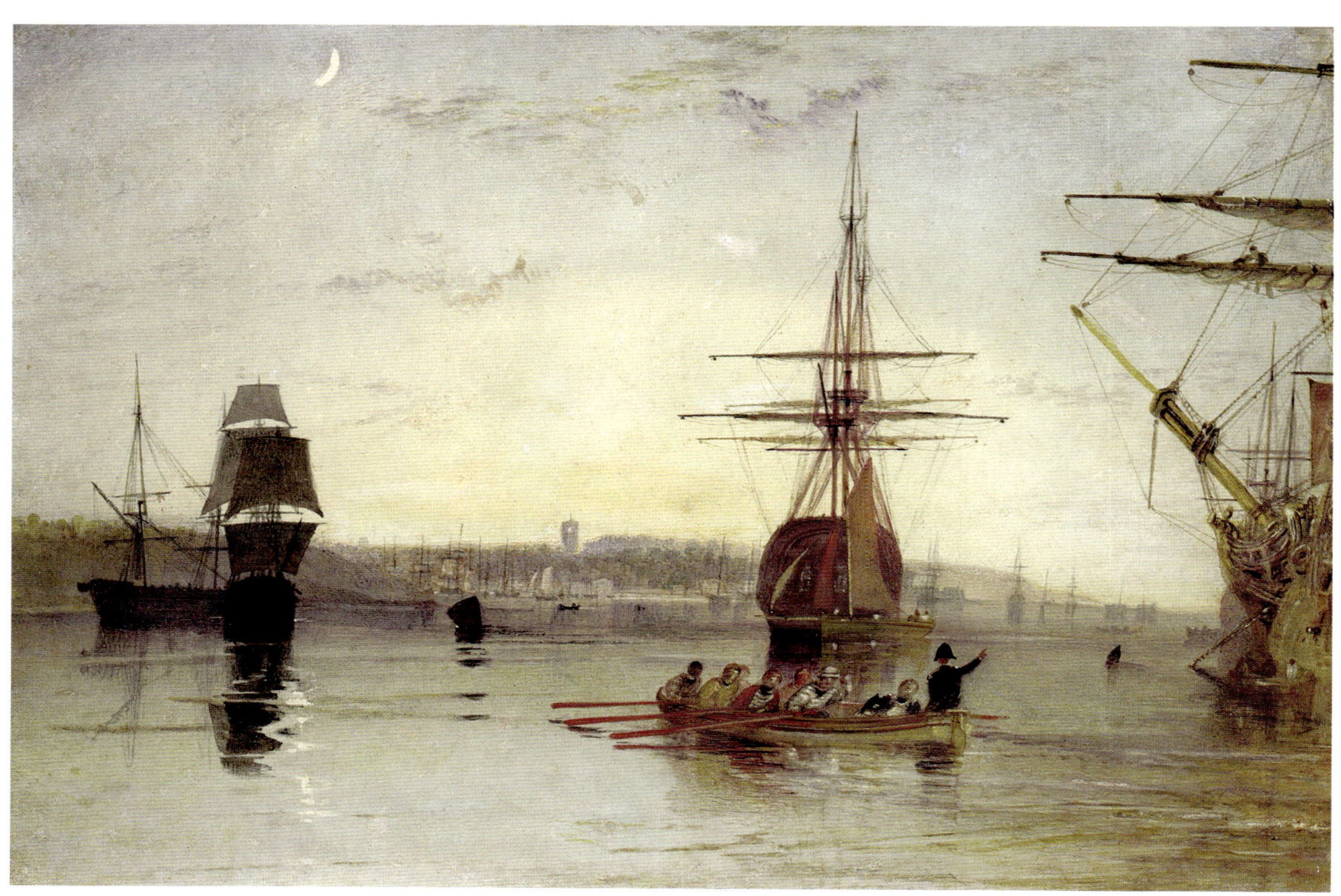

Fig. 162
Cowes, Isle of Wight
*c.*1827–28
Watercolour, 28.6 × 41.9 cm
For *Picturesque Views in England and Wales*
Private collection (W816)

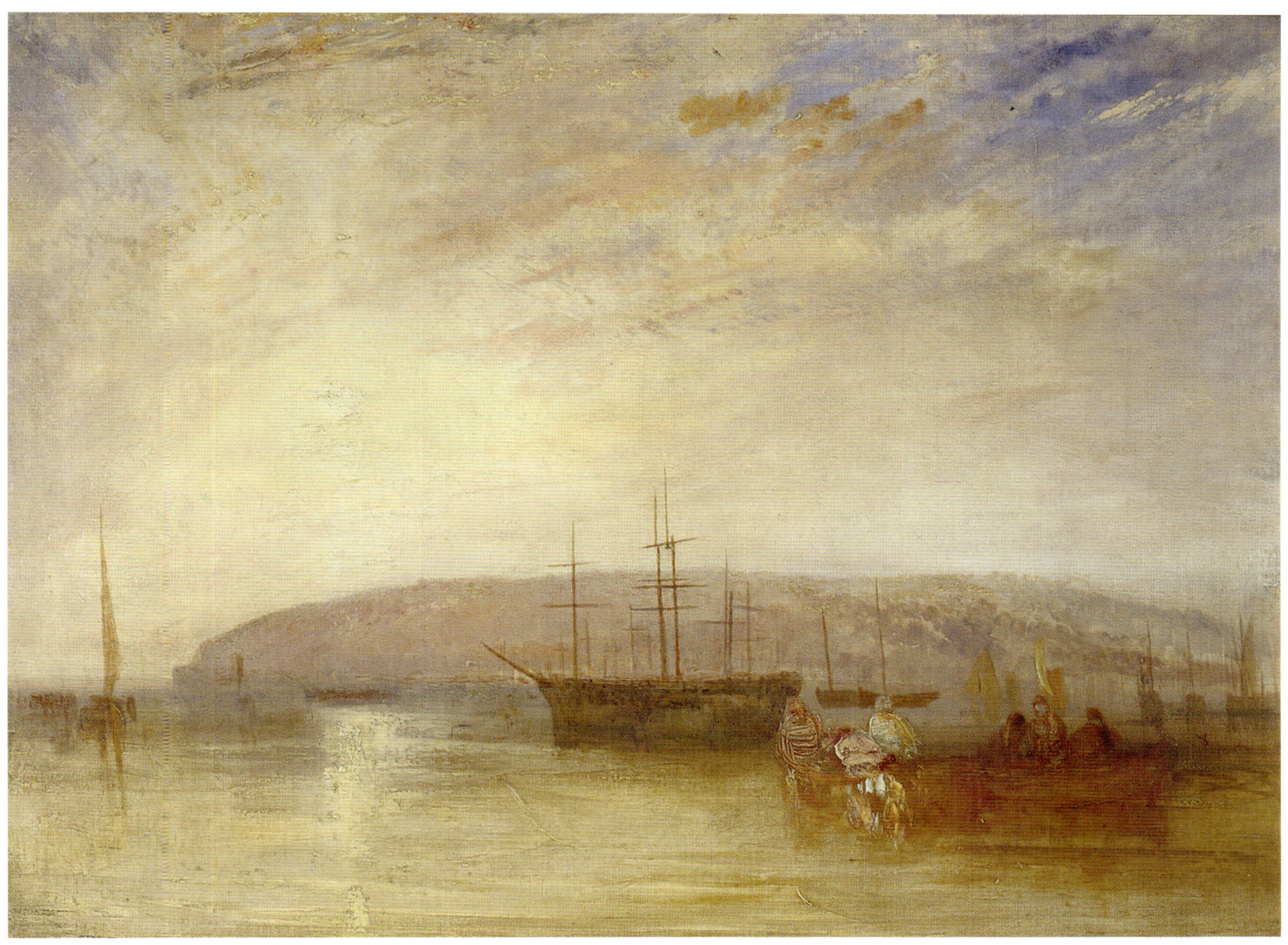

Fig. 163
Shipping off East Cowes Headland

1827
Oil on canvas, 46 × 60.3 cm
Tate (N01999; B&J 267)

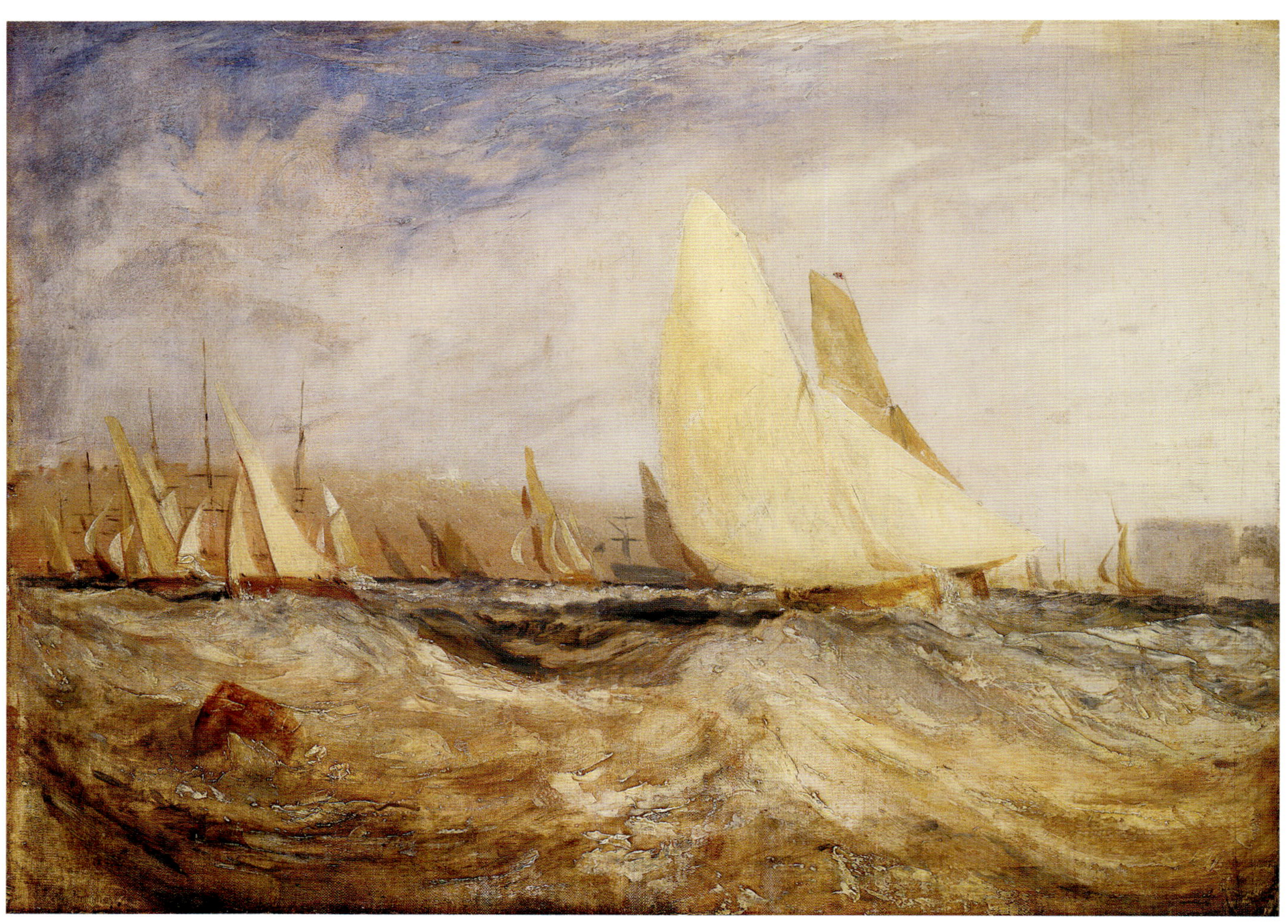

Fig. 164
Sketch for 'East Cowes Castle, the Regatta Beating to Windward'
1827
Oil on canvas, 45.7 × 61 cm
Tate (N01994; B&J 261)

took place from 31 July to 2 August, followed by those of the second regatta from 13 to 17 August, which included the contest for His Majesty's Cup. He made notes of the participants of the first batch of races in one of his sketchbooks.[18] It was evidently a very lively social occasion and the supposedly standoffish Turner rose to the challenge, making presentation drawings as gifts for some of the young ladies also staying with Nash and his famously vivacious wife.[19]

All of this was clearly pleasurable, but possibly also distracting for Turner, who had by then resolved on illustrating the Regatta as a completely new subject. One of the letters he wrote from the castle to his father, back in London, requested a length of canvas and various painting materials.[20] Once it arrived, the canvas was worked on in small sections, like a cartoon strip, allowing Turner to develop his ideas sequentially, all the time modifying and improving his compositions. It was a practice he generally followed when working in watercolour, but more rarely, in such an interrelated way, in his oil paintings. Most of the sketches contributed to the pair of contrasting views he exhibited of the Regatta at the Royal Academy in 1828: one showed the boats in the coastal waters off the Isle of Wight (fig. 164; the

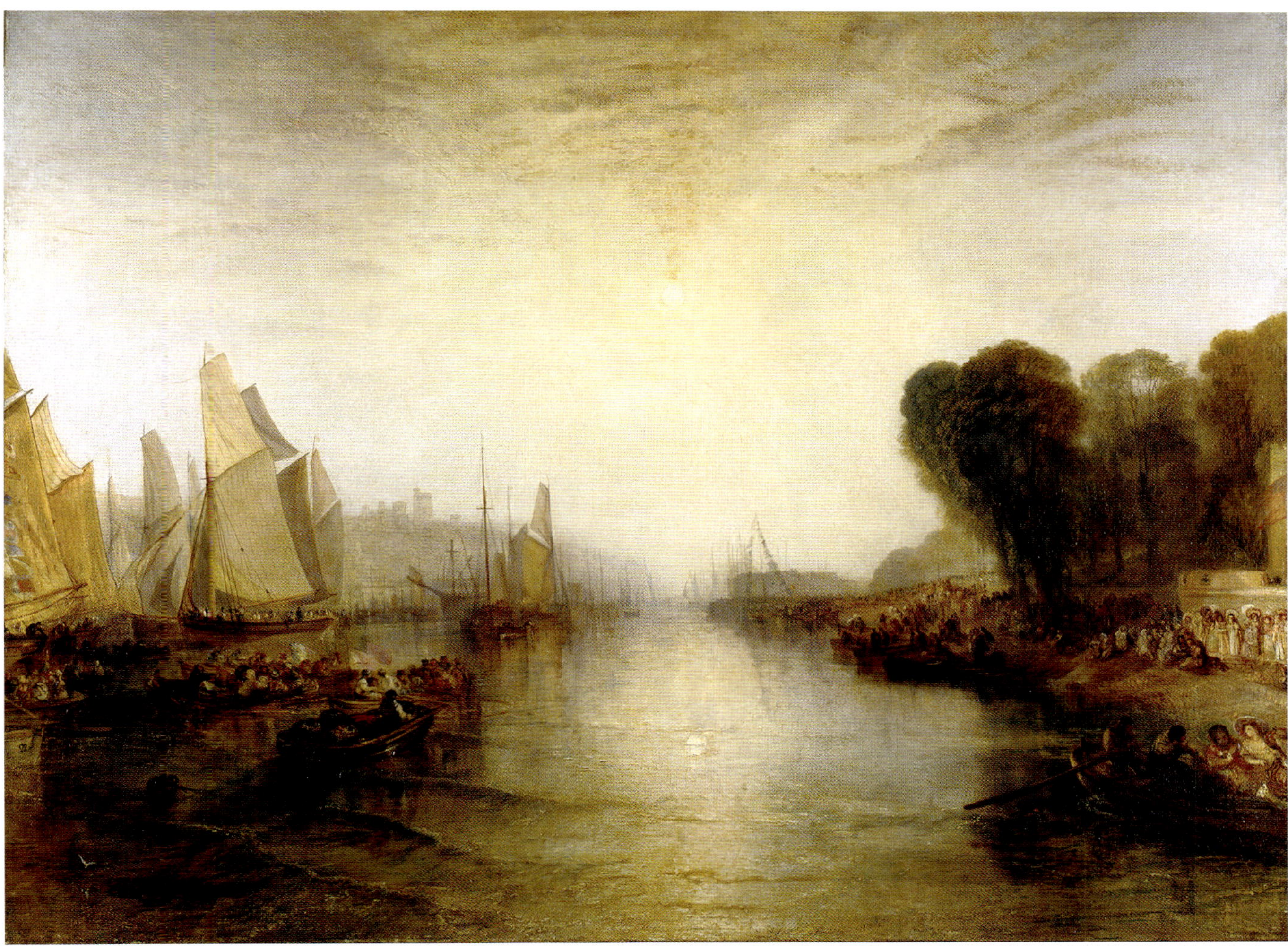

Fig. 165
East Cowes Regatta: the Seat of John Nash, Esq.; the Regatta Starting for their Moorings
Exhibited RA 1828
Oil on canvas, 91.4 × 123.2 cm
Victoria and Albert Museum, London (B&J 243)

finished painting is now at Indianapolis); the other depicted them gathering at their moorings, with crowds of spectators lining the banks of the Medina (fig. 165). Although the titles of the exhibited works suggest the subject was primarily Nash's home, East Cowes Castle appears only as an incidental detail in the distance.

Another of the 1828 exhibits offered a closer impression of the gothic building, entitled *Boccaccio Relating the Tale of the Bird Cage* (1828, Tate). Here Nash's pseudo-medieval structure caused Turner to imagine a bevy of sumptuously-dressed ladies – and a few men – lounging around in a glade below the castle, as if from an earlier age. The idea emanated from a series of pen and ink studies Turner had made on small sheets of blue paper during his stay (figs 166–68).[21] These document the castle from many angles – from the paths in the garden, up on its battlements – as well as recording a few of the interiors. Less well known than the more colourful sequence painted at Petworth House a month or so later, the sketches offer some of the same insights into the informal life of a Regency country house.

In 1831, having already bought the two Regatta subjects, Nash acquired *Life-Boat and Manby Apparatus going off to a Stranded Vessel making Signal (Blue Lights) of Distress*, the

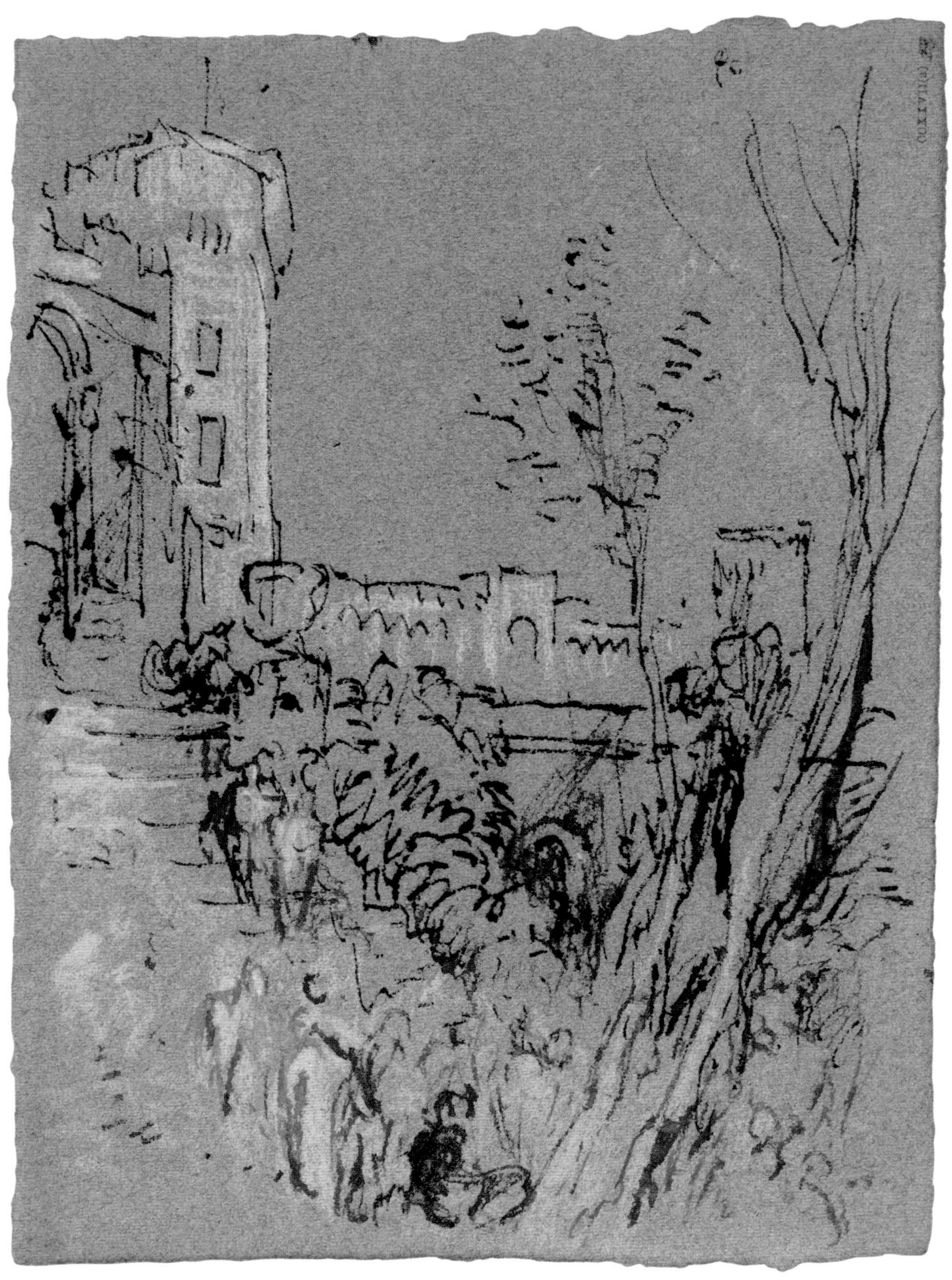

Fig. 166
East Cowes Castle: Figures on the Castle Steps
1827
Pen and ink with chalk, on blue paper, 19.5 × 14.1 cm
Tate (D20826 / TB CCXXVII a 23)

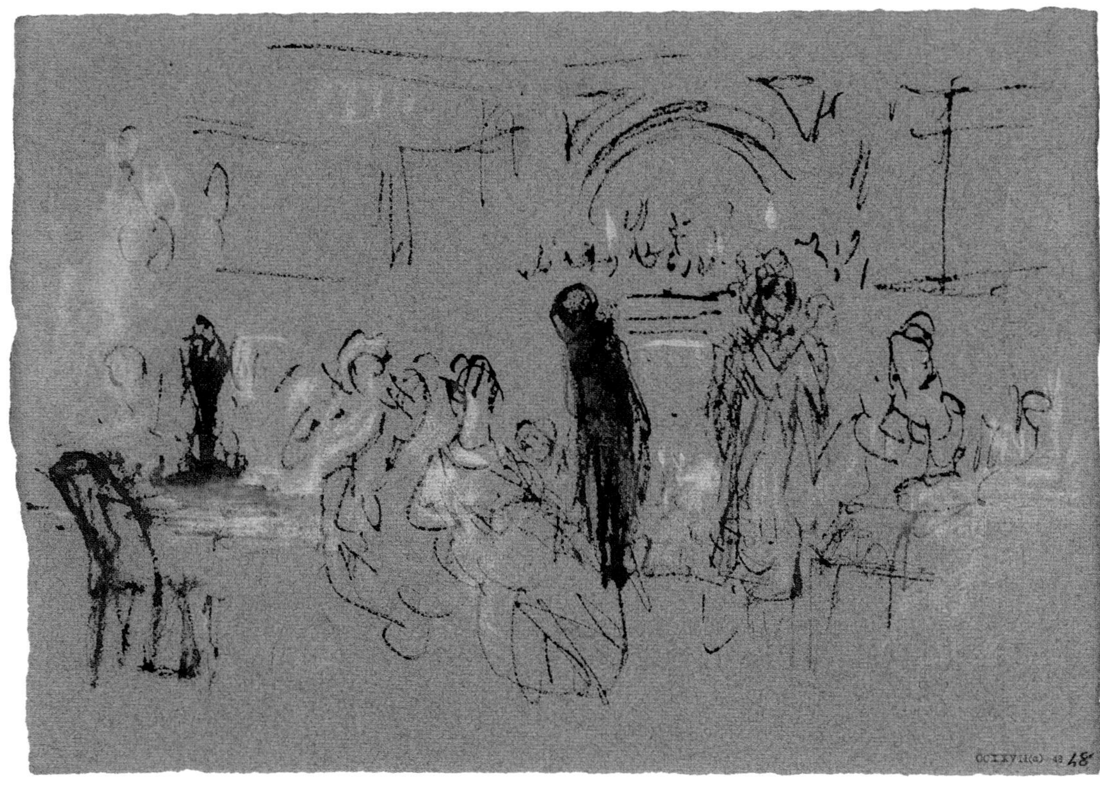

Fig. 167
Interior of the Library, East Cowes Castle
1827
Pen and ink, with chalk, on blue paper, 14.2 × 19.5 cm
Tate (D20851 / TB CCXXVII a 48)

seapiece that possibly prompted Beckford's rant about Turner's new style that year (see p. 117). No correspondence has survived, but Turner undoubtedly remained on good terms with Nash, spending Christmas at East Cowes in 1832. This visit may have been the occasion that stimulated him to paint two unfinished oils recording the Octagonal Room and the Drawing Room.[22] The first room can be seen in the well-known picture *Music Party, East Cowes Castle* (Tate), where a group of people sit around a piano forte. The principal figure is surely Mary Ann, Nash's young wife, who was an entertaining hostess and an accomplished pianist. Behind her stands a man dressed in early seventeenth-century costume. The use of yellow (which Turner habitually joked was a colour he had made all his own because of the mockery he attracted by using it so prominently in his works) perhaps identifies him as a fanciful alter ego. The man's yellow stockings, taken in conjunction with the visit during the 12 days and nights following Christmas, might further link him with Malvolio in Shakespeare's play, *Twelfth Night* – also the subject of Turner's 1822 painting, *What you Will!* (Clark Art Institute).

By contrast with this mood of convivial humour, the other oil painting (fig. 170) presents a more forlorn mood of absence, in which objects are scattered, chairs tumbled and a little dog howls. A feathered cavalier hat suggests the era is later in the seventeenth century, but the lack of any figurative element makes it impossible to determine a narrative; the theme

Fig. 168
The Drawing Room at East Cowes Castle
1827
Watercolour and gouache on blue paper, 13.7 × 19.5 cm
Tate (D22694 / TB CCXLIV 32)

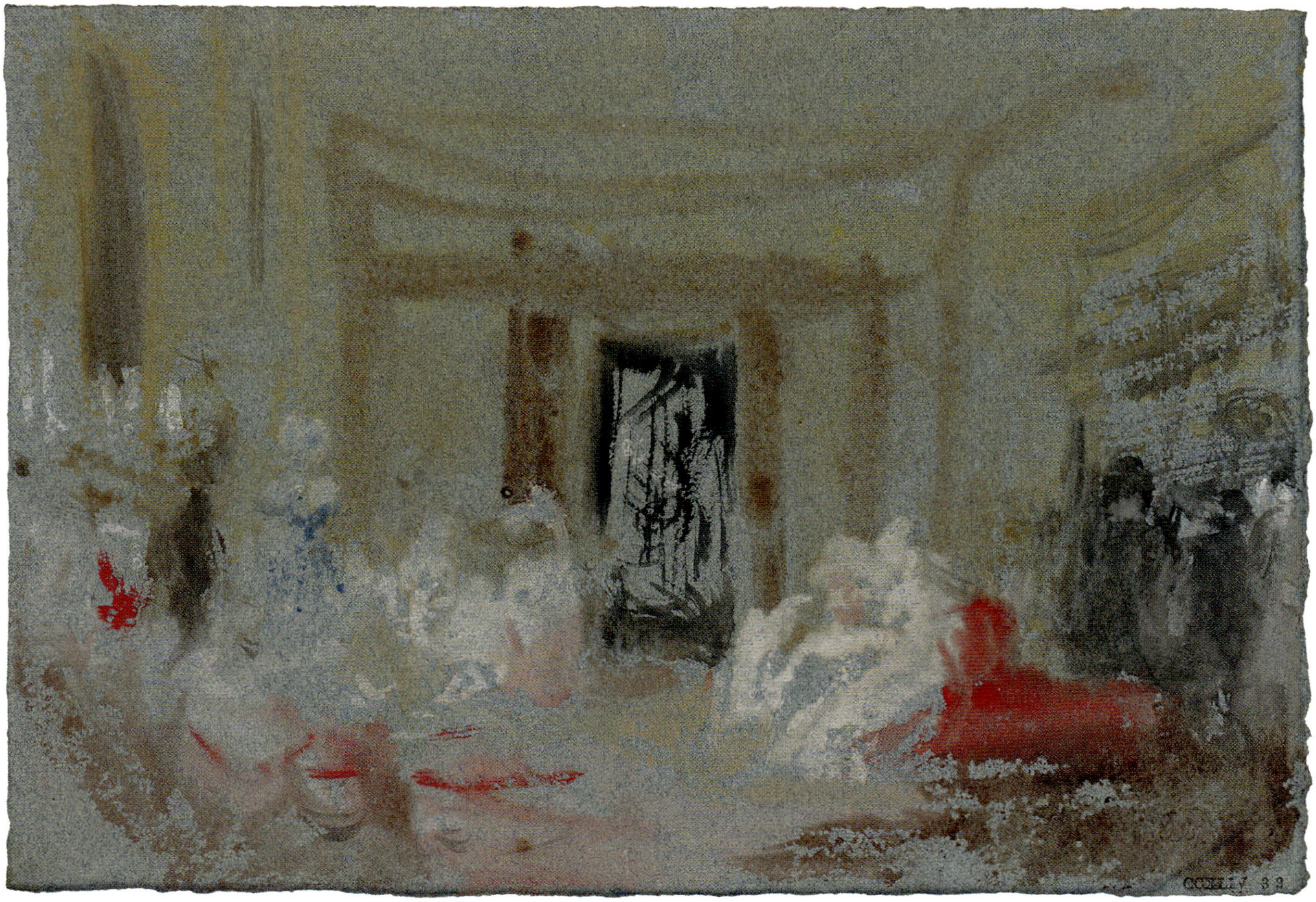

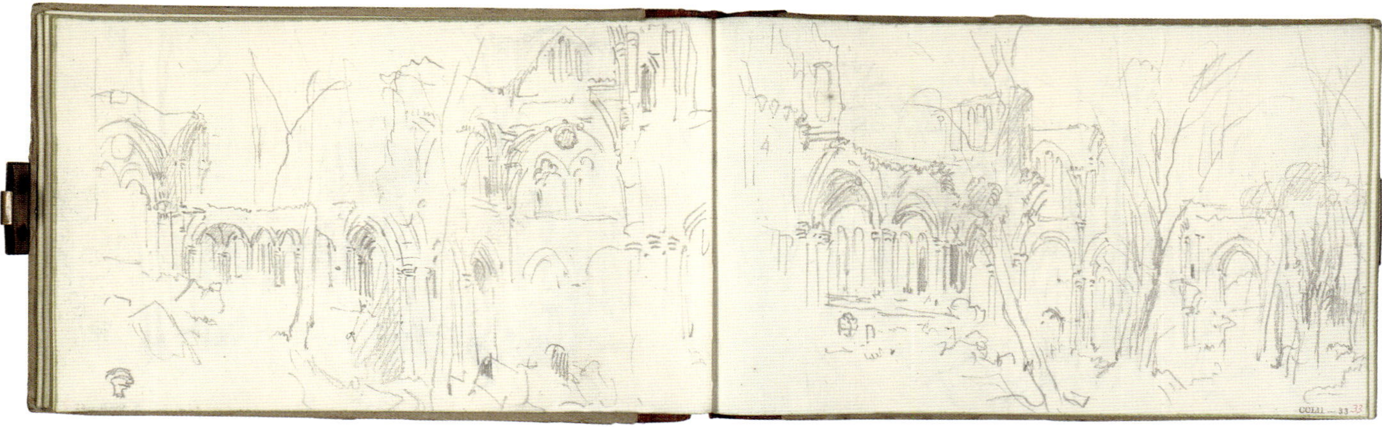

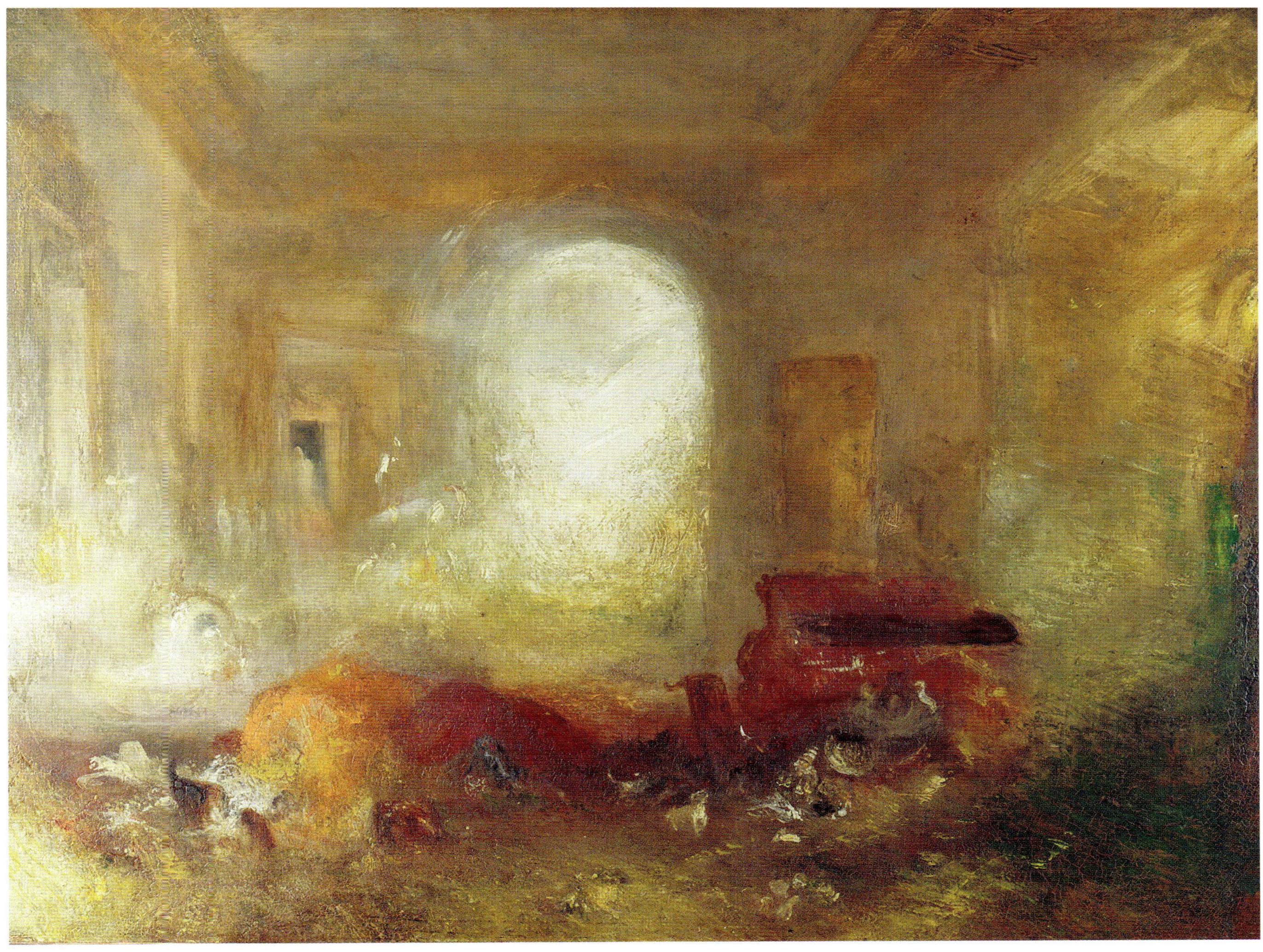

Fig. 170
Interior of a Great House; The Drawing Room, East Cowes Castle
*c.*1830–35
Oil on canvas,
90.8 × 121.9 cm
Tate (N01988; B&J 449)

OPPOSITE BELOW: **Fig. 169**
The Ruins of Netley Abbey
*c.*1832
Pencil, 11.4 × 18.7 cm
From the Guernsey sketchbook
Tate (D23581, D23582 / TB CCLII 32a, 33)

may have grown out of the illustrations Turner had begun to make for editions of Sir Walter Scott's works.

During the summer of 1832, Turner had presumably passed the Isle of Wight on his way to the Channel Islands, before which he also returned to Netley, sketching the abbey and the nearby castle much more fully that year than he had in 1795 (fig. 169). He may also have gone across the Solent once more in November 1833,[23] but after that there are no further records of him visiting the island. He obviously thrived on the social connections he had there, but these also extended into southern England, close to Salisbury.

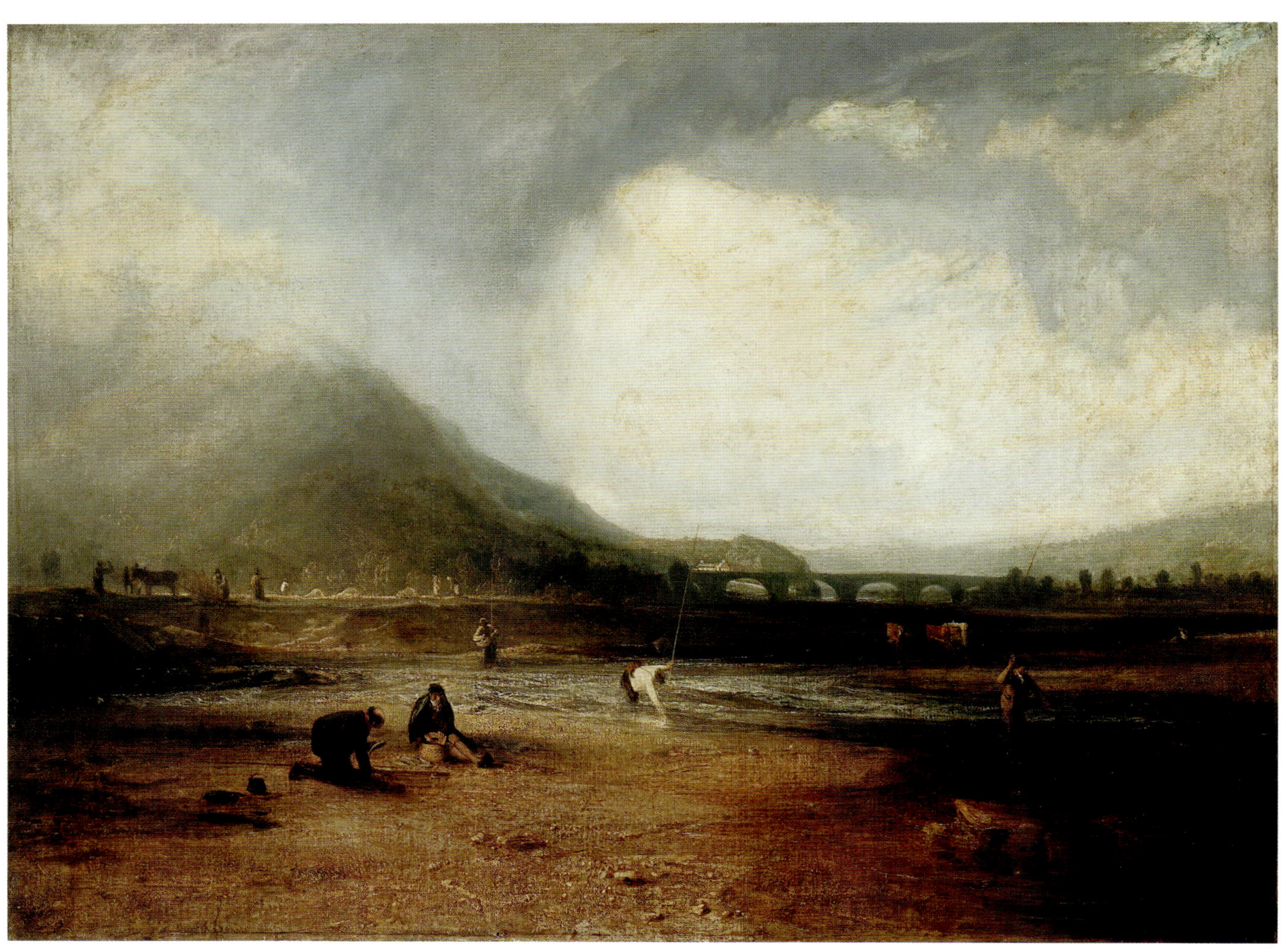

Fig. 171
The Trout Stream ('Trout Fishing in the Dee, Corwen Bridge and Cottage')
Exhibited Turner's Gallery 1809
Oil on canvas, 91.5 × 122 cm
Taft Museum of Art, Cincinnati, Ohio (B&J 92)
Bequest of Charles Phelps and Anna Sinton Taft

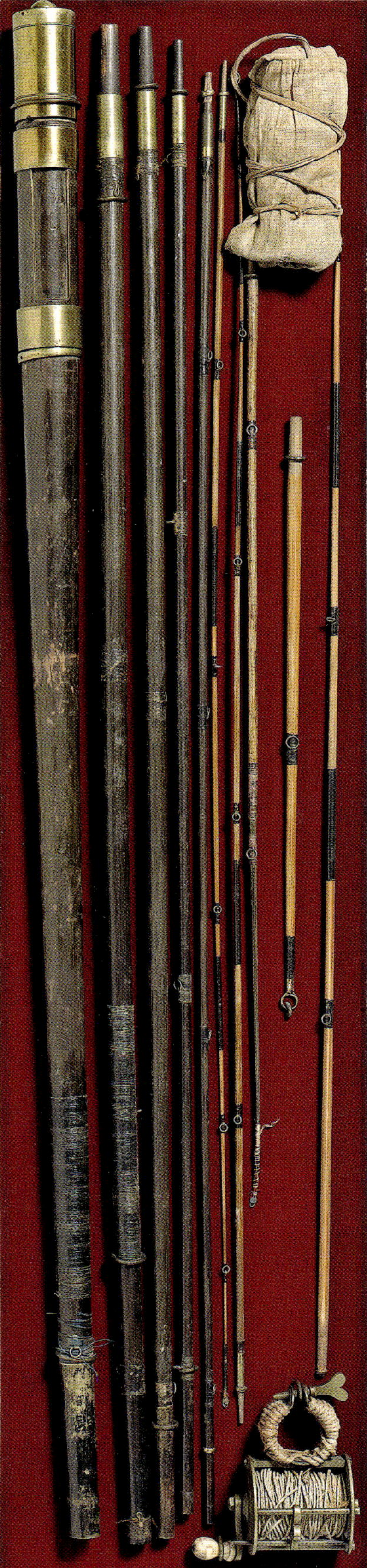

Fig. 172
Turner's fishing rod, made up of five sections, cased
Royal Academy of Arts, London

One of Turner's favourite pastimes, throughout his life, was fishing. He was even considered 'a famous fisherman' in some circles.[24] He shared this passion with many of his patrons and friends – from Colt Hoare and Leicester, who used to fish at Bala in North Wales, near Corwen (fig. 171), to the artist George Jones and the sculptor Sir Francis Chantrey (fig. 174), with whom he jovially competed to catch the biggest pikes while staying at Petworth.

Chantrey was instrumental in the founding of the Houghton Fishing Club, on the River Test, near Stockbridge.[25] The Pickwickian banter and fellowship among the anglers there was something that Turner embraced and contributed to. This can be felt most tangibly in an album compiled by members of the Club, which they filled with mock-heroic accounts of their triumphs that were supplemented by caricatures and sketches; one of these was by Turner (fig. 173).[26] It is derived from an outline in a sketchbook used on a tour of Derbyshire in 1834, when he finally accepted the invitation of his good friend James Holworthy to fish in the waters of the Dove, as immortalised in Isaac Walton's classic, *The Compleat Angler*.[27] Another sketchbook from around that date includes studies of fishermen grouped at a weir (fig. 175); a similar structure can be found in a book Turner used when on a visit to the Isle of Wight, suggesting a familiar place, frequented from time to time, possibly even Houghton.[28] As well as recording the locales he haunted when angling, Turner made remarkable studies of the fish he caught (fig. 176). Looking at the delicate watercolour dating from the early 1820s the otherwise gruff Walter Shaw Sparrow rhapsodised, 'It is evident from this little study that any sort of fish, whether called "coarse" or not, was a romance of colour and shape to this master.'[29]

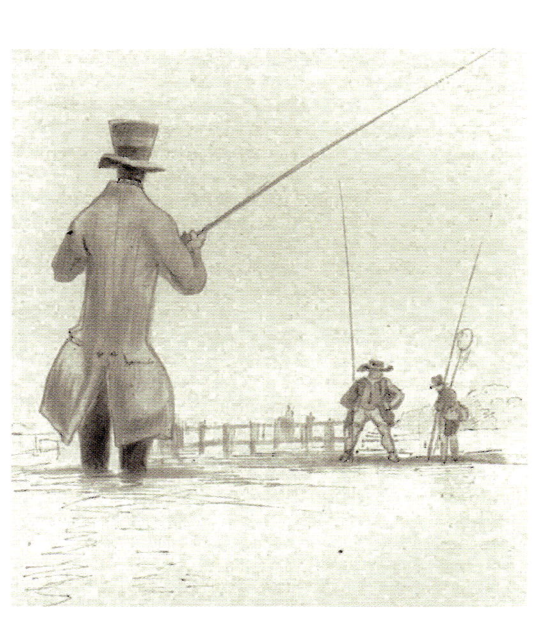

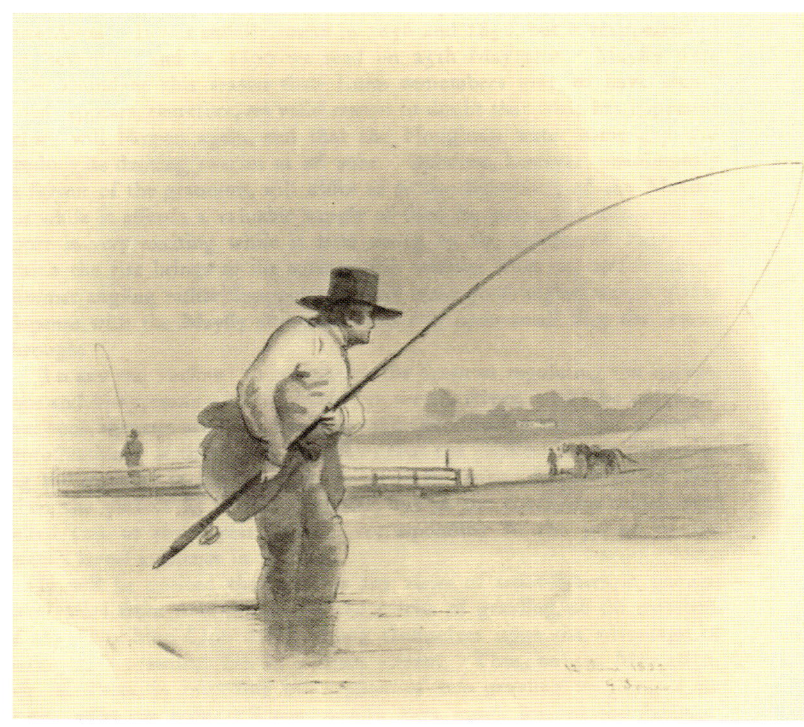

Fig. 173
A Back View of a Man Fishing
*c.*1834
Pencil
From 'The Houghton Club Commonplace Book'

Fig. 174
GEORGE JONES (1786–1869)
Francis Chantrey Blowing
*c.*1830–35
Pencil
From 'The Houghton Club Commonplace Book'

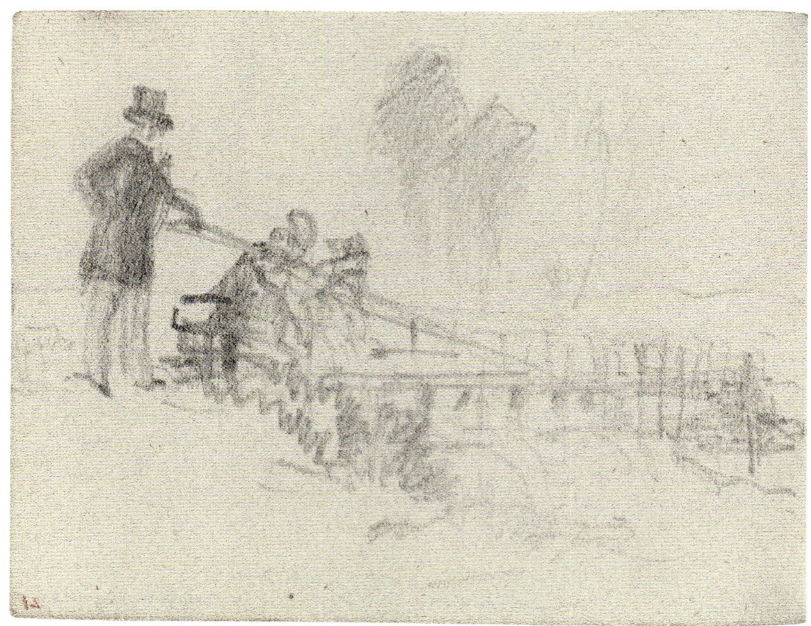

Fig. 175
A Group of Fishermen at a Weir
*c.*1834–36
From the Fishing at the Weir sketchbook
Pencil, 7.9 × 10.1 cm
Tate (D27762 / TB CCLXXXI 20a)

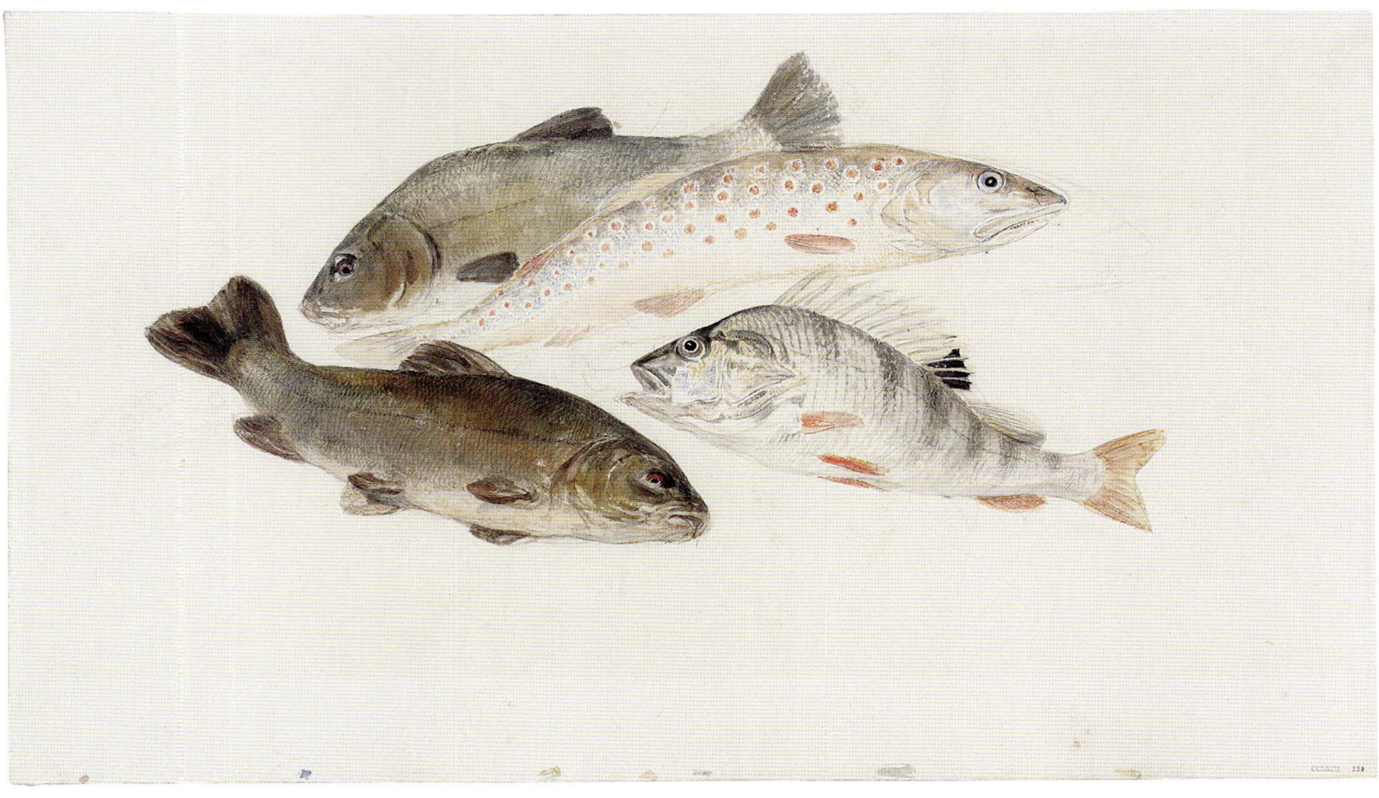

Fig. 176
Study of Fish: Two Tench, a Trout and a Perch
*c.*1822–24
Pencil, watercolour and gouache, 27.5 × 47 cm
Tate (D25462 / TB CCLXIII 339)

There was one final event that brought Turner back to the Hampshire coast in 1884. By then he was 69 and the world he had grown up in was passing away, steadily erased by technology and reform. His patron Colt Hoare had died in 1838, and the aged and tenacious Beckford finally succumbed in May 1844. That October the newspapers were full of excitement at the prospect of the state visit of Louis-Philippe, king of the French.[30] The usual mutual suspicion between Britain and France had recently been tempered as a result of the familial connection that the young Queen Victoria developed with her counterpart. She and Prince Albert had visited Louis-Philippe at his chateau in Picardy the previous September, and it was hoped that the reciprocal visit of 1844 would further strengthen the alliance.

Details of the king's planned arrival at Portsmouth were widely available and it was presumably after reading these that Turner decided to go himself. He was acquainted with Louis-Philippe from the time when the monarch lived in exile near his home at Twickenham. But there was little time for Turner to prepare. He was only just back from his usual late summer trip to Switzerland, and would have needed to travel to Gosport by train and then hire a boat from which to watch events unfold on 8 October.

The arrival of the king certainly proved to be a great naval spectacle. In addition to the numerous flagships stationed at Spithead, there was a vast flotilla of smaller boats to escort the French delegation into the harbour. Louis-Philippe was himself travelling aboard the steam yacht *Gomer*, which was flanked by three other French steamboats. Typically, the handful of pencil sketches that Turner made merely record fleeting traces of all of this, as do some watercolours he painted shortly afterwards (figs 177–78).

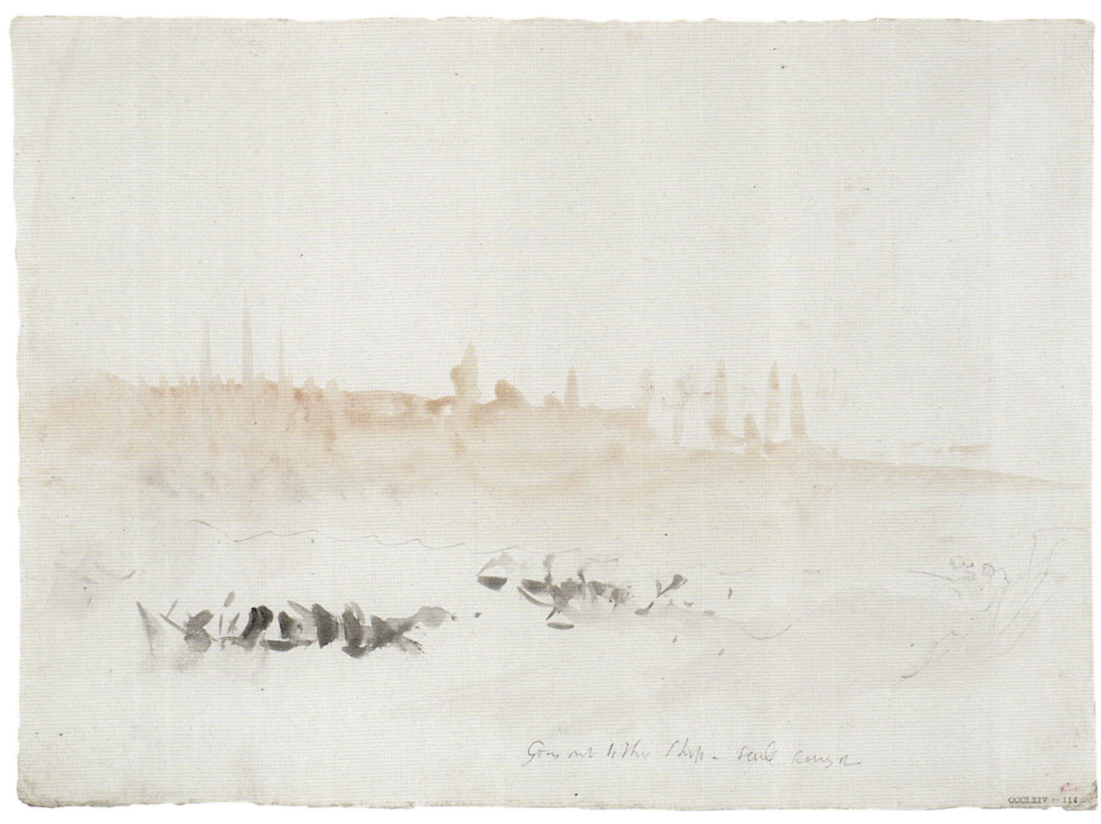

Fig. 177
Portsmouth Harbour: 'Going out to the Ship – Sculls Rough'
1844
Pencil and watercolour, 23.5 × 30.9 cm
Tate (D35957 / TB CCCLXIV 114)

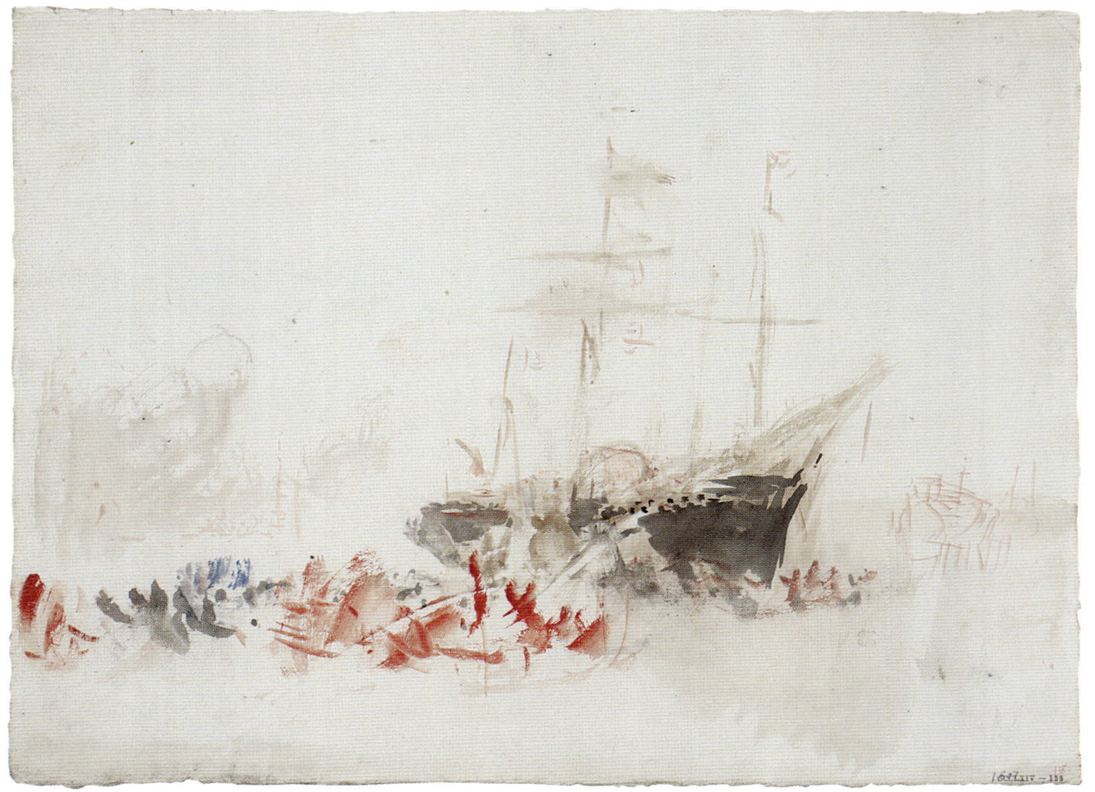

Fig. 178
The Arrival of Louis-Philippe: the Gomer
1844
Watercolour, 23.7 × 31.8 cm
Tate (D35981 / TB CCCLXIV 138)

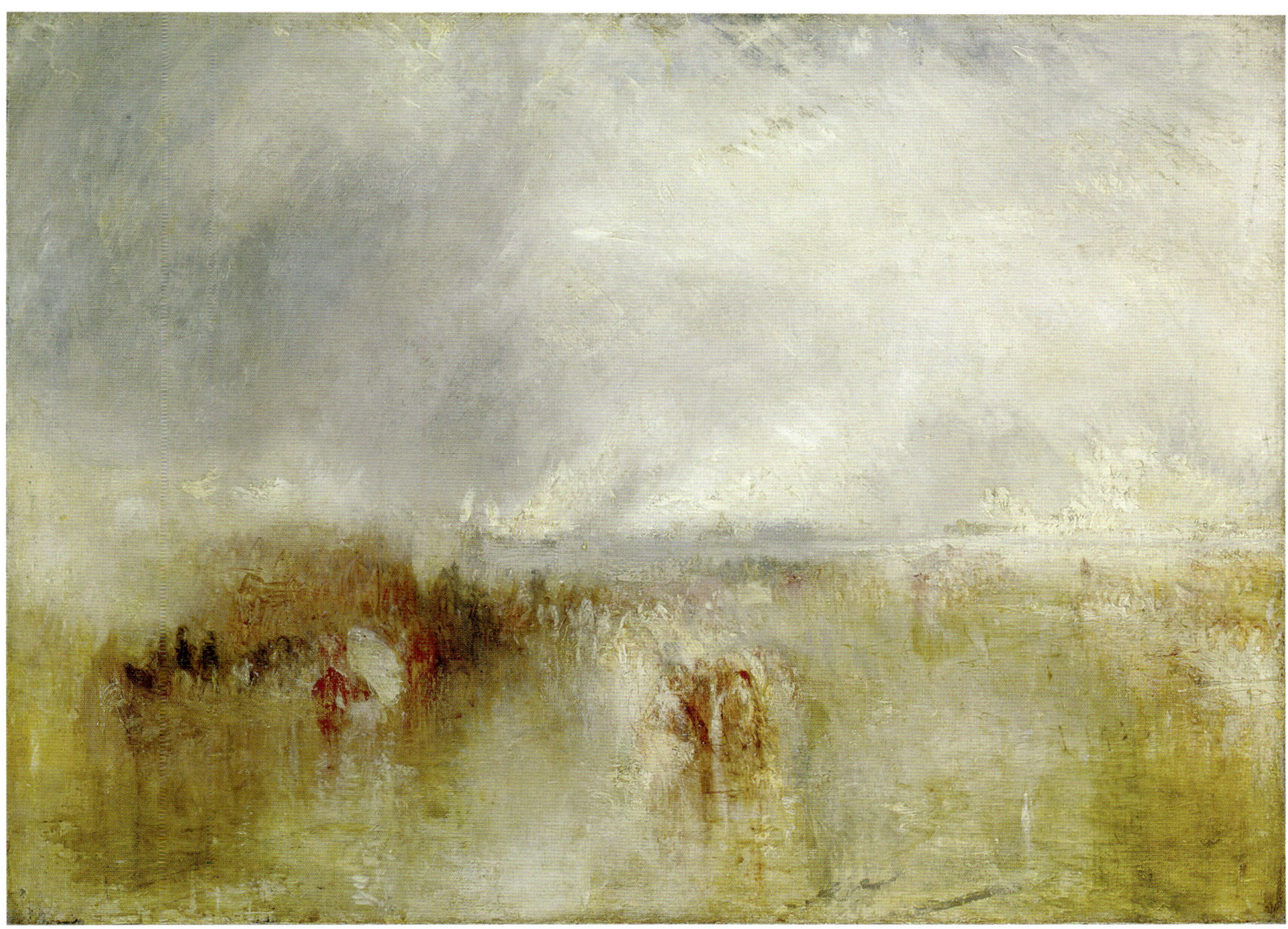

Fig. 179
The Arrival of Louis Philippe, 8 October 1844
c.1844–45
Oil on canvas,
90.2 × 120.6 cm
Tate (N02068; B&J 525)

Turner was, as always, alert to the potential of the scene as a piece of topical contemporary history and he started two canvases that he presumably planned to exhibit at the Royal Academy, perhaps in the hope of winning royal favour (fig. 179). However, his time in the lead up to the following exhibition became more limited after he took on the responsibilities of the ailing President, Sir Martin Archer Shee (1769–1850). He had at last reached the pinnacle of the British art world, but the distinction bestowed with these temporary duties came too late and the additional work contributed to his own ill health later that year. As a result he missed the most opportune moment to complete the pictures, and they then remained abandoned and unidentified in his studio until recently. These unfinished canvases look as though they were painted by a completely different artist from the one who began his successful trajectory with a visit to Salisbury in 1795. Long gone is the straightforward representation of the visible world and in its stead there is something intangible, something new.

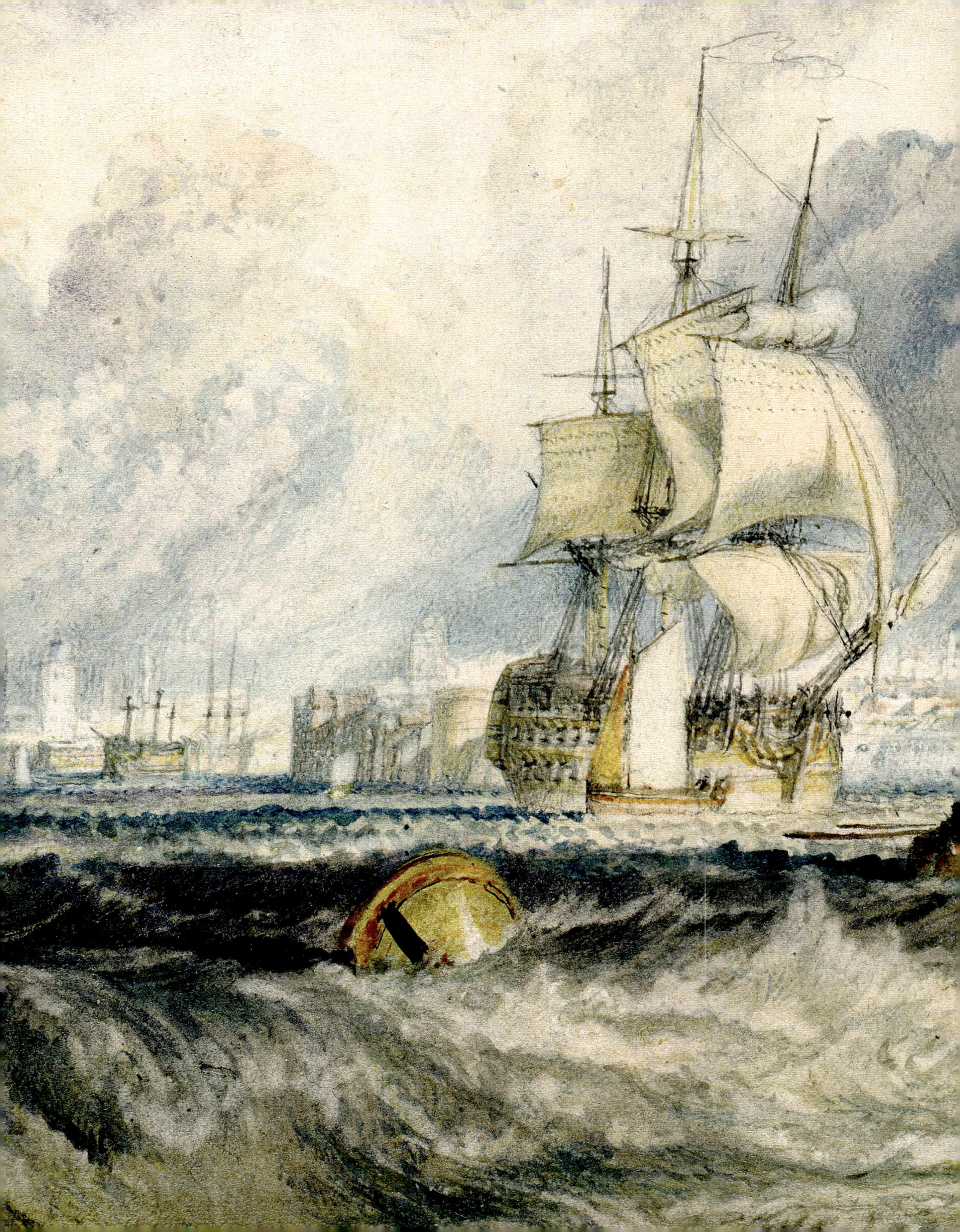

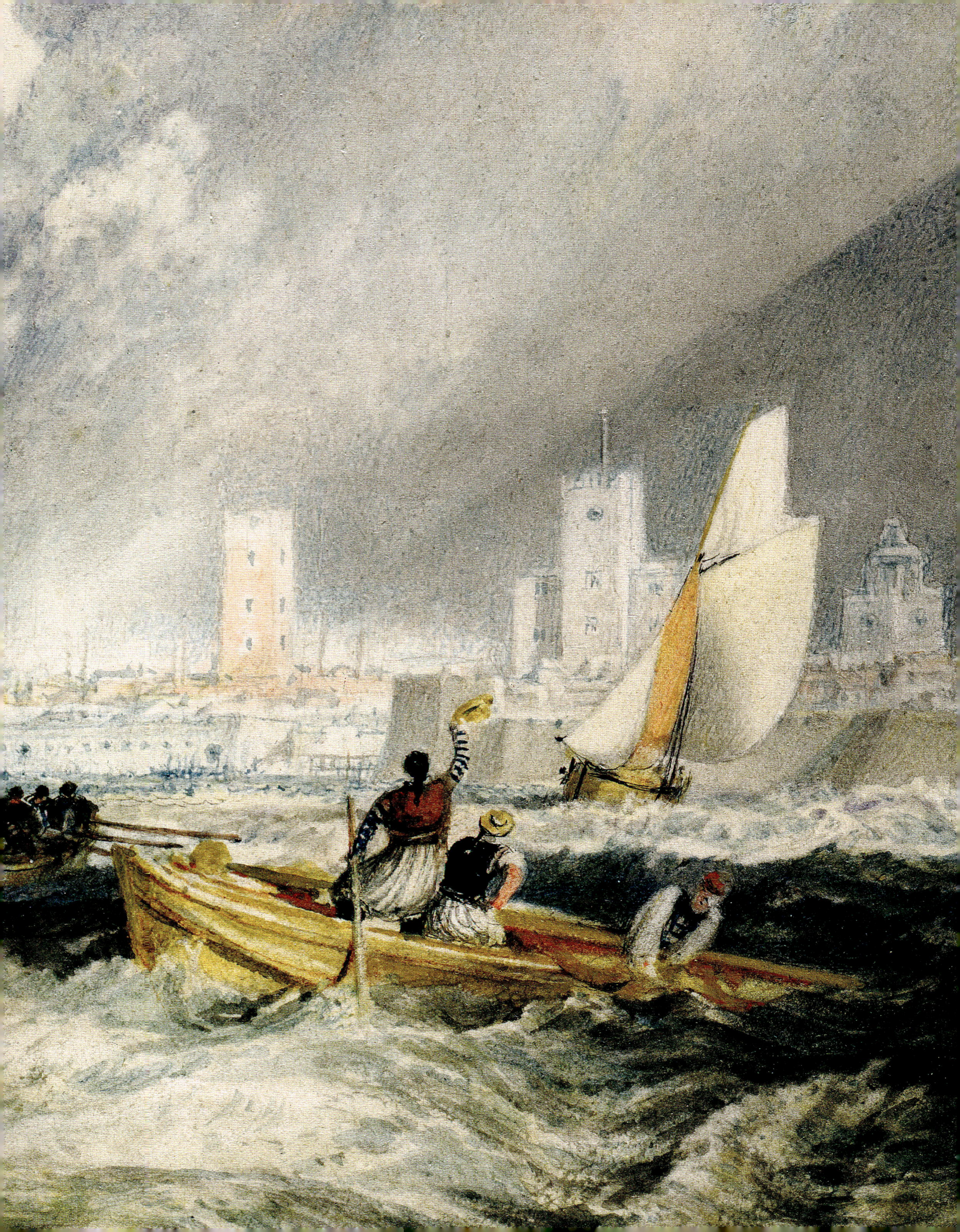

APPENDIX: THE CATHEDRAL SET

Fig. 35
Salisbury Cathedral from the East

*c.*1795–96
Pencil and watercolour, 28 × 23 cm
Tate (D00668 / TB XXVII G)

This small watercolour was made from Bishop's Walk, to the east of the cathedral, and would have been a controversial prospect in the mid-1790s. Its sharp foreshortening emphasises the outer wall of the Lady Chapel, with the faint outline of the newly-installed stained glass based on Sir Joshua Reynolds's *Resurrection* (see also fig. 39). For Turner's contemporaries, it simultaneously highlighted the absence of the flanking Hungerford and Beauchamp chantry chapels.[1] Their recent removal, and the structural restoration of the eastern end, were among James Wyatt's 'improvements' to the cathedral between 1789 and 1792, as sanctioned by Bishop Shute Barrington. Although Colt Hoare requested a watercolour from this viewpoint as no. 5 for his series, a full-scale version was never executed.

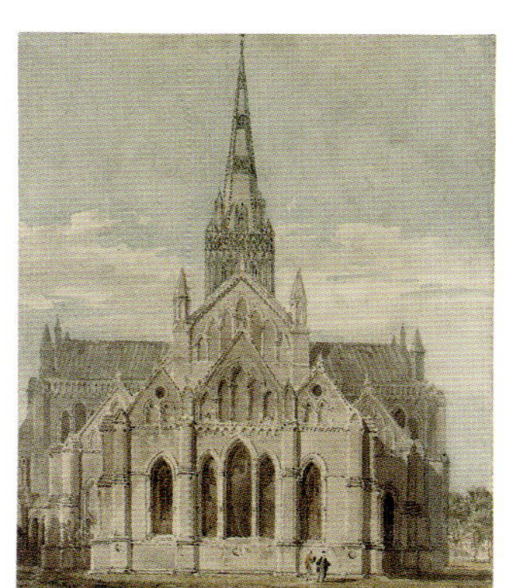

Fig. 37
North Porch of Salisbury Cathedral

Exhibited RA 1797, Council Room (517)
Watercolour, 50 × 65 cm

Provenance: Sir Richard Colt Hoare, 2nd Bt (paid 5 September 1797: £15); by descent to Sir Henry Ainslee Hoare, 5th Bt (1824–94); Christie's, 2 June 1883 (lot 20); bought by Gibbs on behalf of Agnew, for £136.10s (stock no. 7069); sold on 18 December 1884 to A. Crewdoon; ... ; Christie's, 9 July 1985 (lot 98); bought Agnew (stock no. 1485); sold to Salisbury Museum, 17 January 1986; bought with support from the Art Fund.
The Salisbury Museum (W196)

Before the early nineteenth century, when cathedrals became more integrated into national life as symbols of continuity, members of the public were generally only admitted for services. Turner's view of the North Porch depicts assorted citizens – men, women, numerous children and a dog – gathering around the western end of the building. The presence of stonemasons at work to the left, presumably connected with Wyatt's repairs, would seem to indicate that the day recalled by Turner was not a sabbath. None of the human activity appears in the very schematic sketch he made on the spot (fig. 36); he was similarly able to re-create, or imagine, warm light falling across the porch towards the end of a summer's day. This might well be intended to carry a symbolic meaning if the gathering of figures in the far distance is indeed a funeral procession, as proposed in the traditional title for this watercolour. Turner was probably aware of another of the controversies about Wyatt's work at Salisbury, which was the decision to improve the precincts by closing the surrounding cemetery and moving the tombstones aside to line the outer wall.

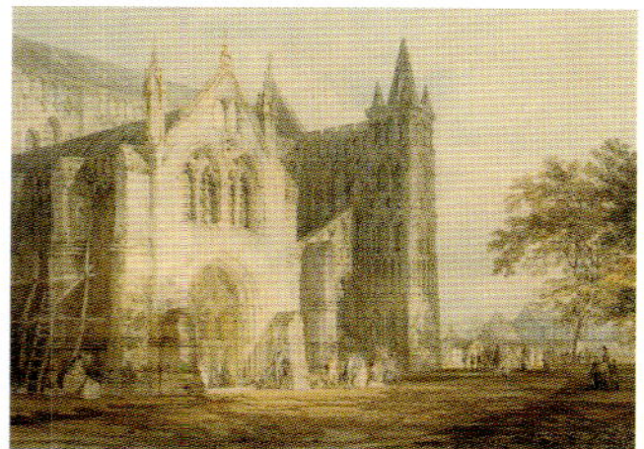

This watercolour was first exhibited in 1797 along with one of Ewenny Priory (National Museum of Wales, Cardiff). It was on visiting that medieval building in 1802 that Colt Hoare forcibly expressed his private reservations about the various transformations he had seen effected in the previous decade by Wyatt: 'the love of innovation and the bad taste, or perhaps I might better say ignorance of the most intelligent of our architects have robbed many of our churches and cathedrals of their original beauties'.[2]

Fig. 39
The Choir of Salisbury Cathedral
Exhibited RA 1797, Council Room (450)
Watercolour, 64.8 × 50.8 cm Inscribed, 'Turner / SARUM', '∑IOV', '1797'

Provenance: Sir Richard Colt Hoare, 2nd Bt (paid 5 September 1797: £15); ... Christie's, 2 June 1883 (lot 23); bought by Gibbs on behalf of Agnew, for £99.15s (stock no. 7072); sold on 23 February 1884 to Fothergill Watson; bought Agnew, 12 May 1924 (stock no. 484); sold to C. Morland Agnew; by descent to Miss E.M. Agnew; bequeathed to Vice-Admiral Sir William Agnew; bequeathed to the museum by his widow, 1977.
The Salisbury Museum (W197)

Fig. 41
The West Front of Salisbury Cathedral
Exhibited RA 1799, Council Room (335)
Watercolour, 48.5 × 66 cm

Provenance: Sir Richard Colt Hoare, 2nd Bt (paid 8 November 1799: £16.5s); ... Christie's, 2 June 1883 (lot 18); bought by Gibbs on behalf of Agnew, for £168 (stock no. 7067); sold 6 March 1884 to Mrs Cash; Christie's, 24 November 1906 (lot 61); bought for £504 by Agnew (stock no. 6090); sold to the Revd John Park Haslam, 13 March 1907; bequeathed to the museum in memory of his father.
Harris Museum and Art Gallery, Preston (W198)

As in the view of the North Porch, which was also exhibited at the Royal Academy in 1797, Turner's depiction of gothic architecture is transformed by his powerful rendering of bright sunlight. In this instance it serves to highlight the uncluttered space at the eastern end of the cathedral's interior created by Wyatt's removal of the altar dais and screens, uniting the Choir with the Sanctuary (or St Mary's Chapel) beyond. Remnants of old ceiling paintings had also been obliterated, all of which had added to the controversies about changes to the cathedral's fabric. The influential sculptor and draughtsman, John Flaxman (1755–1826), was still grumbling about the 'great absurdity' of some of Wyatt's alterations in the Choir in 1811.[3]

On the left the light falls across the chantry chapel of Bishop Edmund Audley (1502–1524), while between the pillars we see the seventeenth-century monument of Sir Thomas and Lady Gorges. Moving past this is a priest carrying a chalice, accompanied by a chanting choirboy, making their way to the high altar, where communicants are already kneeling. These details may reflect the revival of interest in the Sarum Rite at the end of the eighteenth century.

Above the new reredos, an amber light streams into the chapel from Francis Eginton's stained-glass window, designed by Sir Joshua Reynolds. The warm glow surrounding the surging

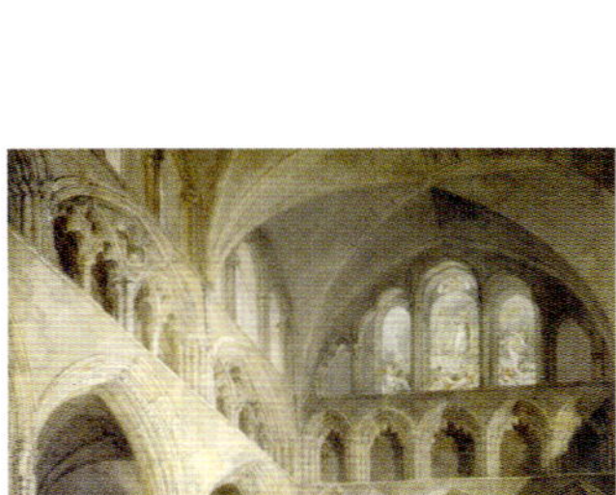

figure of Christ in this depiction of the Resurrection became a distinctive feature of this part of the cathedral and was recorded by other artists.[4] Turner seems to have been especially interested in the intensified colours of stained glass (both at Salisbury and in his depictions of Oxford colleges) and he also noted very precisely the other comparatively recent addition to the glass above the Choir.[5] This shows Moses among the Israelites in the wilderness, with the Brazen Serpent, and was made by James Pearson in 1781, from a design by John Hamilton Mortimer. A contemporary review singled out the 'charming' way Turner re-created the 'light and colour through the painted window', praising the 'true sublimity and grandeur' of effect.[6] As in his depiction of Westminster Abbey (fig. 14), Turner added his name to one of the foreground tombstones.

During his 1795 visit to Salisbury Turner made just two sketches of the cathedral exterior: one of the North Porch (fig. 37); the other of the West Front (fig. 41). Both were approved by Colt Hoare as the first of his commissions for the Salisbury series, but for some reason this watercolour was not exhibited until two years after its pair. By 1799 Turner had otherwise moved on from the detailed rendering of gothic architecture he had previously achieved in his depictions of the west fronts of Bath, Wells and Winchester (figs 8–10). But here he expanded the partial record he had made of the cathedral's main façade to portray the impressively regular patterned wall of ornamented stone and glass (the latter newly replaced by Wyatt).[7] At the peak of the main gable he included the new stone cross, another of Wyatt's restorations, but in his sketchbook he had been forced to

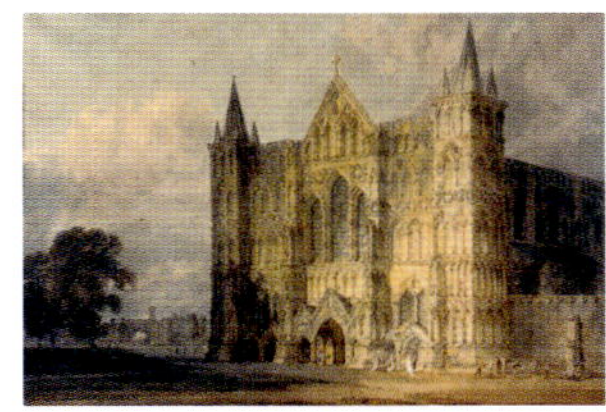

add that detail on the opposite page, having run out of space at the top of his sheet. Curiously, Turner does not show the horizontal line of the Nave roof, which should be visible behind the cross, and the image is cropped on the right just where the tower should rise upwards. Both of these were pragmatic decisions resulting from the absence of this information in his original sketch. Other details that he had recorded only faintly, however, did find a place in the finished design, such as the south side of the Close Gate and the tower of St Thomas's church.

Fig. 42
WILLIAM WOOLNOTH (1780–1837)
after FREDERICK NASH (1782–1856)
The Interior View of Salisbury Cathedral from the West Entrance
1814
For Dodsworth, *An Historical Account of the Episcopal See and Cathedral Church of Sarum, or Salisbury*
Engraving, 21.7 × 16.6 cm
British Library, London

Fig. 43
Inside of the Chapter-House of Salisbury Cathedral
Exhibited RA 1799, Council Room (327)
Watercolour, 66 × 50.8 cm

Provenance: Sir Richard Colt Hoare, 2nd Bt (paid 8 November 1799: £16.5s); ... Christie's, 2 June 1883 (lot 24), bought Agnew, for £110.5s (stock no. 7073) on behalf of the South Kensington Museum (503-1883).
Victoria and Albert Museum, London (W201)

The tenth subject that Turner and Colt Hoare identified for the Cathedral set was intended to be a view of the 'Entrance from West Door', which might well have approximated to this scene by Frederick Nash, engraved for William Dodsworth's authoritative history of the cathedral (1814). However, if Turner made any sketches of this part of the building, they have not survived. The long Nave, then unfurnished, naturally emphasised the new pulpitum, the stone screen across the entrance to the Choir. This had been introduced by Wyatt, using fragments of the Hungerford and Beauchamp chantry chapels, and was surmounted by the organ presented by King George III (later moved to St Thomas's Church); it can also be seen in the watercolour of the crossing and the North Transept.[8]

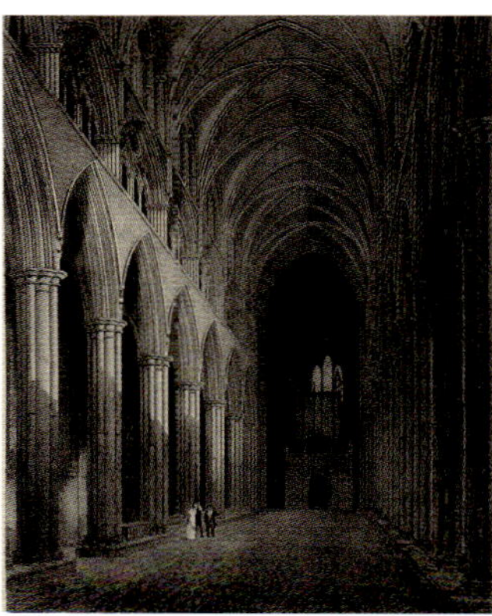

The Chapter House at Salisbury was constructed in the second half of the thirteenth century, after the cathedral was complete, and added an important functional space that was also an architectural marvel. It is defined by its elegant central pillar (shooting up and outwards like a great palm) and complemented by the tall windows on all sides that fill the room with light.

Turner used the doorway into the Chapter House to frame his scene theatrically, heightening the viewer's desire to enter the space. His viewpoint was the adjacent vestibule, which allowed him to study the statues of Virtues and Vices ascending on either side of the arch. Stretching out across the floor into the Chapter Houses are tombstones, or redeployed bits of gothic architecture. These lead the eye towards four boys (possibly absconding choirboys), who look up from their game guiltily. The image presents the diametrically opposite view to that of Turner's later watercolour of the interior (fig. 44). But rather than offering strikingly contrasting effects, both works are illuminated by similar shafts of sunlight. It is only on closer examination that they can be found to represent different times of day; the higher beams of afternoon light cast strong shadows to the left in this work. In painting two views of the Chapter House from different angles perhaps Turner wanted to suggest the timeless nature of the scene: the place and the

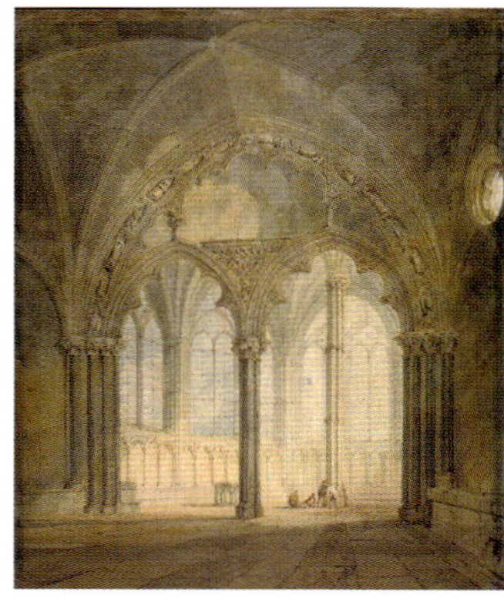

activities remain the same, even as the people come and go. On the facing wall, he took some trouble to record the heraldic shields and other patterns in the stained glass of the east window. This was then the only window to retain its original glass, but it too was replaced in the 1820s.

Given the intricacy of this composition, with its deep perspective, Turner probably worked up the finished image over a very detailed pencil sketch; nearly all of the later watercolours of Salisbury appear to have been developed in this way (figs 63, 66, 68). Note how some features of the finished image do not correspond exactly with the under-drawing. When exhibited at the Royal Academy, it was praised in the *St James's Chronicle* for being 'forcible and rich of colour; very solemn and grand in effect'.[9]

Fig. 44
Chapter-House, Salisbury Cathedral

Exhibited RA 1801, Council Room (415)
Watercolour, 64 × 51 cm

Provenance: Sir Richard Colt Hoare, 2nd Bt (paid 21 November 1801: 25 guineas); ... Christie's, 2 June 1883 (lot 25), bought by Gibbs on behalf of Agnew, for £252 (stock no. 7074); sold to Mrs Mumm, 21 February 1885; Agnew, 5 May 1885 (stock no. 7682); sold to Sir William Agnew, 31 December 1889; presented by him to the Whitworth Institute, 1891 (D.3.1889).
The Whitworth, The University of Manchester (W199)

This later depiction of the Chapter House grew out of some rudimentary notes Turner made in his 'Salisbury' sketchbook, which he used during a visit in August 1799 (figs 45–46). The various elements he noted in detail were no doubt combined with a fairly full outline of the whole composition, which is as complicated as the fish-eye perspective in his depiction of Ely Cathedral (fig. 25). It is not a photographic record of the architecture that has been captured with an optical tool, such as a camera lucida, but one that reflects the experience of inhabiting the space, distorting distances in much the same way that the eye composes a total image.

Turner's viewpoint was from one of the 51 seats that run around the walls to accommodate the bishop and his colleagues (probably that at the juncture of the east and north-east walls). Above these is a frieze illustrating incidents from the first two books of the Bible. In his sketchbook Turner transcribed the last 18 scenes of this cycle, which depict Joseph and his brothers, and the Israelites' escape from Egypt (fig. 45).[10] These studies relate to the sculptures that can be found on the south and south-western sides of the Chapter House, which are the precise focus of the watercolour. On another page he recorded the base of the central column and the encaustic tiles radiating out from it, as seen from his viewpoint at the juncture of the north-east and east bays.[11] A final sketch shows the capital on the pillar dividing the entrance into the Chapter House (fig. 46); the dash of brown paint on this sheet indicates that Turner consulted it while developing the watercolour. Exactly the same warm

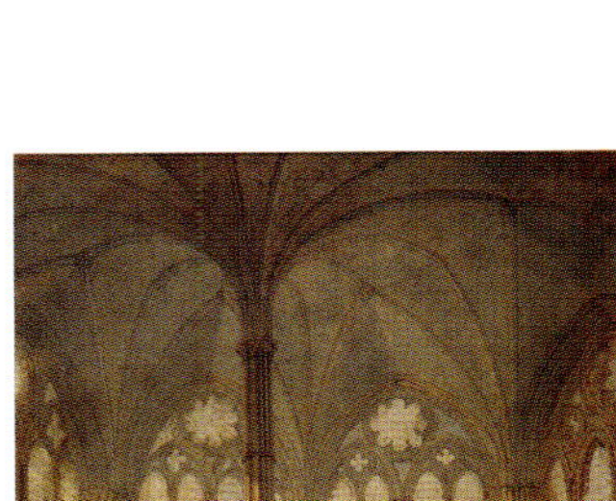

earthy colour can be found throughout the finished work, which has misled some commentators to claim that it now looks very faded. In fact, Turner appears to have been attempting to re-create the appearance of morning sunlight, still gaining in strength as it enters the space from the south-east: a lower and more autumnal effect than that of 1799. His efforts were applauded by the critic of the *St James's Chronicle*, possibly the same reviewer as in 1799, who described the work as 'A clear and beautiful representation of that Edifice; the tints extremely true to nature.'[12]

Lurking in the shadows below the slanting light, a group of boys (dressed in much the same type of clothes as those in the 1799 view – and evidently still shirking two years later) abandon their hoops to play marbles. As well as providing a sense of scale, it has been suggested that the children Turner featured in his cathedral subjects were intended to invoke Christ's decree, 'Suffer little children to come unto me, and forbid them not: for of such is the kingdom of God' (Luke, 18:16).[13]

Fig. 63
Salisbury Cathedral from the South Side of the Cloister

*c.*1801–5
Watercolour, 68 × 49.6 cm
Inscribed, lower left, 'JMW Turner RA'

Provenance: Sir Richard Colt Hoare, 2nd Bt (paid 7 December 1805: 25 guineas); ... Christie's, 2 June 1883 (lot 21), bought Agnew, for £94.10s (stock no. 7070) on behalf of the South Kensington Museum (502-1883).
Victoria and Albert Museum, London (W202)

The large Cloister at Salisbury forms a square running parallel to the full length of the Nave. While many other parts of the cathedral were replaced or restored in the 1790s, the Cloister remained neglected until the 1830s. This was the decade in which the great cedar trees that now spread their shade over the central lawn were planted. Wonderful though they are, their presence makes it difficult to recapture the scene Turner created in this watercolour. They partly obscure the east side of the Cloister, where there is an upper layer, housing the library. This feature was noted by Turner below the gable of the Transept. But everything in his view draws the eye to the celebrated spire, the tallest in England at 123 metres (404 feet), which (this time) he gives in its true proportions, even transcribing the fussy particularities of its ballflower nodules and other decorations.

As in the 1799 view of the Chapter House, he constructed his innovative design through a series of receding planes, framing the view towards the cathedral with some of the broken arcading on the south side of the Cloister. The upper parts of each arch

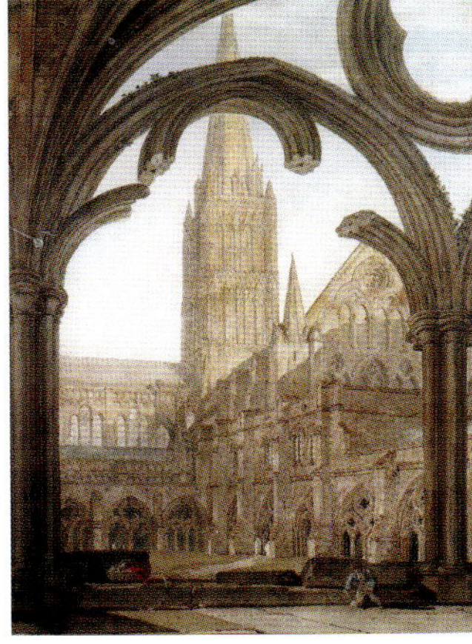

had been glazed until the seventeenth century, but the scale of these openings is somewhat distorted here for artistic effect, and exaggerated still further by the boy, who crouches down in mid throw of his top. This effect can be readily grasped by comparing Turner's stirring image with the more prosaic, and derivative version, by Frederick Mackenzie, published as plate VIII in Britton's *The History and Antiquities of the Cathedral Church of Salisbury* (fig. 65).

Fig. 68

Interior of Salisbury Cathedral, looking towards the North Transept

c.1801–5

Watercolour, 66 × 50.8 cm

Inscribed, 'TURNER / RA', 'EPISOP ... SARUM'

Provenance: Sir Richard Colt Hoare, 2nd Bt (paid 7 December 1805: 30 guineas); ... Christie's, 2 June 1883 (lot 22), bought by Gibbs on behalf of Agnew, £136.10s (stock no. 7071); sold to Mrs Mumm, 21 February 1885; by descent to R.J. Mumm; Christie's, 6 May 1921 (lot 7); bought Agnew (stock no. 9939); sold to C. Morland Agnew , 12 May 1921; by descent to Vice-Admiral Sir William Agnew; bequeathed to the museum, with a life interest to his widow 1977.

The Salisbury Museum (W203)

Turner's skills as an architectural draughtsman were the foundation of his reputation in the 1790s. But few of his earlier representations of ecclesiastical interiors match the audacity and accomplishment of this thrilling view through the very centre of Salisbury Cathedral. The prospect is that seen from the Southern Transept, after entering the building from the Cloister. Here the vast space of the cathedral stretches off the sheet in almost every direction. The strong verticals of the piers supporting the tower rise to an unseen arch, just as the high clerestory level of the Transept is barely glimpsed above the elaborate tracery of the triforium on the upper right-hand side.[14] Yet again, the paving across the foreground asserts the location as 'SARUM' (see fig. 39), and Turner's name finds a place once more among the shields and other heraldic devices. For the first time it is supplemented by the initials 'RA' denoting his status as a full member of the Royal Academy from February 1802.

At the centre of it all is Wyatt's massive neo-gothic screen, topped by the towering new organ (see fig. 42), a feature given further prominence by the great swathe of afternoon sunshine falling across it. Various cassocked clerics and dignitaries walk through to the Choir, presumably to attend evensong. The tall male figure in a green jacket may be intended to represent

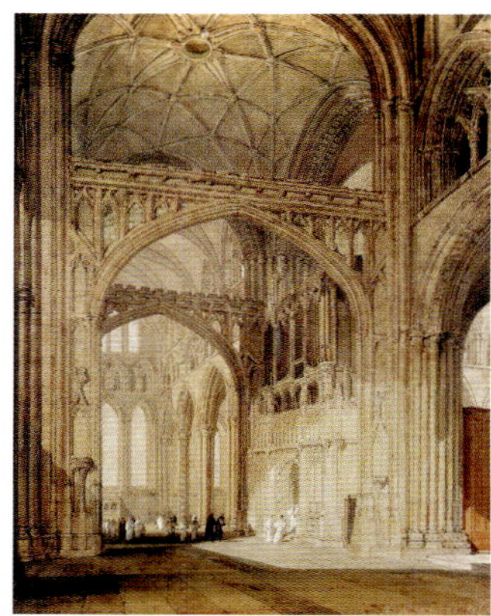

Colt Hoare himself.[15] In Turner's newly-discovered invoice, dated 21 November 1801, he asked Colt Hoare's assistance with a detail in the picture, requesting the loan of what appears to read 'a pair [or 'piece'] of Scipica', although it is unclear what he meant: perhaps it was an attempt at 'Scipio', the Latin name for the baton carried by one of the officials; or possibly he misspelled 'Silica' and was referring to the new glass. The brilliant sunlight visible in the image, no longer dulled by painted glass, was also the result of Wyatt's purification of the building: one account claimed that 'whole cartloads of glass, lead and other rubbish were removed from the nave and transepts, and shot into the town ditch, then in the course of being filled up'.[16]

Fig. 66

A General View of Salisbury Cathedral from the Bishop's Garden

c.1801–5

Watercolour, 51.3 × 67.8 cm

Provenance: Sir Richard Colt Hoare, 2nd Bt (paid 7 December 1805: 25 guineas); ... Christie's, 2 June 1883 (lot 19); bought by Gibbs on behalf of Agnew, for £115.10s (stock no. 7068); sold on 26 March 1884, to Frederick Fish; Christie's, 24 March 1888 (lot 258); bought for £157.10s by Agnew (stock no. 8738); sold 26 March 1888, to Sir John Pender, Foots Cray (1816–96); Christie's, 29 May 1897 (lot 17); bought Agnew, for £173.5s (stock no. 2043); sold to the museum, 31 May 1897 (9'97).

Birmingham Museum and Art Gallery (W200)

It was not until 1805 that Turner delivered this 'General View' (as he called it) along with those of the Cloister and the North Transept (figs 63 and 68). There are no preliminary sketches, so the finished watercolour was presumably developed over the primary record of the scene. Although it has been dated to c.1797–98 by earlier scholars, the landscape Turner depicts does not accord with plans of formal gardens adjoining the Bishop's Palace in a map of 1797, when the kitchen garden wall would also have been visible on the right.[17] The transformation of areas laid out in rigid patterns to a more natural setting is generally credited to Bishop Fisher, Constable's patron, but as he was not translated (or moved) to Salisbury until 1807, two years after this watercolour was acquired by Colt Hoare, it is clear that the landscape was already in transition before that. This is apparent in Turner's image, where felled trees lie across the broadly painted foreground, and a group of labourers take refreshment towards the end of an afternoon. The expanse of grass running up to the path to

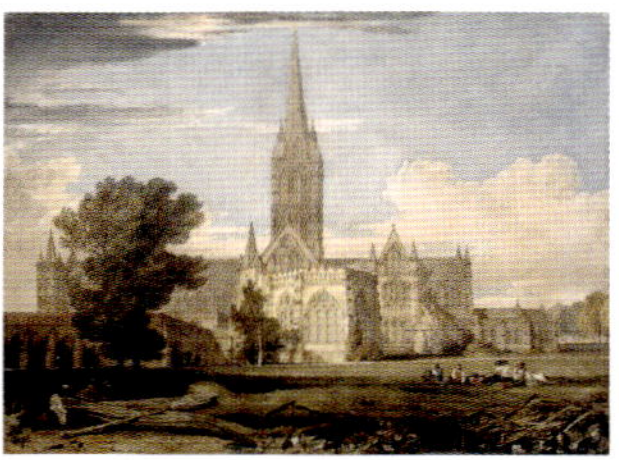

the south of the Cloister is not so different from how it was delineated by Constable in 1811; in fact, allowing for a slight shift in viewpoint to the west, the same trees bordering the path can be found, with rather more growth, in his sketch (Victoria and Albert Museum).[18]

After 1807 Turner spent a great deal of time researching the lectures he eventually gave as Professor of Perspective at the Royal Academy from 1811. One of the diagrams he prepared seems to be related to this watercolour (fig. 67), since both represent the spire of the cathedral as rather stunted, instead of its actual tapering form. Along with another diagram, it was intended to illustrate a discussion of geometric laws of perspective.[19]

THE CITY SET

Fig. 49
The Bishop's Palace, Salisbury
*c.*1799
Watercolour, 28.4 × 35.9 cm
Inscribed, lower right, 'W Turner'

Provenance: Sir Richard Colt Hoare, 2nd Bt (paid 21 November 1801: 7 guineas); by descent to Sir Henry Ainslee Hoare, 5th Bt (1824–94); the Revd John Henry Ellis, MA, of Stourton; by descent to H.A. Steward; Christie's, 28 July 1927 (lot 6); bought Agnew (stock no. 1023); sold on 25 October 1932 to Dr A.W. Young; Fine Art Society, London; bought 30 May 1949 by Agnew (stock no. 5916); sold on 8 September 1952 to the Cecil Higgins Art Gallery (P.97).
The Higgins, Bedford (W204)

This seems to have been one of the earliest completed views of the City set. There are no related sketches, but its style is consistent with Turner's watercolours of the second half of the 1790s, after he first sketched at Salisbury. At this time the incumbent at the palace was Bishop John Douglas (1791–1807). He had succeeded Bishop Shute Barrington, whose controversial restorations at Salisbury included adding the 'Gothick' porch, seen on the right. By choosing to paint the building in the early afternoon, Turner was able to capture the summer sunshine on the mottled surfaces of the east tower. Perhaps the shadows that darken the

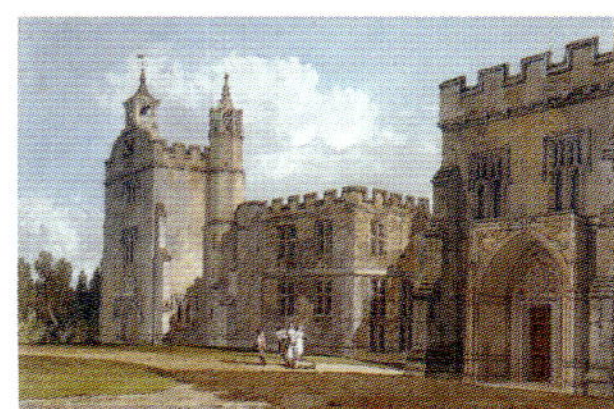

façade were intended to disguise the bright new stone of the porch, although the Barrington coat of arms is readily discernible. In front of the palace some gardeners tug a roller over the carriage turning circle; the same feature can be seen in a watercolour by John Buckler dating from 1804.[20]

Fig. 50
St Edmund's Church, Salisbury
*c.*1799
Watercolour, 38.4 × 27 cm
Inscribed, lower right, 'W Turner'

Provenance: Sir Richard Colt Hoare, 2nd Bt (paid 21 November 1801: 7 guineas); by descent to Sir Henry Ainslee Hoare, 5th Bt (1824–94); the Revd John Henry Ellis, MA, of Stourton; by descent to H.A. Steward; Christie's, 28 July 1927 (lot 9); bought Agnew (stock no. 1026); sold to R.W. Lloyd for £141.15s, plus 5% commission (£7.1s.9d) on 8 August 1927; bequeathed by him to the British Museum, 1958 (1958-7-12-403).
British Museum (W205)

St Edmund's Church lies in the north-east corner of Salisbury, on Bedwin Street, and is now the city's Arts Centre. An earlier church was founded in the thirteenth century by Bishop Walter de la Wyle (1263–1271) to honour Edmund Rich of Abingdon (1175–1240), who had been Treasurer at the cathedral before his elevation to Archbishop of Canterbury in 1234. The original church was part of a larger group of ecclesiastical buildings known as St Edmund's College, though they had separate histories after the Reformation. In 1653 the tower collapsed onto the nave, but remarkably it was rebuilt, one of only two churches granted permission to be reconstructed during Cromwell's Commonwealth.

Turner's depiction shows the west end of the church from the north, which creates afternoon shadows on the side of the tower comparable to those in his

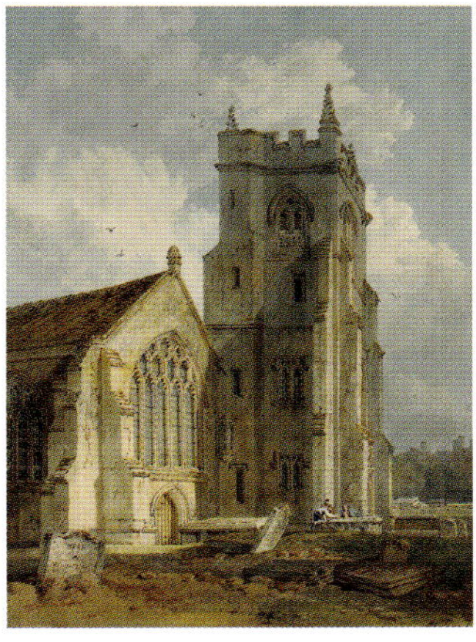

watercolour of the Bishop's Palace (fig. 49). Both of these works, along with fig. 52, are signed using the same simple format ('W. Turner'), linking them as part of the same batch.

Fig. 52
The Ancient Arch in Mr Wyndham's Garden, Salisbury

*c.*1799
Pencil and watercolour, 37.9 × 29.3 cm
Inscribed, lower right, 'W Turner'

Provenance: Sir Richard Colt Hoare, 2nd Bt (paid 21 November 1801: 7 guineas); by descent to Sir Henry Ainslee Hoare, 5th Bt (1824–94); the Revd John Henry Ellis, MA, of Stourton; by descent to H.A. Steward; Christie's, 28 July 1927 (lot 7); bought by Agnew (stock no. 1024); sold to R.W. Lloyd for £68.5s, plus 5% commission (£3.8s.3d) on 8 August 1927; bequeathed by him to the British Museum, 1958 (1958-7-12-404).
British Museum (W206)

Fig. 53
St Thomas's Church from the High Street, looking North

*c.*1799
Pencil, 15 × 12.3 cm
From the 'Salisbury' sketchbook
Tate (D02329, D02330 / TB XLIX 76a, 77)

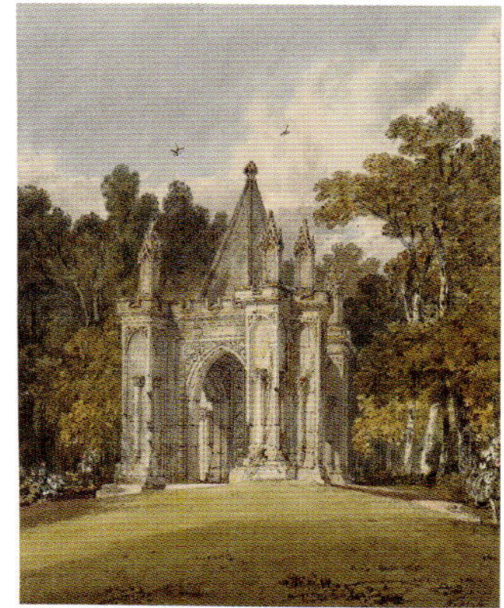

In this watercolour Turner records a curious architectural remnant, which served as the porch to the North Transept until Wyatt began his tidying up of the cathedral. In detaching the structure, it was found to be decorated on all sides with niches, which suggested it had a very specific function in its original setting, apparently at Old Sarum: one theory is that it was a well cover.[21] After the structure was scrapped by Wyatt, the Chapter was lobbied by local antiquarian Henry Penruddocke Wyndham (1736–1819), who sought to move it to the garden of his home, then called Wyndham House, at Bourne Hill, next to St Edmund's Church. Once there, he added what he thought were authentic gothic accretions, including the spire (which is still in place).[22] Wyndham's gardens had been newly landscaped by Richard Woods (1715–1793), followed by modifications to the house, designed by S.P. Cockerell (1754–1827).

Unusually, Turner made two preliminary studies for this image, in which he seems to be experimenting with the fall of light across and through the arch.[23] There is no documentation to confirm the contention made in one account that Turner stayed at Wyndham House,[24] but Colt Hoare would have readily effected an introduction, because many of his interests overlapped with Wyndham's, including the antiquities of Monmouthshire. At the time of Turner's visit to Salisbury in 1795, Wyndham had recently published an account of his travels on the Isle of Wight, which could have informed the artist's tour shortly afterwards.

Of the ten subjects enumerated for Colt Hoare's City set only one was never delivered: that of St Thomas's Church (dedicated to St Thomas Becket). In the list in use around 1801, St Thomas's is clearly itemised as no. 2. But this must be an error, for under no. 7 there are pencil annotations reading 'St Ed[munds] Church, by the Market Place', which is evidently a confusion of St Thomas's Church with the name of the parish to the north-east, as marked on eighteenth-century maps where the parish borders bisect the Market Place. Further muddle arises from the repetition of St Edmund's as no. 9. Compounding all of this is the absence of St Martin's Church on the list, which *was* one of the completed watercolours, and presumably the item intended as no. 2. Given this mess, it is perhaps not surprising that Turner was rather bewildered about which subject he had neglected.

The top of St Thomas's tower can be seen in the view from the Poultry Cross that Turner sketched in 1795. But he depicted its impact on the surrounding streets more dramatically while in Salisbury in 1799 in a sketchbook that he used to record subjects required for the Colt Hoare project.[25]

Fig. 54
The Poultry Cross, with the Tower of St Thomas's Church, Salisbury

c.1799
Watercolour, 36.2 × 48 cm
Inscribed, lower right, 'JMW Turner'

Provenance: Sir Richard Colt Hoare, 2nd Bt (paid 21 November 1801: 7 guineas); by descent to Sir Henry Ainslee Hoare, 5th Bt (1824–94); the Revd John Henry Ellis, MA, of Stourton; by descent to H.A. Steward; Christie's, 28 July 1927 (lot 5); bought Leggatt; Mrs Ether Salter Kerrigan; Park Bernet, 1942; Scott & Fowles, Parke-Bernet, New York, 28 March 1946 (lot 30); John Regina; given to Patrick Sardoni; French & Co., New York, 1977; ... ; Sam Weisbord, Los Angeles; given by him to the American Friends of the Israel Museum, in memory of his mother, Goldie Weisbord. Israel Museum, Jerusalem (W211)

The Poultry Cross, still standing at the western end of Butcher's Row, was the focus of one of the six sketches of Salisbury that Turner recorded in his sketchbook in 1795, and it is possible that he developed this watercolour soon afterwards. The form of the signature – 'JMW Turner' – however, suggests a later date, around 1800; although it may have been added subsequently to be consistent with others in the City set (see also figs 55 and 57). Vegetables and poultry had been sold for centuries near the stone cross, which was the last of four medieval crosses in Salisbury; the others designated the markets

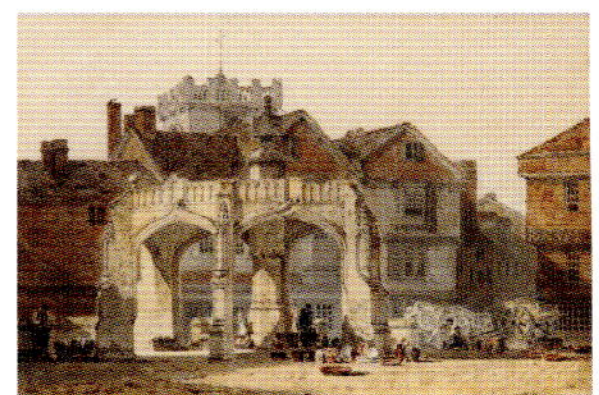

for cheese, wool and cattle.[26] It was not until the mid-nineteenth century that the cross was given its current distinctive crowned roof. In addition to the market vendors, with their clutter of carts and produce, Turner noted the names of several shop-owners, including Evans, a haberdasher.

Fig. 57
The Old Council House, the Market Place, Salisbury

c.1799
Watercolour, 28 × 38.5 cm
Inscribed, 'JMW Turner'

Provenance: Sir Richard Colt Hoare, 2nd Bt (paid 21 November 1801: 7 guineas); by descent to Sir Henry Ainslee Hoare, 5th Bt (1824–94); the Revd John Henry Ellis, MA, of Stourton; by descent to H.A. Steward; Christie's, 28 July 1927 (lot 8); bought Agnew (stock no. 1025); sold on 9 October 1935 to Roland Addy; Mrs Joan Thirsk; bequeathed to the gallery, 1978. Cooper Gallery, Barnsley (W212)

During his visit to Salisbury in 1795 Turner diligently recorded the battered remains of the old timber-framed Council House, which had stood to the north of the Bishop's Guildhall from the 1580s until 1780, when fire swept through its three storeys following the mayor's banquet (presumably a particularly lively occasion). Images of the old Council House prior to this disaster, such as that attributed to Francis Grose, show an attractive building, topped by a central turret and surrounded by a colonnade (The Salisbury Museum). In his finished watercolour Turner placed a group of figures on the steps inside the colonnade, with one of the market traders sitting on the right, selling her wares (market days were Tuesdays and Saturdays). In the far distance a

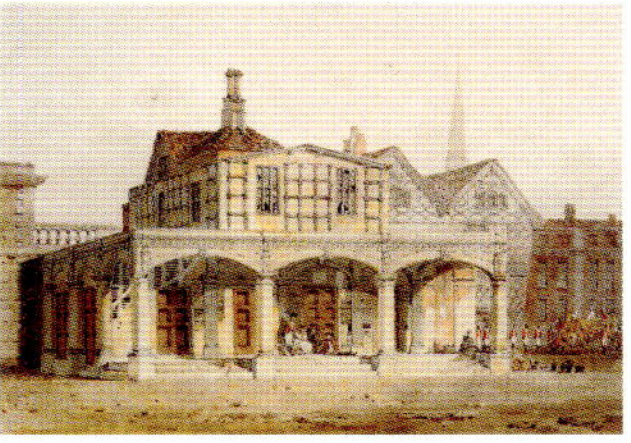

line of redcoats stand on duty, beside figures loading a wagon, indicating that this is very much a garrison town. Their presence may be connected with protests in the years before Turner's 1795 visit about the payment of tariffs by some market traders.[27] Above the old Council House to the right is the spire of the cathedral, while on the left Turner's viewpoint permits a glimpse of the new Council House.

Fig. 55
St Martin's Church, Salisbury
*c.*1800
Watercolour, 31.8 × 43.2 cm
Inscribed, lower right, 'JMW Turner'

Provenance: Sir Richard Colt Hoare, 2nd Bt (paid 21 November 1801: 7 guineas); by descent to Sir Henry Ainslee Hoare, 5th Bt (1824–94); the Revd John Henry Ellis, MA, of Stourton; by descent to H.A. Steward; Christie's, 28 July 1927 (lot 3); bought Permain; P.C. Manuk and Miss G.M. Coles; bequeathed to the British Museum through the NACF, 1948 (1949-10-9-8).
British Museum (W207).

For some reason Turner omitted St Martin's Church from his list of the City subjects for Colt Hoare, despite its historic significance as one of the few buildings pre-dating the construction of the cathedral. He made a pencil sketch in the churchyard, most probably in 1799, when he was rounding up motifs he had not previously studied.[28] In the process of preparing his finished watercolour (which is roughly the same width as that sheet), Turner applied a milky blue wash to the sketch to test his colours. This reveals that, before it faded, the sky would originally have been more modulated to suggest clouds on a sunny afternoon, as in other watercolours in the group.[29]

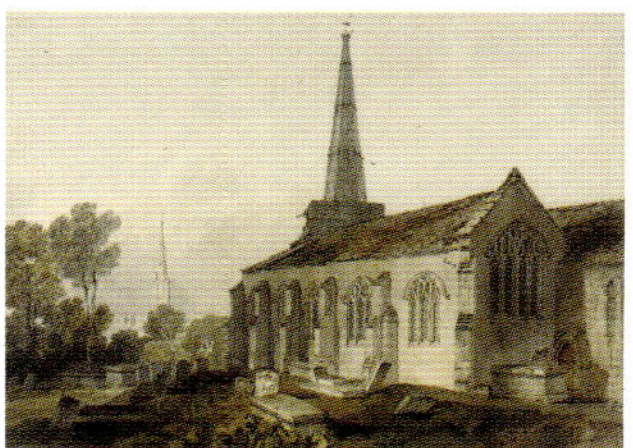

St Martin's Church lies near Milford, to the east, and is divided from the rest of the city by the inner city ring road. Most of the table tombs recorded by Turner have been removed, but it is still a romantic spot. He constructed his composition so that the eye travels from the fourteenth-century spire of the outlying church to that of the cathedral. Constable avoided repeating this neat conceit when he sketched at St Martin's in 1820, choosing a viewpoint where the prospect towards the City is blocked by a line of lime trees (National Gallery of Canada, Ottawa).[30] But his options may have been limited by the fact that these had grown rapidly since they were planted in 1792.

Fig. 59
Gateway to the Close, Salisbury
1802–5
Watercolour, 45.6 × 31.5 cm
Inscribed, lower right, 'JMW Turner RA'

Provenance: Sir Richard Colt Hoare, 2nd Bt (paid 7 December 1805: 10 guineas); by descent to Sir Henry Ainslee Hoare, 5th Bt (1824–94); the Revd John Henry Ellis, MA, of Stourton; by descent to H.A. Steward; Christie's, 28 July 1927 (lot 2); bought Leggatt; P.C. Manuk and Miss G.M. Coles; bequeathed to the museum through the NACF, 1948.
Fitzwilliam Museum, Cambridge (W208)

Turner's first use of the sketches he made during his 1795 visit to Salisbury was a depiction of the crenellated fourteenth-century Close Gate, leading toward the College of Matrons and the cathedral precincts from the High Street (fig. 33). The spire shifts the focus away from the gate, the stonework of which was then rather dilapidated around the Stuart coat of arms. The inclusion of a line of washing further stresses the commonplace current uses of the archway compared with its historic past.

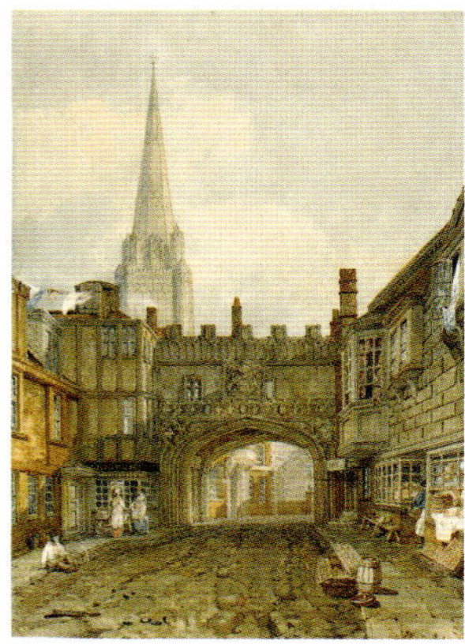

Turner's primary sketch, from which he worked up the 1796 exhibit, and this later version for Colt Hoare, includes the name of the shop owner, 'Fricker', as well as the sign notifying 'Vagrants' of the rules of the Close on the board to the right of the gate. During his travels in 1795 Turner sketched other town gateways at Wells, Monmouth, Gloucester and Southampton (fig. 12), anticipating that such symbols of local pride would prove marketable.

In addition to the two versions of this image already mentioned, there is a third (Private collection), which may have been produced by one of Turner's pupils.

Fig. 62
The New Council House (or Guildhall), Salisbury

c.1805
Watercolour, 30 × 39 cm
Inscribed 'JMWT'

Provenance: Sir Richard Colt Hoare, 2nd Bt (paid 7 December 1805: 10 guineas); by descent to Sir Henry Ainslee Hoare, 5th Bt (1824–94); the Revd John Henry Ellis, MA, of Stourton; by descent to H.A. Steward; Christie's, 28 July 1927 (lot 4); bought Agnew (stock no. 1022); sold on 6 November 1936 to Roland Addy; Mrs Joan Thirsk; bequeathed by her to the gallery, 1978.
Cooper Gallery, Barnsley (W213)

Following the fire in the Old Council House in 1780, Jacob Pleydell-Bouverie, 2nd Earl of Radnor (1750–1828), donated funds for a new building. This act of public-spirited generosity had been encouraged by a promise that he would receive the market tolls recently surrendered by the bishop, but those payments were ultimately secured by the corporation. Rather than beginning work on the site of the previous Council House, permission was gained to demolish the Bishop's Guildhall, which stood behind it, to the south; this curious temporary arrangement can be seen in Henry Brooks's painting of 1795 (fig. 56; Salisbury City Council). The new Council House, containing courts, prison cells, council rooms and a banqueting room, was constructed between 1787 and 1795, using cream brick with stone dressing, to a design by Sir Robert Taylor, with revisions by his pupil William Pilkington.[31] The building was completed on 23 September 1795.[32] Turner's pencil sketch of the façade was made earlier in the summer, while final building work was taking place (fig. 60); indeed, masons and blocks of stone appear in the foreground. It is sometimes unclear whether Turner was simply saving time in not sketching

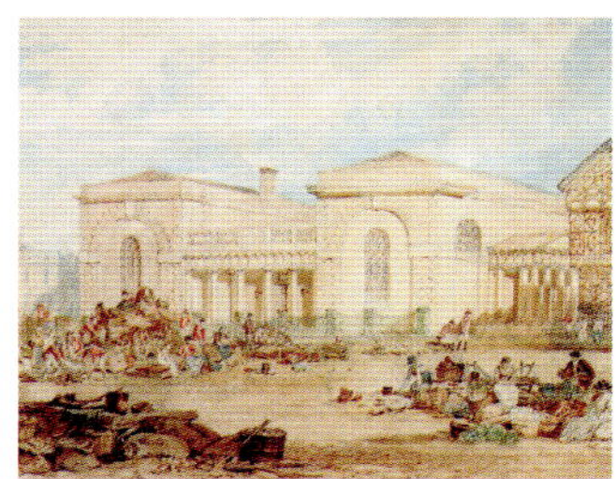

every detail, such the triglyphs on the façade's Doric colonnade, or whether such gaps indicate the actual state of the building. He did not complete his finished watercolour until 1805, and had no doubt revisited the building several times by then, also producing an intermediate study for the image around 1799 (fig. 61). In the finished work, a group of soldiers unloads a wagon piled high with cumbersome packages, transferring them to a wheelbarrow. It is not obvious whether these are related to the market or official matters.[33]

The Council House was later altered, probably in 1889, at which point the portico Turner shows on the west side was moved to the north. After 1927, when the council moved to new premises at St Edmund's College, the building was renamed the Guildhall.

Fig. 58
The East Front of Wilton House

1805
Watercolour, 32 × 46 cm
Inscribed, 'JMWT'
Engraved by Thomas Higham (1795–1844) for Colt Hoare, *History of Modern Wiltshire*, 1825

Provenance: Sir Richard Colt Hoare, 2nd Bt (paid 7 December 1805: 10 guineas); by descent to Sir Henry Ainslee Hoare, 5th Bt (1824–94); the Revd John Henry Ellis, MA, of Stourton; by descent to H.A. Steward; Christie's, 28 July 1927 (lot 1); bought Leggatt; sold to 'Herbert' 1932.
Private collection, whereabouts unknown (W214)

Colt Hoare's decision to commission a view of Wilton House as part of Turner's Salisbury series is intriguing, since the Pembroke family home lies three miles to the west, beyond the city limits. Furthermore, if the remit of the project extended to neighbouring country houses, it is striking that Longford Castle was not also on the list. A possible clue to the exceptional inclusion of Wilton lies in the likely date of the list of agreed subjects, which was in use in 1801, for in that year the architect Wyatt was engaged by the 11th Earl of Pembroke to undertake revisions to his neo-classical mansion. Since Turner's views of the cathedral and the city focus on recent architectural changes, primarily those initiated by Wyatt, it seems reasonable to assume that this was a motive for adding Wilton. Colt Hoare's feelings about Wyatt – 'the modern Goth' – were then running strong and became more trenchantly critical in 1802 when he saw the architect's interventions at Hereford Cathedral.[34] At Wilton, Wyatt eventually transformed the entrance on the north front and in the courtyard created a two-level cloister to

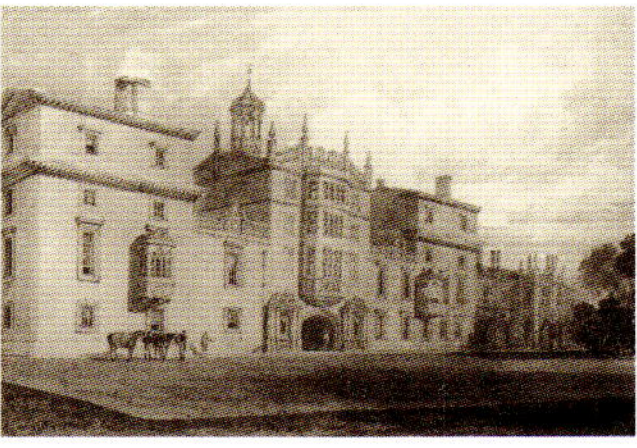

accommodate the collection of antique sculpture. But Turner concentrated in his watercolour on the east front, where at that stage Wyatt had not yet closed and glazed the original gateway to create the Gothic Hall. The façade here is still notably irregular in the number of windows on either side of the entrance, and is also ornamented with two oriel windows, while further along there is a gothic gazebo. These features are likely to have been added by the 9th Earl in the eighteenth century and were subsequently swept away when Wyatt made the façade symmetrical.[35] Turner's watercolour was eventually engraved for Colt Hoare's *History of Wiltshire* in 1825,[36] the only one of the Salisbury set to be published during his lifetime.

TURNER'S FONTHILL EXHIBITS

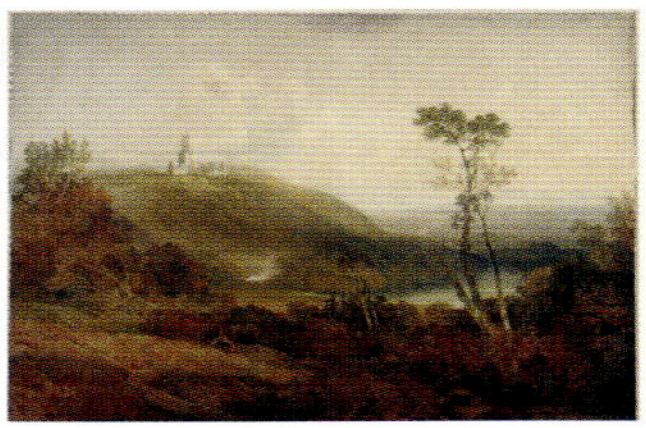

Fig. 81
South-West View of a Gothic Abbey (Morning), Now Building at Fonthill, the Seat of W. Beckford, Esq.
Exhibited RA 1800 (341)
Pencil and watercolour, 69.4 × 102.9 cm

Provenance: Beckford; Christie's, 12 May 1817 (either lot 90, sold for £32.11s, or lot 92, sold for £31.10s; the other view 'Evening'; both bought by Allnutt); John Allnutt (1773–1863), Clapham; Christie's, ?18 June 1863; bought Webb, 260 guineas; ... ; Piers Watt Boulton, Tew Park, Enstone, Oxford; Christie's, 9 December 1911 (lot 7); bought Shepherd, for £168; W.G. Rawlinson (1840–1928); with the Carroll Gallery, London, 1921; John Paris Bickell, by whom bequeathed to the AGO, 1952 (SI/39).
Art Gallery of Ontario, Toronto (W336)

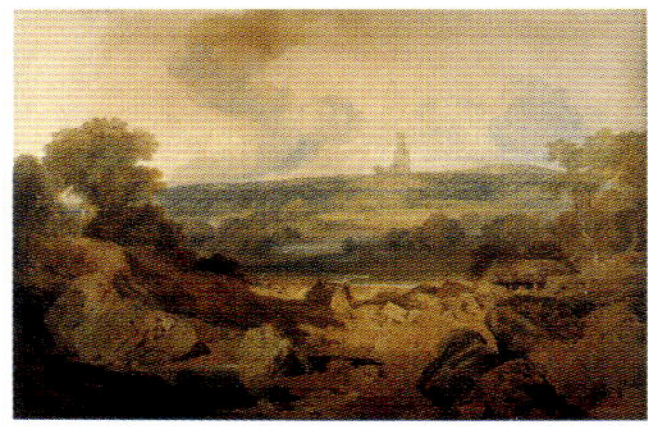

Fig. 85
East View of the Gothic Abbey (Noon) Now Building at Fonthill, the Seat of W. Beckford
Exhibited RA 1800 (663)
Watercolour, 68.5 × 103.5 cm

Provenance: Beckford; probably Christie's, 10 May 1817 (lot 77, A View in Wiltshire, bought in for 33 guineas); Christie's, 1 October 1822 (lot 112, A View of Fonthill from a stone-quarry); probably by descent from Susan Euphemia Beckford, Duchess of Hamilton; to Angus Graham, 7th Duke of Montrose; to the Duchess of Montrose, Brodick Castle, Arran; accepted by the Inland Revenue, in lieu of inheritance tax, 1988.

(NB the provenance of this work has been confused in the past with that of a smaller copy of the image, owned by Ralph Brocklebank, now at The Whitworth, The University of Manchester.)
National Gallery of Scotland, Edinburgh (W338)

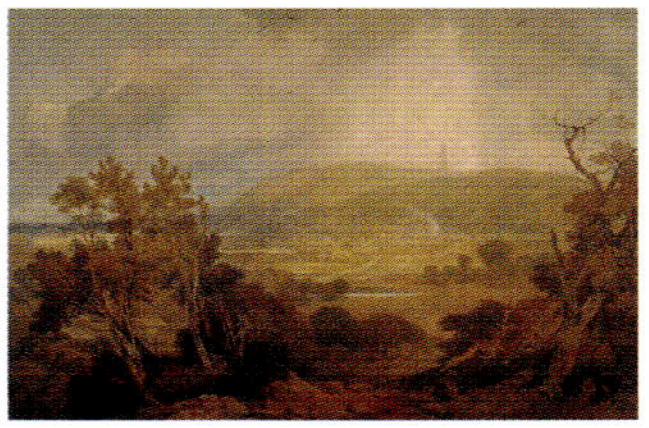

Fig. 87
View of the Gothic Abbey (Afternoon) Now Building at Fonthill, the Seat of William Beckford
Exhibited RA 1800 (328)
Watercolour, 69.5 × 103.5 cm

Provenance: Beckford; Christie's, 12 May 1817 (either lot 91, bought by Franchi for £31.10s; or lot 93, bought by ?Orchard for £38.17s); ... ; Alfred Morrison, Fonthill Bishop; Vokins, 4 March 1870; bought Agnew (stock no. 9633); sold 15 March 1870 to James Worthington, Sale, Manchester; bequeathed by his widow, Mrs Mary Worthington to the Whitworth in 1904 (WAG.1904.19).
The Whitworth, The University of Manchester (W339)

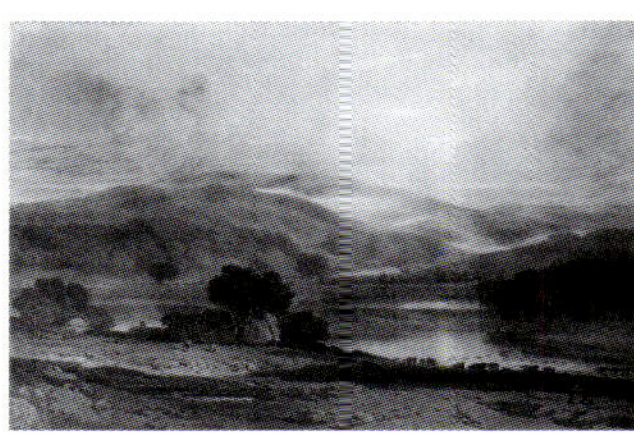

Fig. 89
North-East View of the Gothic Abbey (Sunset), Now Building at Fonthill, the Seat of W. Beckford
Exhibited RA 1800 (680)
Watercolour, 70.4 × 105.3 cm

Provenance: Beckford; Christie's, 12 May 1817 (either lot 91, bought by Franchi for £31.10s; or lot 93, bought by ?Orchard for £38.17s); ... ; Alfred Morrison, Fonthill Bishop; Vokins, 4 March 1870; bought Agnew (stock no. 9634); sold on 19 April 1870 to John Heugh, Holmeswood, Tunbridge Wells; Christie's, 24 April 1874 (lot 100); bought for 700 guineas by Agnew (stock no. 206); sold on 30 June 1877 to C.J. Pooley, Nantwich; Christie's, 6 March 1880 (lot 162); bought for £525 by Agnew (stock no. 5440); sold on to Robert Tennant, MP (1828–1900); Sir Charles Tennant, Bt (1823–1906); his widow, Mrs Geoffrey Lubbock, Greenhill, Sutton Verney; by descent to the Hon. James David Gerald Loder; bought Agnew, 31 January 1978 (stock no. 5889).
Private collection (W335)

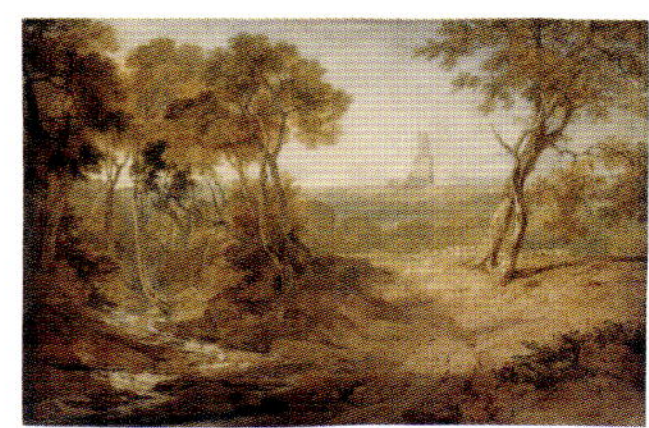

Fig. 91
South View of the Gothic Abbey (Evening) Now Building at Fonthill, the Seat of W. Beckford
Exhibited RA 1800 (566)
Watercolour, 70.5 × 104.4 cm

Provenance: Beckford; Christie's, 12 May 1817 (either lot 90, sold for £32.11s, or lot 92, sold for £31.10s; the other view 'Morning'; both bought by Allnutt); John Allnutt, Clapham; Christie's, ?18 June 1863; bought Cox, 100 guineas; Vokins, 7 June 1870; bought Agnew (stock no. 231); sold on 8 June 1870 to John Heugh, Tunbridge Wells; bought by Agnew, 13 March 1873 (stock no. 1855); sold 11 March 1873 to H.W.F. Bolckow (1806–1878), MP for Middlesborough; Christie's, 18 June 1892 (lot 142); bought by Gooden for £299.5s; ... ; Mr Greenshields, Montreal; by 1906 with Frederick Nichols, Toronto; Sir Henry Pellatt, Toronto; Gordon C. Edwards; bought by the museum, 1963, through the Horsley and Annie Townsend Bequest.
Montreal Museum of Fine Arts (1963.1385) (W337)

NOTES

All volumes published in London unless stated otherwise.

1 ARCHITECTURE AND AMBITION: THE RISING STAR (pp. 8–19)

1. Shanes 1979, p. 16.
2. Thornbury 1862, I, pp. 47–49, 54, 57, 98.
3. Robinson 2012.
4. James Hamilton, *Turner and the Scientists*, 1998, pp. 24–26, and *Turner's Britain*, 2003, pp. 62–63; Harrison 2000, p. 48; Robinson 2012, p. 183; Wilton 2012.
5. Cobb 1980, p. 11; Robinson 2012, p. x.
6. Cobb 1980, p. 12; see also David Starkey, *Making History. Antiquaries in Britain 1707–2007*, 2007, p. 159, no. 115.
7. *The Expedition of Humphrey Clinker*, 1771 (Penguin edition, 2008, p. 202).
8. TB VII A (D00108).
9. TB XXII P (D00369).
10. See Cobb 1980, pp. 77, 87, fig. 128.
11. Tatton-Brown and Crook 2009, pp. 102, 104, 121; see Joan Evans, *A History of the Society of Antiquaries*, Oxford 1956, p. 207 ff.
12. See Wilton 1979, nos 77, 123–24, 126.
13. The size and watermark of the pencil sketch of Bath Abbey, now at Indianapolis Museum of Art, indicate it was formerly a part of the 'South Wales' sketchbook (see TB XXVI).
14. The exception is the view of Gloucester Cathedral, the last in the sequence in the 'South Wales' sketchbook: TB XXVI f.68 verso (D00623).
15. A.J. Finberg first thought the 'Isle of Wight' and 'South Wales' sketchbooks had been used consecutively (*Walpole Society Journal*, I (1909), pp. 41–53, and (1911–12), p. 88). He subsequently reversed the order (1913–14, p. 90). Later again, he proposed that Turner went back to London between the Welsh and the Isle of Wight tours (Finberg 1961, p. 29).
16. TB XXVI, 4th page of itinerary (D40556).
17. Two images in the 'South Wales' sketchbook were also developed as a pair of moonlight subjects: *New Weir on the Wye*, TB XXVI f.59 (D00613) – the original oil painting of this subject is currently untraced, but it was engraved, with its pair, in 1825 (R 776); and *Lime Kiln at Briton Ferry*, TB XXVI f.14 (D00566) – the resulting work is in the YCBA, New Haven, and its current association with Coalbrookdale comes from the 1825 engraving (R 775).
18. Lascelles paid only 3 guineas on 17 May 1797. See David Hill, *Turner in the North*, New Haven and London 1996, p. 3.

2 SIR RICHARD COLT HOARE AND STOURHEAD (pp. 20–39)

1. Woodbridge 1970, p. 145; Woodbridge 1982, p. 30.
2. Woodbridge 1970, p. 96.
3. Farington, XI, p. 3937 (24 May 1811).
4. Woodbridge 1970, pp. 98–99.
5. See Charles Sebag-Montefiore, 'Leicester', in Joll, Butlin and Herrmann 2001, pp. 164–65.
6. Woodbridge 1970, p. 134–35.
7. Colt Hoare, *Recollections*, IV.
8. See Nicholson 1990; or Eric Shanes, *Turner's Human Landscapes*, 1990.
9. Woodbridge 1970, pp. 34–36.
10. Ibid., pp. 147–53.
11. In 1811, the engraver James Heath complained that Colt Hoare's behaviour towards him was typical of 'that to be expected from one who looks down upon you as one not entitled to respect' (Farington, XI, p. 3937, 24 May 1811).
12. Gage 1974, p. 61; and Montefiore, in Joll, Butlin and Herrmann 2001, pp. 164–65.
13. As in Evelyn Joll, 'Hoare', in Joll, Butlin and Herrmann 2001, pp. 141–42.
14. Woodbridge 1970, p. 72. There may be some confusion here in the reference to Blackheath, which was the institution founded by Monro's grandfather. The Monros dominated the mental health profession for several generations, so different members of the family are sometimes mixed up.
15. I am grateful to Kim Sloan for her enlightening comments on Cozens.
16. See Wilton 1979, p. 319 and Hartley 1984, pp. 21–24. There are three at The Whitworth, The University of Manchester: *From the North-West* (W183); *The Oak Tree* (W184); *The Chapel* (W185). Another is at the Victoria and Albert Museum: *The Cascades* (W186). The fifth work, showing the *South Front*, is now untraced, but was engraved in 1797 for the *Copper-Plate Magazine*.
17. TB XXVI, 5th page of itinerary (D40557).
18. See David Hill, 'Lascelles' in Joll, Butlin and Herrmann 2001, p. 161.
19. Thompson 1983, p. 66.
20. Woodbridge 1970, p. 195.
21. See Jan Piggott, 'Britton' in Joll, Butlin and Herrmann 2001, p. 23; Gage 1980, p. 241; Woodbridge 1970, pp. 195–96.
22. Thornbury 1862, I, pp. 389–90.
23. 'Hereford Court' sketchbook: TB XXXVIII ff.66, 67 (D01320, D01321); the finished works are in a private collection and at The Whitworth, The University of Manchester (W182). The second of these was engraved.
24. Jerrold Ziff, '"Backgrounds: Introduction of Architecture and Landscape". A Lecture by J.M.W. Turner', *Journal of the Warburg and Courtauld Institutes*, 26 (1963), p. 141. More surprisingly, Turner also mentioned the painting by Anton Raphael Mengs at Stourhead in this lecture (ibid., p. 142).
25. See, for example, Butlin, Gage and Wilton 1974, p. 40, no. 29; or Anne Lyles, *Young Turner: Early Work to 1800*, 1989, p. 39, nos 42–43. I am grateful to Eric Shanes for discussing this point with me.
26. See Shanes 2000, pp. 13–14.
27. Woodbridge 1970, p. 96; see also Lindsay Stainton, *Images of the Grand Tour: Louis Ducros 1748–1810*, 1985, pp. 26–30.
28. Colt Hoare, *A History of Modern Wiltshire*, 1822, vol. 1, pp. 82–83.
29. Gage 1974, p. 85, n. 18.
30. Ashmolean Museum, Oxford (see Luke Herrmann, *Ruskin and Turner*, Oxford 1968, p. 107, no. 98).
31. See John Gage, *J.M.W. Turner. 'A Wonderful Range of Mind'*, New Haven and London, 1987, p. 103.
32. TB XXIV, List of Ordered Drawings (D41250).
33. Wilton 1979, no. 194; see also no. 193, which is also supposed to have belonged to Colt Hoare.
34. Thompson 1983, pp. 92–103.
35. 'Dinevor Castle' sketchbook: TB XL 5a–6 7a–8, 9a–10, 11a–12, 13a–14, 85, 85a–86, 87a–88, 89a, 90a; 'Hereford Court' sketchbook: TB XXXVIII 1–10, 74, 86.
36. Wiltshire & Swindon History Centre: 383/4/1/folio 198 (March 4 1806); Gage 1980, p. 29, no. 14.
37. Farington, III, pp. 1074–75 (24 October 1798) and p. 1103 (3 December).
38. Chippindale 2012, p. 118.
39. 'Windsor, Eton' sketchbook, *c.*1808: TB XCVII 39a, 40 (D06111/2).
40. For a discussion of Constable's ideas of the need for naturalism, see Michael Rosenthal, *Constable. The Painter and his Landscape*, New Haven and London, 1983.
41. See Woodbridge 1970, pp. 244–48; and Kathleen Nicholson, 'Turner's "Appulia in Search of Appulus" and the Dialectics of Landscape Tradition', *Burlington Magazine*, 122 (1980), pp. 679–86.
42. David H. Solkin, *Richard Wilson, The Landscape of Reaction*, 1982, p. 203, no. 90.
43. N00494, B&J 129; see David Hill, *Turner on the Thames*, New Haven and London 1993, pp. 60, 119.
44. N00463, B&J 34; Nicholson 1990, pp. 30–5; Solkin 2009, pp. 110–13.
45. Woodbridge 1970, pp. 88–89; the work exhibited by Solkin is dated 1790 and was presumably a reworking, painted during the second tour.
46. Colt Hoare's catalogue of his collection appeared in the *Annals of the Fine Arts*, vol. 2, (1817), part v, section xxx, p. 270; see Nicholson 1990, pp. 35, 44 n. 60.
47. TB LI N (D02381); see Nicholson 1990, p. 33, fig. 23.
48. Solkin 2009, p. 112.
49. Farington, IV, p. 1136 (17 January 1799).
50. *Diana and Callisto*, N05490, B&J 43; the image is based on the engraving of Wilson's picture, which reverses the composition.
51. Wiltshire & Swindon History Centre: 383/4/1/folios 200 and 201, both receipts dated 25 February 1815.
52. Colt Hoare, *Annals of the Fine Arts*, 1818, part VII, p. 484.
53. Nicholson 1990, pp. 35–36 fig. 25, 44, n. 62.
54. See Gage 1974, p. 76, which considers the possible influence on Turner's linked Carthage pictures of the pair of works by Claude at Longford Castle, near Salisbury.
55. Powell 1987, pp. 13–14. However, it was in November 1818 that Colt Hoare suggested to Leicester that he should swap a picture by Turner for one by William Collins, who he saw as the more accurate painter of nature (Woodbridge 1970, p. 248).
56. See also the studies, or recollections, of Stourhead in the Fire at Sea sketchbook: TB CCLXXXII 1, 43 (D27792, D27845). Gage (1974, p. 86, n. 33) mentions another possibly related study in the sale of J.E. Taylor's collection (Christie's, 8 July 1912, lot 139, Stourton Park, Wiltshire, 24.1 × 39.4 cm (9½ × 15½ inches)), but this item is no longer known, if it was indeed genuine.

3 THE SALISBURY COMMISSION: 'POEMS IN STONE' (pp. 40–75)

1. Gage 1974, p. 64.
2. *Morning Post*, 24 May 1794.
3. See MS note by C.F. Bell, dated July 1949, in the Print Room at the Fitzwilliam Museum; Woodbridge 1970, pp. 178–85; Whittingham 1972; Cormack 1975, pp. 35–38; Wilton 1979, pp. 320–23.
4. This has been perpetuated by recent authors, but possibly stems from Walter Armstrong 1902, pp. 275–76.
5. Thompson 1983, pp. 143–44.
6. TB XXIV, List of Ordered Drawings (D41250).
7. Hoare's Bank Archive: HFM/11/1. I am grateful to Pamela Hunter for locating this and the other references from this source.
8. Andrew Loukes, *Turner's Sussex*, exh. cat., Petworth House, West Sussex 2013, p. 5.
9. It is notable that the second view on the list is marked as 'Pd' rather than the first, which could support the theory that the titles and dates of these two watercolours have been exchanged.
10. Hoare's Bank Archive: HFM/11/1, 8 November 1799, 'To W Turner – 2 drawings £32-11-0'.
11. Farington, IV, p. 1229 (27 May 1799).
12. Farington, III, pp. 1074–75 (24 October 1798).
13. For the preliminary drawings of Brocklesby, see TB LXXX II, and CXXI U; the completed watercolours were destroyed in a fire. One of Turner's lecture diagrams records the mausoleum's interior (TB CXCV 130). For the Whalley series, see Stanley Warburton, *Turner and Dr*

Whitaker, 1982. The Oxford designs are discussed in Helen Mary Petter, *The Oxford Almanacks*, Oxford 1974, and in Harrison 2000.
14. Wiltshire & Swindon History Centre: 383/4/1/folio 194 (not in Gage). The date in this text appears to read '1802', but the earlier year is corroborated by an entry in Colt Hoare's private account book at Hoare's Bank: see note 15 for this chapter. I am grateful to Eric Shanes for his help with transcribing this letter.
15. Hoare's Bank Archive: HFI/11/1, 21 November 1801, 'To W Turner £70'.
16. Wiltshire & Swindon History Centre: 383/4/1/folio 195; Gage 1980, p. 25, no. 8.
17. I am indebted to Rosy Temple at Christie's for details of the sale. In their catalogue of Cozens's watercolours, C.F. Bell and Thomas Girtin thought Turner acquired the view of Fluelen from Colt Hoare (*Walpole Society*, XXIII (1935), pp. 24, 32–35, no. 32).
18. Woodbridge, who was very familiar with Colt Hoare's handwriting, described it as his (1970, p. 180).
19. Wiltshire & Swindon History Centre: 383/4/1/folio 197; Gage 1980, pp. 27–28, no. 11. This was paid on 7 December, after which Turner wrote from Isleworth to acknowledge it on 14 December 383/4/1/folio 196; Gage 1980, p. 28, no. 12).
20. J.B. Nichols, *Catalogue of the Hoare Library at Stourhead*, 1840, p. 199. The *Gentleman's Magazine* for April 1825, pp. 309–11, discusses the rarity of the 'History of Marden', and other copies.
21. See the letters of 4 March and 19 April 1806; Wiltshire & Swindon History Centre: 483/4/1/folios 198–99; Gage 1980, pp. 29–30, nos 14 and 16.
22. Colt Hoare, *The History of Modern Wiltshire*, I, 1822, p. 82.
23. Wilcox 2011, pp. 22–23, fig. 14.
24. YCBA, New Haven B1981.16.
25. MS notes by C.F. Bell, July 1949, Fitzwilliam Museum. In a separate letter, dated 20 July 1949, Bell mentioned that he had been told by Lady Hoare 'that the drawings were acquired in an extremely underhand way'. I am grateful to Amy Marquis for tracing these documents.
26. 'Camera-work in cathedral architecture', *Camera Work*, 4 (October 1903), p. 17.
27. Anne Hammond (ed.), *Frederick H. Evans. Selected Texts and Bibliography*, 1992, p. 148.
28. Quoted in Anne M Lyden, *The Photographs of Frederick H. Evans*, 2010, p. 3.

4 WILLIAM BECKFORD, AND THE RISE – AND FALLS – OF FONTHILL ABBEY (pp. 76–119)

1. See, for example, Farington, VIII, p. 2888 (16 October 1806).
2. See Mowl 1998, p. 5. Mowl's is the most rounded recent account of Beckford's life.
3. Mowl 1998, p. 27.
4. See Philip Hewat-Jaboor, 'Fonthill House: "One of the Most Princely Edifices in the Kingdom"', in Ostergard 2001, pp. 51–71. Turner's view of the house is TB XLVII 25 (D02202).
5. M. Parker, *The Sugar Barons. Family, Corruption, Empire and War*, 2012, p. 302.
6. Ibid., p. 339; Lord Byron, *Childe Harold's Pilgrimage* (1812), I, stanza XXII.
7. Mowl 1998, pp. 103–4, 109–10.
8. Mowl 1998, pp. 127–28.
9. Mowl 1998, p. 207.
10. Mowl 1998, p. 226.
11. See the sketch recorded by Farington (II, p. 612, 20 July 1796) based on a design dating from four years earlier.
12. The link between Turner's patrons and slavery was explored by Gillian Forrester in her Pantzer lecture, 'Turner and the Course of Empires', in April 2007 at the Paul Mellon Centre, London. See also Sam Smiles, 'Turner and the slave trade. Speculation and representation, 1805–40', *British Art Journal*, vol. 8, no. 3 (winter 2007–8), pp. 47–54.
13. A point first made by John Harris. See Wilton-Ely 1976, p. 41; and Robinson 2012, pp. 220–21.
14. Quoted in Robinson 2012, p. 256.
15. Wilton-Ely 1980, p. 42; Mowl 1998, p. 228.
16. Alexander 1962, p. 159.
17. Wilton-Ely 1980, p. 42. The watercolour was owned by the Duke of Hamilton, so ultimately came from Beckford's own collection.
18. 1797, no. 1143; 1798, no. 955; 1799, no. 1016.
19. See also Susan Morris, '"Two Perspective Views": Turner and Lewis William Wyatt', *Turner Studies*, vol. 2, no. 2 (winter 1983), pp. 34–36.
20. Helmut von Erffa and Allen Staley, *The Paintings of Benjamin West*, New Haven and London 1986, pp. 102, 107, 388–98 .
21. Lees-Milne 1976 [1990 edition], p. 51; Mowl 1998, p. 238–39.
22. Farington, III, p. 880 (6 August 1797).
23. Ibid., III, p. 918 (7 November 1797).
24. Ibid., III, p. 1091 (16 November 1798).
25. John Wilton-Ely, 'Beckford, Fonthill and the Picturesque', in Dana Arnold (ed.), *The Picturesque in late Georgian England. Papers given at The Georgian Group Symposium*, October 1994, pp. 38–39, fig. 3; Ostergard 2001, p. 350.
26. See Jeannie Chapel, 'William Beckford: Collector of Old Master Paintings, Drawings, and Prints', in Ostergard 2001, pp. 239–40.
27. Farington, IV, p. 1219 (8 May 1799).
28. Ibid., IV, p. 1229 (27 May 1799).
29. Ibid., IV, p. 1262 (3 August 1799).
30. TB XLII 12–13 (D01687–8); Wilkinson 1972, p. 98.
31. See Megan Aldrich, 'Fonthill Abbey', in Ostergard 2001, p. 134, n. 56.
32. Farington, IV, p. 1277 (11 September 1799).
33. See, for example, ibid., p. 1175 (16 March 1799).
34. Thornbury 1862, I, p. 200.
35. Farington, IV, p. 1452 (8 November 1800).
36. TB XLVII 6, 7, 9, 10, 11, 12, 13, 46, 47, 51, W340 (Leeds City Art Gallery).
37. TB XLVII 1, 3, 4, 5, 8, 16, W341 (Private collection).
38. *The Times*, 20 May 1800.
39. Britton 1823, p. 28.
40. Accounts appeared in the *Gentleman's Magazine* (March 1801, pp. 206–8; April 1801, pp. 297–98, with an illustration).
41. TB LXX M (D04164).
42. Egyptian Details sketchbook: TB LXVI 126 (D03964); see also TB LXVI 128a, 129, which may depict nearby Old Wardour Castle, the subject of two views in the 'Fonthill' sketchbook (TB XLVII 9, 18).
43. TB XLVIII 1 (D02236).
44. Harrison 2000, pp. 51–52.
45. TB XLVIII 1 verso (D40258).
46. The other records a large mansion, perhaps in the vicinity of Fonthill (TB XLVIII 6, D02241).
47. *St James's Chronicle*, 29 April–1 May 1800.
48. *Recollections of the late William Beckford* [letters written to the author's daughter and published by her], 1893, p. 15.
49. Farington, IV, p. 1418 (10 July 1800). Although the entry for September 1799 definitely reads 'several', it is possible that Farington misremembered Turner saying 'seven' on that occasion. Attempts to account for the seven works have sometimes included the two architectural designs of the abbey.
50. Andrew Wilton pondered whether the traditional title of the Whitworth watercolour was correct in the catalogue of the Royal Academy *Turner* exhibition (1974, p. 42, no. 39), but left the matter unresolved.
51. See Thornbury 1862, I, pp. 199–200 for a description of this work when it was already mistitled as an afternoon scene.
52. See the related sheet from this book in The Whitworth, The University of Manchester, depicting a misty autumn morning (fig. 109).
53. Dolbadarn sketchbook: TB XLVI 106a (Morning), 107 (no. 3), 113 (Afternoon), 111 (Sunset).
54. Farington, IV, p. 1418 (10 July 1800).
55. Egyptian Details sketchbook: TB LXVI 18, 72, 72a, 73, 74, 74a.
56. See the 1823 sale catalogue (p. 83). Turner could also have had access to the images in this book in Colt Hoare's library at Stourhead.
57. See, for example, TB XXXVIII 95; TB XLV 19a; TB XLVI 74a, 79, 116a, 117a.
58. See B&J 13 for contemporary reviews.
59. Smaller South Wales sketchbook: TB XXV 1 (D00462).
60. Butlin and Joll 1984, pp. 13–15, no. 15.
61. TB XLVII 21, 22, 32, 33, 34.
62. See David Hill, *Joseph Mallord William Turner. Le Mont Blanc et la Vallee d'Aoste*, Aosta 2000, p. 279.
63. Lees-Milne 1976 [1990 edition], p. 10.
64. Farington, IV, p. 1554 (26 May 1801).
65. TB XLVII 19 verso (D41265); see Ian Warrell, *Turner et le Lorrain*, Nancy 2002, pp. 56–57, 186.
66. I am grateful to Sidney Blackmore and Rosy Temple for sharing the details of the sale.
67. Wilton-Ely 1980, p. 48.
68. September–December 1844. Reprinted by Jon Millington (ed.), *Conversations with Beckford. Memoirs of William Beckford from the* New Monthly Magazine *1844*, Warminster 2014, p. 24. This article was first brought to my attention by Dr Jan Piggott.
69. E.T Cook and Alexander Wedderburn (eds), *The Works of John Ruskin*, XIII, 1904, p. 161.
70. Butlin and Joll 1984, p. 247.

5 WESTWARD HO! TURNER AND THE PICTURESQUE COAST OF SOUTHERN ENGLAND (pp. 120–39)

1. Shanes 1990, pp. 8–10.
2. I am grateful to Eric Shanes for sharing his discussion of the 1811 itinerary in his forthcoming biography.
3. Devonshire Coast No. 1 sketchbook: TB CXXIII ff.22 (D08403), 24 (D08406), 27 (D08411), 32 (D08421).
4. See Andrew Wilton and Rosalind Mallord Turner, *Painting and Poetry. Turner's 'Verse Book' and his Work of 1804–1812*, 1990, pp. 170–76.
5. TB CXXIII f.52 verso (D08464); the preliminary sketch is f.14 (D08387).
6. Shanes 1990, p. 42.
7. TB CXXIII f.54 verso (D08468).
8. TB CXXIII f.56 verso (D08474).
9. Shanes 2000, pp. 134–37.
10. Edward Yardley, 'Picture Note: "Off St Alban's Head"', *Turner Studies*, vol. 2, no. 2 (winter 1983), pp. 55–56.
11. 'Corfe to Dartmouth' sketchbook: TB CXXIV 22 (D08833).
12. TB CXXIII 58 (D08479).
13. Shanes 1990, p. 58.
14. TB CXXIV 26 (D08837); see also TB CXXIV 27 (D08838).
15. TB CXXIII f.87 verso (D08534); for his verses on Old Sarum, see TB CXXIII f.33 verso (D08424).

16. See also his later watercolour of Lyme Regis, for the *England and Wales* series, in the Cincinnati Art Museum, *c*.1835.
17. Butlin & Joll 1984, no. 80 (Tate, N00481); TB CXXXVI. See also Shanes 1990, pp. 67, 135, 205; and Hamilton 2002.
18. Shanes 1990, pp. 13–14; James Hamilton, *Turner's Britain*, 2003, pp. 139–57.
19. 'Hereford Court' sketchbook: TB XXXVIII ff.1, 86 (D01250, D01340).
20. John Ruskin, *Modern Painters*, V, in *Works* VII, 1905 pp.189–91; Shanes 1990, p. 186; see also TB CXXIII f.29 (D08415).

6 STONEHENGE AND HISTORY (pp. 140–55)

1. Bruce Redford (ed.), *The Letters of Samuel Johnson, 1782–4*, University of Princeton, 1994, IV, pp. 221–22 (9 October 1783).
2. See Sam Smiles, *The Image of Antiquity. Ancient Britain and the Romantic Imagination*, New Haven and London 1994.
3. Chippindale 2012, p. 86.
4. Rosemary Hill, *Stonehenge*, 2008, p. 88.
5. R.B. Beckett (ed.), *John Constable's Correspondence*, 5, Suffolk Record Society, 1967, pp. 84–85.
6. Chippindale 2012, p. 100.
7. See http://calendar-24.co.uk/united-kingdom/moon/phases/1811 or http://eclipse.gsfc.nasa.gov/phase/phases1801.html.
8. TB CXXIII 213 (D08752). See Chippindale 2012, p. 108, fig. 81.
9. For an exploration of what the writer thought of the artist, see J.B. Bullen, 'Thomas Hardy and Turner', *Turner Society News*, no. 50 (November 1988), pp. 11–14.
10. *Quarterly Review*, vol. V, no. 12 (1811); quoted in Woodbridge 1970, p. 231.
11. See Mike Pitts in Starkey 2007, pp. 227–31.
12. Chippindale 2012, p. 98. See also Rosemary Hill, *Stonehenge*, 2008, pp. 86–116.
13. Louis Hawes, *Constable's Stonehenge*, 1975, pp. 6–7.
14. See A.J. Finberg, 'Turner's Newly Identified Yorkshire Sketchbook', *Connoisseur* (October 1935), pp. 185–87; the Salisbury view has previously been identified as Wakefield.
15. Gillian Forrester, *Turner's 'Drawing Book'. The Liber Studiorum*, 1996, p. 145.
16. Shanes 1979, p. 13.
17. John Ruskin, *Works*, VII, 1905, p. 190
18. Eric Shanes, *Turner's Watercolour Explorations 1810–1842*, 1997, p. 15.
19. *The Political Examiner*, issue 106 (11 June 1828).
20. Mike Pitts in Starkey 2007, p. 231; Chippindale 2012, p. 105.
21. John Ruskin, *Catalogue of the Rudimetary Series*, 1872, in *Works*, XXI, 1906, p. 223.
22. Rosemary Hill, *Stonehenge*, 2008, p. 137.

7 CASTLES OLD AND NEW: THE ISLE OF WIGHT (pp. 156–83)

1. *Observations on the western parts of England, relative chiefly to picturesque beauty: To which are added, a few remarks on ... the Isle of Wight*, 1798.
2. Ibid., p. 328.
3. *Tour of the Isle of Wight: The Drawings Taken and Engraved by J. Hassell*, 1790.
4. See John Gage, 'Turner and the Picturesque – I', *Burlington Magazine*, vol. 107, no. 742 (January 1965), p. 22, figs 30–31.
5. Wilton 1979, pp. 318–19, nos 176–81.
6. Selby Whittingham, 'Picture Note', *Turner Studies*, vol. 6, no. 2 (winter 1986), p. 67.
7. Robinson 2012, pp. 154–57, 323.
8. Paul Oppé, 'Talented Amateurs: Julia Gordon and her Circle', *Country Life*, vol. LXXXV (iii) (8 July 1939), pp. 20–22; Hilda Finberg, 'With Mr Turner in 1797', *Burlington Magazine*, vol. 99, no. 647 (February 1957), p. 48; Evelyn Joll, 'Gordon', in Joll, Butlin and Herrmann 2001, pp. 128–29.
9. *Observations on the western parts of England, relative chiefly to picturesque beauty: To which are added, a few remarks on ... the Isle of Wight*, 1798, p. 313.
10. TB CXXI R (D08274): watermarked '1807'.
11. TB CCXX F, G, H (D20212–4); W421, W422.
12. See Ian Warrell, *Turner on the Loire*, 1997, pp. 161–63, figs 156–58; I am grateful to Mr Fox for his helpful correspondence.
13. Ibid., p. 179, fig. 176.
14. Sold at Aldridge's, Devizes, 26 January 2002; now National Art Library, V&A. The Gordons' collection is discussed in Hamish Miles, *Fourteen Small Pictures by Wilkie*, Fine Art Society, London 1981.
15. This may be the focus of the sketches in the Gosport (TB CCVII) and perhaps the 'Isle of Wight' sketchbooks (TB CCXXVII).
16. David Brown, *Turner and Byron*, 1992, pp. 37–38.
17. See Ian Sherfield, *East Cowes Castle. The Seat of John Nash, Esq. A Pictorial History*, 1994; Geoffrey Tyack (ed.), *John Nash. Architect of the Picturesque*, 2013, pp. xiii, 37–40.
18. TB CCCXXVI f.80a (D20730).
19. See Ian Warrell, *Turner. The Fourth Decade, 1820–30*, 1991, pp. 65–66. There are also two related drawings in the Vaughan bequests at Edinburgh and Dublin.
20. Gage 1980, pp. 108–9, no. 124; see Butlin and Joll, pp. 159–61; and E. Joll, 'Cowes', in Joll, Butlin and Herrmann 2001, pp. 66–67.
21. See TB CCXXVII (a); a few related sketches are in TB CCLX and other collections.
22. Butlin and Joll 1984, nos 447 and 449; see Ian Warrell 'Interior of a Great House', in Robert Hoozee (ed.) *British Vision. Observation and Imagination in British Art 1750–1950*, 2007, pp. 325–28.
23. See the ambiguous letter of 30 November published by Selby Whittingham, 'Windus, Turner & Ruskin: New Documents', *J.M.W. Turner, R.A.*, no. 2 (December 1993), p. 90.
24. See *Probe*, 1839, p. 121; Whitley Papers, British Museum, p. 1544.
25. T.C. Hofland, *The British Angler's Manual, or, The Art of Angling in England, Scotland, Wales, and Ireland*, 1841, pp. 261–62.
26. Sir Herbert Maxwell, *Chronicles of the Houghton*, 1908; Walter Shaw Sparrow, *Angling in British Art through Five Centuries*, 1923, p. 155.
27. TB CCXI 42 (D18591), now rebound in TB CCXXXIX.
28. TB CCXXVII f.34 (D20786).
29. Walter Shaw Sparrow, *Angling in British Art through Five Centuries*, 1923, pp. 120–21.
30. See Ian Warrell, '"I saw Louis Philippe land at Portsmouth": Fixing Turner's Presence at the Arrival of the King of the French, 8 October 1844', *Turner Society News*, no. 120 (autumn 2013), pp. 8–15.

APPENDIX (pp. 184–95)

1. See the engraving based on Thomas Hearne's design, published in 1798 (Wilcox 2011, p. 19).
2. Thompson 1983, p. 209.
3. Farington, XI, p. 3937 (24 May 1811).
4. See the watercolour by Frederick Nash of 1814 (Wilcox 2011, p. 103).
5. Wilton 2012, pp. 326–29, fig. 26.
6. *St James's Chronicle*, 20–23 May 1797.
7. Tim Ayers (ed.), *Salisbury Cathedral. The West Front. A History and Study in Conservation*, Guildford 2000, pp. 88–89.
8. See Cobb 1980, pp. 111 and 120, for nineteenth-century photographs of the organ in situ.
9. *St James's Chronicle*, 14–16 May 1799.
10. TB XLIX 80a, 81a (D02336, D02338). See Reverend Canon David Durston, *Salisbury Cathedral. The Chapter House and Medieval Frieze*, 1995.
11. TB XLIX 82a (D02340).
12. *St James's Chronicle*, 12–14 May 1801. I am grateful to Greg Smith for sharing this review and for helping me resolve the dating of the two Chapter House views.
13. Shanes 2000, p. 80.
14. A preliminary idea for the composition may be TB XLIX 83 (D02341). See also Frederick Nash's less inspired view in Dodsworth 1814.
15. Another possible depiction of Colt Hoare, albeit in caricatured form, may be in the 'Studies for Pictures' sketchbook: TB LXIX 131a (D04151).
16. C. Winston, 1849, quoted in Cobb 1980, p. 112.
17. Peter L. Smith, *The Bishop's Palace at Salisbury*, Salisbury 2013, p. 99, fig. 3.16.
18. Wilcox 2011, pp. 22–23, fig. 14.
19. TB CXCV 143 (D17114).
20. Wilcox 2011, p. 15, fig. 4. Note the Benjamin Donn map of 1797 does not include the turning circle (Peter L. Smith, *The Bishop's Palace at Salisbury*, Salisbury 2013, p. 99).
21. Cobb 1980, p. 110.
22. William Dodworth, *A Guide to the Cathedral Church of Salisbury, with a particular account of the late great improvements made therein under the direction of James Wyatt*, II, 1792 (and later editions), p. 34.
23. TB L H (D02349) and TB L I (D02350).
24. See the Wikipedia entry for Henry Penruddocke Wyndham (consulted July 2013).
25. See also the sketch in Wilcox 2011, p. 152, fig. 125.
26. David Hilliam, *A Salisbury Miscellany*, Stroud 2013, p. 79.
27. Elizabeth Crittal (ed.), *A History of the County of Wiltshire*, vol. 6, 1962, pp. 138–41.
28. TB XXVII B (D00663).
29. In fact the blue wash probably relates to the top of the design on TB L P (D02357), which may have formerly been attached to TB XXVII B.
30. See Wilcox 2011, p. 53, fig. 37.
31. Ibid., pp. 86–87.
32. W.C. Oulton, *The Traveller's Guide, or, English Itinerary*, vol. 2, 1805, p. 536.
33. I am grateful to Natalie Murray for help with this and its related image.
34. Thompson 1983, p. 200.
35. I am grateful to John Martin Robinson for clarifying this point. Compare also the view by Conrad Martin Metz for *Picturesque Views of the Principal Seats of the Nobility and Gentry, in England and Wales*, c.1787, which also pre-dates Wyatt's changes.
36. See Armstrong 1902, p. 285, which may be confused in listing a second view of Wilton, seen from the Palladian Bridge, from Colt Hoare's collection.

SELECTED BIBLIOGRAPHY

All volumes published in London unless stated otherwise.

Megan Aldrich, 'William Beckford's Abbey at Fonthill: From the Picturesque to the Sublime', in Ostergard 2001, pp. 117–36

Boyd Alexander, *England's Wealthiest Son*, 1962

Walter Armstrong, *Turner*, 1902

John Britton, *The History and Antiquities of the Cathedral Church of Salisbury*, 1814

John Britton, *Illustrations of Fonthill*, 1823

Martin Butlin, John Gage and Andrew Wilton, *Turner*, exh. cat., Royal Academy, London 1974

Martin Butlin and Evelyn Joll, *The Paintings of J.M.W. Turner*, 2 vols, rev. edn, 1984 (B&J numbers)

Christopher Chippindale, *Stonehenge Complete*, 4th edn, 2012

Gerald Cobb, *English Cathedrals. The Forgotten Centuries. Restoration and Change from 1530 to the Present Day*, 1980

Malcolm Cormack, *J.M.W. Turner, R.A. 1775–1851: A Catalogue of Drawings and Watercolours in the Fitzwilliam Museum, Cambridge*, 1975

E.G. Cundall, 'Turner Drawings of Fonthill Abbey', *Burlington Magazine*, vol. 29, no. 157 (April 1916), pp. 16–21

Dudley Dodd, *Stourhead, Wiltshire*, 1981

William Dodsworth, *An Historical Account of the Episcopal See and Cathedral Church of Sarum, or Salisbury*, 1814

Joseph Farington, *The Diary of Joseph Farington*, MS in Royal Library, Windsor; complete edited edition by Kenneth Garlick, Angus Macintyre and Kathryn Cave, 16 vols, 1978–84

A.J. Finberg, *A Complete Inventory of the Drawings of the Turner Bequest*, 2 vols, 1909 (TB numbers; all these works are at Tate Britain)

A.J. Finberg, *The Life of J.M.W. Turner*, rev. edn, 1961

Amy Frost, 'Beckford's House of Card: An Analysis of the Fonthill Abbey Model', *The Beckford Journal*, vol. 16 (2010), pp. 114–23

John Gage, 'Turner and Stourhead: The Making of a Classicist?', *Art Quarterly*, vol. 37 (1974), pp. 59–87

John Gage, *Collected Correspondence of J.M.W. Turner*, Oxford 1980

James Hamilton, *Our Roaring Channels. Turner, Portsmouth and the Sea*, Portsmouth 2002

Howard J.M. Hanley, *Turner in Dorset*, Weymouth 1992

Colin Harrison, *Turner's Oxford*, 2000

Craig Hartley, *Turner Watercolours in the Whitworth Art Gallery*, 1984

Richard Colt Hoare, *A History of Modern Wiltshire*, 13 vols, 1822–44

Evelyn Joll, Martin Butlin and Luke Herrmann, *The Oxford Companion to J.M.W. Turner*, Oxford 2001

Marin Krause, *Turner in Indianapolis*, 1997

Alastair Laing, *In Trust for the Nation. Paintings from National Trust Houses*, exh. cat., National Gallery, London 1995

James Lees-Milne, *William Beckford*, 1976 [1990]

Alexander Marr, 'William Beckford and the Landscape Garden' in Ostergard 2001, pp. 137–54

Timothy Mowl, *William Beckford. Composing for Mozart*, 1998

Kathleen Nicholson, *Turner's Classical Landscapes: Myth and Meaning*, 1990

Derek E. Ostergard (ed.), *William Beckford, 1760–1844: An Eye for the Magnificent*, New Haven and London 2001

Cecilia Powell, *Turner in the South: Rome, Naples, Florence*, New Haven and London 1987

Graham Reynolds, 'Turner at East Cowes Castle', *Victoria and Albert Museum Year Book*, vol. I, 1969, pp. 667–79

John Martin Robinson, *James Wyatt. Architect to George III*, New Haven and London 2012

John Rutter, *A Description of Fonthill Abbey and Demesne, in the County of Wilts: including a list of its paintings, cabinets, &c.*, Shaftesbury 1822

Eric Shanes, *Turner's Picturesque Views in England and Wales 1825–1838*, 1979

Eric Shanes, *Turner's England 1810–38*, 1990

Eric Shanes, *Turner. The Great Watercolours*, exh. cat., Royal Academy, London 2000

Kim Sloan, *J.M.W. Turner. Watercolours from the R.W. Lloyd Bequest*, British Museum 1998

David Solkin et al., *Turner and the Masters*, exh. cat., Tate Britain, London 2009

David Starkey, *Making History. Antiquaries in Britain 1707–2007*, 2007

Tim Tatton-Brown and John Crook, *Salisbury Cathedral. The Making of a Medieval Masterpiece*, 2009

M.W. Thompson, *The Journeys of Sir Richard Colt Hoare through Wales and England 1793–1810*, Gloucester 1983

Walter Thornbury, *The Life of J.M.W. Turner, R.A.*, 2 vols, 1862 (and revised single volume edition, 1877)

Ian Warrell, '"I saw Louis Philippe land at Portsmouth": Fixing Turner's Presence at the Arrival of the King of the French, 8 October 1844', *Turner Society News*, 120 (autumn 2013), pp. 8–15

Selby Whittingham, *Constable and Turner at Salisbury*, 1972, rev. edn 1976

Timothy Wilcox, *Constable and Salisbury. The Soul of Landscape*, exh. cat., Salisbury and South Wiltshire Museum 2011

Gerald Wilkinson, *Turner's Early Sketchbooks. Drawings in England, Wales and Scotland from 1789 to 1802*, 1972

Andrew Wilton, *The Life and Work of J.M.W. Turner*, Fribourg 1979 (W numbers)

Andrew Wilton, 'Post tenebras lux: J.M.W. Turner, James Wyatt and the importance of stained glass', *Burlington Magazine*, CLIV (May 2012), pp. 322–29

John Wilton-Ely, 'Beckford the Builder', in *William Beckford*, exh. cat., Salisbury and South Wiltshire Museum 1976, pp. 35–62

John Wilton-Ely, 'The Genesis and Evolution of Fonthill Abbey', *Architectural History*, vol. 23 (1980), pp. 40–51, plates 28–36

Kenneth Woodbridge, *Landscape and Antiquity. Aspects of English Culture at Stourhead 1718 to 1838*, Oxford 1970

Kenneth Woodbridge, *The Stourhead Landscape, Wiltshire*, 1982

LIST OF WORKS IN THE EXHIBITION

All works are by J.M.W. TURNER, except where indicated.
(List correct at time of going to press.)

J. POWELL after J.M.W. TURNER
Winchester Cross
1800
Engraving, 21 × 16.5 cm (image); 28.5 × 23 cm (sheet)
Private collection (R51, based on the watercolour, W164)
See fig. 11

Study for 'View over the Lake at Stourhead'
c.1795–96
Pencil and watercolour, 41.9 × 55.3 cm
Tate (D01908 / TB XLIV f)
Fig. 21

View over the Lake at Stourhead, from the South-West
c.1795–96
Pencil and watercolour, 52.8 × 78.1 cm
Tate (D01909 / TB XLIV g)
Fig. 22

The Gothic Cross Above the Lake at Stourhead, with the Pantheon in the Distance
c.1795–96
Pencil and watercolour, 40.3 × 54.1 cm
Tate (D01907 / TB XLIV e)
Fig. 23

Lake with Distant Headland and Palaces; Study for 'Rise of the River Stour at Stourhead'
c.1824–25
Watercolour, 67.3 × 100.5 cm
Tate (D36320 / TB CCCLXV 29)
Fig. 31

Gateway to the Close, Salisbury Cathedral
Exhibited RA 1796
Pencil and watercolour, 50.8 × 37.5 cm
Newnham College, Cambridge (W210)
Fig. 33

Harnham Mill, Salisbury
c.1795
Pencil and watercolour, 35.1 × 27.7 cm
Tate (D00683 / TB XXVII V)
Fig. 34

Salisbury Cathedral from the East
c.1795–96
Pencil and watercolour, 28 × 23 cm
Tate (D00668 / TB XXVII G)
Fig. 35

North Porch of Salisbury Cathedral
Exhibited RA 1797
Watercolour, 50 × 65 cm
The Salisbury Museum (W196)
Fig. 37

The Choir of Salisbury Cathedral, looking East towards the Lady Chapel
c.1796–97
Pencil, 69 × 56 cm
Tate (D02345 / TB L D)
Fig. 38

The Choir of Salisbury Cathedral
Exhibited RA 1797
Watercolour, 64.8 × 50.8 cm
The Salisbury Museum (W197)
Fig. 39

The West Front of Salisbury Cathedral
Exhibited RA 1799
Watercolour, 48.5 × 66 cm
Harris Museum and Art Gallery, Preston (W198)
Fig. 41

Inside of the Chapter-House of Salisbury Cathedral
Exhibited RA 1799
Watercolour, 66 × 50.8 cm
Victoria and Albert Museum, London (W201)
Fig. 43

Chapter-House, Salisbury Cathedral
Exhibited RA 1801
Watercolour, 64 × 51 cm
The Whitworth, The University of Manchester (W199)
Fig. 44

The Bishop's Palace, Salisbury
c.1799
Watercolour, 28.4 × 35.9 cm
The Higgins, Bedford (W204)
Fig. 49

A Study of the Arch in Mr Wyndham's Gardens, Salisbury
c.1799
Pencil, watercolour and gouache, 47.7 × 32.9 cm
Tate (D02350 / TB L I)
Fig. 51

'Isle of Wight' sketchbook (open at *The Poultry Cross, with the Tower of St Thomas's Church, Salisbury*)
1795
Pencil, 20.4 × 26.4 cm
Tate (D00425 / TB XXIV 18)
See fig. 54

St Martin's Church, Salisbury; Preliminary Study
c.1799
Pencil and watercolour on paper, 24.9 × 43.2 cm
Tate (D00663 / TB XXVII B)
See fig. 55

St Martin's Church, Salisbury
c.1799
Watercolour, 31.8 × 43.2 cm
British Museum (W207)
Fig. 55

The Old Council House, the Market Place, Salisbury
c.1799
Watercolour, 28 × 38.5 cm
Cooper Gallery, Barnsley (W212)
Fig. 57

THOMAS HIGHAM (1795–1844) after J.M.W. TURNER
The East Front of Wilton House
Engraving, 16 × 23 cm (image); 30 × 44 (sheet)
from Colt Hoare, *History of Modern Wiltshire*, 1825 (volume II)
The Salisbury Museum
See fig. 58

Gateway to the Close, Salisbury
1802–5
Watercolour, 45.6 × 31.5 cm
Fitzwilliam Museum, Cambridge (W208)
Fig. 59

The New Council House, Salisbury
c.1795
Pencil, 23.1 × 28.2 cm
Tate (D02356 / TB L O)
Fig. 60

The New Council House, Salisbury
c.1799
Pencil and watercolour, 28.4 × 43.1 cm
Tate (D02357 / TB L P)
Fig. 61

The New Council House (or Guildhall), Salisbury
c.1805
Watercolour, 30 × 39 cm
Cooper Gallery, Barnsley (W213)
Fig. 62

Salisbury Cathedral from the South Side of the Cloister
c.1801–5
Watercolour, 68 × 49.6 cm
Victoria and Albert Museum, London (W202)
Fig. 63

A General View of Salisbury Cathedral from the Bishop's Garden
c.1801–5
Watercolour, 51.3 × 67.8 cm
Birmingham Museum and Art Gallery (W200)
Fig. 66

Lecture Diagram. Various Steeples: Salisbury; Christ Church, Oxford; St Giles, London
c.1810–28
Pencil and watercolour, 65.8 × 83.2 cm
Tate (D17113 / TB CXCV 142)
Fig. 67

Interior of Salisbury Cathedral, looking towards the North Transept
c.1801–5
Watercolour, 66 × 50.8 cm
The Salisbury Museum (W203)
Fig. 68

WILLIAM ANGUS (1752–1821)
after J.M.W. TURNER
Fonthill House in Wiltshire, the Seat of William Beckford Esqr. (from *Principal Seats of the Nobility and Gentry in Great Britain and Wales, in a Collection of Select Views*)
1800
Engraving, 13.2 × 18.8 cm (image)
Private collection
(R 62; based on W334)
Fig. 70

Perspective View of Fonthill Abbey from the South-West
*c.*1797, possibly exhibited RA 1797
Watercolour, 49.3 × 75.8 cm
Bolton Museum and Art Gallery (W332)
Fig. 72

Model of Fonthill Abbey
?1806
The Estate of the late Niel Rimington, courtesy of the Beckford Tower Trust
Fig. 74

Ground plan of Fonthill Abbey
From John Rutter, *Delineations of Fonthill and its Abbey*
1823
The Salisbury Museum
See fig. 75

Builders Working on the Construction of Fonthill Abbey
1799
Pencil and grey wash, 25 × 40.5 cm
Trimmed sheet from the Smaller Fonthill sketchbook
Private collection
Fig. 78

A Wooden Shelter, with a Shepherd and his Flock of Sheep; Fonthill Abbey in the Distance
*c.*1799
Pencil and watercolour, 33.3 × 46.8 cm
From the 'Fonthill' sketchbook
Tate (D02224 / TB XLVII 47)
Fig. 79

Fonthill Abbey from the South-West; Study for 'Morning'
1799
Pencil, 33.5 × 43.3 cm
From the 'Fonthill' sketchbook
Tate (D02189 / TB XLVII 12)
Fig. 80

Fonthill Abbey; from the South-West
1799
Pencil, watercolour and gouache, 46.8 × 33.1 cm
From the 'Fonthill' sketchbook
Tate (D02187 / TB XLVII 10)
Fig. 82

An Unfinished View of Fonthill Abbey, with Bitham Lake
*c.*1799–1800
Pencil and watercolour, 104.5 × 71.2 cm
Tate (D04167 / TB LXX P)
Fig. 83

View of Fonthill Abbey from a Stone Quarry near Chilmark; Study for 'Noon'
1799
Pencil and watercolour, 30 × 44.2 cm
From the 'Fonthill' sketchbook
Leeds Art Gallery (W340)
Fig. 84

East View of the Gothic Abbey (Noon) Now Building at Fonthill, the Seat of W. Beckford
Exhibited RA 1800 (663)
Watercolour, 68.5 × 103.5 cm
National Gallery of Scotland, Edinburgh (W338)
Fig. 85

Fonthill Abbey from the North, with the Village of Fonthill Gifford; Study for 'Afternoon'
1799
Pencil and watercolour, 33.2 × 46.9 cm
From the 'Fonthill' sketchbook
Tate (D02188 / TB XLVII 11)
Fig. 86

View of the Gothic Abbey (Afternoon) Now Building at Fonthill, the Seat of William Beckford
Exhibited RA 1800 (328)
Watercolour, 69.5 × 103.5 cm
The Whitworth, The University of Manchester (W339)
Fig. 87

Fonthill Abbey from the East; Study for 'Sunset'
1799
Pencil, 33.5 × 43.3 cm
From the 'Fonthill' sketchbook
Tate (D02184 / TB XLVII 7)
Fig. 88

Fonthill Abbey seen through Trees from the South; Study for 'Evening'
1799
Pencil, 33.5 × 43.3 cm
From the 'Fonthill' sketchbook
Tate (D02190 / TB XLVII 13)
Fig. 90

Fonthill Abbey from the South
*c.*1799
Pencil and watercolour, 33.5 × 43.3 cm
From the 'Fonthill' sketchbook
Tate (D02223 / TB XLVII 46)
Fig. 92

Distant View of Fonthill Abbey, from the North-East, with an Aqueduct
1799
Pencil, 33.2 × 46.8 cm
From the 'Fonthill' sketchbook
Tate (D02183 / TB XLVII 6)
Fig. 93

The Ruins of Old Wardour Castle, with Fonthill Abbey in the Distance
1799
Pencil, 33.5 × 43.3 cm
From the 'Fonthill' sketchbook
Tate (D02186 / TB XLVII 9)
Fig. 94

CHARLES TURNER (1774–1857)
after J.M.W. TURNER
The Fifth Plague of Egypt
(from *Liber Studiorum*; plate 16)
1808
Etching and mezzotint, 18 × 26 cm
Private collection
See fig. 99

WILLIAM SAY (1768–1834)
after J.M.W. TURNER
The Tenth Plague of Egypt
(from *Liber Studiorum*; plate 61)
1816
Etching and mezzotint, 18 × 26 cm
Private collection
See fig. 101

Fonthill Abbey from Bitham Lake
1800
Pencil and watercolour, 31.5 × 45.5 cm
From the 'Fonthill' sketchbook
Private collection, c/o Philip Mould (W341)
Fig. 102

Near View of Fonthill Abbey from the South, with Bitham Lake in the Foreground
1800
Pencil, 43.3 × 33.5 cm
From the 'Fonthill' sketchbook
Tate (D02181 / TB XLVIII 4)
Fig. 103

Fonthill Abbey from the South-West, with the Reconstructed Tower
1800
Pencil, 33.4 × 46.6 cm
From the 'Fonthill' sketchbook
Tate (D02182 / TB XLVII 5)
Fig. 104

The South Front of Fonthill Abbey, with the Reconstructed Tower
1800
Pencil, 46.6 × 32.8 cm
From the 'Fonthill' sketchbook
Tate (D02178 / TB XLVII 1)
Fig. 106

Labourers Sleeping under a Fallen Tree, with Swans Fighting
*c.*1799–1800
Pencil, 33.5 × 43.3 cm
From the 'Fonthill' sketchbook
Tate (D02197 / TB XLVII 20)
Fig. 107

A Fallen Tree, perhaps at Fonthill
*c.*1800–5
Pencil and watercolour, 33.5 × 43.3 cm
Tate (D02225 / TB XLVII 48)
Fig. 110

WILLIAM WESTALL (1781–1850)
after JOHN BUCKLER (1770–1851)
Ruins of Fonthill Abbey: The Tower fell 21st December 1825
Lithograph, 26.5 × 38.7 cm
The Salisbury Museum
See fig. 111

Off St Alban's Head
*c.*1818–22
Watercolour, 39.5 × 67.4 cm
Mercer Art Gallery, Harrogate
Fig. 116

Bow and Arrow Castle, Isle of Portland
*c.*1815
Watercolour, 15.2 × 23 cm
For *Picturesque Views on the Southern Coast of England*
University of Liverpool (W459)
Fig. 122

Bridport, Dorsetshire
*c.*1818
Watercolour, 15.2 × 23.5 cm
For *Picturesque Views on the Southern Coast of England*
Art Gallery and Museum, Bury (W465)
Fig. 124

Lyme Regis, Dorsetshire
*c.*1812
Watercolour, 15.3 × 21.7 cm
For *Picturesque Views on the Southern Coast of England*
Glasgow Art Gallery (W451)
Fig. 125

Portsmouth, Hampshire
1824
Watercolour, 15.2 × 21.8 cm
For *Picturesque Views on the Southern Coast of England*
Lady Lever Art Gallery, Port Sunlight, Liverpool (W477)
Fig. 127

Portsmouth
1824
Watercolour, 16 × 24 cm
For *The Ports of England*
Tate (D18152 / TB CCVIIII S / W756)
Fig. 128

Gosport, Entrance to Portsmouth Harbour
*c.*1829
Watercolour, 28.5 × 41.9 cm
For *Picturesque Views in England and Wales*
Portsmouth Museum (W828)
Fig. 129

Salisbury from Old Sarum, with a Raincloud: Preparatory Study
*c.*1827–28
Watercolour, 34.3 × 48 cm
Tate (D25159 / TB CCLXIII 37)
Fig. 133

Salisbury, from Old Sarum
*c.*1827–28
Watercolour, 27.2 × 41 cm
For *Picturesque Views of England and Wales*
The Salisbury Museum (W836)
Fig. 134

THOMAS GIRTIN (1775–1802)
Stonehenge During a Thunderstorm
*c.*1794
Pencil and watercolour, 10.4 × 14.7 cm
Ashmolean Museum, Oxford (WA 1916.8)
Fig. 136

Stonehenge sketchbook
(open at the view of the ***Inner Sarsen Horseshoe from the South-West***)
1811
Pencil, 18.2 × 22.2 cm
Tate (D41386 / TB CXXV b 13)
Fig. 142

Stonehenge at Sunset
1811
Watercolour, 17.2 × 22.3 cm
From the Stonehenge sketchbook
Private collection
Fig. 147

FRANK SHORT (1857–1945)
after J.M.W. TURNER
Stonehenge at Sunset (previously known as *Stonehenge at Daybreak*; for the *Liber Studiorum*, unpublished plate 81)
1897
Mezzotint , 19 × 26 cm
Private collection
See fig. 151

Passengers Beside a Coach near Salisbury
*c.*1824
Pencil and watercolour, *c.*19.5 × 27 cm
From the Farnley-Munro sketchbook
Private collection
Fig. 152

Stonehenge: Preparatory Study
*c.*1827–28
Watercolour, 34.6 × 48.8 cm
Tate (D25123 / TB CCLXIII 1)
Fig. 153

Stonehenge, Wiltshire
*c.*1827–28
Watercolour, 27.9 × 40.4 cm
For *Picturesque Views in England and Wales*
The Salisbury Museum (W817)
Fig. 154

Carisbrooke Castle, Isle of Wight (formerly identified as Chateau d'Arques)
*c.*1826
Watercolour, 16.7 × 22.8 cm
Fitzwilliam Museum, Cambridge (W421)
Fig. 160

Carisbrooke Castle, Isle of Wight
*c.*1827–28
Watercolour, 29.2 × 41.2 cm
For *Picturesque Views in England and Wales*
Carisbrooke Castle, Isle of Wight (W815)
Fig. 161

Shipping off East Cowes Headland
1827
Oil on canvas, 46 × 60.3 cm
Tate (N01999; B&J 267)
Fig. 163

Sketch for 'East Cowes Castle, the Regatta Beating to Windward'
1827
Oil on canvas, 45.7 × 61 cm
Tate (N01994; B&J 261)
Fig. 164

East Cowes Castle: Figures on the Castle Steps
1827
Pen and ink with chalk, on blue paper, 19.5 × 14.1 cm
Tate (D20826 / CCXXVII a 23)
Fig. 166

Interior of the Library, East Cowes Castle
1827
Pen and ink, with chalk, on blue paper, 14.2 × 19.5 cm
Tate (D20851 / TB CCXXVII a 48)
Fig. 167

The Drawing Room at East Cowes Castle
1827
Watercolour and gouache on blue paper, 13.7 × 19.5 cm
Tate (D22694 / CCXLIV 32)
Fig. 168

Turner's fishing rod, made up of five sections, cased
Royal Academy of Arts, London
Fig. 172

Study of Fish: Two Tench, a Trout and a Perch
*c.*1822–24
Pencil, watercolour and gouache, 27.5 × 47 cm
Tate (D25462 / TB CCLXIII 339)
Fig. 176

Portsmouth Harbour: 'Going out to the Ship – Sculls Rough'
1844
Pencil and watercolour, 23.5 × 30.9 cm
Tate (D35957 / TB CCCLXIV 114)
Fig. 177

The Arrival of Louis-Philippe: the Gomer
1844
Watercolour, 23.7 × 31.8 cm
Tate (D35981 / CCCLXIV 138)
Fig. 178

The Arrival of Louis-Philippe, 8 October 1844
*c.*1844–45
Oil on canvas, 90.2 × 120.6 cm
Tate (N02068; B&J 505)
Fig. 179

OTHER WORKS (not illustrated):

Liber Veritatis; or a Collection of Prints after the Original designs of Claude Le Lorrain; in the Collection of His Grace the Duke of Devonshire, Executed by Richard Earlom, in the Manner and Taste of the Drawings
1777
Volume 2: open at plate 185, ***Landscape with the Arrival of Aeneas before the City of Pallanteum***
Private collection

SIR RICHARD COLT HOARE (1758–1838)
Hints for Travellers in Italy
1815
(Turner's own copy, presented by the author)
Private collection

JAMES HAKEWILL (1778–1843)
Picturesque Tour of Jamaica
1825
(Turner's own copy, presented by the author)
Private collection

ACKNOWLEDGEMENTS

Many people have shared information or helped locate specific works, thereby enriching the exhibition and this accompanying book. I would like to thank all of those listed here for their various contributions:

Julian Agnew; Heather Ault; Christopher Baker; Anne Beckwith-Smith; Kat Berry; Sidney Blackmore; Emily Blanshard; Peter Bower; David Breuer-Weil; Grace Bright; Andrew Brown; Alec Burt; Ann Chumbley; Caroline Collier; Amy Concannon; Oliver Craske: Anthony Crichton-Stuart; Alan Crookham; Anna Cunningham; Caroline Dakers; Julie Dene; Dudley Dodd; Harriet Drummond; Frances Fowle; Mike Fraser; Amy Frost; Hilary Gerish; Mark Griffith-Jones; Vivien Hamilton; Virginia Harrington; Carrie Haslett; Frances Hazlehurst; Rebecca Hellen; Philip Hewat-Jaboor; Stephen Hobbs; Jeannie Hobhouse; Kikuko Iwai; Peter Johnson; Bill Jones; Jill Kelsey; Hope Kingsley; Christopher Kingzett; Nigel Kirk; Sanne Klinge; Martin Krause; Christine Kurpiel; Marcella Leith; Lowell Libson; Katharine Lochnan; Andrew Loukes; Anne Lyles; Linda McLeod; Amy Marquis; Joanna Meacock; Mary Miers; Margaret Moles; Richard Morgan; Philip Mould; Timothy Mowl; Franny Moyle; Jane Munro; Natalie Murray; Seiichiro Nakagawa; Gay Naughton; Gill Neal; Kate Nicholson; Kiko Noda; Yoko Obuchi; Emma O'Neill; Kate Parsons; Bill Perry; Jan Piggott; Naomi Remes; Kathy Richmond; Brenda Rix; John Martin Robinson; Chris Rolfe; Jane Sellars; Nirit Sharon-Debel; Tanya Sirakovich; Kim Sloan; Susan Sloman; Helen Smailes; Gregory Smith; Paul Spencer Longhurst; Joseph Strudholme; Emma Stuart; Stephen Tate; Tim Tatton-Brown; Rosy Temple; Anastasia Tennant; David Thompson; Julia Tregellas; Rosalind Mallord Turner; Tim Unsworth; Georgiana Watt; Tim Wilcox; Theodore Wilkins; Andrew Wilton; John Wilton-Ely; Christie Wyld.

In addition to the assistance of staff at Stourhead, the Wiltshire and Swindon History Centre, and the London Library, I am very grateful to Bonnie Morant and Jim Flower for welcoming me to Fonthill and providing expert guidance. Pamela Hunter has illuminated many important aspects of Colt Hoare's patronage through her knowledge of his records in the archives of Hoare's Bank. I also wish to thank Eric Shanes for helpful advice and for sharing his research on the first half of Turner's working life, which is the subject of his forthcoming book.

At Salisbury, I am grateful to Adrian Green for the invitation to work on this aspect of Turner's career. Kim Chittick has provided invaluable support in the preparation of the book and the exhibition it accompanies. I have also enjoyed working with their colleagues, Sara Willis and Louise Tunnard.

Laura Lappin and Linda Schofield have overseen the production of the book with great dedication and attention to detail, assisted by Sally Nicholls. Nigel Soper has brought it all together effortlessly in his beautiful design.

The book is dedicated to my parents.

IAN WARRELL
August 2014

PHOTOGRAPHIC CREDITS

Fig. 1 Indianapolis Museum of Art, Bequest of Kurt F. Pantzer, 1996.155; fig. 2 Hounslow and Chiswick Libraries; figs 3, 71 © National Portrait Gallery; fig. 4 © Bristol Museums, Galleries and Archives; figs 5, 7, 10, 12–13, 18, 21–23, 26–27, 31, 34–36, 38, 40, 45–46, 51, 53, 60–61, 67, 76–77, 79–80, 82–83, 86, 88, 90, 92–97, 101, 103–4, 106–8, 110, 112, 114, 118, 123, 126, 128, 131–33, 137–46, 153, 155–59, 163–64, 166–70, 175–79 © Tate, London 2014; figs 6, 78, 89, 100, 113, 119, 130, 147–49, 152, 162 Private collection; fig. 8 © Victoria Art Gallery, Bath and North East Somerset Council/Bridgeman Images; figs 9, 127 Courtesy National Museums Liverpool; fig. 11 The Whitworth, The University of Manchester, UK/Bridgeman Images; figs 14, 17, 24, 47, 50, 52, 55, 58–59, 70, 99, 111, 135 © Trustees of the British Museum; fig. 15 © National Trust Images/John Hammond; fig. 16 © National Trust/David Cousins; figs 19, 29–30, 73, 120–21 Yale Center for British Art, Paul Mellon Collection; fig. 20 © National Gallery of Ireland; fig. 25 Corsham Court Collection; figs 28, 42, 65, 75, 150, 173–74, plan on p. 89 © The British Library Board; fig. 32 Courtesy Sudeley Castle; fig. 33 © The Principal and Fellows of Newnham College, Cambridge; figs 37, 39, 68, 134, 154 © The Salisbury Museum; fig. 41 © Harris Museum and Art Gallery, Preston; figs 43, 63, 165 V&A Images; figs 44, 87, 109 The Whitworth, The University of Manchester; fig. 49 Trustees of the Cecil Higgins Art Gallery, Bedford; fig. 54 © The Israel Museum, Jerusalem, by Sara Kopelman-Stavisky; fig. 56 Salisbury City Council; figs 57, 62 Courtesy of the Trustees of the Cooper Gallery, Barnsley; figs 59, 160 © Fitzwilliam Museum, Cambridge; fig. 64 Philadelphia Museum of Art, PA; fig. 66 © Birmingham Museums Trust; fig. 69 City of Salford Museums and Art Gallery; fig. 72 © Bolton Museum and Art Gallery, Lancashire, UK/ Bridgeman Images; fig. 74 Beckford's Tower & Museum; fig. 81 Art Gallery of Ontario, Bequest of John Paris Bickell, Toronto, 1952 (51/39); fig. 84 Leeds Museums and Galleries (Leeds Art Gallery), UK/Bridgeman Images; fig. 85 Scottish National Gallery, National Gallery of Scotland; fig. 91 The Montreal Museum of Fine Arts, Brian Merrett; fig. 98 Indianapolis Museum of Art, Gift in memory of Evan F. Lilly (55.24); fig. 102 © Philip Mould & Company; fig. 105 By courtesy of the Trustees of Sir John Soane's Museum; fig. 115 Imaging Department © President and Fellows of Harvard College; fig. 116 © Harrogate Museums and Arts/Bridgeman Images; fig. 117 Trustees of the Cecil Higgins Art Gallery, Bedford. Acquired with the assistance of The Art Fund; fig. 122 © University of Liverpool Art Gallery & Collections, UK/ Bridgeman Images; fig. 124 © Bury Art Museum, Greater Manchester, UK; fig. 125 © CSG CIC Glasgow Museums and Libraries Collections; fig. 129 Bridgeman Art Library/Christie's; fig. 136 © Ashmolean Museum, University of Oxford; fig. 151 © 2015 Museum of Fine Arts, Boston; fig. 161 Carisbrooke Castle Museum, Isle of Wight, UK/Bridgeman Images; fig. 171 Courtesy of the Taft Museum of Art, Cincinnati, Ohio, photo Tony Walsh, Cincinnati, Ohio; fig. 172 © Royal Academy of Arts, London, photographer: Prudence Cuming Associates Limited.

INDEX

Figures in **bold** type indicate illustrations.

A
Abercorn, 6th Earl of 79
Albert, Prince Consort 179
Altieri collection 6
Anderson-Pelham, Charles 158, 162
Anderson-Pelham, Henrietta 158
Andover, Hampshire 122
Anglesey Abbey, Lode Cambridgeshire 84
Angus, William 85
Angus, William after Turner: *Fonthill House in Wiltshire...* 79, **80**, 85
Annals of the Fine Arts 37
Anthony of Padua, St 81
Antrobus, Sir Edmund 152
Army of the Medes Destroyed in the Desart by a Whirlwind 110, 112
Audley, Bishop Edmund 185
Austen, Jane: *Persuasion* 128

B
Bala, North Wales 177
Banks of the Loire 160
Barrington, Bishop Shute 184, 189
Basire, James after Philip Crocker: *West View of Stonehenge* **151**, 153
Batalha monastery, Portugal 82
Bath, Somerset 117; *West Front of Bath Abbey* **15**, 185
Beaumont, Sir George 35, 37
Beckford, Maria (née Hamilton) 79
Beckford, Alderman William 79, 114
Beckford, William 11, 53, **78**, 86, 88, 112, 179
  Alpine tour 114
  builds Fonthill Abbey 6, 79, 81, 82, 110
  Colt Hoare's near neighbour 56, 79
  and Courtenay 80, 8
  criticism of T's work 39, 117, 119, 173
  and *The Fifth Plague of Egypt* 92, 109
  forced to sell pictures 56, 114, 116
  in Italy 79, 80, 90
  and Nelson 87
  in Portugal 81, 82, 84
  sale of Fonthill Abbey 116–17
  Vathek 80
Bitham Lake, Wiltshire 87, 90, **95**, 112, **113**
Boswell, Henry: *Historical Descriptions of New and Elegant Picturesque Views of the Antiquities of England and Wales, etc.* 10, **11**, 12, 143
Boys, Thomas Shotter 63
Bridport, Dorsetshire **130**
Brighton, East Sussex 130
Bristol 13, 17, 33; *South Porch of St Mary Redcliffe, Bristol* **12**, 13
Britannia Depicta (William Byrne) 35
British Institution 35
Britton, John 25, 26–7
  The Beauties of Wiltshire 26, 63, 145
  The History and Antiquities of the Cathedral Church of Salisbury 187
  Malmesbury Abbey-Church... 34, **35**
Britton, John and Brayley, Edward Wedlake: *The Beauties of England and Wales* 27
Brocklesby Mausoleum, Lincolnshire 53, 196–7
Brooks, Henry: *Salisbury Guildhall from the Square* **65**, 193
Buckler, John **119**, 189
Burke, Edmund: *A Philosophical Enquiry into the Origin of our Ideas of the Sublime and Beautiful* 142
Byron, George Gordon, Lord 80, 116; *Childe Harold* 162

C
Caernarvon Castle, Gwynedd, Wales 87
Cambridge University: King's College 15
Canaletto (Giovanni Antonio Canal) 32
  The Doge Carried Around St Mark's Square, Venice Before his Coronation 24, 32
Carthage 38, 196
Catholic Emancipation (1829) 139
Channel Islands trip (1832) 175
Chantrey, Sir Francis 177
Charmouth 128
Cheddar Gorge, Somerset 130
Chepstow, Monmouthshire, Wales 18
Chichester Cathedral, West Sussex 47, 57
Chippindale, Christopher 143
Christchurch, Dorset 124
  Christchurch: the Ruins of the Constable's House 122
Christie's, auctioneers 117
Clarkson, Thomas 81
Claude Gellée, called Claude Lorrain 6, 32, 38, 42, 84, 114, 116, 196
  The Father of Psyche Sacrificing at the Temple of Apollo 84
  Landscape with the Arrival of Aeneas before the city of Pallanteum 84, **86**
  The Mill 33
Cockerell, C.R. 163
Cockerell, S.P. 190
Collins, William 196
Colt Hoare *see* Hoare, Sir Richard Colt
Coltman, Nathaniel: *British Itinerary* 122
Coningsby, Thomas, Earl 58, 62; *Account of the Manor of Marden* 58
Constable, John 35, 63, 142, 188, 192, 196
Conyngham, William 82
Cooke, George 122
Cooke, William Bernard 122, 124, 132
Corfe Castle, Dorsetshire **124**, 127
Corfe to Dartmouth sketchbook (TB CXXIV) **123**, **126**, **129**
Corsham Court, Wiltshire 33
Corwen, Denbighshire, north Wales: *The Trout Stream* **176**, 177
Courtenay, William (later 9th Earl of Devon) 80, 81
Coventry Cathedral, Warwickshire 139
Coxe, William: *Historical Tour of Monmouthshire* 34
Cozens, Alexander 79
Cozens, John Robert 25, 56, 80; *Fluelen on the Lake of Lucerne* **25**, 57, 197
Crocker, Philip **151**, 153, 154
Cromwell, Oliver 189
Cunnington, William 34, 145
Cuyp, Aelbert 162

D
Dayes, Edward 12
Derbyshire tour (1834) 177
Devonshire Coast No.1 sketchbook (TB CXXIII) **131**, **145**
Diana and Callisto 196
Dodsworth, William 63, 186
Dolbadarn sketchbook **108**
Donn, Benjamin 199
Dorchester from the Frome Valley 128, **129**
Douglas, Bishop John 189
Ducros, Louis 23, 27, 31, 32, 58; *The Valley of the Nera* **23**, 31
Durham Cathedral, County Durham 12, 42
Dynevor ('Dinevor') Castle sketchbook (TB XL) **32**

E
Eginton, Francis 185
Egremont, Lord 35
Egyptian Details sketchbook (TB LXVI) **88**, **108**
Elgin, Lord 84–5
Ellis, Rev. J.A. 64
Ely, Cambridgeshire: *Internal of a Cottage, a Study at Ely* 33
Ely Cathedral, Cambridgeshire 13, 15, 32, 139
  ...South Transept **31**, 33, 45, 47, 187
  Interior of the Galilee Porch... **14**, 15
England and Wales see Picturesque Views in England and Wales
Essex, James 13
Eustace, John Chetwode: *Tours through Italy* 38
Evans, Frederick H. 64, 66
  Gloucester Cathedral: The Cloisters 66, **73**
Ewenny Priory, Vale of Glamorgan, Wales 32, 184

F
Fairfax, Thomas 145
Farington, Joseph 51, 53, 83, 85, 86, 89, 197
Farnley Hall, North Yorkshire 125
Farnley-Munro sketchbook **152**, **153**
Fawkes, Walter 32, 125, 145
  'Book of Birds' 145
  'Historical Vignettes' 145
Fifth Plague of Egypt, The 32, **76–7**, 109–110, **109**, 114
Fisher, Bishop 188
fishing 122, 177
  A Back View of a Man Fishing 177, **178**
  Fishermen at Sea 18, 27, 158
  A Group of Fishermen at a Weir 177, **178**
  Study of Fish: Two Tench, a Trout and a Perch **179**
  The Trout Stream **176**, 177
  T's fish rod **177**
Fishing at the Weir sketchbook (TB CCLXXXI) **178**
Flaxman, John 83, 185
Fluelen **25**, 57, 197
Fonthill Abbey, Wiltshire 11, 51, 53, 142
  chapel 82–3
  collapses of tower 83, 87, 117, 119
  Eastern Transept 84
  Model of Fonthill Abbey **84**
  Revelation Chamber 83, 110
  Stop's Beacon 81
  Western Transept 83, 87, 112
  Autumn Morning near Fonthill **118**
  Builders Working on the Construction of Fonthill Abbey 88, **89**
  Distant View of Fonthill Abbey, from the North-East... 90, **107**
  East View of the Gothic Abbey (Noon) Now Building at Fonthill... 87, 89, 90, **97**, 117, 194
  A Fallen Tree, perhaps at Fonthill 116, **118**
  ...from Bitham Lake 87, 112
  ...from the North, with the Village of Fonthill Gifford; Study for 'Afternoon' 90, **98**
  ...from the North-East; Study for 'Sunset' 90, **100**
  ...from the North-West (with Wyatt) 83
  ...from the South **106**
  ...from the South; Study for 'Evening' **87**, 90, **102**
  ...from the South-West 90, 92, **94**
  ...from the South-West; Study for 'Morning' 87, 90, **93**
  ...from the South-West, with the Reconstructed Tower 87, 113
  Labourers Sleeping under a Fallen Tree, with Swans Fighting 112, **116**
  Near View...from the South, with Bitham Lake in the Foreground **87**, 112, **113**
  North-East View of the Gothic Abbey (Sunset)... 87, 90, **101**, 195
  Perspective View... from the South-West **82**, 83, 197
  The Ruins of Old Wardour Castle, with Fonthill Abbey in the Distance 90, **107**
  The South Front..., with the Reconstructed Tower 87, 113, **115**
  South View of the Gothic Abbey (Evening)... 87, 90, **103**, **104–5**, 195
  South-West View of a Gothic Abbey (Morning)... 90, **93**, 194
  Transcription of the Study for 'View of the Gothic Abbey (Sunset)... 92, **108**
  An Unfinished View of Fonthill Abbey, with Bitham Lake 88–9, 90, 92, **95**
  View of Fonthill Abbey from a Stone Quarry near Chilmark; Study for 'Noon' 90, **96**
  View of the Gothic Abbey (Afternoon)... 87, 90, **99**, 194
  View Towards Fonthill Abbey from the South 87, **88**
  A Wooden Shelter, with a Shepherd and his Flock of Sheep; Fonthill Abbey in the Distance 90, **92**
Fonthill exhibits, Turner's 194–5
Fonthill Gifford, Wiltshire 79, **98**
Fonthill Lake 85, 90
'Fonthill' sketchbook (TB XLVII) 85, 86–7, **93**, **94**, **96**, **98**, **100**, **102**, **106**, **107**, 110, **112–13**, **115**, **116**, **118**
Fonthill Splendens, Wiltshire 79, **80**, 81, 84, 85, 87, 92, 110

Fox, William 159
Frith, William Powell 119

G
Gage, Dr John 42
Geological Society 126
George III, King 11, 127, 186
George IV, King (and as Prince Regent) 23, 130
Gilpin, Revd William 158
Gilray, James: *Barbarities in the West Indies* **81**
Girtin, Thomas 25, 197; *Stonehenge During a Thunderstorm* 142, **143**
Glastonbury: the Abbey and Town, with another study of the Tor, from Wearyall Hill 130, **131**
Gloucester, Gloucestershire 18, 192
Gloucester Cathedral, Gloucestershire 15, 66, 196
Gomer (steam yacht) 179, **180**
Gordon, Colonel James Willoughby 160
Gordon, Lady Julia (née Bennet) 158, 160
Gordon, Lady Margaret 80, 81
Gorges, Sir Thomas and Lady 185
Gosport, Entrance to Portsmouth Harbour 132, **133**
Gosport, Hampshire 132, 179
'Gosport' sketchbook (TB CCVII) 199
Grande-Chartreuse 114
Great Reform Bill (1832) 139
Grose, Francis 191; *Antiquities of England and Wales* 12
Guernsey sketchbook (TB CCLII) **174**

H
Hackert, Jackob 23
Halsewell (wrecked East Indiaman) 124–5
Hamilton, Sir William 79, 85
Hampton Court, Herefordshire 17–18, 26, 27, 62, 196
Hampton Court, Herefordshire, from the South-East **26**, 34, 62
Hardwick, Thomas 11
Hardy, Thomas 198
Tess of the d'Urbervilles 148
Harewood House, Leeds, West Yorkshire 18, 45
Harnham *see under* Salisbury
Hassell, John: *Tour of the Isle of Wight* 158
Hearne, Thomas 199
Heath, Charles 132
Heath, James 196
Henley, Revd Samuel 80
Henry II, King 114
Hereford, Herefordshire 17
Hereford Cathedral, Herefordshire 13, 15
'Hereford Court' sketchbook **33**, 34, 62
Higham, Thomas **66**
Hoare, Henry (1784-1836) **22**, 23
Hoare, Sir Henry Ainslie, 5th Baronet 63
Hoare, Henry 'the Magnificent' (1705-1785) 23, 39
Hoare, Hesther 23
Hoare, Sir Richard Colt, 2nd Baronet **22**, 179, 184, 188, 196, 199
and the British Institution 35
and classical literature 24, 36, 134
fishing 177
High Sheriff of Wiltshire 34, 57
in Italy 23, 24, 25, 27, 37
lives at Stourhead 18
meets Leicester 23
name 25
origin of connection with T 25–7
and Stonehenge 142, 145
and T's Malmesbury views 34, 62
The Ancient History of South Wiltshire 145
Hints to Travellers in Italy 38
History of Modern Wiltshire 42, 153
Villa of Maecenas at Tivoli 36, **37**, 38
Hoare, Sir Richard Colt, 2nd Baronet and Smith, John 'Warwick': *Select Views in Saxony, France, Spain, Elba, Italy, Sicily...* 37–8
Hogg, Thomas 10, **11**, 143
Holworthy, James 177
Hope-under-Dinmore church, Herefordshire 58
Hoppner, John: *William Beckford* **78**, 79
Houghton Fishing Club, near Stockbridge, Hampshire 177
Houghton Hall, Norfolk 79
Hugh of Lincoln, Saint 114
Hugo of Grenoble, Saint 114
Humphry, Ozias **11**
Portrait of James Wyatt **11**

I
Isle of Portland, Dorset **126**, 127
Bow and Arrow Castle, Isle of Portland [Rufus Castle] 127–8, **129**
Isle of Purbeck 124
Isle of Wight 18, 124, 158–81, 190
Appuldurcombe House 158
Bembridge windmill 158
Cowes Regatta 162, 163, 170, **171**
East Cowes Castle 163, 171, 173
Niton 160, 162, 163
Norris Castle 163
The Orchard 160
St Mary's church 163
Boccaccio Relating the Tale of the Bird Cage 171
Carisbrooke Castle... **156–7**, 162, **167**
Carisbrooke Castle... formerly Chateau d'Arques 159, **166**
Carisbrooke Castle from the South-West, with the Church of St Mary in the Distance 158, 159, **163**, **164–5**
Chale Farm 158, **161**
Cowes... 162, **168**
The Drawing Room at East Cowes Castle 171, **174**
East Cowes Castle: Figures on the Castle Steps 171, **172**
East Cowes Regatta... **171**
Fishing Boats in Orchard Bay 158, **162**
Interior of a Great House; The Drawing Room, East Cowes 173, 175
Interior of the Library, East Cowes Castle 171, **173**
Music Party, East Cowes Castle 173
Newport...with Carisbrooke Castle in the Distance 158, 159, **160**
Shipping off East Cowes Headland 162, **169**
Sketch for 'East Cowes Castle, the Regatta Beating to Windward' 170–71
View from the Terrace of a Villa at Niton... from Sketches by a Lady 160
West Cowes Castle... 158, **159**
'Isle of Wight' sketchbook (TB XXIV) **16**, 17, 18, 33, 45, **46**, **50**, **135**, **160–65**, 196, 199
Isle of Wight tours: (1795) 158; (1826) 159-60, 162; (1827) 162-3, 170; (1833) 175

J
Jamaica 81, 82
Johnson, Dr Samuel 142
Jones, George 177
Frances Chantrey Blowing 177, **178**
Juliet and her Nurse (1836) 32

L
Labruzzi, Carlo 23
Lacock Abbey: the Entrance Front **32**, 33
Lake Avernus: Aeneas and the Cumaean Sibyl **20–21**, 35–7, **36**, 130
Land's End, Cornwall 130
Landseer, John 158
Lascelles, Edward 18
Lascelles, Edward, Jr 26
Le Keux, John after Frederick Mackenzie: *View from the Cloisters* 63, **73**, 187
Lee Priory, Kent 82, 83
Leicester, Sir John Fleming, 5th Baronet (later 1st Baron de Tabley) 23, 24, 25, 34, 177, 196
Lettice, Revd John 79
Liber Studiorum 34–5, 110, 122, 152
Lichfield Cathedral, Staffordshire 139
Lichfield Cathedral from the Minster Pool **13**
Life-Boat and Manby Apparatus... 119, 171, 173
Lime Kiln at Briton Ferry 196
Lincoln Cathedral, Lincolnshire 15
Lincoln Cathedral: the South-East Porch with the Chantry Chapel of Bishop Russell **13**, 114
'Little Liber' 152
Llandaff Cathedral, Llandaff, Cardiff, Wales 15
Lloyd, H.E. 152
London
Adelphi Terrace 25
Egyptian Hall, Piccadilly 134, 139
Grosvenor Square 84
Harley Street (No.64) 51, 116
and John Nash 163
Norton Street 53
St Erasmus in Bishop Islip's Chapel, Westminster Abbey 18, **19**, 185
St Giles Church **74**
St Paul's Cathedral 6, 127
Upper Harley Street 115
Westminster Abbey 6, 18, **19**, 185
Longford Castle, near Salisbury 196
Loss of an East Indiaman **125**
Louis-Philippe, King of the French 179, 199
The Arrival of Louis-Philippe, 8 October 1844 181
The Arrival of Louis-Philippe: the Gomer 179, **180**
Loukes, Andrew 90
Loutherbourg, Philippe-Jacques de 114, 158
Eidophusikon 80, 124
Lulworth Castle, Dorsetshire **127**
Lulworth Cove, Dorset 126
Lulworth Cove, Dorsetshire **126**
Lulworth Cove, with the Isle of Portland Beyond **126**
Lupton, Thomas 152
Lyme Regis, Dorset 130, 198
Lyme Regis, Dorsetshire **120–21**, 128, **131**

M
Mackenzie, Frederick 63, **73**, 187
Maiden Castle, near Dorchester 128
Malden, George Capel-Coningsby, Viscount (later 5th Earl of Essex) 18, 25, 26, 27
Malmesbury, Wiltshire 34
Malmesbury Abbey, Wiltshire **35**, 62
The Interior of Malmesbury Abbey from the South Aisle **33**, 34, 62
Malmesbury, Wiltshire 34, 132, **134**
Malton, Thomas, Jr 11
Mengs, Anton Raphael 196
Monmouth, Monmouthshire, Wales 192
Monro, Dr Thomas 25, 28
Turner Working at a Drawing Table, probably at Dr Monro's House **10**, 25
Monro family 196
Montfaucon, Bernard de: *L'Antiquité expliquée et représentée en Figures* 92, **108**
Moore, James 142
Monastic Remains and Ancient Castles in England and Wales 12
More, Hannah: *The Shepherd of Salisbury Plain* 139
Morrison collection 90
Moses 109, 185

N
Nash, Frederick **51**, 63, 186, 199
Nash, John 163, 170, 173
Nash, Mary Anne 173
National Gallery, London 33
Nelson, Admiral Lord Horatio 87
Netley, Hampshire
Netley Abbey: The Interior of the Ruins **18**, 158
The Ruins of Netley Abbey **174**, 175
New Monthly Magazine 117
New Weir on the Wye 196
Nicholson, Francis 38
View of the Lake and Bridge at Stourhead, with the Temple of Apollo and the Pantheon **30**, 38
Nollekens, Joseph 83
Normandy, Brittany and the Loire, tour of (1826) 160, 162

O
Old Sarum, Wiltshire 45, 128, 134, **135**, 139, 190
Old Wardour Castle, Wardour, Wiltshire 90, **107**, 197
Oxford Almanack 35, 53
Oxford University 185
Canterbury Gate 88
Christ Church 18, **74**

P
Peltro, William Tomkins: *Stonehenge* (engraving after Thomas Hogg) 10, **11**, 143
Pennsylvania Castle, Isle of Portland, Dorset 127
Peterborough Cathedral, Cambridgeshire 13, 15
Petworth House, West Sussex 171, 177
Picasso, Pablo 6
Picturesque Views in England and Wales 132, **133**, 134, **138**, 150, 152, **155**, 159, 162, **167**, **168**
Picturesque Views on the Southern Coast of England 35, 122, **123**, 124, **126**, 127, **128**, **129**, 130, **131**, **132**
Pilkington, William 193
Piranesi, Giovanni Battista 18, 24, 32, 109; *Vedute di Roma* 32
Poole, Dorsetshire **123**, 124
Porden, William 11
Portland Bill, Dorset 125
Ports of England 132
Portsmouth, Hampshire 130, 158
Gosport, Entrance to Portsmouth Harbour 132, **133**, 179
Portsmouth 132, **133**, **182–3**
Portsmouth, Hampshire 130, 132
Portsmouth Harbour: 'Going out to the Ship - Sculls Rough' 179, **180**
Powderham Castle, Devon 81, 86
Pyramids: Ancient Chronology 150

Q
Quarterly Review 145
Queensberry, Marquess of 152

R
Radnor, Jacob Pleydell-Bouverie, 2nd Earl of 193
Raphael 42
Reform 139
Rembrandt van Rijn 18
Landscape with the Rest on the Flight into Egypt 18, 27–8, 36
Reynolds, Sir Joshua: *Resurrection* 184, 185
Rhine excursion (1817) 42
Rich, Edmund 189
Risley, Derbyshire 160
Romanticism 79, 142, 154
Rome 32, 109
Doria-Pamphili Gallery 32
founding of 84

Pyramid of Caius Cestius 32, 109
Rome from Monte Testaccio 109, **111**
St Peter's 84
Villa Madama 56
Rossi, John Charles Felix 83
Rotten boroughs 139
Royal Academy of Arts, London 12, 35, 39, 122, 181
exhibitions: (1795) 27; (1796) 33, 45; (1797) 47, 83, 185; (1799) 51, 83, 84; (1800) 87, 88, 89, 109–110; (1826) 160; (1827) 160; (1828) 170–71; (1829) 160; (1887) 64
T elected (1802) 42, 138
T first exhibits (aged 15) 6
T as Professor of Perspective 27–8, 188
Ruskin, John 154; *Modern Painters* 119, 152–3
Russell, Lord John 139
Rutter, John: *Delineations of Fonthill and its Abbey* **91**

S
Saftleven, Herman 33
St Alban's Head, Dorset 124, 125; *Off St Alban's Head* **125**
St David's Cathedral, South Wales 15
St Huges Denouncing Vengeance on the Shepherd of Cormayert... **114**
St James's Chronicle 186
Salisbury, Wiltshire 15, 18, 34, 47, 51, 53, 122, 142, 181
Bishop's Garden 48, 53
Bishop's Guildhall 191, 193
Bishop's Palace 45, 43, 199
City set 47–8, 53, 58, 62, 63–4, 189–93
Close Gate 45, 48, 185, 192
College of Matrons 192
Council House (New) 48, 191
Council House (Old) 45, 191, 193
Guildhall *see* Council House (New)
Harnham Hill 53
Harnham Mill **44**, 45
Market Place 48, 191
Poultry Cross 48, **63**, 190, 191
St Edmund's Church 189
St Martin's Parish Church 48, 190, 192
St Thomas's Church 48, 185, 186
Salisbury Museum 67
T first visits 15, 85
Wyndham's Garden 48, **61**
Wyndham House, Bourne Hill 48, 190
Ancient Arch of Mr Wyndham's Garden... 53, **61**, 189, 190
Bishop's Palace... 53, **53**, 188, 189
Design for a Gothic Frame for Nine Drawings of Salisbury Cathedral **56**, 57
Distant View... from Old Sarum, to the North 45, **135**
...from Old Sarum 45, 132, 134, **136–7**, **138**, 139
...from Sarum, with a Raincloud: Preparatory Study **138**
Gateway to the Close... 45, 55, **67**, 124, 192
New Council House (or Guildhall)... 53, 58, **69**, **70–71**, 193
New Council House... [c.1795] 45, 53, **68**, 193
New Council House... [c.1799] 53, **68**, 193
Old Council House, the Market Place... 53, **65**, 191
Poultry Cross, with the Tower of St Thomas's Church... **40–41**, 45, 53, **63**, 191
St Edmund's Church... 53, **59**, 189, 190
St Martin's Church... 53, **64**, 191, 192
St Thomas's Church from the High Street, looking North 53, **62**, 190
Study of the Arch in Mr Wyndham's Gardens... **60**
View... from Harnham Hill 53, **135**
Salisbury Cathedral, Wiltshire 15, 18, 32, 33, 42, 83
Bishop's Gate 48
Cathedral set 47–8, 53, 57–8, 62–3, 84, 184–8
Chapter House 48, 53, 63
Choir: Audley Chapel 47, 48
Cloisters 48, 55, 188
East Front 48
North Porch 45, 47, 48, 63
Transept 48, 53, 55, 63
West Door 48
West Front 45, 47, 48
Capital in the Chapter House... **55**
Chapter-House... 48, 51, 53, **54**, **57**, 63, 186, 187
Choir... 47, *48*, 57, 64
Choir... looking East towards the Lady Chapel 47, **49**, 51, 56, **57**, 184, 185
...from the East 15, **45**, 184
...from the South Side of the Cloister 55, **57**, 63, **72**, 186, 187, 188
Gateway to the Close... **43**, 45, 124
A General View... from the Bishop's Garden 55, **57**, **74**, 186, 188
Inside of the Chapter-House... 51, **52**, 53, **57**, 63, 186
Interior... looking towards the North Transept 55, **57**, 64, **75**, 186, 188
Lecture Diagram. Various Steeples: Salisbury; Christ Church, Oxford; St Giles, London **64**, 188
North Porch... **47**, **57**, 184, 185
The North-West Corner... 45, **46**, 184
Passengers Beside a Coach near Salisbury 150, 152, **153**
Studies of the Sculptural Frieze in the Chapter House... Joseph and his Brothers; Moses and the Exodus **55**, 187
West Front... [1795] 17, 45, **50**
West Front... [exhibited 1799] **50**, 51, **57**, 185
Salisbury series 42, 47, 56, 184, 185
'Salisbury' sketchbook (TB XLIX) 51, **55**, **62**, **135**, 187
Sarum *see* Old Sarum
'scale practice' 28, 31
Scene in Derbyshire 160, 163
Scotland tour (1801) 53, 55, 87
Scott, Sir Walter 175
Self-Portrait (Tate) 10
Seymour, Lord Henry 163
Shakespeare, William: *Twelfth Night* 173
Shee, Sir Martin Archer 181
Shipwreck 34
Signatures (Turner's) 48, 185, 188, 191, 193
Singleton, Joseph after Ozias Humphry: *Portrait of James Wyatt, RA* **11**
slavery **41**, 42, 81, 197
Smaller Fonthill sketchbook 87, **89**
Smith, J.C. after John Britton: *Malmesbury Abbey-Church, South Aisle &c, Wiltshire* 34, **35**
Smith, John 'Warwick' 31; *72 Select Views in Italy* 38–9
Smollett, Tobias 12
Snow Storm - Steamboat off a Harbour's Mouth 117, 119
Soane, Sir John 163
Society of Antiquaries 12, 15
Solent, the 158, 175
Somerset House, London 12
'South Wales' sketchbook 17, 26, 196
Southampton, Hampshire 192; *The Bargate, Southampton* 18, 158, 192
Southern Coast of England see *Picturesque Views on the Southern Coast of England*
Sparrow, Walter Shaw 177
Spithead, Solent 130, 179
Stonehenge, Wiltshire 6, 34, 130, 142–55
...Preparatory Study **154**
...Inner Sarsen Horseshoe from the South-West [Devonshire Coast No.1 sketchbook] 143, **145**
...Inner Sarsen Horseshoe from the South-West [Stonehenge sketchbook] 143, **147**
...at Sunset [1811] 143, **149**
...at Sunset [c. 1824] 150, **152**
...from the North-East, with the Setting Sun Beyond the Heel Stone 143, **147**
...from the North-West 143, **146**
...from the South, with the Heel Stone Beyond 143, **148**
...from the South-East [pen & ink] 142–3, **144**, 150, 153
...from the South-East [pencil] 143, **146**
...from the South-East, with the Setting Sun 143, **148**
...from the South-West 142–3, **144**
...from the West, with the Heel Stone Beyond 143–4, **149**
...Modern Chronology 150, **151**
Stonehenge, Wiltshire 134, **140–41**, 150, 152–4, **155**
Stonehenge sketchbook (TB CXXV b) **146–7**
Stonyhurst College, Lancashire 127
Stourhead, Wiltshire 6, 18, 20–39, 42, 53, 57, 79, 109, 122, 130
Column Room 31, 58, 62
heirlooms sold off 63
Library 24, 32, 34, 58, 63
Picture Gallery 24–5
Gothic Cross Above the Lake... 28, **30**
Lake with Distant Headland and Palaces; Study for 'Rise of the River Stour at Stourhead' **38**, 39
Rise of the River Stour... (also known as *The Swan's Nest*) 39
Study for 'View over the Lake at Stourhead' 28, **29**
View over the Lake at Stourhead, from the South-West 28, **29**
'Studies for Pictures' (TB LXIX) **86**, **108**, **144**
Studies of Egyptian Figures, copied from Bernard de Montfaucon's 'L'Antiquité expliquée et représentée en Figures' **108**
Studies of Egyptian Gods, copied from Bernard de Montfaucon's 'L'Antiquité expliquée et représentée en Figures' 92, **108**
Study of the Composition of Claude's 'Landscape with the Arrival of Aeneas before the City of Pallanteum' 84, **86**
Stukeley, William: *Stonehenge* 142
Swanage Harbour **123**, 124
Swans sketchbook (TB XLII) 51, 85, **117**
Swinburne, Sir John 158–9
Switzerland 179

T
Tabley House, Tabley Inferior, Cheshire 34
Talbot, William Fox 154
Tatton-Brown, Tim and Crook, John: *Salisbury Cathedral: The Making of a Medieval Masterpiece* **46**
Taylor, Sir Robert 193
Teniers, David and Saftleven, Herman: *Barn with a Still Life of Kitchen Utensils and a Sleeping Cook* 33
Tenth Plague of Egypt 110, **111**
Thornbury, Walter 86
Titian 6
Tresham, Henry 85
Trier (Trèves), Germany 159
Turner, Charles after J.M.W. Turner: *The Fifth Plague of Egypt* 110
Twickenham, Middlesex 179

U
Ultra-Toryism 153
Unknown Artist: *Reform! Reform!! Reform!!! Lord John Stalking Over Boroughmongers, or, the Rotten Prepresentation in Danger* 139

V
Vale of Heathfield sketchbook (TB CXXXVII) **122**
Valle Crucis Abbey, Llantysilio, Denbighshire, Wales 13
Venice 24, 32
Victoria, Queen 179
Views in Sussex 35
Virgil 24; *Aeneid* 36

W
Wallis, Robert 154
Walton, Isaac: *The Compleat Angler* 177
Weld family 127
Weld, Thomas 127
Wells, Somerset 192
Wells Cathedral, Somerset 15, 130
West Front of Wells Cathedral 15, **16**, 185
Welsh sketchbooks 110
Welsh tours: 1795 17, 26; 1796 33; 1798 85, 109; 1799 109
West, Benjamin 83, 85, 109
West Country tour (1811) 142
Westall, William after John Buckler: *Ruins of Fonthill Abbey* 117, **119**
Westmacott, Richard 83
Weymouth, Dorsetshire 127, **128**
What you Will! 173
Whitaker, Thomas Dunham: *History of the Parish of Whalley* 53
Wight *see* Isle of Wight
Wilberforce, William 81
Wild, Charles 84
Williams, Captain Nicholas 86
Wilson, Richard 36, 37; *Lake of Nemi, or Speculum Diana* 35–6, 37
Wilton House, Salisbury, Wiltshire 48, 116, 199
East Front of Wilton House 58, **66**, 116, 193
Winchester, Hampshire 18
Butter Cross, Winchester **17**, 158
West Front of Winchester Cathedral **8–9**, 15, **16**, 18, 158, 185
Windsor Castle, Berkshire 11, 82
Witham, Somerset 114
Woodforde, Samuel 23
Sir Richard Colt Hoare (1758-1838) with Henry (1784-1836), his Son 12, **22**, 23
Woods, Richard 190
Wookey Hole, Somerset 130
Woolnoth, William after Frederick Nash: *The Interior View of Salisbury Cathedral from the West Entrance* **51**, 186, 188
Worcester Art Museum, Worcestershire 160
Worsley, Sir Richard 158
Wren, Sir Christopher 127
Wyatt, James 11–12, 82, 85–6
Appuldurcombe House, Isle of Wight 158
Brocklesby Mausoleum 53
Christ Church, Oxford 88
Durham Cathedral 42
Ely Cathedral 15
Fonthill Abbey 79, 82, 83, 84, 87
Hereford Cathedral 13
Lee Priory, Kent 82, 83
Norris Castle, Isle of Wight 163
Pennsylvania Castle 127
Salisbury Cathedral, Wiltshire 15, 42, 184, 185, 186, 188, 190
Wilton House 193
Windsor Castle, Berkshire 82
Wyatt, James and Turner, J.M.W.: *Fonthill from the North-West* **83**
Wyle, Bishop Walter de la 189
Wyndham, Henry Penruddocke 48, 53, 61, 189, 190

Y
Yarborough, Lord 53

Published on the occasion of the exhibition *Turner's Wessex: Architecture and Ambition*, organised by The Salisbury Museum from 22 May to 27 September 2015.

First published in 2015 by
Scala Arts & Heritage Publishers Ltd
10 Lion Yard
Tremadoc Road
London SW4 7NQ, UK
www.scalapublishers.com

In association with
The Salisbury Museum
The Kings House
65 The Close
Salisbury SP1 2EN
www.salisburymuseum.org.uk

ISBN: 978-1-85759-930-5

Project manager and copy editor: Linda Schofield
Picture researcher: Sally Nicholls
Indexer: Diana Le Core
Designed by Nigel Soper
Printed in China

10 9 8 7 6 5 4 3 2 1

The production of this catalogue has been kindly supported by:

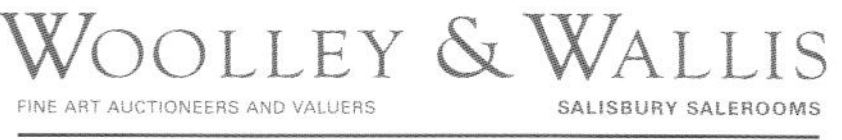

The principal supporters of the exhibition are:

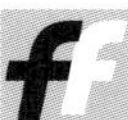
FOYLE FOUNDATION

Woolley and Wallis Fine Art Auctioneers
The Golden Bottle Trust
Arts Council
Smith and Williamson
The Idlewild Trust

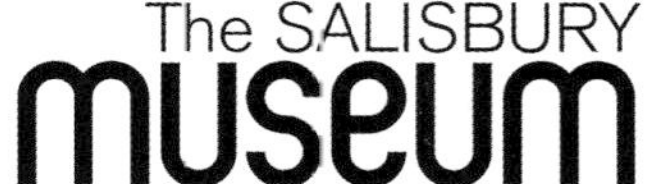

EXPLANATIONS

All illustrations are by J.M.W. Turner unless otherwise stated. References are made to the standard catalogues of Turner's works:

– 'B&J' numbers are those in Martin Butlin and Evelyn Joll, *The Paintings of J.M.W. Turner* (New Haven and London 1984)

– 'TB', accompanied by a Roman numeral, refers to items listed by A.J. Finberg in his *Complete Inventory of the Drawings of the Turner Bequest* (1909). All works on paper in the Bequest are at Tate Britain; quotation marks are used where Turner himself inscribed a sketchbook with its name; supplementary information is available on the Tate website: www.tate.org.uk/art/

– 'W' numbers relate to watercolours outside the Tate, as listed by Andrew Wilton, *The Life and Work of J.M.W. Turner* (Fribourg 1979).

FRONT COVER: *Salisbury, from Old Sarum*, c.1827–28 (fig. 134, detail)
BACK COVER: *Stonehenge, Wiltshire*, c.1827–28 (fig. 154, detail)
INSIDE BACK COVER: The City of Salisbury with the Adjacent Close, Church and River Accurately Surveyed by William Naish. Printed and sold by Benjamin Collins Printer, on the New Canal, 1751 (detail)
PAGES 2–3: *A Wooden Shelter, with a Shepherd and his Flock of Sheep; Fonthill Abbey in the distance*, c.1799 (fig. 79, detail)
PAGE 4: *North Porch of Salisbury Cathedral*, exhibited RA 1797 (fig. 37, detail)